Experimental
Psychology

Experimental
Psychology

Contemporary
Methods & Applications

Irwin P. Levin
The University of Iowa

James V. Hinrichs
The University of Iowa

With Contributions by:

Don C. Fowles
The University of Iowa

John F. Knutson
The University of Iowa

Edward A. Wasserman
The University of Iowa

WCB Brown & Benchmark
PUBLISHERS

Madison, Wisconsin • Dubuque, Iowa

Book Team

Editor *Steven Yetter*
Developmental Editor *Linda A. Falkenstein*
Production Editor *Gloria G. Schiesl*
Designer *K. Wayne Harms*
Art Editor *Kathleen M. Huinker-Timp*
Permissions Coordinator *Mavis M. Oeth*
Visuals/Design Developmental Specialist *Janice M. Roerig-Blong*
Production Manager *Beth Kundert*
Visuals/Design Freelance Specialist *Mary L. Christianson*

WCB Brown & Benchmark

A Division of Wm. C. Brown Communications, Inc.

Executive Vice President/General Manager *Thomas E. Doran*
Vice President/Editor in Chief *Edgar J. Laube*
Vice President/Production *Vickie Putman*
National Sales Manager *Bob McLaughlin*

Wm. C. Brown Communications, Inc.

President and Chief Executive Officer *G. Franklin Lewis*
Senior Vice President, Operations *James H. Higby*
Corporate Senior Vice President and President of Manufacturing *Roger Meyer*
Corporate Senior Vice President and Chief Financial Officer *Robert Chesterman*

The credits section for this book begins on page 399 and is considered an extension of the copyright page.

Cover and interior design by Kay Fulton Design

Cover image by Keith Skeen/Dodge Creative Services

Copyedited by Bonnie C. Gruen

Brief Contents

Contents

SECTION II BASIC AREAS OF RESEARCH

SECTION III APPLIED AREAS OF RESEARCH

SECTION IV CONCLUDING CHAPTERS: LOOKING BACK AND LOOKING AHEAD

Boxes

Preface

We wrote this book for students in research methodology courses in psychology who have completed at least one course in elementary psychology and, ideally, a basic course in elementary statistics. But don't worry, we are not assuming expertise in either psychology or statistics. We will review material you may already have had, but perhaps with a different twist. We will emphasize how something was done and why it was done a particular way, rather than concentrating solely on the outcome. Research findings need to be updated frequently, but the development of sound research methods can lead to a continuous flow of many exciting breakthroughs.

One of our major goals is to make you more informed "consumers" of behavioral research so that you will be able to evaluate research claims in terms of the soundness of the methods used to generate the data that are the source of these claims. Along the way, we hope to instill in you an appreciation of good research and perhaps even "turn on" some of you to consider behavioral research as a worthwhile and enjoyable part of your future.

The book begins with basic issues in research, including the ethical treatment of human and nonhuman research participants, that lay the foundation for developments in all areas of psychological inquiry. But we don't stay at the abstract level very long. Even the beginning chapters include illustrations such as determining the causes of mental illness and examining how our mental processes are affected by changes in mood. Our chapter on statistical inference includes many illustrations of prototypical psychological studies and why the appropriate statistical test provides necessary objective rules for determining the reliability and generalizability of research results.

Later chapters describe how fundamental research principles combine with innovative procedures to address the major issues in the various subareas that constitute contemporary psychological research. Some of these subareas form the traditional "bread-and-butter" topics of experimental psychology because they attempt to uncover the basic processes underlying a variety of human and nonhuman behaviors. These include human and animal learning and memory, and perception and psychophysics.

We then turn to contemporary areas that we know are of interest to students but are often not included in the teaching of experimental psychology (presumably because they are "qualitatively" different from the traditional areas). Our chapters on clinical psychology, social psychology, and judgment, decision making, and problem solving illustrate that advances in applied areas of psychological research can be based on the same standards of scientific rigor as applied to the areas more traditionally thought to constitute the appropriate subject matter of experimental psychology.

Our topical chapters include "classical" studies in each area as well as timely studies dealing with issues such as determining the antecedents of aggressive behavior, measuring the roles of cooperation and competition in response to environmental concerns, examining animal intelligence, and tracking the development of problem-solving skills. Most chapters include a glossary of terms, a set of exercises, and a list of suggested readings for those who want to explore an area in more depth. We conclude with chapters that not only summarize and synthesize the earlier chapters, but also include guidelines and illustrations on how to write a research report, examples of student research, and some helpful hints about graduate school.

We have tried to present the material in a logical order. With the exception of the first two chapters, however, the ordering of chapters is probably not critical. Instructors can pick and choose which chapters to include in which order. In our department, we have found it useful to use a particular topical chapter as the basis for a laboratory course in that area.

Each contributor of a chapter has many years of experience teaching undergraduate students in the Department of Psychology at The University of Iowa. Our department has a long-standing tradition of rigorous, tightly controlled experimental research, often grounded in fundamental theories of behavior, with both humans and nonhumans. While for the most part this book will represent a continuation of this tradition, some may be surprised to see the inclusion of nonlaboratory observational research techniques. We will try to explain why a particular technique is the most appropriate for addressing an important issue in a timely fashion. The authors talk from direct experience in applying these techniques as each is recognized as an active contributor to advancements in his area of research.

In addition to the authors of chapters, we would like to thank our colleagues who contributed valuable suggestions and reactions to the material in this text: Bob Baron, Harold Bechtoldt, Don

Carlston, Allen Hart, Gary Gaeth, Gregg Oden, Milt Rosenbaum, Jake Sines, and the late Charles Spiker. We want also to recognize the influence of those who taught us about research and infected us with their enthusiasm: Norman Anderson, Richard Atkinson, Gordon Bower, William Broen, William Estes, George Mount, and Rudolph Schulz. Various earlier experimental psychology textbooks shaped our thinking, including books by Underwood and by Woodworth and Schlossberg. These and a number of others were considered to be "keepers"— books that you didn't trade in but kept for future reference. In moments of grandeur, we aspire to create a new "keeper."

We benefited from the many helpful comments and suggestions of all the reviewers who saw our manuscript at various stages in the writing process. We'd like to thank the following reviewers:

Ronald Baenninger   *Temple University*
Kate Bruce   *University of North Carolina–Wilmington*
Gerald S. Clack   *Loyola University, New Orleans*
Wendy Idson Domjan   *University of Texas-Austin*
John Jalowiec   *Dartmouth College*
John L. Kibler III   *Mary Baldwin College*
Jerry N. Lackey   *Stephen F. Austin State University*
Mark McCourt   *University of North Dakota*
Leroy Metze   *Western Kentucky University*
Gail Peterson   *University of Minnesota*
Andrea L. Richards   *University of California, Los Angeles*
Lori L. Temple   *University of Nevada–Las Vegas*
S. Lee Whiteman   *Baldwin Wallace College*
J. W. Whitlow, Jr.   *Camden College/Rutgers University*

We also *needed* the continual motivation provided by Brown & Benchmark's team of G. Franklin Lewis, Michael Lange, and Sheralee Connors. We had our own team back home of secretaries who typed the various incarnations of each chapter without once complaining when we labeled a version as "final," only to revise it a half dozen more times. Bev Hamann, Becky Huber, Joyce Paul, and Pam Young, you're the greatest. Finally, we would like to single out our wives and families for their patience, support, and encouragement. We could never have done it without you.

Irwin P. Levin
James V. Hinrichs

SECTION

I

Foundations of Experimental Psychology

Chapters 1 to 3 provide the building blocks for understanding what experimental psychologists do, why they do it, and how they do it. Chapter 1 starts by providing a definition of "experimental psychology" that is perhaps more broad than many would have thought. Our definition would include all systematic research in areas such as cognitive psychology, animal behavior, clinical psychology, child psychology, industrial psychology, and social psychology.

Chapter 1 describes the nature of scientific logic that underlies the search for knowledge and understanding of behavioral phenomena and their causes. Several possible goals of behavioral research are described, along with basic research methods, such as the experimental method and the correlational method, designed to achieve these goals. Chapter 1 concludes with a discussion of ethical issues in conducting behavioral research. Chapter 2 describes common experimental designs used in psychology and the logic behind their use. These descriptions include definitions of basic terms such as independent variable, dependent variable, and confounding, and the use of a variety of control procedures. Descriptions of research methods include illustrative examples of their use, but this text is one of those rare cases where methods are emphasized over results. We want to teach students to critically evaluate research rather than accept results uncritically, so that they can appreciate good research.

Well-designed research should produce results that are easy to analyze and interpret. Before we put much credence on research data we must assess their reliability. This is the purpose of statistical inference, the topic of chapter 3. This chapter describes the critical role of statistical inference in interpreting research data. The logic behind the testing of statistical hypotheses is stressed, along with the nature of statistical errors and statistical power and the factors that affect them. The chapter ends with some typical applications of statistical methods in experimental psychology. These applications are included primarily to help students learn how to match appropriate statistical tests with common experimental design techniques and to illustrate the use of computational procedures. These applications also represent the logical sequence of steps starting from the statement of research questions or hypotheses, to designing the study and collecting the data, to analyzing the data, to using the results of the data analysis to answer the original research questions.

The research methods, experimental designs, and statistical techniques described in chapters 1 to 3 will be illustrated throughout the remainder of the text as we attempt to describe how experimental psychologists address major research questions of historical and contemporary interest in a variety of content areas.

Behavioral Research: Basic Considerations

Irwin P. Levin and James V. Hinrichs

Although speculation about the causes of behavior probably began with human thought and certainly occurs among the earliest documents in recorded history, the scientific study of behavior is much more recent. Scattered systematic investigation of limited aspects of animal and human behavior can be found in early scientific reports in many fields, including physiology and medicine, mathematics, and astronomy. Nevertheless, the origin of psychology as a science is usually traced to the founding of Wilhelm Wundt's (1832–1920) laboratory in 1879 in Leipzig. Since then, the topics and methods of experimental psychology have greatly influenced our understanding of behavior.

The very book you are reading is a product—as well as a description—of behavioral research. The design and display, as well as selection of material, were based on knowledge gained through research on perception, learning, and memory. Perhaps more importantly, experimental psychology can help answer questions such as "How will the caffeine I've been consuming to get through all-night study sessions affect my ability to learn and recall the material?"

The Meaning of "Experimental Psychology"

The label "experimental psychology" has two meanings. First, experimental psychology refers to the application of the experimental method to the study of behavior, where selected factors are systematically manipulated to determine their influence on behavior while attempting to hold all other factors constant. This is to be distinguished from other methods used to study behavior, such as naturalistic observation, case studies, and the use of archival data. Second, experimental psychology refers to a set of basic topics studied in psychology, usually by application of the experimental method, and includes subjects like perception, animal behavior, human learning and memory, and higher mental processes.

Both meanings must be qualified. Experimental psychologists frequently do use methods other than the experimental method. Also, many psychologists in specialty areas other than those listed above use the experimental method. Experimental studies in child behavior, social psychology, and clinical psychology are common. Furthermore, behavioral scientists in many areas outside of psychology such as sociology, law, and marketing have adapted experimental techniques to the study of topics within their own fields.

Nevertheless, the label **experimental psychology** is usually understood to refer to the variety of basic methods, procedures, and analytic tools used in the scientific study of behavior. These methods are basic in the sense that they are fundamental to the analysis of all areas of psychology and other behavioral sciences. In all these fields, tasks originally used to investigate purely theoretical hypotheses can serve as assessment instruments in applied or "real life" settings. For example, a clinical psychologist assessing patients for depression must be aware of possible associated cognitive deficits such as memory loss and therefore must be familiar with techniques used to measure such deficits. The same is true for psychologists studying the effects of addictive or prescription drugs.

Because both meanings of experimental psychology are central to all psychologists, this textbook considers experimental psychology from both points of view. Considerable emphasis is placed on the use of basic research methods in a variety of subareas within psychology and related behavioral sciences. By broadening the topical coverage of experimental psychology to areas such as clinical and social psychology, we are both stressing the common features of the methods of psychological investigation in diverse areas and recognizing the wide application of these methods. Each chapter representing the coverage of a particular content area emphasizes the development of research methodology as a logical progression of steps involved in addressing the major problems in that area. Our goal is for the reader to understand the products of scientific investigation in each specialty area while at the same time learning to evaluate research results in terms of the soundness of the methods used to obtain those results. We think this will make you a more informed "consumer" of research in your area of interest, and we hope it will motivate some of you to conduct research of your own.

The first three chapters will build a foundation for later chapters, concentrating on basic issues in experimental psychology and their origins in the scientific process, including ethical issues in conducting research with humans and nonhumans (chapter 1); issues in the design and conduct of experiments (chapter 2); and the use of statistics to analyze and interpret research results (chapter 3). Later chapters will consider not only subjects usually identified with experimental psychology but also some other topics within psychology that apply rigorous scientific methodology to important and interesting issues that affect us as individuals and as members of society. The last two chapters will briefly review the earlier chapters and will provide you with guidelines for preparing a research report as well as guidelines for those interested in applying to graduate school.

In the rest of chapter 1 we discuss the use of the scientific method in psychological research and the choice between different research methods, and then we turn to some general considerations in formulating a research problem and in designing and conducting an experiment in an ethical and humane manner. Chapter 2 continues these basic themes, describing specific techniques for designing experiments and analyzing experimental results, and concludes with an example of the steps taken in working through a specific research problem.

The Scientific Process in Experimental Psychology

All scientific inquiry centers around the use of systematic and controlled observations. There are a variety of techniques for achieving such observa-

tions. As you go through the examples in this book, consider them in terms of their usefulness in achieving the major goals of any science: *description, prediction,* and *explanation*. Let's say we are interested in studying the causes of schizophrenia. Our goals would include accurate descriptions of the incidence of schizophrenia displayed under varying combinations of genetic and environmental conditions, predicting the likelihood of schizophrenia in an individual or group, and explaining the etiology of schizophrenia in terms of the interrelated factors resulting in a person being classified as schizophrenic. Note that at the heart of these basic goals is the presumption of lawful and systematic relationships between antecedent (prior) conditions and consequent (later) events. Think of your chemistry lab where you had to predict the reactions of a chemical compound based on knowledge of the properties of the ingredients you mixed together. Scientific logic helps us understand these relationships.

Scientific Logic

Suppose that every time researchers in a psychiatric research institute delved into the history of a patient diagnosed as "schizophrenic," they found evidence that one or more of that patient's close relatives also had signs of schizophrenia. They might then come up with a tentative conclusion such as "schizophrenia runs in families" or "schizophrenics have a family history of schizophrenia." In assuming this, they would be applying the logic of **induction**— deriving a general principle from a series of specific observations. This would be a useful thing to do in beginning an investigation into the genetic component of schizophrenia. Note, however, that they have no guarantee that the next schizophrenic patient will have a similar family history. Principles derived from the process of induction are thus subject to continuous confirmation (and possibly refinement). Scientists consider such principles as "true until further notice."

In psychology, as in other sciences, most hypotheses and predictions take the form of "if . . . then" statements. The truth or falsity of such statements is tested using the process of **deduction.**

Consider the above statement derived from induction: "schizophrenics have a family history of schizophrenia." This can be translated into the following: "*if* a person is schizophrenic, *then* he or she will have a family history of schizophrenia." The phrase starting with "if" is called the *premise*, and the phrase starting with "then" is called the *conclusion*. The logic of deduction refers to the relationship between the truth of the premise and the truth of the conclusion. When we find a person who is classified as schizophrenic, we can deduce, "this person has a family history of schizophrenia." The latter statement amounts to a prediction of whether a family history of schizophrenia will be revealed, given that the person is schizophrenic. Scientific advancement through deductive reasoning comes from comparing such predictions with actual data. The original "if . . . then" statement is supported whenever we find a schizophrenic who has such a family history. (Terms like *induction* and *deduction* are briefly summarized in a glossary at the end of each chapter and at the end of the book.)

The one possibility leading to rejection of the "if . . . then" statement is observing a schizophrenic for whom no evidence of family history can be detected. Such an observation would lead us to abandon or modify the original statement, or it would lead us to question our ability to detect a family history of schizophrenia. A reasonable modification of the original statement would be "people who are schizophrenic are more apt to have a family history of schizophrenia than are people who are not schizophrenic." This would recognize a major difference between schizophrenics and nonschizophrenics but would allow for exceptions. Most psychological laws are in fact of this latter type and are tested by statistical measures of the difference between groups.

Let's return briefly to circumstances leading to rejection of the original "if . . . then" statement. Even if family history represents an important "risk factor" in schizophrenia, extreme environmental conditions, including the use of certain drugs, can lead a person with no family history to display behavior leading to the diagnosis of schizophrenia. This is an important point because it illustrates the difficulty of determining the causes of behavior, a primary goal of experimental psychology. Any one outcome can have several possible causes, and it may take extraordinary control measures (in this case, screening out users of certain drugs) to rule out alternative causes of behavior. Theory often plays a role in designing research to understand the causes of behavior.

The Role of Theory

Theory, as used here, has a more concise meaning than the more general terms "explanation" or "prediction." **Theory** in psychology refers to explanations or predictions of observable behavior based on unobservable states such as motivation or arousal. Advocates of the use of theory (e.g., Spence, 1956) have argued that theories are helpful in guiding research and in providing unifying concepts to link together research in different domains. Furthermore, the history of the physical sciences contains many examples of advancement due to theory development. In physics the theoretical construct "gravity" is used to describe, predict, and explain the motion of falling bodies, the flow of blood through the human body, and the orbits of artificial satellites. In psychology the theoretical construct "motivation" has been used to explain the behavior of rats in a maze, the effects of advertising on consumers, and students' choices of college courses. Notice the commonality of these two examples. Neither "gravity" nor "motivation" has any independent meaning, outside of its role in explaining and predicting observable events, but both have been linked to several different observable events.

Some research psychologists such as the well-known behaviorist B. F. Skinner have argued that theories can be overly restrictive and are premature in a relatively young science like psychology where there is great need to accumulate sound empirical data and to categorize empirical relationships (Skinner, 1950). These opponents have been particularly critical of the use of theory to explain observable behavior (e.g., a rat running through a maze to receive food) in terms of unobservable states such as motivation. They prefer to examine directly the relationship between observable stimulus conditions (e.g., hours of food deprivation prior to being put in the maze) and measurable behavior (e.g., time to complete the maze) rather than appeal to intervening states like motivation, which themselves have to be explained.

Consider our interest in the etiology of schizophrenia. There are theories that make specific assumptions about the co-acting of factors that predispose a person to become schizophrenic. For example, Zubin and Spring (1977) developed the "vulnerability-stress model," which starts with the assumption that a predisposition or "vulnerability" to schizophrenia is inherited. This vulnerability, however, can be modified by challenging life events (stressors), particularly those in family life. Whether a person stays well or becomes ill in response to a challenging life event is then assumed to depend on whether a *threshold of vulnerability* is exceeded. (Note that this threshold is not an observable characteristic of a person but is an assumed property to help explain behavior.)

Such theories or models serve the purpose of helping us understand the results of diverse studies—in this case, studies of genetic influences on schizophrenia and studies of the effects of life stressors. Furthermore, these theories have led to new studies that inform us about the interrelated contributions of genetic and environmental factors in the development of schizophrenia. Such studies have implications for identifying persons at risk for schizophrenia and starting preventive treatment.

Other researchers have pursued the study of the causes of schizophrenia without specific theories or models to guide them, other than the general notion that both genetic and environmental factors are logical candidates. Such interests have led to studies that compare the degree of co-occurrence of schizophrenia in monozygotic (identical) and dizygotic (fraternal) twins, and studies that compare the incidence of schizophrenia in adopted children with those of their biological and adoptive parents. In chapter 10 we will see the great care and patience required in conducting these studies and also the exciting results they produce. Such empirical results can, in turn, contribute to the development of refined theories. Scientific progress depends on empirical observations, and theories are constantly updated to accommodate new data. Thus, a theory, in order to be useful, must be testable and flexible, as well as rational and parsimonious.

Note that as we discussed the example of the etiology of schizophrenia we touched on all the scientific goals mentioned earlier. We used induction to gain a better *description* of the conditions of schizophrenia. We cited a theory that attempts to *predict* and *explain* schizophrenic behavior. (A thought question: How are prediction and explanation related?)

Basic Research Methods

All scientific research is based on careful, systematic observation. Field studies, case reports, surveys, and public opinion polls are instances of the method of observation. When an observational study is conducted in a naturalistic setting without any intervention on the part of the investigator, it is usually called **naturalistic observation.** When the object of observational research is to yield quantitative data about the interrelationships between events or factors, the method of observation is also referred to as the **correlational method.** Because we will concentrate on methods that allow psychologists to measure and quantify such relationships, we tend to prefer the term correlational method. When the researcher intervenes with or exercises control over factors that affect the observed behavior, he or she is using the **experimental method.** For reasons that will become clear as we describe the methods, the experimental method is usually preferred whenever possible and will be emphasized throughout the book, but there will be plenty of exceptions.

Observation and Correlation
Researchers using the correlational method rely on careful observation, recording, and classification of behavior in order to determine relationships between variables. (The term *variable* is a general one for any factor that can take on different values or "levels": from characteristics of a person, such as

age; to properties of stimuli, such as brightness of lights; to measures of response, such as reaction time. We will soon describe specific ways of categorizing variables in scientific research.) The correlational method is most often used when manipulation of the behavior of interest is not possible for practical or ethical reasons. For example, there have been a number of interesting studies of how "social support" aids in recovery from illness that did not include manipulation or control of the kind and amount of support a patient gets from family and friends. Careful selection of behaviors to observe and relate to each other can serve many of the same purposes as laboratory research, especially in early or exploratory stages of an investigation. Observed relationships are often the basis for making useful predictions such as a person's chance of becoming mentally ill as a function of family history.

Naturalistic observation may permit investigation of factors over much greater ranges than would be feasible or ethical in the laboratory. For example, we know that stress can have powerful effects on human behavior, but it is extremely difficult to study in a laboratory setting. The levels of stress-producing factors that can be ethically requested of subjects are relatively mild (e.g., giving a speech before a group) compared to "real life" stressors (e.g., automobile accidents or combat situations). Observation of behavior in natural settings has considerable appeal because of its apparent reality. Unlike the restrictions that sometimes must be imposed by a laboratory experiment, there tends to be less concern about the artificiality of results.

Nevertheless, we must avoid being deceived by the apparent reality of behavior recorded in natural settings; several factors can influence or distort naturalistic observations. A primary consideration is whether the setting or individuals in the setting are characteristic of the behavior or attributes being investigated. (Imagine the visitor from outer space who determined the average height and activity patterns of humans from observations of practice sessions in basketball arenas.) Use of proper statistical sampling procedures (chapter 3) can reduce difficulties posed by atypical observations. A second factor is the influence of the observer. The usefulness of

FIGURE 1.1   After many months, wild chimpanzees accept observer Jane Goodall's presence.

Derek Bryceson/© National Geographic Society

naturalistic observation depends on the researcher's ability to avoid intruding on the behavior being observed. Children on a playground will act differently if they know that they are being watched by an adult. Sometimes the use of video recorders with long-range capabilities helps. At other times there is no substitute for patience on the part of the researcher. Animal behaviorists have been known to spend months in the wild becoming acquainted with their subjects before the animals adapt to the observers' presence and act naturally around them (figure 1.1).

The lack of ability to identify cause and effect is the major problem facing users of correlational methods such as naturalistic observation. Many factors vary in an uncontrolled setting and it is difficult, if not impossible, to separate their effects. This leads to problems in interpreting a correlation between A and B: it could be that A influences B, it could be that B influences A, or it could be that a third factor C influences both A and B. For example, consider a major urban problem: overcrowding. Suppose that a correlation is observed between the crime rate in different parts of a city and population density. Is the high crime rate in the areas of highest density due to the direct influence of overcrowding? Or, in a perverse manner, can it be that high crime rate creates high density by driving down property values and housing costs? Or, are factors like poverty, unemployment, and homelessness contributing to both high population density and high crime rate?

Obviously, many important problems cannot be brought under experimental control for practical or ethical reasons, so only correlational methods can be used to investigate them. Outside the behavioral sciences, biology and astronomy provide striking examples of the power of careful observation and systematic cataloging of relationships. Much was known about the phylogenetic relationships among plants and animals long before genetic manipulation became commonplace. The laws of motion of the planets in the solar system were well-described centuries before the first astronaut. Nevertheless, in both sciences, the introduction of experimental methods has increased the rate of gaining new knowledge.

In the history of science, naturalistic observation and correlational methods have often led to hypotheses that are later tested using the experimental method, and vice versa. We will see several examples of studies that combine elements of experimental and correlational methods in order to achieve control over some variables while allowing others to vary naturally. Such methods are sometimes called **quasi-experimental methods** because, like an experiment, they attempt to isolate the effect of one factor by controlling as many other factors as possible.

In an example related to our discussion of the difficulties in interpreting results of a correlational study of crowding in cities, consider the possibility of controlling factors such as educational, recreational, and employment opportunities, which typically co-vary with population density. Several studies compared behavior in dormitories that were at the same university but differed in the number of persons per room. The researchers planted "lost letters" at the different dormitories and found that the lowest rate of return occurred in the highest density dormitories. In such studies, some—but not necessarily all—extraneous

factors can be ruled out as causes of the observed behavior. That is one reason why they are called "quasi" experiments. Can you think of uncontrolled factors in the "lost letters" studies?[1]

Even traditional experimental studies often include variables that describe individual characteristics such as age and gender that are difficult to link causally to observed behavior because they cannot be manipulated. For example, studies of aggressive behavior typically find reliable differences between the sexes, but it is extremely difficult to separate biological and environmental components of these differences. Are boys more aggressive than girls because of differences in brain chemistry or because society is more apt to reward aggression in boys? What studies using the correlational method have in common is that they can identify naturally occurring relationships but they cannot unequivocally determine which factor(s) were directly responsible for the observed behavior.

Experimental Method

By contrast, the experimental method is used to determine **cause and effect.** The experimental method is characterized by the manipulation of one or more variables called **independent variables** and the control of all others. *Manipulation* of an independent variable means creating different levels of that variable to which subjects respond; *controlling* other variables means holding them at a constant level. Techniques for manipulating and controlling variables vary greatly and depend on the behavior or **dependent variables** being studied. Let's say that a researcher is studying aggression in children as a function of crowding. The research could be conducted in a room especially equipped with a one-way mirror, and the researcher could manipulate the number of children in the room during the experimental session, using numbers ranging from 2 to 6. "Number of children in the room" would be the independent variable and that variable would take on the values 2, 3, 4, 5, and 6. (Note that this is *one* independent variable with *five* levels, not five variables.)

Suppose that the children were being observed through the one-way mirror and that objective measures of aggressive behavior had been developed (e.g., the number of times one child pushed, hit,

---

[1]One such factor might be economic background. Students ending up in less expensive but more crowded dormitories might come from poorer families. Different family backgrounds might lead to different attitudes toward handling lost items.

kicked, scratched, etc. another child). "Number of aggressive acts per child" would then be the dependent variable. Variables to be controlled (held constant) might include the size and contents of the room, whether the children were all of the same age and gender, whether they knew each other, and what they were told by the researcher. Differences in number of aggressive acts would be attributed to changes in the number of children in the room because, if the experiment is well controlled, the number of children is the only variable that is changed. We infer that any change in observed behavior is *caused* by the independent variable. What all experiments have in common is the potential ability to define cause-and-effect relationships between the independent and dependent variables.

While the major advantage of the experimental method over the observational method is the ability to identify cause and effect, one must be certain that the plan or design of the experiment is not perturbed by uncontrolled factors that can lead to misinterpretation of causality. Every problem area has special difficulties and concerns that influence the choice of methodology and control conditions; many are discussed in later topical chapters. To a large extent, to become expert in a particular discipline is to become knowledgeable about the particular dangers, pitfalls, and misinterpretations lurking in the shadows for the unwary investigator. In the previous example, children of different ages, gender, or cultural background may not be equally sensitive to the presence of other children.

Another set of concerns is the setting and materials of the experiment and the possibility that the laboratory situation may introduce unintended or unrecognized factors—sometimes very subtle influences—that affect subjects' behavior. One example of a laboratory-induced artifact is **subject bias.** Subjects' beliefs about what they should do in an experiment may affect their responses. There is often a tendency for subjects to try to please the experimenter and comply with what they believe are the experimenter's expectations. An experiment whose goals are transparent may produce **demand characteristics** that lead to biased responding. Good researchers will

thus withhold detailed information about the purpose of their study and their hypotheses until after the subject has completed the task.

One of the authors once conducted an experiment concerned with effects on memory of the tranquilizer Valium in which the research assistant expressed concern about the behavior of one of the obviously drugged subjects. He frequently dozed off and was very uncoordinated—hitting both walls as he attempted to walk down a corridor. In fact, he had received only a placebo, but some of his behavior was influenced by his belief that he had received Valium. This is sometimes called a **placebo effect.** His cognitive performance, however, was not impaired.

In addition to subject bias, **experimenter bias** may render the results of a study useless. Here we are talking about the experimenter's measurement and treatment of the data and other subtle ways in which the experimenter may influence the outcome of research. Examples are given in box 1.1 of experimenter biases known collectively as the "Rosenthal effect" because they have been studied extensively by Robert Rosenthal and his colleagues. Awareness of such potential biasing effects leads good researchers to attempt to eliminate or reduce subject bias and experimenter bias by developing objective measures of behavior and by using **double-blind procedures** whereby neither the subject nor the experimenter knows what experimental condition the subject is in. In a drug study someone other than the experimenter will assign the subject to a drug or a placebo condition and keep account of subject assignments.

An experimental study that permits the introduction of biasing or uncontrolled influences is said to lack **internal validity** because even within its own boundary conditions, the study does not lead to valid inferences about the causes of behavior. Although an experimenter must always be aware of potential uncontrolled or biasing influences, the advantage of an experiment conducted in a well-defined setting (i.e., a laboratory) is the greater degree of control exerted over potential sources of systematic bias compared to real-life settings.

BOX 1.1

Experimenter Bias: The Rosenthal Effect

Robert Rosenthal has written several books dealing with unintentional bias effects in both observational and experimental studies. In Rosenthal's textbook *Experimenter effects in behavioral research* (1966, 1976), he was especially concerned with the demonstration and control of the experimenter's influence on data obtained in psychological research. In *The volunteer subject*, Rosenthal and Rosnow (1975) examine characteristics of individuals who volunteer to serve as subjects in behavioral research. They describe how differences between volunteers and nonvolunteers may affect conclusions and generalizations about the entire population of potential subjects.

One of the most dramatic examples of "experimenter bias" was reported by Rosenthal and Jacobson (1968) in a book titled *Pygmalion in the classroom*. Elementary teachers were told that 20 percent of their pupils had potential for marked intellectual growth during the next school year as indicated by an ability test. In fact, the children were selected randomly. Nevertheless, the selected students exhibited significantly greater gains in IQ than did nonselected children. How did this occur? Quite possibly the teachers treated the supposedly "gifted" students differently from the rest in ways that gave them an advantage on intelligence tests such as spending more time with them and providing them with greater encouragement. This is sometimes referred to as a "self-fulfilling prophecy."

An example of a different type was reported by Rosenthal and Lawson (1964). A group of undergraduate students worked with rats over a period of two months on a series of learning tasks. Half the experimenters were told at the beginning that their rats were "maze-bright" and half were told that their rats were "maze-dull." The rats in fact were randomly selected from the same colony. On some of the tasks, the "maze-bright" animals "learned" faster than the "maze-dull" animals. Can you think of reasons for this?*

How can such effects be avoided? If labels have such a powerful effect, they should be used with caution. In a study comparing performance of subjects receiving a drug and subjects receiving a placebo, neither the subject nor the experimenter should know in which condition, drug or placebo, the subject was placed. A third party should keep account of the assignment of subjects to conditions and reveal this information only when the data for individual subjects have been recorded. This is known as a double-blind technique.

*Reasons given by others range from subtle cuing of the animals by the experimenters to blatant cheating in the scoring of behavior.

Nevertheless, critics may not trust the results of laboratory research because different conditions exist in the laboratory than exist in the real world. The **external validity** or **ecological validity** of the experiment is thus called into question. It is sometimes possible to employ the experimental method in a realistic setting. An example of such **field experiments** might be changing displays in a grocery store to see how that affects shopping behavior. Of course, the experimenter would have to make sure that other factors like prices and promotional strategies (e.g., newspaper ads for the products of interest) are not changed during the study period. It is important to note, however, that experiments can help us learn about *processes* that occur outside

the experimental setting even if the exact conditions are not duplicated. We will see many examples of this in later chapters.

To repeat, the essential characteristic of a controlled experiment is that one or more factors can be varied systematically while all other influences are controlled (held constant). When these conditions are met, we can logically attribute any observed changes in behavior to the factor(s) that were purposely varied. The major challenge for the experimenter is to insure that all requirements for controlled conditions are satisfied. As critics of our own as well as others' experimental research, our task is to search for possible sources of uncontrolled influence, and to find ways to eliminate them.

With the necessary precautions, behavioral research provides many exciting opportunities for understanding how humans and animals perform in a complex world.

Formulating a Research Problem

A key issue in all scientific research is formulating a research question or problem in sufficient detail to permit rigorous and objective testing. As we have seen in the schizophrenia example, research in psychology can be designed to test a theory (the "vulnerability-stress model"), provide an empirical test of a question of interest (the relative contribution of genetic and environmental factors), or address a problem of applied importance (identifying persons in need of preventive measures). As this example illustrates, these goals are often interrelated. Chapter 9 provides another vivid example of the relationship between laboratory-tested theory and contemporary social problems; it describes research to understand how a woman was brutally murdered while bystanders merely watched.

Where Do Ideas Come From?

Experiments often represent attempts to test deductions from theories, i.e., to find out if a prediction made from a prior interpretation of behavior is supported. Research ideas also come from new interpretations of a previous study, extensions of one's own research or pilot work, or merely from attempts to understand one's own or others' behaviors (why do I keep forgetting the names of persons I just met?). Researchers in all fields find a review of previously published research literature particularly helpful in refining their ideas by learning about related research. Fortunately, several shortcuts are available as aids to reviewing the existing research literature. *Psychological Abstracts* cites the titles and authors of articles published in any given year in a particular subject matter and provides an abstract of each article and a reference to where the complete article can be found (see box 1.2). *Psychological Abstracts* is available both "on paper" and as a computer file to permit electronic literature searches. The *Annual Review of Psychology* provides a state-of-the-art summary of progress in a variety of areas. Research in each area of psychology is published in specialized journals. The leading research journals in the chapter's topic area are listed at the end of individual chapters in this text.

A thorough examination of previous research in your area of interest can be particularly helpful in showing what methods and theories have proved successful in the past. Often, prior research results and interpretations can shed light on new research findings. While researchers want to avoid being tied to previous work to the extent that their contributions are only a trivial change from what has already been done, insufficient attention to previous work can lead to "reinventing the wheel" or, worse, repeating the mistakes of the past.

Most leading researchers engage in what is known as **programmatic research.** They conduct a series of studies on a given topic rather than flitting around from topic to topic. In this way, the questions that typically arise at the end of one study are addressed in the next study. Knowledge and expertise are acquired gradually. Progress in scientific research can often be characterized as "slow but steady."

Statement of Hypothesis

The formal expression of a proposal for a research project is usually referred to as the **statement of a hypothesis.** Ideally, it would consist of a clear description of the specific idea to be tested in terms of the variables, procedures, and setting in which the test is to be conducted. "People perform worse when they are under pressure" is too vague to be tested, but the assertion that "reaction time to unsignaled stimuli in the early stages of a drivers' training simulation task is greater when other students are observing than when they are not" can be tested. A major difference between the vague statement and the testable assertion is that the terms have been "operationalized" to make them susceptible to empirical test. (See if you can translate the testable assertion

BOX 1.2

Conducting a Literature Search

Suppose you were interested in the effect of an individual's beliefs on visual perception, especially interpretation and use of colors. There are several methods to determine what information is already available. First, for a general overview of the topic, you might consult a recent textbook or research monograph that reviews the basic principles of the topic. Second, you should also skim the leading publications that periodically survey new developments in the field (e.g., *Psychological Bulletin, Annual Review of Psychology, American Psychologist*) for any relevant, recent reviews. In addition to familiarizing you with current knowledge, textbooks or review articles might immediately give you the answer to your question or provide a reference that does. If you are not so fortunate, the reviews will provide you with keywords and/or technical terms that will aid you in the next step.

The most comprehensive index to research in psychology is provided by *Psychological Abstracts* and its electronic counterparts, *PsychLit* and *PsychInfo*. (Similar indices are provided in most scholarly disciplines.) Printed monthly, with semiannual author and subject indices, *Psychological Abstracts* provides an abstract and complete citation for every article related to psychology printed in approximately 1,200 journals. *PsychLit* is a CD-ROM version of *Psychological Abstracts* that can be searched using a microcomputer with a CD-ROM player and appropriate software. *PsychInfo* is an electronic data service that provides on-line access to the contents of *PsychLit* from a microcomputer or computer terminal. In addition to journal abstracts, *PsychLit* and *PsychInfo* include abstracts of books and book chapters that are not included in *Psychological Abstracts*. The electronic storage systems have the advantage of providing a simple means for combining components of a literature search into

a single step. For example, with the print version, if you wanted to scan the abstracts on a specific topic, by a certain author, and within a range of five years, you would need to examine the indices and abstract volumes for all five years. With either of the electronic systems, you could use a sequence of commands to select the abstracts of interest in a few seconds, and you could view those abstracts on the display screen or transfer them to a disk or printer for later viewing. Regardless of whether you use the printed version or the electronic version to locate an abstract of interest, you should read the complete article in detail to better evaluate its methods and the soundness of its conclusions.

If your research topic overlaps with research in other disciplines, you may find it useful to check other indexing systems in addition to *Psychological Abstracts*. Other abstracting systems that may be useful in psychological research include *ERIC* (education), *Medline* (medicine), and *Biological Abstracts* (biology). Once you have located a few of the most relevant articles, especially "classic" or seminal references, *Science Citation Index* provides a year by year listing of all articles that cite that particular paper. Thus you can quickly determine what recent research has pursued ideas presented in an earlier work.

For other hints in using library materials and reference sources in psychology, consult *Library Use: A Handbook for Psychology*. This manual, published by The American Psychological Association, is specifically written for psychology students. We strongly urge students to use their university librarians as a resource for starting their first literature review. In our own teaching of a research methodology course, we often include a guided library tour as one of the first class sessions.

---

into an "if . . . then" statement.) In this case both a performance measure (dependent variable) and a way of manipulating "pressure" (independent variable) have been operationally defined.

Note that different operational definitions may lead to different conclusions. Table 1.1 provides a number of examples of operational definitions of in-

dependent and dependent variables, as well as previewing material to be covered in later chapters.

These examples raise the issue of the difference between scientific conclusions and more general assertions. We usually express our beliefs and knowledge in grand sweeping statements such as "the harder you try, the better you will do." Unfortunately, such broad

	H Questions	Independent Variables	Dependent Variables
	mount and y of material ing and , now does previous learning affect new learning	Number of words on a vocabulary list; number of commands contained in a new computer program; exposure time (in sec.) of each item shown on computer screen; number of times each item is shown; similarity to previously learned material, as measured by number of common units	Percent of correct responses on each trial; number and type of errors made; time to complete a response; number of trials before the subject performed without error
Animal Learning and Behavior	How do motivation and incentives combine to affect learning; which reinforcement schedules are most resistant to extinction	Task complexity, as measured by number of separate choice points between beginning and end of maze (rats) or number of alternative response keys to choose between (pigeons); amount of food received for making correct response; hours of food deprivation prior to experimental session; how many responses have to be made before a reward is given (schedule of reinforcement)	Number of errors made on each trial; time to reach a goal on each trial (rats); rate of pecking keys (pigeons); number of times response is made after reinforcement is discontinued (trials to extinction)
Perception and Psychophysics	How do thresholds compare for different sense modalities; what are the cues responsible for perceptual illusions	Intensity level of tones or brightness of lights presented on successive trials; concentration of sugar in drinks; relative lengths of intersecting horizontal and vertical lines	Standardized methods of computing thresholds (see chapter 4); percent correct detection of faint signals; judgments of which line appears longer
Judgment and Decision Making	How important are first impressions; when are we apt to make "risky" decisions	Order of presentation of favorable and unfavorable information about a person; presentation of injury rates in auto accidents with and without use of seat belts; description of gambles in terms of "chances of winning" or "chances of losing"	Ratings of likability of a person; stated likelihood of risk; whether or not a person will wear a seat belt; whether or not a person will take a gamble
Social Psychology	How does "crowding" affect interpersonal relations; when will we help our fellow humans; what attracts us to others	Crowding as measured by number of college roommates, or by amount of space for a fixed number of rats; whether or not a person in need of help has a physical stigma; number of shared attitudes by two or more persons in a group	Rate of return of "lost letters"; number and intensity of aggressive acts; rate and latency of seeking help for a victim; ratings of felt degree of responsibility for helping others; ratings of attractiveness of fellow group members
Clinical Psychology	When is therapy effective; how important are early child-rearing experiences; what contributes to interpersonal stress	Number, length, and content of therapy sessions; varying scenarios of child behavior requiring disciplinary action; stress induced by varying forms of peer pressure	Scores on diagnostic test; self-reported improvement; endorsement of items representing "appropriate" parental discipline; electrophysiological recordings of heart rate, blood pressure, etc.

statements are impossible to test because there are too many plausible interpretations of what they mean—some true, others false, and still others uncertain. Translation of a common sense notion into a testable hypothesis is one of a scientist's most creative tasks. The importance of operational definitions in this process will be discussed in more detail in chapter 2.

Sometimes an experiment permits the comparative testing of alternative hypotheses arising from competing theories. Such an experiment is referred to as a **critical test.** For example, the presence of an audience may be seen as a distractor that can interfere with task performance or it may be seen as a motivator that enhances performance. This example will be discussed in our chapter on social psychology.

Choice of Subject Population

After the question or experimental hypothesis to be investigated is clearly stated and the basic research method is selected, the experimenter must address another general issue before attending to the details of designing and completing the study. A target group of subjects for the study must be identified. The choice of **subject population** will, of course, depend primarily on the purpose of the study. However, it will also depend on practical and ethical concerns and issues such as the generality of research findings. Often the initial question is whether to test animals or humans. (Obviously humans are also animals, but the methods of studying behavior are so different that one might say that the psychological laboratory is one of those rare places in science where humans are not treated like animals!)

Animal Subjects
Many people assume that psychology is inherently concerned with human behavior and that research with animals is always directed at learning something that can be applied to humans. Some psychologists, however, are interested in animal behavior for its own sake in the same way that zoologists are interested in the properties and phenomena of animal life. Some psychologists are interested in comparing the behavior of various species, including humans. This branch of psychology, known as comparative psychology, will be described in more detail in chapter 5.

When psychologists with an intrinsic interest in human behavior use animals in their research, it is usually for practical and ethical reasons. Research techniques not suitable to human experimentation include genetic manipulations, surgical procedures, and severe environmental manipulations. The study of hereditary influences on a particular form of behavior is facilitated both by the ability to breed selectively and by the use of species with relatively short life spans. Researchers can then examine behavioral changes across several generations in a single study.

Research on stress, aggression, pain sensitivity, drug-induced changes in behavior, and sensory deprivation can often be more practically and ethically achieved in animals than in humans. Clearly, while knowledge about such conditions is important, the research must be conducted with a sense of concern for the subject's welfare. A careful analysis of benefits vs. costs must be conducted. Animals as well as humans must be protected from capricious research, and, as will be described shortly, a code of ethics has been established for conducting animal research as well as human research.

Experimental psychologists using animal subjects are usually well aware of limitations in generalizing their results to humans. Although some fascinating research related to language has been conducted recently with dolphins, chimpanzees, and gorillas, research interest in areas such as verbal behavior, creativity, and complex problem solving that require language ability usually precludes the use of animal subjects. (See chapters 6, 7, and 8.) When research interest is in the fundamental principles of learning and performance, however, simple animal learning paradigms often provide the most direct test because of the degree of control that can be exercised over genetic factors and environmental factors such as prior learning history. The underlying assumptions are that certain fundamental behavioral processes are common to many different organisms and that the greater degree of complexity of behavior exhibited in some species is built on the shared foundation of common physiological and behavioral processes.

Human Subjects

Many areas of behavioral research such as perception, memory, social psychology, and clinical psychology have relied primarily on human subjects. Even in these areas, however, animals are sometimes used. The choice is based on the researcher's weighing of the relative advantages and disadvantages of using humans versus animals. In these particular areas, need for verbal organisms capable of complex behavior is often the overriding issue.

Once the choice of humans has been made, a more narrow population must be defined. As all students who have taken a course in introductory psychology know, much psychological research is based on the responses of college undergraduates. Of course, the main reason for the popularity of students in psychological research is that they are handy. At the same time, they represent a restricted population and create the usual problem that generalization to other populations may be unwarranted.

Is it desirable to have a wide variety of subjects available for a given study? The answer depends on how you incorporate subject variables—variables such as age, sex, and education level, which may be correlated with performance in the experimental task—into your experimental design. If you were to put subjects with diverse characteristics into the same experimental group, then you might produce results that varied so much between individuals within the same group that you would not be able to detect differences between groups. (Chapter 3 explains how a comparison of differences observed across groups and differences observed within groups forms the basis of tests of statistical significance.) However, if you were to replicate (repeat) the experimental design with each separate classification of subjects, you would then be able to test the generality of your results by comparing the effects of the primary variables across different subject classifications. For example, you could see if the variables that affect memory in college students also affect memory in the same way in grade school children and in older people. Note that when the question is framed this way, it does not matter that the absolute level of performance differs across subject classifications.

In clinical research the appropriate population is often highly specialized and specified as part of the research question (e.g., motivational factors in autistic children, perceptual deficits in children with learning disabilities, memory defects in brain-damaged persons, or personality differences between identical twins reared apart). Research with special populations such as autistic children presents special problems. One such problem is finding a suitable task that can be performed under controlled laboratory procedures and yet represents the type of deficit of interest to researchers and clinicians working with these individuals. Finding appropriate "controls" with which to compare the unique properties of these populations can also be a problem. The latter problem is particularly perplexing because if we find "normal" children who do not match the autistic children on factors such as institutionalization, then we cannot rule out the influence of these factors when comparing the two groups.

A recent dissertation study conducted at our university (Richardson, 1987) illustrates the problem of finding a suitable control group for a special subject population. The researcher was interested in the cognitive deficits (e.g., memory loss) and psychiatric problems of Vietnam combat veterans who contracted a particular form of malaria that affects the cerebral cortex. Because some of the problems suffered by members of this group could come from the combat experience itself, quite apart from the malaria, a control group selected from a population of noncombat veterans would be inappropriate. The researcher selected a control group—more accurately a "comparison group"—of Vietnam veterans who had suffered war injuries but did not contract malaria. These subjects were matched with the experimental subjects on various socioeconomic indexes as well as on amount of combat experience. While this "control" group experienced significant problems, a greater degree of impairment was found in the malaria group.

One final word about special populations. They are often difficult to obtain in large numbers. This reduces the size of potential studies and the ability to conduct a **pilot study** to refine materials and procedures before conducting the main study. Researchers using these populations must be especially knowledgeable about prior research and the success rate of various procedures. Research with special populations often relies on procedures that obtain the maximum information from each individual subject.

Regardless of the subject population selected for study, subjects must be treated humanely. No issue in experimental psychology is more basic than the issue of conducting research in an ethical and humane manner. We turn to this issue next.

Ethical Issues in Psychological Research

Throughout this text, we will see a number of instances in which ethical concerns are raised in psychological research. For example, in studies of therapy outcome in clinical psychology, one or more groups serve as "controls" to be compared with the group who receives a treatment that the investigator believes to be effective. The issue here is whether it is ethical to withhold potentially helpful treatment from those in need. The solution in this case is relatively simple. If the treatment proves to be effective—and this could be learned only by including the appropriate control groups—then the control groups will be given the treatment after the study has been completed. Other situations are not so easy to resolve.

Research using nonhumans sometimes involves painful procedures such as administering electric shock, or surgery, or allowing animals to aggress against each other. It is sometimes necessary to sacrifice the subjects at the end of a study to verify anatomical manipulations requiring precise surgical procedures or to verify changes in the brain resulting from various intervention techniques. Even when more benign procedures such as standard learning or conditioning paradigms are used, there is the issue of handling and housing animals in a humane manner.

Probably the most interesting and controversial issues involving ethical treatment with humans arose in past studies of social psychology where potential damage to research participants was not physical, but "psychological" in nature. These will be described in some detail in chapter 9. Participants in a study of compliance with the orders of an authority figure thought they were administering shock as a punishment to another subject. They were later told that no shock was actually received and that the other "subject" was actually an actor. Nevertheless, many left the experiment knowing that they were capable of inflicting harm on others. Similarly, some participants in a simulated but realistic prison study were asked to play the role of prison guards with authority over other participants playing the role of prisoners. After dealing with a rebellion by the "prisoners," the "guards" were left with the feeling that they will play the role that society provides them, even if it includes brutality and inhumane treatment of others. We now recognize that protecting the feelings of research participants must be an important concern in psychological research.

Box 1.3 represents the ethical principles developed by the American Psychological Association for use of humans and animals in psychological research. Most of these principles serve as reminders of what all fair-minded researchers would regard as humane treatment of research participants. Several of the principles for conducting research with human participants are, however, more subjective in nature and thus worthy of special note. The first concerns the notion of "subject at risk." This can be a judgment call, as in the studies on obedience to authority and role-playing in a prison setting. The researcher may be too invested in the research hypotheses to be objective about possible "psychological" risks such as loss of self-esteem on the part of the participants. Research institutes, government agencies, and colleges and universities now have specially constituted "ethics committees" to make decisions about the acceptability of research

BOX 1.3

Ethical Principles for Use of Humans and Animals in Research*

6.06 Planning Research

a. Psychologists design, conduct, and report research in accordance with recognized standards of scientific competence and ethical research.

b. Psychologists plan their research so as to minimize the possibility that results will be misleading.

c. In planning research, psychologists consider its ethical acceptability under the Ethics Code. If an ethical issue is unclear, psychologists seek to resolve the issue through consultation with institutional review boards, animal care and use committees, peer consultations, or other proper mechanisms.

d. Psychologists take reasonable steps to implement appropriate protections for the rights and welfare of human participants, other persons affected by the research, and the welfare of animal subjects.

6.07 Responsibility

a. Psychologists conduct research competently and with due concern for the dignity and welfare of the participants.

b. Psychologists are responsible for the ethical conduct of research conducted by them or by others under their supervision or control.

c. Researchers and assistants are permitted to perform only those tasks for which they are appropriately trained and prepared.

d. As part of the process of development and implementation of research projects, psychologists consult those with expertise concerning any special population under investigation or most likely to be affected.

6.08 Compliance with Law and Standards

Psychologists plan and conduct research in a manner consistent with federal and state law and regulations, as well as professional standards governing the conduct of research, and particularly those standards governing research with human participants and animal subjects.

6.09 Institutional Approval

Psychologists obtain from host institutions or organizations appropriate approval prior to conducting research and they provide accurate information about their research proposals. They conduct the research in accordance with the approved research protocol.

6.10 Research Responsibilities

Prior to conducting research (except research involving only anonymous surveys, naturalistic observations, or similar research), psychologists enter into an agreement with participants that clarifies the nature of the research and the responsibilities of each party.

6.11 Informed Consent to Research

a. Psychologists use language that is reasonably understandable to research participants in obtaining their appropriate informed consent (except as provided in Standard 6.12, Dispensing with Informed Consent). Such informed consent is appropriately documented.

b. Using language that is reasonably understandable to participants, psychologists inform participants of the nature of the research; they inform participants that they are free to participate or to decline to participate or to withdraw from the research; they explain the foreseeable consequences of declining or withdrawing; they inform participants of significant factors that may be expected to influence their willingness to participate (such as risks, discomfort, adverse effects, or limitations on confidentiality, except as provided in Standard 6.15, Deception in Research); and they explain other aspects about which the prospective participants inquire.

c. When psychologists conduct research with individuals such as students or subordinates, psychologists take special care to protect the prospective participants from adverse consequences of declining or withdrawing from participation.

d. When research participation is a course requirement or opportunity for extra credit, the prospective participant is given the choice of equitable alternative activities.

e. For persons who are legally incapable of giving informed consent, psychologists nevertheless (1) provide an appropriate explanation, (2) obtain the participant's assent, and (3) obtain appropriate permission from a legally authorized person, if such substitute consent is permitted by law.

6.12 Dispensing with Informed Consent

Before determining that planned research (such as research involving only anonymous questionnaires, naturalistic observations, or certain kinds of archival research) does not require the informed consent of research participants, psychologists consider applicable regulations and institutional review board requirements, and they consult with colleagues as appropriate.

6.13 Informed Consent in Research Filming or Recording

Psychologists obtain informed consent from research participants prior to filming or recording them in any form, unless the research involves simply naturalistic observations in public places and it is not anticipated that the recording will be used in a manner that could cause personal identification or harm.

6.14 Offering Inducements for Research Participants

a. In offering professional services as an inducement to obtain research participants, psychologists make clear the nature of the services, as well as the risks, obligations, and limitations.

b. Psychologists do not offer excessive or inappropriate financial or other inducements to obtain research participants, particularly when it might tend to coerce participation.

6.15 Deception in Research

a. Psychologists do not conduct a study involving deception unless they have determined that the use of deceptive techniques is justified by the study's prospective scientific, educational, or applied value and that equally effective alternative procedures that do not use deception are not feasible.

b. Psychologists never deceive research participants about significant aspects that would affect their willingness to participate, such as physical risks, discomfort, or unpleasant emotional experiences.

c. Any other deception that is an integral feature of the design and conduct of an experiment must be explained to participants as early as is feasible, preferably at the conclusion of their participation, but no later than at the conclusion of the research. (See also Standard 6.18, Providing Participants with Information about the Study.)

6.16 Sharing and Utilizing Data

Psychologists inform research participants of their anticipated sharing of further use of personally identifiable research data and of the possibility of unanticipated future uses.

6.17 Minimizing Invasiveness

In conducting research, psychologists interfere with the participants or milieu from which data are collected only in a manner that is warranted by an appropriate research design and that is consistent with psychologists' roles as scientific investigators.

6.18 Providing Participants with Information about the Study

a. Psychologists provide a prompt opportunity for participants to obtain appropriate information about the nature, results, and conclusions of the research, and psychologists attempt to correct any misconceptions that participants may have.

b. If scientific or humane values justify delaying or withholding this information, psychologists take reasonable measures to reduce the risk of harm.

6.19 Honoring Commitments

Psychologists take reasonable measures to honor all commitments they have made to research participants.

6.20 Care and Use of Animals in Research

a. Psychologists who conduct research involving animals treat them humanely.

b. Psychologists acquire, care for, use, and dispose of animals in compliance with current federal, state, and local laws and regulations, and with professional standards.

c. Psychologists trained in research methods and experienced in the care of laboratory animals supervise all procedures involving animals and are responsible for ensuring appropriate consideration of their comfort, health, and humane treatment.

d. Psychologists ensure that all individuals using animals under their supervision have received instruction in research methods and in the care, maintenance, and handling of the species being used, to the extent appropriate to their role.

e. Responsibilities and activities of individuals assisting in a research project are consistent with their respective competencies.

f. Psychologists make reasonable efforts to minimize the discomfort, infection, illness, and pain of animal subjects.

[Continued]

Box 1.3 *continued*

g. A procedure subjecting animals to pain, stress, or privation is used only when an alternative procedure is unavailable and the goal is justified by its prospective scientific, educational, or applied value.

h. Surgical procedures are performed under appropriate anesthesia; techniques to avoid infection and minimize pain are followed during and after surgery.

i. When it is appropriate that the animal's life be terminated, it is done rapidly, with an effort to minimize pain, and in accordance with accepted procedures.

*Standards excerpted from Ethical Principles of Psychologists and Code of Conduct, *American Psychologist,* December 1992.

---

proposals. When in doubt, these committees will disapprove the research or require the investigator to modify procedures to meet ethical standards.

Another important, and relatively new, ethical principle is **informed consent.** The research participant (or the appropriate responsible person in the case of young children or others not able to make informed decisions) must be informed ahead of time about the nature of the study and any possible risks, and has the right to decline to participate or to withdraw at any time. And, unless a prior agreement has been made to the contrary, the confidentiality of each participant's responses must be maintained. Following participation, a clear debriefing is given to clarify the nature of the study and remove any misconceptions (as when deception had been used).

Box 1.4 gives our university's guide for providing information to research participants and the consent form that participants sign.

Before we leave this topic, we should note that for both animal and human research, the "bottom line" for deciding when a study is acceptable is often an assessment of the relative costs and benefits of the research. "Costs" include discomfort, pain, and suffering of the participants. "Benefits" include education and care for the individual participants, and more importantly, possible benefits to society from the knowledge that may be gained. You will probably notice a parallel to medical research where, in some cases, research with intact animals has been replaced with research on samples

of tissue whose removal does not harm the animal. In psychology, however, behavior of the intact organism is usually the target of research, and no such substitutions are possible.

One responsibility of the investigator is to consider alternative research methods and subject populations that will achieve the same goal but with minimal costs. Here again, however, it is important to have an informed but dispassionate group of outside individuals to help the researcher make such decisions. The use of ethics committees, along with the need for informed consent, have been the most important consequences arising from the establishment of formal guidelines for conducting ethical research.

The following is a recent example of an ethical issue dealing with informed consent decided upon by our department's ethics committee: Within a few months after a tragic episode in which several persons were shot and killed on our campus by an emotionally disturbed student, the committee received a proposal to conduct a study to examine the effects of the presence of a weapon on the accuracy of the description of the situation given by eyewitnesses. In one of several contrived scenarios involving the interaction of a subject with an assistant, the assistant was to enter the room brandishing a pistol and verbally threatening the research subject.

Initially, the investigators planned to tell the subject ahead of time only that the purpose of the experiment was to determine how people (the subjects) react to emotional displays by others and

BOX 1.4

Informed Consent Guidelines (University of Iowa)
Information Summary

(Name of Investigator)   (Title of Research Project)

1. Summary of what will be told to the subject about the project (Lay terminology should be used.):
   a. This study involves research. The purpose of the research is (Describe in lay terms.)
   b. You (the subject) are being invited to participate in this research for (expected length of time)
   c. If you agree to participate, these procedures will be followed (list):
   d. Of the procedures listed in 1.c. above, the following are experimental:
2. Foreseeable risk(s) or discomfort(s) to you (the subject):
3. Benefits to you (the subject) or to others that may be expected from the research:
4. Alternative procedures or courses of treatment that might be advantageous to you (the subject):
5. A record of your (the subject's) participation in this research will be maintained, but this record will be kept confidential by (methods).
6. (To be added if the project is an Investigational New Drug study.) The U.S. Food and Drug Administration (FDA) and name of company may inspect and copy your medical records relating to this study, and the results of the study will be reported to the sponsor, the FDA and perhaps to other regulatory agencies. This information will be treated confidentially and, in the event of any publication regarding this study, your identity will not be disclosed.

7. Questions about the research will be answered by
   Project Director _____ _Address_ _____ _(Telephone)_
8. Your (the subject's) participation is voluntary. No penalty or loss of benefits to which you are entitled will occur if you decide not to participate. You may discontinue participation at any time without penalty or loss of benefits to which you are entitled.
9. You will be compensated for time and inconvenience involved in participating in the research in the amount(s) of __$__ per _hr./day_ beginning _date_ and ending _date_ . Compensation will be pro-rated _____ if you withdraw before the research is completed.

Informed Consent Statement
(Department of Psychology)

I agree to participate in the present study being conducted under the supervision of a faculty member of the Department of Psychology at The University of Iowa. I have been informed, either orally or in writing, or both, about the procedures to be followed and about any discomforts or risks that may be involved. The investigator has offered to answer such further inquiries as I may have regarding the procedures. I understand that I am free to terminate my participation at any time without penalty or prejudice.

_____ _Signature_ _____ _____ _Date_ _____

---

that they would be confronted by a person who was angry. Subjects were also advised that ". . . even though all of this just involves role-playing, some people may find this disturbing." The com-mittee requested—and the researcher agreed—to the addition of the following statement to the instructions: "Remember, this whole situation is just make-believe, like theater, you know—props, scripts, etc." The committee hoped the additional statement would reduce the emotional impact of a brandished pistol but not so much as to destroy the attention-getting value of the stimulus.

Ethical issues in animal research often center around health concerns—do the animals have sufficient food, water, space? However, they sometimes involve psychological stress. An example concerns the phenomenon of "learned helplessness." A number of studies have shown that the trauma produced by a noxious stimulus such as electric shock is intensified when the subject cannot escape the stimulus through its own actions. Consequently, investigators examining the effects of electric shock are encouraged to modify their procedures so that following a shock the animal is able to perform some behavior to end the trial by escaping from the shock.

Summary and Conclusions

Experimental psychology uses application of basic research techniques, especially the experimental method, in the study of behavior and in attempts to discover basic principles that apply to a variety of topics in psychology. Much of the research in psychology is guided by theory but some researchers have made substantial contributions by adopting a purely empirical approach. Many sources exist to aid in learning about past research accomplishments.

Rules of scientific logic used in interpreting research findings include induction and deduction. Induction is the process of repeatedly observing an event until you can derive a generalized conclusion. Deduction is the process by which you predict that an event will occur based on the truth of the premises underlying the prediction. Deduction can then be thought of as a process of reasoning that goes from a general principle (an "if . . . then" statement) to a particular instance (e.g., whether a person with a particular family history is at risk for schizophrenia), whereas induction can be thought of as a process of reasoning that goes from particular instances (e.g., observations of the family histories of individual schizophrenics) to a general principle (e.g., all schizophrenics have a family history of schizophrenia). As

we have seen, scientists must understand the limitations of the conclusions they make when applying the processes of induction and deduction. Scientific progress is an evolving process of collecting data and revising explanations and predictions.

Fundamental differences exist between research methods. The experimental method involves the manipulation of one or more variables and the control of all other variables so that changes in behavior can be attributed to changes in the manipulated variables. Control procedures such as the double-blind technique are available for avoiding bias with the experimental method. Cause-and-effect inferences cannot be made with the method of observation or correlational method when naturally occurring phenomena are observed and related to each other without the benefit of experimental control. The method of correlation can be a useful research tool when experimental manipulation is impractical or unethical, but it is important to avoid observer bias and observational techniques that change the behavior under investigation.

Choice of subject population for behavioral research will depend on the nature of the research question and the type of experimental manipulation required. Animal behavior is sometimes studied for its own sake, but animals are also used as surrogates for humans when extreme degrees of environmental or genetic control or manipulation are required that cannot be achieved with humans. Some areas of psychology use human subjects almost exclusively because research questions involve analysis of higher mental processes. Research dealing with special populations presents particular problems such as limited sample size, restricted tasks, and difficulty in finding appropriate "normal controls."

For both human and nonhuman populations, it is imperative to treat subjects in an ethical and humane fashion. Organizations such as the American Psychological Association have established formal guidelines for human and animal research. Universities and other agencies have set up committees for acting on research proposals based on analysis of costs to the participants and benefits to society. Human subjects must be informed of potential risks prior to consenting to participate in research.

Exercises

1. Suppose you are a developmental psychologist interested in children's social interactions with each other. State a specific problem or hypothesis that would be better investigated by use of the observational or correlational method than with the experimental method. Then state another problem or hypothesis that would be more appropriate to study with the experimental method. Explain why each method is more appropriate for each problem.

2. Examples were given throughout this chapter of how the experimental method, the observational or correlational method, and the quasi-experimental method could be used in the study of crowding. Use these examples to summarize the features of each method and to discuss their relative pros and cons.

3. Describe examples of induction and deduction that you use in developing your own theories about human or animal behavior.

4. It has been said that theories are easier to disprove than to prove. Explain this statement in terms of the logical processes of induction and deduction.

5. Find an article in a psychology journal describing a study using the experimental method with animals and an article on the same topic describing a study using the experimental method with humans. Why was each population of subjects chosen? Could the main purpose of each study have been achieved with a different population?

Glossary

cause and effect Identifying factors that determine an observed behavior or change in behavior. (p. 9)

correlational method Observations of behavior aimed at yielding quantitative data about the interrelations between events or factors. (p. 7)

critical test An experiment permitting the comparative testing of alternative hypotheses arising from competing theories. (p. 15)

deduction Process of testing truth or falsity of scientific hypotheses and predictions by going from a general principle (an "if . . . then" statement) to a particular instance. (p. 5)

demand characteristics Those aspects of an experiment enabling subjects to determine what is expected of them. (p. 10)

dependent variable Behavior (response) observed by the experimenter. (p. 9)

double-blind procedures Neither the subject nor the experimenter knows what experimental condition the subject is in. (p. 10)

experimental method Research method characterized by the manipulation of one or more variables and the control of all others. (p. 7)

experimental psychology Basic methods, procedures, and analytic tools used in the scientific study of behavior; sometimes defined as a set of basic topics such as perception, learning, and memory. (p. 4)

experimenter bias How experimenters' expectations about the results of an experiment may affect the measurement and treatment of data (sometimes referred to as "the Rosenthal effect"). (p. 10)

external validity Extent to which the results of a laboratory study apply to conditions that exist in the real world (sometimes referred to as "ecological validity"). (p. 11)

field experiment Use of the experimental method in a realistic setting. (p. 11)

independent variable Variable manipulated by the experimenter. (p. 9)

induction Deriving a general principle from a series of specific observations. (p. 5)

informed consent An ethical principle in research with humans whereby potential participants are informed of the nature of the study before agreeing to participate. (p. 20)

internal validity Extent to which a study is free of biasing or uncontrolled influences. (p. 10)

naturalistic observation Observations of behavior conducted in a naturalistic setting without any intervention on the part of the investigator. (p. 7)

pilot study Preliminary data collected to refine materials and procedures before conducting the main study. (p. 17)

placebo effect How subjects' behavior is influenced by their belief that they are being "treated" (e.g., given a drug). (p. 10)

programmatic research A series of studies on a given topic. (p. 12)

quasi-experimental method Research method characterized by control of some variables while others are allowed to vary naturally. (p. 9)

statement of hypothesis Formal expression of a proposal for a research project. (p. 12)

subject bias How subjects' beliefs about what they should do in an experiment affect their responses. (p. 10)

subject population Target group of subjects for a study. (p. 15)

theory Explanations or predictions of observable behavior based on unobservable states. (p. 6)

Designing Experiments

Irwin P. Levin and James V. Hinrichs

I n this chapter we elaborate on the ideas presented in chapter 1 and discuss specific issues in designing experiments. We include detailed descriptions of commonly used experimental designs. By way of reviewing some of the material in chapter 1 and previewing the material for chapter 2, table 2.1 summarizes the steps in conducting a research study. The chapter concludes with an example that illustrates the various choice points one encounters in designing and conducting an experiment.

Issues in Designing Experiments

After a research idea has been translated into a specific question or hypothesis, the plan for obtaining the data necessary to answer the question must be formulated. The experimenter must anticipate how the data to be gathered can be used to bear directly on the question or hypothesis of interest. The answers to the many decisions involved in planning a study constitute the "design" of the experiment. In this section we describe how research questions and hypotheses can be tested, with an emphasis on manipulation and control of variables with the experimental method. Specific experimental design considerations, such as whether to use the same or different subjects in each experimental condition, choice of experimental tasks, and techniques for analyzing and presenting research results, are also discussed.

Although the decisions are discussed separately, it is important to remember that one decision may strongly affect or change another. Classifying one experimental characteristic as part of the design and another as part of the process of executing the experiment is very arbitrary. Practical considerations such as available subject populations or equipment may also impose constraints on how an experiment is designed.

Our goal here is to outline the primary concerns in designing an experiment and to introduce the most important ways to examine and to control factors that affect behavior. Full understanding of all of the nuances of experimental design is difficult to achieve without working through several examples of each design. We describe a few brief examples in this chapter and present more examples in later chapters.

Manipulation and Control

Manipulation and control are the cornerstones of the experimental method. Suppose that your research question concerns how people react to sounds of different loudness. You could observe an individual at home and at work during specific periods of the day and record his or her reactions to the alarm clock going off, the telephone ringing, a neighbor's stereo being turned on, traffic sounds while driving to work, a jet flying overhead, and so forth. There are several problems here. The first is that it may not be possible to measure accurately the loudness of the different sounds. Even if you could do this, the sounds would differ from each other in ways other than loudness. They would vary in pitch and duration and they would occur with different background noises. Furthermore, the person's level of attention and arousal would differ at the different times when the sounds occurred.

You could, however, *manipulate* loudness (sound intensity) as an independent variable by employing an apparatus that allows you to set specific decibel levels. Experimental subjects would be brought into the laboratory to react to a predetermined sequence of tones of varying intensity. These tones would vary only in intensity (decibel level). Other features such as frequency (pitch) of tone, duration of tone, and level of background noise would be held constant across variations in intensity. Also, because the experimental session would be relatively short, you might assume that factors such as the subject's attention and arousal would be approximately constant throughout. In other words, these various other factors would be *controlled* (held constant) while only the independent variable (sound intensity) was systematically manipulated.

TABLE 2.1   **Steps in Conducting a Research Study**

Step	Comments
Formulating a Research Question	Research questions should be sufficiently specific to be subject to empirical test. Literature review is helpful in revealing earlier theoretical and methodological developments.
Designing the Experiment	
Choice of Subject Population	Nonhuman subjects tend to be used when the research question calls for genetic and environmental manipulations not feasible with humans. Human subjects tend to be used for research questions dealing with verbal behavior or higher mental processes. Both human and nonhuman subjects should be treated in a humane manner, following established ethical guidelines. Generalizing results from one subject population to another requires empirical validation.
Within-Subject vs. Between-Subjects Manipulation	Repeated measure (within-subject) designs provide more control over subject variables but are subject to possibly confounding carryover effects. Control over subject variables in between-subjects designs rests on randomization or matching procedures. Sometimes experimental control over behavior can be demonstrated in single-subject designs.
Choice of Behavioral Measure and Task	Responses recorded in the experimental task must be sensitive to changes in the independent variables.
Data Analysis	Data analysis involves matching the appropriate statistical test (see chapter 3) with the experimental design employed in the study.
Preparing the Report	The research is not complete until it has been communicated to others. (See chapter 12 for a recommended format for preparing a research report.)

The laboratory setting also permits control to be exerted over the type of reaction obtained from the subject. The research question being addressed helps determine which dependent variable measures to take. Here are a few examples. (1) If the purpose is to determine the relationship between subjective estimates of loudness and the actual decibel levels of the tones, then the subject might be asked to rate on a fixed numerical scale how loud each tone was perceived to be. (2) If the question is how the presentation of tones of different intensity affects performance on a mental task, then the subject could be asked to perform arithmetic tasks such as adding columns of numbers while listening to the tones. (3) If the purpose is to examine how subjects react internally to sounds of different intensity, then the subject might sit passively while the experimenter records heart rate, pulse, and so

on. All three measures—and many others that could be devised—are potential indicators of the effect of loudness on behavior, and each addresses a different research question.

Classification of Variables

The variable or variables manipulated in an experiment are called *independent variables*. The independent variable may also sometimes be referred to as the experimental variable and its effect on behavior is sometimes called the "experimental effect" or the "treatment effect." Other variables with potential effects on performance in an experiment are called **extraneous variables.** When extraneous variables pertain to subject characteristics such as age, gender, and educational background, they are sometimes called **subject variables** or organismic variables. When the effects of extraneous variables are held constant across experimental conditions (levels of the independent variable), these variables are said to be *controlled*. Control can be achieved both statistically (e.g., by using random assignment of subjects to conditions—as will be illustrated in box 2.1—so there is no bias for, say, assigning more motivated or more experienced subjects to one condition rather than another) and experimentally (e.g., by keeping background noise constant and sufficiently low so that it does not affect performance in any experimental condition). The behavior or behaviors being measured in an experiment are called *dependent variables*. Note the logic of the terms independent and dependent variables. In a carefully controlled experiment, changes in the observed or measured behavior (dependent variables) will depend on changes in the manipulated (independent) variables.

The potential ability to determine cause and effect is the major strength of the experimental approach. When we can be relatively sure that all extraneous variables have been controlled, we can say that changes in the dependent variables are caused by changes in the independent variable(s).

Operational Definitions

Recall that in our last example a variety of dependent variables were candidates for the general class of behavior "reaction to sounds." Both independent and dependent variables have to be defined explicitly in terms of the operations used to manipulate or measure them. A number of examples were given in table 1.1. Such definitions are called **operational definitions** and they are very important because they communicate exactly what was done in an experiment. A study that defines the dependent variable "aggression" in terms of number of hits to inanimate objects (e.g., children's punching doll) may produce results quite different from a study that defines "aggression" in terms of tissue damage inflicted by one animal on another animal. A study that defines the independent variable "incentive" in terms of monetary rewards may produce different results from a study that defines "incentive" in terms of instructional

appeals to work hard. Even the use of the same type of incentive may produce different results in different studies if different levels of incentive are used in the two studies. After providing the operational definition of an independent variable, the investigator should specify the particular levels selected. While the choice of an operational definition may seem somewhat arbitrary, good operational definitions have several features in common such as objectivity, reliability, validity, and ease of implementation. Most of you have a general notion of the concepts of reliability and validity. You will be given a detailed explanation of their role in experimental psychology later in this chapter. If you notice examples of apparently conflicting results in two studies of the same relationship, you should compare the operational definitions the researchers used and the levels they selected for the independent variables, as well as differences in subject populations.

Confounding

A major concern in designing research is to avoid confounding the effects of two or more variables. **Confounding** is said to occur when changes in behavior are due to the influence of two or more variables whose effects on behavior cannot be separated. A poorly designed experiment is apt to lead to confounding. Its results may be worthless and misleading because you attribute behavior to one cause when it was really another. Consider our hypothetical study of reactions to tones of varying intensity. If louder tones were inadvertently of higher pitch than softer tones, then changes in response as a function of tone intensity would be confounded with changes due to pitch. Such an experiment would lack internal validity because valid inferences of the cause of the observed behavior could not be made. (This does not mean that the effects of two variables can never be separated. The problem of examining both the separate and combined effects of two or more independent variables is a general one discussed later in this chapter.)

Here's another more subtle example that will be developed more fully in the chapter on clinical psychology. For years it was thought that the most appropriate control group to use in a study of the effectiveness of a particular clinical treatment or therapy was a nontreated "waiting list" group—a group of potential candidates for treatment who were willing to wait for a period of time that was equivalent to the time in treatment of the experimental (treated) group. It is now recognized that individuals who are willing to be in such a group may be atypical in their motivation to receive treatment and may in fact be obtaining treatment from a different source. Such treatment would represent a confounding factor when comparing subjects in the experimental and control groups and could lead to rejection of an effective therapy. As we will see in chapter 10, more recent studies of therapy effectiveness include additional control conditions.

Another common source of confounding is subject variables. We want to avoid bias in the assignment of subjects to experimental conditions. For example, if you were obtaining volunteer subjects for an experiment, you would not want to assign the initial volunteers (who might be the most motivated) to one experimental condition (one level of the independent variable) and the later volunteers to another condition (a different level of the independent variable). In such a case the researcher might conclude that the first condition produced superior performance when it really did not. Random assignment of subjects to experimental conditions decreases the likelihood of unnecessary biases. Box 2.1 illustrates the most direct way to assign subjects to conditions so as to avoid confounding subject variables with independent variables.

Randomization

Subjects in a research study will differ in motivation, ability, experience, and attentiveness. All these factors could affect performance on the experimental task. One crucial distinguishing feature of the experimental method is that subjects can be assigned at random to experimental conditions. This is not true of correlational methods or even "quasi-experimental" methods. **Randomization** eliminates systematic biasing effects in the composition of experimental groups by virtue of providing

each subject an equal chance of being selected for any given experimental condition.

In order to highlight the role of randomization in the experimental method, let us briefly discuss a topic that will be covered in more detail in the chapter on social psychology. The topic is "social roles"—the study of how we conform to the roles given us in our society. In one famous study called the "Stanford Prison Study," volunteer subjects were asked to play the role of a prisoner or a guard in a simulated prison setting. Randomization was used to assign subjects to roles. To make a long story short, subjects played their assigned roles all too well. There were actual riots among "prisoners" and cases of brutality among "guards."

Suppose that this study had been conducted by going into an actual prison and observing the behavior of real prisoners and guards. It would have been virtually impossible to separate the effects of subject variables underlying which members of our society end up as prisoners and which as guards from people's adherence to the roles they are assigned in the prison society. Only by assigning subjects at random to roles was the Stanford Prison Study able to determine that individuals who are otherwise indistinguishable act quite differently depending on the roles to which they are assigned. The use of random assignment of subjects to conditions in a naturalistic setting is often referred to as a **field experiment.**

Experimental Design Considerations

A major issue in experimental design is whether to manipulate an independent variable within-subject or between-subjects. **Within-subject manipulations** are those in which each subject receives every level of the independent variable. **Between-subjects manipulations** are those in which different subjects receive each level of the independent variable. The main advantage of a within-subject design is that subject characteristics are held constant across experimental conditions. The main advantage of a between-subjects design is that it rules out possible contaminating influences when a subject goes from one experimental condition to another.

BOX 2.1

Random Assignment to Conditions

Suppose that an investigator wants to assign an equal number of subjects at random to two different experimental conditions, Condition E and Condition C. Random assignment insures that each subject has an equal chance of being selected for Condition E or Condition C. Methods such as drawing names out of a hat or tossing coins can be used, but a table of random numbers (found in virtually all statistics books) is the most convenient method. A table of random numbers has the properties that each numeral between 0 and 9 has an equal chance of falling in each cell of the table and the selection of numbers for any two cells are independent of each other. Portions of such a table (from Snedecor, G. W. (1950). *Everyday statistics*. Dubuque, IA: Wm. C. Brown.) are reproduced below.

39591	66082	48626	95780	55228
46304	97377	43462	21739	14566
99547	60779	22734	23678	44895
06743	63537	24553	77225	94743
69568	65496	49033	88577	98606
68198	69571	34349	73141	42640
27974	12609	77428	64441	49008
50552	20688	02769	63037	15494
74687	02033	98290	62635	88877
49303	76629	71897	30990	62923
89734	39183	52026	14997	15140
74042	40747	02617	11346	01884
84706	31375	67053	73367	95349
83664	21365	28882	48926	45435
47813	74854	73388	11385	99108
00371	56525	38880	53702	09517
81182	48434	27431	55806	25389
75242	35904	73077	24537	81354
96239	80246	07000	09555	55051
82988	17440	85311	03360	38176
77599	29143	89088	57593	60036
61433	33118	53488	82981	44709
76008	15045	45440	84062	52363
26494	76598	85834	10844	56300
46570	88558	77533	33359	07830

Now suppose that the investigator has 50 subjects available for the study. The subjects should be numbered 1 to 50 in any convenient manner (e.g., alphabetically or by order of signing up for the experiment). The first 25 subject-numbers encountered in the table of random numbers can be assigned to Condition E and the rest to Condition C. Because two-digit numbers are involved, adjacent pairs of columns of numerals are scanned from top to bottom. Starting in the upper left-hand corner,* the first two numbers encountered are 39 and 46. These are in the desired set 1 to 50, and the subjects with these numbers are assigned to Condition E. The next number is 99, which is not in the set, so it is skipped. The next number is 06 and the subject with this number is assigned to Condition E. Later we encounter the number 46 for a second time, but it is disregarded because that subject has already been assigned to Condition E. And so it goes until 25 distinct numbers between 1 and 50 have been selected and those subjects have been assigned to Condition E. The remaining subjects are assigned to Condition C.

It should be noted that while this method eliminates bias in the assignment of subjects to conditions, it does not guarantee that the distribution of subject variables will be identical in the two conditions. (Randomness refers to the method of selecting subjects, not the results obtained.) It would be surprising, for example, if the two samples had exactly the same mean IQ. However, as the sample size increases, the closer should be the mean IQ (or the mean of any subject variable) of the two samples.

*Rather than entering the table in this systematic way, you may want to enter it unsystematically. One way to do this would be to arbitrarily pick two cells of the table (without first looking at the numbers in those cells) and use the numbers in these cells to determine the rows and columns marking initial entry into the table. When there are several pages of random numbers, coin flips or the roll of a die can be used to select a page.

Designs using within-subject manipulations are also called *repeated measures designs* because repeated measures, representing different levels of the independent variable, are obtained for each subject. For example, in a study of learning using a fixed number of trials, "trial number" is a repeated measures independent variable because each subject performs on each trial. In a study designed to measure pain sensitivity in rats, "shock level" is a repeated measures independent variable because each rat receives each level of shock. As an example of a between-subjects manipulation, consider the simple comparison of an experimental group to a control group. The two groups of subjects are treated alike except that one group of subjects receives an experimental treatment and the other group of subjects does not. As another example, consider a study designed to examine rate of learning as a function of reinforcement magnitude. Different groups of subjects receive different amounts of reward.

Within-Subject Manipulations

The major strength of within-subject manipulations is that they eliminate the possible confounding influences of subject variables by using the same subjects at each level of the independent variable. Thus, there is no need to be concerned that differences in age, gender, IQ, etc. of the subjects will become confounded with the effects of the independent variables. Because every subject serves in every condition of the experiment, all subject variables are guaranteed to be equally distributed over all levels of the independent variable. In this sense, subjects in a within-subject design are said to serve as their own controls. Another desirable feature is the ability to increase the amount of data provided by each subject and thus reduce the number of subjects needed.

The major concern in using within-subject designs is the potential impact on later behavior of earlier events and reactions to these events. In some studies of learning and transfer of training, **carryover effects** are the object of study. In other cases, however, carryover effects are not of interest but they must be controlled in order to obtain unconfounded measures of the effects of the variables of primary interest. Consider a comparison of the difficulty of learning two different foreign languages such as French and Spanish. If the same person learned both languages during successive eight-week periods, then performance on the second language might suffer because of the confusion caused by mixing up the two languages. If the amount of this confusion is roughly the same when going from French to Spanish as when going from Spanish to French, then a simple procedure can handle the problem. **Counterbalancing** of experimental conditions, with one-half the subjects receiving the AB sequence and one-half receiving the BA sequence, ensures that progressive changes in behavior (sometimes known as "progressive error") are distributed equally across experimental conditions. Expanded discussion and illustrations of counterbalancing are presented in box 2.2.

Now suppose that the carryover effects differ for different sequences, such as when going from French to Spanish causes more confusion than when going from Spanish to French. For a more obvious case, consider that Condition A involves the administration of a drug and Condition B involves the administration of a placebo (e.g., a sugar pill that looks like the drug but has none of its active ingredients), and a motor task is used such as playing a video game. When the conditions are given in the AB sequence, performance in Condition B may be influenced by the physiological carryover effects of the drug administered in Condition A. Even a strong drug effect may go undetected because there might be no differential in performance at the times when Conditions A and B were administered. Of course, no such carryover effects occur in the BA sequence. In this case transfer is different in the AB and BA sequences, and counterbalancing procedures will not solve the problem. Why would you not want to give everyone the BA sequence?[1]

---

[1] The BA sequence may artificially favor Condition A because of the benefits of practice in performing a motor task for the second time.

BOX 2.2

Counterbalancing Procedures

Counterbalancing is a procedure by which the effects of a progressive process such as practice, fatigue, or boredom are equated across experimental conditions. Suppose, for example, that you are conducting an experiment to compare preferences for wines A, B, C, and D. Each subject tastes each type of wine and rates the pleasantness of its taste on a 10-point scale. To reduce "aftertastes" each subject sips water between each taste of wine. However, it is possible that the first wines tasted will have an advantage over the later wines because of the uniqueness of the initial experiences. Another possibility is that wines tasted later will have an advantage because the subject's taste buds have become sensitized. In other words, the order in which the wines are tasted can be a factor. Counterbalancing can handle this problem in one of two ways. Consider the following four sequences of tasting the wines:

1. A B C D
2. B C D A
3. C D A B
4. D A B C

The critical feature of this set of four sequences is that each type of wine appears equally in each position, i.e., A is first in sequence 1, second in sequence 4, and so forth. One way to use this counterbalanced set is to randomly divide the subjects into four groups and assign a different sequence to each group. While each subject could be influenced by the particular position in which wines were sampled, position effects would tend to cancel out when compiling group averages. Another way to use this set of

sequences is to have each subject taste each wine several times and then average the responses. That is, the wines might be tasted first in the sequence DABC. Then the wines would be tasted according to the sequence BCDA, and so forth. This balances position effects for each individual subject—at the possible expense of the subject's sobriety. If only two tastes of each wine are permitted, then the simpler procedure of choosing one sequence and then reversing it (e.g., ABCD, DCBA) can be used.

Similar procedures can be used even when each subject receives only one experimental condition. Suppose four different types of incentives are to be compared in a human learning experiment using one-hour experimental sessions. Suppose also that subject motivation for being in such a study decreases progressively and linearly over the hours 1:00 to 5:00 P.M. Apart from any effect of the incentives used in the study, performance would tend to be better in the early afternoon sessions than in the later afternoon sessions. Now let the letters A, B, C, D stand for the different incentive conditions. The sequences described above would represent the order of testing incentive conditions during a particular day. Counterbalancing would be achieved by using each sequence once during each four-day period. So, on Day 1 you might use the randomly selected sequence BCDA, which means that Incentive B would be given at 1:00, C at 2:00, D at 3:00, and A at 4:00. On Day 2 you might use ABCD, and so forth. You could then compare the mean scores for incentive conditions A, B, C, and D without concern for the possible confounding effects of time of the day when the condition was administered.

Unless the experimental sessions can be spaced far enough apart to insure that drug carryover effects do not occur, the experimenter must abandon the use of a within-subject manipulation of drug versus placebo. Other examples of independent variable manipulations that could lead to differential transfer if used in a within-subject design are the introduction of different learning strategies or motivating conditions. Once subjects discover a

strategy that works or have their motivation peaked, it is difficult to reverse the procedure.

Most research questions are concerned with how the behavior of an individual will vary across levels of an independent variable. The most direct test would then require a within-subject design. This, however, is not always wise because of the possibility of uncontrolled carryover effects. The researcher may then turn to a between-subjects design, making the implicit assumption that *differences observed between groups represent differences that would be observed in an individual's behavior across experimental conditions* if that individual was not affected by prior exposure to other conditions. So, for example, when one group receives a drug and a different group receives a placebo, the research question is really, "If an individual is given the drug, will he or she behave differently than if not given the drug?" The between-subjects design, while changing the question to, "Will individuals given the drug behave differently than other individuals not given the drug?", may still be the best method to use in this case.

Between-Subjects Manipulations

Between-subjects manipulations are, of course, free of the carryover effects that can complicate or invalidate interpretation of results of within-subject manipulations. Also, there are some tasks that do not make sense when repeated several times by the same subject. Learning to drive a car is something that most of us do only once. So, a researcher interested in studying how various factors influence the speed of learning to drive would not use the same subject in more than one experimental condition. Between-subjects manipulations do not have the degree of control over subject variables that within-subject manipulations have. The result is less "statistical power." As is explained in chapter 3, statistical power is the probability that a given experimental effect will be correctly detected. Thus, in situations where power is low because of lack of control over subject variables, there will be a reduced likelihood of detecting the effect of the independent variable. There are, however, ways of reducing differences between subjects when between-subjects manipulations are used. Some methods are extensions of careful thought and common sense: Make the experimental setting as uniform as possible from subject to subject. Use consistent, unambiguous experimental instructions. Use computerized devices to assure uniform presentation of stimuli. Standardize ways of handling animals to minimize differential treatment across subjects. Subject variables such as age, gender, and education level that cannot be manipulated can be controlled

through randomization, matching, and selection of homogeneous subject populations. An example of a homogeneous population would be 4-year-old boys attending a particular preschool. With this population, differences in response to viewing violent vs. nonviolent TV shows could not be due to age, gender, or geographic location.

Matching is a more elaborate way of achieving control of subject variables than is randomization. If two experimental groups are matched on age, IQ, previous experience, and so forth, then differences between the two groups attributable to different treatment conditions will not be confounded with differences in these subject variables. Gender composition can be matched by using the same female to male ratio in each group. Such matching procedures may seem so logical as to make you wonder why they are not always used. However, there are some practical problems. How do you decide what factors to match on? Matching serves no useful purpose if the matching factor is not at least moderately correlated with and predictive of the behavior being measured, and one often does not know this until after the study has been conducted. For example, can you think of tasks in which IQ score should not be a factor? Some information that might be useful for matching purposes, such as IQ scores, may be difficult to obtain and not worth the effort. The result is that the majority of studies using between-subjects manipulations rely on completely randomized assignment of subjects to treatment levels. Random groups and matched groups designs are described in more detail in the next section, which discusses specific experimental designs and how they are used to achieve experimental control.

Alternative Designs for Achieving Experimental Control

In this section we briefly describe several distinct types of experimental design, discuss how they attempt to achieve control of extraneous variables, and preview their role in the various chapters of this text. One basic distinction is whether one variable or "factor" is manipulated or multiple factors are manipulated.

Single Factor Designs

Two Independent Random Groups

In the prototypical **independent random group design,** subjects are assigned at random to one of two conditions, the experimental condition or the control condition. This would be classified as a single factor, between-subjects design, with two levels. The subjects in the first group receive some type of experimental treatment (the administration of a drug or therapy, the presence of a reinforcer, a set of motivating instructions, etc.) while subjects in the other group do not receive the treatment. Control is achieved two ways. First, the two groups are treated alike in all ways except for the presence or absence of the experimental treatment. In that way, comparison of performance in the two groups will reveal the effect of the treatment. While the principle of holding all factors constant except the one being manipulated is simple and straightforward, its implementation may not be so simple. For example, if subjects think they are going to receive a treatment that will affect them a certain way, their expectations may influence their performance and bias the results of the experiment. (Recall the example from chapter 1 of the subject receiving a placebo who thought it was Valium.) Thus, the double-blind procedure described earlier is often applied in such cases. Furthermore, it is sometimes difficult to manipulate just one factor and hold everything else the same. For instance, if rats drink more when they are deprived of food, both thirst and hunger are being varied when amount of food is manipulated by the experimenter. If this fact is critical to the interpretation of the results, additional controls might be included in the design.

The second way in which control is achieved is through the use of randomization. Random assignment of subjects to conditions tends to control for subject variables that may confound the results of an experiment if their distribution differs between experimental conditions. Randomization does not guarantee that the effects of subject variables will be equalized across conditions, but it does eliminate systematic sources of bias that would occur if non-random assignment was used.

The experimental group-control group comparison is not the only example of a two independent random groups design. At a general level, the design is defined as one in which there is a single independent variable with two levels, such as comparison of two types of incentive or two sets of learning instructions. A different group of subjects receives each level of the independent variable. One example illustrated later in this book is an attitude change study in which some subjects are given "one-sided" arguments and other subjects are given "two-sided" arguments. Another example is judgment of medical risk where two different groups of subjects are given the same objective information expressed in different terms: the benefits of performing breast self-examination for some subjects and the dangers of not performing breast self-examination for others. A statistical test for comparing performance in the two conditions is the t-test for independent groups, which is illustrated in box 3.5 in the chapter on statistical inference.

The basic design and statistical analysis become more complicated when we try to deal with the possibility that particular subject variables are related to performance in the experiment. We might, for example, want to see if a treatment effect is different for males and females. Because this interest should have been decided before the experiment was actually conducted, the randomization procedure would have been altered slightly. Assignment of subjects to conditions should have been done separately for males and females so that half of the males were in each condition and half of the females were in each condition. "Gender" then becomes a second factor in the experimental design and statistical analysis.

More than Two Independent Random Groups

Many experiments in psychology utilize the principles of control described for the two independent random groups design but require more than two levels of the independent variable. There may be three, four, five, or more levels of the independent variable and each group of subjects receives a different level. For example, the chapter on social psychology (chapter 9) describes studies aimed at quantifying the effects on helping behavior of variables such as number of bystanders observing a person in need of assistance. In such cases we do not want to limit ourselves to only two levels of the variable. Another example would be dosage of a drug like Valium. We would create a single factor between-subjects design with four or five levels. We determine the number of conditions by the number of levels we want to compare and then randomly assign different subjects to each condition. The usual statistical test for comparing performance between groups is an extension of the t-test for independent groups. It is a one-way analysis of variance, as illustrated in box 3.6.

Matched Pairs

In independent random groups designs the assignment of subjects to one experimental condition is independent of the assignment of subjects to another experimental condition. By contrast, in a **matched pairs design** the assignment of a subject to one condition determines the assignment of a subject to the other condition. This then is a variant of the typical single factor between-subjects design, with two levels. Matched pairs are formed by taking two subjects with the same or similar values on a subject variable such as age, IQ score, or income, and randomly assigning (e.g., by flipping a coin) one member of the pair to one condition and the other to the other condition. Therefore, the two groups are guaranteed to be equated on that subject variable, rather than trusting to complete randomization to accomplish this. That variable can then be ruled out as a cause of any differences observed between the two groups. If more than two experimental conditions are involved, matched triplets, quadruples, and so on can be formed in analogous ways as matched pairs.

The two groups formed in a matched pairs design are compared by taking the difference between the responses of each pair of subjects. In this manner, statistical power can be increased by virtue of factoring out variability due to the matching variable. However, unless the correlation between the matching variable and the dependent variable is of at least moderate value,

statistical power can actually be decreased with this method because the difference scores may be highly variable. The practical problem is determining on which, if any, subject variables to match. For example, it would probably be a waste of time and effort to form matched pairs of subjects based on IQ scores in, say, a visual perception study. Even in a learning experiment, if a homogeneous subject population such as college students is used, there is not likely to be a high correlation between performance and IQ. (See the discussion of the "range effect" in chapter 3.)

In studies of learning and memory, matching can be achieved by providing a pretest of the same task as in the main experiment. Subjects can then be paired on the basis of their pretest scores, which are apt to be highly correlated with performance in the experiment. The main pitfall here is that prior trials of the experimental task can change performance on the experimental task to the extent that differences between groups are reduced or perhaps even eliminated. For example, after practice on initial trials, all groups may perform at near-perfect levels. This is referred to as a "ceiling effect" because factors that might ordinarily improve performance have no room to show improvement.

A popular method of achieving control through a matching procedure is the use of twins, especially identical twins. When one twin is put into one experimental condition and the other twin is put into another condition, the two conditions can be compared with confidence that most subject variables can be ruled out as causes of observed differences in behavior. Of course, a population of twins is not always handy. Nevertheless, some classic studies of the differential effects of heredity and environment have been conducted with twins (see chapter 10).

Randomized blocks design is an extension of the matched pairs design in which subjects are rank-ordered on the basis of a subject variable such as IQ score. Subjects are then arranged in blocks corresponding in size to the number of levels of the independent variable. For instance, if there are three levels of the independent variable, the individuals with the top three IQ scores would constitute the first block, the next three highest would constitute the second block, and so on. Random assignment of subjects to experimental conditions can then be done separately within each block of subjects as illustrated below.

Block	Rank	IQ Score	Condition
1	1	126	A
1	2	125	C
1	3	123	B
2	4	120	C
2	5	119	A
2	6	119	B
3	7	116	B
3	8	113	C
3	9	111	A

Note that this design insures that the average IQ scores will be nearly identical in experimental conditions A, B, and C.

Repeated Measures

A logical extension of the matched pairs design that overcomes some of its pitfalls is the repeated measures or within-subject design. Each subject serves as his or her own matched control by participating in each experimental condition. As indicated earlier, the decision to use such a design may rest on whether or not subjects' performance in one experimental condition will affect their performance in a later condition. However, some studies are inherently of this nature. A common example of this single factor within-subject design with two levels is the **before-and-after design.** In clinical psychology the investigator often needs to compare behavior before and after treatment. In social psychology the investigator may want to examine how a person's attitude changes following a particular persuasive communication.

Sometimes these before-and-after designs take on the characteristics of **longitudinal studies** because they span a considerable length of time. Studies of the effectiveness of a particular clinical treatment may be concerned with the effects of long-term treatment, say six months or a year, as well as the consequences long after treatment has ceased. We will examine in chapter 9 a longitudinal study in which the effects of childhood exposure to violence on TV affects aggressive behavior in adulthood.

In some areas of experimental psychology the use of repeated measures goes beyond before-and-after designs. For example, in chapter 4 we examine studies in which the goal is to determine how perceptions vary over a wide range of stimulus values. In order to control for individual differences in the use of psychological measurement scales, each subject responds to all stimulus values, resulting in a single factor within-subject design with as many as ten levels.

Single Subject

An extreme example of the repeated measures design is the **single subject design,** where each individual subject is treated differently or where there may, in fact, be only one subject. The latter situation is sometimes referred to as a "case study," although this term is often reserved for observations of an individual's behavior without experimental interventions. Traditional statistical tests are, of course, meaningless in such situations. The basic questions here are how experimental control can be exercised for a single subject and how results from a single subject can be generalized to others. Because of these questions, these designs have seen limited use in psychology. There have been, however, some interesting examples such as the famous case of Little Albert (see box 2.3).

While the case of Little Albert is a dramatic example of changing an individual's behavior through controlled laboratory techniques, extraordinary efforts must often be taken in order to infer causality in single subject experiments. Studies of behavior modification in children provide good examples (Bijou & Baer, 1967). Consider the case of a child whose parents were concerned because he did not interact with other children. Researchers attempted to modify the boy's behavior by rewarding him for playing with other children. The boy was given praise by adult supervisors in a playground setting

BOX 2.3

Watson's Study of Little Albert

Perhaps the most famous psychological study using a single subject design was conducted in 1920 by John Watson, the founder of the Behaviorism school of psychology, and his colleague, Rosalie Rayner. Conditioned fear was established in an 11-month-old boy, Albert, by pairing the appearance of a previously unfeared white rat with the striking of a steel bar behind Albert's head. The loud noise produced great fright in Albert. After repeated pairings of the loud noise with the presence of the rat, the fear initially associated with the loud noise came to be elicited by appearance of the rat even when the bar was not struck. Control of behavior was achieved in this study by manipulating the relationship between the presence of the white rat and the sounding of the loud noise. On initial trials with no noise, Albert showed no fear of

the rat and appeared to want to play with it. On trials where presence of the rat was paired with loud noise, Albert showed fear of the rat. The researchers were thus able to conclude that fear of the rat was the result of a conditioning process because no such fear occurred before the pairing of rat and loud noise. On later trials they were even able to show that fear of the white rat generalized to other white furry objects (Watson & Rayner, 1920).

The researchers undoubtedly recognized that the time course of the conditioned fear in Albert may not be the same for all children or for all types of fear, but they felt that the process by which the fear was conditioned represents a model that is common to many kinds of fears and phobias.

---

whenever he approached other children but not at other times. Compared to an initial base rate period when the boy was allowed to choose his own activities, the amount of time the boy spent with other children rose dramatically. Then the researchers did a strange thing. For a period of time they rewarded the child for interacting with adults, not children. They did it to show that the child's behavior was in fact under control of the researcher's reinforcement contingencies. (Can you think of other reasons why the boy started interacting more with other children?[2]) The researchers demonstrated that the boy's behavior was in fact under their control by showing that he interacted more with children when that behavior brought praise and he interacted more with adults when that brought praise. They then went back to reinforcing the boy for playing with other children, eventually removing the external reinforcement when the child no longer needed the external reward the adults were providing.

---

[2] Once the boy started playing with other children, he may have found it enjoyable. This, of course, is the ultimate goal but at this stage of the study the researchers did not want to come to premature conclusions.

Single subject designs are also used in some perception and psychophysics experiments where it can be argued that the responses of any one individual are typical of the population. Actually, two or three subjects may be tested to demonstrate that the pattern of behavior is the same for each one. At the opposite extreme, single subject designs may be used when the tested individual is virtually unique, as in cases of "memory experts" (see chapter 7), persons with "split brains" (disconnected brain hemispheres), or persons purporting "extrasensory perception." Generalization to a population is meaningless in such cases.

Multifactor or Factorial Designs

Despite our description of the "prototypical" experimental group-control group and before-and-after designs, many studies incorporate more than one independent variable manipulation. When all combinations of the selected levels of the independent variables or "factors" are included, the design is called a **factorial design.**

For example, consider the following hypothetical experiment. College students are asked to donate blood on a regular basis during a six-month period.

Half are offered $20 per donation and half are of-
fered $5. Now suppose that within these two groups
half are given a booklet describing the dire need for
blood within the community and half are not given
this booklet. This represents a 2 × 2 factorial design
with each of two factors having two levels each, resulting in four combinations, as illustrated in the
table below.

| | | Written Material | |
		None	Booklet
Monetary	$20	7	12
Incentive	$5	1	10

The average number of donations might reasonably be expected to be greater with a monetary incentive of $20 than with a monetary incentive of
$5, and it might also be expected to be greater for
those receiving the booklet than for those not receiving the booklet. In statistical terms, we would
say that there is a main effect for the amount of
monetary incentive and a main effect for the type
of written material. However, if the booklet is sufficiently compelling, then the amount of monetary
incentive should be less important to those receiving the booklet than to those not receiving the
booklet. This is known as an **interaction** effect, in
this case an interaction between the independent
variables, amount of monetary incentive and type
of written material, on the dependent variable,
number of blood donations. The numbers in the
cells of the above table illustrate such a pattern of
results. Without the booklet, an increase in monetary incentive from $5 to $20 leads to an increase of
6 in the average number of donations; with the
booklet the increase is only 2.

As a second example, suppose that you want to
compare two types of memory aids (e.g., visual imagery and rote memorization) across three levels of
amount of material to be recalled (as operationally
defined by number of items on a foreign language vocabulary list). This would be called a 2 × 3 (or 3 × 2)
factorial design to indicate the number of levels of

each factor. The multiplication sign also has a logical
role—to indicate the number of possible combinations or "cells." There are six possible combinations
of memory aid and list length in this example. In a
complete between-subjects factorial design, each
combination would be administered to a different
group of subjects, requiring six groups of subjects. In
a complete within-subject factorial design, each subject would be tested in each of the six combinations
and only one group would be required. In one possible mixed design, a different group of subjects would
be required for the different levels of one of the variables (e.g., memory aid) but each subject would receive all levels of the other variable (lists of different
lengths). In this example, two groups of subjects
would be required.

In a factorial design, the choices of whether to
use between-subjects or within-subject manipulations and whether to use matching techniques are
governed by the same principles as in single-variable
experiments. Box 3.7 illustrates how to apply analysis of variance to the data of a factorial experiment.
The important new concept in data analysis for factorial designs is that the interaction between variables, as well as the separate or main effect of each
variable, can be assessed.

The interaction between two variables is a measure of the extent to which the effect of one variable differs at different levels of the other variable.
In the preceding example, results might show that
one memory aid is better for relatively short lists
but the other is better for longer lists. We would
then say that there is an interaction between type
of memory aid and amount of material to be recalled. In this case it would not be appropriate to
make a generalized statement about which type of
aid was better; results depend on list length. If results showed that differences between memory aids
were the same for each list length, then we would
say that there is no interaction between the variables. Here we can make a generalizable statement
comparing the two memory aids for recall of foreign
language vocabulary lists.

FIGURE 2.1   Presence (upper panels) and absence (lower panels) of interaction effects as shown in tables and graphs. Note that the lines in the lower graph are parallel but those in the upper graph are not parallel.

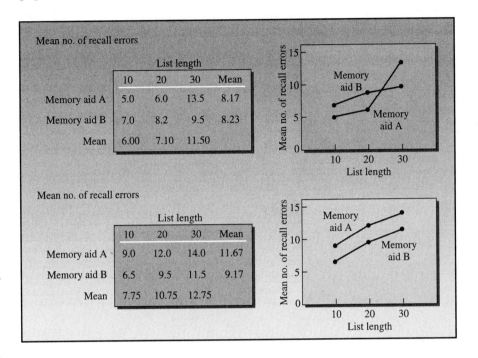

Figure 2.1 shows two ways of displaying the results from an experiment using a factorial design. The left panels give the mean response in each experimental condition in tabular form. Such a table readily shows the structure of the factorial design. A 2 × 3 factorial design corresponds to a table with 2 rows and 3 columns (or vice versa). The right panels plot the mean responses in graphic form.

Being able to read and interpret results provided in tables and graphs is an important skill, especially with factorial designs. Box 2.4 guides you through this exercise. Table 2.2 summarizes the basic characteristics of the various designs.

Choosing Behavioral Measures and Tasks

Having decided on an appropriate design for addressing the research question, the next important issue is what behavioral measures to use. Using the observational or correlational method, the question boils down to one of deciding which types of behavior to record, how to score or code them, and which types of behavior to ignore. For example, consider a developmental psychologist interested in parent-child communications. When observing the family at home or in a more controlled setting, the investigator may be concerned with the frequency and duration of both verbal and nonverbal communication. Who initiates it? Who dominates it? Is it friendly or unfriendly? Who terminates it? Other behaviors such as eating and drinking, watching TV, and playing with toys might be ignored except as they become the focus of parent-child communications. Although observing methods can be standardized and observers trained to perform with high reliability, a certain amount of subjectivity is inevitably involved.

The question is slightly different with the experimental method. Again the researcher selects

BOX 2.4

Tabular and Graphic Displays of Results from a Factorial Design

In the graph one of the independent variables is displayed on the abscissa (the horizontal axis) and the other independent variable is represented by different lines on the graph. In the present case list length is the variable plotted on the abscissa because it is a numerical variable with a logical order of progression. The ordinate (vertical axis) represents values of the dependent variable. (In practice it is not necessary to include both a table and graph of the same results. Try to reconstruct the graphs from the values given in the tables.)

The fact that errors increase with list length can be seen in the tables by comparing means for the three columns, and in the graphs by noting that the lines slope upward. The bottom table and graph clearly demonstrate the difference between memory aids: for each column in the table the mean errors in the top row are higher than the mean in the bottom row; the line in the graph for Memory Aid A is uniformly higher than the line for Memory Aid B. Comparison of memory aids is not so straightforward for the results depicted in the top table and graph.

The upper panels of figure 2.1 show results indicative of an interaction between memory aid and list length. The graphic mode of presentation makes it particularly clear that the comparative effect of Memory Aid A and Memory Aid B on recall errors varies for different list lengths. There is no overall superiority of one over the other; Memory Aid A leads to fewer errors with list lengths 10 and 20; Memory Aid B leads to fewer errors with list length 30.

The lower panels show results indicative of lack of interaction between the two variables. The parallel lines indicate that Memory Aid A leads to more recall errors than Memory Aid B and that this difference is the same for each list length. In the tabular form of presentation this corresponds to differences between rows that are the same for each column. In practice, it would be rare to find differences that are exactly equal; some variability would be expected due to chance factors. The ability to read and interpret such tables and graphs is particularly important when you consult original research reports in psychology journals.

---

which behaviors (dependent variables) to focus on, but the experiment can sometimes be designed to reduce extraneous responding so that recording and scoring are straightforward and possibly even automatic. This, however, is not always possible. Consider the dependent variable "intensity of aggressive acts," which might be of interest in both correlational and experimental research. To deal with the subjectivity in scoring such behaviors it is often desirable to have several independent, trained observer/scorers. The level of agreement between the scorers can be taken as a measure of the reliability of the measurements.

At this point we introduce two important concepts in measuring behavior: reliability and validity. **Reliability** refers to the repeatability of a measure of behavior. The goal is to develop measures that are sufficiently objective and precise that different scorers would arrive at the same results. In some cases this is a simple matter such as counting

the number of errors a subject makes in learning a list of abstract symbols in the laboratory. In other cases it is not so simple. Did the child in the aggression study willfully hit his or her classmate or was it merely a playful act?

We might also ask if our measures of errors in recall and number of times one child strikes another are actually measuring what we want them to—learning and aggression. We are then addressing the issue of **validity.** Number of errors on a list of abstract symbols may be a reliable measure but how revealing is it of the process of learning? What does it say about the way we learn things of importance in our everyday lives? The validity of conclusions based on a study of aggression rests on how realistic the measures are.

As we will see at various points in this text, reliability and validity have special significance in contexts such as clinical diagnosis and measuring attitudes toward important societal issues. (Think

TABLE 2.2   Summary of Experimental Designs

Design	Description	Main Advantages	Possible Pitfalls
Independent Random Groups	Subjects are assigned at random to each level of the independent variable.	Eliminates systematic biases in the assignment of subjects to experimental conditions.	Randomization may not equate all subject variables.
Matched Pairs	Pairs of subjects are matched on a subject variable, and one member of each pair is assigned at random to each level of the independent variable.	Eliminates confounding due to subject variables.	The matching variable must be known to be highly correlated with the dependent variable before increased statistical power is achieved.
Repeated Measures	The same subject receives all levels of the independent variable.	Each subject serves as his or her own control.	Differential transfer may occur where measures of performance in one experimental condition are confounded by performance in earlier conditions.
Single Subjects	Each individual subject represents a separate experiment.	In-depth analysis of a unique individual or situation.	The experimental manipulation must be powerful enough to show an effect in a single subject and be generalizable to other subjects.
Factorial Design	Two or more independent variables are manipulated. All possible combinations of levels of the variables are formed (e.g., 2×3 design means that there are two variables, one with 2 levels and one with 3 levels, forming 6 experimental conditions).	Can examine the separate and combined effects of several variables in a single experiment.	There may be such a large number of combinations that too many subjects would be needed.

about how each of the dependent variables operationalized in table 1.1 might be scored, how reliable each is likely to be, and how valid it is in representing behavior of importance outside the laboratory situation.)

The usefulness of a behavioral measure depends not only on its reliability and validity but on its sensitivity to changes in experimental conditions. The choice of measures usually depends on the research question and the investigator's knowledge of past research addressing similar questions. For example, counting the number of errors in a learning task will not necessarily show which of several incentive conditions is superior. If the learning task is too simple, few errors will be made even in the least effective motivational condition, and if the learning task is too difficult, many errors will be made in all conditions. Neither of these two situations is likely to provide a clear differentiation between experimental conditions. A pilot study is often necessary to determine task characteristics, such as level of task difficulty, that provide a reasonable chance of revealing differences between the experimental conditions.

Analyzing, Interpreting, and Reporting Results

Finally, after an experiment is conducted, the results must be analyzed, interpreted, and reported. Data analysis and interpretation depend on the original hypothesis, the design of the experiment, and on the methods and measures employed.

Data Analysis and Interpretation

Discussion of statistical concepts underlying data analysis and specific analytic procedures will be deferred until chapter 3. By way of a preview of this discussion, let us say that there must be a careful matching of experimental design features and appropriate statistical tests. For example, data obtained in observational or correlational studies are analyzed differently from data obtained in experimental studies. Dependent variables such as response time, which yield continuous, numerical data, are analyzed differently from dependent variables such as "success vs. failure," which take on only two possible values.

Reporting Research Results

Remember the old question about whether the tree falling in the forest made a sound if there was nobody there to hear it? An analogous question is whether research has been completed if it has not been reported. To be sure, the student of experimental psychology will learn from the experience of designing a study, collecting the data, and performing the appropriate statistical analysis. We would argue that the research is not complete until it has been communicated to others in some understandable form. If nothing else, having to make other people understand what you did, why you did it, and how you interpret what you found will help you understand these things better yourself. And, of course, progress in science rests on the ability to accumulate knowledge that has been gained from diverse sources. Chapter 12 will describe a convenient format for writing research reports and will provide several illustrations.

An Example

An experimental psychologist starts with the statement of a problem and then selects those methods that appear to lead to the most direct solution of the problem. Each methodological step must be critically evaluated in terms of its possible advantages and pitfalls. Now let us consider in some detail one example of the design of an experiment to examine a particular research problem.

An area of interest to researchers and students alike is the effect of mood on memory. Do we remember more when we are in a happy mood or in a sad mood, or does it not matter? Let's design a study to get at some aspects of this problem.

First let us consider the choice of subject population. The bulk of research in this area uses college students and there's no reason to believe that their memory would be affected by mood differently than anybody else's. Still, it would be a good idea to start with this handy population and then test the generality of our findings with other groups. (It wouldn't be too far beyond the stretch of imagination to design such a study with nonhumans. As we go through the various steps, think about how they might be done with animals.)

Are we going to use the experimental or correlational method? Perhaps the original idea for such a project came from the observation that when people are in a bad mood—including the researcher—they have great difficulty in remembering certain things. We are at the stage now, however, where we can utilize experimental manipulation and control for variables such as direction and severity of mood, type of material to be recalled, and when the to-be-recalled material was first learned. Thus, we will use the experimental method.

How are we to manipulate the independent variable mood? There are procedures whose reliability and validity have been established over the course of a number of studies, which can be used for our purposes. (No need to reinvent the wheel.) Basically, these procedures involve presenting subjects with either written or videotaped descriptions of happy or sad or neutral events. There are also standardized tests of depression and other moods that can be used to see if subjects' moods were indeed changed by our procedures. (We will see examples of such "manipulation checks" at several points in this book.) Should "mood" be manipulated as a within-subject or a between-subjects factor? There would be several problems with manipulating mood within subjects. First, we would worry about whether the first mood wore off before inducing the next mood. More importantly, a subject who received both a "happy" and a "sad" mood condition would be quite apt to "psych out" the experiment and realize that it was a study of mood effects. The subject might then respond in a biased manner to fulfill expectations. (Recall the discussion of subject biases in chapter 1.) So, we decide to use a between-subjects manipulation where subjects are assigned at random to three groups: happy mood, sad mood, neutral mood. As an ethical consideration we would want to make sure that no subjects will leave the experimental session in a state of depression caused by their participation. Typically, in such a study subjects in the sad mood condition are given a happy mood manipulation at the end of the session.

What materials are we going to ask our subjects to recall? There are a couple of ways we could go here. We could construct new material for them to recall or we could ask them to recall episodes or events in their own life. In order to make the study more lifelike, let's do the latter. What kinds of episodes or events? Here we might well add a second independent variable: the kind of event to be recalled. Because we are dealing with mood effects, why not look for a natural relationship between the mood the subjects are in and the type of material to be recalled? So, we'll ask a randomly chosen half of the subjects in each mood condition to write down as many pleasant events as they can recall in their personal life during the past two weeks (or any convenient period) and the other half to recall as many unpleasant events as possible.

To summarize, we have a 3 × 2 between-subjects factorial design with six different groups of subjects,

each randomly assigned to one combination of mood (happy, sad, or neutral) and type of material to be recalled (pleasant events in their life or unpleasant events). How will we operationally define the dependent variable or variables? In other words, how will we score the data? The most obvious way would be to simply count the number of episodes recalled in each condition. Additional measures could be taken such as asking independent raters to score the intensity of positive or negative feelings conveyed by each recalled episode. For either or both of these measures we would compare average values for positive and negative episodes supplied by subjects in positive, negative, or neutral moods.

One interesting result would be that subjects in a positive mood recalled more pleasant events than subjects in a negative mood, subjects in a negative mood recalled more unpleasant events than subjects in a positive mood, and subjects in a neutral mood fell somewhere in the middle. We leave it to you to guess the results of such a study or search the literature for a similar study. (Some studies like this are described in chapters 6 and 7.)

Note that several of our decisions were quite arbitrary, with suitable alternatives easily available. (Can you suggest what some of these might be?) Many of these choices depend on the knowledge, experience, judgment, and creativity of the researcher.

Summary and Conclusions

The first step in designing and conducting research is formulating a problem in a testable form. A review of the existing research literature can be helpful by pointing out the leading theories in the area and what methods have been used to test them. Steps in designing and conducting an experiment include choice of a subject population and sample, operationally defining the independent and dependent variables, selecting the way in which subjects are to be assigned to experimental conditions, and choosing data analysis techniques appropriate to the design of the experiment.

A problem to be avoided in research is confounding the influence of several variables such that inappropriate causal inferences are likely. Confounding occurs when subject variables or other extraneous variables are correlated with changes in the independent variables. The most basic principle of good experimental design is to eliminate the possibility of confounding by providing maximum control over extraneous variables. Other considerations in experimental design include specifying the most direct test of the research hypotheses and providing sufficient statistical power to detect the presence of experimental effects.

A number of basic experimental designs represent alternative ways of achieving control over extraneous variables by assigning subjects to experimental conditions. Independent random group designs use random assignment of subjects to conditions (levels of the independent variable), with a different group of subjects serving in each condition. Matching techniques are sometimes used as substitutes for complete randomization to insure that the groups are matched on selected subject variables (those subject characteristics that are correlated with performance on the experimental task). Repeated measures designs achieve the greatest control over subject variables by using the same subjects in each condition. The major concern with repeated measures designs is avoiding confounding due to carryover effects from one condition to another. In some cases these can be handled by applying counterbalancing procedures. In the most extreme form of repeated measures design, a single subject may be used or each subject may be treated differently. Such studies provide problems in generalizing the results to other individuals. Studies in which several independent variables are manipulated require special consideration of the way the levels of the various variables are combined. Factorial designs allow an assessment of the interaction between variables.

The choice of behavioral measures for a study should be based on several considerations. Foremost among these are the reliability of the measurements and how sensitive they are to changes in the experimental conditions.

A research project is not complete until the data have been analyzed and interpreted and a clear and concise report has been made. The analysis and interpretation of data are discussed in the next chapter.

Exercises

1. In each of the studies from exercise 5 of chapter 1 identify the independent and the dependent variables. What were the most important extraneous and subject variables and how were they controlled?

2. Think of a behavioral study where you could use yourself as the single subject. How did you arrive at your idea? Describe how you chose the independent and dependent variables. How would you operationally define them? How would you control other variables? What are your hypotheses? How would you test them without introducing personal bias? Do you think that your results would generalize to others?

3. Find two studies in the research literature that found apparently conflicting results. Try to explain the different results in terms of the different methods used, differences in subject populations, and the different ways in which the variables were operationally defined.

Glossary

before-and-after design Comparing subjects' performance before and after an experimental treatment. (36)

between-subjects designs Experimental designs in which different subjects are assigned to different levels of the independent variable. (29)

carryover effects The impact on later behavior of earlier events and reactions to them. (31)

confounding When changes in behavior are due to the influence of two or more variables whose effects on behavior cannot be separated. (28)

counterbalancing Subjects in a within-subject design are assigned to different sequences of experimental conditions such that progressive changes in behavior ("progressive error") are distributed equally across experimental conditions. (31)

extraneous variables Variables other than manipulated (independent) variables with potential effects on behavior. (27)

factorial design More than one independent variable is manipulated and all combinations of the selected levels of the independent variables are included (e.g., 3×2 design means that 6 combinations are formed by combining 3 levels of Variable A with 2 levels of Variable B). (37)

field experiment Use of the experimental method, including random assignment of subjects to conditions, in a naturalistic setting. (29)

independent random group design Between-subjects design in which subjects are assigned at random to different levels of the independent variable. (34)

interaction Statistical measure of the extent to which the effect of one variable differs at different levels of another variable. (38)

longitudinal studies Examples of the use of before-and-after designs when treatment spans a considerable length of time. (36)

matched pairs design Assigning subjects to one of two conditions by taking two subjects with approximately the same value on a predetermined subject variable and randomly assigning one member of the pair to one condition and the other to the other condition. (35)

matching Assigning subjects to conditions in a between-subjects design by equating the conditions on selected subject variables. (33)

operational definitions Explicit definitions of independent and dependent variables in terms of how they are manipulated or measured. (28)

randomization Method of assigning subjects to experimental conditions such that each subject has an equal chance of being selected for any given condition. (29)

randomized blocks design Extension of the matched pairs design to more than two experimental conditions. (35)

reliability Measures of repeatability of experimental results such as the level of agreement between two or more "scorers" of behavior. (40)

single subject design Each individual subject is treated differently or there is only one subject (this latter instance is sometimes referred to as a "case study"). (36)

subject variables Extraneous variables pertaining to subject characteristics. (27)

validity The extent to which a measure used in research is actually measuring what it intends to. (40)

within-subject designs Experimental designs in which each subject receives every level of the independent variable (also known as *repeated measures designs*). (29)

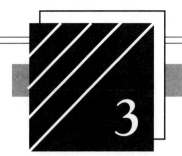

Statistical Inference

Irwin P. Levin

Suppose you start a series of games of handball with a player who you consider to be equal to you in ability. Your opponent wins the first two games. Your confidence is shaken. Should it be? Isn't there a good chance that your opponent will happen to win the first two games, even if you two are equal? What about the first three games? The first four? At what point do you concede your opponent's superiority? Many of you will recognize this as a problem of statistical inference: using a sample of data to form a more general conclusion.

This chapter is designed primarily for those of you who have had an introductory course in statistics. The introductory statistics course was undoubtedly a mixture of descriptive and inferential statistics, statistical concepts and the theory underlying them, and step-by-step development of computational procedures for statistical tests such as t, F, and χ^2. The present chapter is not an attempt to replace a first course in statistics. Rather, it is meant to review and highlight aspects of inferential statistics that are most important and useful to students of experimental psychology and to explain the relationship between statistics and research methods in behavioral science. While specific examples are given to illustrate common statistical computations, the emphasis in this chapter is on the understanding of principles of statistical inference that underlie the design of experiments and the interpretation of research results. Such understanding is crucial not only for those who will someday be designing and conducting research, but also for all of us who are consumers of research and must critically evaluate the latest developments in our fields of interest.

This chapter will focus on the principles and applications of **inferential statistics.** Inferential statistics is the branch of statistics dealing with the process of inference by which we learn about the characteristics of populations by analyzing the behavior of *samples* selected from those populations. The development of inferential statistics is considered one of the major breakthroughs in the history of science because it provides objective rules for reaching scientific conclusions. Because behavioral scientists are typically interested in abstracting generalizable principles of behavior from observations on limited samples, the inferential process takes on special significance. Can the improvement in anxiety level observed for a sample of subjects receiving a particular "anxiety-reducing" treatment be generalized to a broader population? This is one of several illustrative examples to be included in this chapter.

Before one can make meaningful statistical inferences, it is necessary to have accurate, systematic data from a sample of observations. Statistical summaries of data obtained from a sample of observations are called **descriptive statistics** because they serve to describe the sample of observations. Examples are measures of average such as mean, median, and mode, and measures of variability such as standard deviation and variance. At every step it is essential to maintain accuracy. The most elegant experimental test of the most ingenious hypothesis can be rendered worthless by data riddled with errors and/or miscalculations. There are many potential sources of error to plague us all: misreading or transposing numbers, misplacing decimal points or algebraic signs, arithmetic errors, omitting observations in transcribing data, misapplication of statistical formulas, and others that are much more subtle. Computer analysis can reduce the likelihood of some errors but also introduce others, often more difficult to detect. Experienced investigators maintain an attitude of constantly examining and re-examining their data for flaws. Beginning researchers are urged to treat data with meticulous care and to develop habits that ensure accuracy.

I like to play a little game with my laboratory assistants. We have a contest to decide which will be more accurate, calculating by hand or calculating by computer. I use a pocket calculator to get sample means from summary data sheets like those shown later in box 3.5; they enter data into the computer and run the appropriate statistical programs. Then, we compare our answers. When the answers differ, each is double-checked to see if the error was in the hand calculations or in entering data into the computer. A small wager is sometimes made. Over the years, I have won more times than I have lost. Of course, once the sample means are verified, the computer program provides a more efficient way to complete the more complex statistical calculations.

Importance of Statistical Inference in Experimental Psychology

In the physical sciences, observations of behavior of, say, falling bodies can be conducted in such a well-controlled atmosphere that a single observation often can serve to test a theory or define a phenomenon. In psychology, however, behavior is not observed in a vacuum. Each experimental subject is influenced by a unique set of genetic and environmental factors beyond the control of the experimenter. These factors were called *subject variables* in chapter 1. Statisticians sometimes refer to them as *individual difference factors*. Thus, in general, different individuals and different samples of individuals will behave differently in a given experimental condition, apart from the influence of the factors (independent variables) manipulated by the experimenter. When referring to such differences between samples, the term **chance sampling effects** is often used. Therefore, in order to demonstrate that a particular independent variable does in fact influence behavior (the dependent variable), subjects are sampled from the population of interest and *differences in behavior between experimental conditions (different levels of the independent variable) must be shown to be greater than differences attributable to chance sampling effects*.

In order to separate chance and systematic effects, we must have rules for deciding when observed differences in an experiment can be attributed to individual difference factors that vary across experimental conditions and when they can be attributed to real experimental effects. Inferential statistics provide us with such rules. For example, *inferential statistics provide an estimate of the probability or likelihood that a given set of experimental results was due merely to individual difference factors varying randomly among experimental conditions. When this likelihood is estimated to be very low, the most reasonable conclusion is that the differences are due to more than just chance sampling factors and that the manipulation of the independent variable(s) had an effect on behavior.*

Sampling and Probability

Research in psychology almost always entails selecting a representative group of cases (subjects), manipulating some variables, controlling other variables, and determining whether observed differences are meaningful. The first step is concerned with *sampling* and the last with *hypothesis testing*. Probability theory provides a link between these steps.

Sampling
Research psychologists are interested in establishing principles of behavior that have some generality but their experiments are confined to limited samples. If samples are drawn at random from known populations, then observations on the samples can be used to infer characteristics of the population. A **random sample** is one in which each unit (college sophomore, white rat, guinea pig) of the population has an equal chance of being chosen for the sample and each possible sample of a given size has an equal probability of being selected.

Even in cases where the subjects in an experiment do not actually represent a random sample from a readily identifiable population (e.g., "volunteers" from psychology classes), it is critical that the subjects in the experiment be assigned at random to experimental conditions (where each subject has the same chance of being selected for any given condition) so that individual differences do not bias the results of the experiment (see box 2.1). When bias does exist—say, when more highly motivated research participants (e.g., those who volunteer first) are more apt to be placed in the experimental group than in the control group—the effects of the experimental treatment are said to be confounded with the effects of subject variables, so that it is impossible to isolate the effect of the experimental treatment on the results. Such experiments are, of course, worthless.

Even samples chosen at random from the same population will, in general, differ from each other due to chance differences between the individuals selected for each sample. A statistic such as a sample mean will thus differ by an unknown amount from the population mean that it is meant to estimate. Fortunately, statistical theory tells us about the distribution of sample means and how much they are expected to differ from each other. According to the Central Limit Theorem, if the samples are drawn randomly, as sample size increases, the distribution of sample means approaches a normal distribution centered around the mean of the population from which the samples were drawn. As illustrated in figure 3.1, a normal distribution forms a bell-shaped curve with special properties such as having approximately two-thirds of the scores falling within a distance of one standard deviation from the mean.

The distribution of sample means is called a **sampling distribution,** and the standard deviation of this distribution is called the **standard error** of the mean. (Similarly, other sampling distributions and standard errors can be defined for other statistical measures.) As figure 3.1 shows, the standard error ($\overline{\sigma}_M$) decreases with increasing sample size and is equal to the standard deviation of the scores divided by the square root of the sample size.

While sampling distributions are hypothetical rather than "real," in the sense that one doesn't actually generate a distribution of sample means by repeated random sampling from the same population, they do represent a useful concept. Sampling distributions form the basis of evaluating the likelihood that a given set of sample values comes from a population of specified characteristics. Thus, for example, if the population mean is assumed to be 100 with a standard error of 10, then it is unlikely (but not impossible) for a sample with mean of 80 to have come from this population. This principle will be illustrated in the section on hypothesis testing.

Probability

Because statistical inference is based on computing and interpreting probabilities, a basic understanding of the concept of probability and some of the rules governing probability is critical. In this section we will define probability, describe rules for calculating probability, and discuss applications of these rules. **Probability** corresponds to the long-range likelihood that a particular event will occur. Thus, the probability that the outcome of flipping a fair coin will be "heads" is ½ even though any single outcome will be either "heads" or "tails" and any single series of flips can result in an unequal number of heads and tails. Probability theory provides us with rules for generating probability distributions for such cases—i.e., the probability of obtaining any given number of "heads" in n flips of a coin.

Box 3.1 illustrates how probabilities vary in the case of binomial variables: variables that can take on one of two values such as "heads" or "tails," "success" or "failure." The usefulness of such probability distributions is that you can calculate from them the likelihood of obtaining an outcome within a particular range, such as a person guessing correctly 9 or more times in 10 flips of a coin. Then, when you find someone who is actually performing at this level, you can make a judgment about whether that person is just lucky or whether something else is going on. (By the way, the likelihood of someone doing that well "by chance" is about 1 in 100. So, what would you say if you encountered such a person?)

Games of chance provide good examples of how the concepts and rules of probability apply to the analysis of behavioral phenomena. Consider a blackjack ("21") player who regularly and consistently wins at the casino because the player appears to have an uncanny knack for knowing when to "hit" (take another card to get closer to 21 than the dealer without going over 21) and when to "stick" (not take another card). Is the player's success the result of pure luck? More likely, the gambler has remembered something about the cards in the deck

FIGURE 3.1 Variability of sampling distributions as a function of sample size.

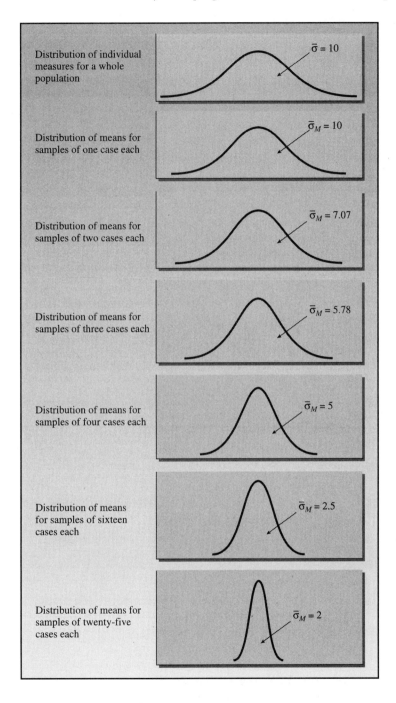

BOX 3.1

Binomial Probability Distributions

The binomial distribution is generated by the formula

$$p\,(X = r) = \frac{n!}{r!\,(n-r)!}\; p^r\,(1-p)^{n-r},$$

where

- n = the number of trials
- p = the probability of success on a single trial
- $1 - p$ = the probability of failure on a single trial
- X = the variable, number of successes in n trials
- r = the value of X in a particular outcome

If $p = \frac{1}{2}$, as in the flipping of a fair coin, the distribution is symmetric and comes closer to being approximated by a normal distribution as n increases. Here are some examples of binomial distributions with varying values of p and n.

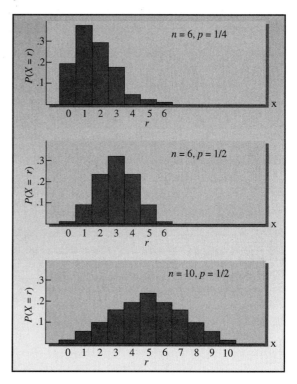

---

that have already been played out and takes into account how removing some cards changes the odds of future draws. For example, remembering that only 5 of the 12 face cards (jacks, queens, and kings) have appeared during the previous 33 draws, provides information about the likelihood of drawing a face card from the remaining 19 cards. The probability of drawing a face card has thus been increased from 12/52 (.23) to 7/19 (.37). In other words, successful players recognize how odds change on successive draws of a card and use the changing probabilities to their own advantage. (Many casinos now employ multiple decks of cards in their blackjack games in order to counter such advantages.)

The rules of probability include the addition rule for mutually exclusive events: If X and Y are **mutually exclusive events** (i.e., events that cannot occur simultaneously, like a coin landing "heads" or "tails" or a response being "correct" or "incorrect"),

then the probability of occurrence of X or Y is $P(X$ or $Y) = P(X) + P(Y)$ where $P(X)$ and $P(Y)$ represent the probability of occurrence of Event X and Event Y, respectively. For example, consider a multiple-choice learning task where each of three alternatives has an equal chance of being chosen on a given trial if the subject has not yet learned the problem. If X is the correct response and Y and Z are incorrect, then the probability of a correct response occurring by chance is 1/3 and the probability that an error will occur (response Y or response Z) is $P(Y) + P(Z) = 1/3 + 1/3 = 2/3$.

Another important rule is the multiplication rule for independent events: If X and Y are **independent events** (i.e., the occurrence of one event does not change the likelihood of the other event, such as whether a baby is born on an even or an odd-numbered day of the month, and its sex), then the probability of both X and Y occurring is

$P(X \text{ and } Y) = P(X) \times P(Y)$. In the previous learning example, if no learning has occurred on the first two trials and responses are independent over trials, then the probability of two successive correct guesses is $(1/3) \times (1/3) = 1/9$. If, on the other hand, two successive events X and Y are not independent, then the probability of Event Y will be *conditional* on Event X. The **conditional probability** of Event Y given Event X is $P(Y|X) = P(X \text{ and } Y)|P(X)$. For example, if making a particular response in a learning task increases the tendency to repeat that response on the next trial, then response probability on Trial 2 will differ for different outcomes on Trial 1.

The concept of conditional probability is important in the inferences made by experimental psychologists. One way to define reinforcement in learning theory is in terms of conditional probability. A stimulus event is said to have reinforcing properties if certain behaviors are more likely to occur following that event than not following that event. In terms of conditional probabilities, this condition is defined by the following inequality: $P(B/E) > P(B/\overline{E})$, where B is the target behavior, E is the occurrence of the stimulus event, and $\overline{E}$ is the nonoccurrence of the event.

To briefly summarize, probability is an important concept in statistics because it allows us to predict the likelihood of a particular event occurring under varying circumstances. Evaluations of probability are based on rules such as the addition rule for mutually exclusive events and the multiplication rule for independent events. Knowing when a particular event is likely or unlikely to occur can be very helpful in reconstructing the circumstances leading to observed data. The next section will describe how evaluations of probability are used to test hypotheses about the outcomes of experiments.

Hypothesis Testing

Experiments are conducted to obtain evidence for answering research questions. The questions may be empirical in nature—Which of three leading behavioral therapies is most effective in treating claustrophobia? The questions may be dictated by theory—Do rats run faster to receive food the longer they have been deprived of food, as "drive theory" predicts? Either type of question reduces to whether or not differences exist between well-defined experimental conditions. The two possible answers—differences or no differences—take the form of competing hypotheses.

The competing hypotheses are referred to as the null hypothesis and the alternative hypothesis. The **null hypothesis** (H_o) is the hypothesis initially assumed true. In most cases, the initial assumption is a hypothesis of no relationship (i.e., the experimental treatment has *no effect*) that the researcher attempts to reject or nullify by providing data that are inconsistent with the assumption. *The strategy underlying* **hypothesis testing** *is thus one of* **indirect proof**—*if the null hypothesis is rejected, support is provided for an* **alternative hypothesis** (H_a), *which typically affirms the existence of differences among experimental conditions.* In other words, the hypothesis that the researcher most likely favors (H_a) is supported indirectly by virtue of rejecting the null hypothesis. Note that the null hypothesis is stated as an equality (i.e., the difference between the population mean scores of the experimental and control groups is zero) and the alternative hypothesis is stated as an inequality (the difference between the means is not equal to zero). This is why only H_o can be tested directly; it has a specified numerical value whereas H_a does not.

Statistical Errors

Hypotheses concern population values but they are tested with data from samples. Recalling our earlier discussion of sampling distributions, the correspondence between a sample value and a population value varies from sample to sample. Sometimes the mean of a sample of scores will be very close to the population mean (i.e., it will fall near the middle of the sampling distribution) and sometimes it will not (i.e., it will fall in one of the tails of the distribution). The latter cases, though rare, can lead to incorrect conclusions when using sample values to test hypotheses about population values. Because H_o may in fact be true or false and the decision made in testing it may be to reject H_o or to retain H_o, there are four possible outcomes in the "truth table" given in box 3.2. Two of the outcomes are errors.

BOX 3.2

Possible Outcomes of Testing Statistical Hypotheses

It should be noted that the probabilities of making Type I and Type II errors are inversely related to each other. The investigator's chosen level of significance (α) determines the risk of making a Type I error. If α is set low (e.g., .01), β will be greater than when α is set higher. Thus, the level of significance should be selected on the basis of an evaluation of the relative consequences of Type I and Type II errors for the particular situation under investigation. However, β is influenced by other factors such as sample size and score variability.

	H_o Is Actually:	
	True	*False*
Retain H_o	Correct decision	Type II error (β)
Reject H_o	Type I error (α)	Correct decision (Power: $P = 1 - \beta$)

Decision Made:

Errors occur when H_o is true but you reject it in favor of H_a or when H_o is false but you retain it. By convention, the two types of errors are labeled **Type I error** and **Type II error,** respectively. Of course, these are not errors in the sense that the researcher did something wrong; the investigator might have just been unlucky in terms of getting an unusual sample (i.e., one whose mean falls in one of the tails of its sampling distribution) that led to the wrong decision even though the methods were perfectly correct. The "error" refers to sampling error not human error. In general, the researcher will not know if a statistical error has been made (although it may become painfully clear later on when no subsequent studies are able to replicate the original findings). However, because hypothesis testing involves "playing the odds," the investigator can achieve some degree of control over statistical errors. The probability of a Type I error (called alpha) and the probability of a Type II error (called beta) vary together; if alpha is reduced, then beta is increased, and if alpha is increased, then beta is decreased. If a strict criterion is set for rejecting H_o, then H_o will seldom be rejected when it is true; but H_o is apt to be retained when it is false, resulting in a low value of alpha and a relatively high value of beta. Conversely, if a lax criterion for rejecting H_o is set, then H_o is more apt to be rejected when it is true, but H_o is less apt to be retained when it is false, resulting in a relatively high value of alpha and a relatively low value of beta.

This is very much like reacting to signals on a radar screen. If you sound the alarm every time there's the slightest blip on the screen, then you'll likely produce some "false alarms" (like Type I errors) but guard against missing a true signal (a "miss" is like a Type II error). The opposite will occur if you use a very strict criterion for sounding the alarm. We will see this example developed further in the section on "signal detection" in chapter 4.

In practice, investigators set their own odds by specifying ahead of time the value of alpha, which is also called the **level of significance.** The level of significance represents the researcher's criterion for making statistical decisions; *if the likelihood of obtaining the observed sample values in the experiment under the assumption that* H_o *is true turns out to be less than alpha, then it is concluded that* H_o *is probably not true and* H_o *is thus rejected. If this likelihood is greater* than alpha, then it is concluded that the population value assumed by H_o is still one of the set of possible values and H_o is thus retained. Retaining H_o is not the same as proving that H_o is true. More about that later when we discuss the concept of the power of a statistical test.

Level of Significance
Choice of level of significance should be based on the investigator's assessment of the relative consequences of Type I and Type II errors in a particular study. For example, suppose an investigation is testing the effectiveness of a new drug. Rejecting H_o in this case may lead to marketing a drug with unknown side effects. So, the investigator will want to set a low level of alpha, say .01 or even smaller, to guard against a Type I error (saying that an ineffective drug has therapeutic properties). If, on the other hand, rejecting H_o is merely the go-ahead for further testing of the drug, then the investigator will want to set a higher level of alpha, say .10, to guard against a Type II error (prematurely abandoning the drug). In practice, a compromise level of .05 is often used to balance the likelihood of making a Type I error or a Type II error. Notice that the choice of alpha is a judgment of the investigator. Different evaluators of the same research may wish to impose different levels and could come to different conclusions about the outcome of an experiment.

Modern computer technology permits the results of a test to be reported by giving the probability value (**p-value**) associated with the results, rather than choosing alpha ahead of time and rejecting or retaining H_o on that basis. The computer output will include the exact probability of obtaining those results if H_o were true (and if the assumptions of the test are met). Nevertheless, we recommend that experimental psychology students think in terms of preset levels of significance rather than p-values, because selecting a significance level requires more careful consideration of Type I and Type II errors and their consequences.

Statistical tables are available for translating the chosen level of alpha into a region of rejection or **critical region** for the particular type of test used. Each test provides a statistical measure of the degree to which the sample data are in disagreement with the null hypothesis. *When the value of a test statistic such as t or F is large enough to fall into the critical region, this means that the sample data are unlikely to have come from a population with the hypothesized value, and the decision is to reject* H_0. The probability of obtaining a test value that falls into the critical region is alpha when H_0 is true.

The critical region will depend in part on whether a **one-tailed test** or a **two-tailed test** is used, corresponding to whether or not a directional inequality is specified in H_a. This is illustrated in box 3.3. Specification of a one-tailed or two-tailed test should be made before the data are collected and should be based on whether or not a particular direction of difference between experimental conditions is predicted or is of special consequence. For example, in a study of the effectiveness of a particular therapy, the investigator will no doubt want to demonstrate that therapy has a beneficial effect and will thus choose a one-tailed test. Conversely, if the experimental question is which of two therapies is the most effective, then a two-tailed test will be chosen.

Statistical Significance and Reliability
When the test statistic falls into the critical region and we reject H_0 for a given level of significance (say, alpha = .05), we sometimes refer to the outcome as a **statistically significant** result. One way to understand an alpha of .05 is that if the null hypothesis were actually true and if the experiment were repeated a number of times, then one would obtain a value of the test statistic large enough to fall into the critical region only about 5 times out of every 100 repetitions of the experiment. Thus, statistical hypothesis testing may be viewed as a substitute for repeating the

The Critical Region for One-Tailed and Two-Tailed Tests

The figures shown are sampling distributions centered around the population mean difference assumed by H_o. The entire critical region is concentrated at one end of the distribution for one-tailed tests and is divided into both ends for two-tailed tests. Note that a particular value of the test statistic (e.g., t) may fall into the critical region (shaded area) for a one-tailed test but not a two-tailed test. Thus, H_o is more likely to be rejected with one-tailed tests than with two-tailed tests when the direction of inequality specified by H_a is correct, but one-tailed tests offer no protection against Type II errors when H_a is in the wrong direction. The investigator must have prior reason for considering a unidirectional alternative to H_o.

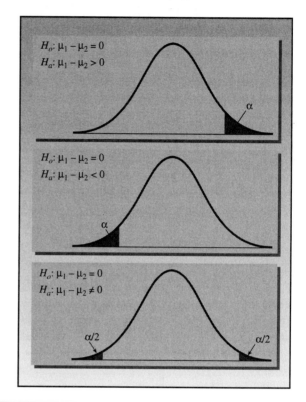

same experiment over and over again with the same population. Like repetition, hypothesis testing tells us something about the reliability of our findings. When we reject H_o we are reasonably confident that H_o is indeed false and that repeated experimentation would bear this out. Of course, if we want to generalize our findings to new populations, then the experiment must be replicated with samples from the different populations. A final note on the use of the term *significance*: statistical significance does not necessarily imply practical significance, theoretical significance, or social significance. With large enough samples, we may detect statistically significant differences that are so small in magnitude they have little meaning.

Power

The major effect of increasing sample size is to increase statistical power. As can be seen in the truth table given earlier (box 3.2), power is the inverse of Type II error. Type II error is the incorrect retention of H_o when it is false. Power is the probability of *correctly* rejecting H_o when it is false. Because the demonstration of an experimental effect requires rejection of H_o, power represents the ability to show that your experiment "worked." Experimenters thus strive to achieve high levels of power.

Although increasing sample size increases power, it has obvious practical limitations, particularly when dealing with a specialized population such as autistic children or identical twins. Even when additional subjects or experimental cases are available, more testing increases the cost and effort of an experiment, so increasing sample size can be an expensive way to increase power.

There are two other ways to increase power. First, because power = 1 – beta and beta decreases when alpha is increased, power will increase when alpha is increased. But, of course, by definition, then the probability of a Type I error increases. A second way to increase power in an experiment is to reduce the variability of scores obtained in each experimental condition. (For a test statistic like t, a measure of variability is contained in the denominator. Thus, decreasing variability leads to a larger value of t, which is more likely to fall into the critical region.) Because behavior is inherently variable across individuals and within individuals on different occasions, there are limits to which variance can be reduced. However, selection of homogeneous subject populations, "matching" procedures, use of repeated measures on the same subjects, reduction of environmental "noise" in an experiment, use of standardized tasks and instructions are some ways in which power can be increased through control of extraneous factors (see chapter 1). These methodological procedures vary in their effectiveness and suitability in different types of research. It is part of the creativity and ingenuity of scientists to devise ways to improve control in their experiments, thereby increasing power and increasing the likelihood of observing reliable differences in behavior. You should take particular note of these procedures as they are illustrated in later chapters.

Finally, power is affected by how seriously H_o is in error. For example, if H_o says that the mean difference in number of errors on a memory test between two experimental groups is zero and the actual (population) mean difference is 0.2 errors, then it is unlikely that H_o will be rejected even though it is, strictly speaking, false. Fortunately, such small differences are usually uninteresting and unimportant.

Small sample size and large variability can reduce power to the extent that Type II errors are likely. Thus, when an investigator fails to reject H_o, firm support for H_o cannot be assumed (this is why we prefer to say H_o is *retained*, rather than H_o is *accepted* in such cases).

Effect Size

One could say that the likelihood of achieving statistical significance in a given study is a function of the size of the effect times the size of the study. A relatively small effect may still be significant if sample size is sufficiently large, while a relatively large effect may fail to reach statistical significance when only a small sample is available. This has led some researchers to suggest that reporting the size of the effect (e.g., the difference between the means of an experimental group and a control group) is more important than reporting whether the results were significant at a particular level of alpha. Furthermore, in areas such as studying clinical populations (e.g., schizophrenics) where it may be difficult to obtain a large sample size in a single study, it is argued that it is especially important to estimate effect sizes *across different studies*. In other words, a more reliable estimate is obtained by combining data from a number of different studies even though each individual study may not have yielded statistically significant results. With newly developed techniques called **meta-analyses,** one can estimate the size of an experimental effect by combining the data from all known studies of that effect. Meta-analysis also allows the investigator to uncover factors such as subject variables that modify the size of the effect but that cannot be detected in a single study.

For example, Smith and Glass (1977) examined the question of whether psychotherapy is effective by conducting a meta-analysis of 375 studies. To compare the results of different studies, they computed a "standard score" for each study by subtracting the mean outcome for the control group from the mean outcome for the treatment group and divided this difference by the standard deviation of the control group. This is their definition of "effect size" for a given study. As a summary measure of treatment effectiveness across studies, they reported that the typical therapy client is better off than 75 percent of untreated (control) individuals. While the magnitude of the effect size correlated with variables such as the estimated IQ of clients and the degree of similarity of therapists and clients, there were negligible differences in the effects produced by different therapy types.

Choice of Test

One of the important steps in hypothesis testing is selecting the most appropriate statistical test for a given problem. Selection is based on the type of data collected and characteristics of their distribution. For example, *t*-tests and *F*-tests are used with dependent variables that are operationally defined by continuous metric measures such as reaction time for each subject in a decision-making task. (Metric measures are scales that have ordinal properties—larger numbers represent greater amounts of the quantity being measured. Chapter 4 will include an expanded description of the properties of various scales of measurement.) Chi-square (χ^2) tests are used with dependent variables that lead to frequency or "count" data such as the number of subjects who correctly solve a complex problem. Even in these cases, however, certain requirements and assumptions have to be met. Chi-square tests require that each observation be independent of every other observation; *t*-tests and *F*-tests are based on the assumptions that sampling distributions for groups to be compared are normal and are of equal variance. When these assumptions are not met, the actual probability of making a Type I error will not be exactly equal to alpha, but minor deviations from normality and homogeneity (equality) of variance will have only slight effects. When deviations are great, "nonparametric" or "distribution-free" tests are available that bypass the distributional assumptions by using only the rank-order information in the data (at the cost of reduced power). One such test will be illustrated later.

To summarize, hypothesis testing is the most common form of statistical inference for experimental psychologists because it permits them to use sample data to come to reasoned conclusions about the effectiveness of their independent variable manipulations. Along the way, several important decisions have to be made: formulation of hypotheses, choice of level of significance based on relative concerns for Type I and Type II errors, and choice of the appropriate test based on the nature of the data. Box 3.4 summarizes the steps in hypothesis testing procedures.

Examples of Hypothesis Testing

The examples that follow were chosen to be representative of the kinds of problems faced by research psychologists in a variety of content areas. Each problem includes a statement of the research question and hypotheses, the logic of the experimental design, a representative (but fictitious) set of data, choice of the appropriate statistical procedure, computational formulas, and conclusions based on the computations. While computational procedures are important, it is more important at this point to pay attention to how the selection of a test is related to the particular problem at hand and how the tests help answer the key research questions. Experimental design and statistics play complementary roles in psychological research.

Use of *t*-Test for Comparing Independent Groups

Suppose a clinical psychologist has devised a treatment for reducing anxiety and wants to demonstrate that the treatment is effective in reducing the anxiety level of highly anxious subjects. He knows that factors other than treatment effectiveness can lead to a reduction in anxiety (see discussion of "regression to the mean" in the later section on Correlation and Regression), so he designs his study as follows: He selects a sample of 50 highly anxious subjects and randomly divides the sample in half into a treatment group and a control group. The treatment group then receives the anxiety-reducing therapy for a period of 3 months while the control group receives no therapy or receives some sort of placebo treatment for 3 months. Measures of anxiety are obtained for each subject at the beginning and at the end of the 3-month period. A difference or improvement score is computed for each subject such that positive differences reflect reduced anxiety. The research question then translates into whether or not the improvement scores are significantly larger for the treatment group than for the control group.

BOX 3.4

Steps in Hypothesis Testing

1. Set up the competing hypotheses, H_o and H_a. In experimental psychology, H_o is typically a statement of no effect (e.g., therapy had no effect) that the investigator wishes to discredit or reject. In the case of a test statistic like t, a choice must be made between a one-tailed and a two-tailed version, depending on whether a particular direction is specified by H_a. In the case of F or χ^2, no such choice need be made because squared values are used and deviations from H_o in either direction are treated alike.

2. Choose a level of significance (α) based on consideration of the relative consequences of a Type I or a Type II error. If the main concern is avoiding Type I errors (e.g., claiming that an ineffective treatment is actually effective), then set α low (e.g., .01). If the main concern is avoiding Type II errors (e.g., failing to detect that a treatment is actually effective), then set α higher (e.g., .10).

3. Choose the appropriate test statistic (t, F, χ^2, etc.) based on the nature of the data (e.g., frequency counts vs. continuous measures; two experimental conditions vs. more than two conditions; independent groups of subjects vs. repeated measures on the same subjects) and the assumptions of the test.

4. Determine the critical region based on the test statistic, the hypotheses, the significance level, and the degrees of freedom.

5. Compute the test statistic and see if it falls into the critical region.

6. Retain or reject H_o on the basis of whether or not the test statistic falls into the critical region. A decision to reject H_o means that the probability of obtaining the observed sample data if H_o were true is so low (less than α) that the investigator concludes that H_o is probably *not* true. A decision to retain H_o means that the probability of obtaining the sample data is sufficiently high (greater than α) that the population value specified by H_o is still tenable. This, however, does not *prove* that H_o is true.

7. The investigator can now make conclusions about the effectiveness of the variables examined in the study. These conclusions must explicitly or implicitly recognize the possibility of Type I or Type II errors and the problem of generalizing beyond the population sampled in the study.

Because this is a between-subjects design with two levels of the independent variable (treatment vs. no treatment), the most direct statistical procedure is the t-test for independent groups. The application of this test to an illustrative set of data is shown in box 3.5.

The calculations shown in box 3.5 use standard computational formulas easily suited to hand calculators, but it should be noted that different statistics books may present slightly different variations of these formulas. The key elements of the computational formulas used here are that they involve: (1) an improvement score for each subject in each group, (2) a sum of the improvement scores in each group, and (3) a sum of the squared improvement scores in each group. From these measures, a mean ($\overline{X}$) and variance (s^2) of improvement scores can be calculated for each group, as well as a t value for comparing the two groups.

The null hypothesis (H_o) to be tested here is that the population mean improvement score of the Treatment Group (μ_T) will be no different from the population mean improvement score of the Control Group (μ_C). Note that Greek letters are used for population values and English letters are used for sample values. Hypothesis testing always uses sample values to test hypotheses about population values. The alternative hypothesis (H_a) in this case is that μ_T will be greater that μ_C. This is, of course, the hypothesis that the clinical psychologist would like to see supported, because he would then be able to claim that his treatment was effective.

BOX 3.5

Calculations for t-Test for Independent Groups

Data

	Treatment Group (T)					Control Group (C)			
Subject Number	Initial Anxiety Score	Later Anxiety Score	Improve-ment X	X^2	Subject Number	Initial Anxiety Score	Later Anxiety Score	Improve-ment X	X^2
T1	88	80	8	64	C1	85	90	−5	25
T2	92	89	3	9	C2	93	91	2	4
T3	90	84	6	36	C3	90	92	−2	4
T4	84	88	−4	16	C4	90	89	1	1
T5	81	70	11	121	C5	88	85	3	9
T6	87	77	10	100	C6	91	91	0	0
T7	93	84	9	81	C7	92	84	8	64
T8	85	85	0	0	C8	80	85	−5	25
T9	90	82	8	64	C9	87	85	2	4
T10	85	73	12	144	C10	94	84	10	100
T11	97	84	13	169	C11	95	90	5	25
T12	95	90	5	25	C12	82	88	−6	36
T13	84	83	1	1	C13	88	85	3	9
T14	80	82	−2	4	C14	92	88	4	16
T15	86	71	15	225	C15	86	85	1	1
T16	85	77	8	64	C16	94	90	4	16
T17	91	84	7	49	C17	95	92	3	9
T18	96	84	12	144	C18	87	96	−9	81
T19	90	80	10	100	C19	87	87	0	0
T20	94	78	16	256	C20	85	86	−1	1
T21	84	85	−1	1	C21	94	81	13	169
T22	95	88	7	49	C22	90	88	2	4
T23	80	72	8	64	C23	92	89	3	9
T24	88	85	3	9	C24	88	90	−2	4
T25	91	81	10	100	C25	86	85	1	1
			175	1895				35	617

Descriptive Statistics

$$\overline{X} = \frac{\Sigma X}{n} \qquad\qquad \overline{X}_T = \frac{175}{25} = 7.0 \qquad\qquad \overline{X}_C = \frac{35}{25} = 1.4$$

$$s^2 = \frac{\Sigma X^2 - (\Sigma X)^2/n}{n-1} \qquad s_T^2 = \frac{1895 - (175)^2/25}{24} \qquad s_C^2 = \frac{617 - (35)^2/25}{24}$$

$$= 27.92 \qquad\qquad\qquad = 23.67$$

Hypotheses

H_o: $\mu_T - \mu_C = 0$

H_a: $\mu_T - \mu_C > 0$

Assumptions for Applying t-Test

1. Independent random samples.
2. The two populations of improvement scores are each normally distributed.
3. The two populations of improvement scores have equal variances.

Note: According to the Central Limit Theorem, sampling distributions are approximately normal even when the populations are not normally distributed. Thus, Assumption 2 can be relaxed to some extent. Also, slight variations from Assumption 3 have only small effects.

Degrees of Freedom

$df = n_T + n_C - 2 = 48$

Critical Region

For $\alpha = .01$ and $df = 48$, the critical value of t for a one-tailed test is approximately 2.41 (obtainable from any standard statistics text). Therefore, the decision rule is to reject H_o if the value of t computed from the data is greater than or equal to 2.41.

Calculation of t

$$t = \frac{\text{difference between sample means}}{\text{standard error of the difference}} = \frac{\overline{X}_T - \overline{X}_C}{\sqrt{\dfrac{s_T^2}{n_T} + \dfrac{s_C^2}{n_C}}}$$

$$= \frac{7.0 - 1.4}{\sqrt{\dfrac{27.92}{25} + \dfrac{23.67}{25}}} = \frac{5.60}{1.435} = 3.90.$$

Decision

Reject H_o in favor of H_a and conclude that the treatment was effective in reducing anxiety because the mean improvement in the treatment group was significantly greater than the mean improvement in the control group.

However, as an objective scientist he is cautious about claiming success prematurely, so he sets a stringent significance level (α = .01) to guard against Type I errors (claiming there is a difference between treatment and control conditions when there actually is not). Nevertheless, for these data, H_o is rejected in favor of H_a and the effectiveness of the treatment is supported. (Note that statistical support is only one part of the story. The clinical psychologist would also have to convince his peers that the experimental test of the effectiveness of his treatment was free of potential artifacts such as biased measures of anxiety or anxiety-raising components of the procedure used for the control group.)

Testing Hypotheses about More Than Two Means

Suppose that an experiment is conducted where three randomly formed groups of 20 moderately food-deprived rats each are put in a complex maze and have to find the goal to receive food. The groups differ in the amount of reinforcement at the goal—2 food pellets, 4 food pellets, or 6 food pellets. Data are recorded in terms of the number of trials for each rat to reach a criterion of two consecutive errorless runs. The research question is twofold: Does the amount of reinforcement affect the rate of learning the maze and, if so, what is the function relating the dependent variable (number of trials to each criterion) to the independent variable (number of food pellets). Illustrative data and calculations are given in box 3.6, using analysis of variance and trend tests to answer the research questions. This is called a "one-way" analysis of variance because it applies to a design with one independent variable. In this case, it is a single-factor between-subjects design with three levels.

One-way analysis of variance is like an extension of the t-test illustrated earlier, but t-tests can compare only two groups at a time. Say, for example, that there are 6 groups to be compared. The number of t-tests comparing two groups at a time is equal to the number of *combinations* of 6 things taken 2 at a time (the number of possible pairs). The formula for computing the number of combinations of n distinct objects taken r at a time is nCr = n!/r!(n − r)!. In this

case, n = 6 and r = 2, so the number of tests is 6!/2!4! = 15. If each t-test is conducted with α = .05 (i.e., 1 out of 20 chance of a Type I error), it is easy to see that 15 different tests could well lead to one or more Type I errors. A single analysis of variance test is thus preferred on the grounds that it does not inflate the likelihood of making a Type I error. In the hypothetical experiment with varying amounts of reinforcement, analysis of variance confirmed that the means of the three groups differed significantly, and the trend tests indicated that performance improved linearly as amount of reinforcement was increased from 2 to 4 to 6 food pellets.

In the present example, the independent variable (amount of food reinforcement) had numerical properties and was varied systematically (in arithmetic progression). Thus, trend tests are an integral part of the statistical analysis and may be considered as **planned comparisons.** In other cases, comparisons between certain experimental conditions become of interest only after the data have been collected. These are called **post hoc comparisons.** For example, suppose that there were five independent experimental groups and inspection of the data revealed that only Groups 3 and 5 differed appreciably from each other. It would be a simple matter to run a t-test to compare these groups. However, such a test would violate statistical assumptions and would have an inflated probability of a Type I error. (To exaggerate this point, suppose there were 100 groups, each representing a different random sample from the same population. If you picked out the two groups with the highest and lowest mean scores, they would be bound to look different from each other even though only chance factors were operating.) There are tests for making such post hoc comparisons that tend to be "conservative" by adjusting the critical region to compensate for the increased likelihood of a Type I error as the number of possible group comparisons increases.

For example, in the Tukey method an "honestly significant difference" (HSD) between any two means is computed by the following formula:

$$HSD = q_\alpha \sqrt{\frac{MS error}{n}}$$ where MS error is the analysis of variance term for mean square within groups,

BOX 3.6

Calculations for One-Way Analysis of Variance and Trend Tests

Data Summary

Group	n	ΣX	ΣX^2	$\overline{X}$	s
A: 6 pellets	20	111	657	5.55	1.47
B: 4 pellets	20	142	1046	7.10	1.41
C: 2 pellets	20	165	1441	8.25	2.05
	60	418	3144		

Hypotheses

H_o: $\mu_A = \mu_B = \mu_C$
(H_a is simply that the three group means are not all equal.)

Assumptions

Same as for *t*-test for independent random samples.

Analysis of Variance Table and Computational Formulas

Source of Variance	df	Sum of Squares (SS)	Mean Square (MS)
Between groups	$(k-1)$	$\sum_{j=1}^{k} \dfrac{T_j^2}{n} - \dfrac{T^2}{N}$	$SS_{\text{Between}}/(k-1)$
Within groups	$k(n-1)$	$SS_{\text{Total}} - SS_{\text{Between groups}}$	$SS_{\text{Within}}/k(n-1)$
Total	$N-1$	$\sum_{j=1}^{k} \sum_{i=1}^{n} X_{ij}^2 - \dfrac{T^2}{N}$	

where

k = number of groups
n = number of subjects per group
$N = kn$ = total number of subjects
T_j = sum or total of scores in Group j
T = sum of scores in all groups
X_{ij} = the score for the ith subject in Group j
$\sum_{j=1, \, i=1}^{k} \sum^{n} X_{ij}^2$ = sum of squared scores for all subjects in all groups

Computations

Source	df	SS	MS
Between groups	$3 - 1 = 2$	$\dfrac{111^2 + 142^2 + 165^2}{20} - \dfrac{418^2}{60} = 73.43$	$\dfrac{73.43}{2} = 36.72$
Within groups	$3 \times 19 = 57$	$231.93 - 73.43 = 158.50$	$\dfrac{158.50}{57} = 2.78$
Total	$60 - 1 = 59$	$3144 - \dfrac{418^2}{60} = 231.93$	

The statistic for testing H_o is the F-test, where

$$F = \frac{MS_{\text{Between groups}}}{MS_{\text{Within groups}}}$$

$MS_{\text{Between groups}}$ represents the differences in scores between individuals in different groups and includes both sampling error and the experimental effect; $MS_{\text{Within groups}}$ represents differences in scores between individuals in the same group and is thus a measure of sampling error. The larger the ratio of these two variances, the more likely that there is an experimental effect.

In the present case, $F = \dfrac{36.72}{2.78} = 13.21$, with $df = 2$ and 57.

The critical value for $\alpha = .05$ and these df is 3.16.

Decision

Reject H_o and conclude that the rats learned the maze faster the greater the amount of food reinforcement.

Trend Analysis

In order to test for a linear component of the difference between three group means, group totals are multiplied by the linear coefficients -1, 0, 1. The resulting difference score (D) is squared and divided by n times the sum of the squared coefficients to yield SS_{Linear}.

$$D = (-1)(111) + (1)(165) = 54$$
$$SS_{\text{Linear}} = \frac{(54)^2}{20[(-1)^2 + (1)^2]} = 72.90, \text{ with } df = 1$$

The linear component is tested for significance by dividing MS_{Linear} by $MS_{\text{Within groups}}$.

$$F = \frac{72.90}{2.78} = 26.22, \text{ with } df = 1 \text{ and } 57$$

The critical value for $\alpha = .05$ and these df is 4.01. Because our computed value of F is larger than this critical value, we conclude that there is a significant linear component of the difference between the three group means.

[*Continued*]

Box 3.6 continued

In order to support a linear trend across the three group means, it is also necessary to show that deviations from linearity are nonsignificant. (It is possible to have a more complex function, describable by both linear and quadratic components.) To do this, we compute SS for deviations from linearity by subtracting SS_{Linear} from $SS_{Between\ groups}$.

$$SS_{Deviations\ from\ linearity} = 73.43 - 72.90 = 0.53, \text{ with } df = 1.$$

Then, $F = \dfrac{0.53}{2.78} = 0.19,$

which is obviously not significant.

So, in this case, we can conclude that there is a linear trend between the specified levels of amount of reinforcement and number of trials to learn the maze.

---

n is the sample size per group, and q_α is the "studentized range statistic" whose table of significant values for a given level of α is adjusted for the number of groups to be compared. The greater the number of groups, the larger the required value. For the data in box 3.6, $q_\alpha = 3.40$, MS error = 2.78 and $n = 20$, leading to HSD = 1.27. This means that any two group means differing by 1.27 or more are significantly different. All the means in box 3.6 are significantly different from each other. A good empiricist will follow up an unexpected finding by designing a new study to directly investigate and, if possible, explain this finding.

Testing Interaction Effects

Suppose a sports psychologist designs a study to determine the combined effects of natural athletic ability and training. She starts with a group of high school sophomores who are interested in competing in the high jump but who have had no prior formal training. She classifies them as high or low on athletic ability on the basis of a battery of physical performance tasks. She then randomly divides each group in half and assigns one half to a 1-month program of high jump training led by a professional coach. The students in the other half are instructed to spend an equivalent amount of time practicing the high jump but are given no formal training. High jump scores at the end of 1 month are recorded. Formal training procedures are predicted to be superior to no formal training and high-athletic-ability subjects are expected to do better

than low-ability subjects, but these predictions border on the trivial.

A more interesting research question is whether the beneficial effects of training differ for high-ability and low-ability subjects. It could be that formal training produces an equivalent improvement for both types of subjects; it could be that training allows the low-ability subjects to catch up with the high-ability subjects; or it could be that training has its greatest effect on those with more natural ability. The statistical test illustrated in box 3.7 is an analysis of variance that includes a test for interaction effects. (The term "higher-order" analysis of variance applies here because it deals with the effects of more than one variable.) The presence of an interaction would indicate that the effect of one variable (i.e., the independent variable, formal training vs. no formal training) differed for different levels of the other variable (the subject variable, high vs. low athletic ability).

In a completely analogous fashion, data can be analyzed for a 2 × 2 factorial design with two manipulated independent variables. For example, instead of the subject variable, athletic ability, the second variable could be whether or not subjects were given a special diet for enhancing strength. The presence of an interaction would then indicate that the effect of training depends on whether subjects are given the special diet.

For a student who has never done such a problem before, the computational formulas used in box 3.7 may seem a bit forboding. However, after

BOX 3.7

Calculating Interaction Effects with Multifactor Analysis of Variance

Data Summary

	Athletic Ability	
	Low (L)	High (H)
Yes (Y)	n: 10 ΣX: 560 in. ΣX^2: 31,552	n: 10 ΣX: 706 in. ΣX^2: 50,164
No (N)	n: 10 ΣX: 496 in. ΣX^2: 24,888	n: 10 ΣX: 552 in. ΣX^2: 30,800

Formal Training (row label)

Plot of Mean Values

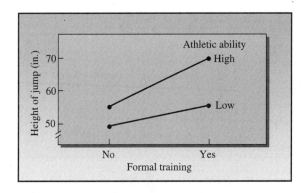

(Note: The nonparallelism of the lines suggests the presence of an interaction effect, but its reliability has to be tested statistically.)

Null Hypotheses

1. Effect of athletic ability: $H_o: \mu_H - \mu_L = 0$
2. Effect of formal training: $H_o: \mu_Y - \mu_N = 0$
3. Interaction: $H_o: \mu_{H,Y} - \mu_{H,N} = \mu_{L,Y} - \mu_{L,N}$

[*Continued*]

Box 3.7 continued

Analysis of Variance Table and Computational Formulas

Source of Variance	df	Sum of Squares (SS)	Mean Square (MS)
Row variable (R)	$(r-1)$	$\dfrac{\sum_{j=1}^{r} T_{Rj}^2}{cn} - \dfrac{T^2}{N}$	$SS_R/(r-1)$
Column variable (C)	$(c-1)$	$\dfrac{\sum_{k=1}^{c} T_{Ck}^2}{rn} - \dfrac{T^2}{N}$	$SS_C/(c-1)$
Interaction (R × C)	$(r-1)(c-1)$	$\dfrac{\sum T_{jk}^2}{n} - \dfrac{T^2}{N} - SS_R - SS_C$	$SS_{R \times C}/(r-1)(c-1)$
Within groups	$rc(n-1)$	$SS_{Total} - SS_R - SS_C - SS_{R \times C}$	$SS_{Within}/rc(n-1)$
Total	$N-1$	$\sum_{k=1}^{c} \sum_{j=1}^{r} \sum_{i=1}^{n} X_{ijk}^2 - \dfrac{T^2}{N}$	

where

r = number of rows
c = number of columns
n = number of subjects per cell
$N = rcn$ = total number of subjects
T_{Rj} = sum of scores in Row j
T_{Ck} = sum of scores in Column k
T_{jk} = sum of scores in the cell formed by the intersection of Row j and Column k
T = sum of scores in all cells of the design
X_{ijk} = the score for the ith subject in the cell formed by the intersection of Row j and Column k
$\sum_{k=1}^{c} \sum_{j=1}^{r} \sum_{i=1}^{n} X_{ijk}^2$ = sum of squared scores for all subjects in all cells

Computations

Source	df	SS	MS
Athletic Ability (A)	$2-1$ $=1$	$\dfrac{1056^2 + 1258^2}{20} - \dfrac{2314^2}{40}$ $= 1020.1$	1020.1
Training (T)	$2-1$ $=1$	$\dfrac{1266^2 + 1048^2}{20} - \dfrac{2314^2}{40}$ $= 1188.1$	1188.1
Interaction (A × T)	$(2-1)(2-1)$ $=1$	$\dfrac{560^2 + 496^2 + 706^2 + 552^2}{10} - \dfrac{2314^2}{40} - 1020.1 - 1188.1$ $= 202.5$	202.5
Within groups	$2 \times 2 \times 9$ $= 36$	$3539.1 - 2410.7$ $= 1128.4$	$1128.4/36$ $= 31.34$
Total	$40 - 1$ $= 39$	$137{,}404 - 133{,}864.9$ $= 3539.1$	

- F ratios: MS_A, MS_T, and $MS_{A \times T}$ are each divided by $MS_{\text{Within groups}}$.

- To test H_o for athletic ability, $F = \dfrac{1020.1}{31.34} = 32.55$, $df = 1$ and 36.

- To test H_o for training, $F = \dfrac{1188.1}{31.34} = 37.91$, $df = 1$ and 36.

- To test H_o for interaction, $F = \dfrac{202.5}{31.34} = 6.46$, $df = 1$ and 36.

- The critical value for $\alpha = .05$ and these df is 4.11.

The summary analysis of variance, as it might appear in a journal article would look like this:

Source	df	Sum of Squares	Mean Square	F Value
Athletic Ability	1	1020.1	1020.1	32.55*
Training	1	1188.1	1188.1	37.91*
Athletic Ability x Training	1	202.5	202.5	6.46*
Error	36	1128.4	31.34	

*$p < .05$.

Decision

Each H_o is rejected.
The conclusion regarding the interaction is that the effect of training is greater for high-ability subjects than for low-ability subjects.

doing a few problems of this type, a certain "logic" in the formulas should be detected. For example, in terms like $\frac{T^2}{N}$, $\frac{T_{Rj}^2}{cn}$, $\frac{T_{Ck}^2}{rn}$, the squared total is always divided by the number of individual scores that made up that total. The (fictitious) data and calculations shown here detect an interaction indicating that the effect of training was greater for high-ability subjects than for low-ability subjects.

Another question that can be addressed in an experimental design such as this is to what extent variations in the dependent variable (height of jump) can be accounted for by each of the independent or subject variables and by their interaction. A simple descriptive statistic is provided by taking each sum of squares and dividing by the total sum of squares. In the present case, the resulting "proportions of variance" are .29 for athletic ability, .34 for training, and .06 for the interaction. Thus, in this case, the systematic features of the experiment accounted for over ⅔ of the variance in the high jump scores. (What accounts for the rest of the variance?)*

Role of the Subject Variable

Now recall our discussion in chapter 2 of how the inclusion of a subject variable in the design and analysis of an experiment can lead to increased power for detecting an experimental effect. The above example can be used to illustrate this point. We had examined high jumping performance as a function of the independent variable, training vs. no training, and the subject variable, athletic ability. This resulted in $F = 37.91$ for the training effect. Let's reanalyze the data comparing height of jump with and without training when the subject variable, athletic ability, is not considered. We then have a two independent groups design in which the groups can be defined as "formal training" and "no formal training." From the data summary already given we can compute the respective means of the two groups to be 63.3 in. and 52.4 in., with variances equal to 83.06 and 40.67. Using the procedures described in box 3.5, we get $t = 4.38$ with $df = 38$. (As an exercise, check these calculations for yourself.)

To get the equivalent value of F with $df = 1$ and 38, we square the value of t. The resulting F ratio of 19.21 is about half the value as when the subject variable, athletic ability, was included. (The small change in df from 36 to 38 is due to the lack of a test of the main effect of athletic ability and the lack of a test of the interaction between athletic ability and training.) While the recomputed value of F for the training effect is still statistically significant, its reduced value reflects a substantial reduction in power. Furthermore, exclusion of the subject variable would have concealed an interesting interaction between the subject variable and the independent variable.

This illustration should help you see the logical connection between experimental design and statistical analysis. The appropriate inclusion of a relevant subject variable into the design of an experiment not only makes sense as sound experimental practice, it also has desirable statistical effects. We will see additional examples in later chapters such as the differential effects of one-sided vs. two-sided arguments on people who initially agreed or disagreed with a persuasive message.

Test of Independence between Categorical Variables

Suppose a social scientist wants to determine if males and females in a particular district differ in their political party affiliation. He selects a random sample of 300 registered voters in the district and determines their preferred political party. Data are summarized by frequency counts cross-classified by sex and political party affiliation. The research question translates into whether or not the relative proportion of Democrats, Republicans, and Independents is different for males and females. Because frequency or "count" data are involved and because each sample voter can fall into one and only one cell of the resulting contingency table, the appropriate statistical test is chi-square (χ^2). The application of chi-square to an illustrative set of data is shown in box 3.8. In this case, the relative proportion of registered voters preferring each party is not significantly different for the two sexes, so there is no evidence that sex and political party affiliation are related in this population.

---

*A likely guess is uncontrolled subject variables such as motivation and participation in other athletic activities involving running and jumping.

BOX 3.8

Calculation of χ^2 Test of Independence

Data

Observed Frequency Counts:

Political Party

		Democratic	Republican	Independent	
Gender	Male	63	67	30	160
	Female	67	53	20	140
		130	120	50	

Hypotheses

H_o states that the proportion of males in the population who affiliate with the Democratic party is the same as the proportion of females in the population who affiliate with the Democratic party. Likewise, for the Republican and Independent parties; the proportion of males in the population who affiliate with that party should be the same as the proportion of females in the population who affiliate with that party. H_a merely states that this equality of proportions does not hold.

Degrees of Freedom

$df = (r-1)(c-1)$, where r = the number of categories in the row variable (gender) and c = the number of categories in
$= 1 \times 2 = 2$ the column variable (political party).

Critical Region

For α = .05 and df = 2, the critical value of χ^2 is 5.99. Therefore, the decision rule is to reject H_o if the value of χ^2 computed from the data is greater than or equal to 5.99.

Calculation of χ^2

$$\chi^2 = \sum_{i=1}^{k} \frac{(O_i - E_i)^2}{E_i}$$

where O_i is the observed frequency in cell i of the contingency table and E_i is the expected frequency (frequency predicted from H_o). In the present case there are 6 cells in the table, so k = 6.

The key to any χ^2 problem is computing the values of E_i. Consider the upper left-hand cell of the table (males who affiliate with the Democratic party). According to H_o, the proportion of male Democrats in the sample should be 130/300 because this is the proportion of Democrats observed for the whole sample, irrespective of gender. To convert this *proportion* into an expected *frequency*, we merely multiply it by the total number of males in the sample (160). To compute the expected number of female Democrats, we take the same proportion and multiply it by the total number of females in the sample (140). For the expected number of male and female Republicans we use the proportion 120/300 and for the expected number of male and female Independents we use the proportion 50/300. Calculation of all E_i's is shown on the following page. Note that the row sums and column sums must be the same for the O_i's and the E_i's.

[*Continued*]

Box 3.8 continued

Expected Frequency Counts:

		Political Party		
Gender		Democratic	Republican	Independent	
	Male	$\frac{130}{300} \times 160$ $= 69.33$	$\frac{120}{300} \times 160$ $= 64.00$	$\frac{50}{300} \times 160$ $= 26.67$	160
	Female	$\frac{130}{300} \times 140$ $= 60.67$	$\frac{120}{300} \times 140$ $= 56.00$	$\frac{50}{300} \times 140$ $= 23.33$	140
		130	120	50	

The tables of observed frequency counts and expected frequency counts must be aligned so that the corresponding O_i's and E_i's can be compared.

O_i: 63   67   30   67   53   20

E_i: 69.33   64.00   26.67   60.67   56.00   23.33

$$\chi^2 = \frac{(63 - 69.33)^2}{69.33} + \frac{(67 - 64.00)^2}{64.00} + \frac{(30 - 26.67)^2}{26.67} + \frac{(67 - 60.67)^2}{60.67} + \frac{(53 - 56.00)^2}{56.00} + \frac{(20 - 23.33)^2}{23.33}$$

$$= 2.44$$

Decision

Retain H_o and conclude that there is no evidence to indicate that sex and political party affiliation are related in this population.

Use of χ^2 in Nonparametric Tests

Recall that when the assumptions of tests such as t are seriously violated, alternative tests have to be employed that reduce the data to their rank-order properties. These tests are called **nonparametric or distribution-free tests** because they do not rely on assumptions about the shape and variance of sampling distributions. The simplest of these tests, called the Sign Test or the Median Test, involves the use of χ^2. Suppose that there are four independent groups (samples) of scores to be compared but that they differ greatly in variance. The procedure is as follows: (1) compute the median score of all groups combined; (2) count the number of scores in each separate group that are above (+) and below (−) the joint median and construct a frequency table based on these numbers; (3) use χ^2 to compare these observed frequencies with frequencies based on the assumption (null hypothesis) that half the scores in each group are above and half below the overall median. This is illustrated in box 3.9.

Confidence Intervals

Sometimes it is not enough to test whether a hypothesis is supported by sample data. For example, in addition to testing whether a treatment for depression is effective, we may want to estimate the amount of improvement produced by the treatment. Even though we know that sample data may vary from the true population value, we can use them to pin down a plausible range of values for the

BOX 3.9

Calculation of χ^2 for Nonparametric Test

Observed Frequency Counts:

	Group 1	Group 2	Group 3	Group 4	
+	12	11	15	12	50
−	8	14	10	18	50
	20	25	25	30	

Comparison to Joint Median

Expected Frequency Counts:

+	10	12.5	12.5	15
−	10	12.5	12.5	15

$$\chi^2 = \frac{(12-10)^2}{10} + \frac{(8-10)^2}{10} + \frac{(11-12.5)^2}{12.5} + \frac{(14-12.5)^2}{12.5} + \frac{(15-12.5)^2}{12.5} + \frac{(10-12.5)^2}{12.5} + \frac{(12-15)^2}{15} + \frac{(18-15)^2}{15}$$

$\chi^2 = 3.36$, with $df = 3 \times 1 = 3$

For $\alpha = .05$ and $df = 3$, the critical value of χ^2 is 7.82. Thus, in this case, the null hypothesis that the four groups come from equal populations would be retained.

population. A **confidence interval** is a range of values within which we can establish with a certain degree of confidence that a population parameter will fall. For example, because we know that 95 percent of the scores in a normal distribution fall within 1.96 standard deviations of the mean, we estimate the 95 percent confidence interval for the mean of a normally distributed population (μ) with known variance (σ^2) as the mean computed from a sample ($\overline{X}$) ± 1.96 standard errors ($\sigma\sqrt{n}$ where n = sample size). When the population variance is unknown and must be estimated from sample data (which is usually the case), the t-distribution rather than the normal distribution is used. The sample variance (s^2) is substituted for the population variance.

Use of confidence intervals to compare conditions can be illustrated by computing the 95 percent confidence interval (CI) for the data presented in box 3.5. In this case, the population parameter of interest is the difference between the population means of the treatment and control conditions, and the relevant data values are the differences between the sample means and the standard error of the difference.

$$95\% \text{ CI} = (\overline{X}_T - \overline{X}_C) \pm t \times \sqrt{\frac{s_T^2}{n_T} + \frac{s_C^2}{n_C}}$$

where $(\overline{X}_T - \overline{X}_C) = 5.6$ from box 3.5, and $\sqrt{\frac{s_T^2}{n_T} + \frac{s_C^2}{n_C}}$

is the estimated standard error of the difference = 1.435 from box 3.5. The appropriate value of t is that for 48 df and alpha = .05/2, which approximately equals 2.01.

So, the 95 percent CI = 5.6 ± 2.01 × 1.435 = 2.72, 8.48. In words, the 95 percent CI for the population mean difference between the Treatment condition and the Control condition is the interval 2.72 to 8.48.

Confidence intervals are sample statistics because different samples from the same population will in general lead to different values for the limits (end points) of the confidence interval. If we were to generate a number of estimates of the 95 percent confidence interval by taking repeated random samples of the same size from the same population, then 95 percent of these would contain the population value of interest. Thus, in some sense, we have pinned down the plausible values of the population value by virtue of having computed a sample value. Of course, other levels of confidence (say 90 percent or 99 percent) can be established, population values other than means can be estimated, and the intervals can either be bounded on both ends or on only one end. The greater the degree of confidence required (e.g., 99 percent as opposed to 95 percent), the larger the range of possible population values that must be admitted.

Confidence interval estimation and hypothesis testing can be considered as opposite sides of the same coin. In hypothesis testing we start with assumptions (H_o and H_a) about population values and use sample data to assess these assumptions. In confidence interval estimation we start with sample data and use these to establish plausible ranges for the population values. The two approaches can serve the same purpose. If the 95 percent confidence interval for the difference between two population means, $\mu(1) - \mu(2)$, does not contain the value 0, this is equivalent to rejecting (with alpha = .05 in a two-tailed test) the hypothesis that the population means are equal. The two approaches can serve complementary purposes. Hypothesis testing is likely to be an important first step in theory evaluation—e.g., is there really a difference between the experimental condition and the control condition? Following rejection of the null hypothesis, confidence intervals can be computed to provide more information about the magnitude of the difference.

Some journals that publish psychological research now strongly suggest that authors report standard errors along with mean values. Interested readers can then readily compute confidence intervals. Some authors even provide confidence bands rather than points in presenting their results on graphs.

Correlation and Regression

Sometimes a research psychologist is faced with a problem that does not involve the effects of variables under experimental control. For example, the researcher might be interested in the relationship between amount of television viewing by grade-school children and their grades. The researcher will not be able to determine the direction of causality between these variables (see chapter 1) but will be able to measure the strength of association or **correlation** between them. In this section we examine ways of quantifying the relationships between two or more variables that are not under experimental control and use this information to predict future values of one of the variables.

Correlation Coefficient

In discussing the computation of correlation and regression, only the case of linear relationships will be considered—i.e., situations where a "scatter diagram" plotting each pair of values (e.g., X_i, Y_i for individual i) as a point in two-dimensional space has the form of an ellipse with its axis serving as "the line of best fit," "the prediction line," or "the **regression line.**" Linear relationships are common in psychological research and are the simplest to deal with mathematically. When the variables are linearly related, Pearson's correlation coefficient is a measure of the degree of relationship present. The definitional formula for the correlation coefficient is

$$r = \sum_{i=1}^{n} Z(X_i)Z(Y_i)/n$$

where $Z(X_i)$ and $Z(Y_i)$ are the standard score transformations of the scores X_i and Y_i, respectively, and n is the number of paired observations of X and Y. The standard score transformation,

$$Z(X_i) = (X_i - \bar{X})/s_x \text{ or } Z(Y_i) = (Y_i - Y)/s_y,$$

FIGURE 3.2   Scatter diagrams depicting relationship between correlation and prediction. Note that as the absolute value of r increases, the scatter about the regression line decreases and the more accurately one can predict Y from X.

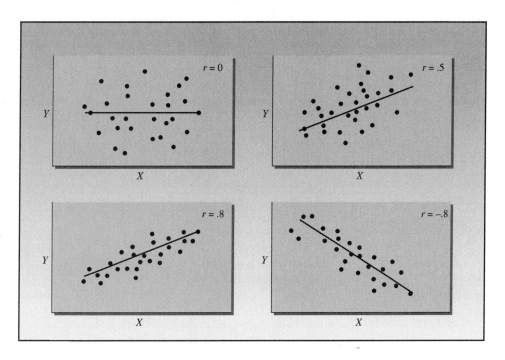

expresses each score in units of standard deviation from the mean rather than in physical units so that a correlation between, say, height and weight will be the same if the measures are expressed in metric units or in U.S. customary units. The formula can then be stated simply as the mean of the cross product of standard scores.

While conceptually simple, the standard-score form of the formula is awkward to work with and other, mathematically equivalent, computational formulas are usually substituted, as illustrated in box 3.10. Besides being unit-free, the correlation coefficient has the desirable property of being bounded by +1 (for a perfect positive correlation where $Z(Y) = Z(X)$ for each pair of values) and –1 (for a perfect negative correlation where $Z(Y) = -Z(X)$ for each pair), with $r = 0$ representing no relationship between the variables. These values of r represent the extremes of the elliptical nature of the scatter diagram: for $r = \pm 1$ all points fall on a straight line, and for $r = 0$ the points form a circular array. The

higher the absolute value of r, the "tighter" the ellipse and the closer the points lie, on the average, to the line of best fit.

A graphical description also indicates the relationship between correlation and prediction. If one uses the scatter diagram of paired values of X and Y to predict the value of Y for a new value of X, then the regression line will give the best prediction. The less the scatter or variability of points around the line—i.e., the higher the absolute value of r—the more accurate the prediction. The stronger the relationship, the greater the extent to which knowing X reduces our uncertainty about Y, as illustrated in figure 3.2.

Suppose a clinical psychologist wishes to examine the relationship between the degree of emotional disturbance of her new inpatients and their required length of hospitalization. She devises a battery of tests leading to a composite score of emotional disturbance and hopes eventually to use this to predict the required length of hospitalization of her patients. While this problem bears some

BOX 3.10

Calculation of Correlation Coefficient and Regression Line

Data

Patient Number	Emotional Disturbance (X)	Days of Hospitalization (Y)	X^2	Y^2	XY
1	10	26	100	676	260
2	11	18	121	324	198
3	6	12	36	144	72
4	10	20	100	400	200
5	13	35	169	1225	455
6	20	38	400	1444	760
7	9	21	81	441	189
8	12	7	144	49	84
9	8	10	64	100	80
10	18	42	324	1764	756
11	13	25	169	625	325
12	14	20	196	400	280
13	7	9	49	81	63
14	15	30	225	900	450
15	10	25	100	625	250
16	11	14	121	196	154
17	7	16	49	256	112
18	16	32	256	1024	512
19	8	18	64	324	144
20	15	40	225	1600	600
	233	458	2993	12,598	5944

Scatter Diagram:

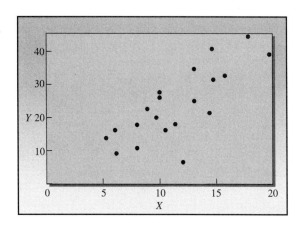

Calculation of Correlation Coefficient (r)

A version of the computational formula for r that uses raw scores (and thus is ideally suited for hand calculator use) is

$$r = \frac{\Sigma XY - (\Sigma X)(\Sigma Y)/n}{\sqrt{[\Sigma X^2 - (\Sigma X)^2/n]\,[\Sigma Y^2 - (\Sigma Y)^2/n]}}$$

where all the appropriate sums are given at the bottom of the data table and n = number of pairs of scores. Substituting in these values,

$$r = \frac{5944 - (233)(458)/20}{\sqrt{[2993 - (233)^2/20]\,[12{,}598 - (458)^2/20]}}$$

$$= .79$$

($r^2 = .63$ represents the proportion of the variance in Y explained by variations in X.)

Assumptions

1. X and Y are linearly related.
2. For each value of X, Y is normally distributed.
3. The variance of Y for a given value of X is the same for all values of X.

Test of Significance of r

If we want to test the hypothesis that the population correlation is zero (i.e., that the variables are not linearly related), we use the following t-test:

$$t = r\sqrt{\frac{n-2}{1-r^2}}\,,\text{ with } df = n - 2.$$

In our case,

$$t = .79\sqrt{\frac{20-2}{1-.63}} = 5.51, \text{ with } df = 18.$$

For $\alpha = .01$ (or any higher level), we would reject H_o in favor of the alternative that there is a positive correlation between X and Y.

Calculation of Regression Line

$$Y = a + bX$$

$$\text{where } b = \frac{\Sigma XY - (\Sigma X)(\Sigma Y)/n}{\Sigma X^2 - (\Sigma X)^2/n} = \frac{608.3}{278.55} = 2.18$$

Note that the computational formula for b contains the same terms as the formula for r, thus minimizing the additional calculations required.

$$a = \overline{Y} - b\overline{X} = 22.90 - 2.18 \times 11.65 = -2.50$$

The value of Y for a new value of X can then be predicted from the equation, $Y = 2.18X - 2.50$. (e.g., if $X = 10$, $Y = 2.18 \times 10 - 2.50 = 19.30$)

resemblance to the chi-square problem described earlier, the data in the present case are pairs of continuous scores (degree of emotional disturbance and length of hospitalization) rather than cross-classified frequency counts. The appropriate statistical procedures here are correlation and regression. These are illustrated in box 3.10 for data from 20 hypothetical patients who were given the battery of tests and whose length of hospitalization was recorded.

For these data, a moderately high positive correlation (r) was obtained such that over half the variance in length of hospitalization could be accounted for by the composite score of emotional disturbance. This, of course, still leaves a substantial portion of the variance unexplained, so that predictive accuracy is less than perfect. Nevertheless, such data would indicate that the battery of tests developed by the clinical psychologist is useful for anticipating approximately how much hospitalization is required for a particular patient. The logic here is that data from past subjects summarizing the relationship between an initial measure (test scores of emotional disturbance) and a later measure (required length of hospitalization) can be used to predict the second measure from the first for a new subject. The higher the correlation, the more accurate the predictions. Note, however, that these tests do not tell us *why* the two measures are related. Unknown subject variables may underlie both measures of emotional disturbance and required length of hospitalization.

Range Effects

One statistical phenomenon associated with correlation and regression that could affect the interpretation of psychological research is the "variance" or "range" effect. Suppose that the correlation between reading ability and arithmetic ability is near 0 for a group of students at the same grade level. If a group is formed by combining third, fourth, and fifth grade students, then a positive correlation between reading ability and arithmetic ability will emerge, as illustrated in figure 3.3. Note that several partially overlapping circular scatter plots can have the appearance of a single ellipse.

FIGURE 3.3   Effect of score variability on correlation.

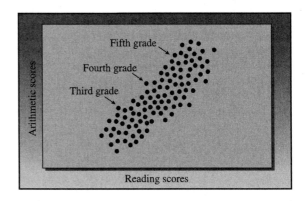

The main point of this illustration is that the correlation between X and Y will increase as the variance of X-scores and the variance of Y-scores increase. Researchers must thus be cautious in interpreting differences in correlation between conditions that may also vary in score variability.

Regression

The standard score form of the formula for the regression line is simply $Z(Y) = rZ(X)$. This formula states that when X and Y are expressed in standard scores, then the regression line passes through the origin, with slope equal to r. However, if one wants to use the relationship between high school grade point average and college grade point average to predict college grades for a current high school graduate, then a computational formula in actual grade-point units is needed (see box 3.10).

The standard-score regression formulation does illustrate an important statistical phenomenon that has implications for designing experiments in psychology. The phenomenon is known as **regression to the mean.** Suppose that the correlation between "degree of emotional disturbance" at one time (Time X) and "degree of emotional disturbance" six months later (Time Y) is .75. Now suppose that a sample of the most severely disturbed patients (e.g., those who are 3 standard deviations above the mean on a test of emotional disturbance) is chosen for a study of therapy effectiveness. The equation $Z(Y) = rZ(X)$ tells us that, on the average, the patients will be less severely disturbed six months later (2.25 rather than 3 standard deviations above the mean), apart from any beneficial effect of therapy, because factors other than X that affect Y are not likely to be as extreme as the selected values of X. (In other words, in selecting extreme values of X, we "capitalize on chance" by including all factors, even random ones, that produce high values. On a later test, these random factors, on average, will be less extreme, lowering the mean score for the sample.) A good clinical researcher will thus include an untreated control group (matched to the treatment group on "degree of emotional disturbance") to test whether the improvement shown by the treatment group is due to more than just a regression effect. Effectiveness of therapy will then have to be demonstrated by significant improvement above and beyond that shown in the control group. Another example to which we will return concerns the "slippage" often found when a baseball player receives a high salary for one year's performance only to perform worse the following year.

Multiple Regression

If a variable Y can be predicted from a single variable that is known to be correlated with Y, then it stands to reason that better predictions of Y can be made from several variables that are correlated with Y. The **multiple regression equation,** $Y = a + b(1)X(1) + b(2)X(2) + \ldots + b(k)X(k)$, predicts the value of Y from a weighted linear combination of the variables $X(1), X(2), \ldots, X(k)$. In the equation, a is the intercept and $b(1), b(2), \ldots, b(k)$ are coefficients corresponding to the weights or contributions of each of the X variables. When $k = 1$, the formula reduces to the simple regression case described above. Corresponding to r in the single-variable case is the **multiple correlation coefficient,** which is the correlation between the observed values of Y and the predicted values of Y based on the weighted linear combination of X scores. Computational formulas (translated into computer programs) have been developed to find the values of a, $b(1), b(2), \ldots, b(k)$ that will result in the highest possible correlation between the observed and predicted values of Y. Since there is no guarantee that

the relationship between Y and the Xs is actually linear, a linear regression analysis will not necessarily lead to a good fit but research in a variety of areas supports the usefulness of the linear regression method.

For example, success in graduate school has been predicted with reasonable accuracy by a multiple regression equation that includes factors such as undergraduate grade point average, graduate record exam scores, and quality of undergraduate institution. Predictions based on multiple regression equations are more accurate the higher the correlations between the individual X variables and Y, and the lower the correlations between the various X variables (i.e., it does little good to add "class rank" if it measures almost the same thing as "grade point average"). In research, multiple regression is often used when a variety of subject variables such as age, income, and education level are related to some measure of behavior. Hypothesis testing procedures are available for testing the significance of the effect of each X variable on Y, as well as for testing the significance of the combined effects of the several variables.

Summary and Conclusions

Statistics are used in two ways: (1) descriptive statistics summarize the behavior observed in a psychological study; (2) inferential statistics permit generalization of the results from a particular sample of individuals to the population from which the sample was randomly selected. Even in those instances where the population is not well defined, randomization of subjects to experimental conditions permits a statistical assessment of the reliability of the results of an experiment. This assessment is made by carrying out the steps in formal hypothesis testing (box 3.4).

Hypothesis testing applies probability theory to a random sample of behavior. The probability relationships among events can be mutually exclusive (additive), independent (multiplicative), or conditional. An observed sample statistic such as a sample mean is assumed to be only one instance taken from a sampling distribution of the statistic.

Hypothesis testing proceeds from statements of null and alternative hypotheses for a population value to a test of data based on a sample drawn from the defined population. Hypothesis testing is based on a method of indirect proof whereby a null hypothesis is tentatively assumed to be true until the data lead to its rejection. The allowable probability of rejecting the null hypothesis when it is true is the level of significance of the experiment (also called Type I error) and is chosen by the experimenter. The chosen level of significance also affects the probability of retaining the null hypothesis when it is false (called Type II error). The power of an experiment is the probability of correctly rejecting the null hypothesis and is equal to one minus the probability of a Type II error. Statistical power is a major consideration in experimental design. Experiments should be designed to provide sufficient power to reject the null hypothesis if it is indeed false. Because of lack of statistical power, an experimental effect may go undetected in a single study. Reliable estimates of effect size can be obtained through a technique known as meta-analysis, which combines the results of many studies.

A number of statistical tests are available for testing hypotheses about population values, and confidence intervals can be estimated to describe the location of the population value. A variety of examples were used to illustrate the continuity between formulating a research problem in psychology, generating hypotheses, selecting a suitable experimental design, applying the appropriate statistical test, and providing answers to the research questions.

The degree of relationship between two covarying factors is described by the correlation coefficient, r. Establishing that two variables are correlated does not tell us about causality but it does tell us about the accuracy of predicting the value of one variable by knowing the value of the other. The higher the absolute value of the correlation coefficient, the more accurate is the prediction of one variable from the other. Several variables can be combined in a multiple regression equation to predict the dependent measure with greater accuracy than when only one predictor variable is included.

The statistical procedures described in this chapter are common in experimental psychology and will apply to many of the examples given in later chapters. However, the particular illustrations included do not describe all the statistical analyses used in the diverse studies cited in this book. The list of suggested readings at the end of the chapter includes books that provide statistical procedures appropriate to more complex experimental designs than those illustrated in this chapter. However, the logic behind these tests is a direct extension of the logic described here.

Exercises

1. Test yourself or a friend for ESP (extra-sensory perception). Use a task where you can compute the expected number of correct and incorrect responses by chance alone (e.g., a coin-flipping or dice-throwing task). Then use chi-square to compare observed and expected frequencies. Choose a level of significance (alpha) and defend it. What outcome would support ESP? What did you find?

2. Devise a hypothetical experiment to test the hypothesis that behavior is directly related to the *product* of heredity and environment ($B = H \times E$). Describe the appropriate statistical test and the expected outcome of the test. Graph the expected results.

3. Suppose you were interested in the relationship between phases of the moon and abnormal behavior. How would you investigate this? What statistical test would you use? What are its limitations? Can you think of ways to overcome these limitations?

4. Find recent journal articles that illustrate the use of each of the following statistical tests: t-test, χ^2, analysis of variance. In each case indicate why that particular test was chosen and how it contributed to the conclusions drawn from the research.

5. Recall the opening example in this chapter. How many consecutive games would your opponent have to win before you would concede his or her superiority? (Relate your answer to the laws of probability and to choice of a level of significance.)

Glossary

alternative hypothesis Hypothesis that affirms the existence of differences between experimental conditions. (53)

chance sampling effects Differences in subject variables between samples taken from the same population. (49)

conditional probability The probability of one event given that another event has occurred. (53)

confidence intervals Range of values within which we can establish with a certain degree of confidence that a population parameter will fall. (71)

correlation Measure of the degree of covariation or strength of association between two variables. (72)

critical region Extreme values of the distribution of a statistical test; the probability is α that sample data will lead to these values if the null hypothesis is true (also known as *region of rejection*). (55)

descriptive statistics Statistical summaries of data obtained from a sample of observations. (48)

hypothesis testing Using data from samples to test whether populations are the same or different. (53)

independent events Events for which the occurrence of one does not change the likelihood of another. (52)

inferential statistics The process of inference by which characteristics of populations are learned by analyzing the characteristics of samples taken from the populations. (48)

level of significance Choice of acceptable Type I error rate (designated α) based on consideration of relative consequences of Type I and Type II errors. (54)

meta-analysis A quantitative method for combining the results of many different studies of the same phenomenon. (57)

method of indirect proof Strategy underlying hypothesis testing, by which the alternative hypothesis is supported when the null hypothesis is discredited. (53)

multiple correlation coefficient Correlation between the observed values of Y and the values of Y predicted by the multiple regression equation. (77)

multiple regression equation Equation predicting the value of a criterion variable (Y) on the basis of a weighted linear combination of predictor variables (Xs). (77)

mutually exclusive events Two events that cannot occur simultaneously. (52)

nonparametric tests Statistical tests of significance that do not rely on assumptions about the form of sampling distributions (also called *distribution-free tests*). (70)

null hypothesis Hypothesis initially assumed true; usually the hypothesis of no effect of the variable of interest. (53)

one-tailed test The critical region is concentrated at one end of the distribution of a statistical test. (55)

p-value Probability that the results of a statistical test were due to chance. (55)

planned comparisons Statistical tests designed to answer specific questions about differences between experimental conditions; trend tests relating mean values on the dependent variable to successive levels of the independent variable are examples. (62)

post hoc comparisons Statistical comparisons between experimental conditions that arise after the data have been collected. (62)

probability The long-range likelihood that a particular event will occur. (51)

random sample Sample in which each individual in the population has an equal chance of being selected. (49)

regression line Line that best fits a "scatter diagram" plotting pairs of values on a two-dimensional graph (also known as *prediction line* or *line of best fit*). (72)

regression to the mean When predicting Y from X based on the correlation between X and Y, the predicted value of Y will be less extreme (fewer standard deviation units from the mean) than the value of X. (76)

sampling distribution Distribution of values of a statistic such as the mean for different samples from the same population. (51)

standard error Standard deviation of a sampling distribution. (51)

statistically significant Results of a statistical test leading to rejection of the null hypothesis. (55)

two-tailed test The critical region is divided between both ends of the distribution of a statistical test. (55)

Type I error Rejecting a true null hypothesis. (54)

Type II error Retaining a false null hypothesis. (54)

Suggested Readings

Those of you who have already had a course in elementary statistics will have used a textbook. If you liked it, you probably kept it for future reference. If you continue on in psychology, you will have plenty of occasion to refer to your statistics book. Most elementary statistics texts cover the same basic topics—descriptive statistics, probability theory, sampling, hypothesis testing and confidence interval techniques, and correlation and regression. The texts will differ in the extent of mathematical development included, the relative emphasis on descriptive and inferential statistics, the areas from which examples are drawn, and the inclusion or exclusion of specific topics such as trend tests, multiple regression, nonparametric tests, higher-order analysis of variance, and experimental design.

For those of you who will need to go to the library on occasion to check on a particular issue in statistics, the following comprehensive texts are considered classics and have gone through several editions:

Edwards, A. L. *Statistical analysis*. New York: Holt-Rinehart-Winston.

Hays, W. L. *Statistics for psychologists*. New York: Holt-Rinehart-Winston.

Winer, B. J. *Statistical principles in experimental design*. McGraw-Hill.

For selected topics, the following texts are recommended:

Probability Theory

Feller, W. (1968). *An introduction to probability theory and its applications Vol. 1* (3rd ed.). New York: Wiley.

Parsen, E. (1960). *Modern probability theory and its applications*. New York: Wiley.

Mathematical Statistics

Dixon, W., & Massey, F. (1957). *Introduction to statistical analysis* (2nd ed.). New York: McGraw-Hill.

Hoel, P. G. (1971). *Introduction to mathematical statistics* (4th ed.). New York: Wiley.

Hogg, R. V., & Craig, A. T. (1970). *Introduction to mathematical statistics* (3rd ed.). New York: MacMillan.

Experimental Design

Cochran, W. G., & Cox, G. M. (1957). *Experimental designs* (2nd ed.). New York: Wiley.

Kirk, R. (1968). *Experimental design: Procedures for the behavioral sciences*. Belmont, CA: Brooks-Cole.

Nonparametric Statistics

Siegel, S. (1956). *Nonparametric methods for the behavioral sciences*. New York: McGraw-Hill.

Statistical Tables

Beyer, W. H. (1968). *Handbook of tables for probability and statistics* (2nd ed.). Cleveland: The Chemical Rubber Co.

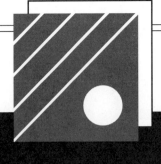

SECTION

II

Basic Areas of Research

These chapters describe content areas in psychology that are "basic" in the sense that they formed the foundation of psychology as a science. Yet they themselves rely on the building blocks described in chapters 1 to 3. These areas include perception and psychophysics, animal learning and comparative cognition, human learning, and memory. Modern day applications of "behavior modification" techniques, "motivational" procedures, behavioral medicine, and "artificial intelligence" systems owe their existence to a solid research base in these key areas.

The chapters in this section and the next section provide a sampling of research issues in the various topic areas. By no means are these meant to replace a complete course devoted to a particular area. Rather, we hope that in many cases our relatively brief coverage will serve to make you want to learn more about it.

The chapter on perception and psychophysics addresses basic issues in relating the physical world to the "psychological" world. The need for quantification in addressing these issues has led to the development of methods for measuring the capabilities and limits of the sensory system. We will describe these developments and their applications.

The chapter on animal learning and comparative cognition describes reasons for using nonhumans in behavioral research. These include both practical and ethical reasons. This chapter includes basic learning and conditioning paradigms, representing the continuum from simple to complex behaviors, stressing the unique purposes served by each paradigm. Research in this area demonstrates both the unique and the shared learning processes of different species.

The chapters on human learning and memory deal with topics that are fundamentally "human" in that they require complex verbal behavior. Basic topics include determining whether learning, at the microscopic level, is an all-or-none or a gradual process, studying the acquisition of skills such as those involved in reading comprehension, separating passive (decay) and active (interference) effects in memory, deciding whether the memory system can be broken down into component parts such as short-term and long-term memory, and analyzing the role of experience in complex tasks such as chess playing. Emphasis here will be on the development of methods to address these issues.

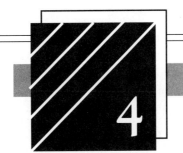

Perception and Psychophysics

Irwin P. Levin

Basic Issues in Perception
> Innate Processes
> Learning Effects
> Depth Perception
> Selective Attention
> Illusions

The Psychophysical Problem
> Thresholds
> Applications of Threshold Measures
> Relative Constancy of the DL:
>> Weber's Law
> The Psychophysical Law
> Theory of Signal Detection
> Signal Detection Tasks
> Applications of Signal Detection
>> Theory

Scaling and Measurement
> Properties of Scales
> Scaling Methods
> Tests of the Validity of Scaling
>> Methods
> Applications of Scaling Techniques

Summary and Conclusions

Exercises

Glossary

Suggested Readings

Boxes
> 1. Construction of Spatial Illusions
> 2. Formalization of Signal
>> Detection Theory
> 3. Computation of d'
> 4. Reliability and Validity

To set the stage for thinking about the issues discussed in this chapter, let us consider some simple demonstrations that can be done with everyday coins. Take a coin and move it close to your eyes and then farther away. View it in varying lighting conditions. Turn it in your fingers so that it varies from a circular image to an ellipse to a straight edge. Throughout all these permutations, you still see it as a coin. This phenomenon is known as **perceptual constancy** and has been considered one of the most impressive achievements of living organisms and one of the most important for survival.

Now, without looking at the coin, identify the president pictured on the coin and which direction he is facing. What else is printed on that side of the coin? Although you've handled and looked at coins countless times, you may not have paid much attention to these details because they weren't important to your use of coins. **Selective attention** is another crucial component of how we deal with the world.

Move the coin to a distance of arm's length and then bring it closer and closer to your eyes. At what point can you read the date on the coin? This would represent a crude measurement of *threshold,* an index of the capacity of our sense organs. Auditory as well as visual thresholds can be calculated. Have a friend drop the coin at varying distances from you. How close does it have to be before you hear the coin hit the floor?

Now take three coins of different sizes, such as a dime, a nickle, and a quarter. Trace them to form solid and dotted circles as shown below, where the dotted circles are of the same size.

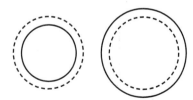

Do the two outlines of the dotted lines appear to be of the same or different sizes? If they appear different, then you've demonstrated an *illusion* (See box 4.1 on p. 91.)

Now take out a handful of coins that are otherwise identical except that one is newer and shinier than the rest. Have a friend dim the lights and spread the coins out on the floor, moving them around from trial to trial. On some trials the shinier coin is included and on some trials it is not included. Your task, called *signal detection,* is to indicate on each trial whether the shiny coin (the signal) is present or not. To make the task more interesting, suppose you were given monetary rewards for being correct and penalties for being incorrect where, for example, the penalty for not detecting the presence of the signal is higher than the penalty for saying it was there when it really wasn't. This would force you to consider the consequences of your response when you are unsure. Thus, we have injected "psychological" factors into a perceptual task.

Finally, examine coins of varying denomination and compare their physical sizes. One way to do this would be to assign a number between 1 and 100 to represent the sizes of a penny, a nickel, a dime, and a quarter. This would be an example of **psychophysical scaling,** assigning subjective values to physical dimensions. Note that persons with different characteristics—e.g., children of different ages or people above and below a certain income level—might respond differently in the coin size task.

In this chapter we will describe some rather sophisticated techniques for studying perceptual constancy, selective attention, illusions, thresholds, signal detection, and scaling. A warning: the techniques and theories developed to address issues in perception and psychophysics are more quantitative in nature than those for most other areas in psychology. The issues themselves, however, are among the most basic and fundamental in all of psychology.

Basic Issues in Perception

Probably the most basic of issues in perception is **nativism** vs. **empiricism**—the extent to which our perceptions are guided by innate processes and past experiences (sometimes referred to as "nature vs. nurture"). In 1690 John Locke proposed that the mind at birth is a blank page or "tabula rasa." The sense organs were thought to be the suppliers of all knowledge. This led to great interest in the functioning of the sense organs and the relative contributions of past experience and innate processes to perception.

Theories of perception differ in the extent to which they stress innate or learning effects. Indirect perception theories assume that the senses receive an impoverished description of the world. The stimuli do not provide accurate, complete information about objects or events and thus we must enrich stimuli with associations and expectations through learning. Direct perception theories, by contrast, stress that all the information we need is in the stimulus itself. According to this conceptualization, our perceptions are rich and elaborate because the stimuli in our environment are rich with information, rather than because our thought processes or experiences provide that richness (Gibson, 1979). Research guided by this latter approach is more apt to concentrate on real-world perception rather than sterile laboratory phenomena. Notice how several studies described in this section stress the importance of how persons interact with their environments.

Innate Processes

Several methods have been developed to study the role of innate processes in perception. What these methods have in common is the ability to demonstrate that organisms can recognize and discriminate stimuli without prior opportunities to learn them. Human infants and animals are preferred subject populations for such research because, in the one case, they have little prior exposure to selected stimuli and, in the other case, they can be deprived of stimulation.

In a classic study, Lashley and Russell (1934) compared a group of rats who were reared in the dark with a group reared under normal conditions on a distance discriminating task. The animals were placed on a high pedestal and taught to jump across a gap to a platform on which food was placed. The distance between the pedestal and platform was varied from a few inches to several feet. Both groups accurately gauged their jumps to discriminate the different distances between pedestal and platform, with the dark-reared animals performing at the same level as the control group. This showed

FIGURE 4.1   The "Visual Cliff"

© William Vandivert

that the capacity to discriminate distance in the rat was not dependent upon prior learning.

The use of children, as well as young animals, is illustrated in a series of studies using the famous "visual cliff." As shown in figure 4.1 the apparatus consists of a runway across the edge of a "cliff" (apparent sharp drop-off). A sheet of nonreflecting glass prevented the subject from actually falling off the deep side. In an early study by Gibson and Walk (1960), infants ranging in age from 6 to 14 months were tested on the visual cliff by placing them on the shallow side and having their mothers call them from the deep side. While 27 of 36 infants crawled off the runway at least once on the shallow side, only 3 crawled over the edge on to the glass. These results with human infants were duplicated by Gibson and Walk with young rats, kittens, puppies, chicks, turtles, and other animals.

Because these young subjects would still have had some visual experience, Gibson and Walk also tested dark-reared animals with no prior experience. Results were the same—preference for the shallow side over the deep side. This series of experiments supports the view that vertical depth discrimination is an innate capacity.

Learning Effects

While the case for unlearned influences on perception is clear, so also is the case for learning effects. Think of the highly paid "experts" who make their living as wine tasters or ice cream tasters. To be sure, these individuals probably started with better equipped sensory apparatus than most of us, but observation of them at work would reveal highly stylized ways of practicing their crafts, which utilize cues of aroma, color, texture, and so forth. Extended prior exposure or training has been shown to increase ability to discriminate such cues. Another example is Eskimos' ability to discriminate many more different kinds of snow than the rest of us. J. J. Gibson (1950) attributes this "perceptual learning" to the perceiver's discovery of new properties—new variables—which are present in a complex stimulus.

Another learning process is represented in figure 4.2. This ambiguous figure developed by Bugelski and Alampay (1964) can be seen as either a human profile or a rat. If prior to seeing this figure subjects are exposed to a series of unequivocal animal figures, most will perceive it as a rat. If, instead, they are shown outlines of human profiles, most will see it as a human. In this case, subjects' prior expectancy or **set** influences their perceptions. Study of the role experience plays in perception goes back to 1896 when Stratton developed an optical device for rotating the retinal image 180° so that the subject—Stratton himself—saw the world upside down. After a period of three days, he learned to adjust to his reversed visual world and move about with ease and proficiency.

Depth Perception

An important function in learning to adjust to the visual world is the ability to perceive space in three dimensions. Understanding this function has been a central problem for perception since the nineteenth century, and the topic provides some excellent examples of how researchers who were

FIGURE 4.2   An ambiguous figure (Bugelski & Alampay, 1964).

fascinated by how we perceive the world around us were able to devise apparatus and procedures for controlled study of the process.

As reported by Dember and Warm (1979), Charles Wheatstone (1838) was a pioneer in this investigation. Wheatstone observed that the image falling on one eye is slightly different from the image falling on the other eye, due to the physical separation of the eyes. This came to be known as "retinal disparity," "binocular disparity," or "stereopsis." Wheatstone was able to study this phenomenon under laboratory controlled conditions by developing an apparatus known as a "stereoscope." This apparatus, depicted in figure 4.3, permitted two slightly disparate versions of the same two-dimensional drawing to be presented separately to the two eyes. The resulting vivid three-dimensional effect demonstrated that retinal disparity is a primary determinant of the experience of depth. Stereoscopes much like those designed by Wheatstone are still in use in the study of depth perception and some families still own "Viewmasters," which project three-dimensional pictures using the same principle.

More recent research has shown that the "binocular" cues provided by retinal disparity are not the only cues in depth perception. Note by closing one

FIGURE 4.3   The Wheatstone Stereoscope. Panels E′E house slightly different drawings of a common object. Images of the drawings are reflected into each eye as an observer faces the instrument by the mirrors, AA. The instrument can be calibrated for use by different observers by sliding E′E in the uprights D′D and by adjusting the distance between D′D and the mirrors by turning the screw, p (Dember & Warm, 1979).

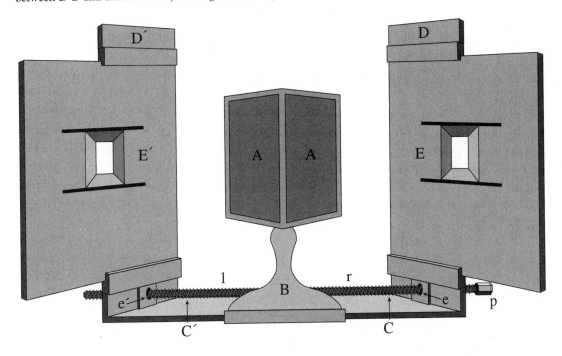

eye that objects are perceived three-dimensionally with one eye ("monocularly") almost as vividly as with two. The two-dimensional projection of three-dimensional space onto the retina of an eye provides a number of cues useful in perceiving depth. For example, as the distance of objects of the same size increases, their image on the retina becomes progressively smaller (a property which, as we will see, allows clever researchers to construct visual illusions). Notice in figure 4.4 that railroad tracks seem to converge in the distance and the railroad ties appear to be closer together near the horizon, giving a finer texturing with distance.

When comparing two otherwise identical objects, the object that casts the retinal image having the larger visual angle appears nearer. A clever study by Ittelson and Kilpatrick (1951) known as the "balloon experiment" provided a dramatic

FIGURE 4.4.   Monocular cues to depth perception

demonstration of this. Two partly inflated balloons were illuminated by a concealed source and were viewed monocularly in a dark room. The relative size of the balloons was controlled by bellows. When the balloons were of equal size, they appeared as glowing spheres at equal distances from the observer. When their relative size was continuously varied, the balloons appeared to move in a dramatic fashion back and forth through space. At any one time, the balloon that was larger seemed to be nearer than the smaller one.

Movements of the observer, the object, or the observer's eyes and head result in another stimulus property that contributes to three-dimensional space perception. Near objects appear to move more rapidly than far objects because the nearer objects move over a greater distance in the same amount of time. Watch a car coming toward you. It appears to be traveling faster the closer it comes to you. This provides yet another cue to depth or distance.

If an object hurtles toward you, it is accompanied by a rapidly expanding retinal image that signals an impending collision. This phenomenon, known as "looming," has been studied under controlled conditions by using shadow-casting devices to project the silhouette of an object onto a screen. Human infants and a variety of animals react with avoidance responses when such "looming" configurations are presented (Schiffman, 1976).

The eyes are not the only sense organs that contribute to space perception. One way to study the role of the other organs is to use blind subjects. For example, Ashmead, Hill, and Talor (1989) tested obstacle perception and navigation in 4- to 12-year-old congenitally blind children. In one task subjects walked along a sidewalk toward a target location. A box was placed along the path on some trials. Subjects spent more time in front of the box than behind it, indicating that they perceived the box and acted so as to navigate around it. In another task subjects attempted to discriminate whether a nearby disk was on their left or their right. They performed at above-chance levels. The researchers concluded that blind children with little or no visual experience use nonvisual information to perceive objects. In this case, the information they used was presumably auditory. Subjects typically talked during the trials and nearly always turned their heads from side to side, which is consistent with the hypothesis that they were using auditory information such as reflected sound from the object to be detected. Such studies clearly demonstrate nonvisual spatial ability.

Selective Attention

Another important process in learning to respond to the world is selective attention, the ability to focus on one channel of information while ignoring others. Most conceptualizations of human and animal perception consider that the capacity to process information is limited and that a filtering mechanism operates by selecting information on the basis of separate channels or classes of information. For example, auditory and visual stimuli may be considered different classes of information, and stimuli coming from different directions could be considered as different channels.

A useful experimental task for studying selective attention is the visual search task. The search task has been used to study differences in the detection of a single property of an item versus the recognition of an item having two or more properties. This is a particularly important issue because it gets at fundamental processes underlying the way we perceive the world. In a study by Treisman and Gelade (1980), subjects had to search through a series of alphabetical letters written in different colors. On each trial a card was shown bearing an array of 1, 5, 15, or 30 items consisting of the letters S, T, and X printed in the colors blue, green, and brown. In one condition subjects had to search for the letter S or any letter written in blue. In the other condition subjects had to find a green T. Each condition included some trials where the target was present and some where the target was absent. Note that the first condition required detection of a single property, "S" or "blue," while the second condition required detection of two simultaneous properties, "T" and "green." (Why do you think the single-property condition included two choices?)[1] In each condition the nontarget or "distractor" items were green Xs and brown Ts.

---

[1] The single-property condition included two choices in order to equate the relevant dimensions (letter and color) for each type of search.

Subjects were instructed to press a response key with their dominant hand if they detected a target and with the nondominant hand otherwise, and to respond as quickly as possible without making any errors. Reaction time was selected as the dependent variable because it is particularly sensitive to differences between "parallel" and "serial" search processes. A parallel process is one that allows all the properties of a target to be processed simultaneously. A serial process requires the properties to be processed one at a time.

The main finding was that an increase in the number of distractor items had a much more detrimental effect on searching for the item with two features than on detecting an item based on one feature. The authors concluded that attention can only be directed at one feature at a time and that search time for a multifeature item grows linearly with the number of items in the display because the features are searched for in serial fashion. (What result would have supported a model in which features are searched for in parallel [simultaneous] fashion?)[2]

In most cases selective attention is an important survival mechanism—we must focus our attention to avoid responding to irrelevant stimuli. Occasionally, however, it can work in the opposite direction. Consider the jogger wearing a Walkman who may be "tuned in" to the music but "tuned out" to traffic hazards. Consider also the present author who, after a lifetime of driving in the United States, had to adjust to driving in England. When negotiating a right turn in the United States, you have to attend to the cross-traffic on the street to which you are turning but you can more or less ignore the traffic on the street you are currently traveling. Think of what would happen if you did the same thing in England. Do you wonder why so many American tourists stay off the roads and in the pubs?

A variant of the visual search task has been used to study the effects of conflicting features or cues on perception of stimuli. In a classic study, Stroop (1935) asked subjects to name a series of colors as quickly as possible. In one condition, subjects were shown different colored squares. In another condition, the colors were printed on words that named another color (e.g., "green" printed in red ink). Times to name colors were approximately 75 percent longer when colors were printed on incongruent color-words than when they were printed in squares. This phenomenon, known as the "Stroop effect," has been replicated many times with various procedural modifications. It has been attributed to the interference effect of learning to associate word stimuli and reading responses. This task has proved sufficiently frustrating to subjects that medical scientists sometimes use it as part of their "stress tests."

Note that the last two cited studies used **reaction time** (RT) as the primary dependent variable. Among the reasons why RT can be a useful dependent measure are its reliability and its sensitivity to changing stimulus conditions. Sometimes a mean difference between experimental conditions of .2 seconds or less is sufficient to produce a statistically significant result.

Simon (1990) describes a series of such studies concerning the effects of an irrelevant directional cue on selective attention with auditory information. For example, in one experiment subjects wore earphones and sat at a table with their right and left index fingers each resting on a telegraph key. They were instructed to press the right-hand key as quickly as possible after hearing the word "right" and to press the left-hand key as quickly as possible after hearing the word "left." A timer started when a command was presented and stopped when the subject pressed the key. The commands were presented to either the right ear or the left ear, in random sequence. The RT was found to be significantly faster when the command "right" was presented in the right ear and when the command "left" was presented in the left ear than when the command did not correspond to the ear in which it was presented. Simon interpreted results such as these to reveal a stereotypic tendency to respond initially to the directional component of a stimulus rather than to its symbolic content. Probably no other dependent variable would have enabled Simon to reach these conclusions.

---

[2] If features are searched for in parallel fashion, then increases in search time as the number of distractor items increased would be the same in both conditions.

Illusions

The classic example of providing conflicting cues in the study of perception is constructing perceptual illusions. There are several reasons why the study of illusions has been an important part of the area of perception and psychophysics. First, it is intriguing to study when and why our senses let us down and lead to distortions. More importantly, the study of illusions allows us to better understand the cues that govern the perception of the world around us.

Illusions represent one of those topics in which naturalistic observation was followed by controlled experimentation. Consider the "moon illusion." We have all observed that when the moon is closer to the horizon it appears larger than when it is high in the sky. One explanation is that the apparent distance of the moon from us is greater when it is on the horizon. Under normal viewing conditions the size of the image of an object on the retina decreases with increases in viewing distance. The principle of "size constancy" is fundamental to the perception of depth. It follows that when there are two objects whose retinal images are of the same size, the one at the greater distance will appear larger. Thus when the moon appears to be farther away (i.e., when it's on the horizon), it also appears to be larger.

While the moon illusion itself is based on observational data, the experimental method has been applied to investigate issues related to the moon illusion. For example, Suzuki (1991) presented subjects with two pairs of light points, separated by a visual angle of 3.5 degrees, on the dome screen of a planetarium. One pair of light points was presented in the horizontal direction and the other was at the zenith. Subjects' comparison of the distances between the two pairs produced a size discrepancy comparable to the moon illusion: as long as the room was darkened, the horizontal points were seen as farther apart than the points at the zenith.

Another likely cue in the moon illusion is the terrain at the horizon. When the image of the moon is superimposed on a background of houses, trees, etc., the contrast in size makes the moon seem especially large. After many years of debate, there is still no single universally accepted explanation of

FIGURE 4.5   The Müller-Lyer Illusion

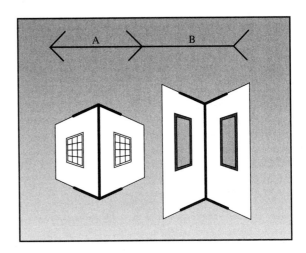

the moon illusion. Nevertheless, interest in the moon illusion led to many interesting studies of visual perception.

The Müller-Lyer illusion illustrated in figure 4.5 is also useful for understanding the principles of perception. In the upper portion we all see the line enclosed by diverging markers as longer than the line enclosed by converging markers. This perception remains even after we assure ourselves that the two lines measure the same. Now note in the lower portion that the longer-appearing line segment more closely resembles the back edge of a rectangular object while the shorter-appearing line segment more closely resembles the front edge of a rectangular object. By the same principle used by some to explain the moon illusion, the line that appears farther away also appears larger. By pitting against each other the cues used for size estimation and the cues used for depth perception, an illusion is created. Box 4.1 describes several other common illusions.

While we take it for granted that studies such as those cited above use overt behavior as the ultimate unit of measurement—whether or not the child crosses the "cliff," which brand is preferred by the wine taster, whether the ambiguous figure is identified as a rat or a human, time to identify the color—this has not always been the case. As

BOX 4.1

Construction of Spatial Illusions

As was seen in the Müller-Lyer illusion, illusions are constructed by providing cues that conflict with one another. A research goal is to separate their effects. Included here are several additional examples. Orientation of the line is shown to be a cue for perception of length. In the horizontal-vertical illusion, the vertical line will appear to most of us to be the longer. Using psychophysical methods to be described later in this chapter, the magnitude of the illusion can be measured (e.g., how much one line has to be altered before it appears equal in length to the other), and various independent variables and subject variables can be examined for their effects. Independent variables of interest include the relative positions of the two lines (e.g., to what extent is the vertical line centered over the horizontal line, do the two lines intersect) and whether the lines are tilted. (Try these variations for yourself.)

A common subject variable in studies of illusions is age, with the usual finding that the magnitude of illusions decreases with age. This suggests that the capacity to perceive objects in terms of their true physical properties is to some extent learned. In the case of the horizontal-vertical illusion, cross-cultural studies are also of interest. One hypothesis is that the illusion is due to our experience with horizontal and vertical expanses. Thus, city dwellers who are constantly looking up at tall buildings whose images are foreshortened should be more apt to "adjust" vertical images upward than are ocean dwellers or desert dwellers. Data tend to bear this out.

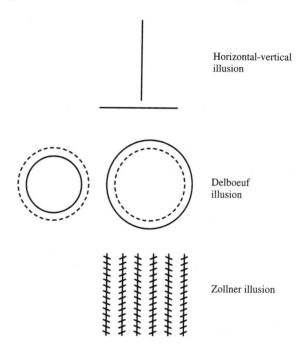

Horizontal-vertical illusion

Delboeuf illusion

Zollner illusion

In the Delboeuf illusion, the two dashed circles of equal diameters appear different when one is inside a larger circle and the other is outside the smaller circle. The one surrounded by a large circle appears larger. In the Zollner illusion, parallel lines no longer look parallel when they are cross-hatched in opposite directions. Can you develop your own hypotheses for these effects? How would you test them?

---

reviewed by Day (1966), the nineteenth century conception of psychology was as the study of conscious experience, as exemplified by the writings of Wilhelm Wundt. In this view, sensations were thought of as the raw material of experience and perceptions as their meaningful synthesis. Wundt developed a refined method of introspection by training observers to report their experiences under various conditions of stimulation. "Analytical introspection" requires observers to

take apart their total experience and analyze the sensations that constitute it. This method lacks the objectivity of more recent methods and has largely been replaced by psychophysical methods designed to quantify the data of perception. In later chapters we will see that "think aloud" techniques, which attempt to go beyond the earlier introspection methods, have a role in understanding human thinking, problem solving, and decision making.

The Psychophysical Problem

The term **psychophysics** implies a relationship between internal sensations ("psycho") and external properties of stimuli ("physics"). In exploring this relationship we will examine a variety of ingenious methods developed by experimental psychologists to uncover the processes by which the "external" world is translated into the "internal" world. The area of psychophysics goes far beyond qualitative, intuitive analyses, and is noted for its quantitative approach. A key issue here is finding appropriate measurement or scaling techniques.

The historical development of psychophysics parallels the development of experimental psychology itself because some of the first experimental methods applied to behavior came from psychophysics. Many of these methods are attributed to Gustav Fechner (1801–1887) whose background in philosophy and physics led him to become involved in the mind-body problem. In 1860, he published his *Elemente der Psychophysik*, which developed the thesis that the mind can be measured by measuring how changes in "physical energy" lead to changes in "mental energy." During the course of this chapter we will describe methods for measuring thresholds that can be traced back to Fechner, and we will describe his development of a mathematical equation that became known as "the psychophysical law." As we will see later, this equation was based on the concept of the "just-noticeable difference," which was first expressed by another founding father of psychophysics, Ernst Weber (1795–1878).

Thresholds

Definitions

The measurement of sensory thresholds is important because it defines the capabilities (to accentuate the positive) or the limitations (to accentuate the negative) of our sensory system. Sensory thresholds are of two types: those measuring the boundary between sensation and its absence, and those measuring the minimal change in stimulus intensity that can be detected. The first type is exemplified by asking what is the softest tone that can be detected by an observer. The second type is exemplified by asking how many additional candles must be lit before an observer detects an increase in illumination in a room already lit by 100 candles. These two questions correspond, respectively, to the measurement of absolute thresholds and the measurement of difference thresholds. Let us now define these terms more precisely.

Absolute threshold is traditionally defined as the minimal physical stimulus value that will produce a response 50 percent of the time. (Occasionally, as in pitch of tone, an upper threshold must also be defined.) **Difference threshold** is defined as the change in value of the physical stimulus that is noticeable 50 percent of the time.

Why the 50 percent figure in these definitions? We all recognize that species differ in their ability to detect stimuli (dogs can respond to high-frequency tones that are inaudible to humans) and that individuals within a species differ in, say, visual acuity. A little more thought will reveal that the same individual varies from moment to moment—sometimes we hear the alarm clock go off and sometimes we do not; sometimes the smell of food cooking in the next room goes unnoticed and sometimes it drives us to distraction. Because of these moment-to-moment variations, thresholds must be defined statistically. The 50 percent figure is arbitrary but it has a ready analog in the use of the median as a measure of average or central tendency.

Methods

The classic methods of measuring thresholds differ in terms of how the stimuli are presented (in random order or in systematically ascending or descending order), who manipulates the stimulus levels (the experimenter or the subject), and the type of response required (judgments of equality or judgments of inequality). To give you a feel for how thresholds are calculated, we provide a detailed description of one of these methods. We then refer briefly to other methods.

The Method of Limits. If you were asked to devise a method for determining thresholds, you just might come up with the method of limits. In this method stimuli are presented in systematic order. In determining absolute thresholds, the level of intensity of

TABLE 4.1 The Measurement of Absolute Threshold by the Method of Limits.

Stimulus Value	Asc.	Des.	Asc.	Des.	Asc.	Des.	Asc.	Des.	Asc.	Des.	Stimulus Value
20								+			20
19								+			19
18		+				+		+			18
17		+				+		+		+	17
16		+				+		+		+	16
15		+		+		+		+		+	15
14		+		+		+		+		+	14
13		+		+		+		+		+	13
12		+		+	+	−		−		+	12
11	+	+		−	−				+	−	11
10	−	+	+						−		10
9	−	−	−				+		−		9
8	−		−				−		−		8
7	−		−				−		−		7
6	−		−				−		−		6
5	−						−				5
4	−						−				4
3	−										3
Individual thresholds	10.5	9.5	9.5	11.5	11.5	12.5	8.5	12.5	10.5	11.5	

Mean threshold value: 10.8   Standard deviation: 1.27

the stimulus is sometimes started low and then increased gradually until the subject is able to detect it; and it is sometimes started high and then decreased gradually until the subject is no longer able to detect it. (Of course, the experimenter must determine through pilot work the range of stimuli to be employed.) On each trial the subject responds whether the stimulus was "present" or "not present." The first type of series is referred to as an ascending series and the second type of series is referred to as a descending series. A threshold measurement is obtained for each series by recording the value on which the series ends (i.e., when the subject first detects the stimulus in ascending series or when the subject first fails to detect the stimulus in descending series). In practice, the average of an equal number of ascending series and descending series is often used to estimate the stimulus value that is detected

50 percent of the time. This is illustrated in table 4.1 for determining the absolute threshold for brightness of light (Underwood, 1966).

Measurement of difference thresholds requires a comparison of two stimuli—the standard stimulus and the variable stimulus. A fixed value of the standard is used on each trial and the variable stimuli range from values that can be clearly detected to be less than the standard to values that can be clearly detected to be greater than the standard. Difference thresholds can be calculated with the method of limits by presenting ascending series in which the variable stimulus is initially much lower in intensity than the standard and is increased gradually until it is clearly greater in intensity than the standard, and by presenting descending series in which the variable stimulus is initially higher than the standard and is decreased gradually until it is clearly lower

TABLE 4.2   **The Measurement of Difference Thresholds by the Method of Limits.**

STIMULUS VALUE	ASC.	DES.	ASC.	DES.	ASC.	DES.	ASC.	DES.	ASC.	DES.	STIMULUS VALUE
58				+						+	58
57		+		+				+		+	57
56		+		+		+		+		+	56
55		+		+		+		+		+	55
54		+	+	+		+		+	+	+	54
53	+	+	=	+	+	=		+	=	+	53
52	=	+	=	+	=	=		=	=	+	52
51	=	=	=	+	=	=	+	=	=	+	51
50	=	=	=	=	=	=	=	=	=	=	50
49	=	=	=	=	=	=	−	=	=	=	49
48	−	=	−	=	−	=	−	−	=	−	48
47	−	−	−	=	−	−	−	−	−	−	47
46	−		−	−	−	−	−				46
45	−		−		−	−	−				45
44	−		−		−	−	−				44
43	−				−	−					43
42					−						42
Upper threshold	52.5	51.5	53.5	50.5	52.5	53.5	50.5	52.5	53.5	50.5	
Lower threshold	48.5	47.5	48.5	46.5	48.5	47.5	49.5	48.5	47.5	48.5	

Mean upper threshold: 52.1   Upper difference threshold: 52.1 − 50 = 2.1
Mean lower threshold: 48.1   Lower difference threshold: 50 − 48.1 = 1.9

than the standard. When comparing the variable and standard stimulus on each trial, the subject is asked to respond that the first stimulus is "less than," "equal to," or "greater than" the second stimulus.

On each series of trials there are two transition points. In ascending series there is a change from "less than" responses to "equal to" responses (this is the lower threshold of change) and a change from "equal to" responses to "greater than" responses (the upper threshold of change) as the value of the variable stimulus level is increased. In descending series there is a change from "greater than" responses to "equal to" responses (the upper threshold of change) and a change from "equal to" responses to "less than" responses (the lower threshold of change) as the value of the variable stimulus is decreased. There are thus two thresholds of change

(or DLs, from "difference limen," the original Latin term). These are the difference between the upper threshold of change and the *point of subjective equality* (or PSE, which is defined as the mean stimulus value of the "equal to" responses) and the difference between the lower threshold of change and the PSE. This is illustrated in table 4.2 for measuring the difference thresholds for brightness of light, with a standard stimulus value of 50.

Other Methods. Other methods of calculating absolute and difference thresholds vary somewhat from the method of limits. Most notable among these are the *method of constant stimuli* and the *method of adjustment* (also known as the *method of average error*). Table 4.3 summarizes these methods and shows how they differ from the method of limits. The interested

TABLE 4.3   Methods of Measuring Thresholds

Method	Manner in which Stimuli Are Presented	Subject's Response		Threshold Measure	
		Absolute Threshold	Difference Threshold	Absolute Threshold	Difference Threshold (DL)
Method of Limits	Stimuli presented in ascending series or descending series of magnitudes	Stimulus is "present" or "not present"	One stimulus (e.g., the variable stimulus) is "less than," "equal to," or "greater than" the second stimulus (e.g., the standard)	Average of values of when subject first detects the stimulus in ascending series and when subject first fails to detect the stimulus in descending series	Difference between value when subject changes from "less than" response to "equal to" response and mean stimulus value of "equal to" responses (upper DL, for ascending series); difference between value when subject changes from "greater than" response to "equal to" response and mean stimulus value of "equal to" responses (lower DL, for descending series)
Method of Constant Stimuli	Stimuli of varying intensity are presented in random order	Stimulus is "present" or "not present"	Which stimulus—the "standard stimulus" or the "variable stimulus"—is greater in magnitude	Stimulus value detected 50% of the time	Difference between 75th percentile[1] and the "point of subjective equality" (upper DL) and the difference between the 25th percentile[2] and the "point of subjective equality" (lower DL)
Method of Adjustment or Average Error	Subject adjusts the stimulus level upward or downward	Detect or not detect the stimulus	Match or reproduce a standard stimulus value	Average of values of when subject first detects the stimulus for upward adjustments and when subject first fails to detect the stimulus for downward adjustments	Average of distribution of errors for upward adjustments (upper DL) and downward adjustments (lower DL)

[1] Level of the variable stimulus judged greater than the standard 75 percent of the time.
[2] Level of the variable stimulus judged greater than the standard 25 percent of the time.

95

reader can find the procedural details for applying these methods in a number of texts, including Underwood (1966) and Candland (1968).

Applications of Threshold Measures

Age-Related Differences in Threshold

In a study by McFarland, Warren, and Karis (1958), *critical flicker frequency thresholds* were obtained from subjects ranging in age from 13 to 89 years. Critical flicker frequency thresholds are measures of how close together rapid flashes of light must be before they "blend together" and are perceived as a single steady light. The methodology is aimed at distinguishing between the perceptions of flicker and fusion. In this study subjects were seated in a modified dentist's chair to regulate their position and eye fixation. A flicker fusion apparatus was employed that was capable of varying flash frequency from 1 to 125 flashes per second.

The method of limits was employed where frequency was continuously increased in steps of 1 cycle per second until the response changed from "flicker" to "steady" (ascending series) or frequency was continuously decreased in steps of 1 cycle per second until the response changed from "steady" to "flicker" (descending series). The major finding concerning the age factor was that the critical flicker frequency threshold decreased linearly with age—i.e., the older the person, the farther apart the light flashes had to be before he or she could distinguish between flicker and fusion.

Perception of Taboo Words

In a classic study, McGinnis (1949) presented subjects with words flashed for brief periods on a tachistoscope. The subject was asked to identify each word by saying it aloud. Each word was presented repeatedly using the method of limits. The exposure time was made progressively longer until the subject was able to say the correct word. Eleven of the words were neutral in affect such as "apple" and "river," but seven were emotional or taboo words such as "whore" and "raped." Results showed that longer exposures were needed for the subjects to correctly report the emotional words. However, galvanic skin response (GSR) recordings showed that subjects were affected by the emotional words even before they reported them correctly. (Note the relevance of this to "subliminal perception.")

A popular theoretical account at that time was called "perceptual defense." Perceptual defense was said to be based upon conditioned avoidance of unpleasant or dangerous stimulus objects. According to this account, subjects tend to repress (not perceive) things that are threatening. However, a more recent account is based on response bias. Subjects set a higher criterion for taboo words than for neutral words such that they have to be surer of them before saying them out loud. The theory of signal detection to be described in a later section explicitly includes response bias as a component of signal detection.

Relative Constancy of the DL: Weber's Law

Consider the example of lighting additional candles in a room already illuminated by many candles. Intuition tells us that the larger the number of candles already lit, the more additional candles will be needed before an increase in illumination is detected. In other words, the *just-noticeable difference* will depend on the original stimulus value. The methods described above allow us to quantify this relationship. Recall that the difference threshold is calculated as a change in stimulus intensity (ΔS) from the value of some standard stimulus (S). Across a wide variety of stimulus dimensions and methods of measuring DLs, the following simple equation approximates the relationship between ΔS and S: $\Delta S/S = k$, where k is a constant for a given observer and is known as **Weber's fraction.** The entire expression is known as *Weber's law* in honor of the man who originally postulated the law in 1834 to account for results with lifted weights. In words, it says that the DL is a constant ratio of the stimulus value at which it is measured. The simplicity of this formulation attests to the orderliness of our perceptions.

Perhaps the main use of Weber's law has been for comparing the sensitivity of different types of stimulation. The smaller the value of Weber's fraction, the greater the sensitivity of the observer in detecting differences along that stimulus dimension. Table 4.4 provides estimates of Weber's

TABLE 4.4 Weber's Fraction. Values of Weber's fraction obtained under ideal laboratory conditions for various sensory discriminations. The smaller the fraction, the greater the differential sensitivity.

SENSE MODALITY	WEBER'S FRACTION
Pitch of a tone	1/333
Deep pressure, from skin and subcutaneous tissue	1/77
Visual brightness	1/62
Lifted weights	1/53
Loudness of a tone	1/11
Cutaneous pressure	1/7
Taste for saline solution	1/5

Adapted from E. G. Boring, H. S. Langfeld, and H. P. Weld, *Foundations of Psychology*. 1948: John Wiley & Sons, Inc., New York.

fraction for a variety of types of stimulation. It can be seen, for example, that sensitivity to changes in pitch of a tone is much greater than sensitivity to changes in loudness of a tone.

The Psychophysical Law

Fechner's Law

Fechner (1860) used Weber's law to develop a more general law relating changes in stimulus intensity to changes in sensation. Whereas Weber's law applies only to difference thresholds, or just-noticeable differences (jnd's), Fechner's law addresses changes of any magnitude. The usefulness of such a law is that for a given sense dimension the response to any stimulus value can be predicted.

The basis of the mathematical derivation of Fechner's law is that Weber's law can be used to specify the value of the jnd at any stimulus value and thus the jnd can be used as a unit of sensation. Fechner reasoned that the greater the number of jnd's apart two stimuli are, the farther apart they will seem on a psychological scale. He then assumed that a change in stimulation of a given number of jnd-units will always lead to a fixed change in sensation. However, these units are not equal. They increase proportionately as the stimulus value increases. Equal proportional changes in stimulus intensity are paralleled by equal arithmetic changes in sensation. For example, every time the stimulus is doubled, the response should increase by a constant amount. Thus, Fechner's

Law states that sensation increases in equal arithmetic steps as the magnitude of the stimulus increases in ratio steps.

The resulting equation can be expressed as follows: $R = k \log S$, where R is the psychological scale value, S is the physical scale value, and k is a constant of proportionality. The equation states that the psychological scale value equals a constant times the logarithm of the physical scale value. You will recall that one of the functions of logarithms is to change multiplicative relationships to additive or linear ones ($\log XY = \log X + \log Y$). For example, the Richter scale of earthquake intensity is a logarithmic scale in which an increment of 1 on the scale (e.g., from 6.0 to 7.0) represents a 10-fold increase in amplitude of ground movement. A graphic test of Fechner's law would be to plot stimulus values in log units, and the corresponding responses should plot as a straight line. The slope of the line is k, and this value will generally vary as a function of the stimulus and response dimensions.

The Power Law

About 100 years after the formulation of Fechner's law, S. S. Stevens (1961) developed a revised formulation of the psychophysical law based on his own research findings. Rather than a logarithmic function, Stevens proposed a power function. The power law is given by the following equation $R = kS^n$, where R, S, and k are the same as in Fechner's law; n is the exponent of the power function. In words, the law states that sensation is proportional to the stimulus magnitude raised to the *n*th power. It also implies that equal stimulus ratios are paralleled by equal sensation ratios. For example, if $n = .5$, quadrupling the stimulus value should lead to a doubling of response. Graphically, this formulation predicts that when both stimulus and response values are logged (i.e., the data are plotted on log-log coordinates), a straight line with slope *n* will result. This, of course, provides a ready means for estimating *n*. The value of *n* will generally differ for different sense modalities and this value can be used to categorize different sense modalities in much the same way as with Weber's fraction.

While the classic methods of measuring thresholds have produced interesting results and have furthered the development of laws of psychophysics, they have concentrated more on the properties of stimuli than on the characteristics of individuals. We now know that subject characteristics or "nonsensory processes" play a major role in perceiving the world.

Theory of Signal Detection

A fundamental problem in psychophysics is separating the effects of sensory processes (vision, audition, etc.) from the effects of nonsensory processes (response biases, expectations, motivations, etc.). A classic contemporary solution involves the combination of theory development and experimental methodology.

Overview of Theory

The name "signal detection theory" or "the theory of signal detectability" (Green & Swets, 1966; Swets, Tanner, & Birdsall, 1961) reflects the presumed pervasiveness and importance of situations in which a physical signal must be detected in the presence of background noise. (Picture, for example, a radar operator during wartime having to detect the presence of enemy aircraft, or a new parent listening for baby cries in another bedroom.) For situations in which the signal clearly stands out from the noise, the detection task is trivial. But if there is any overlap between the potential range of signal intensities and the range of noise values (in-

cluding external sources of noise and internal sources such as heartbeat), there will be instances in which the observer cannot be sure whether or not a signal was present. Here, some rule must be adopted for reporting the possible presence of a signal, even though the observer knows that the rule may generate errors. This then is an ideal situation for examining the subjective factors in dealing with an uncertain world.

Consider the two kinds of errors possible in signal detection. The observer can report a signal when in fact none was present. For obvious reasons, this is called a "false alarm." (Think of the embarrassed radar operator or the parent getting out of bed in the middle of the night.) The observer can fail to report a signal when in fact there was one. This is called a "miss." (Again, think of the radar operator, but also think of the possible victims of a sneak enemy attack, and think of the parent whose baby may really be in distress.) The four possible outcomes are given in table 4.5.

According to signal detection theory, sensory and nonsensory factors can be represented by two separate components of the signal detection process. The sensory or "sensitivity" factor is represented by the difference between a distribution of stimulus values arising when a signal is actually presented and a distribution of values when only noise is present. The greater this difference, the more likely it is that the signal will be correctly detected. The nonsensory factor is represented by a cutoff point indicating how certain the observer must be that a signal was actually presented before reporting the presence of a signal.

The placement of the cutoff point is purely subjective. The observer should take into consideration both the expected probability of a signal during any given time period and the relative consequences arising from "false alarms" and "misses." In the latter regard, the situation is analogous to that involving the setting of a significance level (alpha) in statistical hypothesis testing. Note the similarity between the possible outcomes in table 4.5 and the "truth table" given for possible outcomes of hypothesis testing in the chapter on statistical inference (box 3.3). If we assume that the

TABLE 4.5   Possible Outcomes in Signal Detection

		Signal is: Absent	Signal is: Present
Observer's Response	Yes	false positive ("false alarm")	correct positive ("hit")
	No	correct negative	false negative ("miss")

event "H_o is true" corresponds to "no signal pres-ent," then a Type I error is like a "false alarm" and a Type II error is like a "miss." In the same way that setting the value of alpha (and the resulting "criti-cal region") affects the relative probability of Type I and Type II errors in hypothesis testing, setting the value of the cutoff point in signal detection affects the relative probability of misses and false alarms. A liberal criterion of saying "yes" when uncertain will result in few "misses" (not responding to the baby's cries) but many "false alarms" (getting out of bed for nothing); a conservative criterion of saying "no" when uncertain will have the opposite effect.

Box 4.2 provides a more formalized description of the theory. The mathematical details are not as important as is gaining a basic understanding of the distinction between the observer's "sensitivity" to a signal (the sensory component) and the observer's "decision criterion" for reporting a signal (the non-sensory component). If, after going through the boxed material, you can understand the essential features of figure 4.6, then you will be in good shape for the rest of the section on signal detection theory and its applications.

The assumptions of signal detection theory are illustrated in figure 4.6. There is no intent to imply that the observer is literally performing the mathe-matical operations. Rather, the assumptions repre-sent an idealized conception of the process by which observers perceive stimulus intensity and

translate their perceptions into overt responses. This is typical of the use of mathematical models in psychology.

Separating Sensory from Nonsensory Factors

The two key parameters, d' and c, provide a con-ceptual way of separating sensory from nonsensory factors in signal detection. However, because these cannot be observed directly (remember that they are merely mathematical abstractions from a theo-retical model), they must be inferred from observ-able data. Fortunately, signal detection theory pro-vides means of doing this. The key data are expressed in the form of conditional probabilities: the conditional probability of reporting a signal when there actually was one presented (a "hit") and the conditional probability of reporting a signal when there was no signal (a "false alarm").

For any given value of the observer's cutoff point, the two conditional probabilities can be esti-mated empirically as the observed hit rate and false alarm rate. Note that while these two values are in-dependent of each other, neither by itself conveys much information about the signal detection process. A high hit rate could mean that the ob-server was quite able to detect a signal when it was presented or it could mean that the observer adopted a relatively lax criterion for reporting a sus-pected signal. A low false alarm rate could mean that the observer was able to discriminate between

BOX 4.2

Formalization of Signal Detection Theory

The theory of signal detection makes the following assumptions.

1. At any point in time, the observer converts the sensory input (perceived stimulus intensity) into a random variable, X, located on a continuum. The significance of this assumption is that sensory processes are implied to be continuous rather than discrete. This is contrary to traditional threshold theory, which assumes that the signal on a given trial either does or does not exceed the threshold and that the output of the sensory system thus can take on only one of two values. By contrast, signal detection theory assumes that the output of the sensory system can take on a whole range of values. (Listen for your own heartbeat. Even though it may be constant, it will likely appear to wax and wane in loudness.)

   The nature of the conversion of perceived stimulus intensity into a value X is based on a fundamental concept of *decision theory* (Egan & Clarke, 1966). If one of two events (A and B) can arise from the same stimulus value (S_i), then the ideal observer is assumed to be sensitive to the likelihood ratio, $P(S_i | A)/P(S_i | B)$, in deciding which event has occurred. In signal detection, Si is the perceived stimulus value at time i and A and B are the events "signal presented" and "no signal presented"; $P(S_i | A)$ and $P(S_i | B)$ then represent, respectively, the probability that the perceived stimulus value occurred on a "signal" trial and on a "no-signal" trial. X corresponds to the likelihood ratio—to be exact, it is the log of the likelihood ratio. In simpler terms, the observer is assumed to consider a stimulus input in terms of the relative likelihood that it arose from signal plus noise or from noise alone.

2. Signal presentations against a background of noise will generally lead to higher values of X than will noise alone, but for faint signals the distribution of X values for signal plus noise and the distribution of X values for noise alone will overlap. If a signal is presented, X is normally distributed with mean μ_n and variance σ^2. If only noise is presented, X is normally distributed with mean μ_s and variance σ^2, where $\mu_s \geq \mu_n$. (The assumption of equal variance for both distributions is an idealized one for purposes of simplification.) Thus, the effect of presenting a signal above and beyond the background of noise is to shift the distribution of values of X upward by an amount equal to the difference, $\mu_s - \mu_n$. If we let $d' = \frac{\mu_s - \mu_n}{\sigma}$, which is the standardized mean difference, then d' is known as the *sensitivity* measure, or the ability of the observer to discriminate between the two classes of events (noise alone vs. signal plus noise).

3. There exists on the continuum a cutoff point X_c, such that if $X > X_c$, then a signal is reported and if $X < X_c$, then no signal is reported.

   In addition to the sensitivity parameter, d', which represents sensory factors, the cutoff point defines a second parameter of signal detection theory, which is a measure of the observer's decision criterion. This second parameter represents the degree of bias present in the observer's responses. Mathematically, this parameter is usually defined as the standard score transformation of the observer's cutoff point: $c = \frac{X_c - \mu_n}{\sigma}$. In words, c represents the location of the cutoff point in terms of standard deviation units above the mean of the noise distribution.

FIGURE 4.6   Graphic representation of assumptions of signal detection theory

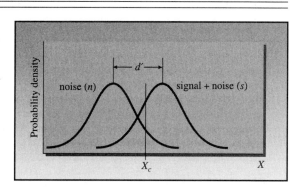

signal and noise or it could mean that the observer adopted a strict criterion for reporting a signal. Taken together, however, these two values can be very informative. For example, the combination of a high hit rate *and* a high false alarm rate suggests that a lax criterion (low value of Xc) was used; the combination of a high hit rate and a low false alarm rate suggests a high degree of sensitivity (high value of d'). It is thus logical that data analysis focuses on the relationship between these two values.

ROC Curves

Hit rate and false alarm rate can be plotted as a single point on a two-dimensional graph with hit rate on the ordinate and false alarm rate on the abscissa. Suppose now that the experimenter increases the reward for hits and decreases the penalty for false alarms. This should induce the observer to change the decision criterion (cutoff point). In this case, the subject would reduce the value of Xc and thereby increase both conditional probabilities. The two new conditional probabilities are represented by a second point on the graph. By successively inducing changes in the observer's decision criterion, a new point on the graph is produced by each new criterion. When these points are connected, the result is called a **receiver-operating-characteristic curve,** or ROC curve. The ROC curve describes changes in the observer's performance for constant signal and noise levels and a continuously changing decision criterion. This is illustrated in Figure 4.7.

The form of the ROC curve can be used to both test the adequacy of signal detection theory and estimate the key parameters. The degree of curvature of the ROC curve is positively related to the value of d' for an observer (Green & Swets, 1966). This can be seen in figure 4.7. The diagonal line represents chance performance where $d' = 0$ the probability of a hit and the probability of a false alarm are equal and the likelihood ratio is 1.0. For likelihood ratios that are nearly 1, the ROC curves lie close to the chance line. As it becomes easier to discriminate signal and noise, the ROC curve leaves the origin with steeper slope and deviates more from the chance line. Because d' is independent of the

FIGURE 4.7   ROC Curves

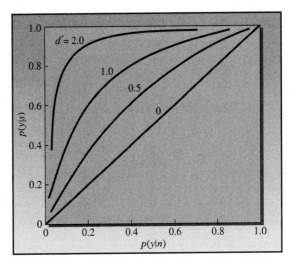

From J. P. Egan and F. R. Clarke, "Sensation and Perception" in J. B. Sidowski, Ed., *Experimental Methods and Instrumentation in Psychology.* Copyright © 1966 McGraw-Hill, Inc., New York. Reprinted by permission.

observer's response bias, it provides a "pure" measure of the sensory process, with nonsensory factors removed mathematically. Researchers can then study how sensory processes vary as a function of physical variables such as signal intensity and background noise level or subject variables such as age and attentional factors. As shown in box 4.3, the value of d' can be computed algebraically with the aid of a table of areas of the standard normal distribution.

Signal Detection Tasks

The prototypical signal detection task involves a series of "yes-no" decisions with auditory stimuli. Each trial is represented by a single well-delimited interval of time in which a signal may or may not be presented against a background of continuous white noise. The signal is a tone of fixed amplitude, frequency, and duration. On each trial the observer must report "yes, I detect it" or "no, I do not detect it"—usually by pressing keys labeled "yes" and "no." While the introduction of background noise is intended to provide a test of the

BOX 4.3

Computation of d'

Suppose that the hit rate is .80 and the false alarm rate is .40. The .80 hit rate means that the cutoff point is located where 20 percent of the area of the signal plus noise distribution lies below that point. This corresponds to a normal deviate (z-score) of −0.84. In other words, the cutoff point is .84 standard deviation units below the mean of the signal plus noise distribution. The .40 false alarm rate means that the cutoff point is located where 40 percent of the area of the noise distribution lies above it. This corresponds to a z-score of +0.25. The cutoff point is thus .25 standard deviation units above the mean of the noise distribution. Because the same point is both .84 standard deviations below the mean of the higher distribution and .25 standard deviations above the mean of the lower distribution, it follows that the difference between the means of the two distributions is .84 + .25 = 1.09 standard deviation units. This difference between the means of the noise and the signal plus noise distributions defines d'. Thus $d' = 1.09$. These calculations are illustrated here.

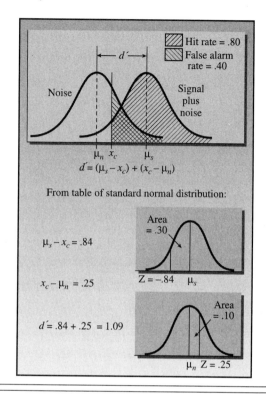

theory of signal detection, it also serves as an analog for the detection of stimuli in everyday life. Physiological processes such as breathing and circulation represent a continuous source of noise so that even in a "quiet" environment, noise is always present. Thus, information gained from a signal detection experiment conducted in the laboratory should be generalizable to the detection of signals in a variety of settings.

The laboratory task itself requires a great deal of care. Equipment is necessary to generate signals and background noise with fixed properties such as the distribution of amplitudes over time. Signal levels must be adjusted for individual subjects such that

the observer can perform at better-than-chance, but less-than-perfect levels. Because interest usually centers on the detection process rather than the learning process, observers must be well practiced. The listener may be brought to a near-asymptotic level of performance in a single session of about one hour. Later sessions can then be used to manipulate the criterion adopted by the observer so the ROC curves can be generated. For example, the observer can be induced to change from a "lax" to a "strict" criterion by changing the instructions from "press the 'yes' key each time there was any indication that a tone was presented" to "press the 'yes' key each time that you are fairly sure that a tone was presented." The criterion can also be manipulated by varying the rewards and costs of the various possible outcomes on a given trial. (How would you change your criterion if the reward for a hit increased while the cost of a false alarm decreased?) Finally, the criterion can be manipulated by varying the proportion of trials on which a signal is presented. (How would you respond if you knew that signals occurred only 10 percent of the time?)[3] Because so much information is obtained from each individual observer, studies of this type usually do not require many subjects. Sample sizes of less than 10 are common.

A variant of the "yes-no" method is the rating method. The observer is asked to rate the likelihood that the signal occurred on each trial. This provides more information than a simple "yes-no" response. The conditional probabilities represented by hit rates and false alarm rates can be computed separately for each point on the rating scale. A response of "1" is reserved for judgments of near certainty that the signal was presented and corresponds to a strict criterion (high cutoff point) and should be associated with relatively low hit and false alarm rates. A response of "2" corresponds to a somewhat more lax criterion (lower cutoff point), which leads to somewhat higher hit and false alarm rates, and so on. This procedure can thus be used to generate an ROC curve directly because each different value along the rating scale represents a different response criterion and defines a separate point.

A variety of problems in psychophysics and perception have been studied within the framework of signal detection theory, including speech perception, vigilance behavior, and pattern recognition. In addition, the theory's ability to separate sensory and nonsensory factors has led to its application in studying the sensitivities of adult and infant humans and animals to a variety of sources of stimulation.

---

[3] When unsure, you should respond "yes" more often when the reward for a hit increases and the cost of a false alarm decreases, but you should respond "yes" less often as the percentage of trials with a signal decreases.

Applications of Signal Detection Theory

Medical Diagnosis

The ROC procedure has been used to test the accuracy of medical diagnostic technologies. In one study (Swets et al., 1979), twelve radiologists using different methods were asked to examine brain images of over 100 patients in whom a tumor had been suspected. For each patient the radiologist responded on the following rating scale: definitely, or almost definitely, abnormal; probably abnormal; possibly abnormal; possibly normal, probably normal; definitely, or almost definitely, normal. Points on an ROC curve for each radiologist were obtained by plotting the proportion of hits against the proportion of false alarms for each category on the scale. As measured by the elevation of the ROC curve, the technology known as "computed tomography" was found to be more accurate than other techniques for detecting tumors.

Pain Sensitivity

A fundamental question in the area of pain perception is to what extent observed differences in response to pain are due to differential sensitivity to pain-producing stimuli and to what extent they are due to a differential tendency to report pain. Signal detection theory, by virtue of its ability to separate measures of stimulus sensitivity from response biases, is ideally suited for addressing this question.

Goolkasian (1980) used signal detection theory and methodology to compare pain sensitivity between the sexes and to compare pain sensitivity at different phases of the menstrual cycle for women. During a series of experimental sessions over a four-week period, subjects had radiant heat of varying intensities applied for 3 seconds each to a spot on the right forearm. Pain stimuli of different intensity were presented in random order in each session. Subjects were instructed to assign each stimulus to one of the following response categories: (1) nothing, (2) warm, (3) hot, (4) faintly painful, (5) moderately painful, (6) strongly painful. Subjects were given practice trials to acquaint them with the range of stimulus levels before each set of experimental trials.

Subjects were college students in good health who were taking no drugs or medication. The women in the sample were selected from those who had a regular menstrual cycle and were classified in terms of their own menstrual cycle: onset of menstruation, menstrual, postmenstrual, ovulatory, and premenstrual. Onset of experimental sessions was counterbalanced across menstrual phases.

ROC curves were generated from the rating data and used to compare pain sensitivity (estimates of d') between the sexes and at different phases of the menstrual cycle. Sex differences were found only when men were compared with women who were ovulating. Women with normal menstrual periods experienced a heightened sensitivity to pain during ovulation. The researcher concluded that past reports of pain threshold changes in association with menstrual phase were due to sensory effects and not due to differences in criteria for reporting pain.

Facial Recognition

A study by Tooley and associates (1987) illustrates how signal detection analysis can help us understand people's sensitivity to "social" situations as well as traditional psychophysical tasks. A group of white female college students were asked to simulate eyewitnesses in a trial by identifying faces they had seen before. Each subject saw a total of 24 target photos: six black persons holding a weapon in their hands, six white persons holding a weapon in their hands, and six of each race holding objects other than weapons. After inspecting each of these photos they were asked to view 72 facial photographs including the 24 target persons (but in different clothing and surroundings) plus 48 distractors (half of each race). The target persons constitute the "signals" and the distractors constitute the "noise." The subject's task was to indicate whether each face was a target person by checking *yes* or *no* on an identification form.

Two dependent variables were recorded: number of correct identifications (hits) and d' scores, which take into account both hits and false alarms (where a false alarm is described as responding *yes* to a new face). The data from both measures revealed a significant "weapon effect": subjects were better at identifying photos of persons who were not holding a weapon than they were at identifying photos of persons who were holding a weapon. This demonstrates the distracting role of the weapon. There was an interesting difference between the two dependent variables in revealing the effect of the race of the target person. Facial recognition rates were significantly higher for black persons than for white persons but there was a higher false alarm rate for black persons (i.e., the criterion cutoff for making a "seen before" response was lower for other-race [black] faces than for same-race faces). The result was that the d' scores were significantly higher for white faces than for black faces. (Which of the two dependent measures—hit rates or d' scores—do you think was most informative in this case?)[4]

Signal detection theory and the other psychophysical laws described in this chapter are summarized in table 4.6.

Scaling and Measurement

The way we react to objects in the environment is governed more by our perceptions than by objective reality. Reliable and valid measures of our perceptions are crucial. The measurement problem in psychology is particularly interesting and challenging because experimental psychologists not only work with well-defined objective stimulus dimensions, but they also work with abstract affective dimensions. Interest in one study may focus on how tone intensity in decibels affects perceived loudness, and interest in another study may focus on how personality trait characteristics affect a person's likableness. In the first case, the measurement problem can be described as a problem in *psychophysical scaling*; and in the second case, the

---

[4] d' scores are generally considered to be better measures of accuracy because they take into account both types of errors—misses and false alarms.

TABLE 4.6   Psychophysical Laws and Theories

LAW/THEORY	DESCRIPTION	COMMENTS
Weber's Law	$\Delta S/S = k$; the difference threshold is a constant ratio of the stimulus value at which it is computed.	Holds for the middle ranges of most stimulus dimensions. Is useful for comparing the sensitivity of different sense modalities.
Fechner's Law	$R = k \log S$; sensation is proportional to the logarithm of stimulus intensity.	Fechner's law was derived from Weber's law, using the jnd as the unit of sensation.
Steven's Power Law	$R = kS^n$; sensation is proportional to the nth power of stimulus intensity.	The power law tends to be supported in studies using direct scaling methods.
Signal Detection Theory	In a detection task the observer evaluates the relative likelihood that the perceived stimulus level comes from signal plus noise rather than noise alone. A cutoff point is established for reporting whether or not a signal was presented.	This theory is especially useful for separating the influence of sensory and nonsensory factors. It differs from classic threshold notions by assuming that sensory processes are continuous rather than discrete.

measurement problem can be described as a problem in *psychometric scaling*. As we shall see, the same methods can be applied to both types of problems. In psychophysical scaling, interest centers on the relationship between the obtained scale values and the corresponding physical measurements; in **psychometric scaling,** scale values may represent the only metric information available.

Properties of Scales

The three properties that are used to classify scales of measurement are whether or not they contain any *quantitative information* for comparing objects, whether or not they possess an *absolute zero* value, and whether or not they have a *constant unit*. Scales possessing an absolute zero must have a zero value indicating a zero amount (absence) of the quantity being measured. Physical dimensions such as height and weight clearly possess this property; IQ scores and most attitude measures do not. When a scale possesses a constant unit, a change of a given number of scale units has the same absolute magnitude at all points along the scale. Many physical scales have this property but many psychological scales do

not. A change from 70 degrees to 80 degrees F represents the same increment in heat as a change from 80 degrees to 90 degrees F, but does it represent the same change in "comfort"?

Four major classifications of scales based on these properties are described in table 4.7. These scales are labeled *nominal, ordinal, interval,* and *ratio,* and their different properties lead to different permissible statements about the underlying dimension being measured. For example, nominal scales merely identify or name different objects and say nothing about their relative magnitudes on any dimension. At the other extreme, ratio scales allow meaningful statements about the sum, difference, ratio, or product of two or more values.

Table 4.7 provides examples in the physical world of these different types of scales. Various psychological scales have also been presumed to fall into these different categories. In some cases this is relatively straightforward. For example, methods that require subjects to rank-order a set of stimuli generally lead to ordinal scales. However, methods that instruct subjects to sort stimuli into numerical categories or to judge the ratio of stimulus values

TABLE 4.7   Properties of Scales

Type of Scale	Quantitative Information?	Constant Unit?	Absolute Zero?	Examples of Permissible Statements	Examples
Nominal	No	No	No	$A \neq B$	Numbering of football jerseys, social security numbers
Ordinal (or Rank-Order)	Yes	No	No	$A > B$	Rankings of football teams, military ranks
Interval (or Difference)	Yes	Yes	No	$(A - B) = (C - D)$	Temperature in °C, time of day
Ratio	Yes	Yes	Yes	$A = 2B$	Height, weight, cost

may or may not lead to sets of numbers that meet the criteria of interval or ratio scales. After we describe the various scaling methods, we will describe ways to test their properties.

Scaling Methods

The Method of Paired-Comparisons

The method of paired-comparisons developed by Thurstone (1927) is one of the oldest scaling methods and is based on the notion that the psychological difference between two stimuli can be specified by the ease with which they can be discriminated from each other. Because subjects do not directly assign values to individual stimuli, this is called an "indirect" scaling method. Subjects are presented with pairs of items from a set and asked to compare the two members of each pair on a single dimension. The items might be tones to be compared for loudness or photos of persons to be compared on attractiveness. Subjects are presented one pair at a time. During the course of the experimental session all possible pairs are presented several times each. The key data are the frequencies of response for each item. In the tone loudness example, the tone that was judged louder than its paired comparison the most often receives the highest scale value, the

tone with the second highest number of "louder" responses is given the second highest scale value, and so forth.

In order to convert the raw frequencies into actual scale values with interval properties, Thurstone developed the *Law of Comparative Judgment*. Among the mathematical assumptions comprising this law is the basic assumption that the momentary subjective difference between two stimulus values is normally distributed. The standard normal table can then be used to convert the relative proportion of times one tone is judged louder than another into the difference in scale value, expressed in standard deviation units, between the two tones. (See the earlier derivation of d' in the signal detection example.) Note that this method then requires that stimuli be chosen so that there will always be some confusability between any two paired stimulus values.

In cases where there is no confusability—e.g., subjects can always tell which tone is louder or which photo is more attractive—and the Law of Comparative Judgment cannot be applied, the method can still generate an ordinal scale of values. However, a practical limitation of the method of paired comparisons is that the number of possible pairs may become prohibitively large when the number of values to be judged is 10 or more. (If n is the number of different values, the number of pairs is given by the formula $n(n-1)/2$.)

Ratings and Rankings

In situations where the number of items to be scaled is too large for paired comparisons, rating and ranking methods have often been used. Although these methods can be used in both psychophysical and psychometric scaling, their use in psychometrics is particularly prevalent. Here, subjects directly assign values to individual stimuli. Hence these methods are referred to as "direct" scaling methods.

The methods are relatively straightforward and familiar to most people. Rankings usually require subjects to assign "1" to the most extreme (longest, loudest, best-tasting, most attractive, most likable, etc.) item, "2" to the next-most extreme item, and so forth. Typically, ties are not allowed. Ratings require the prior definition of the range of permissible values. Here, more than one item can be assigned the same value.

While it is a simple matter for a researcher to apply one of these methods, several important questions must be addressed when deciding which method to use. What are the properties of the resulting scales? How reliable are the scale values? How difficult is the task for the subject?

In many applications it is sufficient that ranking and rating methods produce data with no more than ordinal properties. What is the most preferred (first ranked or highest rated) item and what is the least preferred (bottom ranked or lowest rated) item? In other cases, interval properties are desirable. Users of rating scales often treat their data as if they represent direct measures with interval properties. There is, however, no guarantee that, say, a difference between 9 and 10 in judging a dive in Olympic competition is the same as the difference between 8 and 9. The judge may require a smaller increment in perceived quality to change from a response of "8" to a response of "9" than to change from a "9" to a "10." In such cases a "10" may be rarely given.

Studies have been conducted to compare the reliability and relative difficulty of ranking and rating methods. For example, Tharp and associates (1978) asked subjects to rank or to rate (on the ubiquitous 10-point scale) the desirability of alternative apartment descriptions, where the alternatives varied in terms of attributes such as rent and size. The number of apartments to be judged was 18 or 36. Subjects came back two days later to repeat the procedure with the same set of apartments as they judged initially. **Reliability,** as defined by the mean correlation between each respondent's two sets of data, was higher for the ranking method than for the rating method. However, time to complete the task was greater with ranking than with rating, especially when the number of items to be judged was 36. (Picture the amount of scanning back and forth that would be required to assign ranks 1 through 36.)

In order to compare the *predictive validity* of the methods, people actually seeking apartments would be used as subjects. The different methods would then be compared in terms of their ability to predict actual choices. Box 4.4 further describes the concepts of "reliability" and "validity" as they apply to psychological scaling.

Category Scaling

Numerical rating methods are an example of **category scaling:** the sorting of items into a fixed number of categories. For example, in psychophysical scaling the items might be a series of tones varying in intensity. The experimenter specifies a number of labeled categories into which these tones should be placed—e.g., "very loud," "loud," "moderately loud," "moderately soft," "soft," "very soft." (Experimenters often recategorize these verbal labels into numbers 1–6.) Note that, in contrast to ranking or paired-comparison methods, category scaling involves *absolute* judgments. A respondent might feel that all the tones presented are at least "moderately loud" and that respondent would then never use the bottom half of the scale.

In psychometrics, category scaling has taken a variety of forms and, as we will see in later chapters,

Reliability and Validity

Reliability and validity are related but separate concepts. Consider, for example, a method for assigning grades to students' term papers on the basis of the length of the paper: a paper of over 20 pages gets an A, a paper of 15 to 20 pages gets a B, etc. That would be a highly reliable method of measuring student performance because once the rule is stated, a given student would always receive the same grade no matter who did the grading or when. But this method would not be apt to provide valid measures of what the student had learned. A student who rambled on and on without ever making a relevant point would score better than a student who knew the material well enough to state things correctly and concisely.

Reliability of a scaling or measurement technique then represents the replicability or repeatability of the resulting measures. Will the same judge's rank-ordering of 10 table wines be the same this week as it was last week? As we saw in the text, the test-retest correlation between scale values obtained on two separate occasions can be used as a measure of reliability. One problem with this measure, however, is that stimuli that are difficult to

discriminate can lead to relatively low test-retest correlations even if the method is reliable.

Validity of a scaling or measurement technique deals with its ability to tap the underlying process it claims to measure. Validity is not as easily assessed as reliability. For example, controversy surrounds the question of just what is being measured by so-called "intelligence tests." Some claim that these tests possess "construct validity," the ability to measure a construct such as "capacity to learn." Others claim that the tests are contaminated by cultural and experimental factors and thus lack "construct validity." Others merely state that whatever the tests measure, they are useful as predictors of academic performance. They are then said to have "predictive validity" or "criterion-oriented" validity.

Later chapters will provide examples of reliability and validity in different contexts such as attitude measurement and clinical assessment. Because the concepts of reliability and validity are especially critical for establishing the usefulness of diagnosing clinical problems such as depression and anxiety, chapter 10 includes a detailed discussion of the reliability and validity of clinical assessment techniques.

---

has been employed frequently in social psychology and clinical psychology. For example, social psychologists are interested in measuring the similarity of attitudes among different people, and clinical psychologists are interested in measuring a variety of personal traits. Category scaling techniques such as described below are often the methods of choice.

Use of the *semantic differential* (Osgood, Suci, & Tannenbaum, 1957) requires the subject to rate an item or issue (e.g., "abortion") on each of several bipolar scales such as "good-bad," "soft-hard," "moral-immoral," "important-unimportant." Seven-point scales are typically employed, with the anchor words representing the extremes. A complete description of any item consists of the profile of the item on all the scales and different items can be compared on their configuration.

Likert scales (Likert, 1932) require subjects to respond to each item on a 5-point scale of agreement or approval (e.g., "strongly agree," "agree," "neutral," "disagree," "strongly disagree"). Sometimes the scale is reduced to just 2 points, "agree" and "disagree." The items can represent attitudinal statements such as "I believe abortion is immoral" or person descriptions such as "President Clinton is trustworthy." As with the semantic differential, an attitude can be expressed as a profile of responses to specific items. Sometimes a single summary attitude score is obtained by assigning the numbers 1 through 5 to the response categories for each item and summing the numbers for all items that pertain to the same attitude. This is often preceded by pilot work designed to eliminate specific items that are not positively correlated with the total attitude score.

Magnitude Estimation

One scaling method assumed to be capable of producing data with ratio properties is **magnitude estimation.** In the most common form of the method (Stevens, 1956), subjects are instructed to assign numbers to stimuli such that the ratio of any two number responses corresponds to the ratio of the stimulus magnitudes. For example, if a subject in a loudness scaling experiment assigns a particular number to the first tone in a series and the next tone appears twice as loud, then he or she should assign it a number twice as large. Sometimes, in order to restrict the range of numbers given, the experimenter assigns an a priori value (e.g., 100) to the first stimulus and repeats this frequently as a standard of comparison or "modulus." The variable stimuli are presented in random order.

Several interesting variations of magnitude estimation have been developed. In the method called cross-modality matching, numbers are eliminated altogether. For example, subjects might be instructed to draw lines of different length to match lights of different brightness, or adjust tones of different loudness to match weights of different heaviness. When each paired value of one mode with another is expressed as a point in two-dimensional space, the dots typically fall close to a linear array, showing that subjects can in fact match sensory experiences in two different modalities.

Magnitude estimation and its derivative methods can be applied to psychometric as well as psychophysical scaling problems, but the task tends to be quite difficult. For example, subjects could be asked to assign numbers to persons with varying characteristics such that if one person is "liked twice as much" as another person, a number twice as large should be chosen. If responses in such a task were to conform to the requirements of a ratio scale, subjects would have to conceptualize the notion of "zero likability."

Multidimensional Scaling of Similarity Judgments

When stimuli differ along several different dimensions, the primary goal of scaling is to disentangle the contribution of each dimension in perceiving and evaluating the stimuli. One popular method, called **multidimensional scaling,** requires subjects to judge the *similarity* of multidimensional stimuli and then the researcher searches for those underlying dimensions which best account for the similarity judgments. This can be done with well-defined physical stimuli such as geometric figures of different size, shape, and color. It can also be done with stimuli such as personality descriptions, which vary in ways that cannot be described by physical dimensions.

Primary data are measures of similarity for all pairs of stimuli. Each stimulus is conceptualized as a point in n-dimensional space with the similarity measures representing the distances between the points. Data are analyzed with computer programs that generate a series of multiple regressions based on varying numbers and placements of stimulus dimensions. The goal is to find a solution that accounts for a high percentage of the variance in the similarity or distance measures (see the discussion of multiple regression in chapter 3) on the basis of a relatively small number of interpretable dimensions. While statistical tests are available for comparing solutions based on varying numbers of dimensions, a certain amount of subjectivity is involved in selecting and labeling the dimensions. This will be illustrated shortly.

The various scaling methods described in this chapter are summarized in table 4.8.

Tests of the Validity of Scaling Methods

The validity tests described in this section examine the "quality" of the data produced by different scaling methods. The tests are of two types. In the first type of test the data arising from psychological scales will be compared to the predictions of well-known theories of the perceptual process. Proponents of a particular theory tend to accept as valid those methods that lead to data consistent with the theory and they tend to refute methods that lead to data at variance with the theory. In the second type of test the properties of a particular scaling method are evaluated in terms of subjects' abilities to combine scale values appropriately in a stimulus integration task. If the data do not conform to the algebraic properties of the task requirement, then the method of obtaining these data is questioned.

TABLE 4.8 Summary of Scaling Methods

METHOD	DESCRIPTION	COMMENTS	EXAMPLES
Paired-Comparisons	Subject is presented all possible pairs of stimulus values and compares the stimuli within each pair on some dimension. Scale value positions are based on the frequency of "greater than" responses to each stimulus.	Thurstone's Law of Comparative Judgments is used to convert frequencies into scale values with interval properties. This requires that there must be some confusability between any two paired stimulus values.	Measuring relative attractiveness of political candidates, defining visual illusions.
Rankings	Subject is presented all stimulus values and must rank order them in terms of some specified characteristic.	Highly reliable technique, but task becomes difficult when the number of stimulus values is large. Assumed to produce ordinal scales of measurement.	Scaling preference for different jobs, wine/food preferences.
Category Scaling *Ratings*	Subject assigns a number in a specified range to each stimulus according to the amount of some specified characteristic it possesses.	Category scaling methods may produce interval scales of measurement if procedural precautions are taken such as the use of "end anchors." These methods tend to be highly subject to context effects.	Scaling brightness of lights, judging athletic performance, physical attractiveness.
Semantic Differential	Subject rates an item or issue on a series of bipolar scales such as "good-bad," "soft-hard."		Comparing preferences for different kinds of music, measuring perceptions of people.
Likert Scales	Subject rates each item on a 5-point scale of agreement or approval.		Measuring attitudes toward abortion, affirmative action programs.
Magnitude Estimation	Subject assigns numbers to stimuli such that the ratio between the numbers assigned to any two stimuli corresponds to the ratio of their perceived magnitudes.	Magnitude estimation and its derivative methods are assumed to be able to produce ratio scales of measurement. However, the task can become difficult, especially for qualitative variables with undefined "absolute zero."	Scaling loudness of tones, brightness of lights.
Cross-Modality Matching	Subject selects or produces a value in one stimulus mode to match the level of another stimulus mode.		Scaling perceptions of brightness of lights by adjusting loudness of tones.
Multidimensional Scaling	Subject judges similarity of pairs of stimuli that differ along several dimensions. Statistical methods used to locate each stimulus in n-dimensional space.	Method especially useful when dimensions cannot be defined on an a priori basis. Some subjectivity involved in identifying dimensions.	Defining the dimensions of color perception, defining the dimensions by which people's likability is judged.

Tests Based on Psychophysical Theory

Recall that there are two major candidates for "the" psychophysical law—Fechner's law based on Weber's law of just-noticeable-differences, and Stevens' power law. The corresponding equations are $R = k \log S$ and $R = kS^n$, respectively.

You may have noticed that the symbol R in both Fechner's law and Stevens' power law has been referred to alternately as "sensation" and the "psychological scale value." Theoretically, the laws are meant to apply to sensation. But sensation has to be measured on some psychological scale. The question then is which scale provides the "true" measure of sensation. Whereas Fechner's law was derived from indirect methods of scaling, such as paired-comparisons, the more recent direct methods of scaling, such as magnitude estimation, tend to give results that fit Stevens' power law better than Fechner's law. It should be noted, however, that while the two equations look quite different, they can make rather similar predictions when their parameters (k and n) are derived from empirical data. If frequency of usage is taken as a measure of acceptance, direct measures of scaling seem to be preferred by most contemporary psychophysicists, and the power law is recognized as a reasonable representation of the psychophysical law.

However, different forms of direct scaling can produce different results. When the same stimuli are scaled by both category and magnitude estimation methods, the resulting scale values are typically not linearly related (Gescheider, 1988). This should not be surprising when one considers the different response requirements. For example, the response scale is open-ended in magnitude estimation, whereas it has a fixed upper limit in category scaling. According to Banks and Coleman (1981), subjects use numbers differently when there is an upper limit and when there is not. In addition, the use of numbers to scale successive stimulus presentations is subject to context effects that need to be taken into account.

Context Effects

Both magnitude estimation and category scaling procedures tend to be subject to **context effects.** Many studies have shown that when people have to judge individual stimuli that are imbedded in a larger set, their responses depend in part on what

occurred on earlier trials. For example, King and Lockhead (1981) reported the presence of **assimilation** and **contrast** effects in magnitude estimation of tone loudness. When no feedback was given, responses on one trial were found to be positively correlated with responses from preceding trials. This context or sequential effect is called assimilation. When feedback was given after each response, responses were negatively correlated with responses from earlier trials. This is called a contrast effect.

Examples of context effects abound with category judgments as well. Helson (1964) developed **adaptation-level theory** to account for the fact that category judgments are influenced by past experiences. The same tone may seem louder when it follows a series of softer tones than when it follows a series of louder tones. A "good" dive may be rated lower when it follows a "great" dive than when it follows a "mediocre" dive. According to adaptation-level theory, all judgments are made in comparison to a single stimulus value, the adaptation level (or AL). The AL is the value of the stimulus judged "average." Judgments are linearly related to the difference between each of the stimuli being judged and the AL. However, the AL varies with the stimulus context. A series of loud tones will shift the AL upward and will thus lead to a decrease in the assignment of a response to the next stimulus.

Parducci (1965) developed an alternative theory of context effects in category scaling that places more emphasis on the psychological representation of the range of stimuli experienced by the subject. According to this *range-frequency theory*, subjects divide their psychological range into subranges (e.g., "loud" vs. "soft") whose relative sizes are independent of the stimulus conditions. They use the alternative categories with approximately equal frequency. So, for example, if louder stimuli were presented with greater frequency than softer stimuli, subjects would adopt a narrower subrange for the category "loud" and an intermediate stimulus might shift from the "loud" to the "soft" category.

Similar effects are found in psychometric scaling. For example, in a study of personality impression formation, Levin and others (1973) found that presentation of an unfavorable personality trait adjective lowered ratings of likableness more if the subject had been exposed to a prior series of favorable adjectives than if the subject had been exposed to a prior series of unfavorable adjectives.

The ever-present context effects in psychophysical and psychometric scaling studies present the researcher with an interesting dilemma. Should these effects be considered as an integral part of the psychophysical process and be studied in their own right, or should they be considered as artifacts to be eliminated or controlled for in order to get on with the business of developing a law of psychophysics? What do you think?

The following section describes how scaling methods can be evaluated on the basis of subjects' ability to use psychological scale values in a manner consistent with the requirements of a stimulus integration task.

Tests Based on Stimulus Integration Tasks

In **stimulus integration** tasks (also known as information integration tasks) the subject has to make a single judgment based on several stimulus values. The use of stimulus integration tasks with known algebraic requirements affords an excellent opportunity to examine the properties of psychological scales.

An interesting example is Anderson's (1972) study of weight judgments. In each of two tasks weight judgments were made on a 20-point rating scale. In the weight averaging task subjects lifted two weights in succession and rated their average heaviness. Each weight had one of five values: 200, 300, 400, 500, and 600 grams. This 5 by 5 factorial design yields 25 different weight pairs. In addition, two end anchor pairs were presented: both 100 grams or both 700 grams. Subjects were instructed to give these pairs the ratings "1" and "20," respectively. End anchors serve an important function in rating tasks. The purpose of such end anchors is to provide examples of the most extreme values so that subjects can distribute their responses across the range of numbers without running into instances where they have already assigned a stimulus the highest (or lowest) possible rating and later encounter a more extreme stimulus. (This is why "10s" are rarely given in judging athletic events, especially in early competition.)

FIGURE 4.8   Weight averaging (Anderson, 1972).

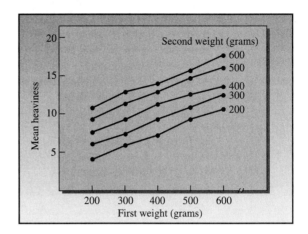

If, in fact, subjects were able to meet the demands of the task, then the rating data should conform to the predictions of an averaging model. Graphically, this translates into the prediction of five parallel curves. However, verification of the parallelism prediction requires an interval response measure. If the response was not on an interval scale, then the curves would not be parallel even if the subjects were using an averaging model. This is so because the parallelism prediction requires that equal-appearing stimulus differences lead to equal response differences. The parallelism prediction was confirmed both visually (see figure 4.8) and by statistical analysis showing no interaction between the value of the first weight and the value of the second weight.

Anderson (1972) concluded that rating data—when obtained in carefully designed experiments (e.g., with the appropriate use of end anchors)—are valid measures of sensation and that simple rating methods can produce interval scales. The point of this illustration is not to present results that permanently settle the issue of which types of scaling methods are valid and which are not, but to describe methods for addressing this important issue.

Applications of Scaling Techniques

Scaling of Taste

In a study of sensory judgments of sweetness, Moskowitz (1970) used magnitude estimation procedures to examine the function relating sweetness to

FIGURE 4.9   Data from a multidimensional scaling task (from Rosenberg et al., 1968).

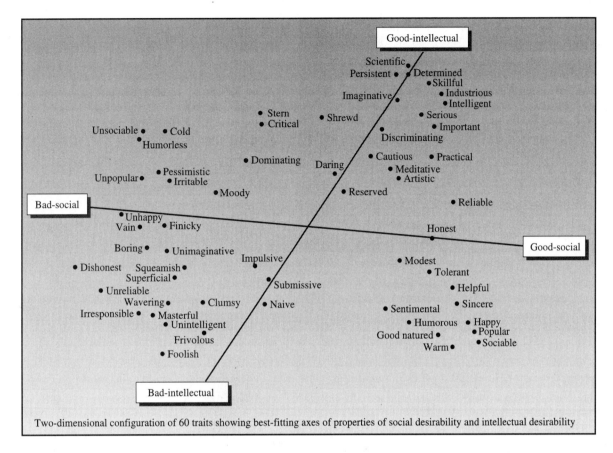

Two-dimensional configuration of 60 traits showing best-fitting axes of properties of social desirability and intellectual desirability

concentration of sugar and to compare different types of sugar. Subjects were instructed to assign numbers to stimuli in proportion to their perceived sweetness. Various types of sugars (sucrose, fructose, lactose, glucose, etc.) were mixed with water in varying concentrations. Subjects were presented the various solutions to taste in irregular order, rinsing their mouths with water following each trial. Results showed that intensity of sweetness for a given type of sugar grows as a power function of concentration—in agreement with Stevens' power law. The parameters of the power function differed for different types of sugar. Sucrose and fructose were the sweetest sugars.

Multidimensional Scaling of Personality Impressions

Rosenberg, Nelson, and Vivekananthan (1968) showed how multidimensional scaling can be used to study how we form impressions of other people.

The stimuli were personality trait adjectives. A sorting task was used to define a measure of dissimilarity or "disagreement score" for each pair of traits. Subjects were instructed to think of approximately 10 people they knew and consider each person as a different category. Each of 64 traits was to be placed in one of these categories. The disagreement score for each pair of traits was obtained by counting the number of subjects who ascribed the two traits to two different persons. For example, 9 out of 69 subjects assigned "warm" and "intelligent" to the same person so the disagreement score for this pair is 60. The idea here is that traits that are perceived to be similar will tend to go together in the same person and traits that are perceived to be dissimilar will tend to be ascribed to different persons.

Figure 4.9 plots these data in two-dimensional space. The axes represent the optimal placement of the two dimensions. Note that they are approximately but not exactly orthogonal to each other, indicating that the two dimensions are not quite independent of each other. For example, the adjectives "scientific" and "foolish" are at the opposite extremes on one dimension and they each tend toward neutral on the other dimension but they still differ somewhat. In this case, the labels "intellectual desirability" and "social desirability" seem reasonable as a description of the dimensions or factors underlying judgments of other people.

Summary and Conclusions

The area of perception and psychophysics can be characterized by the attempt to measure and quantify the relationship between the external and internal worlds. Problems studied in this area include separating innate and learned influences on perception, understanding optical illusions, measuring thresholds, describing the relationship between sensation and stimulus intensity for a variety of stimulus dimensions, separating the effects of sensory and nonsensory factors in signal detection, measuring qualitative as well as quantitative stimuli, scaling each separate dimension in a multidimensional stimulus, examining context effects in scaling, and validating scales of measurement.

Experiments that employ techniques such as raising animals in the dark or subjecting human infants to "visual cliffs" demonstrate perceptual adequacy with minimal learning, while other experiments show improved discrimination with learning and experience. Reaction time is often a sensitive measure of our ability to discriminate stimuli. Our perceptions are influenced by learned expectancies or "sets" and by the mechanism of "selective attention," which channels our processing of information.

Illusions arise when cues such as the relative size of the retinal images produced by two objects and their apparent distances from the observer are in conflict. Experiments designed to understand the causes of illusions shed light on the basic mechanisms of perception.

Thresholds are statistical measures of the capabilities and limitations of the sensory system. Absolute thresholds measure the minimal or maximal stimulus values that will produce a response 50 percent of the time and difference thresholds measure the change in stimulus value that is noticeable 50 percent of the time. The various methods for measuring thresholds differ in terms of the manner in which the stimulus values are presented and the type of response required of the subject.

According to *Weber's law*, the value of the difference threshold is a constant fraction of the value of the standard stimulus at which it is measured. The size of this fraction as a measure of sensitivity to changes in stimulus magnitude has been used to compare different sense modalities. While Weber's law deals with threshold values, it was used by Fechner to develop a psychophysical law relating above-threshold changes in stimulus intensity to changes in sensation. *Fechner's law* states that sensation is proportional to the log of stimulus intensity. An alternative law developed by Stevens is the *power law* which states that sensation is proportional to stimulus magnitude raised to a particular power. These laws allow prediction of responses to various stimulus intensities.

Signal detection theory was developed to account for the fact that nonsensory factors such as response biases can affect reports of sensation. In a typical signal detection task the subject or observer must decide on each of a series of trials whether a signal or only background noise was presented. Each type of trial—signal or no signal—is assumed to generate a distribution of values for the likelihood that a signal was presented. Signal detection theory assumes that the observer establishes a subjective cutoff point or criterion for deciding when to report that a value comes from the "signal plus noise" distribution rather than the "noise" distribution.

Separation of the sensory factor (difference between the noise and signal plus noise distributions) and the nonsensory factor (criterion cutoff point) can be accomplished by examining *receiver-operating-characteristic (ROC) curves*. These curves plot "hit" rates against "false alarm" rates to describe changes in the observer's performance as a function of changing criterion values for constant signal and noise levels. Methods developed to induce the observer to change criterion values include varying rewards and penalties for hits and false alarms, and varying the probability that a signal will be presented.

The *scaling* or *measurement* problem is especially important in perception and psychophysics because conclusions about how subjects react to stimuli of varying magnitude will depend on the methods used to define and measure reactions. When stimulus dimensions are objective and well-defined, the methods are called *psychophysical scaling;* when the dimensions are abstract and qualitative, the methods are called *psychometric scaling. Paired-comparisons* is a method that uses comparative judgments to scale stimuli. *Magnitude estimation* is a method whereby subjects are asked to assign numbers to stimuli such that the ratio between any two numbers corresponds to the ratio of the stimulus magnitudes. *Category scaling* is a method that requires the sorting of items into a fixed number of categories. There are a number of variations for use in areas such as attitude measurement and clinical diagnosis. Rating tasks are an example of category scaling.

Different scaling methods can differ in several important ways: *reliability*, which represents the replicability or repeatability of the resulting measures; *validity*, which represents the ability of a scale to tap the underlying process it claims to measure; *scale properties*, which indicate whether scale values for different stimuli can be compared in terms of their ratio, their difference, or just their rank ordering; and *context effects*, which indicate how the value assigned to a given stimulus varies as a function of the magnitude of the stimuli presented earlier.

The area of perception and psychophysics provides good examples of how advances in methodology lead to the accumulation of knowledge needed for theory advancement in experimental psychology. The "visual cliff" was a method for determining the role of innate factors in perception. Fechner's methods for measuring thresholds led to the original formulation of a law of psychophysics. Stevens later refined the law based on more recent developments in psychological scaling. The development of multidimensional scaling techniques and stimulus integration tasks led to further refinement in theory and an examination of the crucial issue of validity of psychophysical methods. Analysis of context effects in a variety of tasks revealed the existence of nonsensory factors in psychophysical judgments. Signal detection theory served the purpose of separating sensory from nonsensory factors in detection tasks in which signals are imbedded in a background of noise. Resourceful researchers have been able to apply the methods and theories of perception and psychophysics to a variety of problems of contemporary interest.

Exercises

1. What additional independent variables and subject variables would you want to test using the "visual cliff"?

2. Consider one of the illusions described in this chapter. Devise a study to test a hypothesis concerning the cause of the illusion.

3. Using the method of limits, compare the difference threshold for length of lines of different color.

4. Describe how the theory of signal detection might be applied to study sex discrimination in job hiring. Devise an appropriate experimental task.

5. Examine how the effects of order of presentation of lines of different length affect magnitude estimation of line length. Do you get contrast or assimilation effects? How do you explain these effects?

Glossary

absolute threshold Minimal physical stimulus value that will produce a response 50 percent of the time. (92)

adaptation level The value of the stimulus judged "average," to which other stimuli are compared in scaling. (111)

assimilation Context effect in which responses on one trial are positively correlated with responses from earlier trials. (111)

category scaling The sorting of items into a fixed number of categories. (107)

context effects The manner in which judgments of individual stimuli are affected by earlier trials with different stimulus values. (111)

contrast Context effect in which responses on one trial are negatively correlated with responses from earlier trials. (111)

difference threshold Change in value of a physical stimulus that is noticeable 50 percent of the time (sometimes referred to as just-noticeable difference). (92)

empiricism The view that our perceptions are derived from learning experiences. (84)

magnitude estimation Scaling method where subjects assign numbers to stimuli such that the ratio of any two numbers corresponds to the ratio of the stimulus magnitudes. (109)

multidimensional scaling Measuring the contribution of each dimension in perceiving and evaluating stimuli that differ along several different dimensions. (109)

nativism The proposition that our perceptions are guided by innate processes. (84)

perceptual constancy Recognizing an object in different perspectives. (84)

psychometric scaling Measuring abstract affective dimensions with no well-defined physical values. (105)

psychophysical scaling Measuring the relation between subjective scale values and corresponding physical values. (84)

psychophysics Relation between internal sensations and external properties of stimuli. (92)

reaction time (RT) Measure of speed of responding to stimuli of varying properties. (89)

receiver-operating-characteristic (ROC) curve Plot of hit rate against false alarm rate in signal detection for varying decision criteria. (101)

reliability In scaling or measurement, the replicability or repeatability of measures. (107)

selective attention Focusing of attention on one channel of information while ignoring others. (84)

set Prior expectancy based on repeated experience with a class of stimuli. (86)

stimulus integration Tasks in which the subject has to make a single judgment based on several stimulus values (also known as *information integration* tasks). (112)

validity The ability of a scaling or measurement technique to tap the underlying process it claims to measure. (108)

Weber's fraction Ratio of the value of a difference threshold to the value of the standard stimulus. (96)

Suggested Readings

It should come as no surprise that a leading journal that publishes research in the area of this chapter is called *Perception & Psychophysics*. Other leading journals include *Journal of Experimental Psychology: Human Perception and Performance*, *Perception*, *Acta Psychologica*, *Vision Research*, *Journal of the Acoustical Society of America* and, because of the quantitative nature of much of the research in this area, *Journal of Mathematical Psychology*.

There are many excellent contemporary textbooks in perception and psychophysics such as *Fundamentals of sensation and perception* by M. W. Levine and J. M. Shefner (2nd ed., 1991, published by Brooks/Cole). For historical perspectives on some of the major topics in this area, the following books are recommended:

Boring, E. G. (1942). *Sensation and perception in the history of experimental psychology*. New York: Appleton-Century-Crofts.

Broadbent, D. E. (1958). *Perception and communication*. New York: Pergamon Press.

Gibson, J. J. (1950). *The perception of the visual world*. Boston: Houghton Mifflin.

Green, D. M., & Swets, J. A. (1966). *Signal detection theory and psychophysics*. New York: Wiley.

Animal Learning and Comparative Cognition

E. A. Wasserman

Introduction

Why Study Animal Behavior?

Animals have always been vitally important to us. They serve as sources of food, fuel, and clothing. They provide us with transportation, companionship, and amusement. More recently, animals have become fascinating objects of study to behavioral and biological scientists.

What we learn about animals could contribute to their further usefulness to humans and also aid our efforts to protect animals from rapidly changing environments. But, the study of animal behavior is interesting and justifiable as an intellectual activity without concern for application or utility. To the experimental psychologist, the two main reasons for investigating animal behavior are: (a) to compare the actions of humans and animals, and (b) to study basic laws of behavior within the constraints that are imposed by society on experimentation with human beings.

Comparative Psychology

The evolutionary basis of behavior (see box 5.1) provides one major reason for comparing human and animal behavior. (Obviously, humans are also animals; nevertheless, we will adopt the convention of using "animal" as shorthand for "nonhuman animal.") Similarities in biological function provide another compelling reason. To the extent that behavior is influenced by common physiological structure and function, we can expect similar behavior to occur.

For some psychological processes, it is of considerable interest to determine whether the principles governing behavior are universal or species specific. For example, it has often been a strong assumption of some learning theorists that the laws of learning hold across all animal species. If so, then the choice of which animal to investigate in the study of learning is one of convenience or cost. Consequently, rats and pigeons have inhabited learning laboratories for decades. Alternatively, biological factors may greatly affect the nature or the expression of fundamental learning principles (see *Specializations in Learning*, later in this chapter).

Finally, a particular animal may permit the study of a psychological process in isolation. Just as pigs may be useful subjects for physiologists studying the digestive system because their digestion is so similar to humans', so too may some animal's behavior serve as a special preparation or analog of human action (see box 5.9 on learned helplessness and depression). Selection of animals for such "analog" studies can be closely linked to issues of control and manipulation of variables. For example, to return to the example of learning, in order to understand learning without the influence of prior experience, it is almost essential to use animals. Control of prior learning history (or other relevant experience) is a major advantage of animals in behavioral research.

Animal Behavior and Societal Ethics

Ethical issues sometimes limit the nature of the research that can be conducted on human subjects and provide still another reason for the use of animals in the study of behavior. One obvious constraint that is imposed on the researcher of human behavior involves irreversible bodily interventions, like brain surgery. So drastic an intervention as neurosurgery is not an ordinary practice of the experimental psychologist, although collaborative research with neurosurgeons performing therapeutic procedures is not uncommon. However, the experimental psychologist interested in the bodily bases of behavior is not without recourse. Humane surgery on animal subjects can be conducted and, to the extent that similar processes participate in human and animal behavior, some understanding of the biology of human behavior can be gleaned from the study of animals.

A second area of ethical concern involves the use of potentially traumatic aversive events. Although there are theoretical and clinical reasons to believe that strong noxious events are critical in molding an individual's behavior, the experimental psychologist faces many moral and legal challenges in administering such events to human subjects. Thus, researchers may accept animals as reasonable experimental substitutes if research interests require the use of strong aversive stimuli.

BOX 5.1

Comparative Psychology and Evolution

In 1859, Charles Darwin published his revolutionary account of the forms of life on earth, *The Origin of Species*. As opposed to the Biblical view of creation—in which all species of plants and animals were simultaneously and divinely created—Darwin proposed a gradual, natural process of species development, change, and extinction. According to Darwin, natural factors such as geography, climate, and predation select from among genetically diverse individuals those that are best suited to survive and reproduce. Under constant conditions, natural selection will tend to maintain the fitness of a species; however, under altered environmental conditions, a change in the species might result in evolution.

In his careful observations, Darwin was greatly impressed with the success of farmers and commercial breeders in bringing about rapid and dramatic alterations in the appearance and actions of animals and plants. If humans could artificially select breeding stock to bring about profound modifications in populations of living beings, he reasoned, then why couldn't natural selective factors operating over hundreds of generations also shape the morphology and physiology of organisms?

Darwin's account of evolution through natural selection was bold and controversial, as it challenged nearly 2,000 years of Biblical teachings. But even Darwin initially hesitated in applying his theory to humankind. It was not until 1871 that he first explicitly extended his naturalistic notions to the human species.

Darwin's writings on the evolution of humankind centered on two major psychological matters: emotion and intelligence. Darwin was a keen observer of animal and human behavior under natural circumstances. He noted that certain conditions tended to arouse in people particular emotional feelings that were accompanied by highly stereotyped facial expressions. The strong similarity of these facial displays from individual to individual and from culture to culture suggested to Darwin that there was a large genetic or innate component to emotional expression. Furthermore, the similarity of human facial displays to those of nonhuman primates implied that common ancestry may underlie this resemblance. A full understanding of human emotions would then require the systematic study of animal behavior.

Darwin not only held that our emotional outbursts may be shared by animals, but our intelligence as well. Accounts of extraordinary behavioral feats persuaded Darwin that animals possessed keen intellects, in some cases even rivaling human cognition. A protégé of Darwin, George J. Romanes, later collected literally hundreds of such tales of intelligence in most animal groups—from protozoans to primates. He too construed this evidence as supporting an evolutionary thesis linking human beings and our behavior to the animal kingdom.

Darwin's evolutionary thesis strongly contradicted the traditional view that humankind was special and could lord over the earth and its other inhabitants. Our very nature—our thoughts and feelings—was rooted in an archaic past and was netted together with living animal species. To understand the emotions and intelligence of animals was necessarily to shed light on human nature as well. Thus, Darwin's theory of evolution through natural selection made the study of animal behavior a particularly important field of scientific inquiry.

A third factor that limits the investigator of human behavior is experimental control. In attempting to delineate the laws of behavior, the experimentalist tries to narrow the range of possible variables as tightly as possible. This quest is made easier if the variables of interest are controlled by the investigator. However, as we noted above with human subjects, it is often impractical to accomplish such experimental control. Even when it could be done, ethical considerations affect the choice of subjects. For instance, suppose a researcher hypothesizes that the age at which a child is weaned will affect the speed of learning in adulthood. It would not be wise to use the retrospective reports of mothers to assess the correctness of the hypothetical relation; so much time will have passed between their children's weaning and adulthood that the mothers' recollections may be grossly

BOX 5.2

Myths and Facts about Research with Animals

Myth: Other research methods can replace the use of animals in behavioral research.

Fact: There are no real alternatives to animal research. Complex behavior is only now beginning to be carefully and scientifically documented in animals, and the environmental and biological determinants of behavior remain to be systematically and experimentally delineated. Thus, computerized models of complex behavior are truly decades away.

Myth: Much research with animals is unnecessary.

Fact: In addition to humane concerns, there are strong economic pressures against the unnecessary use of animals in research. There are extremely limited funds available to defray the very high costs of animal research. Funding agencies, therefore, must severely restrict support to those projects that are deemed to be the most likely to contribute to basic scientific knowledge or to solve a pressing applied problem. For example, the National Institute of Mental Health is able to support fewer than one-fifth of all research proposals that have been judged to be scientifically worthy. This selection process minimizes the possibility that animals will be used for trivial purposes.

Myth: Most research animals are dogs and cats.

Fact: Nearly 90 percent of the animals used in research are rats, mice, and other rodents. Dogs and cats account for less than 1 percent of the total. Nonhuman primates, too, represent less than 1 percent of the total number of animals used in research.

Myth: There are no laws or regulations protecting research animals.

Fact: A federal law, the Animal Welfare Act, sets forth standards for the care and treatment of laboratory animals, including housing, feeding, cleanliness, ventilation, and veterinary care. The law also contains provisions for the use of anesthesia or pain-killing drugs for potentially painful procedures and for postoperative care. In addition, the United States Public Health Service requires adherence to its Animal Welfare Policy by all institutions receiving research grants from the National Institutes of Health. Under the terms of the Animal Welfare Policy, institutions must follow the detailed recommendations on animal care and treatment that are contained in a book entitled the *Guide for the Care and Use of Laboratory Animals*. The policy also mandates the review of all research by an animal care and use

---

inaccurate. Nor would it be ethically possible to assign mothers of infants to different experimental conditions randomly and to require them to wean their babies at different times. Any proper evaluation of this particular experimental hypothesis would seem to require the kind of control that can only come from the study of animal subjects, where the conditions of postnatal care and weaning can be dictated by the researcher. (See box 5.2 for more information on the use of animals in behavioral research.)

How Should Animal Behavior Be Studied?
Scientists often debate the merits of different approaches to a particular problem area. The study of animal behavior is no exception. Here, as in all

behavioral research (see chapter 1), two rival strategies are often distinguished: (a) **naturalistic observation** and (b) **controlled experimentation.** We next consider what distinguishes naturalistic observation from controlled experimentation in studies of animal behavior and assess the particular virtues of each.

Naturalistic Observation
The oldest form of scientific inquiry involves observing events as they occur in nature. As the well-known cave paintings of primitive humans reveal, our species has been observing the behavior of other species for many thousands of years. Even today, zoo attendance suggests that humans derive great pleasure from watching animals. Most of what

committee in each institution, in order to insure that laboratory animals are being used responsibly and cared for humanely. Each committee comprises at least three members and must include at least one individual who has no association with the institution and at least one veterinarian. (For the American Psychological Association's guidelines for humane treatment of animal subjects, please refer back to box 1.3.)

Myth: Animals in research suffer great pain and distress.

Fact: Most behavioral and biomedical research does not result in pain or significant distress to the animal. A survey of research facilities released in 1985 by the United States Department of Agriculture showed that the majority of experiments using animal subjects (62 percent) involved no pain for the animals. In another 32 percent of the studies, the animals felt no pain because they received either anesthesia or pain-killing drugs. In a small number of experiments (6 percent), anesthesia or pain-killers were withheld, because they would have obscured the results of the research. An example of such research is the study of pain, itself a major human health problem.

Myth: Researchers are indifferent to the well-being of research animals.

Fact: Responsible researchers are quite concerned about the condition of the animals they study. Such concern arises from both humane and scientific considerations. Scientists cannot afford to mistreat research animals. To be a good research subject, the animal must be adequately fed and housed and kept free of any disease. Poor care and treatment will reduce the reliability of the results of the study, something that researchers do everything they can to prevent.

Myth: Research on animal subjects yields results of no practical value.

Fact: Research on animal subjects has produced findings that have benefited both animals and human beings. As one example, knowledge of animal sexual and feeding behavior has permitted zoos to save species from extinction and to breed endangered species for repopulation in new habitats. As another example, the principles of learning, derived largely from research with animals, have enabled workers to fashion particularly effective behavior therapies to alleviate the intense embarrassment associated with enuresis. Many more examples of the benefits of behavioral research on animals are to be found in an important paper by Miller (1985).

we know about the behavior of animals—their patterns of feeding, mating, aggression, migration, and so on—has come from carefully watching animals behave in their natural, or near natural habitats.

When we consider our knowledge of animal learning, we should not be surprised to discover that our earliest information about animal intelligence came from naturalistic observation. Many of the stories of animal intellect collected by Darwin and Romanes arose from the systematic observations of naturalists. Still other accounts came from zoo attendants and pet owners; these individuals related the cognitive accomplishments of animals behaving in comfortable, seminatural conditions. (See box 5.3 for one such amusing anecdote.)

Descriptions of animal intelligence as it is manifested in nature provide important basic data. Seeing how animal learning occurs naturally can give important clues as to the survival advantages of this capability. Observing behavior in naturalistic conditions imposes few constraints on the behaving animal, thus providing an uncontaminated picture of its intellect. Finally, the interaction of learned and instinctive actions may perhaps best be seen when an animal is behaving in naturalistic circumstances.

These benefits notwithstanding, many scientists interested in animal behavior have pointed out a number of problems or limitations associated with naturalistic observation as the sole method of investigation: First, although naturalistic observation may tell us *what* an animal is doing, it cannot tell us *how* the animal is doing it. Isolating the causes of an animal's actions requires more than simply noting the antecedents to those actions. Thus, knowing that

BOX 5.3

An Anecdote of Animal Intelligence

The following tale of feline guile was related by one of Romanes' friends:

> Our servants have been accustomed during the late frost to throw the crumbs remaining from the breakfast-table to the birds, and I have several times noticed that our cat used to wait there in ambush in the expectation of obtaining a hearty meal from one or two of the assembled birds. Now, so far, this circumstance in itself is not an "example of abstract reasoning." But to continue. For the last few days this practice of feeding the birds has been left off. The cat, however, with an almost incredible amount of forethought, was observed by myself, together with two other members of the household, to scatter crumbs on the grass with the obvious intention of enticing the birds. (Romanes, 1883/1977, p. 418)

Believe it or not!

---

pigeons are remarkable homers provides few clues as to how they are able to navigate from remote release sites to their home loft.

Second, merely recording remarkable behavior on the part of an animal does not necessarily provide us with adequate information for correctly interpreting the behavior. If the observer is unfamiliar with the natural behaviors of the species or is unacquainted with the prior history of the particular animal, incorrect inferences may be drawn. Thus, were a naive individual to see a pigeon fly to its loft after being transported several miles away, that *one* bird might wrongly be judged to have a special homing ability when in fact *all* pigeons possess this skill. Or were one to see a dog jump through the vertical bars of a gate while holding a stick endwise in the mouth, it might erroneously be concluded that the dog was uncharacteristically insightful, instead of being the recipient of many painful lessons that came from trying to jump through the gate with the stick held crosswise in the mouth.

Third, observing learning in the natural environment may not disclose the *limits* of an animal's intelligence. More demanding testing conditions may have to be imposed on the subject if we are to define the boundaries of its cognitive capabilities. Special tests would thus seem to be necessary in order to determine whether animals can count, an ability rarely if ever observed in the natural environment. Such tests may best be conducted in the laboratory, where appropriate control and precision can be imposed.

Controlled Experimentation

One of the first individuals to see problems with naturalistic observation was C. Lloyd Morgan. In his 1894 text, *An Introduction to Comparative Psychology*, Morgan described several of his own investigations, which represented an advance beyond mere observation. In much of this work, Morgan studied newly hatched chicks. Because of their young age and limited post-hatching experience, Morgan could be confident that their learned behaviors were not the result of prior training under similar circumstances. And, because the chicks had been hatched in an incubator, he could be sure that they were not imitating the behavior of the mother hen. Concern with eliminating confounding factors is a hallmark of the experimental method. Morgan's effort to disentangle learning from transfer and imitation sets his research apart from the work of other investigators of animal behavior and makes him a pioneer in the study of animal learning.

Morgan's interest in bringing the experimental method to animal learning actually stemmed from the same anecdotes that persuaded Darwin and Romanes of the high intellects of animals. Morgan was much more critical and conservative in his

BOX 5.4

Morgan's Canon in Action

Early in the history of comparative psychology, research was begun on animal memory. Hunter (1913) devised a delayed response task for this purpose. Here, an animal was placed an equal distance from two potential food sites. The animal could see the experimenter bait one of the two sites. Some time later, the animal was released to see if it would go to the baited site rather than to the unbaited one. Many different animals succeeded in this task, but Hunter was unwilling to conclude that memory of the baited site was necessarily responsible for their success. Perhaps accurate responding was accomplished by the animal's maintaining its orientation toward the baited site during the retention interval, in much the same way that a hunting dog maintains its "point" toward potential prey.

To test this notion, Hunter took the animal out of the room during the retention interval, thus eliminating postural mediation of performance, but still allowing the animal to retain some central representation of site baiting to guide its later choice behavior. Hunter's skepticism was justified; only a fraction of the animals who performed accurately when they were permitted to stay in the room during the delay interval performed accurately when they were removed from the room during the delay interval.

---

own assessments of animal intelligence. As a counterweight to what he perceived to be uncritical acceptance of tall tales of animal genius, he proposed his famous **canon of parsimony:** In no case may we interpret an action as the result of a higher cognitive capability, if it can be interpreted as the result of one which is less complex or advanced. (See box 5.4 for an example of Morgan's canon in action.) Preference for simplicity over complexity is another hallmark of the experimental method.

Beyond experimentalists' concerns with eliminating confounding factors and their preference for elegant theories is the matter of direct participation in the phenomenon of interest. Whereas naturalists who observe behavior do everything they can not to disturb their animal subjects, experimentalists directly manipulate the animal's environment. Here, too, Morgan led the way in the study of animal behavior and learning.

Morgan occasionally fed his chicks fuzzy worms about an inch long. These worms were a favorite food and Morgan sought to determine whether the visual properties of the worms were sufficient to trigger the chicks' feeding responses. To do this, Morgan engaged in a bit of deception; he gave his chicks similar sized pieces of reddish brown worsted wool. The chicks accepted these snippets as readily as they did real worms, avidly pecking and swallowing the "worsted worms." To see the effect of size on the chicks' feeding, Morgan snipped off "worms" of still greater lengths. He found that longer woolen lengths were less readily pecked than were lengths approximating those of real worms. By directly intervening into the chicks' environment, Morgan was able to determine that visual properties of prey objects strongly influenced the chick's feeding behavior.

We began this section by noting a debate between individuals dedicated to the naturalistic observation of animals and individuals committed to the experimental analysis of animal behavior. Historically, those of the former persuasion were **ethologists** and those of the latter were psychologists. More recently, the boundaries between the disciplines have been breaking down, because of a growing awareness that our understanding of animal behavior and learning will be needlessly incomplete if we fail to take into account the important information gathered by researchers in one tradition or the other. Contemporary workers are more likely than ever to incorporate into their research aspects of both naturalistic observation and controlled experimentation. However, because most of the data on the comparative psychology of learning has come from controlled laboratory experiments, our review of the area will focus on that literature. A list of further readings on the ethological approach (as well as the psychological approach) can be found at the end of the chapter.

Classic Methods in the Study of Animal Learning

As the study of animal behavior moved from naturalistic observation in the field to experimental investigation in the laboratory, two approaches can be distinguished, historically and methodologically. These two approaches each have several labels (see box 5.5), but are most clearly identified by their originators, Pavlov and Thorndike. The basic procedure, empirical results, and control groups will be described for each approach before turning to a consideration of theoretical issues. As we shall see, the most hotly debated controversy is over whether the two procedures for studying learning involve the same fundamental principles or whether they entail two different kinds of learning obeying different laws.

Pavlov's Procedure

I. P. Pavlov was a Russian physiologist whose place in twentieth century science was already secure after winning the Nobel Prize in 1904 for his studies of the biology of digestion. Yet, to experimental psychology, Pavlov was to report even more important

discoveries later in his long and distinguished career. Pavlov's 1927 book, *Conditioned Reflexes,* is best known to Western psychologists.

Rather serendipitously, Pavlov found that the dog's gastric secretions could be stimulated not only by food in the stomach, but by the sights and sounds that ordinarily preceded routine feedings. Pavlov initially termed the latter reaction "psychic secretion," reasoning that the response was not innate, but learned by the dog during its extended stay in the laboratory. Although the term "psychic secretion" was not retained, Pavlov's scientific analysis of the phenomenon was upheld in a long series of careful and incisive experiments.

In a typical Pavlovian investigation, a dog would first be given minor surgery to redirect the secretions of one of its salivary glands from inside the mouth to outside the cheek. By means of a specially devised hydraulic system, Pavlov was able to monitor the flow of saliva from the everted gland without discomfort to the alert animal. Thus, the dog's reactions to food and other stimuli could be precisely measured (figure 5.1).

Using this system, Pavlov was able to ascertain that hungry dogs avidly salivated to food in the mouth and that the reaction was not the result of prior learning; young puppies responded as readily as adults. Pavlov also determined that salivary secretion to the stimuli that regularly preceded feeding was the result of prior learning; adult animals with extensive feeding histories responded to the sight and smell of food, but puppies lacking this experience did not.

FIGURE 5.1 Pavlov's research apparatus for studying conditioning.

FIGURE 5.2 The events of a Pavlovian conditioning trial both before a conditioned response is established (left) and after (right).

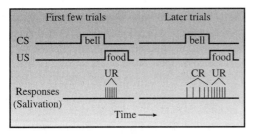

From James E. Mazur, *Learning and Behavior*, 2e, © 1990, pp. 56, 65, 109, 125, 126. Reprinted by permission of Prentice-Hall, Englewood Cliffs, New Jersey.

Pavlov did not extensively explore the development of the dog's feeding responses from infancy to adulthood. Instead, he examined the role of learning by employing stimuli that the dogs had never before experienced. For instance, just before feeding, a bell would be sounded. Because the bell is a novel stimulus, the dog might initially react to the bell by turning toward the sound source and perking its ears. However, after prolonged training with bell-food pairings, the dog came to salivate to the bell in advance of food's presentation (figure 5.2). Because the condition of pairing with food was necessary for the bell to acquire the ability of evoking salivation, Pavlov called such signals conditional

stimuli; because no special conditions were necessary for food in the mouth to elicit salivation, Pavlov called such events unconditional stimuli. Due to a curious translation error, we now refer to conditionally effective stimuli as **conditioned stimuli** (CSs) and to unconditionally effective stimuli as **unconditioned stimuli** (USs). In a parallel fashion, we call the reaction originally evoked by the US the **unconditioned response** (UR); we call the newly acquired reaction to the CS the **conditioned response** (CR).

Pavlov's discovery of conditioning and his development of a laboratory paradigm for its experimental study are landmarks in the comparative psychology of learning. In the first place, Pavlov provided us with an objective means of studying association formation. In the eighteenth century, British philosophers had written extensively on the importance of mental connections in human thought and action. Yet, in their hands, the introspective study of one thought suggesting another constituted the primary data of associationistic theories. With Pavlov's procedure, the evidence of association was now objective, in the form of the conditioned response. In the second place, this objective indicant of association was as readily utilized in the study of animal behavior as in the study of human behavior. Thus, a prerequisite to a comparative psychology of learning—similar and objective methods of study—was also provided by Pavlov's procedure.

Basic Empirical Results

Pavlov and his collaborators collected a vast array of facts concerning the determinants of conditioned responses. The key findings are now familiar to students of behavior.

The **acquisition** of the conditioned response is the most basic of all facts. Here, the tendency for the CS to evoke the CR increases in probability or strength as a function of the number of CS-US pairings (figure 5.3). In Pavlov's research, for example, the number of drops of saliva evoked by a CS such as a bell increased the more often the CS was paired with a food US. So long as the food US followed the bell CS, the CS continued to elicit a

FIGURE 5.3   **Idealized changes in the strength of a CR across one day of acquisition followed by four days of extinction.**

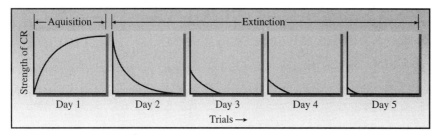

From James E. Mazur, *Learning and Behavior*, 2e, © 1990, pp. 56, 65, 109, 125, 126. Reprinted by permission of Prentice-Hall, Englewood Cliffs, New Jersey.

BOX 5.6

Spontaneous Recovery

Other evidence exists which indicates that extinction does not eradicate the CS-US association. Suppose that a single session of extinction training follows a long period of acquisition training. The probability of a CR might be .90 at the beginning of the extinction session and .10 at its end. Now, suppose that a second session of extinction is given the next day. Although you might expect the probability of a CR at the beginning of the second session of extinction training to be .10 or lower, empirically the probability of a CR is often much higher, in the order of .40 to .50 (figure 5.3). This resurgence of an extinguished CR without the reintroduction of CS-US pairings is called **spontaneous recovery.** Had extinction eradicated the CS-US association, there would have been no way for responding at the beginning of the second session of extinction to have exceeded responding at the end of the first session of extinction.

---

strong flow of saliva. However, when Pavlov later repeatedly presented the CS alone without following it with the US, the flow of saliva to the CS progressively dropped. Such a decrease in responding to a previously effective CS due to CS alone presentation is called **extinction** (figure 5.3). Because acquisition of a CR and its continuation require that the US follow the CS, the US is often called the **reinforcer** of the CS-US association.

If extinction is carried out long enough, then the CS may come to elicit as little salivation as it did on its very first presentation (figure 5.3). Does this mean that CS alone presentation has completely eradicated the effects of earlier CS-US pairings? No. When Pavlov later followed the CS with the US, salivation again rose to the CS, but now more rapidly than during initial acquisition. Because

reacquisition may be faster than original acquisition, Pavlov concluded that extinction did not erase the association between the CS and the US—it only suppressed it. (See box 5.6 for related evidence on spontaneous recovery.) Paralleling the case for CR increases, **reextinction** may proceed more quickly than extinction.

Other work in Pavlov's laboratory concerned the specificity of conditioned behaviors. For instance, Pavlov wondered if reinforced training with a bell of a particular pitch would lead dogs to respond exclusively to that bell. To test this notion, Pavlov sounded a number of bells of both higher and lower pitch, after CS-US training with only one bell pitch. The result was that maximal responding occurred to the bell previously paired with the US. However, responding also occurred to the untrained

FIGURE 5.4 The percentage of eyeblink CRs made to tones of five different auditory frequencies after training with a CS of 1,200 Hz (cycles per second).

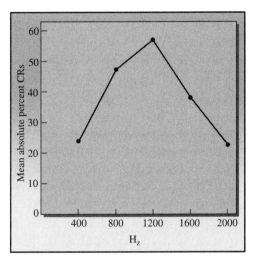

From Moore, in A. H. Black and W. F. Prokasy, Eds., *Classical Conditioning II: Current Research and Theory*. Copyright © 1972 Appleton-Century-Crofts. Reprinted by permission of Simon & Schuster, Englewood Cliffs, New Jersey.

auditory stimuli; such responding increased as their pitch approached that of the reinforced CS. The term for responding to similar, but untrained stimuli is **generalization** (figure 5.4).

Although there may be substantial generalization from an established CS to similar test stimuli, it would be wrong to conclude that the animal is incapable of distinguishing among them. Prolonged training with the US following one stimulus but not following other similar stimuli may lead to much more responding to the reinforced stimulus. So, a dog might avidly salivate to a bell of middle pitch, but not as much to bells of higher or lower pitch. Such selective responding after selective reinforcement is called **discrimination** (figure 5.5). Many theorists now believe that generalization and discrimination are two sides of the same psychological coin. To the extent that an organism reacts similarly to different stimuli it is generalizing among them; to the degree that an organism responds differently to different stimuli it is discriminating among them.

Thus far, we have been primarily concerned with discrete CSs eliciting CRs. Pavlov referred to this brand of stimulus control as **excitation.** However, CSs may also acquire the ability of suppressing CRs due to a process known as **inhibition.** Consider as an example a situation in which food invariably follows the presentation of a bell, but does not follow the same bell if it is accompanied by illumination of a light bulb. Initially, the dog salivates to the bell, whether presented alone or combined with the lighted bulb; the bell excites salivation. Ultimately, however, the dog salivates only if the bell is presented alone and refrains from responding when the bell and the light occur together—the lighted bulb inhibits salivation. Although more research has been conducted on conditioned excitation than on conditioned inhibition, Pavlov considered both processes to be critical in the control of conditioned responses.

Finally, we must consider among the basic results of conditioning the role played by time. To this point, the CSs we have considered have been briefly presented external stimuli, such as lights and sounds. However, the passage of time may also serve a discriminative function. Two results from Pavlov's laboratory support this conclusion. First, if the duration of the CS is gradually lengthened from a short value of say 5 sec to a long value of say 30 sec, then salivation comes to increase to high levels only toward the latter portions of the CS, when food is about to be presented. Pavlov reasoned that the dog could discriminate the passage of time during the CS and that, because food was unlikely to occur during the early portions of the CS, the response of salivation was inhibited during that period. Pavlov termed such reduced responding in the early parts of the CS-US interval **inhibition of delay.** Second, Pavlov was able to demonstrate successful conditioning without any extra external CS. The trick here was to present the food US at regular temporal intervals, say every 15 min. Under such a regular feeding schedule, Pavlov found that salivation tended to rise as the time of the next scheduled feeding approached. This tendency was termed **temporal conditioning.**

FIGURE 5.5   The percentage of eyeblink CRs made to CS+ (1,200 Hz) and to CS– (2,400 Hz) of a Pavlovian auditory discrimination procedure.

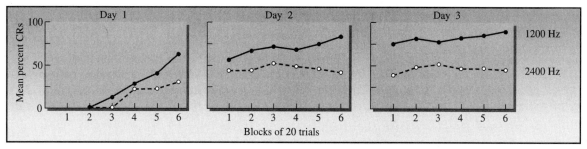

From Moore, in A. H. Black and W. F. Prokasy, Eds., *Classical Conditioning II: Current Research and Theory.* Copyright © 1972 Appleton-Century-Crofts. Reprinted by permission of Simon & Schuster, Englewood Cliffs, New Jersey.

Control Groups and Conditioning

Pavlov's research in conditioning was quite thorough and most of the basic findings that he obtained can be readily replicated, even with other CSs, USs, and species of animals. Such robust results are in no small measure a testimony to Pavlov's skills as an experimenter. For example, Pavlov went to great lengths to minimize the possibility that incidental stimuli would distract his subjects. To do so, Pavlov placed the dogs in an isolation chamber that shielded them from extraneous sights, sounds, and smells.

Yet, ironically, Pavlov did little to control for the prior conditioning histories of his canine subjects; many of the dogs were participants in dozens of different experiments! With such apparent disregard for transfer of training effects, it is all the more remarkable that as many of Pavlov's findings are as reliable as they are. Today, researchers of acquisition processes use experimentally naive subjects to eliminate the involvement of prior conditioning experience.

Another matter that was of little apparent concern to Pavlov was the possibility that factors other than CS-US association produce responding to the CS. Consider the following comparison involving two groups of subjects. One group, like Pavlov's, receives CS (bell)-US (food) *pairings*. The other group receives presentations of the *CS alone*. We should not be surprised to learn that the bell comes to evoke much more salivation in the first group than in the second. But does this result unequivocally prove that CS-US association was responsible for the difference in salivation to the CS? Not necessarily. Suppose that the mere presentation of food in the experimental situation broadened the range of stimuli that could trigger salivation. This enhanced responsivity, quite independent of CS-US association, could support greater responding in the group receiving CS-US pairings than in the group receiving the CS alone; only the first group receives the US in the experimental setting. Were these the only two groups in our investigation, we might be mistaken in interpreting the results as due to associative mechanisms.

In answer to this particular interpretive ambiguity, several additional control procedures have been proposed. One is the *US alone* control. The logic here is that presenting the US alone in the experimental context might be sufficient to broaden the range of effective stimuli. After such training, presentation of a novel CS might then provoke as much responding as does the prior pairing of the CS and the US with one another. Although a familiar control, the US alone procedure has two drawbacks. First, it is very inefficient; one has but a single chance to compare responding to the novel CS here with responding to the US-paired CS from the experimental group. Second, the US alone control differs from the CS-US group not only in terms of CS-US pairings, but also in terms of number of CS presentations. Thus, there is a confounding of potentially relevant factors.

Another control procedure takes into account the number of CS and US presentations by giving exactly the same numbers of each as are scheduled in the CS-US group. However, in this **explicitly unpaired** procedure, CS and US can never occur in close temporal proximity to one another. Thus, an event series might run "CS, CS, US, CS, US, US" with at least 30 seconds separating stimulus presentations. If temporal contiguity of CS and US is necessary for conditioning to occur, then this factor should have been removed from the explicitly unpaired group while equating all other factors, including the number of presentations of CS and US.

Yet another control procedure addresses problems with the CS alone and US alone controls in a different way. Here, the experimental subject serves as its own control. Following Pavlov's *discrimination* regimen, one conditioned stimulus (CS+) is paired with the US, but another conditioned stimulus (CS–) is not. If CS+ comes to elicit more responding than CS–, we can be confident that the mere presence of the US in the situation is not the critical factor; if it were, then CS+ and CS– should have been equally effective. And, by presenting CS+ and CS– an equal number of times, we can be sure that differential responding is not the result of differential stimulus exposure. The most plausible reason for CS+ evoking more responding than CS– in the discrimination procedure is its pairing with the US.

A final control procedure is the **random control.** As with the explicitly unpaired control, the random control procedure arranges the same numbers of stimulus presentations as the CS-US group. Here, however, no temporal constraints are placed on when CSs and USs can be presented: either may occur at any moment in time, thereby generating a random series of CS and US events. Note that this may be a more conservative control than the explicitly unpaired procedure. When CSs and USs are presented randomly in time, CS-US pairings may occasionally happen, thus potentially raising responding to the CS. Still, if responding to

the CS here is less than in the CS-US group, then we can be confident that association is the most likely reason for this performance differential.

What should be made of all these various controls? First, the sheer number of proposed controls indicates that researchers subsequent to Pavlov have been much more interested than was he in distinguishing associative from nonassociative contributions to learning. Second, some disagreement exists as to the best control(s) to employ in conditioning experiments. Third, given the interest in and debate surrounding proper control procedures, the prudent investigator will employ as many controls as possible in a conditioning experiment, particularly when controversy exists, as when learning in invertebrates is being explored (see ahead).

Thorndike's Procedure

As we saw earlier, the basic condition for learning to occur in Pavlov's procedure is that the CS and the US be sequentially paired. We might also say that presentation of the US is contingent on presentation of the CS. A related contingency is the basis for learning in another procedure, initially developed by the American psychologist, E. L. Thorndike.

Thorndike was an early researcher of animal learning, who turned to this topic after an unsuccessful attempt at demonstrating telepathy in children. Thorndike was especially interested in bringing experimental rigor and interpretive caution to the issue of animal intelligence. Like Morgan, Thorndike was quite skeptical of the kind of evidence accepted by Darwin and Romanes as proof of great intelligence in animals. Thorndike demanded clear and replicable results under tight experimental control. To collect such data, he devised the **puzzle box** (figure 5.6).

As described in Thorndike's 1911 book, *Animal Intelligence*, the puzzle box was a very simple apparatus indeed—basically a small enclosure into which an animal such as a cat, dog, or chick could be placed. Once there, the animal would be required to operate a device such as a button or a lever in order to be released. To insure his animals' interest in the problem, Thorndike deprived them of food

FIGURE 5.6   Puzzle box used by Thorndike in his conditioning research.

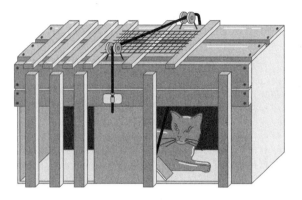

FIGURE 5.7   The number of seconds required by one of Thorndike's cats to escape from a simple puzzle box on 24 consecutive trials.

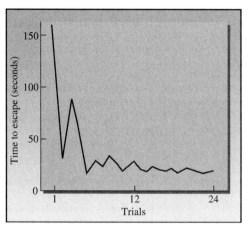

From James E. Mazur, *Learning and Behavior*, 2e, © 1990, pp. 56, 65, 109, 125, 126. Reprinted by permission of Prentice-Hall, Englewood Cliffs, New Jersey.

for several hours and gave them a tasty tidbit on their release from the box. Therefore, the important experimental contingency was between the performance of a simple act and release from the box and the subsequent receipt of food.

Thorndike recorded the time taken by the animal to escape from the puzzle box on each learning trial. The time systematically decreased as more and more learning trials were given (figure 5.7). In addition, Thorndike observed that his cats' initial, frantic efforts to escape from the box by random clawing and biting gradually dropped out, to be supplanted by more economical actions directed toward the release device. Thorndike reasoned that the consequences of an act determined its future probability in that situation. This result was so basic that it has come to be called the **law of effect.** Some consequences, like food, increase the later likelihood of a response; other consequences, like continued confinement or a brief electric shock, decrease the later likelihood of a response. Effects that increase prior behaviors we call reinforcers; effects that decrease prior behaviors we call **punishers.**

In any problem situation, Thorndike proposed that both reinforcement and punishment may participate in determining the resulting behavior. Thus, if a cat must press a button to escape from the puzzle box, then button pressing should be strengthened by

release and feeding. Any other responses should be weakened, because their performance is unsuccessful and adds to the time elapsing before a successful response can be made. Although both processes may operate in a learning situation like Thorndike's, it is important to note that the explicit response-reinforcer contingency is the only one arranged to change the animal's environment: press→release and food. The implicit response-punisher contingency represents the status quo in the animal's environment: no press→no release and no food. Other versions of Thorndike's procedure (discussed later) receive their definition from the explicit or environment-altering contingency.

Skinner's Variation
Thorndike's puzzle box was an important innovation in the study of animal learning. Yet, it had an important drawback: after each successful escape, the experimenter had to return the subject to the enclosure. Such handling might introduce an unnecessary

FIGURE 5.8   A rat pressing a lever in a Skinner box. The food delivery mechanism is located to the left of the box.

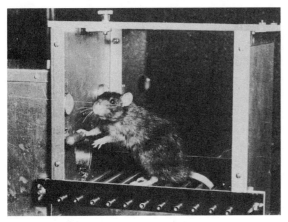

B. F. Skinner

confounding factor affecting the animal's behavior. For example, if the experimenter was uncharacteristically rough or returned the animal to an unusual part of the box, then the escape time on that trial might be extraordinarily long.

To eliminate this confounding, the late B. F. Skinner invented the now famous **Skinner box.** His apparatus, too, was a small enclosure. It contained a response mechanism, like a lever, plus a food tray, into which small pellets of food could be given to one of Skinner's favorite experimental subjects—the rat (figure 5.8). When the rat pressed the lever, it could receive a food pellet; after its consumption, the rat was free to respond again, without any handling by the experimenter. Skinner measured the time between successive responses in a manner similar to Thorndike's recording the time to escape from the puzzle box (figure 5.9). The reciprocal of

FIGURE 5.9   A simplified drawing of a cumulative recorder and the type of graph it produces.

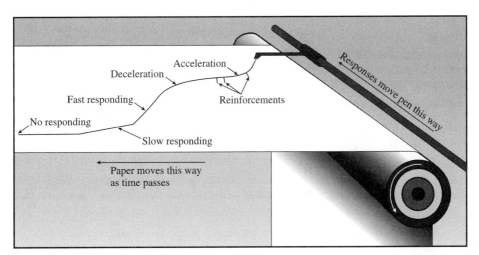

From James E. Mazur, *Learning and Behavior,* 2e, © 1990, pp. 56, 65, 109, 125, 126. Reprinted by permission of Prentice-Hall, Englewood Cliffs, New Jersey.

the interresponse time, response rate, was Skinner's prime behavioral measure. In most situations, response rate is simply the total number of responses divided by the total session time, typically 1 hour. The rate of response (in responses per hour) might well be expected to rise as an animal learns the connection between lever pressing and food delivery. Such a result would be analogous to a progressive reduction in escape latency in Thorndike's procedure.

Basic Empirical Results

Skinner reported the results of an extensive series of experiments in his 1938 book, *The Behavior of Organisms*. Much of that work addressed the basic phenomena of conditioning.

When he arranged each lever press to produce a pellet of food, Skinner observed that the rat's rate of lever pressing rose as training continued—acquisition. When Skinner later disconnected the lever and the feeder, he observed that the rat's rate of lever pressing fell as time progressed—extinction.

The rat's behavior can also come under the control of external stimuli. Thus, an animal initially trained to press in the presence of a flickering light bulb might later be found also to respond to both faster and slower flicker frequencies—generalization. The rat's rate of response is usually greatest at the trained frequency and falls as the testing value becomes progressively remote from the training value. Differential reinforcement in the presence of distinctive environmental stimuli often supports different rates of response to those stimuli—discrimination. Thus, responding might be higher during a discriminative stimulus (S+) in whose presence responses are reinforced than during a discriminative stimulus (S−) in whose presence responses are not reinforced.

The four phenomena—acquisition, extinction, generalization, and discrimination—are readily observable in both Pavlov's and Skinner's procedures. Other aspects of conditioning are more specifically affiliated with Skinner's technique. In Skinner's procedure (and Thorndike's too), the response of central interest usually has some nonzero likelihood

of occurring prior to the animal's learning the linkage between the response and the reinforcer (or punisher). Thus, Skinner's rats and Thorndike's cats could be expected to operate the critical mechanism if the experimenter were willing to wait a rather long time for the animals to do so. Because the response was of low initial probability, it was easy to discern if the reinforcer was effective in strengthening the response. And, because the response was of nonzero initial likelihood, it was guaranteed that the animal's behavior would eventually contact the explicit experimental contingency. However, in Pavlov's procedure, special care is ordinarily taken to insure that the CS does *not* evoke the CR prior to the CS being paired with the US; if it were to do so, then a serious question would be raised as to whether the reaction to the CS after pairings was a CR or a UR.

Saying that Skinner's procedure customarily begins with a response of preexisting strength should not be construed to mean that brand-new responses cannot be conditioned with this method. Indeed, they can. Imagine that a rat is placed in a more or less typical Skinner box. However, unlike the conventional box, this one contains a lever that is 6 inches above the floor; this height essentially insures that the rate of lever pressing will be zero prior to conditioning. How then can lever pressing be conditioned? Skinner's answer was to take the animal through a series of successive approximations to the desired act—**shaping.** Thus, the rat might first be trained to orient toward the lever. Then, the rat could be taught to rise toward the lever. Finally, the rat could be conditioned to jump at the lever and to depress it with the forepaws.

Shaping through successive approximations is obviously an important technique to employ in teaching very difficult or improbable behaviors. The method can be seen to involve the familiar processes of reinforcement and extinction. Only responses exceeding a certain criterion qualify for reinforcement; all others may undergo extinction (or punishment according to Thorndike's analysis). As

FIGURE 5.10   Idealized cumulative records showing the typical patterns of behavior generated by the four simple reinforcement schedules.

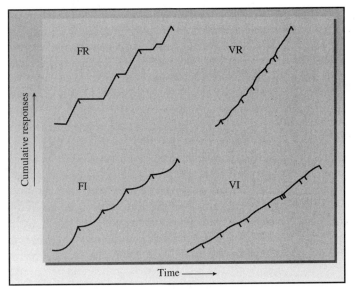

From James E. Mazur, *Learning and Behavior*, 2e, © 1990, pp. 56, 65, 109, 125, 126. Reprinted by permission of Prentice-Hall, Englewood Cliffs, New Jersey.

performance improves at one stage of training, the experimenter adjusts the criterion to a more advanced level. The speed and magnitude of the transition from one step to another may importantly influence the effectiveness of shaping. Steps that are too large or sudden may lead to the extinction of earlier-learned behavior; steps that are too small or gradual may lead to behavior that is too inflexible to meet new demands later. Because shaping is a matter of considerable care, patience, and experience, it justifies the salaries that are earned by animal trainers, tennis instructors, and speech therapists—all expert practitioners of shaping.

Another distinctive aspect of Skinner's procedure is the large literature on **schedules of reinforcement** that it has spawned (figure 5.10). Schedules are simply rules that specify how and when reinforcers can be earned. Some basic schedules that are studied in the conditioning laboratory have obvious counterparts in the extralaboratory world.

Ratio schedules are purely number based. In our original example, each lever press of the rat produced a pellet of food; this schedule is called fixed ratio 1 (FR 1). But not every response need deliver a reinforcer. If only every fifth response produced a reinforcer, then we would have an FR 5 schedule. Fixed ratio schedules are common in everyday life. Salespeople often earn extra money if their sales meet a quota, or they may get a prize for every *n* items they sell. Besides schedules that fix the number of responses required for reinforcers to be earned, there are also schedules where the required number of responses varies from reinforcer to reinforcer. A variable ratio 5 (VR 5) schedule would be one in which, *on average*, five responses would be required, the exact number varying from say one to nine in a random fashion. The most familiar example of a variable ratio schedule is the slot machine. Jackpots on the slot machine are scheduled to occur after so many plays on average, with the number changing from jackpot to jackpot. Ratio schedules usually support high rates of response. Variable ratios often support more sustained and consistent responding than fixed ratios, perhaps because of the greater unpredictability of reinforcers on that schedule.

Another kind of reinforcement schedule is based on the passage of time—an **interval schedule.** In a fixed interval (FI) schedule, reinforcers become available only after the passage of a fixed period of time. Thus, the rat might earn a pellet of food for the first lever press that occurs t second after the last food delivery. Commonly, college students are tested at fixed intervals—midterm and finals week. The accelerated rate of studying that this examination schedule supports has its match in the laboratory, with the rat increasing its rate of response as the time of food availability approaches. Variable interval (VI) schedules also make reinforcers available after the passage of time; here, however, the time interval varies from reinforcer to reinforcer. The variable interval schedule supports a far steadier rate of response than the fixed interval schedule. Students tested with "pop" quizzes rather than with regularly spaced examinations can testify to this fact. A further feature of the variable interval schedule is that, of all four basic schedules, it engenders the most resistance to experimental extinction. This fact is often exploited by experimenters who must study behavior at times when reinforcers are no longer available.

Finally, four different conditioning paradigms are definable in either Thorndike's or Skinner's procedures. (Within any of these paradigms, responses may have consequences that are arranged according to any of the above schedules.) Two have already been mentioned: reinforcement and punishment. In **positive reinforcement,** the criterion response is raised in likelihood by the outcome that it produces; in **positive punishment,** the criterion response is lowered in likelihood by the outcome that it produces. Thus, the explicit contingency in reinforcement and punishment is the same: response → outcome. What distinguishes the two is whether future responding is strengthened (in the case of positive reinforcement) or weakened (in the case of positive punishment). Two other paradigms involve the opposite explicit contingency: response → no outcome. In the case of **negative reinforcement,** the criterion response is raised in likelihood by removing an event; in **negative punishment,** the criterion response is lowered in likelihood by removing an event. Again, the same explicit contingency can either strengthen (in the case of negative reinforcement) or weaken (in the case of negative punishment) a criterion response (see box 5.7). So, rats will increase their rate of lever pressing when presses decrease the incidence of electric shock and they will decrease their rate of lever pressing when presses decrease the incidence of feedings.

In analyzing these four conditioning paradigms, it becomes apparent that we may be able to understand them better if we use them to define appetitive and aversive stimuli. Thus, an **appetitive stimulus** can be defined behaviorally as one that serves to strengthen responses that produce it (positive reinforcement) and that serves to weaken responses that remove it (negative punishment). A rat will then increase lever pressing if such responding produces food; the rat will also decrease lever pressing if such responding removes food from the situation. Food is thus an appetitive stimulus. An **aversive stimulus** can be defined behaviorally as one that serves to weaken responses that produce it (positive punishment) and that serves to strengthen responses that remove it (negative reinforcement). A rat will then decrease lever pressing if such responding produces electric tail shock; the rat will also increase lever pressing if such responding removes shock from the situation. Electric shock is thus an aversive stimulus.

Why should we go to the trouble of supplying these behavioral definitions of appetitive and aversive stimuli? First, requiring two behavioral tests better bolsters our confidence in classifying potentially hedonic stimuli than does only a single test. It is conceivable that a stimulus could decrement behaviors that produce it (positive punishment), but not increment behaviors that remove it (negative reinforcement). Second, overt behavior may be the best guide to sound scientific conclusions. Although our intuitions and introspections lead us to believe that food is invariably appetitive and that

BOX 5.7

Conditioning Paradigms

Some students are confused by the terms positive reinforcement, positive punishment, negative reinforcement, and negative punishment. The adjectives "positive" and "negative" have nothing to do with the hedonic character of the relevant consequence; instead, they refer to the correlation between response and consequence. Positive contingencies involve a positive correlation between response and consequence, with increases in responding increasing the incidence of the consequence; negative contingencies involve a negative correlation between response and consequence, with increases in responding decreasing the incidence of the consequence. The nouns "reinforcement" and "punishment" refer to the behavioral result of the contingency. Reinforcement is said to occur when the contingency increases the incidence of behavior, whereas punishment is said to occur when the contingency decreases the incidence of behavior.

---

electric shock is invariably aversive, such inferences may be wrong. In many situations, humans and animals work to produce stimuli that most would suspect are strongly aversive. Such "masochistic" or "self-punitive" behavior is difficult to comprehend. Proper understanding may well require that we abandon our intuitions and introspections in favor of a more objective and operational approach.

Controls for Conditioning

Earlier, we saw that modern researchers have been concerned with controlling for nonassociative contributions to responding in conditioning procedures. With Pavlov's procedure, we saw that many different controls have been proposed. With Thorndike's and Skinner's procedures, less interest has centered on the problem of nonassociative influences on behavior. However, in the case of potentially weak reinforcers or species that were generally suspected to be incapable of associative learning, the issue of a control for conditioning became salient. To address these issues, the so-called **yoked control** was invented.

The easiest way to think of the yoked control procedure is to imagine two subjects in two separate Skinner boxes. The first, or master, subject has outcomes contingent on its behavior; the second, or yoked control, subject receives outcomes at the same time as the master subject, but not contingent on its own behavior. Thus, were the

master subject to be placed on an FR 1 reinforcement schedule, each response it made would deliver a reinforcer to itself and to the yoked control subject. In so doing, we insure that the frequency and timing of reinforcers would be the same for both subjects. Should the master subject respond more than the yoked control, we could be confident that response-outcome association is the most straightforward interpretation of the result.

Conceptions of Conditioning

Research with Pavlov's and Thorndike's conditioning procedures has generated a great deal of theory and analysis. In order to round out our consideration of Pavlovian and Thorndikian conditioning, we examine a few of the theoretical issues involved in the analysis of associative learning. In particular, we explore contiguity and contingency as explanatory devices. Finally, we discuss whether one or two kinds of learning are involved in Pavlov's and Thorndike's paradigms.

Pavlovian Conditioning

Theories of **Pavlovian conditioning** have been based on two contrasting notions: contiguity and contingency. We develop explanations of learning based on the two different ideas in the following discussion (see box 5.8).

BOX 5.8

Contiguity vs. Contingency

Much debate has centered on the question of whether contiguity or contingency is the critical condition for learning to occur. However, this may not be the best way to conceptualize the problem. Writing in the mid-eighteenth century, the Scottish philosopher David Hume suggested that both contiguity and contingency might be important in causal perception. For one event to be considered a cause for another, it should shortly precede the other. Furthermore, the "cause" should not

fail to be followed by the "effect" (this would reduce the sufficiency of the cause) nor should the "effect" occur without being preceded by the "cause" (this would reduce the necessity of the cause).

Hume's analysis of causal perception suggests that contiguity and contingency may be independent contributors to conditioning. Thus, prior efforts to prove one factor to be of preeminent importance may be misguided (see Papini & Bitterman, 1990, for more on this issue).

Contiguity

Pavlov held that the essential condition necessary to support learning was temporal **contiguity.** Thus, in his procedure, the CS and the US had to occur in close temporal proximity for the CS to come to evoke a CR. Substantial delays between the CS and the US did not support conditioning, although they might be sufficient to maintain responding that had earlier been established with contiguous stimulation (see the earlier description of inhibition of delay).

Why was temporal contiguity necessary for learning? To answer this question, Pavlov developed a largely speculative neurophysiological theory. To begin, Pavlov proposed that sensory stimuli briefly excite localized regions of the cerebral cortex. For example, a tone might excite one region of the cortex and acid on the tongue might excite another. The size of the region that was excited was, he believed, a direct function of the intensity of the stimulus, and this in turn determined the magnitude of the response that was elicited. With respect to the present example, the reaction to acid is stronger than that to a tonal stimulus. Thus, Pavlov assumed that the corresponding cortical regions would show differential degrees of excitation, the gustatory locus being more broadly excited than the auditory locus.

In his studies, Pavlov tried to select CSs that did not initially elicit responses like those evoked by the US. In this way, he could be confident that there was no preexisting connection between the neural CS center and the neural US center. Connection between the originally isolated regions was possible, Pavlov said, through a "drainage-like" process. According to this notion, an area of intense cerebral excitation tended to attract or to drain any weaker excitation toward it. Thus, after repeated temporal pairings, a new pathway was paved for excitation to flow from one formerly unconnected area to another, a pathway that could be established only if the region of CS excitation were still active when excitation of the US region began.

Pavlov's theory had a number of attractive features besides its ability to account for conditioning. First, it explained why the CR often involved the same motor systems as the UR; excitation in the CS locus flowed to the US locus, thus exciting those URs innately connected with this area. Second, it accounted for the fact that CRs are often smaller in magnitude than URs; CSs are generally less intense than USs, thus leading to weaker excitation of the neural US center through presentation of the CS than by presentation of the US. Third, increases in the intensity of either the CS or the US result in stronger conditioning; increases in

CS intensity should lead to greater neural excitation of the US center via the conditioned connection, and increases in US intensity should lead to more effective drainage of excitation from the CS region to the US region. Finally, presenting stimuli similar to the CS should lead to substantial, though weaker conditioned responding; generalization is to be expected because excitation in neighboring cortical regions overlaps the cortical area of the CS to varying degrees.

These positive features notwithstanding, Pavlov's theory has not been very seriously considered. There is little independent evidence that excitation in one cortical area drains excitation toward it from distant cortical regions. Nor is it likely that new, stable neural connections are formed through the "erosion-like" process that Pavlov imagined. Pavlov's theory is best viewed as a metaphorical rather than a mechanistic interpretation of conditioning.

Contingency

A rather different analysis of the Pavlovian experiment is traceable to the ideas of the well-known American psychologist Edward C. Tolman. Writing principally in the 1930s, Tolman and his proponents argued that learning was basically a matter of discovering "what leads to what." Applied to Pavlovian conditioning, the thesis holds that the animal learns the relationship between the CS and the US.

Just how Tolman's approach might be developed can be seen by considering the concept of **contingency,** a more precise rendering of the notion of relationship. A contingency can be said to exist between variables if knowing the state of one enables you to predict the state of the other. Thus, if a contingency holds between cloudiness and rain, then you are in a better-than-chance position of predicting rain when you know the existing cloud conditions than when you do not. In Pavlovian conditioning, the presence of a contingency between the CS and the US enables the subject better to predict the US by attending to the CS than by ignoring it.

This emphasis on CS-US contingency greatly broadens the scope of the Pavlovian procedure, because it specifically acknowledges that events may be both positively and negatively related to one another. Positive CS-US contingencies are more frequently studied; they involve CSs predicting the *occurrence* of US. Negative CS-US contingencies are, however, also possible (as in conditioned inhibition); they involve CSs predicting the *nonoccurrence* of US. Thanks largely to the efforts of the contemporary investigator Robert A. Rescorla (1978), we now know that animals learn about negative CS-US contingencies as well as about positive ones. Thus, contiguity of CS and US is not the only temporal arrangement between the events that can support learning.

In this context, it is useful to return to our earlier discussion of controls for Pavlovian conditioning (pp. 128–129). We saw that, of many possible controls, the random control procedure had much to recommend it. With regard to contingency theory, the random control is the ideal procedure to select; when CSs and USs are presented independently of one another, CS presentation conveys no information about US delivery, i.e., there is no contingency. From the contingency analysis, however, the explicitly unpaired procedure should not be selected as a control for conditioning. Because the explicitly unpaired procedure arranges a negative CS-US contingency, it is a method that should support learning, not preclude it.

We see, therefore, that the choice of a "proper" control for conditioning is not a simple matter. Depending on one's theoretical assumptions, different controls could be deemed appropriate or inappropriate. Controversies like this one are not unusual in science. Although they make textbooks like the present one difficult to write, they excite a great deal of novel and interesting experimentation. Because of the debate between contiguity and contingency theorists, we are learning a great deal more about Pavlovian conditioning than we would know otherwise.

Thorndikian Conditioning

The notions of contiguity and contingency can be applied to **Thorndikian conditioning** as well as Pavlovian conditioning.

Contiguity

Thorndike, himself, proposed that response-reinforcer contiguity was responsible for conditioning. When it closely followed a response, a reinforcer made it more likely that the situation would again elicit that kind of response. Punishment worked in the opposite manner. When it shortly followed a response, a punisher made it less likely that the situation would again evoke that class of response.

Skinner, too, believed that contiguity was a sufficient condition for learning. The basis for this conclusion was an investigation that he reported in 1948, provocatively entitled " 'Superstition' in the pigeon." In this work, Skinner simply presented food to pigeons every 15 seconds—no matter what they were doing. Although the rational and energy-saving thing for them to do was to wait calmly in front of the feeder, six of the eight birds that Skinner studied developed idiosyncratic, stereotyped patterns of behavior that were energetically performed during the intervals between feedings. The birds behaved, Skinner said, as though they thought that their responses were necessary for reinforcer presentation. This constitutes **superstitious behavior.**

Do these observations refute the laws of adaptive behavior? Of course not; but, they do underscore the power of contiguity. When a response accidentally happens to be followed by a reinforcer, the response is automatically strengthened. A single response-reinforcer pairing may be sufficient to raise the likelihood of the response to such a high level that, when another reinforcer is delivered "by the clock," it again is the response most contiguous with the reinforcer. In this way, Skinner proposed, responses unrelated to reinforcement can arise and continue, whether these responses are the bobbings and swayings of pigeons or the contortions and gesticulations of human athletes (watch the "body English" of bowlers and golfers).

Why are procedures that require responses to produce reinforcers so effective in modifying behavior? They work because such procedures guarantee that responses and reinforcers will be contiguous with one another. When responses must be performed in order to produce reinforcers, but delays longer than 1 second are imposed between them, conditioned responding may be greatly reduced or even eliminated.

Contingency

Tolman's suggestion that animals learn "what leads to what" is applicable to Thorndikian conditioning as well as to Pavlovian conditioning. Here, animals may learn the relationship between their behavior and environmental outcomes.

As was the case earlier, the concept of contingency is a useful one. If a contingency holds between a response and an outcome, then the frequency of the outcome can be altered by the response. If a positive contingency exists, then relative to not responding, making the response will increase outcome frequency; if a negative contingency exists, then relative to not responding, making the response will decrease outcome frequency; and if no contingency exists, then relative to not responding, performing the response will not affect outcome frequency.

Do animals learn the contingency between their behavior and an environmental event? Yes, say Seligman, Maier, and Solomon (1971). More specifically, these authors argue that a prior history of uncontrollable aversive events may render organisms "helpless"; when later given control over aversive events, animals with such prior training may be inferior to unpretrained subjects in learning to escape or to avoid noxious events (see box 5.9).

Do Pavlov's and Thorndike's Procedures Involve Different Kinds of Learning?

For many years, theorists have hypothesized that Pavlov's and Thorndike's techniques involve different kinds of learning. As noted before (box 5.5), it is in the context of different learning processes that students often hear the terms classical (Pavlovian)

BOX 5.9

Learned Helplessness

Learned helplessness was confirmed in research with dogs. When dogs with a prior history of inescapable electric shock (i.e., they were shocked at random points in time) were given shock-escape training to jump a low hurdle to terminate shock, most did not acquire the hurdle-jumping response. This result contrasted with the rapid response acquisition of animals that had never before received electric shock.

To prove that it was the inescapability of electric shock and not its familiarity that was responsible for the negative transfer effect, later research in this area has used a so-called triadic design (Seligman, 1975). In addition to the untreated control group, another control group is studied, in which pretraining involves electric shock that is escapable by means of some response other than the one used in the transfer phase.

To guarantee that exposure to shock is the same in this escapable condition and in the inescapable condition, the latter group is yoked to the former (p. 135). To demonstrate "learned helplessness" now requires that the inescapably shocked animals learn more slowly than either the escapably shocked animals or those never receiving pretraining with shock. Even with this more conservative control condition, learned helplessness has been demonstrated.

Beyond the possibility that learned helplessness may support a contingency theory of conditioning, some believe that the phenomenon may be important in the etiology of clinical depression in humans (Seligman, 1975). Perhaps the negative affect associated with this disorder is, like the learning deficit, a by-product of prior uncontrollable aversive events.

---

and instrumental (Thorndikian) conditioning. We will see, however, that this **two-process view of learning** is controversial and that the evidence in support of it is problematical. Therefore, the present chapter has quite cautiously described and discussed Pavlovian and Thorndikian conditioning *procedures,* and has steered clear of the issue of two conditioning *processes.* To conclude this section, we now consider that controversy.

In Pavlovian conditioning, the experimenter arranges a stimulus-stimulus relation, e.g., light→shock. The animal's behavior cannot affect stimulus presentations. In Thorndikian conditioning, the experimenter arranges a response-stimulus relation, e.g., press→shock. The animal's behavior here does affect stimulus presentations. Thus, in Thorndike's procedure the animal has control over important events in its environment, whereas in Pavlov's procedure the animal is powerless to control its environment. The ability to control one's environment is obviously of enormous practical advantage to a human being or to an animal (again,

see box 5.9). But does this mean that different processes are responsible for learning when control is possible and when it is precluded?

One way to evaluate two-process theory is to look at the empirical results that are supported by Pavlovian and Thorndikian procedures. We have already seen that parallel basic effects occur in both paradigms: acquisition, extinction, generalization, and discrimination. Furthermore, as best we know, variables such as the amount of reinforcement, the delay of reinforcement, and the schedule of reinforcement have generally similar effects in the two procedures (Mackintosh, 1974). Thus, there appears to be little empirical reason to assume that different processes are at work in Pavlovian and Thorndikian conditioning. Alternatively, proponents of two-factor theory emphasize some specific differences in responding produced by the two procedures.

It has been argued that different neurological systems mediate learning in Pavlov's and Thorndike's procedures. Although it is surely inefficient to have different learning principles for each system, several influential psychologists including Skinner have suggested that the autonomic nervous system mediates Pavlovian conditioning and that the somatic nervous system mediates Thorndikian conditioning. But, the alignment of physiological and psychological functions is flawed. Many skeletal responses—like eyeblinking in humans, pecking in birds, and leg flexion in goats—have been reported to be conditionable with Pavlov's procedure; and, many autonomic responses—like changes in heart rate, intestinal contraction, and salivation—have been reported to be conditionable with Thorndike's procedure (Macintosh, 1974; Miller, 1969).

Finally, consider the implications of the important learning phenomenon of **conditioned reinforcement.** Conditioned reinforcement is observed in a Thorndikian-Skinnerian procedure when an initially indifferent stimulus acquires an ability to reinforce responses on which its presentation is contingent. Thus, a rat will learn to press a lever to present a tone, if the tone was previously paired with food, in much the same way that a child will work for her mother's praise, if such verbalizations were earlier paired with biological satisfactions. Although conditioned reinforcement is observed in the Thorndike-Skinner procedure, it is clear that Pavlov's procedure is an important ingredient for establishing a stimulus as a potential conditioned reinforcer. Thus, pairing a tone with food will, on the one hand, cause an animal to salivate to the tone—Pavlovian conditioning. The same stimulus pairing procedure will, on the other hand, cause the stimulus to function as a conditioned reinforcer, if the animal's behavior is arranged to present the tone contingently—Thorndikian conditioning. It is unparsimonious to believe that different psychological or neurological processes are responsible for each change in behavior just because different conditioning methods were used in the two cases. It is more likely that a single associative process is responsible for behavior change in both Pavlov's and Thorndike's conditioning procedures. Nevertheless, we can expect advocates of two-process theory to continue the argument.

Broader Views of Learning and Cognition in Animals

It is common in textbooks like the present one to examine the methods, results, and theories of Pavlovian and Thorndikian conditioning in animals such as pigeons, rats, cats, and dogs. Although such treatments are representative of most work in the comparative psychology of learning, they fail to do justice to the full breadth of animal learning, either in terms of the diversity of learned modifications in behavior or in terms of the range of species capable of adjusting to environmental change. To gain a better sense of the breadth of animal learning, we must also consider other kinds of learning and less familiar species of animals.

Both Pavlovian and Thorndikian conditioning are forms of **associative learning.** In associative learning, at least two classes of events are functionally linked. Thus, in Pavlovian conditioning CS and US are connected with one another, whereas in Thorndikian conditioning response and consequence are connected with one another. The critical feature distinguishing Pavlovian and Thorndikian conditioning is not whether they are associative in nature (both are), but rather the character of the events that enter into association with one another (two different stimulus classes in the case of Pavlovian conditioning; stimulus and response classes in the case of Thorndikian conditioning).

Despite experimental psychologists' primary interest in associative learning, we must also appreciate that **nonassociative learning** may play an important role in promoting adaptive behavior. In the clearest example of nonassociative learning (*habituation*), relatively enduring changes in behavior result from presentation of only one class of events, thus precluding the obvious involvement of associative processes.

Not only are there instances of animal learning that appear simpler than Pavlovian and Thorndikian conditioning, there are also examples of extremely complex changes in behavior that greatly eclipse the intelligence that we commonly attribute to animals and that exceed the requirements of standard laboratory tasks. Such examples of extraordinary intelligence also demand attention.

Finally, in surveying the domain of animal learning, it happens that animals often learn with such ease that one wonders whether they may be predisposed to react in special ways to certain environmental exigencies. Such behaviors may be called instinctive, species-specific, or species-typical. Special preparedness may also be revealed by learning that is limited to certain phases in the life history of an individual organism (such as imprinting; see ahead). Specializations in learning must thus be examined if we are to gain a comprehensive understanding of learning within the general context of adaptive behavior.

Nonassociative Learning

Habituation

We are all familiar with the fact that repeatedly presenting a stimulus may reduce the reaction to the stimulus. The new urban dweller eventually becomes accustomed to street noises; she ultimately gets used to frequent jostling in the subway; and she becomes less tempted by the tantalizing aromas emanating from snack wagons scattered along the walk to and from the office.

Reduced responsivity to eliciting stimuli is a hallmark of the phenomenon of **habituation.** However, experimental psychologists and neuroscientists insist that, if habituation is to be considered a bona fide case of learning, then the change in behavior must be mediated by the central nervous system (Thompson & Spencer, 1966). Such insistence effectively eliminates two other reasons for response decrements resulting from repetitive stimulation: sensory adaptation and motor fatigue. In **sensory adaptation,** the receptor organs themselves become less able to respond to previously effective stimulus energy. For instance, the photoreceptors in the retina of the eye become less able to react to a repeated visual stimulus the more often it is presented. In **motor fatigue,** the muscles

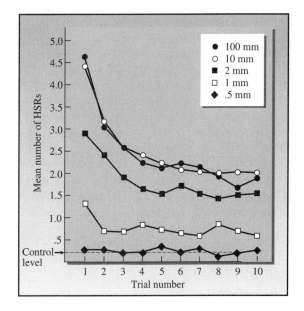

FIGURE 5.11 Effects of increasing stimulus intensities and repetition on habituation of the headshake response of rats to air puff stimulation of the ear (Ratner 1970).

themselves become increasingly unable to perform the same amount of work, given a particular level of stimulus energy.

Granting that sensory adaptation and motor fatigue are very real reasons for responding to decline when eliciting stimuli are regularly repeated, we must be prepared to show that habituation is something above and beyond these other two processes. Just how this can be done will be discussed shortly.

Many different responses in many different species of animals have been shown to be subject to habituation (Ratner, 1970), including bodily contraction in the earthworm, headshaking in the rat, leg flexion in the cat, and the startle response of the human infant. As a concrete example, take the headshake response of rats (figure 5.11). If a jet of air is blown into a rat's ear, the rat vigorously shakes its head from side to side. Repeated applications of the air puff lead to a reduction in the number of to and fro motions of the rat's head—habituation.

Like other forms of learning, habituation may be retained over substantial intervals of time. Even the lowly earthworm has been shown to retain the effects of repeated vibratory stimuli for up to 96 hours. Longer and shorter intervals have been reported as boundaries for the duration of habituation for other responses and other species.

How do we distinguish habituation from unlearned sources of response reduction? The answer comes from applying other principles of learning to habituation. Consider the phenomenon of **dishabituation.** If, after habituation has proceeded to its limit, a novel stimulus in another modality accompanies the habituated stimulus, then the compound stimulus may actually produce a *stronger* response than that to the habituated stimulus alone, even though the new stimulus itself does *not* evoke a response like that under study. Thus, for example, after habituating the rat's head shake response to an air puff, a bright light can be flashed along with the next air puff. The response on this occasion may be much larger than that on the prior series of trials. If so, then we have an instance of dishabituation.

Does dishabituation effectively eliminate sensory adaptation and motor fatigue as possible reasons for the original habituation result? Yes. Suppose that during the habituation series, the tactile receptors in the rat's ear had become progressively less sensitive to air puff stimulation. Flashing a light should not affect sensory adaptation. Thus, dishabituation should not occur. In an analogous vein, suppose that during the habituation series, the rat's neck muscles had tired due to extensive exertion. Flashing a light should do nothing to motor fatigue. Again, dishabituation should not occur. The occurrence of dishabituation suggests that some other process—probably operating in the central nervous system—is mediating the behavioral result we call habituation.

Because habituation is a relatively enduring change in the central nervous system that occurs in a broad range of species and response systems, it demands much greater attention by experimental psychologists than it has received so far. Associative learning may not be the most prevalent or important form of behavior change in the animal kingdom. Indeed, the ability of organisms to disregard often-repeated, unimportant stimuli may be of far greater survival value. Habituation may pave the way for the animal to attend to more important events: novel stimuli or those heralding biologically significant events like food, mates, and predators.

Sensitization

Although reduced responsivity is the most frequent and best understood behavioral consequence of repeated stimulation, it is not the only possible result. Repeated stimulation may also occasion enhanced reactivity to a stimulus—**sensitization.** A familiar example of sensitization is the case of a dripping faucet. The constant plop of water drops hitting the sink can become an incredibly irksome irritant to the fitful sleeper.

Despite our everyday familiarity with sensitization, very little experimental effort has been addressed to the phenomenon (Fantino & Logan, 1979; Groves & Thompson, 1970). We remain largely ignorant as to why repeated stimulation sometimes yields reductions in responding (habituation) and why at other times it yields augmentations in responding (sensitization).

Complex Forms of Learning and Cognition

Learning Sets

If nothing else, psychologists since Pavlov have been scrupulous in their efforts to control the prior experience of their experimental subjects. Thus, in most research, animal subjects are experimentally naive; they have never before participated in an investigation like that being conducted. This practice of using inexperienced subjects has the strong virtue of reducing generalization from prior learning as a serious confounding factor in the obtained results. The influence of past experience was, you will recall (p. 122), a major reason why Morgan concentrated his experimental energies on newly hatched chicks.

FIGURE 5.12   The Wisconsin general test apparatus.

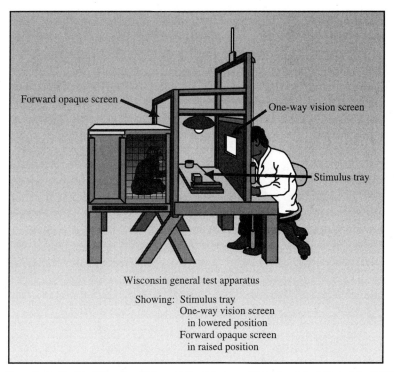

Forward opaque screen

One-way vision screen

Stimulus tray

Wisconsin general test apparatus

Showing: Stimulus tray
One-way vision screen
in lowered position
Forward opaque screen
in raised position

From G. A. Kimble, Hilgard and Marquis' *Conditioning and Learning,* 2d ed. Copyright © 1961 Appleton-Century-Crofts. Reprinted by permission of Simon & Schuster, Englewood Cliffs, New Jersey.

However, there is a very serious danger that accompanies the use of experimentally naive subjects: namely, most individual animals who survive an appreciable time in the wild are the beneficiaries of numerous learning experiences. Thus, learning in nature is more often accomplished by practiced than by unpracticed animals. If prior learning experience changes the way in which animals learn, then by using only inexperienced subjects, we may greatly limit the generality of our empirical results. Harlow (1949) has very clearly shown that prior practice dramatically changes *how* animals learn tasks of many different kinds.

In one line of work, Harlow trained rhesus monkeys on two-object discriminations (figure 5.12). In such tasks, two different objects—such as a box and

a cylinder—simultaneously cover two recessed wells in a board that can be slid within the monkey's reach. When the monkey pushes aside one of the objects, it might find food in the exposed well. Assuming that the correct object to displace is the box, the monkey can receive food on each trial if it selects the box, regardless of its position over the left and right wells of the tray. (From trial to trial, the location of the two objects is irregularly varied by the experimenter.) Selection of the incorrect object, here the cylinder, results only in the sight of an empty food well.

Initial exposure to this kind of problem results in a slow and steady rise in the percentage of correct choices as the number of training trials increases. Thus, on Trial 1, the percentage of correct choices

FIGURE 5.13 Monkeys' performance on Trials 1 to 6 in a series of 344 separate discriminations. The improvement with practice depicts the development of a learning set.

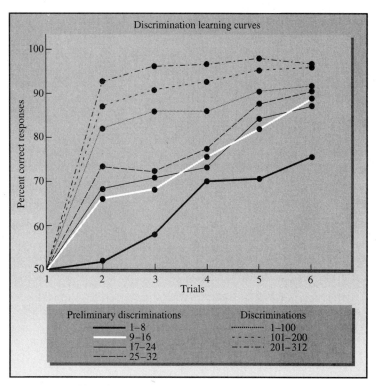

From G. A. Kimble, Hilgard and Marquis' *Conditioning and Learning*, 2d ed. Copyright © 1961 Appleton-Century-Crofts. Reprinted by permission of Simon & Schuster, Englewood Cliffs, New Jersey.

for a group of animals would be a chance score of 50, with the score rising progressively to Trial 6 (and beyond), where well more than 50 percent correct choices would be recorded (figure 5.13).

In striking contrast to this portrait of discrimination learning as slow and steady, well-practiced animals learn two-object discriminations in one trial! Thus, an animal who has mastered several hundred discriminations based on different objects in each problem can use the result of a single trial as a guide to impeccable future performance. Should the monkey select the correct object on Trial 1, it will *stay* with that choice on later trials; should the animal select the incorrect object on Trial 1, however, it will *shift* to the other alternative on later trials. This "win-stay, lose-shift" pattern produces an abrupt rise in choice accuracy from 50 percent to almost 100 percent from Trial 1 to Trial 2 (figure 5.13).

Harlow reasoned that something beyond the specifics of any particular problem had been learned by his highly experienced subjects. Here, the animals seemed to have learned the general rules of the game: for any two objects, only one will have food beneath it, no matter where on the food tray it is located. The well-practiced subject is thus prepared or set to deal with any two objects, needing only the information on Trial 1 to direct it toward the correct object on all later trials. In short, a disposition or set to learn the two-object task had been acquired. Harlow called this propensity a **learning set.**

Learning sets can be shown in even simpler Thorndikian situations than Harlow's. Thus, rats can be trained on successive discrimination reversals where, for example, left button presses first produce food, then right button presses do so, then left presses, and so on. A single nonreinforced response can thus signal the rat to choose the other button. Animals exposed to their first reversal may perseverate on the initially reinforced, but now nonreinforced button for some time; however, animals exposed to many prior reversals rapidly abandon an ineffective button in favor of the now-effective one—a reversal learning set (Mackintosh, 1974).

Even the Pavlovian situation can support learning sets. Thus, alternating long blocks of CS-US pairings with blocks of CS only presentations amounts to successive acquisitions and extinctions. Initially, acquisition and extinction are slow, progressive changes in behavior. However, after many successive exposures to each type of training, a single CS-US pairing can reinstate responding to a very high level; and a single CS alone presentation can decrement responding to a very low level—an acquisition-extinction learning set (Mackintosh, 1974).

Learning sets thus cut across both Pavlovian and Thorndikian tasks. They represent the learning of general properties of the conditioning situation that transcend the specifics of any one particular problem. Consistent with Harlow's speculations, learning sets suggest that learning in experienced animals may differ qualitatively from learning in experimentally naive subjects. (We will see this principle at work again in later chapters on human learning and thinking.) We must therefore be extremely careful in making sweeping statements about the nature of learning from the study of either highly practiced or unpracticed animals.

Conceptual Behavior

Reacting to relatively stable features of a situation (e.g., two-object discriminations), while accepting some measure of variability in those features (e.g., any two objects covering the food wells) is not unique to learning sets. In fact, we see these same aspects of performance in cases we are apt to term **conceptual behavior.** Take the word "chair." We use this word to denote objects having: one or more legs, a resting place for the buttocks, and an upright support for the back. Such objects are quite distinct from others we call "lamps," "automobiles," and "coats." Yet, despite the common properties shared

by most chairs, this class of objects is an impressively large one, comprising dining chairs, armchairs, and highchairs. Somehow, we are able to distinguish chairs from nonchairs and also to disregard great differences among individual chairs. How is correct classification accomplished?

One useful way to think about conceptual behavior is in terms of two now-familiar phenomena of stimulus control: discrimination and generalization. As children learn to label objects, they are reinforced by parents and teachers for saying "chair" to some stimuli but not to others—discrimination. Furthermore, applying the word "chair" to new, but similar stimuli also yields reinforcers—generalization. Thus, discrimination and generalization provide for the establishment of stimulus classes that permit means for excluding some objects from the class and for including others, even those that have never before been encountered. Such learned stimulus classes enable organisms to respond to abstract and general relations of objects, rather than to concrete and specific stimuli.

As we will see in the next chapter, this analysis of conceptual behavior makes good sense when applied to the verbal behavior of humans. But what about animals? Do nonverbal animals also behave in ways that convince us that they possess some measure of conceptual ability?

To answer this question in the pigeon, a technique was devised to train it concurrently to discriminate stimuli from several human language categories. The specific method (Bhatt et al., 1988, Experiment 1) was based on the technique that parents often use to teach their children to label objects in a picture book—the "name" game. When the page is turned, the child is asked to look at the object and then she is requested to name it. If she is correct, she is lavished with praise. If she is incorrect, she is gently told "no" and is encouraged to try again. And, if self-correction fails, she is provided with the correct name. To implement this method with pigeons, a color snapshot was displayed on a 3-inch square frosted plastic screen and the pigeon was required to peck a clear plastic key covering the screen 30 times to ensure the subject's seeing the stimulus. Completing this observing response requirement led to the illumination of four differently colored keys just beyond the corners of the viewing screen. The different colors were used simply to make the keys easy to discriminate. A single choice response was then permitted. If it was to the *correct* key for reporting the stimulus on the viewing screen, then all of the visual stimuli were turned off and the pigeon was fed mixed grain; if the response was to any of the three *incorrect* report keys, then all report key lights were turned off and the trial was repeated. Only the first choice response of a trial was scored; correction trials were not considered in analyses of performance. In several studies, the 40 slides seen in each daily session depicted 10 different examples each of cats, flowers, cars, and chairs. The pictures contained one or more instances of the critical stimulus object; the objects were indoors or outdoors, near or far away, centered or off center, and in different colors, orientations, and backgrounds. The subject's task was to peck the key corresponding to the object shown on a given trial; for example, the top left key for cats, the top right key for flowers, the bottom left key for cars, and the bottom right key for chairs.

In one representative experiment (Bhatt et al., 1988, Experiment 1B), a group of four pigeons attained a mean level of discriminative performance of 76 percent correct during Days 26 to 30 of training, after beginning the investigation near the chance level of 25 percent correct. Also noteworthy were the results of two later days of test performance with the 40 original training slides and with 40 brand-new slides of cats, flowers, cars, and chairs. Mean accuracy to old slides was 81 percent and to new slides it was 64 percent. Although test performance was highly discriminative to both sets of stimuli, accuracy was reliably higher to old than to new pictures, perhaps because the birds remembered some or all of the old slides. Finally, there was no evidence for any of the stimulus categories being harder or easier for the pigeons to discriminate (contrary to the suggestion made by Herrnstein, 1985, that pigeons cannot categorize humanmade stimuli). Thus, pigeons are able concurrently to categorize stimuli from four classes of natural and artificial objects, and also to extrapolate that categorization to completely novel test stimuli, albeit at a somewhat lower level of accuracy. (See box 5.10 for further data on natural concepts in pigeons.)

Beyond animals' acquisition of such object or **natural concepts,** we might ask whether they can learn more artificial relations or properties of objects, so-called **arbitrary concepts.** One property of objects that is particularly arbitrary is whether two or more objects are the same or different from one another. Here, one can train animals to select the one of several choice stimuli that is the same as some standard or sample stimulus. The animal then receives reinforcement for correctly **matching-to-sample.**

Many different species of animals have learned matching-to-sample tasks with Thorndikian and Skinnerian procedures. However, correct performance on a single matching-to-sample task does not establish the acquisition of an arbitrary matching concept. Selecting the triangle over the circle when the sample is the triangle and selecting the circle over the triangle when the sample is the circle could represent the learning of individual stimulus-response rules that would show little generality beyond those specific stimuli. Again, what must be done in order to demonstrate that a concept has been learned is to show that correct matching performance extends to new stimuli that were never used in prior training. When generalization tests of this sort have been performed with pigeons, only weak support has been found for their acquiring a concept of stimulus matching (for reviews and critical analyses see Carter & Werner, 1978; D'Amato et al., 1986; Edwards, Miller, & Zentall, 1985; Premack, 1978). Compared to pigeons, both new- and old-world monkeys more readily generalize their visual matching-to-sample performance to novel stimuli (e.g., D'Amato & Salmon, 1984), as does the bottlenose dolphin in an auditory matching-to-sample task (Herman & Gordon, 1974).

However, the clearest evidence of spontaneous transfer of matching-to-sample performance comes from chimpanzees. Oden, Thompson, and Premack (1988) taught four infant chimpanzees to match-to-sample using a set of only two objects: a lock and a cup. In the simultaneous matching-to-sample procedure that they employed, the chimpanzee was handed a sample object; it was then required to choose from the set of two test objects the one that was the same as the sample object on that trial. A

BOX 5.10

Further Data on Natural Concepts in Pigeons

Perhaps even more important were the results of a later investigation (Bhatt et al., 1988, Experiment 3) in which a large pool of 2,000 unique snapshots—500 from each of four categories—were shown to pigeons on a one-time-only basis. Without the benefit of *any* stimulus repetition, the birds attained a mean accuracy level of 70 percent correct on Days 46 to 50. Either the pigeon has an undocumented ability to remember a rather large number of stimuli it has seen only *once* (cf. Vaughan & Greene, 1984 who showed that pigeons can remember up to 320 pictures seen at least 28 times each) or it can abstract some kind of generic or prototypical information from varied stimuli, as implied by several models of conceptualization (Smith & Medin, 1981).

It is surely no small matter to demonstrate that nonverbal animals like pigeons are so adept at categorizing snapshots of real objects (also see Herrnstein, 1985). Yet, one is bound to wonder just how similar this feat is to the conceptual behavior of human beings. Here, an additional project suggests that the similarity may be more than accidental.

In that investigation (Wasserman, Kiedinger, & Bhatt, 1988, Experiment 2), two groups of four pigeons were trained to categorize the same set of 80 snapshots. The first (or true category) group had to peck one of four keys to report each of 20 stimuli from four human language categories: cats, flowers, cars, and chairs. The second (or pseudocategory) group had to classify the same slides into random assortments, in which each of the four pseudocategories comprised equal numbers of cat, flower, car, and chair slides. In this latter case, each of the four keys served as the correct key for a mixture of stimuli from the four true categories; thus, there is no perceptual "glue" to bind stimuli in pseudocategories. Over Days 37 to 40 of training, pigeons on the true categorization task averaged 79 percent correct whereas pigeons on the pseudocategorization task averaged only 44 percent correct (a small, but reliable rise from 25 percent). Thus, learning proceeded far faster when the to-be-trained categories coincided with human language classes than when they did not. These and other results (Astley & Wasserman, 1992; Edwards & Honig, 1987; Herrnstein & de Villiers, 1980; Wasserman et al., 1988, Experiment 1) suggest that *to pigeons* members of human language categories resemble one another more than they resemble members of other language categories. The pigeon's categorization behavior thus confirms the nonarbitrary nature of human language terms, at least for the object categories they have thus far been given.

---

correct choice resulted in social and gustatory reinforcement, whereas an incorrect choice did not. After reaching a criterion of 83 percent correct, the animals were given a series of tests with novel objects and fabrics. Test accuracy on these trials averaged 85 percent. Thus, the chimpanzees transferred their matching-to-sample performance *without decrement* to brand-new stimuli, suggesting that they had strongly conceptualized the same-different relation.

It is surely noteworthy that dolphins and primates more readily generalize their matching-to-sample behavior than do pigeons. But does this mean that pigeons are completely unable to appreciate the abstract relation of sameness-difference? Other evidence suggests not.

Yet another procedure has been used to assess control over behavior by same and different stimuli. In the paired comparison procedure, two stimuli are either spontaneously or successively exposed. Then, two response alternatives are afforded to subjects: one for reporting that the stimuli were the same and the other for reporting that they were different. Correct choices occasion reinforcement, whereas incorrect choices do not.

In a project by Santiago and Wright (1984), pigeons were trained on a simultaneous visual paired comparison procedure. During original training, 105 color slides of fruit, flowers, animals, people, and other natural and humanmade objects were shown in pairs on a horizontally split screen. After making an observing response to a clear panel covering the split screen, two choice keys were lighted: the left for reporting that the two slides were different and the right for reporting that they were the same. Half of the trials involved "same" stimuli and half involved "different" stimuli. The large number of training stimuli that were employed guaranteed that no stimulus occurred on more than one trial in a session, in the hope that the birds' behavior would more likely come under control of the same-different relation than under control of the specific features of the stimuli. After training to over 80 percent correct on the original set of slides, the pigeons were shown 105 brand-new slides. First session transfer performance averaged 70 percent correct. This score was a bit lower than that to the training slides; but, it was much higher than the 50 percent score expected by chance, and it compared quite favorably with the 72 percent score of rhesus monkeys trained and tested under virtually identical circumstances (Wright, Santiago, & Sands, 1984). (See box 5.11 for further data on arbitrary concepts in pigeons.)

Besides the case of same-different concepts, other arbitrary concepts in animals have been studied. These include: perceiving the number of stimuli, discriminating the duration of stimulus presentation, and detecting melodic patterns of auditory stimuli (Honig & Fetterman, 1992; Roitblat, Bever, & Terrace, 1984; Wasserman, 1993). The positive results of many of these investigations are prompting today's psychologists to reconsider earlier claims by Morgan (1894) and others that conceptual behavior is a unique ability of human beings. As often happens to sweeping claims, more recent research focuses on which concepts can be acquired or on the relative difficulty of different kinds of discriminations, rather than on assertions of uniqueness.

Specializations in Learning

Experimental psychologists have, since beginning their study of animal learning, arranged laboratory paradigms to model rather general contingencies for survival that animals confront in their natural habitats. Thus, in Pavlov's work, one stimulus signaled another, enabling the animal to react in advance of an important biological event. Signalization of one event by another is a very general feature of natural learning situations: lightning signals thunder, a scent signals a mate, and the sight of a flower signals pollen. In Thorndike's work, a response caused the presentation of an appetitive or an aversive event. Control over the environment too is a general property of natural contingencies: beavers alter the flow of streams by building dams, hunting wolf packs can cut off the flight of a lamb from the rest of the herd by special stalking techniques, and bees cool the interior temperature of the hive by rapidly fanning their wings.

However general we think our laboratory learning tasks are, we must be ever alert to the possibility that we are tapping in on some species-typical behavior pattern or potentiality (see Shettleworth, 1993). The case of rats' avoidance of tainted food is a good example of this point.

Food Aversion Learning

When a rat eats food and later becomes ill, it subsequently shows a strong reluctance to eat that food again (Revusky & Garcia, 1970). Superficially, a **learned food aversion** hardly questions the principles of associative conditioning. However, the robustness of the result is especially noteworthy. A single pairing of a novel taste or odor with gastrointestinal distress is sufficient to support a strong food aversion. Commonly, tens or even hundreds of trials may be required for animals to learn standard laboratory problems. Furthermore, delays of several hours intervene between ingestion of the tainted substance and the later illness that it causes. Ordinarily, delays of consequence that exceed only a few seconds preclude the occurrence of association formation (Mackintosh, 1974). Finally, the animal preferentially associates the flavor or odor of the food with illness over other potential cues such as the food's size and location. This selectivity is uncommon in typical laboratory tasks.

BOX 5.11

Further Data on Arbitrary Concepts in Pigeons

Further evidence that even pigeons can appreciate abstract stimulus relations comes from a report by Macphail and Reilly (1989). In this project, pigeons were shown a series of color slides depicting indoor scenes, outdoor scenes, objects, faces, and so on. Each slide was shown twice in each daily 48-trial session, and slides were never reused from one session to another. Pecks to the *first* presentation of a given slide were reinforced with food, whereas pecks to the *second* presentation were not. After only four sessions of discrimination training, pigeons pecked much more often on the first presentation of a slide than on its second presentation. Because of the continually changing composition of the slide sets, these results suggest that the pigeons were readily able to discriminate "familiar" from "novel" stimuli, quite apart from the specific attributes of each stimulus display. Macphail and Reilly proposed that earlier difficulties in training highly general same-different or familiar-novel reports in pigeons may have been due to procedural factors rather than to any cognitive limitations of the species.

These results suggest that food aversion learning may be a specialized form of conditioning, one particularly suited to the environmental and biological exigencies operating in the domain of ingestive behavior (Rozin & Kalat, 1971). Thus, a rat might not survive long enough to profit from its eating experiences if it does not: learn very quickly, remember what it last ate for a rather long time, and more strongly affiliate the source of its illness with gustatory and olfactory stimuli than with other, less ingestionally relevant cues in the environment.

Imprinting

Another possible case of a specialized learning ability is that of **imprinting,** a phenomenon brought to our attention by the ethologist Konrad Lorenz. Soon after hatching, young birds of many species form strong social attachments and faithfully follow their parents wherever they go (Hess, 1973; Sluckin, 1965). We know that learning is involved in the attachment process because socially isolated animals can be imprinted to such odd foster parents as toy trains, footballs, and sneakers! Importantly, however, imprinting is often most likely to occur within certain **sensitive periods** in the animal's development. Mallard ducklings, for example, have been reported to imprint maximally within the range of 5 to 24 hours after hatching; attempts to imprint younger or older animals meet with much less success.

We still do not know why social attachments are constrained by the age of the animal. If it is adaptive to learn which object to follow at 16 hours, then why would it not also be adaptive to learn which object to follow at 36 hours? Perhaps the young animal's neural machinery is best equipped to learn only a few things at a time. Assuming that in the course of normal development the young animal has already imprinted to its parents by 24 hours, it now becomes more efficient for it to switch its intellect to other tasks, like what to eat and drink. And, because the parents are the natural tutors of the young, learning who mom and dad are should take initial precedence over any other learning the young has to do.

Instinctive Drift

Still other evidence underscores the importance of species-typical behavior patterns in the results of conditioning research. Here, it has been found that well-learned response sequences may break down due to the intrusion of species-specific or instinctive reactions.

Breland and Breland (1961) reported several examples of this effect in their business enterprise of training animals for zoos, state fairs, and television commercials. One particularly graphic case was their training a raccoon to deposit disks into a metal box:

Raccoons condition readily, have good appetites, and this one was quite tame and an eager subject. We anticipated no trouble. Conditioning him to pick up the first coin was simple. We started out by reinforcing him for picking up a single coin. Then the metal container was introduced, with the requirement that he drop the coin into the container. Here we ran into the first bit of difficulty: he seemed to have a great deal of trouble letting go of the coin. He would rub it up against the inside of the container, pull it back out, and clutch it for several seconds. However, he would finally turn it loose and receive his food reinforcement. Then the final contingency: we put him on a ratio of 2, requiring that he pick up both coins and put them in the container.

Now the raccoon really did have problems (and so did we). Not only could he not let go of the coins, but he spent seconds, even minutes, rubbing them together . . . , and dipping them into the container. He carried on this behavior to such an extent that the practical application we had in mind—a display featuring a raccoon putting money in a piggy bank—simply was not feasible. The rubbing behavior became worse and worse as time went on, in spite of reinforcement.

This and other cases where reinforcement did not sustain the desired behavior patterns shocked and surprised the Brelands, who had expected no problems in training their animal partners in profit. What had gone wrong?

The Brelands suggested that the learned responses they were trying to condition were simply weaker than the natural food-getting behaviors of the animal. Although the learned behaviors might emerge and continue for a while, unlearned reactions might, if the circumstances were right, gradually overwhelm and replace those conditioned responses. Thus, because food-washing is a natural behavior of the raccoon, food-washing became coin-rubbing and slowly intruded into the coin-depositing sequence planned by the Brelands. As a name for this phenomenon, the Brelands suggested **instinctive drift.**

The Brelands believed that the phenomenon of instinctive drift represented a flagrant failure for learning theory to predict animal behavior. Although Thorndikian conditioning does not lead one to expect learned behavior patterns to disintegrate, Pavlovian conditioning may provide a ready account for the intrusion of food-related behaviors, like those the Brelands saw. Thus, the disks may have become CSs for food and elicited rubbing behaviors by the raccoon. Regardless of the correct interpretation of instinctive drift, however, the phenomenon certainly emphasizes that we should look very carefully at the natural behaviors of an animal before undertaking elaborate experimental work with it. Failure to do so could lead to improper inferences about the species in question.

Less Common Experimental Animals

As noted earlier, the most common animals studied in the experimental analysis of learning are pigeons, rats, cats, and dogs. No matter how much we discover about the nature of learning in these species, we run the risk of being too narrow in our overall perspective of animal intelligence. In order to round out our survey of animal learning, we should consider the intelligence of lower and higher species than those usually studied in the laboratory.

Learning in Invertebrates

Even though more than 99 percent of all living animals on the earth are invertebrates, fewer than 5 percent of the published studies of animals by experimental psychologists have used invertebrate subjects (McConnell & Jacobson, 1973). Why have these animals been so neglected? One possibility is that most invertebrates are quite small. True, single-celled creatures like the protozoa require a microscope to be seen. Yet, several invertebrates like the beetle and the squid are quite large and their behavior is easily observed. A second possibility is that we are strongly biased toward animals like ourselves. Such an anthropocentric bias does indeed appear to be one reason for the disproportionate attention given to mammalian species. Finally, there may be a strong preconception that the behavior of invertebrates is much simpler and less modifiable than that of vertebrates. If our primary interest is in animal intelligence, then it would be particularly unwise to look for learning in invertebrates. As it turns out, there is a growing

FIGURE 5.14 CRs to light (solid line) and vibration (dashed line) CSs during Pavlovian discrimination training with a shock US in six planaria (Fantino and Logan, 1979).

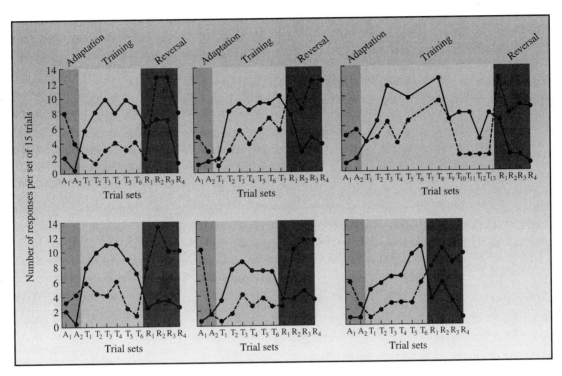

body of evidence (Carew & Sahley, 1986; Eisenstein, 1967; Fantino & Logan, 1979; McConnell & Jacobson, 1973) that invertebrates are capable of showing many modifications in behavior, some of them quite complex and comparable to vertebrates.

Although most invertebrates that have been studied have evidenced the phenomenon of habituation (as illustrated before in earthworms), clear cases of associative learning have been more elusive. Indeed, associative learning in invertebrates has been a hotly disputed topic. After years of sometimes acrimonious debate, there is an emerging consensus that invertebrates can acquire associations, not unlike those formed by vertebrates. Rather than simply listing examples of successful associative learning, it might be more instructive here to examine two often cited reports of conditioning: one using Pavlov's procedure and the other using Thorndike's procedure.

The planarian flatworm is usually less than an inch long and lives in both fresh and salt water. The animal is the simplest to be bilaterally symmetrical,

to have neural synapses, and to possess a clearly defined brain. These features, plus others such as regeneration after segmentation and being hermaphroditic, make planaria particularly interesting to comparative psychologists and neuroscientists. Most important to us is the reported ability of planaria to condition under Pavlov's procedure. When given a brief electric shock, the animal contracts its body. If a brief stimulus such as an overhead light or vibration regularly precedes the electric shock, then these shock-paired stimuli become increasingly able to elicit a contraction response.

Several control procedures have been used to show that these changes in responsivity to the CS are truly associative. Thus, groups given CS only and US only were included in the initial studies of planarian learning. However, because of the less conclusive character of these controls, random control and discrimination procedures (p. 129) were added to later studies (Corning & Freed, 1968; Jacobson, Horowitz, & Fried, 1967; Levison, 1979)—(figure 5.14). Even with the inclusion of

FIGURE 5.15   The arrangement of the connections to the Positional (P) and Random control (R) animals from the stimulator. (a) In initial training, the two animals are arranged in series and both animals receive shocks when P lowers its leg below the critical level. (b) In testing, the animals are connected so that each receives a shock whenever it lowers its leg below the critical level. (Eisenstein, 1967).

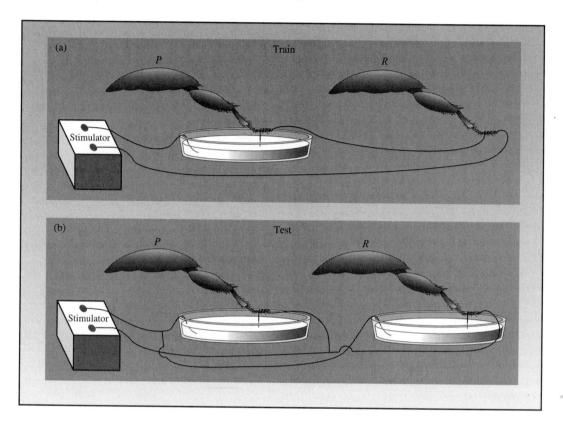

these more stringent controls, positive evidence for Pavlovian conditioning in planaria has been found. Thus, the results of these reports suggest that planaria are capable of associative learning.

The cockroach and the locust are, of course, better-known species than planaria. Some remarkable investigations of learning in these species have been conducted. Of special note are provocative reports of Thorndikian conditioning using electric shock as the contingent consequence.

The general plan of this work (Eisenstein & Cohen, 1965; Horridge, 1962) was to deliver electric shock to the leg of an animal whenever the appendage dropped to a particular level. As long as the leg was held above the criterion height, no shock was

delivered. This Thorndikian contingency led to an increased tendency to hold the leg above the criterion level. To guarantee that this change in behavior was associative, a yoked control group was also included. Here, electric shock was given to the leg of another animal, but independent of its leg position (figure 5.15). Yoked controls failed to hold the leg as high as did experimental subjects (figure 5.16).

Finally, to underscore the amazing nature of this report of Thorndikian conditioning, it must be revealed that the learning took place in headless animals! Indeed, all that was necessary for learning was the thorax, one leg, and the affiliated neural tissue. Learning may not only take place in invertebrates, but also in isolated portions of these

FIGURE 5.16   The left curve illustrates the decrease in the median number of shocks received by the P animals during training. The right curves show the difference in the median number of shocks received by the P and R animals during testing (Eisenstein, 1967).

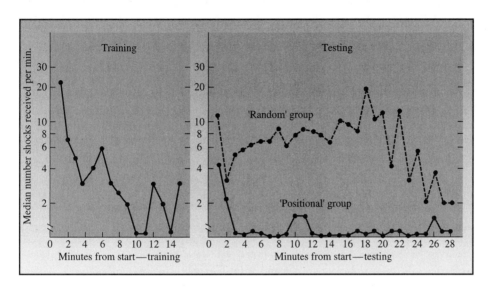

animals (see box 5.12). Note that this experiment raises the issue of central nervous system involvement (Thompson & Spencer, 1966) mentioned before (p. 141).

Language in Apes

Moving from the ridiculous to the sublime of nonhuman animal species, we come to our nearest evolutionary neighbors—the apes. The almost human anatomical features of these animals plus the fact that a 99 percent genetic similarity exists between human beings and chimpanzees prompt the inevitable question of how similar in intellect they are to us. In this context, such prosaic forms of learning as habituation, Pavlovian conditioning, and Thorndikian conditioning are largely taken for granted; instead, the issue of intelligence in apes jumps to the most advanced of human competencies. Now, we will concentrate on what have historically been held to be two uniquely human skills: language and self-awareness.

The ability of humans to communicate verbally with one another is truly an amazing gift. From a rather limited set of vocal sounds, words are formed, which acquire meaning by representing objects and relations among objects in the environment. These words can, in turn, be organized by prescribed rules of grammar to generate novel sentences, which refer to objects and ideas often remote in time and space from the speaker and the listener. With the recorded word, individuals may communicate across both continents and generations. Can any nonhuman species begin to approximate this extraordinary achievement?

Famous work with chimpanzees suggests that apes may very well share some of the skills necessary for verbal communication, although they lack the vocal means for uttering words. Although several techniques for investigating conceptual knowledge in apes have been developed, the most provocative line of investigation has been the Gardners' (1975) teaching a manual sign language for the deaf to an infant chimpanzee, Washoe. Beginning before Washoe was a year old, the Gardners trained her to communicate in American Sign Language (Ameslan), using a variety of teaching

A Cellular Analog of Thorndikian Conditioning

Neuroscientists have also studied the principles of Thorndikian conditioning in biologically reduced preparations from the nervous systems of vertebrate animals. In one of the most interesting cases to date, Stein, Xue, and Belluzzi (1993) have reported the conditioning of activity in a single neuron from a slice of tissue take from the brain of a rat. This *in vitro* preparation keeps cells alive for many minutes while it also detaches the cells in the slice from many of their distant interconnections.

Conditioning proceeds after a spontaneously active cell is isolated. Then, contingent on the cell's pattern of neural firing, minute quantities of neurotransmitters or artificial drugs are given. Individual cells have been found that increase their rates of firing when microinjections of, for example, the neurotransmitter dopamine are given after the cells fire. Rates of firing decrease under extinction procedures and when the injections are given independently of the cell's firing. The rate of firing is also an inverse function of the delay between firing and drug administration, with little effect of the drug being seen at delays in excess of 200 ms.

All of this evidence closely parallels the data obtained from the behavior of intact vertebrates, thus raising the possibility of neuroscientists' ultimately identifying the cellular substrates of learning.

---

techniques, typically by physically manipulating her fingers and hands ("molding"). After four years of training, Washoe was reported to have learned 132 signs of Ameslan.

The signs that Washoe learned fell into several categories: proper names (e.g., Susan, Washoe), pronouns (e.g., me, you), common nouns (e.g., bug, hat), possessives (e.g., mine, yours), traits (e.g., hungry, funny), colors (e.g., green, red), verbs (e.g., hug, go), and locatives (e.g., in, up). Not only did Washoe learn these many signs, but she apparently used them grammatically. She could, for example, respond appropriately to who, what, and where questions.

Washoe's performance led the Gardners to conclude that chimpanzees can learn a bona fide human language and use that language in two-way communication with human beings. When Washoe was five years of age, the Gardners would have rated her linguistic competence at the advanced end of the preschool range.

With so much at stake in the debate over ape language, it is no surprise that the Gardners' work with Washoe has come under intense scrutiny and criticism. The greatest challenge to this work has come from Terrace and his colleagues (Terrace et al., 1979). This team of researchers trained another infant chimpanzee, Nim, to use Ameslan via methods like those used by the Gardners. During his first four years, Nim learned 125 signs, a number similar to that of Washoe. However, despite this extensive vocabulary, Nim's trainers failed to find any compelling evidence that he could produce sentences comprising three or more signs. Furthermore, Nim was a poor conversationalist, often repeating the words of the speaker and interrupting the speaker's sentences. Finally, in re-examining the films and writings of the Gardners, Terrace and associates also failed to find evidence that the signing of Washoe was in any way superior to that of Nim.

Where does this work leave us in evaluating the linguistic competence of chimpanzees? First, a manual language does appear to be an excellent one for chimps to learn. It exploits the dexterity of their arms and digits, thus bypassing any limitations in their vocal apparatus. Second, isolated signs are readily acquired. Little doubt now exists that these signs are effective representations of real-world objects and relations. But third, doubt still exists that chimps can combine groups of signs into grammatical strings. Part of the limitation is in the weak structure of sign language; but, until evidence of syntactical control is provided, many will deny that nonhuman primates have mastered a human language. We hope that research along these intriguing lines will continue, so that a more decisive resolution of this controversy is in hand.

Self-Concept in Apes

As if the question of language in animals were not controversial enough, imagine the debate that surrounds the issue of self-awareness in animals. What is self-awareness? How do we measure self-awareness? How can we begin to compare self-awareness in humans and nonhuman animals? These are difficult questions indeed; but some say that there may be objective measures in the offing for answering them (Griffin, 1981; Povinelli, 1993).

Consider the research of Gallup (1977). Here, the problem of self-awareness was made a bit more manageable by asking whether chimpanzees could recognize their own reflections in a mirror. The initial step in the study was to give preadolescent chimps a full-length mirror for ten days. Over this period, two trends were noted. First, the incidence of vocalizing, bobbing, and making threatening gestures toward the mirror all declined. Second, the frequency of picking at bits of food between the teeth, blowing saliva bubbles, and using the mirror to groom parts of the body that could not be seen directly all rose. If the first set of responses represent "other-directed" behaviors and the second set of responses represent "self-directed" behaviors, then these data give us some reason to believe that the chimps were also learning to use that reflection to guide their behavior.

A more definitive test came in the second step of the study. The chimps were anesthetized and a bright red, odorless, nonirritating dye was painted on the animals' ear and forehead. After they recovered from anesthesia, the chimps were again given the mirror. The animals not only looked at the reflection of the red spots in the mirror, they touched and rubbed these spots on their bodies with their fingers, and then brought their fingers up to the nose for a sniff. These actions clearly reveal that the chimps had come to expect a particular image in the mirror and that, when something novel appeared in that image, it prompted directed exploratory behavior.

As a check against the possibility of some unknown confounding, Gallup gave the dye test to a group of chimps who did not have the ten days' experience with a full-length mirror. When these animals recovered from anesthesia and were given a mirror for the first time, they showed no tendency to direct grooming behaviors to the red spots. Why should they? Without any prior experience with the mirror, they should have had no expectation of how they looked. For all they knew, they had been born with those red spots! These interesting results led Gallup to conclude that humans may not have a monopoly on self-awareness, to the extent that mirror recognition implies a rudimentary concept of self.

Not surprisingly, others balk at attributing things like self-concepts to animals, when possibly simpler interpretations may suffice. Thus, Epstein, Lanza, and Skinner (1981) successfully trained pigeons to use their reflected image in a mirror to peck at blue spots that had been stuck on their body, but were out of direct view. Epstein and colleagues argued that the series of steps that they used to shape this final behavior pattern was the cause of the pigeons' actions, not any mentalistic notion of self. Contingencies of reinforcement are, they proposed, the source of complex behavior patterns, such as mirror recognition. Therefore, our understanding of these behavior patterns may better be gained by elucidating the laws of reinforcement than by postulating the operation of mysterious inner causes.

Who is correct in this debate? Are contingencies of reinforcement all that we need to explain self-recognition and language acquisition? Or do we profit by postulating the involvement of unobservable psychological processes? These fundamental questions are best addressed in our consideration of the contemporary status of comparative cognition.

Comparative Cognition

In the 100 years of its existence, comparative psychology has made substantial progress. Empirically, we have learned a great deal about the intelligence of animals, the evidence coming mostly from laboratory studies of conditioning. However, somewhat less progress has been made in understanding the evolution of intelligence. Also, as the debate over self-awareness reveals, we are still uncertain as to how best to deal with complex behavioral capacities. In the following sections, we will briefly discuss these continuing controversies that are at the heart of a new area called **comparative cognition:** the field of psychological science concerned with comparing the process of cognition in different species, including human beings (also see Wasserman, 1981, 1982, 1993). We will conclude with a little speculation about the direction of future research.

The Evolution of Intelligence

Romanes (1883, 1887) was one of the first to propose a clear scale of intelligence along which existing animal species might be placed (figure 5.17). Beginning with memory (the lowest mental faculty), his scale progressed through association formation, reasoning, communication, tool use, reflection, and self-consciousness. Not only did Romanes feel that this mental scale permitted the *linear* ordering of living species, he also felt that the scale was a useful means of tracing the ontogenetic development of the human being. As the human infant matures, his or her intelligence progresses linearly along the scale. By 15 months of age, the child has reached the same point of mental development as the anthropoid apes and the dog. Thereafter, the maturing human eclipses all other species in terms of intellectual and language abilities. However, Romanes was careful to note that the psychological faculties often graded into one another, thus making firm divisions between species or ages of human beings difficult. Romanes saw mental evolution as analogous to physical evolution; a continuous process, but one capable of producing abrupt changes in biological functioning. His mental scale

can thus be seen to be a unidimensional ordering, where each step in the scale is both the culmination of preceding steps and the preparation for ensuing steps.

Naturally, Romanes had very little experimental evidence at his disposal with which to compare the intelligence of animal species; Thorndike (1911) had a bit more. On the basis of the evidence available to him, Thorndike concluded that most vertebrates learn in the same general way. Species differences were best thought of as being matters of degree: associations increasing in number, being formed more quickly, lasting longer, and becoming more complex. Growth in the number, speed of formation, permanence, and complexity of associations reaches its high point in the case of human beings. Thorndike also noted the parallel between ontogeny and phylogeny: the development of the infant's intelligence to an adult condition progressing from the animal to the human type of cognition.

Thus, both Thorndike and Romanes held that there was phylogenetic and ontogenetic development of intelligence. Although both accepted a continuity between humans and animals, Romanes saw more diversity in animal intelligence than did Thorndike. Romanes was more attuned to the emergence of new mental faculties throughout phylogenesis than was Thorndike, who spoke more about quantitative differences among animals than about qualitative differences.

Despite the rather large amount of experimentation since Thorndike involving quantitative comparisons among animal species, most reviewers (e.g., Brookshire, 1970; Warren, 1973) have concluded that this research has not been productive. Quite simply, performance is affected by so many other factors—variations in motivation and reward or punishment, and differences in sensory and motor capabilities—that valid quantitative cross-species comparisons of intelligence are virtually unattainable.

More along the lines of Romanes than Thorndike, Bitterman (1960, 1965 a & b, 1975) for some years investigated qualitative differences in learned performance among different species of animals.

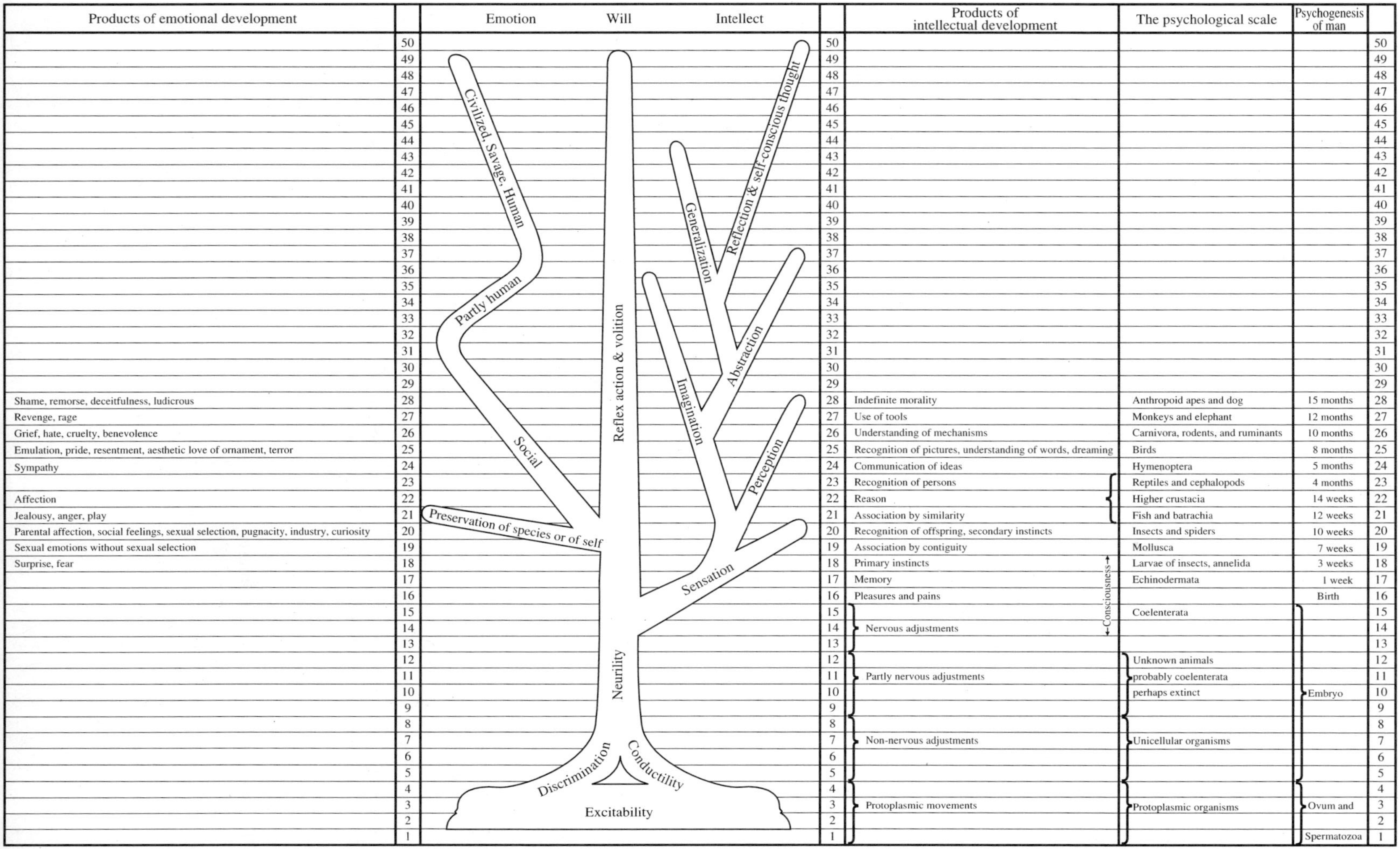

FIGURE 5.17 — Romanes' tree of mental evolution with accompanying scales to illustrate the relative intelligence of different species and stages of mental development in humans (Boakes, 1984).

Tree labels: Excitability — Conductivity — Discrimination — Neurility — Sensation — Reflex action & volution — Imagination — Perception — Abstraction — Generalization — Reflection & self-conscious thought — Partly human — Social — Preservation of species or of self — Civilized, Savage, Human. Column group headings: Emotion — Will — Intellect. Consciousness (bracketed range).

Scale	Products of emotional development	Products of intellectual development	The psychological scale	Psychogenesis of man
28	Shame, remorse, deceitfulness, ludicrous	Indefinite morality	Anthropoid apes and dog	15 months
27	Revenge, rage	Use of tools	Monkeys and elephant	12 months
26	Grief, hate, cruelty, benevolence	Understanding of mechanisms	Carnivora, rodents, and ruminants	10 months
25	Emulation, pride, resentment, aesthetic love of ornament, terror	Recognition of pictures, understanding of words, dreaming	Birds	8 months
24	Sympathy	Communication of ideas	Hymenoptera	5 months
23		Recognition of persons	Reptiles and cephalopods	4 months
22	Affection	Reason	Higher crustacia	14 weeks
21	Jealousy, anger, play	Association by similarity	Fish and batrachia	12 weeks
20	Parental affection, social feelings, sexual selection, pugnacity, industry, curiosity	Recognition of offspring, secondary instincts	Insects and spiders	10 weeks
19	Sexual emotions without sexual selection	Association by contiguity	Mollusca	7 weeks
18	Surprise, fear	Primary instincts	Larvae of insects, annelida	3 weeks
17		Memory	Echinodermata	1 week
16		Pleasures and pains		Birth
15		Nervous adjustments	Coelenterata	
14				
13				
12			Unknown animals	
11		Partly nervous adjustments	probably coelenterata	
10			perhaps extinct	Embryo
9				
8				
7		Non-nervous adjustments	Unicellular organisms	
6				
5				
4				
3		Protoplasmic movements	Protoplasmic organisms	Ovum
2				
1				Spermatozoa

(Scale runs 1–50 on both numeric columns; rows 29–50 are blank across all columns.)

Bitterman's primary approach was to compare species according to their orderly responses to parametric changes in the environment. For example, some animal species may come to learn discrimination reversals faster than they learned the original problem (p. 144), whereas others may not. Such a dramatic difference in the functional relation holding between number of discrimination reversals and trials to discrimination mastery suggests that qualitatively different learning processes may be producing these effects. As another example, some species may exclusively select the response alternative associated with the highest payoff probability ("maximizing"), whereas other species may match their choice probabilities to the payoff probabilities ("matching"). These two patterns of choice may represent qualitatively different decision strategies—again, an inference derived from a comparison of functional relations.

Even comparing the functional relations of two or more species presents interpretive hazards; differences in motivation and reward as well as sensory and motor differences may confound cross-species comparison when studying a range of independent variable values, just as when only one parameter value is being studied. Noting the virtually impossible task of equating situational and biological factors in learning problems for any two species (what is called **control by equation**), Bitterman proposed the idea of **control by systematic variation**. According to this notion, any suspected confounding factors can be systematically varied in order to see if such systematic variation produces qualitatively different results. Thus, should one species show progressive improvement in discrimination reversal learning and another not, the factors of motivation and reward could be systematically varied to see if, under *any* conditions, the characteristic performances of the two species ever change.

Bitterman's ideas of comparing the functional relations that characterize the behavior of different species and controlling cross-species comparisons by systematically varying possible confounding factors are important contributions to comparative psychology. As more workers explore the species

generality of psychological processes, these ideas should help to improve the validity of their comparative conclusions.

Rival Approaches to Animal Intelligence

Today, two different theoretical orientations oppose one another on the issue of animal intelligence. Cognitive psychologists (Hulse, Fowler, & Honig, 1978; Roitblat, 1987) propose that we can gain a deeper understanding of animal intelligence by considering those unobserved processes—cognitions—that intervene between stimulus and response. Radical behaviorists (Skinner, 1977) counter with the position that such mediating processes really explain nothing, and that valid behavioral laws need refer only to objective environmental and behavioral events. It is unlikely that the debate will end soon. The lines of the controversy were drawn long ago.

Because of these deep historical roots, we can gain a better understanding of these feuding factions by going back to Tolman's early work on **intervening variables.** Tolman stated that intervening variables are defined wholly operationally—that is, in terms of the actual experimental operations whereby their presence or absence and their relations to the controlling independent variables and to the final dependent behavior are determined. Tolman provided us with a host of objectively inferred intervening variables, of both the cognitive and motivational varieties.

One example of considerable contemporary interest is that of memory. According to Tolman (1925), memory

may be conceived . . . as a purely empirical aspect of . . . behavior. To say that an animal remembers "such and such" is merely another way of saying that . . . behavior is then and there a function of a now absent object. But this tempero-functional dependence of behavior is a purely objective fact and all that need be meant by memory.

In other words, the term memory merely names a functional relation between an independent variable and a dependent variable. There are, of course, many empirical relations that might be said to define or to involve memory. If they all could be subsumed in some way with a single theoretical concept, then we might greatly simplify a wealth of isolated facts. One theory of animal memory attempted to do just that.

Roberts and Grant (1976) proposed that the concept of the **memory trace** might be able to comprise many empirical relations found with delayed matching-to-sample procedures. Two such relations are: (a) the longer the sample stimulus is presented, the better is discriminative test performance, and (b) the longer the time since offset of the sample stimulus, the poorer is discriminative test performance. The memory trace, argued Roberts and Grant, grows with sample exposure and decays after sample offset. Because delayed matching-to-sample procedures necessarily present and remove the sample stimulus prior to the discrimination test, trace theory provides the potential of embracing *two* sets of empirical relations with *one* theoretical notion.

Unlike Tolman's earlier definition of memory that simply *named* an empirical relationship, the memory trace of Roberts and Grant truly *intervenes* between the objective procedural and behavioral variables. Roberts and Grant hypothesized precise quantitative relations between sample exposure and trace strength and between delay length and trace strength. By using the intervening variable as a theoretical mediating device, workers endeavor to reduce the number of factors they must entertain in order to predict and control behavior. Who could reasonably object to this? Skinner, for one.

Skinner (1964, 1977) noted problems with postulating intervening cognitive variables in the analysis of behavior. First, Skinner believed that the use of intervening variables encourages individuals to treat these ideas as "mental way stations," in which environmental variables induce certain subjective states that then are causally linked to behavior. But how can we ever measure or manipulate these nonphysical states? A second danger noted by Skinner is that cognitive theories may seduce workers into stopping at these "mental way stations," believing that their job is now complete. The very ease of inventing intervening cognitive processes might deter researchers from the important activity of carefully delineating the environmental variables of which behavior is a function. This concern was a very real one for Skinner and others committed to applying the principles of behavior to human and environmental problems.

For now, whatever one's theoretical orientation, the work of today's comparative and cognitive psychologists is broadening our understanding of environment-behavior interrelations. Interest and research in comparative psychology may have never been greater (Wasserman, 1993). Skinner himself was drawn into this arena and he reported the results of thought-provoking research on animal "self-awareness," largely in response to those espousing a cognitive orientation. The science of behavior has surely benefited from the controversy.

Future Directions

As we embark on our second century of study in comparative psychology, what trends do we see ahead? First, it is likely that most work on animal cognition will continue to be conducted in highly controlled laboratory settings. Field studies may represent an increasing percentage of the effort; but, because they are much more difficult to conduct and because they involve far less experimental control, these studies will still be less common than laboratory investigations.

Second, although investigators have become a bit more likely to adopt unconventional views of animal behavior and to accept that animals may have complex cognitive processes like our own (Griffin, 1981), we can expect workers to continue to adhere to Morgan's canon of parsimony in interpreting the results of their research. The prominence of radical behaviorism as an active school in psychology should serve as a strong counterweight to uncontrolled speculation by cognitive theorists. The tension between the camps should generate thought-provoking studies.

Third, the influence of human cognitive psychology and its methods will continue to increase. Already, there are signs that problems comparable to complex human tasks are being posed to and solved by animal subjects: probed recognition of serially presented stimuli has been learned by rhesus monkeys (Sands & Wright, 1980; for human data, see Sternberg, 1969); pigeons apparently forget prior information if later instructed to do so (Roper & Zentall, 1993; for human data, see Bjork, 1972); and pigeons seem to be able to mentally rotate complex visual stimuli (Hollard & Delius, 1982; for human data, see Shepard & Metzler, 1971). Demonstrations that animals can solve comparable cognitive tasks is obviously an excellent way to show that their intelligence may approximate our own. They may, however, master these problems in a fundamentally different manner than we do. Here, the best technique to assess the extent of the resemblance is to see whether a *variety* of independent variables have equivalent effects with both humans and animals. If so, then our confidence would be raised that like processes were mediating both species' behavior.

Finally, although not now prominent in the field, two other trends may have an impact on comparative psychology. One is the surge of interest in developmental psychology and the other is the rapidly emerging field of artificial intelligence. Despite efforts to relate the development of intelligence in the human child to the evolution of intelligence in the animal kingdom there has been little direct effort to examine the plausibility of this hypothesis. Perhaps the growing body of data on learning in infants and children will permit useful comparisons to be made with animal intelligence. And, although there has been great interest in simulating human intelligence with computer programs, there has been no concerted effort in simulating animal intelligence. If animals are simpler information processors than humans, then it should be easier to simulate animal intelligence than human intelligence. Perhaps some will try.

Final Remarks

What we learn about animals may tell us a great deal about the nature of intelligence and its evolution on the planet. Also, we may better understand what it means to be human by studying others who are not. Better understanding could help us deal with the problems that now plague us, for effective solutions will certainly influence not only ourselves, but every other living thing on the earth.

Summary and Conclusions

The study of animal learning and cognition is important for comparing the actions of humans and animals, and for developing basic laws of behavior. Constraints imposed on the researcher of human behavior—such as avoiding irreversible bodily interventions and controlling prior learning history—sometimes make research with animals a more attractive alternative. Yet, research on animal behavior and learning is important and interesting in its own right. Darwin's theory of evolution through natural selection originally made the study of animal behavior an important area of scientific inquiry.

Naturalistic observation of animals, including the pioneering work of Darwin and Romanes, has suggested some fascinating possibilities of what an animal can do. Isolating the causes of an animal's actions, however, requires controlled experimentation. Early work by C. L. Morgan with chicks led the way. Classic methods of studying animal learning in the laboratory came from I. P. Pavlov's work on conditioned reflexes and E. L. Thorndike's development of the "puzzle box."

Pavlov's procedure provided objective evidence of associative learning: a previously neutral stimulus (e.g., the sound of a bell as a "conditioned" stimulus or CS) when paired in time with another stimulus (e.g., food in the mouth as an "unconditioned" stimulus or US) acquired the ability to evoke a response (salivation) normally produced by the US. Later researchers were concerned with the possibility that factors other than CS-US association produced responding to the CS. In order to test this possibility, they developed control procedures such as CS-alone presentation, explicitly unpaired CS and US presentations, and random presentations of CSs and USs. Comparison of responding between these conditions and the paired CS-US condition provided evidence of the crucial role of the CS-US relation in Pavlovian conditioning.

Thorndike's puzzle box provided another vehicle for studying associative learning. Animals such as cats performed an act like pressing a lever in order to be released from the box and to receive food. Successive decreases in the time to escape from the box over trials led Thorndike to reason that the consequences of an act determined its future probability in that situation. This law of effect was used to classify events as "reinforcers," which increase prior behaviors, and "punishers," which decrease prior behaviors.

B. F. Skinner's modification of Thorndike's procedure was to minimize handling the animals (and thereby eliminate a possible confounding factor in the experiment) by using an automated box—the "Skinner box"—in which the subject's responding led to reinforcement without removal from the box. The four basic phenomena observed in Thorndike's and Skinner's settings—acquisition, extinction, generalization, and discrimination—are the same as those observed in Pavlov's procedure. In addition, the Skinner box permitted the extensive study of "shaping" through successive approximations of very difficult or improbable behaviors, and "schedules of reinforcement," which relate responding to rules specifying how and when reinforcers can be earned. In order better to understand the conditioning phenomena studied with Skinner's procedure, a special control condition was invented: the yoked control. While the "master" subject receives outcomes contingent on its behavior, its "yoked control" subject receives outcomes at the same time as the master subject, but not contingent on its own behavior. Differences in response rate between the subjects reveal the role of the response-outcome relation.

Various theories have been developed that postulate different psychological or neurological processes to be operating in different conditioning procedures. This chapter, however, stresses differences in procedure and what can be learned from each one, and concludes that it is unparsimonious to believe that different learning processes are responsible for changes in behavior with each procedure.

Traditional treatments of conditioning procedures often fail to do full justice to the breadth of animal learning, so this chapter included examples as far-reaching as headshaking in the rat, pigeons' ability to discriminate human language categories, and chimpanzees' use of sign language.

The headshake response of rats to a puff of air into the ear is an example of a response that has been shown to be subject to "habituation." Repeated applications of the air puff lead to a reduction in the number of head movements. If a novel stimulus is later introduced along with the original stimulus, headshaking increases again. This phenomenon, known as "dishabituation," is important because it helps us understand the processes that mediate habituation. These processes may be important to the animal's survival because the ability to disregard often-repeated, unimportant stimuli may prepare the animal to attend to more important, novel events.

More complex forms of learning and cognition are exhibited by different species if the experimenter is clever enough to devise tasks that allow the species to disclose their learning potential. For example, Harlow demonstrated "learning sets" in monkeys by showing that prior practice dramatically changes how the animals learn tasks of many different kinds. Among the several tasks developed to illustrate "conceptual behavior" in animals is "matching-to-sample," where the animal is trained to select the one of several choice stimuli that is the same as some standard or sample stimulus. This and other tasks permit investigators to determine those properties or categories of stimuli for which an animal is capable of distinguishing "same" from "different." Pigeons, for example, have been shown to master "natural concepts" such as cats and flowers and "arbitrary concepts" such as "novel" or "repeated" snapshots. To demonstrate that a concept has been learned, investigators must find that correct performance extends to new stimuli never used in prior training. Earlier claims that conceptual behavior is uniquely human have now been refuted.

Undertaking laboratory research with animals must be accompanied by careful observation of the natural behaviors of a species. Examples of research that taps into species-typical behavior include "food aversion learning" in rats and "imprinting" in young birds. Research with the nearest evolutionary neighbors of humans—the apes—raises an interesting question: how similar are they to us in intelligence? Studies showing that chimpanzees can learn sign language take advantage of their natural manual abilities and suggest that they possess at least some of the skills necessary for verbal communication. Other research using procedures like noting chimps' reactions to seeing themselves in a mirror suggests that they possess the "human-like" quality of self-awareness. However, some scientists consider that complex behaviors such as these can be explained by simple contingencies of reinforcement.

Debate about the comparative intelligence of different species often focuses on the role of unobserved processes—cognitions—that intervene between stimulus and response. Differences in motivation and reward as well as sensory and motor differences may confound cross-species comparisons of intelligence. Future research may help unravel some of the age-old questions about the evolution of intelligence by controlling these confounding factors and by adding a richer variety of independent variables whose effects can be compared between humans and animals.

Exercises

1. Summarize the purposes behind the various control conditions used in the basic conditioning paradigms. What was learned from their use?

2. Discuss how Darwin's notions of evolution and natural selection apply to the study of animal behavior. Include discussion of the evolution of intelligence.

3. Describe a variety of learning or conditioning studies that could be done with "simple" forms of animal life, such as earthworms or cockroaches. Include the phenomena of acquisition, extinction, generalization, and discrimination.

4. List the natural skills possessed by various species such as birds, fish, and reptiles, and indicate how a researcher might tap into these skills in devising learning tasks appropriate to each.

5. Describe the steps you would go through in "shaping" a complex behavior such as having a dolphin "shoot baskets" or getting your dog to bring you the newspaper.

6. In your own personal experience, what is the most extraordinary feat of animal intelligence that you have observed? How do you explain it in light of what you have learned in the present chapter?

7. What animal is more intelligent, the horse or the pig? How would you go about addressing this question?

Glossary

acquisition An increase in the strength of a learned response due to reinforced practice. (p. 125)

appetitive stimulus One that serves to strengthen responses that produce it and that serves to weaken responses that remove it. (p. 134)

arbitrary concept A tendency for responding to be controlled by stimulus relations—like same, larger, inside—that can be instantiated by objects from many natural classes. (p. 146)

associative learning Behavioral change that results from the contingent occurrence of two classes of events: two classes of stimuli in Pavlovian conditioning and responses and stimuli in Thorndikian conditioning. (p. 140)

aversive stimulus One that serves to weaken responses that produce it and that serves to strengthen responses that remove it. (p. 134)

canon of parsimony (Morgan's canon) The stricture to be extremely conservative in interpreting behavior. (p. 123)

comparative cognition Comparative study of higher forms of learning, memory, and problem-solving. (p. 156)

conceptual behavior Responding that extends beyond the conditions of training and that suggests the acquisition of rules or regularities to guide behavior. (p. 145)

conditioned reinforcement An initially indifferent stimulus may acquire the ability to strengthen responses that produce it. (p. 140)

conditioned response A response to a conditioned stimulus in Pavlovian conditioning that is the product of the pairing of that stimulus with an unconditioned stimulus. (p. 125)

conditioned stimulus A stimulus that is arranged to occur in conjunction with an unconditioned stimulus in Pavlovian conditioning. (p. 125)

contiguity The notion that mere coincidence in time of events is responsible for associative conditioning. (p. 136)

contingency The notion that the relationship between events is responsible for associative conditioning. (p. 137)

control by equation In comparative behavior analysis, the method of equating situational and biological factors in learning problems for two or more species. (p. 158)

control by systematic variation In comparative behavior analysis, the method of varying potential confounding factors to see if they materially change the behavioral differences between or among species. (p. 158)

controlled experimentation The method of carefully changing the situation in order to determine its effect on the phenomenon being observed. (p. 120)

discrimination The narrowing of learned behavior to stimuli associated with reinforcement. (p. 127)

dishabituation Restoration of responding to a habituated stimulus by introducing a new stimulus that does not itself elicit the target response. (p. 142)

ethologist Scientist who specializes in the naturalistic observation of behavior. (p. 123)

excitation Stimulus control that produces learned behavior. (p. 127)

explicitly unpaired control A suggested Pavlovian conditioning control procedure in which CSs and USs can never co-occur. (p. 129)

extinction A decrease in the strength of a learned response due to the discontinuation of reinforcement. (p. 126)

food aversion learning A tendency to form a reluctance to eat foods paired with illness—even with long delays between eating the foods and the later sickness that ensues. (p. 148)

generalization The spread of learned behavior to untrained stimuli. (p. 127)

habituation Reduced reactivity to a repeated stimulus. (p. 141)

imprinting The formation of a strong attachment to the parents often shown by young birds shortly after hatching. (p. 149)

inhibition Stimulus control that reduces learned behavior. (p. 127)

inhibition of delay The hypothesized tendency for the early portion of a long CS-US interval to suppress the incidence of Pavlovian CRs. (p. 127)

instinctive drift The breakdown of well-learned response sequences due to the apparent intrusion of species-typical behaviors. (p. 150)

interval schedule Consequences follow the first response after finite periods of time. (p. 134)

intervening variable A theoretical or mediating process between manipulated independent variables and recorded dependent variables; e.g., hunger might be hypothesized to bridge changes in food deprivation and amount of food eaten. (p. 158)

law of effect Responses in some situations are strengthened or weakened by their consequences. (p. 130)

learned helplessness A hypothesized psychological state that results from the prolonged receipt of aversive stimuli independent of behavior. (p. 139)

learning set A propensity to learn that itself is acquired through specific experience. (p. 144)

matching-to-sample A procedure in which the correct choice alternative is the one that matches a prior or present stimulus called the sample. (p. 146)

memory trace A hypothesized process that may link prior presentation of an event with the later behavioral control that it exerts; the trace may grow as stimulus presentation time increases and fade as the time since stimulus offset increases. (p. 159)

motor fatigue Reduced responsivity of muscles after repeated exertion. (p. 141)

natural concept A tendency for responding to be controlled by classes of objects—like cats, flowers, cars, and chairs—that are both broad (they comprise limitless individual influences) and circumscribed (they are readily distinguishable from other categories of objects) and are labeled by humans with simple (unmodified) nouns. (p. 146)

naturalistic observation The method of observing events as they occur in nature without direct intervention. (p. 120)

negative punishment A response is weakened by its removing an event. (p. 134)

negative reinforcement A response is strengthened by its removing an event. (p. 134)

nonassociative learning Behavioral change that results from the repeated occurrence of only one class of events, as in habituation and sensitization. (p. 140)

Pavlovian conditioning An associative learning procedure in which two different kinds of events are temporally paired with one another irrespective of the organism's behavior. (p. 135)

positive punishment A response is weakened by its producing an event. (p. 134)

positive reinforcement A response is strengthened by its producing an event. (p. 134)

punisher A consequence of responding that makes the response less likely to recur. (p. 130)

puzzle box Thorndike's original conditioning apparatus in which performance of the required response permitted the animal to escape from the box and get food. (p. 129)

random control A suggested Pavlovian conditioning control procedure in which CSs and USs are presented independently of one another; unlike the explicitly unpaired control, occasional co-occurrence is possible. (p. 129)

ratio schedule Consequences follow finite numbers of responses. (p. 133)

reacquisition Acquisition of a conditioned response that follows previous acquisition and extinction. (p. 126)

reextinction Extinction that follows previous acquisition, extinction, and acquisition. (p. 126)

reinforcer A consequence of responding that makes the response more likely to recur. (p. 126)

schedule of reinforcement An explicit rule according to which consequences follow responses. (p. 133)

sensitive period A period of development during which experiences are particularly likely to change behavior. (p. 149)

sensitization Increased reactivity to a repeated stimulus. (p. 142)

sensory adaptation Reduced responsivity by sensory receptors after repeated stimulation. (p. 141)

shaping The conditioning of rare behavior through a series of successive approximations to the final act; reinforcement is contingent on responses increasingly like the target topography. (p. 132)

Skinner box Skinner's modification of the puzzle box that permitted responses to have consequences without requiring the animal to leave the conditioning chamber. (p. 131)

spontaneous recovery Resurgence of an extinguished CR without the introduction of CS-US pairings; a period of time away from the conditioning situation may bring about spontaneous recovery. (p. 126)

superstitious behavior Apparent Thorndikian conditioning without any real connection between response and consequence. (p. 138)

temporal conditioning A Pavlovian conditioning procedure in which the US is delivered at regular temporal intervals without any external CS being given. (p. 127)

Thorndikian conditioning An associative learning procedure in which an organism's own behavior affects the occurrence of events of potential importance to it. (p. 138)

two-process theory The idea that there are two different kinds of learning that eventuate from Pavlovian and Thorndikian conditioning procedures. (p. 139)

unconditioned response A response that is unconditionally elicited by an unconditioned stimulus. (p. 125)

unconditioned stimulus A stimulus that unconditionally elicits a response. (p. 125)

yoked control A control procedure for Thorndikian/Skinnerian conditioning in which the same pattern of stimulation is given to a control subject that is given to a master subject, but without the yoked control subject exerting any influence on the pattern of stimulation. (p. 135)

Suggested Readings

A general introduction to animal learning and comparative cognition is M. Domjan's *Principles of learning and behavior* (1993, 3rd ed.), Pacific Grove, CA: Brooks/Cole. Recent research in conditioning and its biological bases is contained in I. Gormezano and E. A. Wasserman's *Learning and memory: The behavioral and biological substrates* (1993), Hillsdale, NJ: Erlbaum. Recent research in comparative cognition is presented in T. R. Zentall's *Animal cognition* (1993), Hillsdale, NJ: Erlbaum.

Prime scholarly journals in the field include: *Journal of Experimental Psychology: Animal Behavior Processes, Journal of Comparative Psychology, Journal of the Experimental Analysis of Behavior, Animal Learning and Behavior,* and *Learning and Motivation.*

Human Learning

James V. Hinrichs

It is likely that all the laws, principles, variables, and problems that apply to animal learning as described in the previous chapter also apply to human learning. Likewise, research methods involving Pavlovian, Thorndikean, and Skinnerian conditioning procedures can be—and have been—extended to human behavior. The reader should easily be able to visualize procedures for conditioning of human eyeblink responses and payoff schemes in the workplace that mirror the schedules of reinforcement described in the previous chapter.

In this chapter, however, we will stress research methods that are unique to humans, often involving an additional major complexity—language. For this reason, many of the topics discussed in this chapter are often referred to as verbal learning. We will consider other topics as well that do not necessarily involve the use of language but are almost certainly complicated by the human ability to use language even in nonlanguage learning tasks. For example, it would be difficult to prevent humans from using language for self-instruction, remembering cues, or rehearsing strategy as they learn a spatial task.

Another unique quality of the human species is its propensity to ask questions about its own thought processes. Throughout the Egyptian, Greek, and Roman periods, as well as during the Renaissance, philosophers have been concerned with the origins and bases of human thought. In this chapter we will start by examining the development of research tools for studying basic verbal learning in humans, and then proceed to methods for studying transfer-of-training and mediational processes in human verbal behavior. We then show how progress in these areas leads to the study of more complex mental activities such as classroom learning and skill acquisition.

Analysis of human learning involves the consideration of ancient philosophical questions as well as the use of modern research techniques. We will briefly trace the history of these philosophical questions and consider some problems of definition before turning to a consideration of the various categories of human learning. Then we will describe the major procedures (or paradigms) used to study verbal learning. An important controversy concerning the nature of the acquisition process (incremental versus all-or-none) will be used to illustrate methods, controls, and pitfalls in studying human learning. We will end the chapter by considering transfer of training, examples of complex learning, and some new theories of learning.

Background

The Definition of Learning

Consider first how to characterize and define the topic of learning. Although useful, definitions of learning must be treated with caution for they may impose unnecessary limitations and restrictions. Attempts to provide definitions of learning have ranged from very simple to very rigorous and complex definitions (see box 6.1 for examples).

One definitional issue is distinguishing between learning and memory. It is convenient to think of learning and memory as two separate processes, acquisition and retention. Acquisition and retention are not quite synonymous with learning and memory, but both are always required in order to demonstrate that learning or memory has occurred. The labels of learning and memory reflect different emphases on the processes of acquisition and retention. Generally, when we speak of learning, we place major emphasis on the investigation of the problems of acquisition. When we study memory, we are concentrating primarily upon the problems of retention. However, it must be recognized that every test of acquisition also involves a test of retention and every test of retention also necessitates some prior adequate acquisition. For learning to be demonstrated, some new information must be acquired and retained until tested. Similarly, for memory to be examined, some information must first be acquired. For example, in Kimble's definition of learning (box 6.1), he leaves open the question of what is meant by "more or less permanent" changes in behavior. In fact, specifying learning as

BOX 6.1

Definitions of Learning

". . . learning refers to a more or less permanent change in behavior which occurs as a result of practice." (Kimble, 1961, p. 2)

"a change in probability of response. . . ." (Skinner, 1950, p. 193)

". . . any relatively enduring change in behavioral dispositions which occurs as a result of previous experience." (Estes, 1970, p. 8)

"Learning refers to the change in a subject's behavior or behavior potential to a given situation brought about by the subject's repeated experience in that situation, provided that the behavior change cannot be explained on the basis of the subject's native response tendencies, maturation, or temporary states (such as fatigue, drunkenness, drives, and so on)." (Bower & Hilgard, 1981, p. 11)

"The kind of ignorance distinguishing the studious." (Ambrose Bierce, 1941, p. 76)

---

relatively permanent, as many definitions do, is a statement about the retention part of learning. We will use the labels learning or memory depending upon which process, acquisition or retention, is being emphasized more strongly. Consequently, this chapter is primarily concerned with acquisition of new information and the next (Memory) with retention of old information.

Another definitional concern is with distinguishing learning from other psychological and physical processes. Changes in behavior can occur as a result of changes in physiological state, motivation, maturation, injury, and other factors as well as learning. A major problem for any investigator is separating learning from nonlearning processes and is often the major reason for including control groups in learning experiments.

As you saw in the previous chapter, reinforcement is a major theoretical concern in learning. Identification of the conditions and processes sufficient to induce or "stamp in" changes in behavior are a major concern of learning theorists and investigators, especially in animal learning. Investigators of human learning appear to have been less concerned with this issue, primarily because humans can be instructed to learn and will learn with much

weaker inducements than those required in many animal experiments. Indeed, knowledge of results, or "feedback," appears to be sufficient to motivate and reward learning in many laboratory and everyday situations. Nevertheless, identification of the minimal conditions to induce learning remains as a thorny theoretical issue.

British Empiricism

Although similar ideas can be found in the writings of earlier philosophers, the historical beginning of most contemporary issues in human learning and memory can be primarily traced to the **British empiricist school of philosophy** in the eighteenth century. Among the contributions of this revolutionary philosophical movement was the strong rejection of the necessity of using nonphysical principles to explain mental phenomena like learning and memory. Instead, the claim was advanced that the study of mind can be reduced to "movements," that is, physical activity within the brain. This assertion was a radical departure from previous beliefs that mind and body were separate entities. Although stated as components of larger philosophical systems, the British empiricists' interpretations can be thought of as an early theoretical attempt to explain the physical basis of learning and memory. They particularly emphasized the way ideas become connected or associated (the laws of association).

For these philosophers, psychology was concerned with the study of mind or mental life. The basic unit of the mind is the *idea,* an irreducible unit of thought or knowledge; mental activity could be analyzed into collections of ideas. The mind starts out as a **tabula rasa**—a blank slate—upon which experience writes its messages. In short, all ideas are derived from experience—none is innate. In addition to obtaining ideas directly from the external world through sensations, it was also possible to generate ideas through self-reflection (later called introspection).

The most important contribution of the British empiricists was their concern with the various laws of association. As we shall see in more detail later, contemporary verbal learning and memory still have very strong ties to associationistic principles of learning, which can be traced to their philosophical origins in the work of the British empiricists. The language has changed, and the evidence is now empirical rather than "logical" or introspective, but the three most basic laws still occur in contemporary theory. They are: (1) *similarity*—the greater the similarity of two ideas on some dimension, the greater the likelihood of their association; (2) *frequency* or *repetition*—the more often two ideas are paired, the greater their strength of association; (3) *contiguity*—the closer together in time or space two ideas occur, the greater their associative strength or probability. James Mill culminated most of the British empiricists' tradition, and his views closely resembled most of the former points of view except that he reduced the many association rules to one of passive association by spatial or temporal contiguity alone. He also proposed criteria by which the strength of associations may be measured, for example, (1) *permanence*—the longer an association lasts, the greater its original strength; (2) *certainty*—the greater the individual's confidence in a particular association, the stronger it is; and (3) *facility*—the faster an association is produced, the greater its strength. These suggestions for measuring the strength of associations are

only a short step away from an empirical study of learning and memory, but the philosophers never gathered any data!

John Stewart Mill criticized his father's ideas, as sons will do, as being too mechanical. His own view of mind and memory is a more dynamic one, summed up in the phrase "mental chemistry." By this, Mill meant a process by which sensory elements become so fused in a new compound that they must be considered to constitute an essentially new entity which is "more than the sum of its parts." His interpretation was the forerunner of all modern views of memory traces as being dynamic rather than static structures. The differences between the Mills—father and son—foretell and summarize a debate that has raged throughout the history of investigation of human memory: static behaviorism versus dynamic cognition.

In a more negative vein, it must be recognized that the British empiricists' view was still essentially a mentalist concept with no empirical foundation. A physical basis of memory and sensation was assumed, but most of the philosophers' discussion emphasized that memory was a property of mind, and all the concomitant difficulties in discussing "mind" as a nonphysical entity resided in the British view. The philosophers had good hypotheses but no evidence (data).

As is usually the case, empirical science grew out of the fertile soil of philosophical inquiry. However, the major impact of the British empiricists' school of philosophy was not upon British scientists, but upon German scientists. One German scientist in particular was strongly influenced by British philosophy and has since been recognized as the founder of the empirical study of human learning and memory. He made the step from philosophical inquiry to empirical investigation; his name was Herman Ebbinghaus.

Herman Ebbinghaus

It is probably impossible to overestimate the contribution of Herman Ebbinghaus to the development of human learning and memory. His contributions are many, but by far the most important was his initiation of the *empirical* investigation of learning and memory. In order to do this, Ebbinghaus had to reject assertions that it was impossible to study higher mental processes scientifically. He invented new methods, used himself as his only subject, and spent years investigating the temporal course of acquisition and retention of verbal materials. He published his work in 1885 in a book entitled *Uber das Gedachtnis* (*On Memory*). Excellent reviews of Ebbinghaus' many contributions are found in Postman (1968) and in Hilgard's introduction to a reprint of Ebbinghaus' own book (1964). The Ebbinghaus tradition still has a strong influence on current views of verbal learning. Certainly the Ebbinghaus view held a dominant position for more than 50 years in the development of verbal learning and memory. More recently, there have been some striking departures from the Ebbinghaus tradition, but his influence is still very strong, particularly in the methods used to study human learning and memory.

Over a six-year investigation, Ebbinghaus learned and relearned many lists of nonsense syllables. He manipulated retention interval, list length, and many other variables in his attempt to describe the course of human acquisition and retention. (Can you imagine spending several years learning lists of nonsense syllables? It is no wonder that Ebbinghaus' work has also been described as the first experimental study of masochism!) To merely list Ebbinghaus' original contributions is impressive: (1) Invention of the nonsense syllable, (2) the use of statistical techniques to test the significance or reliability of his results, (3) invention of the serial learning task, (4) the use of criterion measures of performance, (5) the invention of the savings method as an objective means of scoring retention, and (6) the empirical description of the temporal course of forgetting. It is possible to make many serious criticisms of Ebbinghaus' methods and measures after a century of succeeding investigations, but these criticisms cannot negate the value and the originality of Ebbinghaus' contribution.

Verbal Assessment

In order to study learning, Ebbinghaus made the simplifying assumption that the nonsense materials he used in his experiments had no prior associative history and could be used to study the course of learning from the very beginning. This assumption is certainly false. Even the most artificial of nonsense material will invoke some associations to an individual's previous experiences. A more reasonable assumption is that materials used in learning tasks vary in their tendency to evoke associations, with nonsense material being on the low end of the continuum. Since Ebbinghaus, considerable research has demonstrated that the nature of the materials used in verbal learning experiments exerts a strong influence over the speed and efficiency of later learning. Consequently, before we can introduce experimental manipulations, it is necessary to know something about the characteristics of the materials used to study verbal learning and memory. The primary reason for **verbal assessment** is to measure and control the prior verbal habits and experiences that may affect later experimental manipulations. Some examples of verbal assessment measures are described in box 6.2.

When subjects give their personal idiosyncratic impressions about verbal materials, we call such measures subjective. By contrast, objective measures do not depend on the impressions of individual subjects, but only on the physical characteristics of the materials being assessed. Depending on the purpose intended by the experimenter, a number of physical characteristics of verbal materials can be identified and measured, the most common being the frequency of usage. The best known word frequency count is that of Thorndike and Lorge (1944), which presents the approximate frequency of usage of individual words in the English language as determined by counts of words in selected examples of English texts. New computer technology and the invention of optical scanning devices resulted in an update of the Thorndike-Lorge

Objective Measures of Verbal Materials

The most commonly used measure of *word frequency* was developed by Thorndike and Lorge in 1944. It includes, for thousands of English words, the mean frequency of occurrence of that word per one million words. Part of one page is reproduced below. The column headed G is based on the frequency of occurrence of the word in general and is the index usually used. The other columns refer to specialized counts. The number under G is the mean frequency of occurrence per one million words; an A means that the frequency was 50–99; an AA means 100 or more per million.

	G	T	L	J	S		G	T	L	J	S
oxford	2	13	22	0	7	painting (n.)	45	212	220	212	174
Oxford	13	77	29	33	108	pair	AA	700	374	466	325
oxidation	2	28	0	0	25	pajamas	6	18	95	1	0
oxide	4	12	1	18	51	pal	7	14	112	0	6
oxidize	3	28	2	2	28	palace	A	360	104	360	369
oxygen	25	50	30	189	197	palatable	1	8	16	1	6
oyster	23	130	175	45	67	palate	3	18	21	13	6
oz.	7	115	2	0	20	palatial	1	7	7	2	5
						palatine (P)	1	10	3	2	10
						pale	A	300	413	300	209
pa	8	57	92	1	2	paleface	1	12	1	3	15
pace	A	260	264	260	202	paleness	1	18	1	5	5
pacific	14	78	53	49	177	Palermo	2	3	1	34	8
Pacific	25	82	54	51	270	Palestine	6	57	18	15	28
pacifism	1	0	4	0	20	palette	1	5	4	4	6
pacifist	1	1	11	0	22	palfrey	3	16	3	43	3
pacify	3	16	14	8	26	paling	1	2	14	6	0
pack	A	330	469	330	188	palisade	2	16	4	10	6

Individual *letter frequencies* have also been measured. The rank order (from most common to least common) of the 26 letters of the English alphabet for five different samples are shown below (from Underwood & Schulz, 1960). The absolute frequency from the U count is shown in the next-to-last column. Note the very close agreement among the five counts.

Letter	Americana	Lysing	Attneave	T-L Count	U Count	Absolute f
A	3	3	3	2	3	5417
B	21	20	20	19	20	1049
C	13	12	12	10	13	1893
D	10	11	10	14	11	2697
E	1	1	1	1	1	8532
F	15	15	17	17	15	1494
G	19	17	15	15	16	1433
H	8	9	9	12	9	3596
I	4	5	6	5	5	4993
J	23	24	24	24	24	119
K	22	22	22	22	22	493
L	11	10	11	9	10	2761
M	14	14	14	16	14	1751
N	7	6	4	6	6	4820
O	6	4	5	7	4	4982
P	18	19	18	13	19	1308
Q	24	25	26	25	26	61
R	9	8	7	4	8	4217
S	5	7	8	8	7	4578
T	2	2	2	3	2	5983
U	12	13	13	11	12	2085
V	20	21	21	20	21	688
W	16	16	16	21	17	1378
X	25	23	23	23	23	132
Y	17	18	19	18	18	1331
Z	26	26	25	26	25	67

[*Continued*]

Box 6.2 continued

Finally, counts for individual letters can be extended to strings of letters. Two counts for two-letter strings (bigrams) are shown (from Underwood & Schulz, 1960).

The T-L count is for a random sample of individual words from the Thorndike and Lorge table and the U count is based on 15,000 words of running text.

	T-L	U	Total		T-L	U	Total		T-L	U	Total
IL	796	287	1083	LW	—	13	13	OM	448	292	740
IM	262	179	441	LY	846	254	1100	ON	2321	786	3107
IN	2637	1265	3902					OO	510	206	716
IO	1366	249	1615	MA	921	289	1210	OP	149	119	268
IP	198	36	234	MB	232	56	288	OQ	—	1	1
IQ	12	1	13	ME	761	400	1161	OR	1605	655	2260
IR	857	204	1061	MF	—	5	5	OS	442	150	592
IS	1467	584	2051	MI	548	172	720	OT	492	246	738
IT	680	654	1334	ML	1	3	4	OU	1428	690	2118
IU	7	4	11	MM	12	40	52	OV	693	73	766
IV	442	152	594	MN	3	1	4	OW	446	230	676
IW	1	—	1	MO	648	204	852	OX	27	11	38
IX	110	14	124	MP	273	109	382	OY	89	22	111
IZ	17	33	50	MR	1	10	11	OZ	1	4	5
				MS	8	41	49				
JA	66	17	83	MT	—	1	1	PA	917	181	1098
JE	70	23	93	MU	73	75	148	PB	4	—	4
JI	—	2	2	MY	17	60	77	PE	1033	230	1263
JO	157	47	204					PF	14	—	14
JU	133	30	163	NA	505	132	637	PH	125	32	157
				NB	16	—	16	PI	206	75	281
KA	47	4	51	NC	661	134	795	PK	—	1	1
KB	5	2	7	ND	870	780	1650	PL	342	156	498
KD	1	1	2	NE	1242	447	1689	PM	9	3	12

Combinations of letters can be scaled for their *association values* as well as their frequency. Kruger (1934) asked subjects if they "had an association" to each of a number of three-letter nonsense syllables (trigrams). The column headed G is the percent of 15 subjects who "had an association" to the trigram (Glaze, 1928). The K column is the percent of about 250 subjects who actually reported an association (Kruger, 1934). The correlation between the two measures is .86 (from Underwood & Schulz, 1960).

Syll	G	K	Syll	G	K	Syll	G	K	Syll	G	K
HIZ	60	84	JEH	13	61	JUZ	20	75	KIL	93	99
HOB	100	87	JEK	40	79	JYB	27	65	KIM	60	89
HOD	87	93	JEL	100	98	JYC	0	42	KIP	80	91
HOF	87	86	JEM	80	94	JYF	40	76	KIQ	53	82
HOK	73	91	JEN	87	93	JYG	47	77	KIR	73	78
HOL	100	98	JEP	47	77	JYH	7	45	KIS	87	99
HOM	100	99	JEQ	7	48	JYK	13	54	KIW	33	48
HON	100	98	JER	93	93	JYL	47	91	KIX	47	80
HOR	87	95	JES	93	95	JYM	87	96	KIY	27	56
HOS	93	90	JEV	47	56	JYN	87	95	KIZ	20	78
HOV	87	90	JEX	0	58	JYP	67	94	KOB	53	83
HOX	73	91	JEY	33	65	JYQ	0	41	KOC	47	73
HOZ	33	83	JEZ	20	82	JYR	33	74	KOF	80	89
HUC	7	80	JIB	60	84	JYS	7	69	KOG	40	74
HUD	87	93	JIC	0	51	JYT	27	77	KOH	40	68
HUF	87	93	JID	0	64	JYV	0	46	KOJ	7	50
HUJ	53	72	JIF	67	96	JYW	7	51	KOL	80	91
HUK	60	81	JIH	20	44	JYZ	0	49	KOM	80	89
HUL	80	98	JIK	13	45				KON	53	86
HUP	80	97	JIL	87	98	KAB	47	87	KOP	67	98

Meaningfulness, often abbreviated as *m*, is a psychological construct with a precise operational definition—the mean number of associations presented in 60 sec. (Noble, 1952). The "meaning" of a word, however, is much less precise. Rather than grapple with the definitional problem of meaning, most experimentalists have preferred to concentrate their efforts on more explicit properties of words like meaningfulness, association value, and frequency.

Word association tests are also useful in scaling the relative strength of various responses to specific stimulus words. As reported by Postman and Keppel (1970), responses to a stimulus can be scaled in terms of the proportion of individuals giving that response. So, for example, the word *stomach* produces the associations "food" and "ache" with much greater frequency than the associations "intestine" and "ulcer."

While most of these verbal assessment techniques go rather far back in origin, the care and objectivity with which they were obtained led to their wide use, and they served as models for later techniques. The important thing to remember is that studies of human learning conducted in the laboratory must take into account the subjects' prior history of use of the task material. The measures described here provide tools for this assessment. Researchers wishing to conduct a learning study using words, letters, or nonsense syllables are well advised to consult these original sources. See Brown (1976) and Bradshaw (1984) for lists of available ratings for verbal material.

count (e.g., Kucera & Francis, 1967). The word is not the only possible unit for frequency counts; Underwood and Schulz (1960) provided frequency counts for **bigrams** (2-letter units) and **trigrams** (3-letter units) in the English language, as well as reviewing the existing frequency counts for individual letters.

A different approach to the scaling of nonsense and meaningful material was introduced by Noble (1952). Noble used a continuous association procedure to gain an index of what he called *m* or meaningfulness. Noble's materials and procedures are still widely used, so it is useful to consider his technique in some detail. His stimulus list consisted of 96 items including some **paralogs** (pronounceable syllables such as "neglan" that look like words but are not), some very low frequency words, and some high frequency words. All these units (words and nonwords) are collectively referred to as **dissyllables.** As each dissyllable was presented, the subject was given 60 sec to write down as many associations as possible. To reduce the likelihood of chained associations, that is, giving associations to prior responses rather than to the presented dissyllable, Noble printed a column of the dissyllables and asked the subject to give a new response to the dissyllable on each line. Later research demonstrated that the greater the number of associations that come to mind, the more meaningful is the material and the easier it is to learn. Noble's dissyllables have been used in a large number of studies and a variety of indices have been scaled using his dissyllables as stimuli.

Perhaps the most familiar verbal assessment measure is the word association test (WAT) introduced by Kent and Rosanoff (1910) and updated by Russell and Jenkins (1954). In the WAT subjects are asked to respond with "the first word they think of," e.g., table-chair, black-white, run-walk. The WAT now exists for several other languages as well as English (Postman and Keppel, 1970) and is often used in clinical settings in an attempt to reveal disturbed thought processes.

In the typical word association test a stimulus word is presented to the subject who is required to give a single word response (discrete association)

or, sometimes, several words (continuous association). The most typical dependent measure is a response frequency commonality count. The words given as responses to the stimulus words are arranged in a descending order and referred to as the response hierarchy. The relative strength of an item in the hierarchy is the proportion of occasions in which that response is given to the stimulus. The difficulty of learning associations can then be manipulated by selecting items from different parts of the hierarchy.

Finally, a more sophisticated technique for assessing word associations is provided by the **semantic differential** invented by Osgood, Suci, and Tannenbaum (1957). The goal of the semantic differential is to provide a measure of the connotative meaning of the word. The subject's task is to rate a word on a series of subjective polar opposite scales, such as bad-good, black-white, sharp-dull, loud-soft. These anchor words provide the endpoints on a seven-point rating scale. The stimulus word is to be rated on each one of these scales even though the scale may seem to be completely unrelated to the attributes of the word. The composite rating to each of the stimulus words is referred to as a "profile" for that particular word. These scales may be used to assess similarities or differences in affective responses. (In a later chapter we will see the use of this technique in attitude measurement.)

Basic Verbal Learning Paradigms

As noted before, the study of human verbal learning has closely followed the associative tradition of the British empiricists. The methods for studying verbal learning also closely follow these traditions by emphasizing techniques that would reveal the associations between individual ideas or items. Although we shall consider four basic methods for studying human learning, two methods dominate: serial list learning and paired-associate learning. The other two methods to be illustrated are multiple-trial free recall and verbal discrimination learning.

Although these methods were developed many years ago and seem the essence of simplicity, they have been proven valuable over the years in providing new information about the acquisition process. Note the logical development of each paradigm for uncovering a particular learning process and how the processes studied with the different paradigms differ from each other.

Of course, there are many possible methods for studying the acquisition process. A learning paradigm in psychology is somewhat analogous to a laboratory preparation in biology. In biology, considerable research is conducted with relatively few species, for example, fruit flies, frogs, and mice, because so much information has accumulated about their physiology and genetics. Similarly, much is known about serial list and paired-associate learning that aids the design and interpretation of future experiments. Although use of standard, familiar procedures can be more efficient, each investigator is free to invent new methods as the need arises.

Serial List Learning

One of the basic facts about behavior is that it is serially organized. Events occur in a specific order, and learning the order of events is an important component of much learning. The **serial list learning** task is designed to study the acquisition of items in serial order. It is the oldest task in the study of classical verbal learning, dating back to the original experiments by Ebbinghaus.

In serial list learning a list of verbal items is displayed, one at a time, in a fixed order (see box 6.3). The items are usually presented at a regular fixed rate of presentation, say 2 seconds per item. After the list is presented, a short intertrial interval occurs, say 4 seconds or so, and then the list is repeated in exactly the same order. Serial list learning is usually conducted by the **anticipation method,** which requires the subject to attempt to respond with the succeeding item as each item in the list is presented. In other words, as the first item is shown, the subject is to respond with the second item in the list, then the second item is shown, reinforcing the correct response to the first, and the third item is required as a response, and so forth, to the end of the list. Notice that the first and last items in a serial list learning task differ from the rest of the

items in the list. Except for the first and last items in the list, all items in a serial list function both as a stimulus for the next item and as a response to the prior item. The first item, however, functions only as a stimulus and the last item functions only as a response. The presentation of each item in the serial list is called a *trial;* the interval between successive presentations is called the *intertrial interval.*

Although the anticipation method is the most common method for studying serial list learning, the **recall** or **study-test method** may also be used. In the study-test method, the subject studies each item in the serial list without responding, then recalls all items in the serial list in the appropriate order, without being prompted. The subsequent study trial provides feedback for responses on the test trial.

Many task variables can and have been studied within the context of serial list learning. Some of these include the number of items in the list, rate of presentation, and type of stimulus material. Acquisition of a serial list is usually measured in terms of the number of trials necessary to learn the list to a criterion of one perfect recitation. Other measures might include the total number of errors before obtaining the criterion or the number of errors within a fixed number of trials.

The most noteworthy characteristic of serial list learning is obtained by plotting the acquisition data in terms of the serial position of each item in the list. The **serial position curve** is obtained by plotting the number of errors or the number of correct responses for each serial position of the list. When this is done, a characteristic bowed serial position curve emerges showing a point of maximum difficulty, that is, the greatest number of errors, toward the center of the list, but somewhat displaced toward the end of the list (see panel 1 of figure 6.1). The first third of the list produces the fewest errors, the last third is intermediate, and the middle third always has the greatest number of errors.

The bowed serial position curve is almost always obtained in list learning experiments and occurs in other behavior as well, for example, most spelling errors are in the middle of words, recitation of the alphabet slows down in the middle, and so on. Because

BOX 6.3

Serial List Learning

Sample Instructions (Anticipation Method)

In this experiment, you are to learn a list of English words. Please listen to the instructions carefully and be sure you understand the task before we begin. If anything is unclear, ask questions before we start because we cannot stop once we begin.

The words will appear one at a time—here [point to appropriate location]. The list will begin and end with an asterisk. Your job is to learn the list so that you can say each word just before it appears. When you have learned the list, you will say the first word when the asterisk appears, say the second word when the first word is shown, and so forth. The words will be shown for only a short period of time, so be alert and respond quickly.

The first time you see the list, you do not have to respond. Just study the words and try to remember as many as possible. On the second and all later presentations, when the first asterisk and words appear, try to say *out loud* the next word in the list. You do not have to say anything about the asterisk at the end of the list. The words will always be presented in the same order.

It is very important that you try your best to learn the list as rapidly as possible. Even if you are not sure, you may guess. It is OK to guess.

Do you have any questions?

[Answer questions by repeating or paraphrasing previous instructions.]

Procedure

The list of items, words in this case, are presented one-by-one at a fixed rate, say, 2 seconds each. On early trials, subjects may give few responses; later, they may anticipate items too soon. A word list (the words are the 12 highest m dissyllables on Noble's list) and typical response pattern on the fifth or sixth trial might be:

Stimuli	Response	Score
*	heaven	+
heaven	wagon	+
wagon	garment	+
garment	army	−
office	army	+
army	(no response)	0
dinner	(no response)	0
village	(no response)	0
kitchen	jewel	−
money	jewel	+
jewel	insect	+
insect	jelly	+
jelly		
*		

Analysis

One simple scoring scheme is to assign a + to correct anticipations, a − to incorrect anticipations, and 0 to omissions.

---

it is such a strong and pervasive effect, it is not surprising that it has attracted the efforts of many learning theorists over past decades. In serial list learning experiments, one of the most outstanding characteristics of the bowed serial position curve is its relative invariance. This invariance was not recognized in some of the early research and one textbook on human learning (McGeoch & Irion, 1952) presented a long chapter primarily concerned with describing the effect of different variables upon the bowed serial position curve. As they noted, the absolute magnitude and the absolute shape characteristics of the curve change as a function of several variables including the type of practice, rate of presentation, amount of previous learning, and the

difficulty of the material. The older literature contains several attempts to account for the differences in the serial position effect as a function of these independent variables.

However, all these explanations were made obsolete by a clever analysis by McCrary and Hunter (1953). They reviewed a number of experiments and showed that the large differences in the serial position effect could be completely removed by a different method of plotting the data. Previously, the serial position effect had been demonstrated by plotting the mean number of errors per serial position. McCrary and Hunter plotted performance in terms of the *percent* of total errors occurring at each serial position (see panel b of figure 6.1). Although

FIGURE 6.1   Serial position curves for two 14-item serial lists: (a) Illustrates the functions for a relatively easy list (names) and a relatively difficult list (syllables) when absolute frequency of errors is measured. (b) Shows the same functions when relative errors (percent of all errors) are plotted (McCrary & Hunter, 1953).

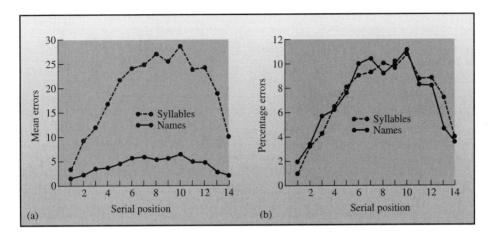

serial position functions may vary in their absolute level of performance, once the performance is adjusted for level of difficulty by measuring performance in terms of relative rather than absolute error, the relative serial position curves are almost perfectly identical for all conditions. With this single insight, McCrary and Hunter accounted for much of the previous literature merely in terms of the absolute level of performance as controlled by the relative difficulty of the material.

In spite of the reliability of the serial position curve, one way to disturb the shape of the serial position curve is to introduce a novel item into the list. This effect is called the **isolation** or **von Restorff effect.** For example, if a word occurs in place of a nonsense syllable in a list of such syllables, or if one word in a list or a set of words is printed in red and the others in black, the distinctive item will be learned much more rapidly than would be predicted by its relative serial position.

Paired-Associate List Learning

As we have noted, in serial list learning each item except the first and last serves both as a stimulus and a response item. In **paired-associate learning** an attempt is made to separate these two aspects of the learning situation and a separate stimulus is

provided for each response. Pairs of items are presented to the subject with one item of the pair serving as the stimulus and the other item in the pair as the response. Within a paired associate list, a number of pairs are presented and the subject's task is to learn to give the appropriate response to each stimulus as it is presented. A familiar example is provided by simple foreign language vocabulary learning, where the student attempts to learn the English response to each foreign word stimulus or vice-versa. To eliminate serial list effects on the paired-associate task, the order of presentation of the stimulus-response words is usually randomized from one trial to the next. The third pair on one trial may be the eighth pair on the next trial, and the sixth on the next, and the first on the next, and so on. See box 6.4 for an example. (Interestingly, constant serial order paired associate lists do not seem to be acquired much more rapidly than varied order lists, Williams, Hinrichs, and Henigbaum, 1971.)

As with serial lists, two variations of the paired-associate method have been used. The first is the *anticipation method*, in which each stimulus is presented by itself and the subject must learn to say the response before some exposure interval elapses and the response is automatically shown to the

BOX 6.4

Paired-Associate Learning

Sample Instructions (Study-Test Method)

In this experiment, you are to associate a letter with a nonsense word. The list will contain 10 pairs of nonsense words and letters. The letters will either be an A or a B. All 10 pairs will be presented, one pair at a time, then only the nonsense words will be shown. You are to say the letter, A or B, that was paired with that word. The items will be shown here [point].

The pairs will be shown in a different order each time, so you must learn what letter goes with each nonsense word. You should study each pair when they are shown together. On test trials, when only the nonsense word is shown, you must say *out loud* the letter that goes with it before the word disappears. Try to say a letter on each trial even if you must guess.

Do you have any questions?

Procedure

On study trials, the pairs are presented at a fixed rate, say, 3 seconds per pair. On test trials, the stimuli alone may be presented at the same rate, a different rate, or in some

cases, responding may be self-paced, that is, the subject is given as much time as necessary. A representative study and test trial might look like this (using the 10 lowest *m* dissyllables from Noble's list as stimuli):

Study	Test	Response	Score
latuk-A	quipson-?	A	1
neglan-A	tarop-?	B	0
byssus-B	balap-?	A	0
volvap-A	neglan-?	A	0
gojey-B	gojey-?	B	0
tarop-B	xylem-?	B	1
quipson-B	meardon-?	B	0
xylem-A	latuk-?	A	0
balap-A	byssus-?	A	1
meardon-B	volvap-?	B	1

Analysis

In the scoring procedure shown above, errors are scored as 1 and correct responses as 0. This type of scheme facilitates counting of errors and is used in assessment of all-or-none models of learning (see Box 6.7).

---

subject. A trial consists of the presentation and the anticipation of all of the stimulus-response pairs in the paired-associate list. A trial is usually followed by a short intertrial interval, and then the list is presented again in a new random order until the subject responds correctly to all stimuli or meets some other performance criterion. In the second method, the *study-test* or *recall method,* each pair in the list is presented for a brief period of time and the subject is instructed to study each pair as it is presented. Then each stimulus item is shown and the subject attempts to make the appropriate response but without the response term being shown on the test trials. After the subject has attempted to respond to each stimulus item, a new round of study trials begins. In the anticipation method, the acquisition and test phases are mixed, but they are separated in the study-test or recall method.

Multiple-Trial Free Recall

The **free-recall procedure** is primarily a technique for assessing retention when only a single trial is presented. The subject is presented with a list of items and then asked to recall as many of the items as possible in any order in the time allowed (see box 6.5). Order and pacing requirements during recall are usually minimized. The procedure becomes an acquisition procedure by presenting the same list several times, either in the same order or in a new order on each trial. The multiple-trial free recall method (MTFR) is especially appropriate for studying associations and interrelations among words in the presented list.

One example of the use of MTFR is Tulving's investigation of **subjective organization (SO)** in learning. Even though words may be chosen randomly, subjects can impose their own organization

BOX 6.5

Multiple-Trial Free Recall

Sample Instructions

In this experiment you are to learn a list of words. The words are all common English words. You will see [or hear] the list several times. Each time after the list of words is presented, you will be given two minutes to recall as many as possible. You may recall the words in any order.

Please pay careful attention as the words are presented. After the last word is shown, write down as many words from the list as you can on the sheet provided. Then the list will repeat but in a different order. You can write the words in any order. If you are not sure of a word, you may guess. Try to remember as many words on each attempt as possible.

Do you have any questions?

Procedure

The words may be presented visually (e.g., on slides) or aurally (via tape recorder) at rates ranging from two words per second to one word every 5 seconds; one word every 2 seconds is a common, moderate rate of presentation. Many word lists with special features are available (see Brown, 1976). Because subjects usually write their responses, multiple-trial free recall is suitable for testing groups of subjects.

Analysis

One special problem of scoring the free recall of words is how to handle misspellings. Experimenters must adopt a consistent rule throughout; possibilities range from accepting only exactly correct spelling (as presented) to accepting responses that are phonetically correct. Otherwise, scoring depends on the purposes of the study, ranging from simple counts of the number correct per trial to complex clustering or serial position analyses.

---

on the list, making use of the relationships that occur among any set of words. The concept of SO refers to the tendency to recall items together in the same order even when they are presented randomly and in different orders on each trial (Tulving, 1962). The amount of SO is measured by the ratio of the number of repeated pairs from Trial n to Trial $n + 1$ to the maximum number of possible repetitions. As recall increases, so does SO. The two are highly correlated, raising questions about the causal relationship between the two.

Verbal Discrimination Learning

The **verbal discrimination** method, so called because of its similarity to the discrimination task in animal experiments, requires the subject to select the appropriate response from a set of stimulus items. Usually pairs of items are presented to the subject who must choose which member of the pair has arbitrarily been designated by the experimenter as the correct response (see box 6.6). Level of performance may be reduced by either employing very long lists or by increasing the number of alternatives within the set. The experimenter usually provides feedback to the subject by simply saying right or wrong after each response. Learning trials are repeated until a performance criterion is reached.

The verbal discrimination task is especially useful for studying the effects of frequency on learning. Ekstrand, Wallace, and Underwood (1966) argued that the way subjects learned verbal discrimination lists is to increase the subjective frequency of the correct items relative to the incorrect items. By pronouncing and rehearsing the correct item the subject increases its frequency. The difference in frequency of experience then becomes the cue for selecting the correct item and the list is learned. By manipulating the number of times an item was used in a list and whether it was designated as correct or incorrect,

BOX 6.6

Verbal Discrimination Learning

Sample Instructions

In this experiment, you will see pairs of nonsense syllables, and your task is to learn which one is the correct choice.

The pairs will be shown here [point to location]. Each time a pair is shown, you are to choose one, and spell it out loud. I will then say either "correct" or "wrong" and go on to the next pair. You will see all the pairs before they repeat. The order of the pairs and the location of each nonsense syllable within each pair will vary.

The first time you see each pair, you must guess. Thereafter, try to remember which member of the pair was correct and choose it. The correct member of each will always be the same.

Please try to choose the correct nonsense syllable each time.

Do you have any questions?

Procedure

The pairs can be presented at a fixed rate on a display apparatus, or simply on cards with pacing controlled by the subjects. Two sample trials are illustrated here with six pairs; usually the lists would be longer. The items are all trigrams with medium-level meaningfulness (Archer, 1960).

Stimuli Presented	Subject's Response	Experimenter's Feedback	Score
BEH-LUQ	LUQ	correct	+
FOH-YUH	YUH	wrong	−
GEZ-VEM	GEZ	wrong	−
PIF-JAT	PIF	correct	+
NEQ-BOH	NEQ	correct	+
RAJ-DEH	DEH	wrong	−
JAT-PIF	PIF	correct	+
NEQ-BOH	BOH	wrong	−
LUQ-BEH	LUQ	correct	+
DEH-RAJ	DEH	wrong	−
GEZ-VEM	VEM	correct	+
FOH-YUH	FOH	correct	+

Analysis

Scoring and data reduction are very similar to paired-associate analysis. The major differences are that subjects almost always respond and the chance level of performance is 50 percent.

---

impressive support was found for the frequency theory of verbal discrimination learning in several experiments (Ekstrand et al., 1966; Underwood & Freund, 1969; Underwood, Jesse, & Ekstrand, 1964). This series of experiments also demonstrates the fate of a very successful theory. Ironically, although frequency continues to be a much investigated variable in other paradigms and certain aspects of frequency are still debated in the discrimination task, research in the verbal discrimination task is currently at a low ebb. Just as research declines when a theory fails, it also decreases when a theory succeeds.

Two Interpretations of Acquisition

The most fundamental question about learning is how does one item or idea become associated or connected to another? If we examine the course of learning over several attempts (learning trials) either in real life (for example, improvement of typing skills) or in the laboratory (increase in correct responses in a paired associate task), performance generally shows a regular pattern of improvement. Examination of a single individual's performance will exhibit considerable variability, as in all behavior, but when averaged over several subjects, the

FIGURE 6.2   Mean learning curve. An idealized mean learning curve: the increase in the probability of a correct response on each trial is a constant proportion of the amount left to be learned. Here the value of the increment is .5; one-half of the unlearned material is learned on each attempt.

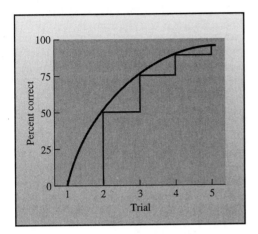

pattern of learning is clear. The **mean learning curve** is typified by a negatively accelerated increasing performance function, that is, the absolute improvement in learning scores becomes smaller as the number of trials increases. The general course of learning is so consistent over a wide range of tasks that it is sometimes referred to as the **law of constant proportionality**. That is, as shown in figure 6.2, the average amount of increase on each trial is approximately a constant fraction of the amount left to be learned.

The observed regularity in learning that yields the law of constant proportionality is merely descriptive and tells us nothing about the learning process that produces the function. A central question is whether the mean learning curve is also the typical curve, in other words, does the description of average performance represent the learning of a single item by a single individual?

Most early theories assumed that learning was an **incremental process** with gradual improvement in the associative connection between items. The incremental assumption was challenged in many experiments that supported an alternative interpretation called **all-or-none learning**. Examination of this issue gives us a good chance to illustrate the use of experimental design and analytic procedures in addressing conflicting theories.

Rock's Experiment

The basic idea of all-or-none learning was first proposed by Rock (1957). In his original experiment, two conditions of paired-associate learning were compared. In a control condition, the procedure was conventional: subjects learned 12 randomly selected letter-number pairs by repeated study-test trials. On study trials, each pair was shown for 5 seconds; on test trials the stimulus term was shown and the subject tried to provide the response term. The same 12 pairs were repeated in scrambled order through a number of study-test trial cycles until the subject answered all 12 items correctly on a given trial. In the experimental condition, Rock used the novel procedure of replacing any item the subject missed on a test trial with a new item. If at any time during the learning trials, the subject gave the wrong response to the stimulus term, the pair was replaced with a new stimulus-response pair. In effect, the subject had to start over on that item. Each subject in this replacement group was also continued until achieving one errorless test on all 12 items.

Rock's surprising finding was that the mean learning curve and average trials to reach criterion were nearly identical for the control (repetition) and experimental (replacement) groups. Apparently an item that has been responded to incorrectly several times has no advantage in learning over an item seen for the first time. He concluded that repeated reinforcement of a missed item must have had about the same effect as the first rein-forcement of a new item. The results contradict the assumption of gradual learning that every reinforced trial increases associative strength even if an incorrect response is made. From the point of view of incremental theory, acquisition of the experimental list should be severely impaired if not impossible because only one opportunity was provided to learn each item. All other things being equal, the results were inconsistent with an incremental theory and consistent with the assumption of all-or-none learning, with the probability of learning being constant on any one trial and independent of the number of prior repetitions and failures to learn.

The methodological question is, of course, whether "all other things are equal" is a valid assumption for the repetition and replacement groups. Specifically, there is the possibility, as critics were quick to point out, that subjects in the experimental group were at an advantage because the replacement procedure selectively removes the most difficult items for each subject, so they end up with an easier list of items to learn. If so, the replacement group would learn more quickly after the hard items are dropped out and replaced with easier ones. (Note that Rock had selected items that were of approximately equal difficulty according to group norms, but that does not mean that they were of equal difficulty for any individual subject or that the items that were the most difficult for one subject were the same as the items that were the most difficult for another subject.) Rock also recognized this possibility and performed several experiments attempting to reduce or eliminate selection artifacts.

The question was raised, however, whether these experimental controls on item selection succeeded (Postman, 1962). Of the many subsequent experiments, we will only note that the evidence does support the contention that item selection was operating and that Rock's "drop-out" procedure does result in lists that are easier to learn than the original lists (e.g., Underwood, Rehula,

& Keppel, 1962). Nevertheless, it is still noteworthy that Rock's subjects did learn in "one trial" at least in the descriptive sense that an item was replaced unless it was acquired the first time it was shown. Some countercritics also feel that the incremental theorists must invoke rather implausible coincidence to argue that the benefit of item selection occurs in just the right amount to offset the benefit of repetition.

Model-Building Approach

Another approach to the controversy is to state assumptions of alternative theories as explicitly as possible, often in the form of mathematical models, and compare the predictions with data. One particularly elegant approach was the "one-element" model proposed by Bower (1961, 1962), which is a direct formalization of the all-or-none assumption. As shown in box 6.7, the axioms of the one-element model can be used to generate quantitative predictions that summarize a large amount of data.

One particularly interesting prediction derivable from the simple all-or-none formulation is the prediction of so-called **precriterion stationarity** (e.g., Bower, 1961). The procedure consists of examining backward learning curves. A backward curve is obtained by averaging responses from each sequence across successive trials back from the trial of last error (TLE) on each sequence. Alternatively, one may plot a forward "prelearning" curve starting from trial 1 but dropping out items after the last error occurs. If the one-step process of the simple all-or-none learning model is correct, then the prelearning or backward learning curves will be horizontal; that is, there is a constant (chance) level of probability of being correct prior to the last error. Incremental theories, on the other hand, would predict a gradual increase in the likelihood of a correct response prior to the last error. A test of these differential predictions requires examination of the sequence of correct responses and errors for each item in the list for each individual subject. Since different items could be learned on different trials, averaged data such as typically plotted in a mean

BOX 6.7

Bower's One-Element Model

Basic Assumptions

Bower's model is based on the representation of each stimulus item in a list as a single "element" to be associated with an appropriate response. The assumptions of Bower's (1961) one-element model for paired-associate learning can be stated as five axioms:

1. *Representation:* Each stimulus item is represented by one element that is sampled (studied) by the subject every time that the stimulus is presented.

2. *States:* On each trial, an element is in one of two states. The element is either associated to the correct response ("learned," State L) or not associated to the correct response ("unlearned," State UL).

3. *Transition:* On every trial, there is a constant probability c of the element moving from State UL to State L. If the element is in State L, the probability of staying in State L is one. These assumptions can also be stated as

    $Pr(UL \rightarrow L) = c$; $Pr(L \rightarrow L) = 1$.

Corollary:

   $Pr(UL \rightarrow UL) = 1 - c$; $Pr(L \rightarrow UL) = 0$.

4. *Performance rule:* If the element is in State L when the stimulus is presented, the probability of a correct response is one. If the element is in State UL, the subject guesses with the probability of a correct guess equal to g. Restated:

   $Pr(\text{Correct} \mid \text{State } L) = 1$; $Pr(\text{Correct} \mid \text{State } UL) = g$.

Corollary:

   $Pr(\text{Wrong} \mid \text{State } L) = 0$; $Pr(\text{Wrong} \mid \text{State } UL) = 1-g$.

5. *Starting state:* The element always begins in State UL on the first trial, i.e.,

   $Pr(UL_1) = 1$ or $Pr(L_1) = 0$.

One way to represent these assumptions is a "transition" diagram, where an element begins in a starting State S and then moves to State UL and State L according to the probabilities shown:

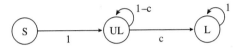

Prediction of the Mean Learning Curve

An equation for the mean learning curve can be derived from the assumptions of the one-element model. The mean learning curve is the probability of a correct response on any Trial n, or $Pr(C_n)$. Because there are two ways to be correct (by being in State L or being in State UL and making a correct guess), but only one way to be wrong (being in State UL and making a wrong guess), it is easier to derive $Pr(E)$, the probability of an error on Trial n. First, note that $Pr(E_n)$ has two parts: $Pr(UL_n)$ and $Pr(\text{Wrong} \mid \text{State } UL)$. The second part we know from Axiom 4 to be $1-g$, therefore we need only to find $Pr(UL)$. The proof is by induction, examining the states from Trial 1 to Trial 2 to Trial 3, etc.:

$$Pr(UL_1) = 1 \quad \text{(from Axiom 5)}$$
$$Pr(UL_2) = Pr(UL_1)Pr(UL \rightarrow UL)$$
$$= 1 \times (1-c) = (1-c) \quad \text{(from Axiom 3)}$$
$$Pr(UL_3) = Pr(UL_2)Pr(UL \rightarrow UL)$$
$$= (1-c) \times (1-c) = (1-c)^2$$
$$Pr(UL_4) = Pr(UL_3)Pr(UL \rightarrow UL)$$
$$= (1-c)^2 \times (1-c) = (1-c)^3$$
$$Pr(UL_n) = Pr(UL_{n-1})Pr(UL \rightarrow UL)$$
$$= (1-c)^{n-2} \times (1-c) = (1-c)^{n-1}$$

[Continued]

Box 6.7 continued

(The above result depends on the fact that the only way that the element can be in State UL on Trial n is by failing to be learned, i.e., failing to make the transition to State L, on every one of the $n-1$ previous attempts.)

Now, recall that an error occurs only if a wrong guess is made:

$$Pr(E_n) = Pr(UL)Pr(\text{Wrong } UL)$$
$$= (1-c)^{n-1} (1-g)$$

Subtracting from 1 gives the probability of a correct response:

$$Pr(C_n) = 1 - Pr(E)$$
$$= 1 - (1-g)(1-c)^{n-1}.$$

Analysis

To ensure that learning has occurred when there is a high probability of a correct guess, a high-performance criterion of four or more perfect trials in a row is usually required. To compare the predictions of the one-element model with data, it is necessary to conduct an experiment like the one described in box 6.4 and organize the data into trial-by-trial protocols. The mean number of errors for each subject-item protocol $\bar{E}$ can be used to estimate the value of the learning parameter, c:

$$c = (1-g)/E.$$

In the typical application of the model, only two responses are used and $g = 1/2$. Substituting the estimated value of c into the equation for the mean learning curve allows the comparison of observed results with the predictions of the model. In a similar fashion, a large number of other predictions can be generated such as the trial of the last error, the probability of exactly n errors before learning, and the number of times that alternations between errors and correct responses occur.

A critical prediction of this model, which contrasts directly with the predictions of any model assuming gradual learning, is that the probability of a correct response is constant for all trials within a sequence prior to the last error. This is the "stationarity" prediction described in the text.

---

learning curve are useless for examining the acquisition process at the level of an individual subject learning a particular item. Among other contributions, Bower's model has served to focus our attention on the detailed analysis of learning.

Initial tests of the precriterion stationarity prediction for verbal learning situations involving two response alternatives gave encouraging results for the all-or-none theory. However, it immediately became clear that stationary prelearning curves are not obtained under any circumstances but the simplest. Indeed, the requirements seem to be that the stimuli be very discriminable and the responses be very familiar and not greater than two in number.

It is clear that models based on the all-or-none interpretation of learning and applied to quite simple situations allow a description of the learning process in far greater detail than that permitted by any other learning interpretation. Obviously, there will be situations in which the assumptions of the mathematical models become inappropriate, but it is an important theoretical exercise to attempt to extend and push the models as far as possible. A great deal can be learned from those situations where the models fail. Today, elaborate three- and four-stage learning assumptions are incorporated into mathematical models along with assumptions about the memory process and various control procedures. These assumptions, in combination with sophisticated mathematical techniques, can produce very detailed interpretations of the learning process.

Transfer: Basic Paradigms and Theories

Of all the topics within the confines of human learning, transfer of training may be the most basic to practical applications of the principles of human learning. Educational systems assume that skills learned in the past may be applied in future learning situations. In modern society, it is not uncommon for a person to work at a number of increasingly demanding jobs during a career. Consequently, it is not surprising that a major effort of learning theorists has been to understand and apply the principles of transfer of learning.

Therefore, the laboratory study of transfer of training is intermixed with very practical educational questions. Indeed, educational ideas about transfer of training are older than the experimental study of human learning. The first educational theory of transfer of training was the notion of **formal discipline.** Slightly overstated, the basic idea was that simple mental exercise was beneficial to mental functioning—and American and British nineteenth century school curricula reflected this idea. The unfortunate student was expected to learn Greek, Latin, rhetoric, and geometry, not because there was any special value to these studies, but because it was believed that learning would exercise and sharpen the mind. The basis for this contention appears to depend upon a poor analogy with the effects of physical exercise on muscular development.

The doctrine of formal discipline was an early battleground for verbal learning and educational theorists. Although it took some time, the more empirically minded investigators were finally able to convince educators that if the final goal was improved use of the English language by their students, they would be better advised to study English directly rather than achieve the smaller indirect benefits from the study of Latin or Greek.

Recall that in chapter 2 we discussed the general need to control for carryover effects when the same subjects perform two or more successive tasks. By contrast, understanding these carryover effects is precisely the goal of studying transfer of training. In the study of transfer of training, the general experimental objective has been the identification of the components or subprocesses of transfer. In discussing transfer, a basic distinction is made between two broad classes of transfer: specific and nonspecific. **Specific transfer** usually refers to the consequences of identifiable previous learning and in particular to the processes that depend on the similarity relationships between the stimuli or the responses in the two tasks. **Nonspecific transfer** refers to the facilitative effects of experience regardless of the type of task or the nature of the materials in the prior task and is usually attributed to the acquisition of highly generalizable habits and skills. The methods used to evaluate transfer of training are similar in both specific and nonspecific cases.

Design and Methodology in Specific Transfer of Training

Two basic designs are used to study transfer. The first (see box 6.8), called the **proactive transfer design,** evaluates the effect of a prior task on the acquisition of a second task. The second, less frequently employed paradigm, called the **retroactive transfer design,** evaluates the effect of an interpolated task upon the further practice or retention of the first task. Although "transfer of training" is, by definition, a within-subject phenomenon, the basic designs use between-subjects manipulations. For example, the first procedure is one of the simplest arrangements for the study of transfer and one of the most basic. The comparison is between two groups of subjects: The experimental group practices Task I and is then tested on Task II. The second group of subjects, the control group, is tested only on Task II. The amount of transfer is defined as the difference in performance between the experimental and the control group. Transfer effects may be either (1) positive, when the experimental group is superior to the control group so that training in the first activity facilitates the performance on the second or (2) negative, when the control group is superior to the experimental group, so that training on the first task inhibits or retards learning or performance of the second task, or (3) zero, or indeterminant, when there is no significant difference in the performance of the two groups. A major issue is defining relationships between Task I and Task II that lead to these different transfer effects.

In the retroactive design the experimental group learns Task I and then practices Task II and then is tested on Task I. The control group practices only Task I and then is tested on it after the same period

BOX 6.8

Transfer Designs

The proactive transfer design is outlined below for the A-B, A-C paradigm. Note the sources of transfer contributing to each learning situation and the appropriate comparisons that can be made. Only the modified design provides an unconfounded estimate of specific transfer.

Group	List 1 Content	List 2 Content	Type of Transfer	E-C Contrast
Traditional Design				
E	A-B	A-C	nonspecific and specific	nonspecific and specific
C	none	A-C	none	
Modified Design				
E	A-C	A-B	nonspecific and specific	specific
C	D-C	A-B	nonspecific	

of intervening time as the experimental group. It should be clear that this design is most appropriate for studying the effects of retention of the original learning as a function of the amount or kind of interpolated learning. This will be further illustrated in the next chapter.

In order to describe transfer further, we need to be more specific in our designation of the learning of the items in the two tasks. Assume that the two tasks are paired-associate lists. The stimuli of the first list are usually referred to as A terms and the responses as B terms. Collectively, the items in List 1 are designated as an A-B list. Depending upon the object of the experimenter's investigation, a wide range of possibilities exists for the second list. For example, if we wish to examine the transfer relationships involved in learning to make the same responses to new stimuli, then we would construct a so-called C-B list, and the overall transfer paradigm would be labeled as an A-B, C-B paradigm. An example would be learning the English equivalents of a list of Greek words after having mastered the same vocabulary list in Latin. Another common transfer problem would be to retain the same stimuli but to change the responses. This arrangement is called an A-B, A-C paradigm. Changing from one automobile to another often provides a vivid example of A-B, A-C. The demands of the roadway (the stimuli) remain the same but many responses are different, occasionally resulting in a wild thrust of a hand or foot into empty air for a lever or pedal that isn't there.

Do these common transfer situations facilitate or retard learning in the second task? Before examining specific relationships between the first and second tasks, it is necessary to introduce a control for nonspecific sources of transfer. To control for nonspecific sources of transfer, it is necessary to include a control group that also receives two lists. For this group an equivalent task experience is introduced that is not systematically related to the test task. For example, consider the A-B, A-C paradigm. Analysis of specific transfer effects depends on the common stimuli in the A-B and A-C lists, but if performance by the experimental group on the A-C list were compared to A-C performance by the control group with no prior list (a so-called "rest" control), then the first list experience is a potential source of nonspecific transfer. The appropriate control is to have the control group learn an unrelated D-C list, equating for learning experience but with no specific relationship between the two lists. If we wish to have an exact comparison in the learning of the second task, one additional complication remains in comparing the A-B, A-C and the A-B, D-C groups. If exactly this order of events were followed, then the two groups of subjects would learn the same first list but two different second lists. In order to secure a more exact description of the transfer effects, we would prefer that they have the same second list and the difference in the two groups occur only in the learning of the first list. This is easily arranged by simply reversing the order of the two lists, producing as the actual paradigms for comparison A-C, A-B and D-C, A-B. Although this is the correct way to conduct these transfer experiments, the labels applied to these paradigms retain the usual alphabetical ordering.

The Stimulus-Response Analysis of Transfer

The early study of transfer of training was primarily a search for basic principles and general laws of transfer. Many of these early studies manipulated the degree of similarity among the response terms or among the stimulus terms of the various lists. For example, the application of the principle of stimulus generalization to transfer defines the case of changing the stimulus slightly while holding the responses constant, i.e., A-B, A'-B. The change from A to A' could be along a dimension of meaning, e.g., cold-icy, bed-cradle, or amount of physical agreement in trigrams, e.g., AZL-AZT, MQR-MQF. By extrapolation from other conditioning and learning paradigms one would expect that the more similar the test stimulus is to the original training stimulus, the more similar would be the responses to the two stimuli, i.e., greater positive transfer. Such results have been replicated several times in learning experiments as well as in retention studies.

In a similar fashion we can test the results if the stimuli are held constant and the response members are changed. When compared with an A-B, D-C control, an A-B, A-C condition shows a great deal of negative transfer. Even more negative transfer is exhibited in an A-B, A-Br paradigm in which the stimuli and the responses in the original A-B list are the same but re-paired in the second A-Br list. One example would be learning to type at a keyboard where some of the characters are in a different position than originally learned. The characters are the same (stimuli) and the keyboard design or locations are the same (responses), but some of the S-R pairings are changed.

Mediation

The operation of **mediation** also may be invoked as an explanatory device for some transfer effects. For example, the A-B, A-B' transfer paradigm in which responses similar to those used in the first list are acquired in the second list, (e.g., "baby" and "cold" in the first list, and "cradle" and "icy" in the second list) can be interpreted as involving three stages. According to this interpretation, A-B' is learned using the existing B-B' association (e.g., "baby-cradle" learned from prior associations). After A-B is learned, a subject in the experimental group has forged an A-B-B' chain that greatly facilitates performance in the A-B' list compared to a control group for which the material does not provide a B-B' link. (As we will see in the next chapter, memory aids are sometimes built on this principle.) When analyzed in this fashion, the A-B, A-B' paradigm may be interpreted as a three-stage paradigm, A-B, B-B', A-B', in which B-B' is the mediating link.

In the case of A-B-B', the source of mediation is the set of natural language habits that the subject brings to the learning situation. Obviously, such **natural language mediators** are not under the control of the experimenter. In order to study mediational paradigms at a more formal level, it is necessary to bring all three stages under the control of the experimenter. For example, an analog to the hypothetical B-B' link described above can be investigated by requiring subjects to learn the link in the laboratory. The A-B, B-C, A-C paradigm can be compared with the A-B, D-C, A-C control list, which has a comparable learning history without a mediational link like the A-B-C chain learned by the experimental subjects.

Nonspecific Sources of Transfer

As we have already observed, nonspecific sources of transfer usually lead to overall positive transfer. In considering possible nonspecific sources of transfer from one task to another, there are at least two that might be expected to produce negative effects: fatigue and boredom. Nevertheless, positive factors appear to dominate. It may be the case that negative factors do reduce the influence of the overall positive factors, but there is little convincing evidence for overall nonspecific negative transfer. Two positive sources of nonspecific transfer are usually distinguished: warm-up and learning-to-learn. The concept of warm-up refers to the development of postural and perceptual set or attention that is required for the efficient performance of a given task. In verbal tasks, it is assumed that familiarization with the apparatus and the temporal order of events will contribute to the development of an effective set. In other words, warm-up refers to the subject's adjustment to receive the relevant stimuli and the adoption of the required rhythm of responding. The attentional and postural adjustments made by subjects are usually temporary, appearing to dissipate when the individual leaves the situation, and must be reestablished when the subject returns to practice a new task.

On the other hand, learning-to-learn usually refers to the acquisition of higher order habits and skills that produce more or less permanent changes in the subject's mode of attack on the task. These habits and skills are still nonspecific in that they do not refer to the particular characteristics of the task involved but to general verbal intellectual performance. Therefore, as Postman (1969) notes, the distinction between warm-up and learning-to-learn is based on two criteria: (1) the nature of the changes in a subject's behavior that serve to facilitate performance, and (2) the degree of temporal persistence after the practice has ended. Again, the important point is that these nonspecific sources must be controlled for when studying specific sources of transfer.

Complex Learning

Our previous discussion of basic human learning paradigms, theories of acquisition, and transfer lays the foundation for considering more complicated

FIGURE 6.3 Sample trials from concept formation task. Shape is the relevant dimension; squares are correct; + refers to correct response.

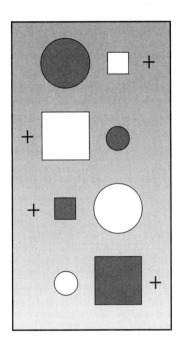

forms of human learning like concepts and categories, skill acquisition, and classroom learning. These are only a few examples of how elementary learning processes can be applied and extended to current practical and theoretical issues.

Concept Learning

A concept is the association of a single response with a set of different stimuli on the basis of some identical or similar elements. At its simplest level, concept learning is a form of discrimination learning; at its most complex, particularly when we attempt to understand the use of natural categories like cats, trees, games, and furniture, concept learning draws upon language, logic, and knowledge of the real world.

In **concept formation** or concept identification tasks, subjects are typically presented with simple stimuli like the geometric forms shown in figure 6.3. The forms can vary along several dimensions like size, color, and shape; and have several attributes within each dimension, for example, square or circle for the dimension of shape. In an example of

FIGURE 6.4   Conceptual rules with two dimensions. Positive and negative examples for four logical rules—conjunctive, disjunctive, conditional, and biconditional. The relevant attributes are *striped* and *square* (Bourne, 1970).

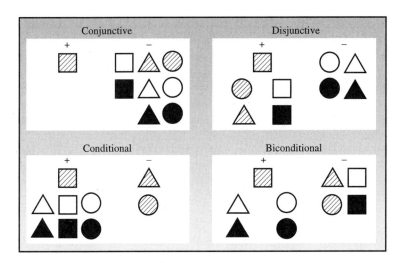

a simple concept identification experiment, subjects would be shown a series of pairs of items, like geometric forms, and asked which of the presented items in a pair is a member of the experimenter-designated correct category. After each response, the experimenter tells the subject whether his or her choice is correct. The subject's task is to discover the basis for identifying the "correct" instances among the presented choices. The task may be as simple as discovering the single identifying feature that classifies items as members of the correct category, for example, all square objects. If square is the basis for identifying correct concepts, then shape is the relevant dimension for concept learning and square is the correct attribute within the shape dimension; the other dimensions are irrelevant to the classification.

Concept learning becomes more difficult and more interesting when concepts involve more than one relevant dimension and subjects must discover the rule combining the correct attributes from two or more dimensions. Consider the possible rules for combining attributes from the two relevant dimensions of pattern and shape. If the correct concept is "striped square," then the presented object must have the attribute "striped" on

the pattern dimension and the shape "square" on the shape dimension; all other characteristics are irrelevant to identifying the correct concept or label. When two attributes (call them A and B) must both be present for a concept, the relationship for combining them is called the **conjunctive rule,** or simply conjunction, and is described by A *and* B. (See figure 6.4 for a visual display of each of the rules.) If the presence of either of the two is sufficient, the rule is the **disjunctive rule,** or disjunction, and is equivalent to the logical relationship A *or* B. A somewhat more complicated case holds when the concept follows the **conditional rule,** where the concept is valid when A occurs only if B occurs; if A does not occur, then all instances are members of the concept. The logical relationship is *if* A, *then* B. Note that invalid instances of the concept occur only when A is presented without B. With our original attributes, if A stands for striped objects and B for squares, then striped squares are valid instances of the concept, all squares are valid, and all non-striped objects. The only exceptions are striped nonsquares. Finally, the **biconditional rule,** usually stated as A *if and only if* B, holds when both A and B occur, and when both non-A and non-B

FIGURE 6.5 Intradimensional and extradimensional transfer shifts. (Refer to figure 6.3 for samples of training trials.) Shape was the original relevant dimension; square was correct. For the intradimensional shift group, shape is still the relevant dimension; circles are correct. For the extradimensional shift group, size is now the relevant dimension; the large figures are correct.

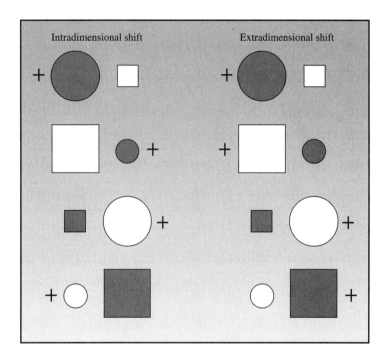

occur. With our attributes, striped squares and objects that are not striped and not squares are instances of the concept; if an object is either striped or a square (but not both), it is not an instance. Confusing? Study figure 6.4 carefully. You can image how difficult some of these rules are to learn when possible instances are presented one at a time. Bourne (1970) has shown that the difficulty of learning increases in the order that the rules have been described here.

In one of the most famous experiments in concept learning, Kendler and Kendler (1962) examined how past experience affects new concept learning. As shown in figure 6.5, their study involved the use of a two-stage transfer design. Subjects first learned a simple attribute identification task where, for example, shape was the relevant dimension and several other

dimensions, including size, were irrelevant. Only two attributes were used for each dimension, say large and small for size and square and circle for shape, and all items were classified as correct or incorrect. (For simplicity, only size, shape, and shading are illustrated in figure 6.5; other dimensions could also have been manipulated.) After all subjects reached a specified learning criterion (e.g., being correct on eight consecutive trials) with all square objects being designated as correct, they were switched to one of two tasks in the second stage of the experiment. For half of the subjects, the relevant dimension was switched from shape to size, called an **extradimensional shift,** making large and small the basis for responding. For the other half, shape remained the relevant dimension, but the correct response switched from square to circle—an **intradimensional shift.**

Which group should learn the second stage faster? Consider the two shifts according to two interpretations of learning: From a simple stimulus-response view, the subjects in the extradimensional shift condition have already learned one-half of the correct associations, only half of the previous acquired responses must be changed to the other response. For the intradimensional shift condition, however, all of the responses must be reversed. From a mediational point of view, we can make a different prediction. If subjects first identify the relevant dimension and then make the correct attribute-response pairing, subjects in the intradimensional condition need only to relearn the pairings; they are already attending to the relevant dimension. Subjects in the extradimensional shift condition, on the other hand, must now discover the relevant dimension and then learn the pairings.

The Kendlers were primarily interested in young children and how their performance in this task might change with age, but variations of their study have been conducted with many kinds of subjects, animal and human, with a vast range of abilities. At the risk of oversimplifying, animals and preverbal children perform better on the extradimensional shift and verbal children and adults perform better on the intradimensional shift, suggesting the employment of a mediational strategy based on language skills.

This interpretation can be extended by assuming that subjects actively formulate and test hypotheses about relevant dimensions, attributes, and rules that lead to correct concept identification. Trabasso and Bower (1968) formulated a model, using mathematics similar to that employed in the one-element model of paired-associate learning (box 6.7), for a hypothesis-testing interpretation of concept identification. Their model assumes that a subject attends to, or samples, one stimulus dimension at a time and uses that dimension to generate a response to the presented stimulus item. As long as the sample dimension leads to a correct response it is maintained by the subject; if an incorrect response occurs, the subject discards the current hypothesis about the relevant dimension, and draws a new sample dimension. The process of sampling, testing, and resampling is called the "win-stay, lose-shift" strategy and suggests that subjects are very active participants in the process of learning new concepts rather than passive recipients of information.

The investigation of concept learning becomes more complicated when we consider real world, or natural categories like furniture, animals, and faces. As with more artificial stimuli like nonsense syllables and geometric forms, the first step in analysis entails an assessment of how we use everyday language to understand natural categories. Rosch and her colleagues (1976) have gathered evidence for the hierarchial nature of real-world concepts by asking subjects to list attributes for categories at three levels: superordinate (e.g., furniture, tool), base (e.g., chair, saw), and subordinate (e.g., kitchen chair, hacksaw). Members of superordinate categories have few attributes in common while subordinate items are very similar and have many specific attributes. Base level categories are quite differentiated, but share many attributes. Rosch argues that base categories are most fundamental to understanding the world, and the best examples of categories, that is, the most frequently generated in word association tests, define category *typicality*. The most typical members of categories share the most attributes (Rosch & Mervis, 1975).

One way to test these conjectures about the learned relationships among natural categories is to employ semantic or sentence verification tasks. For example, Collins and Quillian (1969) suggest that we store attributes in memory in close association to the hierarchical level of the critical features of the category. That is, canaries are birds and birds are animals, the attributes of "singing" and "yellow" are more closely linked to canaries than "flying," which is associated with birds, and "eating," which is derived from the fact that canaries are birds, which are animals, and animals eat. In fact, if given a series of short, simple, factual statements (propositions) such

FIGURE 6.6 Faces as perceptual categories. The upper five faces represent category 1, and the lower five faces represent category 2 (Reed & Friedman, 1973).

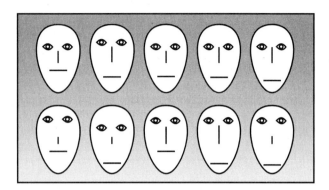

as "Canaries sing," "Canaries fly," and "Canaries eat," the time to verify the accuracy of the proposition increases as the distance from the associative link increases. To conduct these experiments, subjects are presented with a series of statements on slides or a computer display and asked to push a button indicating whether the statement is true or false. Some statements are false ("Canaries have gills"), but comparisons are usually made only among true propositions.

Finally, one of the most important kinds of concepts that we acquire are perceptual categories such as faces. The ability to recognize many different faces, or the same face under extreme variation in lighting, is a remarkable skill that we all share. One interpretation of this learning ability is that we form prototypes of faces or other visual patterns (Posner & Keele, 1968). For example, Reed (1972, Reed & Friedman, 1973) showed that subjects asked to classify new faces into one of two categories of faces like those shown in figure 6.6 appear to form a pattern that averages over the most frequent features of each category. The average pattern or prototype may not be identical to any presented face but is used to classify new instances; for example, the shape of the nose and the mouth that occurs most often for one face will be part of the pattern even if they never occur together in any particular face.

Notice how far we have come from simple association theory and experiments. Instead of examining the ease of learning a discrete verbal response to a simple stimulus, in some concept learning tasks we appear to respond on the basis of a prototypic stimulus that we may have never seen! We will examine some of the new theories that attempt to explain these more complicated concepts in the next section. Nevertheless, the experimental methodology and the logical structure of hypothesis testing are consistent over both older and more recent theories of human learning.

Skill Learning

Another important domain of human learning is in skills ranging from juggling and golf swings in athletics, to assembling components in factory work, to recognizing cancer cells in lung X-rays. Although we usually think of skill learning in terms of motor skills and physical tasks, it also involves perceptual and cognitive abilities. Indeed, probably the most important skill we learn—and the one that has received the most attention in the skill literature—is the ability to read.

Skill learning is usually concerned with **procedural learning**—"learning how"—rather than **declarative learning**—"learning what." An example of procedural learning comes from considering how you would teach someone how to tie her shoelaces.

FIGURE 6.7   An example of skill learning: Reading upside-down text (Kolers, 1976).

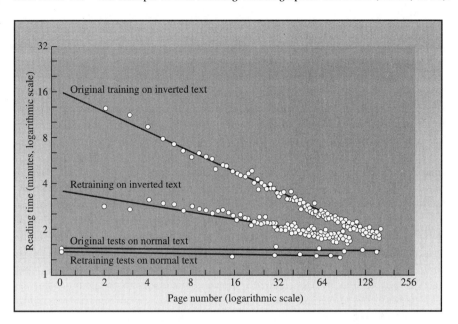

It is much easier to demonstrate the skill than to tell another how to do it. In teaching a young child how to tie shoelaces, we ask her to perform the action with us and then correct her actions rather than giving verbal instructions. With continued practice, the slow careful steps soon become fast and skillful. After considerable practice we may even lose the declarative knowledge that originally preceded the procedural skill. For example, when you first learned to type, you probably could visualize and locate the position of every letter on the keyboard (declarative knowledge). As an expert typist (or even modestly skilled typist), you now know the position of the letter "k" only by imagining typing a word with the "k" in it and observing which finger moves when you think "k" (procedural knowledge).

Even more than declarative learning, procedural learning depends on practice. As with other kinds of learning, the most rapid improvements occur in the first few practice trials, but gains in skill continue even with years of practice. The difference between the best musician, athlete, or chess player

and the talented amateur is often the amount of practice that the professional performer has devoted to his or her talent. Consider the skill of reading that we have all practiced: Kolers (1976) measured the improvement in reading upside-down printed text. Over many hours subjects read 200 pages of inverted text, showing gradual improvement (see figure 6.7). When they were brought back a year later, they exhibited some loss of skill, but considerable savings, and further gains with renewed practice. (Note the use of the log-log scale in figure 6.7 to compress the range of the practice effect and to demonstrate a linear relationship with the logarithmic transformation.)

When skills become highly practiced, they seem almost effortless. The study of such **automatic processing** has become an area of intense interest in recent years with several competing interpretations and definitions (Hasher & Zacks, 1979; Posner & Snyder, 1975; Shiffrin & Schneider, 1977). Although the details differ, all interpretations of automaticity agree that automatic processes can be conducted with minimal attention and no interference with other activities. The skilled juggler can keep three balls in the air while carrying on a conversation while the beginner requires full concentration. You and I can walk and talk at the same time, but the toddler just beginning to walk will sit down at the mention of his name.

One of the first detailed applications of automaticity was by LaBerge and Samuels (1974) to the analysis of reading. Readers must learn and practice the identification of perceptual elements into single letters, letters into words, words into phrases and concepts, and finally, comprehension of the printed ideas. Only when the lower order skills become automatic, can attention become fully engaged in the comprehension of text.

Interestingly, the acquisition of procedural knowledge appears to involve different mechanisms than declarative learning. One illustration of this difference comes from the investigation of amnesic patients who cannot ordinarily acquire new information. One famous patient known as H. M. has been unable to learn new facts for more than 30 years, but was able to improve in mirror reading (Cohen & Squire, 1980) and in playing a game (Cohen & Squire, 1981) while having no memory of engaging in either activity. The mirror reading task is a particularly good illustration of both the distinction between declarative and procedural learning and a control procedure.

Over many weeks, amnesic patients and normal control subjects practiced reading words that were presented in mirror-image form. Half of the words were repeated in every block of trials; the other half were always new words. The amnesic patients improved in reading the nonrepeated words at the same rate as the control subjects, but lagged well behind the controls in reading the repeated words. Both groups were faster reading repeated words, but control subjects were much better at remembering the repeated words both within each test session and between sessions to improve their reading times. By varying the content of the reading text (old and new words), the experimenters were able to separate the effects of procedural learning from declarative memory.

Classroom Learning

Most students think about learning in the context of their education and classroom learning. Obviously, most of the principles of learning that we have considered up to now apply equally well to formal education as to the laboratory and everyday learning, but there are some special considerations and strategies as well. One of the most fundamental observations is that formal education is based on the assumption of positive transfer from previous learning. Effective instruction uses past knowledge and preparation as a foundation for new information and skills. Consequently, one way to apply learning principles to the classroom is to examine methods of maximizing positive transfer.

One approach is to use analogies between familiar situations or problems and new ones. Unfortunately, this turns out to be much more difficult than it might appear. Evidence from problem-solving research shows that individuals are very poor at noticing relationships among problems unless the analogies are explicitly pointed out (Gick & Holyoak, 1980). This may be because they do not bother to think about possible analogies, especially if the problem appears to be solvable without it, or because the conceptual basis of the two domains are so different that the relationships are not easily perceived (Johnson-Laird, 1989).

Consider, for example, an experiment by Reed and Evans (1987) to teach chemistry students to estimate acid concentrations resulting from mixtures of two solutions with different initial concentrations. The students were taught general principles for estimating concentrations, but the estimates were not very good. However, when mixtures were compared to mixtures with different temperatures and the principles were explained in terms of temperatures, estimates improved significantly. Use of a familiar situation (temperatures) aided the comprehension of the principles of blending unfamiliar components (acid concentrations). Use of analogies in the classroom must be very explicit and well understood to be effective.

Another approach to improved classroom learning is to teach explicit strategies for efficient learning and memory. Mnemonics, or the "art of memory," refers to various strategies and devices for improving retention. Mnemonic devices are most effective when they substitute for organization or understanding of the material to be remembered (see chapter 7). Because students often do not have a good understanding of a new topic until well into the study of the subject, mnemonic aids may facilitate the early memorization necessary until comprehension catches up with factual information.

For example, one of the impediments to learning a foreign language is building an adequate vocabulary with which to learn grammatical rules and motivate continued interest in the new language. Atkinson (1975) developed a "keyword" system using an "acoustic link" to facilitate the pronunciation of the word and an "imagery link" to aid the retention of the meaning of the word. Experimental evidence indicates more rapid acquisition and better retention of vocabulary lists than leaving the students to their own memorization methods.

The development of cognitive skills and expertise in academic subjects has sparked considerable interest in several domains (e.g., Anderson, 1981; Elstein, Shulman, & Sprafka, 1978; Larkin et al., 1980), but we have only begun the application of learning principles to classroom instruction.

Network Models of Learning

Early in this chapter simple learning was described as the formation of associations or connections between ideas. From early philosophers to midtwentieth century psychological researchers, these associations were viewed as direct connections, like links in a chain; there was little concern with the pattern or structure of the connections. Over the past two decades, inspired by computer models of human behavior and the need to explain the variety and complexity of human learning and memory, elaborate associative network theories of learning and memory have been developed. As a final section on human learning we outline some of the features and

varieties of these **network models,** introducing the basic concepts and some of the research issues raised by the new theories.

Semantic Network Models

Within network models, the facts and concepts (the "ideas" of the philosophers) are called **nodes** and they are connected by **associative links.** The number of nodes and their interconnections can be very large, but they define the nature of the relationships among the concepts. Learning is represented by the growth of the network as new nodes and links are added. Most of the theoretical interest, however, has focused on retrieving information from the network by answering questions.

One early example of a semantic network underlying category membership and features was proposed by Quillian (1969) to answer questions about canaries singing, flying, and eating as described in the last section. Part of a memory structure is illustrated in figure 6.8. Note that Quillian's network is hierarchical: larger, superordinate categories are represented by nodes at the top and smaller, subordinate nodes branch off below. Features or properties of each category are linked to the appropriate level, illustrating the property of **cognitive economy,** that is, attributes of concepts are stored at the highest level to which they generally apply, eliminating the necessity of storing that information at lower levels, and saving memory.

Later network models were less structured, but introduced other features. Semantic distance was used as a measure of the degree of association among related concepts with highly related ideas located close to each other and less related concepts separated by greater distance. Collins and Loftus (1975) introduced the concept of **spreading activation** to explain how networks are searched to retrieve information: when a node is stimulated, nearby nodes are also activated with the amount and speed of activation depending on the distance from the stimulated node.

Meyer and Schvaneveldt (1971) tested some of the predictions of spreading activation by use of

FIGURE 6.8   Answering questions about concepts stored in a semantic network. (a) An example of a part of a three-level hierarchical memory structure for fish and birds. (b) Time required to verify statements about category membership and properties of category members as a function of hierarchical level (Collins & Quillian, 1969).

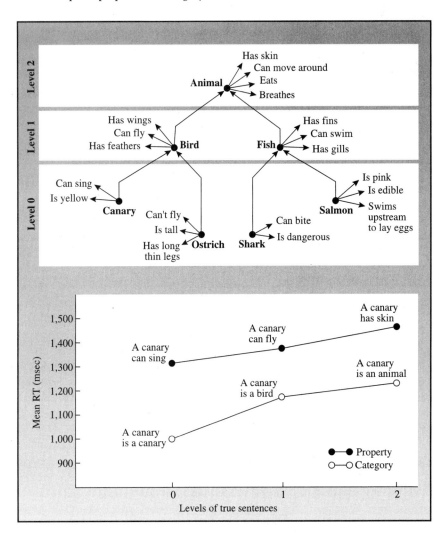

priming in a **lexical decision task.** Subjects were asked to decide as quickly as possible whether a string of letters (e.g., NURSE or NERSE) was a word. Decision times were generally faster when the test word was primed, that is, it was preceded by exposure to a closely related word like DOCTOR. (See Ratcliff and McKoon, 1988, for an alternative interpretation.)

Propositional Networks

More structure can be contained in network models with nodes that represent propositions as well as single concepts or attributes. A proposition is the smallest unit of information that has a truth value; the statement can be clearly decided to be either true or false. Examples of propositions include "birds have wings," "cows fly," and "water is wet,"

FIGURE 6.9   A propositional-network representation of the sentence *Children who are slow eat bread that is cold* (Anderson, 1990).

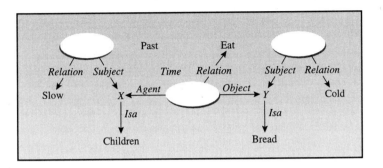

but not "blue coats," "summer," or "flying birds." In several variations (called HAM and ACT), Anderson (1983) and others have used propositional and syntactical relationships to represent semantic knowledge. One example of a propositional-network representation of the sentence "Children who are slow eat bread that is cold" is shown in figure 6.9. The sentence contains three propositions represented by the ovals, eight other nodes represented by words, and ten links represented by the italicized words. Note that the propositions state relationships (e.g., "object-agent," "isa") and are interconnected, forming more complex relationships and ideas. Even more elaborate network models and structures have been proposed in the form of frames (Minsky, 1975), schemas (e.g., Rumelhart, 1975), and scripts (Shank & Abelson, 1977).

How do we test these models? Although some experiments have been conducted to test predictions generated by the theories, generally the network models have been represented as computer programs that specify the structure of the propositional knowledge for comparison to human representations or recall of the same information. The comparisons are often very general and problems are not difficult to detect. At this early stage of theory development, discrepancies between human data and computer model are frequent, leading to revisions in the theory.

Connectionism

Most recently, network models have been proposed in a new form that minimizes structure, but has enormous predictive power by using **parallel distributed processing (PDP).** These PDP or **connectionist models** do not associate a single node with a concept or proposition, a concept known as local representation. Instead, ideas are associated with patterns of activation referred to as distributed representation. The pattern of activation must occur in parallel, that is, a number of nodes must be activated together to represent a particular idea or concept. Individual nodes may be randomly connected, perhaps in several layers, from stimulus ("input") to response ("output"). Learning occurs as connection weights, the strength of the associative links between nodes, are adjusted with repeated trials and correction from the results ("feedback") until the input pattern produces the correct output pattern. Clearly, some of the inspiration for connectionist models comes from the analogy to neural networks in the brain. Box 6.9 shows an outline of how a connectionist model would handle the problem of word identification in reading.

The proceeding oversimplified description cannot capture the incredible power of connectionist models. By "tuning" the weighting parameters and the assumptions about the connections, the system can gradually improve with experience—exactly

BOX 6.9

A Connectionist Interpretation of Reading

Identification of words during reading illustrates the interactive, parallel nature of processing in connectionist models. In the figure below (from McClelland, 1985), the black arrows at the bottom represent the excitatory connections through three layers of processing for the components of the word *TIME*. Four copies of the feature and letter units permit parallel testing of each feature and letter. Processing proceeds through three interactive layers analyzing the sensory input from the external world to the word identification level.

Physical features of individual characters are recognized and passed on to several alternative possibilities at the next layer for identification as possible letters. Note that each rectangle contains a different set of feature units activated by the input stimulation, which in turn activate only some of the possible letters. The bidirectional arrows represent the mutual influence that possible words have on letter identification and that letters have on word recognition. Each rectangle at each level represents a set of incompatible alternatives, i.e., excitatory input for *T* is inconsistent with *A* at the same letter position.

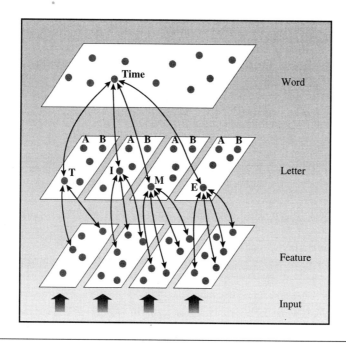

The figure below (from McClelland & Rumelhart, 1981) conveys the same general model, but emphasizes the array of features that combine to produce recognition of the letter *T*. Note that the *T* unit is activated (represented by the arrowhead) both from below by the horizontal and vertical lines in the feature units and from above by words with *T* in the first position. The *T* letter unit itself also activates words beginning with *T*. Other letter units would be operating in parallel and have patterns of activation for each of the other three letters, providing simultaneous activation for the word *TIME*.

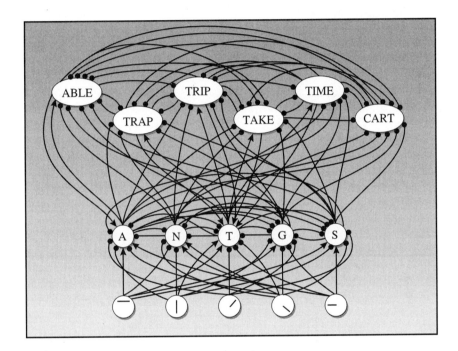

what we expect of a learning device. At this time, PDP models can be tested by comparing the output of a computer program with human data, usually after considerable adjustment in the program's assumptions. The process is so powerful and successful that one criticism of connectionist models is that they may not be falsifiable. In other words, they can never be incorrect because they can always be adjusted to predict any set of data. Future theorizing with network models is likely to be concerned with determining what amount of structure is necessary to describe human learning and memory.

Summary and Conclusions

There are many definitions of learning and a long history of philosophical thought and empirical research on human learning and thinking. In this chapter we focused on research methods for studying the variety of learning phenomena in humans. In most cases what sets these methods apart from those used for studying learning in nonhumans is the emphasis on language. Because language habits are built up over a lifetime, laboratory studies of the acquisition of verbal material must either control for or manipulate the level of prior learning represented in the task materials. Thus, the early history of research in verbal learning is marked by the development of a variety of methods of verbal assessment. These include measures of frequency or familiarity with words, letters, or letter strings known as nonsense syllables. Additional assessments for words include meaningfulness and strength of association between a stimulus word and a variety of possible responses.

Many verbal learning tasks have been developed to identify the processes that underlie human learning and thinking. Serial list learning is designed to uncover the sequential associations that are acquired when information is received one item at a time. The serial position curve is obtained by plotting the number of errors or the number of correct responses for each serial position in a list. The typical result is a bowed curve with the most errors occurring on the middle items.

In paired-associate learning, one item in a pair serves as the stimulus and the other as a response. This method is designed to study the acquisition of stimulus-response associations. Item-pairs can be presented with the *anticipation method,* in which each stimulus is presented by itself and the subject must respond before the correct response is given, or with the *study-test* method, in which all stimulus-response pairs are shown and then only the stimuli are presented and the subject must give the response to each one.

In multiple-trial free recall, subjects learn as many items as they can in a list in any order. The object is to study subjective organization and associations when no order is imposed by the task requirements.

Verbal discrimination learning is similar to discrimination tasks used in animal learning. Pairs of items are presented and subjects must learn which item in the pair is correct. This task is especially useful for studying the effects on learning of frequency of exposure.

Research methods were described for addressing the issue of whether the learning of a single stimulus-response association occurs on an all-or-none or an incremental basis. Mean learning curves that plot the proportion of correct responses over successive trials for a group of subjects do not provide this microscopic analysis. Rock's paradigm for detecting all-or-none effects in paired-associate learning used an item replacement technique where, for some subjects, a missed item was replaced by a new item on the next trial. The object was to see if missed items were partially learned. Critics of this method argued that items missed by an individual subject on a given trial represent a subset of items of greater difficulty for that subject, thus biasing the results. A model building approach by Bower provided stronger evidence for all-or-none learning. Here, the sequences of correct responses and errors for individual items received by individual subjects were used to compare the assumptions of all-or-none and gradual learning. These sequences were characterized by a period of random responding with no apparent learning followed by an immediate transition to a state of learning.

The effects of transfer of training are important to study because they show the extent to which we are influenced by our prior learning experiences. Transfer paradigms must separate the effects of specific sources of transfer such as the similarity between stimuli and responses on two consecutive tasks, and nonspecific transfer such as the acquisition of generalizable habits and skills sometimes called "learning-to-learn." While the focus of most transfer studies is to identify and compare specific sources leading to positive or negative transfer, nonspecific transfer must be controlled by including a condition with unrelated tasks.

Extension of transfer paradigms to more than two tasks is used when the process of mediation is of interest. Mediational paradigms examine how the transfer relationship between a first list and a third list is affected by the characteristics of a second list that may be related in some manner to the other two lists. Of particular interest are mediational conditions leading to positive transfer.

Analyses of transfer effects, particularly mediational processes based on natural language habits, lead to the study of more complex human learning phenomena based on the accumulation of prior knowledge. In concept formation subjects learn to provide a single response to a whole class of stimuli. Concepts may vary on physical dimensions such as size and color and may be defined by logical relationships (rules) among particular attributes. Experiments that shift the relevant and irrelevant dimensions demonstrate that what is learned can depend on the language skills of the learner.

Learning of natural categories like tools and animals is tested by semantic verification tasks that measure the time required to determine the accuracy of simple factual statements.

Skill learning focuses on procedural learning such as typing or juggling and improves with extended practice, until the skill becomes automatic. Automatic processing appears to require no attention and depends on different learning mechanisms than declarative learning.

Classroom learning often applies learning principles like positive transfer and mediation. Research

with analogical reasoning suggests that relationships between familiar and new problems must be clearly specified to be effective.

The future of research on human learning will use more concepts from computer simulation and artificial intelligence such as semantic networks, spreading activation, and connectionism. These powerful new models treat learning as changes in strength of associative connections among nodes in a distributed representation of concepts and ideas. The computer programs are very sophisticated extensions of philosophical speculations raised more than two centuries ago by the British empiricists.

Exercises

1. Use any of the sources in this chapter to construct a list of 15 nonsense syllables. Use yourself as a subject in a free recall task and practice the list for as many trials as it takes to give one perfect recitation. After you've finished, write down observations of your own behavior: Did you use any strategies or shortcuts? Did you exhibit the usual "bowed serial position effect"? Plot how your errors change over trials.

2. Again, use one of the sources in this chapter to construct a list of 20 words of high meaningfulness. Assign at random the number "1" as the correct response to half the words and the number "2" as the correct response to the other half. Test one subject in this task using the study-test method of paired-associate learning. Perform Bower's analysis of the data (box 6.7) and see if you support all-or-none learning.

3. Reproduce the Von Restorff effect by giving a serial learning task to several subjects but make one of the items in the middle of the list qualitatively different from the others. Plot your serial position curve and discuss it.

4. Choose material for constructing two three-stage transfer paradigms: one expected to lead to positive mediation effects and one expected to lead to negative mediation effects.

5. Describe a situation where past learning enabled you to learn a new topic quickly and another where past learning slowed your progress.

6. Using materials like those in figure 6.3, make up flash cards with one stimulus per card. For example,

the three dimensions of color, number, and form, which have two attributes each (e.g., red or green, one or two, circle or triangle), would yield eight possible stimuli (e.g., a single red circle). Test a friend on speed of learning a simple one-dimension task (e.g., red), a conjunctive task (red circles), and a conditional task (if red, then circle; if not red, then any shape).

7. Do you learn a new skill faster or slower if you distribute the practice time? Choose a new task such as an unfamiliar computer game, juggling three tennis balls, or writing the alphabet backward. Decide on a unit of analysis, e.g., score of each game, number of drops in five minutes of juggling, or number of letters written in two minutes. With a partner compare improvement in performance over five to ten practice trials. One partner has no rest between trials, the other has ten minutes between trials. What would happen if the test periods were longer, say one day? Does the rest period have a different effect depending on the task?

Glossary

all-or-none learning Assumption that learning of the associative connection between items occurs on a single trial. (p. 181)

anticipation method List learning method in which the subject responds with the succeeding item as each item in the list is presented. (p. 175)

associative links Connections between nodes (facts and concepts) represented in semantic network models; used to explain how knowledge is organized. (p. 195)

automatic processing Highly practiced skills that do not require attention to perform. (p. 193)

biconditional rule A concept defined by the joint occurrence or joint nonoccurrence of a specified level of two relevant dimensions (e.g., objects that are striped squares or nonstriped nonsquares); defined by the "if . . . and only if" relationship, as in if "striped" and only if "squares." (p. 189)

bigrams Two-letter units used in verbal learning studies. (p. 174)

British empiricism Philosophical school of the eighteenth century that claimed that the study of mind can be linked to physical activity within the brain and that ideas (thoughts) depend on experience. (p. 167)

cognitive economy Saving memory by storing the attributes of concepts at the highest level to which they generally apply. (p. 195)

concept formation Learning to make a common response to each of a class of objects. (p. 188)

conditional rule A concept defined by the occurrence of a specified level of one relevant dimension if a second level also occurs (e.g., if the object is striped then it must be a square to be a valid instance); defined by the "if . . . then" relationship, as in if "striped," then "square." (p. 189)

conjunctive rule A concept defined by the joint occurrence of specified levels of each of two relevant dimensions (e.g., striped square); defined by the relationship "and," as in "striped" *and* "square." (p. 189)

connectionism An idea or concept is understood through its pattern of associations to other ideas or concepts. (p. 197)

declarative learning Acquisition of factual knowledge that can be stated as specific verbal propositions or clear visual images; compare with procedural learning. (p. 192)

disjunctive rule A concept defined by the occurrence of a specified level of either of two relevant dimensions (e.g., objects that are either striped or square); defined by the relationship "or," as in "striped" *or* "square." (p. 189)

dissyllable Label applied to both words and nonwords used in verbal learning studies. (p. 174)

extradimensional shift A two-stage concept transfer task in which the relevant dimension is changed from the first task to the second task (e.g., from shape to size). (p. 190)

formal discipline Early theory of learning stating that simple mental exercise sharpens the mind. (p. 185)

free recall The subject is presented with a list of items and is asked to recall as many of the items as possible in any order. This task is especially useful for studying how subjects organize material. (p. 178)

incremental learning Assumption that learning of the associative connection between items improves gradually over trials. (p. 181)

intradimensional shift A two-stage concept transfer task in which the relevant dimension is the same for both tasks but the correct attribute of that dimension is changed (e.g., from square to triangle). (p. 190)

isolation effect See von Restorff effect. (p. 177)

law of constant proportionality The average amount of increase in performance on each trial of a learning task is often approximately a constant fraction of the amount left to be learned. (p. 181)

learning-memory distinction The study of learning emphasizes the acquisition of new information; the study of memory emphasizes the retention of old information. (p. 166)

lexical decision task Subjects are asked to decide as quickly as possible whether a string of letters is a word. (p. 196)

mean learning curve Plot of mean performance level over successive learning trials, usually showing that absolute improvement in learning scores becomes smaller as the number of trials increases. (p. 181)

meaningfulness A measure of the extent to which a word or syllable evokes associations (e.g., the mean number of associations produced in 60 sec). (p. 173)

mediation Use of an interpolated association learned or naturally occurring to facilitate later learning. (p. 187)

multiple-trial free recall (MTFR) Presentation of the same free recall list several times, usually in a different presentation order each time, to study associations and interrelations among words in the list. (p. 178)

natural language mediators Natural language habits (e.g., learned associations between words) that help subjects in new learning situations. (p. 187)

network models Models of learning based on the interconnections between concepts. (p. 195)

nodes Facts and concepts represented within semantic network models. (p. 195)

nonspecific transfer Facilitative effects of prior experience on new learning attributed to the acquisition of highly generalizable habits and skills. (p. 185)

paired-associate list learning Pairs of items are presented with one item of the pair serving as the stimulus and the other item as the response. This task is especially useful for studying the formation of associations between stimuli and responses. (p. 177)

parallel distributed processing (PDP) In network models of memory based on the principle of

"connectionism," a number of nodes must be activated together to represent a particular idea or concept. (p. 197)

paralogs Pronounceable syllables that look like words but are not. (p. 174)

precriterion stationarity If learning of a stimulus-response association is all-or-none, then for each item there is a constant (chance) level of probability of being correct prior to the trial of last error. (p. 182)

priming Prior exposure to a stimulus item (usually a word) or a closely related associate facilitates later processing (e.g., identification of a word in a lexical decision task) or memory of the item. (p. 196)

proactive interference/facilitation The effect of a prior task on the retention of a second task, studied by comparing the performance of an experimental group that receives both tasks with the performance of a control group that receives only the second task. (p. 185)

procedural learning Acquisition of a skill or action such as typing or juggling; knowledge is demonstrated by performance rather than by descriptive statements; compare with declarative learning. (p. 192)

recall method See study-test method. (p. 175)

retroactive interference/facilitation The effect of an interpolated task on the later retention of a task learned earlier, studied by comparing the performance of groups that do and do not receive the interpolated task. (p. 185)

semantic differential A measure of the connotative meaning of a word based on ratings of the word on a series of bipolar scales. (p. 174)

serial list learning Task designed to study the acquisition of items in serial order. Subjects have to learn a list of items in the exact order in which the items are presented. (p. 175)

serial position curve The number of errors or correct responses in a serial list learning task is plotted for each serial position. The typical result is a bowed curve where performance is best for the items at the beginning of the list and at the end, and worst for items in the middle. (p. 175)

specific transfer Effects of prior experience on new learning attributed to the similarity between the stimuli or the responses on the two tasks. (p. 185)

spreading activation In explaining how information is retrieved in memory, the assumption in network models that when a node is stimulated, nearby nodes are also activated. (p. 195)

study-test method List learning method in which the subject studies each item in the list without responding and is then asked to recall all items in the list without being prompted (also called the **recall method**). (p. 175)

subjective organization (SO) The tendency to recall items in a free-recall list together in the same order even when they are presented in a different order on each trial. (p. 178)

tabula rasa John Locke's assertion that the mind starts out as a blank slate upon which experience writes its messages. (p. 168)

trigrams Three-letter units used in verbal learning studies. (p. 174)

verbal assessment Measurement of the characteristics (e.g., frequency) of the materials used to study verbal learning and memory. (p. 169)

verbal discrimination The subject is presented with a set (e.g., a pair) of stimulus items and is asked to pick out the item that the experimenter designates as correct. This task is especially useful for studying the effects of frequency on learning. (p. 179)

von Restorff effect A distinctive item within a list (e.g., one printed in a different color from the rest) is generally learned more rapidly than adjacent items (also called the **isolation effect**). (p. 177)

word association tests Used for testing verbal associations to words, usually the first response, e.g., table-chair, black-white, up-down. (p. 173)

Suggested Readings

The study of human learning is closely associated with research on human memory and cognition, so references at the end of the next chapter are also relevant to learning. Some textbooks combine consideration of human learning with learning in other species, so references from the previous chapter may also be helpful.

Leading specialty journals that report contemporary research in this area include *Cognition; Cognitive Psychology; Journal of Experimental Psychology: Learning, Memory, & Cognition; Journal of Memory and Language; Memory & Cognition.*

Annual series that often present reviews of topics in human learning include the *Annual Review of Psychology,* and *The Psychology of Learning and Motivation: Advances in Research and Theory.*

Historical reviews and analyses of theories of human learning can be found in standard textbooks such as Bower and Hilgard (1981), Crowder (1976), Kausler (1974), Schwartz and Reisberg (1991). In addition to the preceding, widely used textbooks that cover the material of this chapter, primarily from a cognitive point of view, include Anderson (1990), Baddeley (1990), Leahey and Harris (1993), Matlin (1994), and Reed (1992). For the ambitious, an introduction to connectionist models can be found in a 1986 two-volume tutorial monograph by Rumelhart and McClelland (Vol. 1) and McClelland and Rumelhart (Vol. 2).

7

Memory

James V. Hinrichs

In the last chapter, we emphasized the acquisition process in learning. We now turn our attention to the opposite side of the coin and the study of retention. Once again we must emphasize that retention and acquisition are both components of learning and memory processes. One cannot be studied without involving the other. As noted before, however, by labeling "memory" our focus of concern, we are focusing on retention and emphasizing the changes in performance that occur after the initial acquisition of the material.

From Ebbinghaus' (1885) pioneering experiments until about 1960, the study of human learning and the study of human memory were closely intertwined. Most of the research was concerned with what we would today call long-term, rote, verbal memory, usually the recall of lists of random words after retention intervals of several hours to several days. The primary explanation of memory loss was in terms of interference theory, which is related to the principles of transfer of training. A dramatic shift in research emphasis can be traced to a pair of papers, Brown (1958) and Peterson and Peterson (1959), independently documenting the rapid loss of information over very brief intervals of time. The Brown and Peterson experiments coincided with development of information processing theories of perception, attention, and memory, resulting in a marked change in the nature of research on human memory.

One of the contributions of the information processing interpretation was the now fundamental distinction between long-term and short-term memory. Also, where earlier investigations of memory employed a few standard experimental paradigms and mostly measures of accurate recall, later research exhibited an explosion of creative methods of studying human memory abilities and a variety of dependent variables. More recently, memory theorists have introduced a host of interesting distinctions and dichotomies among various types of memory, including semantic and episodic, implicit and explicit, declarative and procedural, visual and verbal, among others.

In addition, modern investigations of memory have shown considerable interest in what might be called the practical or applied aspects of memory. Think of the times you tried in vain to come up with a crucial name, date, or other fact that you were sure you knew, and wondered what mysterious forces were at work to thwart your best efforts. The study of mnemonics, the "art" of memory, provides many useful strategies for enhancing retention of difficult material. On the other hand, think of all the trivial facts that you are exposed to that have no essential function in your life—the number of pages in this book, the brand of pen you are using to take notes, and so forth. Forgetting, as well as remembering, has an adaptive function. We will examine some of the factors that influence the rate of forgetting like brain injury, drugs, and aging. We will also take a brief look at some of the exceptional cases that make us wonder about the limits of human memory, like Luria's patient who apparently could not forget.

Exploring the full range of contemporary memory theory is beyond the scope of this introductory chapter (consult the references at the end of the chapter for current textbooks), but we will examine the major concepts, focusing on the methods used to provide evidence for the validity of the concepts and to distinguish between types of memory. First, we will review pre-1960 verbal memory, focusing on interference theory. Then we will examine the evidence and the methods used to generate the evidence for the distinction between short-term (STM) and long-term (LTM) memory. This will lead us to a variety of means of testing how information is stored and retrieved from STM, particularly from an information-processing perspective. After a similar review of how information is stored and recovered from LTM, we will consider a few selected topics that show some exceptional memory abilities and some applications of memory processes.

FIGURE 7.1 Typical decay curve. The retention interval could be in units of seconds, hours, or days. The shape of the curve remains approximately the same over long and short intervals.

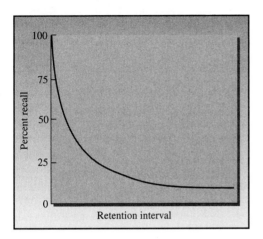

Rote Verbal Memory

Beginning with the work of Ebbinghaus, the typical study of human memory required learning a well-defined set of verbal material, usually a paired-associate or serial list of common words or nonsense syllables, and then testing the retention of that material after some period of time, usually several hours or days, either by recall or by relearning the list. Performance was measured in terms of percent of the items recalled or percent of savings of the number of trials required for relearning. For example, if it originally took 10 trials to learn a task to a given criterion of performance, and later, on a second relearning effort, it took only 5 trials to relearn the same task, then the number of trials saved in relearning is 5. The **savings score** in this case is 50 percent.

Plotting performance as a function of length of the retention interval yielded a standard retention curve that usually showed a sharp initial drop and then a gradual decline (figure 7.1). There is some evidence (Woodworth & Schlosberg, 1954) that a log function describes these long-term retention functions, which are sometimes called "decay curves."

Law of Disuse

The primary issue for early theorists was how to account for forgetting. The leading prescientific theory of forgetting is sometimes called the "law of disuse." This "law" is primarily a statement of the old folklore that "if you don't use it, you lose it," and it follows the reasoning that learning occurs because of practice and that forgetting occurs because of the lack of practice of the material (McGeoch, 1932).

There are several problems with the law of disuse as an explanation of forgetting. First, it is not really an explanation at all so much as it is a tautological restatement of the fact of forgetting. It merely asserts that a decrement in performance occurs over retention intervals; it proposes no mechanisms for the decrement. Second, forgetting and disuse are not really correlated to the high extent assumed by this law; rather, forgetting seems to depend very heavily on the type of intervening event between the initial learning and later retention tests. (Indeed, recency is not always a good predictor of memory: older individuals often complain that they remember events from their early life better than what happened a few days before.)

The "law" of disuse may be viewed as a prescientific anticipation of a physiological explanation of memory. That is, some (unknown) change occurs in the brain that results in decreased ability to remember past events. Such interpretations are today labeled **decay** theories and imply that retention loss is the result of internal biochemical or neurological events and relatively independent of intervening behavioral events. The opposing point of view, usually labeled **interference** theory, ascribes the major role in forgetting to the nature or content of other behavioral events. Interference interpretations have been most prominent in long-term verbal memory experiments; decay theories have been applied more often in studies of short-term memory.

Neuroscientists continue to search for the physiological basis of memory storage, while cognitive psychologists seek descriptions in terms of behavioral manipulations. Some physiological change must occur in order to produce the observed decrement in performance, but knowledge of these physiological changes would not necessarily give us the behavioral explanation and laws that we need to understand forgetting at the observed behavioral level. Even if we knew the neurological changes that occur with acquisition and forgetting, we would need to translate these biological states into behavioral laws.

Interference Theory

The search for the behavioral laws of forgetting have focused on the conditions necessary to produce the decrement in performance that we call forgetting. These conditions are specified in terms of intervening activities either before or after the event to be tested for retention, providing an active account of forgetting as opposed to the more passive interpretation of the law of disuse. Whereas decay theory or the law of disuse says that the memory trace fades automatically over time unless it is renewed (e.g., rehearsed), interference theory assumes that forgetting occurs when a stimulus-response association is weakened by the learning of another association.

The focus of interference research has been upon the conditions and activities that produce a decrement in memory performance after some period of time. The sources of interference may be identified as either proactive, occurring before the learning event; retroactive, occurring after the learning event; or extraexperimental, which refers to the sources of interference not under the control of the experimenter, generally stemming from language knowledge and habits acquired outside of the laboratory environment. The interference interpretation of forgetting is a basic extension of the principles of transfer in that acquired information is assumed to interfere with other learned material and produce forgetting through response competition.

The study of forgetting caused by interference occurs within the context of two experimental designs very similar to transfer designs. These two designs are used to study the two assumed sources of interference in forgetting: **retroactive inhibition** (RI) and **proactive inhibition** (PI). Both designs call for the comparison of an experimental group with a control group (see boxes 7.1 and 7.2 for more details). In both, the experimental group learns two successive lists; the control group learns only one. The difference between the RI and the PI design lies in the temporal location of the list to be recalled. In the RI design, recall is measured for the list learned first. In the PI design, the recalled list is learned second. The decrement in performance as compared with the control groups is attributed to the inhibitory effect of either proactive or retroactive sources of interference.

You may have a personal sense of how RI affects you if you study a new language in college, say French, after learning a different language in high school, say Spanish. Now when you visit Mexico, you are likely to find that some Spanish words and phrases that you once knew so well now pop out in French! A familiar example of how PI can influence everyday memory occurs in trying to remember where you have parked your car in an often-used parking lot. On the first occasion, remembering the car's location is easy, but with each successive day, the shifting locations become more and more difficult to recall when you return to the lot—perhaps explaining why people like to park in the same place every day.

The major difference between these designs for studying interference effects in memory and transfer designs is, of course, that the emphasis in performance is on the later retention tests rather

BOX 7.1

Retroactive Inhibition Paradigm

The experimental design for demonstrating retroactive inhibition (RI) may be diagrammed as follows:

	Learn Task X	Learn Task Y	Recall Task X
Control Group	Yes	No	Yes
Experimental Group	Yes	Yes	Yes

If the recall performance on task X is significantly poorer for the experimental group than for the control group, then retroactive inhibition is operationally defined. Maximum RI is produced when tasks X and Y bear the relationship described earlier for negative transfer, such as learning new responses to the same stimuli (A–B, A–C). A variety of other variables affect the amount of RI: number of trials on task X, number of trials on task Y, similarity of the two tasks, length of retention interval.

Several control features are critical with this paradigm. Learning and recall of task X must be conducted in exactly the same manner for the experimental and control groups. More importantly, while the control group does not receive the interpolated task Y, the length of time between learning task X and being tested for recall of task X—the retention interval—must be exactly the same for the experimental group and the control group. The retention interval for the control group has to be filled with a task that prevents rehearsal; otherwise, quite apart from interference effects, the control group will have an artificial advantage over the experimental group. Choice of a filler task should be based on two criteria: (1) it sufficiently occupies the subject's attention to prevent (as much as possible) rehearsal of task X; (2) the filler task material should be unrelated to the material in task X so that neither positive nor negative transfer effects occur. When task X material consists of words, nonsense syllables, or letters of the alphabet, numerical tasks such as counting backward or summing columns appear to satisfy these criteria.

In an interesting extension of the RI paradigm, two groups of subjects were given a serial list to be recalled 12 hours later (Ekstrand, 1972). One group was presented the material in the morning and was tested for recall in the evening. The other group was presented the material at night and was tested for recall the next morning. It was predicted that the morning-evening group would show greater RI than the evening-morning group because there would be more interfering events during waking hours than during sleeping hours. This prediction was confirmed when the morning-evening group was found to commit more recall errors than the evening-morning group.

---

than on the acquisition of the second or common list. It should be clear, therefore, that interference in recall is closely tied to the concept of negative transfer in acquisition, both in terms of experimental operations and hypothetical mechanisms. For example, McGeoch (1942) attributed RI in the recall of the first list to competition from second list responses just as negative transfer in acquisition was a result of competition from previous habits—as, for example, in the A–B, A–C negative transfer design.

From Ebbinghaus through the 1950s, much of the research concerned with human learning and memory focused on developing and refining the principles of interference theory with special emphasis on the similarity relationships between lists. There is no question that inference is a powerful influence on our ability to recall learned material, particularly information that is not well organized or meaningful. Around 1960 the question was raised about the sufficiency of interference theory to account for all forgetting.

BOX 7.2

Proactive Inhibition Paradigm

The experimental design for demonstrating proactive inhibition (PI) may be diagrammed as follows:

	Learn Task X	Learn Task Y	Recall Task Y
Control Group	No	Yes	Yes
Experimental Group	Yes	Yes	Yes

If the recall performance on task Y is significantly poorer for the experimental group than for the control group, then proactive inhibition is operationally defined. Note the logic of the term proactive inhibition. The prefix "pro" (like "pre") designates the influence of a prior event, in this case learning task X, on the recall of a later event (task Y). By contrast, the prefix "retro" in retroactive inhibition designates the influence of a later event (learning task Y) on the recall of an earlier event (task X). Hopefully, this mnemonic device will help you keep straight PI and RI. We will discuss more such devices later in this chapter.

While the amount of PI is influenced by much the same factors as influence the amount of RI, one factor has a particularly critical role on PI—the length of the retention interval. So while we do not have to be concerned with a special task to replace task X for the control group in the PI paradigm (why not?), it is very important that the interval between task Y presentation and task Y recall test be equated for the experimental group and the control group. It is still possible to manipulate the retention interval in studies of PI, but each level of that variable should be represented by both an experimental group and a control group. And, of course, the retention interval should be comparably filled with a distractor task for each group. By comparing the difference in recall performance between the two groups at each level of retention interval, the effect of this variable on PI can be documented.

Separating Long-Term and Short-Term Memory

One of the most important issues in the investigation of human memory over the past three decades has been the distinction between short-term memory (STM) and long-term memory (LTM). Theoretical concerns have dominated the research literature, and we will discuss some of those arguments, but we will use the controversy to focus on a number of research methods and paradigms used to distinguish between the two kinds of memory. In many cases, the experiments represent an attempt to demonstrate **functional dissociation,** that is, a clear difference in the influence of independent variables on two theoretically distinguishable types of memory.

In the study of the acquisition and retention of verbal lists, as we have seen in this chapter and the last, a few standard paradigms are used repeatedly. In contrast, a large number of different techniques have been used to study STM and LTM. A brief survey of these methods serves to introduce both the topic and the problems that are confronted in investigating memory.

Distractor and Probe Techniques

The year 1960 marked a major shift in the study of human memory, both in terms of theory and methodology. Experiments by Brown (1958) and Peterson and Peterson (1959) demonstrated rapid forgetting over the course of a few seconds and suggested that interference principles were insufficient to account for the rapid loss of memory. The goal of both studies was to examine retention of a small amount of information (letter pairs or trigrams) when subjects were prevented from rehearsing (i.e., repeating the items to themselves) the to-be-remembered (TBR) material. Rehearsal-preventing procedures, also called **distractor techniques,** have many variations and are essential if we are to study the causes of forgetting.

The procedure used by Brown (1958) was to require subjects to read two-digit numbers during a

FIGURE 7.2 **Immediate recall of letter diagrams (Peterson & Peterson, 1959). Compare the shape of the retention function with figure 7.1.**

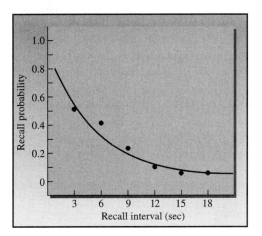

5-second retention interval after seeing a TBR letter pair or series of pairs. Performance was compared with a control condition in which the numbers were not presented. Without the intervening numbers, retention of the letters was virtually perfect. With interpolation of the numbers between the letters and recall, performance showed a dramatic decline.

In the Peterson and Peterson experiment, the amount of TBR material was held constant at a single item—a set of three consonants (CCC trigram)—and the duration of the rehearsal-prevention was varied from 3 to 18 seconds of counting backward by threes or fours. The Petersons found a sharp decline in the retention of the trigram from approximately 50 percent correct after 3 seconds to about 10 percent correct after 18 seconds (see figure 7.2). Brown presented his results as evidence for a decay component in short-term memory separate from the interference principles that control long-term memory.

There are some important differences in the implementation of the distractor technique in the two experiments. Brown presented his filler material at a fixed rate of presentation, and the subject was merely required to read it. Peterson and Peterson, on the other hand, presented a single number to the subjects and required them to count backward by threes from that number at a fixed rate. There would appear to be very great differences in the demands on the subjects by these different tasks. Subjects in the Peterson and Peterson experiment are required to be much more involved in the distractor task and much greater demands are made on their performance. In the Brown experiment, subjects can be much more passive and the response demands made on them are not as great. Furthermore, the Peterson task is partially self-paced by the subject (the rate of counting backward cannot be completely controlled), while the Brown procedure is paced by the experimenter. Both procedures potentially allow some rehearsal by the subject. In the Brown procedure the subject may be rehearsing between presentations of the items to be read and in the Peterson experiment the subjects may vary their rate of counting backward and steal time to rehearse in between responses. In other words, although it is certain that rehearsal is diminished by these procedures, it cannot necessarily be claimed that it is removed entirely.

In addition to these methodological concerns, there were many theoretical objections to the Brown-Peterson-Peterson experiments, particularly the claim that the results could not be explained by interference principles. Eventually, Keppel and Underwood (1962) demonstrated that previous tests of letter trigrams earlier in the experimental session provided a source of proactive interference, a phenomenon that they referred to as "build-up of PI." Nevertheless, interest in short-term memory phenomena increased and other investigators invented new techniques to study rapid forgetting. One of these other methods is called the **probe technique.**

In the probe technique, a single list of homogeneous items is presented to the subject and one member, or in some cases a small subset of members, of the list is tested. The probe technique represents a sampling procedure in which different parts of the list are tested at different times. There are a number of ways in which an item within the list may be probed. For example, Anderson (1960) presented 12 digits in three blocks of 4 digits each, separated by periods of temporal spacing. After the items were presented, the subjects were cued to recall either the first, second, or third block of 4 digits after intervals of 0, 5, or 30 seconds.

There are other variations on the probe technique: Murdock (1961) presented a list of six paired-associate items for a single study trial and then tested one of the six pairs by presenting the stimulus term alone and requiring the response term. Waugh and Norman (1965) used a slightly different procedure in which they present a list of digits and used one digit as a cue for the following one. Notice that this procedure places a restriction on the probe digit; it can be used only once in the sequence.

Both probe and distractor methods represent an attempt to keep the subject busy and reduce the amount of rehearsal before a subsequent recall test. However, the two tasks differ in at least two different ways (Keppel, 1965; Murdock, 1967). First, they differ in the similarity of the filler material. In the distractor technique, the filler material is very dissimilar from the TBR material, and in the probe technique, it is derived from the same set of material. Second, the two tasks differ in the requirements to remember the filler material. In the distractor technique it is very clear that the filler need not be remembered, but in the probe technique there is no distinction between the TBR item and the filler material. As Keppel has pointed out, the difference in material and in the need to remember could produce very different sets of results for the two techniques. On the other hand, Murdock has presented data from the two types of procedures that show similar form and suggest that both techniques give equivalent results. Generally, the differences do not appear to be large although it is possible that they may influence the magnitude of the retention effect. (A question for further thought: given the strong emphasis on similarity by interference theory, what are the implications for an interference explanation of immediate forgetting when distractor and probe experiments yield similar results?)

Multiple-Item Tasks

The second class of immediate memory tasks are tests in which the subject is asked for retention of all of the items presented in a short list. The best-known of these procedures is the classical **memory span** in which the subject is presented with a short list of items, usually digits or letters of the alphabet, and asked for recall of all of the items in either forward or backward order. Since the memory span test was introduced by Jacobs in 1887, it has been widely used as a simple and quick estimate of memory, including its use as one item on IQ tests. A large number of variables have been manipulated in the context of memory span, including type of material, rate of presentation, and differences among types of subjects. However, a rule of thumb is that the average memory span is about seven unrelated items whether these are digits, letters, or words (Miller, 1956). (Because it appeared so pervasively in sensory judgment and memory experiments as a limit on human discriminability, Miller referred to it as the "magical number seven, plus or minus two.")

There are a large number of procedural and scoring variations possible in the memory span test. For example, in IQ testing, subjects are usually given credit for the longest string of items they can recall without an error 50 percent of the time. In most laboratory experiments, however, the emphasis is on the number of items recalled at each serial position. Items may be scored in terms of the number correct in the correct serial position, or the number correct regardless of serial position.

Memory span performance resembles serial list learning especially with respect to the serial position curve. There is a typical bowed serial position curve for the memory span just as there is for serial list learning although the two shapes are different largely because the serial learning curve is based on several recall trials and the memory span curve on only one. The serial position curve for the memory span task can be changed markedly by task demands. For example, very different serial position curves are produced by requiring either forward or backward recall of the memory span items. When order of recall is not stipulated, the memory span task becomes a free recall task (see below).

The second type of multiple-item test is a variation of the classical memory span called the **running memory span** (Pollack, Johnson, & Knaff, 1959). Subjects are presented with a list of items, stopped at some point, and then asked to recall as many items backward in the list as possible. This experiment examines a number of characteristics. One of the most interesting is the comparison of list length with the subjects either informed or uninformed of the number of items to be presented to them. Across a wide number of experimental conditions, subjects informed of length performed much better than subjects uninformed of the length of the sequence to be presented. They also found as the length of the message increased, the average number of items recalled by the subjects first increased, then decreased with very long sequences. Waugh (1960) applied the concept of the running memory span in her analysis of the classical memory span. She considered the classical memory span to be composed of two separate spans: an initial and a terminal span. In other words, the ends of the list may be considered anchor points from which the subject remembers a sequence of items. Using this analysis she was able to predict performance on the retention of a 12-item span.

The third type of multiple-item memory test may also be considered a **continuous** or **steady-state memory test.** In tasks of this type, the subject is required to make repeated continuous demands on memory, constantly updating categories or testing old items. This procedure is somewhat similar to the probe technique in that items are tested individually without the subject being informed of which item is to be tested. But it differs from the probe technique in that the presentation of new items and tests of old items are continuously mixed. The procedure is a fairly efficient way to test memory under continuous demand and without the artificiality of the stop and start short-list procedures.

One of the simplest types of steady-state recall tasks is the one used by Atkinson and Shiffrin (1965) in which a long series of study-test paired-associate pairs are presented to the subject. Each presentation may be the presentation of a new item or a test of an old one. Each stimulus term appears at most twice: once for its initial presentation and once for its later test. (Some "filler" items may be presented only once and never tested.) Subjects see a mixture of tests and new presentations and must respond to each test as it occurs with what they remember as the correct response. A list of 200 or 300 test and study trials may be presented this way, abandoning the usual list structure in paired-associate experiments. A recognition steady-state memory task is described in the section on recognition memory.

Free Recall Methods

Although distractor/probe and multiple-item techniques suggested that the STM-LTM distinction was a useful one, they provided no clear evidence of a functional dissociation between the two types of memory. Better evidence was obtained from a number of experiments using free recall procedures. Free recall tests differ from other multiple-item tasks by allowing subjects to recall the items in any order. For example, subjects may be given a list of familiar words presented at the rate of one word every 2 seconds and then are required to recall as many words as possible. Typical response curves are plotted in figure 7.3 for different list lengths.

For obvious reasons these are called **bowed-serial-position curves.** Note that performance in figure 7.3 is plotted in terms of the original presentation position in the list, but the subject may have recalled the items in any order; in fact, typically, the items presented last are recalled first. The higher recall of the initial items is called the **primacy effect** and better performance of the last few items is called the **recency effect.** The relatively flat portion of the curve in the middle of the list is sometimes referred to as the "plateau" or "asymptote." Because the initial items were acquired earlier in time than

FIGURE 7.3   Serial position curves for three different list lengths (from Murdock, 1962).

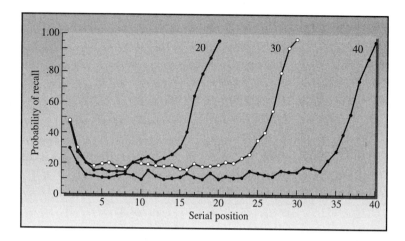

FIGURE 7.4   Serial position curves for (a) 20-word lists presented at 3 or 9 seconds per word, and (b) 15-word lists with 0 or 30 seconds of filled delay between the end of the list and recall (Glanzer & Cunitz, 1966).

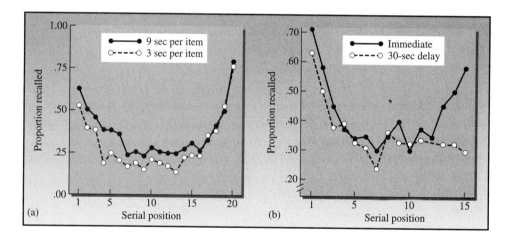

the others, whereas the last items were acquired more recently than the others, the primacy effect has been associated with long-term memory and the recency effect has been associated with short-term memory. However, to consider these as distinct processes, it must be shown that they are affected by different variables.

In a study of free recall by Glanzer and Cunitz (1966), the authors compared the effects of two manipulations on the serial position curves (see figure 7.4). The first independent variable was rate of presentation of items on the list. The prediction here is that faster presentation rates reduce or slow processes such as storing the meaning of items that

FIGURE 7.5   Typical modality effect in (a) serial recall and (b) free recall (Gregg, 1986).

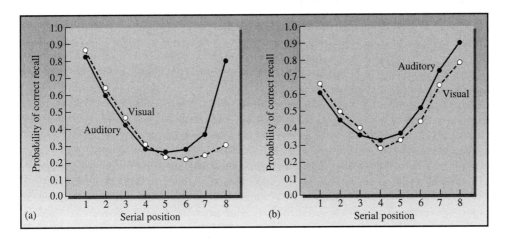

are assumed to occur in long-term but not short-term memory. Confirming this prediction, the manipulation of presentation rate had its greatest effect on the primacy portion of the curve, leaving the recency portion relatively intact. The second independent variable was length of the **retention interval**—the time between the end of the presentation phase and the beginning of the recall test phase—either 0 or 30 seconds. Note that this manipulation requires an important control feature. If subjects were allowed to do whatever they wanted during the retention interval, they could rehearse the items to be recalled and maintain their recall performance over long retention intervals. So, instead, the researchers gave their subjects a distractor task to perform during the interval (a simple counting task). Results showed that the recency part of the curve disappeared with longer retention intervals but the primacy part was left relatively intact. This finding was taken as evidence that the usual good recall of items at the end of the list is due to short-term memory, which is negated by a long retention interval.

A related phenomenon is the **modality effect** in serial recall (see figure 7.5). It involves a comparison of the serial position curve when items are presented in the auditory or visual mode. While recall of earlier items is little affected by the mode of presentation, performance of the last few items is typically superior when presentation is auditory rather than visual. This supports the view that short-term memory store of words is based on the sound of the word, not its meaning, and that matching of presentation mode and storage mode facilitates short-term memory.

Other evidence for the distinction between STM and LTM was found in clinical studies of unusual patients (see box 7.3).

Theories of STM and LTM
Studies like the ones described above and many others tend to support the theoretical distinction between STM and LTM first proposed by Atkinson and Shiffrin (1968) and Waugh and Norman (1965). Both theories view STM as a limited capacity, short duration memory store that operates either by decay or displacement of items, while LTM is a relatively permanent, apparently unlimited capacity memory store controlled by interference principles and other language- and meaning-based operations.

Multistore Models
The proposed distinction between short-term and long-term memory led many researchers to conceptualize a **multistore model** or a multistructure memory storage system. A prototypical example (from

BOX 7.3

A Clinical Study of Separate Short-Term and Long-Term Memory Processes

A dramatic illustration of a dichotomy in the memory system comes from a study of patients with lesions in the hippocampus region of the brain (Milner, 1966). Surgical lesions in this region produce a severe and persistent memory disorder. Patients with these lesions show no loss of preoperatively acquired skills but they seem largely incapable of adding new information to long-term memory. This was found with measures of recall, recognition, and relearning. Nevertheless, the immediate registration of new information—as in digit span tests—appears to take place normally. Material can be held in memory for many minutes if rehearsal is permitted, but if rehearsal is interrupted with a distractor task, immediate forgetting occurs, and, if simple material is not easily categorized in verbal terms, it decays rapidly.

Apparently these patients retain short-term memory, but are incapable of retaining new material on a long-term basis. The lesions seem to have produced a breakdown either in the ability to store new information in long-term memory or to retrieve new information from it. It would be difficult to account for the highly specific memory loss in these patients without assuming a separation of the memory system into short-term and long-term components.

FIGURE 7.6   Atkinson and Shiffrin's model of short-term memory (adapted from Atkinson and Shiffrin, 1971).

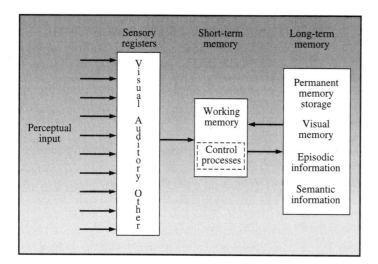

Atkinson & Shiffrin, 1971) is illustrated in figure 7.6. While we won't discuss all the details of this model, it will be useful to review its basic structure.

In the Atkinson and Shiffrin conceptualization, the memory system is divided into three components: the sensory register, the short-term store, and the long-term store. When a stimulus is presented there is an immediate registration of that stimulus within the appropriate sensory dimension. Independent evidence of the existence of a sensory register comes from studies of the visual system where an accurate visual image is shown to occur after a several hundred millisecond delay (Sperling, 1960).

The second basic component of the system is the short-term store. Atkinson and Shiffrin consider this to be the subject's **working memory.** Information entering the short-term store is assumed to decay and disappear completely, but the time for this to occur is considerably longer than for the sensory register. It is assumed here that information from one sense modality, say vision, may be encoded from the visual sensory register into an auditory short-term store. (Errors at the end of a serial list are often soundalikes of the correct response.) The rate of decay of information in the short-term store is influenced by subject-controlled processes such as rehearsal. However, most accounts are that information in this store is lost within 15 to 30 seconds.

Continued rehearsal is one of the so-called "control processes" that lead some information in the short-term store to be transferred to the long-term store. The long-term store differs from the other components in the system in that information stored here does not decay and become lost in the same manner as the other components. All information eventually is completely lost from the sensory register and the short-term store, but information in the long-term store may be maintained indefinitely. As we have seen, however, interference effects from other stored information can make some information temporarily irretrievable. As noted before, many experiments support the distinction between STM and LTM stores and processing.

Levels of Processing

The information processing interpretation of the STM-LTM distinction did not go unchallenged, of course. An important alternative explanation of STM phenomena is provided by the **levels of processing** theory proposed by Craik and Lockhart (1972) and Craik and Tulving (1975). The major assumption of the levels-of-processing model is that memory is dependent on the level (or depth) of processing imposed on the incoming information. The critical difference between STM and LTM is provided by the kind of processing that occurs at presentation and the extent to which this processing provides adequate cues for later retrieval. Items that receive only "shallow" processing based on physical features can be maintained briefly but are not easily retrieved after long retention intervals. Recall after long periods of time requires "deep" processing that insures contact with the meaning or semantic content of the TBR items.

In one experiment conducted within the levels-of-processing framework, Craik and Tulving (1975)

presented subjects with a series of words and asked questions about the meaning of a word; other subjects were asked only about superficial aspects such as whether it has capital letters or what rhymes with it. After subjects went through a series of test words, they were given a surprise recognition memory test. The test consisted of going through a new list with old and new items and indicating whether each word was on the original list. Consistent with predictions, recognition performance was a direct function of the depth of the question asked by the experimenter.

(Before reading further, you might pause and reexamine the previously described experiments in terms of the levels of processing interpretation and decide how the results are consistent or inconsistent with that explanation. What difficulties do you see with the levels of processing view?)

The levels-of-processing framework could be used to reinterpret the standard serial position curve without referring to short-term and long-term memory. The items at the end of the list may have been processed at a more superficial level than items at the beginning of the list. This fits the observation that subjects tend to produce the final items first in attempting to recall the entire list.

Despite the intuitive appeal of the levels-of-processing viewpoint, it was found to be difficult to test. The basic difficulty is that there is no independent assessment of depth of processing other than by memory performance (Baddeley, 1978). You should recognize the circularity of the argument: deep processing leads to improved memory, but you only know how deep something is processed by how well it is remembered.

Nevertheless, the research generated within the levels-of-processing framework had interesting consequences. It raised questions about the viability of multistore models of memory and clearly demonstrated that emphasizing meaningful processing at the time of presentation markedly improves memory. (Later we will discuss other methods for improving memory performance.) Other more recent theories and interpretations of memory have also questioned the need for a sharp distinction between STM and LTM, but the dichotomy has become firmly entrenched in the memory literature. We will use this distinction to continue our examination of memory processing.

Storing and Retrieving Information from Short-Term Memory

Information processing models of memory suggest that sensory information is perceived and held briefly in a sensory register, before being passed to STM. What is the capacity and duration of the sensory registers? Do they differ by sensory modality? New experimental techniques were designed to address such questions.

Storing Sensory Information

Sperling (1960) tested the amount of information available in very brief visual displays by using a variant of the probe technique, with presentation of a letter matrix consisting of three rows of four letters each (e.g., SQHM). The matrix was presented for a few hundred msec and then removed, followed by a high-, medium- or low-pitched tone, indicating which row of letters was to be recalled. Note that the tone serves as a *poststimulus cue* because the subject does not know what is to be tested until after all items have been presented. The results, using this partial report procedure, indicate that subjects have more information available immediately after presentation than they are able to produce before losing part of it. Sperling found average recall of slightly more than 3 letters out of a line of 4 letters, suggesting that 9 to 10 items are available in memory from the three by four matrix immediately after presentation. This number contrasts with the whole report procedure of approximately 5 items recalled when subjects are asked for all 12 letters and shows the rapid loss of information while subjects are attempting to produce their responses (sometimes referred to as output interference). However, the information retained in visual sensory memory, or **iconic memory,** is held for only a very brief period. Within approximately 500 msec, one-half of a second, the partial report method falls to about 1.5 items, equivalent to the 5 items observed with the whole report procedure. Apparently, during the short period of time that an item or set of items is held in the iconic store, the information must be transformed into a representation that can be maintained in STM.

Does a similar process occur with auditory sensory information? Darwin, Turvey, and Crowder (1972) answered this question by constructing an auditory analogy to Sperling's experiment. They presented sets of four rapidly spoken single-digit numbers over each of three speakers located to the left, directly in front of, and to the right of the subjects. The spatial locations of the speaker correspond to the three rows in the visual matrix. After the auditory presentation of the numbers, partial report of one set was cued by a flashing light over the speaker location from which the numbers were to be recalled. As with visual presentation, recall accuracy for the whole report of the entire set of 12 numbers was about 5. Compared to iconic memory, the advantage of immediate partial report of only a subset of the items was small, equivalent to only about one-half of an item. However, the duration of auditory sensory memory, or **echoic memory,** was much longer than iconic memory, extending for 2 to 4 seconds after presentation. Consequently, echoic memory appears to have a smaller capacity, but longer duration, than iconic memory. This result is consistent with what might be called the "huh" experience, familiar to everyone: a friend says something to you when you are not listening and you respond with an intelligent "huh?" but before your friend can repeat the comment, you "hear" the original remark (like an echo).

Transfer to STM

As we have noted before, in some theories, STM is also referred to as "working memory." Information processed through the sensory registers must be actively maintained and manipulated as it is being used to handle other cognitive demands or being transformed for long-term storage. How does this temporary storage system work? Both auditory and visual rehearsal mechanisms have been proposed.

Many models of memory have incorporated an auditory or speech mechanism as part of working memory, with the most common label being the **phonological loop** (Baddeley, 1990), in which input sensory information is coded in terms of speech that can be repeated or rehearsed. The evidence for phonological coding and rehearsal comes from many sources, including the modality effects described before. In early experiments on STM, it was noted that the shorter the verbal description of the TBR material, the better the recall (Glanzer & Clark, 1963). In memory span experiments, letters that have similar-sounding names (B, C, E) are more often confused in recall even when they are presented visually (Conrad & Hull, 1964).

Baddeley (1990) has proposed a visual working memory system that he calls the "visuo-spatial sketch pad," which maintains visual imagery and spatial information. Supporting evidence comes from the ability to rotate three-dimensional figures mentally and choose between normal and mirror-image alternatives (Shepard & Metzler, 1971).

Retrieval from STM

Once information is stored in STM, how is that information used to answer questions? A variant of the "yes-no" recognition procedure known as **memory scanning** has been developed to study retrieval from STM (Sternberg, 1966, 1969). The memory scanning procedure also illustrates the use of response or **reaction time** (RT) to measure variation in memory performance even when recall is perfect. In Sternberg's procedure, subjects are given a brief list of items called a "memory set" (e.g., the digits 8, 5, 2, 7). Because the number of items in the set is chosen to be well within the memory span of approximately seven items, the subject can easily hold them in memory. Instead of asking the subject to recall all the items from the memory set, the experimenter shows a single item and the subject must push a button to respond "yes," indicating that the number was one of the items in the set or another button to respond "no," it wasn't.

Because most subjects can perform this task without making any mistakes, accuracy data are not very informative. So, the subject's reaction time—the time between presentation of the test stimulus and the response (usually pushing one of two buttons

marked "yes" and "no")—is the primary dependent variable. RT is a common response measure in other areas of psychology like perception and psychophysics, problem solving, and decision making. (See box 7.4.)

Sternberg was interested in how variations in RT correspond to variations in the number of items in the set as a way of telling him about the processing that goes on in retrieval from STM. He suggested three processing strategies that might be used by subjects to decide if a presented number was a member of the memory set (see figure 7.7). According to a **parallel processing** hypothesis, the subject can examine everything in STM at one time with no more effort than it takes to look at part of it. This hypothesis leads to the prediction that variations in the number of items in the set will not affect RT as long as the memory span is not reached (panel a of figure 7.7). According to the **serial processing** hypothesis, the subject can examine only one item in the memory set at a time. This hypothesis predicts an increase in RT as the number of items in the set increases. On trials where the test item is not part of the original set, the subject must compare the items in the set one at a time with the test item before responding "no." However, on positive trials where the test item is one of the items in the set, the subject must compare individual items in STM with the test item before coming up with a "match" and responding "yes." Sternberg's (1966) data support the serial hypothesis and reject the parallel processing interpretation by showing that RT does increase as the size of the memory set increases, but there is still an additional question about the nature of the serial scanning process.

Clearly, a subject must check every item before responding "no." But if the memory set does contain a match to the test item, does the subject stop the scanning process and respond as soon as the match is encountered (a "self-terminating" search) or complete the scanning process and check all items before responding (an "exhaustive" search)? The two possibilities produce two clearly different predictions about the relation between RTs for positive and negative responses as shown in panels

Use of Reaction Time (RT) Measures

When the ultimate response to a stimulus varies little across experimental conditions, reaction time (RT) measures often provide the best means of understanding the processes governing the response. In recognition memory tasks the RT may include the time required to perform such processes as perceiving a test stimulus and comparing it to items in the memory set. RT should reflect the time to perform these processes.

The use of RT measures can be traced back to the early work of Donders (1862), who devised a "subtractive procedure" for using RT to investigate psychological processes. Suppose there are two tasks, X and Y, in which task Y includes all of task X plus some other component Q (i.e., Y = X + Q). If we measure RT for the completion of tasks X and Y, and then subtract the two, we can derive the time it took for component Q even though Q

was not directly observable. In order for this logic to be correct, the time to complete each component must not overlap, a requirement that is often difficult to prove. (See Sternberg, 1969, for a sophisticated, modern treatment of the Donders method.)

In the Sternberg (1969) memory-scanning example in the text, the assumption of separate time for each step is easier to accept because the same task (matching target and memory set numbers) must be repeated for each number held in memory. Therefore, the difference in RTs for different set sizes can be subtracted to estimate the time for each comparison. The linear increase in RT as the number of items held in STM increases gives us more confidence that the function describes how items in STM are scanned.

---

b and c of figure 7.7. For the exhaustive search, "yes" and "no" responses should show the same increase in RT as the set size increases because the same number of items must be checked in both cases. However, for a self-terminating search, only about half of the items must be checked before a "yes" response, so positive responses should be faster than negative responses with the difference between "yes" and "no" responses increasing as the set size increases. For example, if the set size is four, all four must be checked before a "no" response is made. If the memory set contains the test item, one-fourth of the time it will be in each of the four possible positions. Hence, one-fourth of the time only one item must be checked, producing a very fast "yes," and one-fourth of the time, all four items must be checked, producing a "yes" as slow as a "no" response. On average, 2.5 items must be checked before a positive response can be made. (Thought question: If the set size is N, what is the average number of items that must be checked to find a positive match?)

Although it may seem more efficient to use a self-terminating search, Sternberg's and hundreds of later experiments clearly indicate that we scan STM with a serial, exhaustive search as demonstrated by the parallel RT functions for positive and negative responses as a function of set size (as shown in panel b of figure 7.7). Note that the slope of the function can be interpreted as the rate of scanning STM, in the range of 40–50 msec/item, and the intercept represents all other information processing components including perceiving and encoding the stimulus and executing the response.

Storing and Retrieving Information from Long-Term Memory

At the beginning of this chapter, we examined one kind of long-term memory and how it was affected by interference from similar materials. Because early memory theorists from Ebbinghaus on were primarily interested in the origins of memory and the most

FIGURE 7.7 Three possible outcomes of the Sternberg memory-scanning experiment: (a) parallel processing of all items in STM, (b) serial exhaustive processing, and (c) serial, self-terminating search of STM.

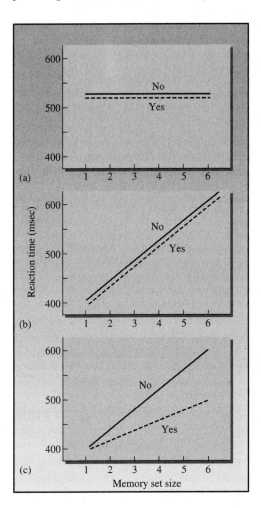

a discussion of organizational factors, we will briefly consider methods for studying state-dependent memory, imagery, and implicit memory.

Episodic and Semantic Memory

In the last section, figure 7.6 showed a model of memory in which the long-term store included both "episodic" and "semantic" information. According to Tulving (1972) who made this distinction, **episodic memory** refers to the records of an individual's personal experiences, whereas **semantic memory** refers to the accumulated information and rules necessary for the use of language. Tulving further described semantic memory as "a mental thesaurus, organized knowledge a person possesses about words and other verbal symbols, their meaning and referents. . . ." Thus semantic memory is involved in the understanding of the meaning of the language contained in episodic memory. Semantic memory is less prone to forgetting: you may forget the distinction between retroactive and proactive inhibition but you are able to reread boxes 7.1 and 7.2 and understand the meanings of the definitions contained there. In contrast, episodic memory requires a personal record of experience. Knowing the meaning of "horse" is a reflection of semantic memory; knowing the last time you saw a horse or encountered the word "horse" is an example of episodic memory. Therefore, most of the early research with interference theory was concerned with episodic memory.

A critical component of semantic memory is that it depends on understanding and meaning. Because information we understand well appears to be resistant to loss, semantic information is easier to acquire and more slowly forgotten than episodic material. Semantic knowledge also appears to be relatively independent of contextual situation; we know the meaning of the word *horse* regardless of where we are or what we are doing. Box 7.5 describes an interesting real-world phenomenon of long-term memory when semantic memory momentarily fails us, the "tip-of-the-tongue" phenomenon, and how it can be studied in the laboratory.

basic phenomena of retention, they tended to ignore complex factors that shape human cognitive abilities. In particular, by concentrating on verbal, rote retention, they minimized the influence of organization and meaning in increasing our ability to retain large amounts of factual information. After introducing the fundamental distinction between episodic and semantic memory, and continuing with

BOX 7.5

The "Tip-of-the-Tongue" Phenomenon

A phenomenon of long-term memory that we have all experienced is the **"tip-of-the-tongue"** phenomenon. This occurs when you are unable to recall a name, word, or other fact that you're sure you know but just can't seem to be able to get out. You may be able to recall it at a later time and you would almost surely recognize it if you heard it. You may even be able to recall the first letter or initial sound.

As we are seeing throughout this text, a particularly interesting—in this case, even tormenting—real-world phenomenon often motivates controlled research. Such is the case with tip of the tongue (TOT). Brown and McNeill (1966) successfully induced the TOT state in some subjects by presenting them with a definition of an uncommon English word and asking for the word. The researchers then encouraged the subjects who experienced the TOT state to give all of the words that come to mind. Typically, some of the words given were similar

in meaning to the target (e.g., "protractor" for "sextant") and others were similar in sound and spelling to the target (e.g., "sextet"). Subjects often remembered the first letter or the number of syllables in a word.

The semantic confusions show that words with similar meaning can be thought of as being stored and/or retrieved together or substituted for each other. The similar sounding items show that perceptual descriptions of words are stored along with their meaning. In sum then, a laboratory study was able to demonstrate that we can have partial information—either perceptual or conceptual—about an item to be recalled and that this underlies our common experience of having the correct answer "on the tip of our tongue." The nature of this partial information provides insight into long-term memory. Retrieval of information from long-term memory may occur on a piece-by-piece basis and sometimes not all the pieces can be found.

Cues and Context

Studies on retrieval from memory often focus on the process of **cuing**—the role of cues in retrieving information. These studies manipulate the relationship between cues present at the time of information acquisition and cues present at the time of recall. For example, in a study by Thomson and Tulving (1970), subjects were presented with a list of to-be-remembered words, either presented alone (e.g., BLACK), or paired with a weak associate (e.g., train, BLACK), or paired with a strong associate (e.g., white, BLACK). At recall each group was divided into three subgroups based on whether they were to recall the words without cues, recall them cued with the weak associates, or recall them with the strong associates. Free recall performance is summarized in table 7.1. Note that when the cues were the same at presentation and at recall, performance was better; when the contextual cues were

changed, even to stronger associations, recall decreased. This principle, known as **encoding specificity,** is a powerful factor in recall. (Thought question: Contextual cues have very little effect on recognition performance. Why?)

(If you expected your final exam to cover largely lecture material, would you want to take it in the regular classroom or somewhere else?)

The influence of cues and context applies to internal states such as emotional mood and drug use as well as external states such as whether acquisition of material and recall testing are conducted under the same physical conditions. These effects are called **state dependent retrieval** and refer to the improved memory when recall and learning occur in the same context. A favorite example comes from a 1931 Charlie Chaplin movie called *City Lights*. Charlie's depression-era character, the Little Tramp, helps an inebriated millionaire return home

TABLE 7.1   Cuing Effects in Free Recall

| | NUMBER OF ITEMS RECALLED | | |
| | CUES AT RECALL | | |
Presentation Condition	No Cues	Weak Associates	Strong Associates
No Associates	14.1	11.1	19.0
Weak Associates	10.7	15.7	13.9
Strong Associates	12.2	9.2	20.2

From: Thomson and Tulving, 1970.

safely after a particularly adventurous night on the town. The millionaire rewards Charlie by making him an honored guest in his home. The next morning, the now sober millionaire spots Charlie wearing his pajamas and sleeping in his bed, and unceremoniously throws him out. As a "running gag" throughout the movie, every time the millionaire is drunk and sees Charlie he treats him like a long-lost friend, and every time the millionaire is sober he treats him with disdain, much to Charlie's continuing confusion.

State-dependent retrieval has been demonstrated with many drugs (Eich, 1980) and with emotional states (Bower, 1981). One of the most unusual and dramatic controlled studies was in an experiment by Godden and Baddeley (1975), in which they had deep-sea divers memorize a list of words either on dry land or underwater. They later recalled the words in the same or opposite environment. As shown in figure 7.8, the learning and recall context significantly affected memory performance.

Interaction of Episodic and Semantic Information
One of the noteworthy features of the cuing data is that the effectiveness of a cue supplied at retrieval depends critically on the circumstances of encoding, suggesting that the interaction of semantic and episodic memory may play a role in everyday memory function. Consider a study of eyewitness testimony by Loftus and Palmer (1974). Students were

FIGURE 7.8   State-dependent memory (Godden & Baddeley, 1975).

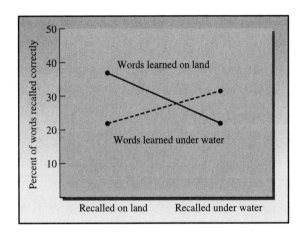

shown a film depicting a multiple-car accident and then questioned about what they had seen. One group was asked, "How fast were the cars going when they smashed into each other?" Another group was asked the same question, but with the word "hit" substituted for "smashed into." One week later the two groups were asked, "Did you see any broken glass?" The group given the verb "smashed" reported higher estimates of speed and were more apt to report seeing broken glass. The cue provided in the question thus altered—or became incorporated into—the memory trace at the time of retrieval. In other words the semantic knowledge implied by the difference between the words "smashed" and "hit" influenced the quality of episodic memory. A similar process has been suggested to play a role in a recent controversy: the question is whether "repressed" memories of childhood abuse brought out in therapy sessions are actual episodic memories or are influenced by suggestions or questions from therapists, distorting later recall.

Recognition Memory

As we have just seen, recall performance depends on the quality of the contextual cues provided to aid retrieval of information from memory. To take the argument to its extreme, we can also test memory by providing the strongest cue of all—the TBR item itself. In a **recall test,** the subject must generate the correct response; in a **recognition test,** possible responses are provided and the subject must decide whether or not any particular item was previously learned.

One way to think of these two measures is to consider "fill-in-the-blank" questions and "multiple-choice" questions on an examination. With recall, you have to produce or fill in the appropriate response. With recognition, you must pick out the appropriate response from a list or set of possible responses. Conventional wisdom says that multiple-choice (recognition) tests are easier than fill-in-the-blank (recall) tests. This also jibes with theories of memory that assume that recall is a two-stage process of generating possible responses and selecting one, compared to recognition, which involves only the selection stage. Nevertheless, there are examples of tests of retention where more errors occur with a recognition procedure than with a recall procedure using the same material. In these instances, the alternative responses on the recognition test are so similar to each other as to cause great confusion or misleading associations.

The characteristics of recognition tests have been examined by Murdock (1963). As Murdock's analysis shows and as any student who has taken a multiple-choice test realizes, performance in a multiple-choice recognition test is not simply a matter of picking the correct response from the list of alternatives. Murdock suggests that subjects often behave as if they first eliminate wrong alternatives and then randomly select an answer from the remaining ones. Subjects' partial knowledge may help them to eliminate some alternatives and change the characteristics of the multiple-choice recognition task.

A common recognition procedure in studies of memory is to present a list of items to be remembered with some items later repeated, mixed with new items. The subject's task is to recognize which items are "old" and which are "new." For example, in a procedure developed by Shepard and Teghtsoonian (1961), subjects are presented with a long list of three-digit numbers. To each number subjects are required to respond "old" or "new" depending on whether or not they remember having seen that item before. Each three-digit number in the sequence was presented twice with the number of intervening items varied between the first and second presentation. They found that the probability of a correct response to an old item was a decreasing function of the number of interpolated items. But even after 60 interpolations, performance was still well above chance. They also found that the false alarm rate, saying "old" to a new item, also increased across trials from 0 percent to an asymptote of approximately 30 percent. The false alarm rate may be taken as an indication of the subject's response bias to saying "old."

The two kinds of errors in a task like this are akin to "misses" and "false alarms" in studies of signal detection. In fact, a variant of signal detection analysis has been useful in analyzing performance in recognition memory. In this conceptualization, discriminating between old and new items is based on perceptions of "familiarity." In general, old items will seem more familiar than new items but there will be some overlap between the perceptions of familiarity for old and new items. The subject is assumed to adopt a criterion cutoff point for responding "old" or "new." (Look back at figure 4.7 in the chapter on Perception and Psychophysics and compare it with figure 7.9. Consider the old items as

FIGURE 7.9   A representation of signal detection theory applied to recognition memory.

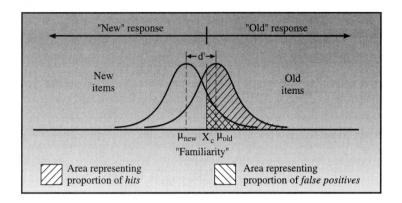

"signals" and new items as "noise." How do you think "similarity" would affect the separation of the two curves?)

Organization in Memory

As should be clear from both personal experience and studies cited previously, subjects bring to the learning laboratory skills and habits that they attempt to use in the learning of the experimental task. The free recall memory task and the free recall learning task are most useful in analyzing a subject's individual characteristics. As we noted earlier, in free recall, subjects are permitted to recall lists of words presented to them in any order they wish. If the items are presented once and only once and then recalled, we usually call this a free recall memory experiment. If the items are presented and recalled several times then it is a learning experiment.

The defining characteristic of free recall tasks is the removal of any restriction on the order of output of the responses. When the lists are presented more than once they may be in either the same or a varied order, although the varied order is more common. The subjects are not required to reproduce the items in the same order as they were presented. Therefore, the groupings that do occur in the output sequence reflect the subject's manipulations of the material. The researcher's task is to analyze response patterns to discover the origins of organizational strategies. At least four sources of subjects' preexperimental habits and cognitive skills that influence free recall performance can be identified: inter-item associations, clustering, subjective organization, and contextual constraints.

Inter-Item Associations

One basis for organization of memory flows from the simple word associations that we considered in the last chapter. Verbal associations among words may both facilitate and impair memory performance. On the one hand, strong associations between items may lead to a false recognition or recall of an item that was never presented. By the same means, inter-item associations may also facilitate and help organize the recall of material that was presented. For example, inclusion of three of the four compass directions (e.g., north, south, east) will both aid recall of the presented three and increase the likelihood of false recall of the fourth.

Clustering

Closely related to the influence of inter-item associations is the influence of clustering in free recall. **Clustering** refers to the categorical grouping of items in recall and may occur for reasons other than simple inter-item association. For example, suppose a list to be recalled is composed of several groups of words, each of which falls into a distinct separable category, such as animals, minerals, countries, and names of presidents. The items may be presented in a random order so that members of the same category follow each other with no more than a chance probability. However, in recalling the list, most subjects will show a pronounced tendency to group the words by category. The occurrence of clustering in response output can be taken as an index of organization by subjects of the presented items. However, if response clustering does not occur in recall this does not necessarily indicate a failure to organize the materials. Instead, the categories used by the subject may be different from those defined by the experimenter.

Bousfield and Cohen (1953) found an increase in the amount of clustering as the number of presentations increased. What about the number of different clusters used in recall? It might be expected that recall would decline as the number of categories increase due to the difficulty in remembering all the categories. On the other hand, if the total list length is held constant, increasing the number of categories means decreasing the number of instances per category, which would tend to reduce the amount of interference within the same category. To the extent that items within the same category compete with each other at the time of recall, one might expect that a fewer number of items per category would increase the overall retention. Generally, both number of categories and number of items per category have been shown to be important (Bousfield & Cohen, 1956).

In a study by Mandler (1967), subjects were asked to sort a set of randomly selected words into as many subsets as they wished based on any conceptual relations they could discover among them. Performance on a free recall task was found to increase as a direct function of the number of sets used for sorting, up to about 7 sets. Mandler concluded that while there are upper limits on long-term storage, the amount of stored material can be increased by organizing or chunking items into functional units.

Subjective Organization

Subjective organization (Tulving, 1962) refers to the tendency of unrelated items to be recalled together on repeated trials. Subjective organization (SO) differs from category clustering in that the organization that occurs in category clustering can be identified and measured because the categories are known to the experimenter. In SO the response groupings that define the organization are generated and known only to the individual subjects. The amount of SO can be inferred from the consistency in the order of recall, either for a group of subjects on a single trial or more commonly for a single subject across trials. Because the organization depends only on the characteristics provided by the subject, there is a great deal of difficulty in measuring SO. The index of SO devised by Tulving is based on concepts derived from information theory and is essentially a measure of redundancy. It asks how predictable the sequence of items is from one output to the next given the number of words the subjects is able to recall. Tulving shows that the index of subjective organization increases as a function of trials and subjects are highly redundant from one trial to the next in the order of recall. Tulving has argued that the development of subjective units is responsible for the progressive improvements in recall. Subjects are able to improve their recall performance by clustering their items into categories and recalling the categories.

Contextual Constraints

The fourth organizational factor in free recall is provided by contextual constraints. Contextual constraints refer to the limitations placed on performance by the language knowledge that the subject brings to the laboratory. Language constrains the choice of particular words as a function of the preceding verbal context. The longer the prior sequence, the greater is the degree of constraint on the word that may follow. Hence, as Miller and Selfridge (1950) demonstrated, by scrambling the order of words in a sentence, the closer the approximation of a sequence of words to actual language, the better is the free recall of that sequence.

The lowest approximation to natural language is constructed by a completely random sequence of words, the next highest by maintaining pairs of words, the next by word triplets, and so forth. The effect of contextual constraints on memory appears to be most evident at the lower levels of approximation to English. There appears to be very little difference in free recall between English text and higher order approximations to it. Apparently, linguistic habits are most important in maintaining and facilitating the short range associations that occur between the most adjacent words. However, when order of presentation must be maintained, English text is better than the higher order approximation to it (Marks & Jack, 1952).

Imagery

Much of the modern research in the area of **imagery** began with Allen Paivio who theorizes that there are two basic cognitive systems for encoding, organizing, storing, and retrieving information, one verbal and the other imaginal (Paivio, 1969). According to this theory, words that readily evoke distinct images are better remembered because they are readily encoded in both a verbal and an imaginal representation system, whereas words that do not evoke ready images are coded only in the verbal system. In one test of this theory, Paivio and Csapo (1969) employed pictures of nameable objects, concrete words, and abstract words in a variety of memory tasks. (Note that in comparing materials that vary on imagery, it is important to control—hold constant—other features such as meaningfulness and frequency of everyday usage.) On free recall tasks, pictures and concrete words were recalled better than abstract words and this superiority increased with slower rates of presentation, presumably because of the increased opportunity to access imaginal codes. In tasks dependent on serial order (memory span and serial learning), pictures were

inferior to words at fast rates of presentation but not at slow rates, presumably because of the comparative difficulty of gaining access to verbal codes with pictorial stimuli.

Research on the effect of imagery on memory has produced a controversy about the fundamental basis of knowledge representation in human cognition. On the one side, we have growing evidence that properties of mental images influence what we know, remember, and decide about concepts. Consider, for example, experiments by Kosslyn (1975; 1983) in which subjects were asked simple "yes-no" questions about properties of pairs of familiar animals. Before they answered the questions, the subjects were told to imagine the two animals, say an elephant and a rabbit, next to each other, on a television screen. Obviously, the larger elephant would occupy more of the space on the screen than the smaller rabbit. In another condition, a rabbit and a fly were compared, so that the rabbit was the larger of the two images. The subjects were asked a number of easy questions about the animals: "Does an elephant have ears?" "Does a rabbit have a tail?" "Does a fly have wings?" Questions about the rabbit were answered much faster when the rabbit was imagined next to a fly than next to an elephant, suggesting that relative image size affected the ease of retrieving information from memory. Other theorists, like Pylyshyn (1981), argue that subjects do not directly examine mental images, but maintain propositional information in memory and compute how the visual information should be available as a function of size.

Questions about the nature of processing mental images raise an important concern about *demand characteristics* in cognitive experiments. Consider a study by Intons-Peterson and Roskos-Ewoldsen (1989) in which students were instructed to take an imaginary walk around campus and to signal by pushing a button when they arrived at a particular location. In one condition, they were to imagine that they were carrying a balloon, in another, that they were carrying a cannonball. Not too surprisingly, the subjects took longer to report traveling the same distance in their imaginary trip when they were carrying the cannonball than when carrying the balloon. Is the time difference a result of the differences in the images or because the subjects used semantic information about the difference in weight of cannonballs and balloons and adjusted their reports? In other words, do subjects use semantic knowledge to infer what the "proper" response should be and respond to that implicit "demand" from the experimenter? What control procedures might be used to eliminate demand characteristics as an explanation for the observed behavior?

Implicit versus Explicit Memory

A more recent distinction in memory is between "explicit" and "implicit" memory (Roediger, 1990). **Explicit memory** refers to the conscious recollection of specific events in one's life. **Implicit memory** refers to information from the past that influences later behavior without being directly retrieved. Most of the studies described so far in this chapter are tests of explicit memory because they ask people to consciously recall or recognize specific material. By contrast, implicit memory tests attempt to show the effect of material learned in the laboratory in the absence of overt recall.

Tests of implicit memory use a priming procedure that often resembles word puzzles. For example, subjects might be given the first three letters of a word, such as THI _____ , and be asked to complete the fragment with the first word that comes to mind, or they might be asked to name five animals that begin with the letter "A." Before the priming test, subjects are exposed to a list of words that contains a word like THINK or "antelope," which fits the test stimulus. Results show that subjects' performance is spontaneously improved by the prior exposure even though they were not asked to remember the studied words and may not even be aware of their influence. Compared to other subjects who are asked to recall the presented words (explicit memory), subjects tested with the fragment completion task show less decrease in performance days later, demonstrating a functional dissociation between the two types of memory (Tulving, Schacter, & Stark, 1982). Even

more amazing is the observation that individuals suffering from severe amnesia, who could not recall words presented earlier in explicit tests, performed as well as normal subjects in implicit tests of fragment completion (Graf & Schacter, 1985).

Selected Topics in Memory

The use of implicit memory testing in amnesia patients is an example of how special populations can sometimes be used to reveal fundamental differences in behavioral processing. We turn now to a consideration of situations in which special subjects, testing conditions, or environmental demands can be used to gain new knowledge about memory processing. Because our emphasis is more on methodology than on theory, the examples are selected to illustrate a variety of methods rather than a comprehensive review of memory processing.

Case Study 1: The Mind of a Mnemonist
Sometimes, analyzing the behavior of a memory expert or **mnemonist** can provide helpful hints. In one of the classic examples of a "case study" in psychology, Alexander Luria in 1968 provided a detailed report compiled over a period of years of the unusual memory of a Russian newspaper reporter referred to as "S." S was observed to remember an incredible amount of information on a variety of topics and retain it for long periods of time without much apparent effort. For example, he was able to remember a long grocery list by imagining himself walking down a familiar street and visualizing each item at some specific point along the way. He might "see" the bacon lying in a patch of grass. In order to remember the list at a later time, he simply repeated his imaginary walk to take a look at the objects where he had placed them. In a similar vein, he was able to memorize a complex mathematical formula by placing each successive symbol in a story with strong visual content. While only studying the formula for seven minutes, he was able to recall it perfectly some *fifteen years later*!

Would we all want to become like S? Probably not. His heavy reliance on mental imagery often interfered with S's ability to function in the world. His

BOX 7.6

Memory Aids

Here is a sample of well-known mnemonic devices.

Use of the *method of loci* was bolstered by recent research on memory, but this mnemonic device was actually developed around the year 500 B.C. by the Greek poet Simonides. This method involves forming an image of a familiar room or other space, and imagining the to-be-remembered items each in a specific location. You will of course recognize this as the method used by Luria's subject S. Demonstrations of the effectiveness of this method in college students utilized instructions to use familiar places on a mental walk around their campus as loci to learn a list of words presented only once. Recall rates of as high as 95 percent were found after 24 hours for lists of 40 words.

The *pegword* method also relies on imagery, but employs familiar objects rather than spatial locations. This method starts by teaching subjects to associate familiar words or "pegwords" with numbers by means of a rhyme such as "one is a bun," "two is a shoe," "three is a tree," "four is a door," and so-forth. The to-be-remembered words can then be "hung" on the pegs through visual images. For example, if the required list begins with the words "plate, flower, snake," the images could be a bun on a plate, a flower growing in a shoe, a snake in a tree. The idea is that you can remember the list by going

through the pegwords and noting what object you placed on each peg. The pegwords, like the loci in the previous method, then serve as *mediators* just as in the A–B, B–C, A–C positive transfer paradigm described in the preceding chapter. In this case, A refers to the serial position of the to-be-remembered word, B is the pegword, and C is the target word.

Another kind of mnemonic which relies on imagery is the *keyword* method. This method uses visual imagery to link a keyword with another word. Suppose that you meet a man named Gus and you want to remember his name for future occasions. A useful keyword here would be one that rhymes with Gus and conjures up a distinct visual image that you can link with Gus. Suppose you notice that Gus has the habit of running his fingers through his hair. The keyword "muss" could then help you remember Gus as the man who musses his hair. Of course, it might not always be as easy to come up with a good keyword as in the "Gus-muss" example. But given the difficulty most of us have with remembering names, it may be well worth the effort.

Creative individuals can construct their own memory aids based on the basic principle of using images to facilitate retrieval of required information.

---

tendency to conjure up a long chain of thoughts often made it difficult for him to understand simple communications. After failing at several jobs, S, not surprisingly, became a professional theatrical memory performer.

Nevertheless, the dramatic use of imagery by S and others like him illustrate the extreme range of human memory abilities and encouraged the study and development of highly stylized memory aids or **mnemonics.** A few of these are described in box 7.6. Try them for yourself.

Case Study 2: Learning a Memory Skill

It is not clear how Luria's S developed his extraordinary mnemonic skill, but one very devoted undergraduate student at Carnegie Mellon University has

demonstrated what concentrated effort over a long period of time will accomplish. As we have observed earlier, the average memory span for numbers is about seven. We have also discussed the use of organization to enhance recall of information. One simple form of organization is called **chunking** and refers to reorganizing sequences of items, say numbers like 7-2-5-8-1-3-3-9-4 into units like 7-2-5, 8-1-3, 3-9-4, which may be more meaningful and more easily remembered.

Chase and Ericsson (1981) reported on a student called SF who used a chunking strategy and much practice to increase his memory span from 8 to 80 numbers! SF was a runner who used his knowledge and interest in running times to make sense of clusters of 3-, 4-, and 5-digit numbers, translating them into sensible running times for various events. Over the course of almost daily practice sessions for two years, SF developed an organizational scheme for classifying random numbers into running times for events, then using the race events as a retrieval system for recalling the numbers. His incredible effort shows how average human memory can be greatly extended under special circumstances.

Special Circumstances: Flashbulb Memories

There are times, however, when our memories are enhanced not by training or great effort, but by unusual circumstances beyond our control. Consider the phenomenon of **flashbulb memory**—the registration in long-term memory of irrelevant detailed information associated with an event of enormous importance. In 1977, Brown and Kulik asked Americans, "Do you recall the circumstances in which you first heard that John F. Kennedy had been shot?" A high proportion of respondents recalled with confidence the circumstances in which they had received the news some 14 years earlier, and were able to do so with great clarity. Try this example on your parents and try it on yourself using more recent examples such as the shooting of John Lennon or the Challenger disaster. Likely factors in the creation of such memories are the level of surprise, the intensity of the emotional reaction, and the personal consequences to the individual. However, there is one inherent difficulty in doing research on flashbulb memory—verifying the accuracy of the subject's descriptions. What other factors can you think of that would influence the vividness of flashbulb memories?

Age-Related Changes in Memory

It is commonly assumed that as we get older we will experience greater difficulties in learning new information and recalling past events. However, apart from the obvious effects of diseases such as Alzheimer's, the influence of the aging process on memory is not so easy to assess. A major methodological issue in all studies on aging is whether to conduct a **longitudinal study,** in which the same individual is

studied over a long period of time, or a **cross-sectional study,** in which groups of varying ages are compared at the same time. The first approach is the most direct but, with some notable exceptions, requires more time and patience than most researchers are willing to spend. The second approach poses some problems in interpretation of data. For example, if an older group shows poorer memory, is it because they were more poorly educated in memorial skills than the younger group, because their skills deteriorated over time, or because the TBR material is more familiar to the younger group?

Converging evidence from studies with varying techniques is especially important in this area. One consistent pattern of findings seems to be that short-term memory for verbal material does *not* deteriorate with age but that the long-term memory store or the ability to store material in long-term memory does deteriorate with age. Consider a study by Heron and Craik (1964) comparing memory for Finnish and English digits in groups of young and old English-speaking subjects. First, the two age groups were matched on their digit span for the unfamiliar Finnish digits. Then, when the two groups were compared on their memory span for English digits, the performance of the older subjects was worse than the younger subjects. Even when the ability to remember meaningless material was held constant, older subjects apparently made less effective use of familiar information.

Now consider a study using the **dichotic listening task.** In this task subjects wear earphones connected to a stereo tape recorder. One message is played through one earphone and a completely different message is played through the other earphone. (Imagine being at a noisy party and having conversations going on both sides of you.) The subject is asked to pay attention to one of the messages and to repeat it back aloud as it is being played. As you might have guessed, subjects are stopped unexpectedly in the middle of the task and asked to recall the "unattended" message. This recall is typically poor, suggesting that the unattended message decays rapidly. Age-related differences on this task were investigated by Inglis and Caird (1963). As age varied from 20 to 60, no difference was found in recalling items in the attended ear, but recall from the unattended ear grew progressively worse with age.

Both sets of results can be interpreted to mean that old subjects are just as good as young ones at retaining sensory information such as sounds on a short-term basis but are less able to process information for long-term memory. Supporting these conclusions are results showing different serial position curves for younger and older subjects. Older subjects perform as well as younger subjects on the last few items on a list but older subjects perform worse on the beginning and middle items suggesting a greater deficiency with age in long-term memory (Kaszniak, Poon, & Riege, 1986).

Drug-Induced Memory Impairments

Similar effects on STM and LTM have been found when comparing sober and intoxicated subjects' performance on a free recall task (Jones & Jones, 1977). Subjects given alcohol prior to presentation of a list of 12 words recalled the last items as well as subjects given a placebo, but the alcohol group did poorer on the initial and middle items. Alcohol in the bloodstream apparently leads to difficulty in the transfer of information into long-term memory.

The effects of another drug, the tranquilizer diazepam (Valium), were investigated by Hinrichs, Ghoneim, and Mewaldt (1984) in a series of experiments. In one experiment, subjects studied and recalled one list of words prior to ingesting either a drug or placebo capsule, were then given a second list to study and recall, and then finally given a recall test of the first list. On the postdrug list, placebo subjects recalled significantly more words than diazepam subjects. However, diazepam subjects actually made significantly fewer errors than placebo subjects on delayed recall of the predrug list. In other words, diazepam reduced memory of information presented after its administration but it improved memory of predrug information. In another experiment in the series, subjects were given the predrug task and were later given a delayed recall test of that task following drug administration,

but were not given a second (interpolated) task. In this case there was no improved memory for the predrug task after receiving diazepam. This finding demonstrates that a source of interference is necessary to produce a reliable difference in predrug recall. A third experiment showed that learning of new materials was inhibited following administration of diazepam. The researchers concluded that it was the poor learning following administration of the drug that reduced the amount of new information available to interfere with prior learning. What started out looking like improved retention processes as a result of taking diazepam turned out to be due to a drug-induced learning deficit.

Memory-Based Social Judgments

There is growing interest in how memorial processes affect later impressions, judgments, and decisions. N. H. Anderson refers to this as **"functional memory."** The distinction can be understood by considering the following scenario. You meet someone at a party and in the course of conversation learn that they are committed to the same environmental causes that you are. You immediately like the person. The next time you see the person is six months later. You may recall the conversation on the environment and thereby renew your feeling of liking the person. On the other hand, you may retain only the recollection of liking the person, without remembering the reasons. In the latter case, the original conversation functioned to form an initial impression that may have a lasting effect.

Anderson (1991) summarizes a series of studies in which subjects are presented a series of person descriptions each composed of a set of personality trait adjectives. Each set consists of a unique sequence of positive traits (e.g., honest) and negative traits (e.g., deceitful). Subjects are asked to rate how much they would like or dislike each hypothetical person described by a set of adjectives. In one experiment subjects were also asked to recall the adjectives in a set. As shown in figure 7.10, the recall curve shows the traditional bowed serial position effect. By contrast, the judgment curve—a plot

FIGURE 7.10   **Evidence for separate judgment and verbal memories. Recall curve for adjectives in person description shows strong recency over the last six serial positions. Judgment curve for effect of these same adjectives in person impression shows marked primacy, with decreasing effects over serial positions. Contrast between recall recency and judgment primacy implies that person memory differs from verbal memory (Anderson, 1991).**

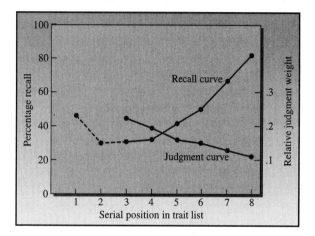

of the relative impact of adjectives at each serial position within a set—shows only a primacy effect. The earlier in the sequence an adjective appears, the greater the impact of that adjective on the likability judgment. It is therefore not the case that more easily recalled information necessarily has greater effect.

Anderson concludes that verbal stimuli function as momentary carriers of information or meaning that are integrated into the current judgment. Once this integration occurs, the verbal stimulus itself is no longer needed and is stored in a separate memory system.

In a second line of research a distinction is made between "on-line" and "memory-based" judgments. **On-line judgments** are those made immediately following presentation of the relevant information. **Memory-based judgments** are those in which judgments are required at a later time based on information that the subject does not originally think requires a judgment. In the one case, for example,

subjects read about different makes of cars while trying to decide which one they favor. In the other case, subjects read about the cars as an incidental task and then are later asked to compare them. In studying memory-based judgments, it is important to disguise the task so subjects do not realize that they will have to use the information at a later time. Hastie and Park (1986) found that judgments and recall of information were correlated in memory-based judgments but not in on-line judgments. In other words, when task demands do not force the subject to rely on memory to make judgments, there is no relationship between the judgment and what is recalled. These results, like Anderson's, reinforce the notion of two memory processes, one for reproductions and one for judgments.

Summary and Conclusions

In this chapter we emphasized methods for studying remembering and forgetting. From the early work of Ebbinghaus until about 1960, most of the research on memory emphasized retention of word lists over relatively long periods of time and the primary source of forgetting in long-term memory was thought to be interference from competing material.

Methods for studying interference are similar to transfer paradigms. The retroactive inhibition (RI) paradigm was developed to study the influence of acquiring new material on the ability to recall old material. This paradigm requires a control condition in which acquisition of new material is replaced by a neutral filler task. The proactive inhibition (PI) paradigm was developed to study the influence of prior learning on the recall of new material. A control condition is needed here to account for the effects of varying retention intervals. Both paradigms show that as the similarity increases between the two sets of material, the greater the decrement in recall for the experimental group compared to the control group.

An important issue in memory research is separating the influences of short-term and long-term memory processes. A popular method for studying short-term or immediate memory is the distractor technique, in which varying lengths of the retention interval are compared and the interval is filled with a task that prevents the subject from rehearsing the material to be remembered. The resulting plot of recall performance as a function of length of the retention interval is called a decay curve. Another method for studying short-term memory is the probe technique where the subject is stopped at various points in a list and asked to recall a subset of items or a single item such as the item that immediately followed the current item the last time the list was presented. A method for studying how much information is contained in short-term memory is the "memory span" method, which requires immediate recall of as many items as possible from a list of numbers or letters.

The bowed serial position effect in free recall is a reliable phenomenon that is thought to involve both short-term and long-term components. Enhanced recall of the last few items on a list is called a recency effect, which is thought to represent short-term memory. The recency effect disappears when a long retention interval is included. Superior recall of items at the beginning of the list is called a primacy effect, which is thought to represent long-term memory. This effect is reduced by factors that interfere with the ability to process the meaning of the to-be-remembered material.

One way to conceptualize the human memory system is to think of it as a succession of discrete stages such as sensory register, short-term store, and long-term store. This conceptualization provides a framework for studying processes related to the storage and retrieval of information from different sense modalities. An alternative conceptualization focuses on levels of processing. This framework has been used to distinguish between the effects of processing information at a deep level based on its meaning and the associations it produces, and processing information at a shallow level based on its sound or spelling.

Long-term memory can be divided according to many different characteristics, including episodic and semantic memory, explicit and implicit memory, recognition and recall features, and organizational strategies. As reflected in these distinctions, contemporary researchers are interested not only in the ability to reproduce to-be-remembered material, but in the role that prior learning plays on later recollections and actions.

Methods for studying how people organize information in free recall and how individuals develop extraordinary memories are useful for prescribing memory aids or mnemonics. Imagery is an important component of these aids. Memory as a dependent variable has been used to understand the effects of aging and the action of drugs such as alcohol and diazepam. Memory-based judgments have been used to study how information presented earlier in time affects later judgments and decisions.

Exercises

1. From a table of random numbers, pick out several sequences of 10 two-digit numbers. Investigate the effects on free recall of degree of learning by varying the amount of time you spend studying each sequence. How would you control for "learning-to-learn" effects (see chapter 6)?

2. Devise a procedure for studying "selective forgetting." That is, how would you teach someone to forget material that you don't want them to retain?

3. Construct a recognition memory test that you think would be more difficult than a recall test of the same material.

4. Note the difference in figure 7.5 between the serial position curves for serial recall (where subjects have to recall the items in the order presented) and free recall (where subjects can recall the items in any order). Describe and try to explain the difference.

5. Think of several "distractor" tasks to use when the main task consists of recalling a list of two-digit numbers. Use the criteria described in box 7.1.

6. Investigate the modality effect by giving two acquaintances the same free recall task presented in the visual mode to one person and the auditory mode to the other. Compare the serial position curves and compare the kinds of errors made by each respondent.

7. Using the same material and the same subjects as in number 6, devise and test memory aids like those described in box 7.6.

8. Which do you think affects you more in your personal life, retroactive inhibition (RI) or proactive inhibition (PI)? Explain why.

9. Discuss the pros and cons of the "longitudinal" approach and the "cross-sectional" approach to studying the aging process.

10. Describe examples in your own life of "on-line" and "memory-based" judgments.

Glossary

bowed-serial-position curve Plot of recall errors following a single trial on a free recall task; recall of the initial items (a primacy effect associated with long-term memory) and recall of the last items (a recency effect associated with short-term memory) are better than recall of the middle items. (p. 213)

chunking Reorganizing sequences of items into larger units or "chunks" that may be more meaningful and more easily remembered. (p. 229)

clustering In responding to items in free-recall, subjects tend to group the items by category. (p. 225)

cross-sectional study Study of age-related differences in memory in which groups of varying age are compared at the same time. This is to be contrasted with longitudinal studies in which the same group is examined at different points in time. (p. 230)

cuing The use of specific cues to aid in retrieving information. (p. 222)

decay Retention loss assumed to be due to internal biochemical or neurological events independent of intervening behavioral events. (p. 207)

dichotic listening task One message is presented to one ear and a different message is presented to the other ear. The subject is asked to pay attention to one of the messages but is unexpectedly asked to recall the "unattended" message. (p. 230)

distractor techniques Use of an irrelevant activity (such as counting backward by 3s) following presentation of the to-be-recalled material; designed to prevent rehearsal during the retention interval. (p. 210)

echoic memory Information retained in auditory sensory memory. (p. 218)

encoding specificity The relation between cues at presentation and cues at recall; when the cues are the same, performance is better and when the cues are changed, recall decreases. (p. 222)

episodic memory The records of an individual's personal experiences. (p. 221)

explicit memory The conscious recollection of specific events in one's life. (p. 228)

flashbulb memory The long-term retention of detailed information associated with an event of extreme importance. (p. 230)

functional dissociation Distinguishing between different types of memory by showing that they are influenced by different independent variables. (p. 210)

functional memory How memorial processes affect later impressions, judgments, and decisions. This is to be distinguished from reproductive memory, which is the literal reproduction or recognition of the to-be-remembered material. (p. 231)

iconic memory Information retained in visual sensory memory. (p. 218)

imagery Words that readily evoke distinct images are better remembered because they are easier to encode. (p. 227)

implicit memory Information from the past that can be retrieved without making any conscious effort. (p. 228)

interference Retention loss due to learning other material. (p. 207)

levels of processing The assumption that memory is dependent on the level or depth of information processing; deep processing leads to good memory. (p. 217)

longitudinal study Study in which the same individual is followed over a long period of time. (p. 230)

memory scanning Procedure for studying recognition memory in which the experimenter shows a single test item and the subject indicates whether it was one of the items from a previously presented list. (p. 219)

memory span Subjects are asked to recall all of the items on a short list of items. (p. 212)

memory-based judgments Judgments are required at a later time based on information that the subject does not originally think requires a judgment. This is to be contrasted with on-line judgments, which are made immediately following presentation of the information. (p. 232)

mnemonics Highly stylized memory aids such as the method of loci, the pegword method, and the keyword method. (p. 229)

mnemonist A memory expert. (p. 228)

modality effect Comparison of recall when items are presented in the auditory or visual mode. (p. 215)

multistore models Conceptualization of a multistructure memory storage system, such as a three-component model of sensory register, short-term store, and long-term store. (p. 215)

on-line judgments Judgments made immediately following presentation of the relevant information; to be contrasted with memory-based judgments, which are required at a later time. (p 232)

parallel processing Hypothesis that the subject can simultaneously examine all of the items in short-term memory at one time. (p. 219)

phonologic loop Hypothesized component of working memory in which sensory information is coded in terms of speech that can be repeated or rehearsed. (p. 219)

primacy effect In free-recall, performance is better on the initial items than on later items. (p. 213)

proactive inhibition Decrement in recall of a second list attributed to the prior learning of the first list. (p. 208)

probe techniques Sampling procedures in which different parts of a list of to-be-recalled material are tested at different times. (p. 211)

reaction time Time between presentation of a test stimulus and the response. (p. 219)

recall tests Tests of memory in which the subject has to produce the appropriate response. (p. 224)

recency effect In free-recall, performance is better on the last few items than on the preceding items. (p. 213)

recognition tests Tests of memory in which the subject has to pick out the appropriate response from a set of possible responses. (p. 224)

retention interval The time between the end of the presentation of a to-be-recalled list and the beginning of the test of recall. (p. 215)

retroactive inhibition Decrement in recall of an initial list attributed to the interpolated learning of a second list. (p. 208)

running memory span Subjects, presented with a list of items, are stopped at some point and asked to recall as many items backward in the list as possible. (p. 213)

savings score Percentage reduction in number of trials to relearn a task that was previously learned. (p. 207)

semantic memory The accumulated information and rules necessary for the use of language. (p. 221)

serial processing Hypothesis that the subject can examine only one item in the memory set at a time. (p. 219)

state dependent retrieval Memory is improved when recall and learning occur in the same context such as the same emotional mood or drug state. (p. 222)

steady-state memory test Subjects are required to make repeated continuous demands on memory, such as being presented with a long series of paired-associate items. (p. 213)

"tip-of-the-tongue" When you are unable to recall something that you're sure you know but can't seem to produce. (p. 222)

working memory Another name for short-term memory store; emphasizes manipulation of current information. (p. 216)

Suggested Readings

Most of the readings and resources suggested at the end of chapter 6 are also relevant here, but the past two decades have seen an emphasis on human memory with many textbooks using that title. Some recent excellent textbooks include: Baddeley (1990), *Human memory: Theory and practice*, a chatty review of theories and applications; Ellis and Hunt (1993), *Fundamentals of cognitive psychology* (5th ed.), a scholarly systematic treatment of memory in the context of larger cognitive issues; and Klatzky (1980) *Human memory*, an older, but solid presentation of fundamental theory and data.

SECTION

III

Applied Areas of Research

The distinction between "basic" and "applied" research can be quite arbitrary. However, we have chosen for this section three content areas that provide contemporary applications of the methods described in chapters 1 through 3 and that often rely on specific techniques and behavioral measures from basic content areas described in chapters 4 through 7. For example, social psychological studies of "audience effects" use simple learning tasks to provide measures of behavior that are sensitive to the effects of being observed and evaluated. Nevertheless, some new research techniques have been devised in these "applied" areas as responses to research questions that require innovative approaches. These new techniques will be of particular interest to us.

As was the case with chapters in the previous section, the chapters on judgment, decision making, and problem solving; social psychology; and clinical psychology will make no attempt to be comprehensive in coverage. In picking topics for these chapters, we asked ourselves the following questions: (1) Do current researchers think the topic is important enough to be the subject of continuing investigation? (2) Is it a topic of interest to students? (This is a judgment call. We hope that we've been at least partially successful.) (3) Does this topic illustrate a fundamental research principle developed earlier in this text? or (4) Does it illustrate a *new* research method

or issue? And, as before, we will stress method over results, with particular attention to the reasons behind the methods.

The chapters on clinical psychology and social psychology will rely heavily on psychometric techniques from the chapter on perception and psychophysics to measure such subjective constructs as depression, anxiety, and attitude. The clinical psychology chapter will also illustrate subtleties involved in selecting appropriate control groups and the need for "analog" studies when the target population is difficult to obtain. The social psychology chapter develops new methods for creating situations involving social interactions. These methods sometimes include the use of deception such as making subjects believe that they administer electric shock to others in response to the request of an authority figure. Such methods raise ethical issues concerning the impact of experimental procedures on research participants. We will thus return to the discussion of research ethics introduced in chapter 1. The chapter on judgment, decision making, and problem solving also involves new issues and methods, such as developing tasks that help us determine when people are rational in their decisions and choices or when past habits interfere with solving new problems. This particular area is especially known for its interdisciplinary applications and various of these will be illustrated.

8

Topics in Human Cognition: Judgment, Decision Making, and Problem Solving

Irwin P. Levin

The branch of contemporary psychology dealing with processing of information (i.e., how knowledge is acquired and used) is called **cognitive psychology.** The chapters preceding this one focused on the acquisition and basic use of information. This chapter focuses on the use of information in complex but commonplace situations such as making decisions and solving problems.

The study of perception and psychophysics and learning and memory paves the way for investigating more complex phenomena. In this chapter we will describe research methods for two important areas in cognitive psychology: (1) human judgment and decision making and (2) thinking and problem solving. These areas of research are often referred to as the study of "higher-order" mental processes because they build onto basic information processing components such as perception, learning, and memory. Methods will be described for examining how people break down the information needed for making decisions and solving problems. These methods will allow us to identify variables that affect decision making and problem solving in everyday life. Thus the tasks used to illustrate research methodology in this chapter are often closer to those we encounter in the real world than were those of earlier chapters.

The two areas of human judgment and decision making and thinking and problem solving have much in common and that's why we treat them together in a single chapter. Both areas are interested in the rationality of human behavior, thus causing researchers to search for tasks and measures in which "rational" behavior can be defined and used as a standard to which actual behavior can be compared. Both areas are concerned with uncovering the processes or strategies used enroute to a final decision or solution, thus leading researchers to develop analyses based on techniques such as requiring subjects to "think aloud." Both areas are interested in the use of shortcuts or "heuristics" in reaching decisions or solving problems. Nevertheless, some of the issues and techniques described in this chapter will be unique to the study of judgment and decision making or unique to the study of problem solving.

Judgment and Decision Making

Human judgment and decision making comprise one of the most rapidly growing areas of interest in contemporary experimental psychology, although scholars throughout the ages have been interested in how people make judgments and decisions. For example, Aristotle expressed one of the first formal models of human judgment 23 centuries ago. He took the proposition, "Awards should be according to merit," and operationalized it by defining an equitable state for two persons as one in which the ratio of one person's outcome to the other person's outcome is equal to the corresponding ratio of their inputs (Ross, 1966). Twentieth century social scientists are still investigating alternative mathematical models of how judgments of equity are made and applied (Walster, Walster, & Berscheid, 1978; Mellers & Hartka, 1989). Given the wealth of judgments and decisions that face us in everyday life, experimental psychologists have developed a variety of methods and tasks to understand the processes underlying judgments and decisions. A major premise of this chapter is that human judgment and decision making can be subject to rigorous scientific investigation.

A recent dramatic example illustrates this point. In July 1988 an Iranian domestic airplane was accidentally shot down by the U.S. Navy ship, *Vincennes.* In the excitement of the moment, the aircraft was mistaken for an attacking fighter plane. A hearing was conducted by the U.S. House Armed Services Committee in which several judgment and decision-making researchers were brought in to provide expert testimony.

The researchers related the decision faced by the ship's captain to the type of decision-making task so often studied in the laboratory. In particular, they pointed to results of various studies showing that unaided diagnostic judgments are seriously deficient because of the inability to weigh and integrate information of less than perfect validity. Various biases were suggested as possible in this case, including an "expectancy bias," in which the data at hand were distorted to fit expectations (e.g., that the *Vincennes* was a target for Iranian fighter planes). One recommendation from the hearing was that further studies of decision making under stress be conducted.

We will see in this chapter that the principles of experimental design, the behavioral measures, and the analytic methods of experimental psychology illustrated in earlier chapters can be used to uncover the laws or rules by which judgments and decisions are made. This is an extremely important concern because decision-making analysts need to go beyond the point where each individual judgment or choice must be analyzed on a case-by-case basis. If we understand how a particular type of decision is made, then questions such as why the ship's captain fired on the plane, or why you were accepted for graduate school while your classmate was not, or why some people wear automobile seat belts while others do not, become far less mystical.

Here are some of the major problems addressed by researchers in the area of human judgment and decision making, along with examples of specific questions that will be answered in this chapter.

1. Are humans rational in their judgments and decisions? Can we identify situations leading to rational and irrational judgments and decisions? For example, when do we ignore important sources of information while judging guilt in a court case?

2. Can we identify general strategies used in judgment and decision making? What are the factors influencing the way we process information used in judgment and decision making? For example, how does reliance on memory of specific instances affect judgments of the frequency of occurrence of events such as airline disasters?

3. How do people perceive and deal with risks in making decisions that could lead to unfavorable outcomes? For example, how does the manner of presenting information (emphasizing positive or negative consequences) affect the likelihood of seeking medical treatment or using seat belts?

4. Can we develop rules to aid people in making decisions? An example will be developed for aiding students in the selection of courses.

In this chapter we will discuss these problems and the research strategies and methods used to address them. We will emphasize those research methods and tasks that are used primarily to study judgment and decision making. These include both tasks in which mathematically correct responses can be computed for comparison with subjects' responses and completely subjective tasks in which there are no correct responses. Some tasks are designed explicitly to uncover biases in judgment or decision making. We will present examples of how the problems of judgment and decision making are studied in a variety of areas of application, including forming impressions of other people, judgments made by children, gambling, evaluating judicial evidence, making consumer choices, and making risky medical decisions.

Normative vs. Descriptive Analysis

Normative Analysis

The notion of **normative** or "rational" decision making can be traced back to the economic principle of **utility maximization.** This principle states that a rational decision maker will choose the alternative with the highest expected value or average outcome. According to the original formulation of this principle, a gamble providing a 50 percent chance of winning $20 (expected value = $.50 \times \$20 = \$10$) should be equally attractive to a gamble with a 10 percent chance of winning $100 (expected value = $.10 \times \$100 = \$10$). However, a person for whom the pleasure of winning $20 is more than one-fifth the pleasure of winning $100 may well prefer the former gamble; and a person who finds intrinsic value in taking risks (going for the "long shot") may prefer the latter gamble.

Modern day researchers recognize that "value" is subjective and cannot be measured solely in monetary terms. Thus, they often include measures of individual difference in their studies. For example, Lopes (1987) used verbal protocols—a method to be illustrated later in this chapter—to identify some persons who are motivated by a desire for security and thus avoid risks, and other persons who are motivated to exploit the potential for gain in a situation and are thus risk seekers.

To complicate things further, we are often faced with choices where the alternatives are not so well defined as in the above example. Consider a study by Shanteau and Nagy (1979) of college students' dating choices. Female college students were shown photos of seven possible dates. The students rated each photo on a scale of physical attractiveness, estimated the probability of being accepted by each date, and made preferential choices between the two dates in each of the 21 possible pairs of dates. Rated attractiveness and estimated probability tended to be negatively related. The more attractive the date, the less they thought their chances were. Of primary interest was examining how choice of a date is related to rated physical attractiveness and estimated probability of being accepted by the date.

A number of students preferred dates of intermediate physical attractiveness. For these subjects, preferences could be described as a multiplicative function of attractiveness and probability. This would be consistent with the notion of utility maximization if we assume that the "expected value" of choosing a date is the product of his attractiveness and the likelihood of being accepted by him. The product of high probability and intermediate attractiveness may be larger than the product of low probability and high attractiveness. Thus the choice of a lower-rated option may be seen as perfectly rational. For those subjects who consistently preferred the most attractive dates,

their choices could be described on the basis of physical attractiveness alone, as if they ignored the possibility of being turned down or believed in going for the "long shot."

To deal with situations in which there are many options to choose from, Nobel Prize winner Herbert Simon made an important contribution to both economic and psychological theories of decision making by introducing the concept of **bounded rationality.** Simon (1956) found that decision makers often search through a set of alternatives until they find one that satisfies their aspiration level. They then terminate their search rather than continuing on to compare all possible alternatives to find the "best" one (i.e., the one that maximizes utility). The rationality of such choices is thus "bounded" by factors such as the cost (in time and effort) of continuing a search. Of course, for something like choosing a date—or a mate—the decision maker may be more patient.

One job of the researcher investigating the issue of whether or not humans are rational in their judgments and decisions is to find or create laboratory-controlled tasks in which rational or correct judgments or decisions can be prescribed, and then collect data to compare actual behavior with rational behavior. A task of this type favored by some experimental psychologists is the "bookbags-and-pokerchips" task (Edwards, 1962). In this task a subject is shown two bags, each containing a different mixture of poker chips of two different colors. For example, Bag 1 might contain 70 blue chips (Bs) and 30 white chips (Ws), while Bag 2 contains 30 Bs and 70 Ws. The experimenter then draws chips, one at a time, from Bag 1 or Bag 2. The experimenter specifies that the same bag is sampled on each trial and that the drawn chip is replaced and the chips are shuffled before each new trial. The subject's task on each trial (each draw of a chip) is to specify the probability that a particular bag is being sampled. Consider the following sequence of draws: BWBBWBWBBBWB. Virtually all subjects will realize that such a sequence is more apt to arise from sampling Bag 1 than from sampling Bag 2. Subjects will vary in assigning probabilities to their selection of Bag 1, but a typical mean outcome would be about .75.

There is, in fact, a correct probability value that can be calculated by a statistical law known as Bayes' Theorem. In words, Bayes' Theorem states that odds should be changed following each new event (draw) by multiplying the prior odds by the relative likelihood that the event could have occurred under the two competing assumptions (e.g., sampling from Bag 1 vs. sampling from Bag 2). Bayes' Theorem thus provides a "normative" model for prescribing accurate judgments in the "bookbags-and-pokerchips" task. That is, if subjects used the appropriate laws of probability for this problem, then their behavior would conform to that predicted by Bayes' Theorem.

In our case, every time a blue chip is drawn, the relative likelihood that sampling is from Bag 1 rather than from Bag 2 is 7/3; every time a white chip is drawn, the relative likelihood is 3/7. Assuming a 50-50 chance of starting with Bag 1 or Bag 2 and applying the multiplication rule for independent events (you may wish to refer back to the rules of probability in chapter 3), the odds that the above sequence of 8 Bs and 4 Ws was generated by drawing from Bag 1 can be calculated as $(7/3)^8 \times (3/7)^4$. This comes out to be about 30 to 1, corresponding to a probability of about .97. The typical probability judgment of .75 would thus contain a large error of underestimation. Such an error has been labeled "conservatism" to indicate people's reluctance to make extreme judgments (Phillips & Edwards, 1966), and the reliability of this finding has been used to illustrate that human judgments are often not rational or accurate.

Studies designed to test a person's ability to estimate event likelihood need not be limited to traditional (and sometimes boring) laboratory tasks such as "bookbags-and-pokerchips." For example, Tversky and Kahneman (1980) asked subjects to evaluate eyewitness testimony on the basis of so-called base rate information and observer reliability. Subjects were told that a cab was involved in a

hit-and-run accident at night. Two cab companies, the Green and the Blue, were said to be operating in the city. The following data were provided: (1) 85 percent of the cabs in the city are Green and 15 percent are Blue (this is the base rate information); (2) A witness identified the cab as a Blue cab; (3) When the court tested the witness's ability to identify cabs under the appropriate visibility conditions, the witness made correct identifications 80 percent of the time and erred 20 percent of the time.

Subjects were asked the following question: "What is the probability that the cab involved in the accident was Blue, rather than Green?" The modal and median response was .80. However, the probability as calculated by Bayes' Theorem is .41. (As an exercise, you should try to compute this yourself. Then check your computations against those shown in box 8.1.)

Why the large discrepancy? According to Tversky and Kahneman, subjects gave too little weight to the base rate information about the proportion of Green and Blue cabs in the city, presumably because this information is not causally related to the occurrence of accidents. In order to test this interpretation, the researchers devised a slightly different version of the task. Instead of being told that 85 percent of the cabs are Green and 15 percent are Blue, subjects were told that the two companies are roughly equal in size but that 85 percent of cab accidents in the city involve Green cabs and 15 percent involve Blue cabs. The median answer dropped from .80 to .60, much closer to the "correct" answer. The relevant information was the same in each case, but subjects in the second problem placed more weight on the base rate information, presumably because it was more easily linked to the cause of an accident. Drivers of Green cabs were seen as more reckless and more likely to be involved in an accident.

Consider another example of judging the likelihood of events. Suppose you were asked to rank-order the likelihood of a series of events that include the following: (1) There will be a large earthquake in the Los Angeles area in the next two

BOX 8.1

Testing Normative Models of Human Judgment

One approach to the study of human judgment and decision making is to develop tasks that possess a model or criterion of correctness, optimality, or rationality. Observed behavior can then be compared to the model or criterion to assess the rationality or correctness of human judgment. Bayes' Theorem provides such a model for tasks in which subjects are required to assess subjective or personal probabilities for testing two competing hypotheses (e.g., which of two possible bags is being sampled in the "bookbags-and-pokerchips" task described in the text). The model in this case takes the following form:

$$\frac{P(H_1 \mid D)}{P(H_2 \mid D)} = \frac{P(D \mid H_1) \times P(H_1)}{P(D \mid H_2) \times P(H_2)}$$

where D is the datum (e.g., what color chip is drawn); $P(H_1 \mid D)$ and $P(H_2 \mid D)$ are the posterior probabilities that H_1 or H_2 is true, taking into account the new datum as well as all previous data (previously drawn chips);

$P(D \mid H_1)$ and $P(D \mid H_2)$ are the conditional probabilities of obtaining the given datum under each of the competing hypotheses; and $P(H_1)$ and $P(H_2)$ are the prior probabilities that H_1 or H_2 is true, given all information prior to the new datum.

If all this terminology seems abstract and confusing, let's try the "Blue cab/Green cab" data as an example. H_1 and H_2 are the hypotheses that the cab in the accident was blue or green, respectively. $P(H_1)$ and $P(H_2)$ are the prior probabilities based on base rates and have the ratio 15/85. $P(D \mid H_1)$ and $P(D \mid H_2)$ are the conditional probabilities based on the reliability of the eyewitness testimony and have the ratio 80/20. The ratio of the probability that the cab was blue, given the eyewitness testimony; to the probability that the cab was green, given the testimony, is computed as $15/85 \times 80/20 = 12/17$. The required probability is then $12/(12 + 17) = 12/29 = .41$.

---

years. (2) A number of homes will be destroyed in the Los Angeles area in the next two years. (3) A number of homes will be destroyed in the Los Angeles area in the next two years following a large earthquake. Most people will rank #3 ahead of #2. In fact, the likelihood of two things both happening cannot be greater than the likelihood of any one of the things happening. This **conjunction fallacy** (Tversky & Kahneman, 1983), like the Blue cab/Green cab example, is related to people's attempts to find logical relationships. Can you think of other examples?

Descriptive Analysis

Having reached the somewhat oversimplified conclusion that many judgments are less than optimal, the researcher can go further by attempting to describe how judgments and decisions are made, regardless of their accuracy or rationality. Most recent research by psychologists on human judgment and

decision making can be categorized as **descriptive** rather than normative in nature, and this chapter will emphasize this approach. Furthermore, this approach removes research on judgment and decision making from restriction to situations where models for correct or rational decisions are available (Who is to specify the "correct" choice of a mate?).

A task commonly used in the development of descriptive models of human judgment is **personality impression formation.** Who would you like more: a person described as *sincere, honest,* and *kind,* or a person described as *truthful, intelligent, warm, poised, agreeable,* and *modest?* Subjects are presented person descriptions, each consisting of a series of personality trait adjectives varying in favorableness from traits like "cruel" to traits like "kind," and are asked to rate each hypothetical person on "likableness." Rather than relying on intuition to assess trait values, we can use norms developed from an extensive study by Anderson (1968)

TABLE 8.1 Personality Trait Adjectives Used in Studies of Personality Impression Formation (from Anderson, 1968)

Adjective	Mean Rating*	Adjective	Mean Rating*	Adjective	Mean Rating*	Adjective	Mean Rating*
Sincere	5.73	Relaxed	4.39	Skeptical	2.64	Gloomy	1.36
Honest	5.55	Rational	4.38	Opinionated	2.57	Aimless	1.22
Truthful	5.45	Nice	4.36	Dependent	2.54	Deceptive	1.17
Intelligent	5.37	Agreeable	4.34	Self-conscious	2.49	Incompetent	1.10
Considerate	5.27	Modest	4.28	Frivolous	2.37	Prejudiced	1.06
Warm	5.22	Practical	4.25	Forgetful	2.24	Unpleasant	1.04
Kind	5.20	Self-confident	4.21	Indecisive	2.19	Abusive	1.00
Humorous	5.05	Studious	4.18	Clumsy	1.99	Unethical	.97
Broad-minded	5.03	Easy-going	4.12	Nervous	1.96	Unkindly	.96
Courteous	4.94	Scientific	4.00	Inefficient	1.78	Hostile	.91
Respectful	4.83	Religious	3.87	Reckless	1.78	Annoying	.84
Efficient	4.82	Obedient	3.73	Noisy	1.73	Narrow-minded	.80
Witty	4.80	Fearless	3.66	Unintelligent	1.68	Greedy	.72
Courageous	4.71	Reserved	3.48	Domineering	1.67	Insincere	.66
Neat	4.66	Shrewd	3.28	Unsociable	1.61	Unkind	.66
Tolerant	4.61	Quiet	3.11	Short-tempered	1.59	Malicious	.52
Amusing	4.60	Aggressive	3.04	Neurotic	1.52	Dishonest	.41
Independent	4.55	Shy	2.91	Finicky	1.50	Cruel	.40
Diligent	4.49	Average	2.84	Stingy	1.43	Mean	.37
Poised	4.48	Naive	2.70	Negligent	1.39	Liar	.26

*Ratings were made on a 7-point scale, ranging from 0 to 6.

in which 555 personality trait adjectives were rated singly on the dimension of "likableness." (See table 8.1 for examples. Note the similarity of this research strategy to the use of word frequency counts in the study of verbal learning, chapter 6.)

Results typically conform to a model that describes the overall judgment of a person as an *average* of the values of the various traits describing the person. This is in contrast to a model that describes the judgments as the *sum* of the values. Thus a person described by three extremely favorable traits (*sincere, honest, kind*) will generally be rated higher than a person described by three extremely favorable traits plus three moderately favorable traits (*truthful, intelligent, warm, poised, agreeable, modest*). Note the relevance of this finding for putting together a resume or creating an advertisement. Instead of an exhaustive list of statements, you might want to concentrate on the ones that compare most favorably with your likely competition.

The personality impression formation task is ideal for studying **order effects**—whether the same set of information is responded to differently depending on the order of presentation. For example, a person description consisting of half positive traits and half negative traits can be alternatively presented with the favorable information first or the unfavorable information first. Hogarth and Einhorn (1992) conducted a meta-analysis (see chapter 3) to examine the reliability of order effects under varying circumstances. For tasks like the personality impression formation task where a sequence of simple stimuli are responded to at the end of the sequence, a *primacy* effect is typically found, where the initial stimuli have more impact than the later ones. Other circumstances lead to different results. For example, belief updating tasks in which subjects revise their judgments following each of a short series of complex information presentations (e.g., several narratives or scenarios) lead to a *recency* effect, where the most recent information has the greatest impact. Thus the study of order effects involves systematic variation in task characteristics as well as information sequences. Results of such studies have important implications for understanding jury decisions, teachers' evaluations of students, stock market investments, and other situations in which we respond to sequences of information of varying value.

Heuristics

Some psychologists have focused on the issue of identifying strategies or **heuristics** used in human judgment and decision making. As illustrated in the Green cab/Blue cab example, these strategies often involve selective attention to some factors in a decision-making task and lack of attention to other factors. Such simplifying strategies are most apt to be used when the task is complex and the decision maker is under some time pressure (recall the incident of the *Vincennes.*) Studies designed to uncover the use of heuristics tend to use tasks in which biased judgments are expected. The logic here is like that of using illusions to study perceptual processes. By taking factors that are usually in agreement and making them conflict, we can isolate their effects. The researcher's ingenuity in designing novel experimental tasks has been the key to advances in this area. For example, Kahneman and Tversky (reported in Kahneman, Slovic, & Tversky, 1982) devised experiments to demonstrate

that intuitive predictions follow a judgmental heuristic they labeled **representativeness.** By this heuristic, people predict the outcome that appears most representative of the evidence. While this would seem to be a reasonable strategy, Kahneman and Tversky devised tasks to show that people tend to rely solely on this heuristic while ignoring important factors such as information reliability and prior probability of outcomes.

In a classic experiment, Kahneman and Tversky presented the following personality sketch of a student: "Tom W. is of high intelligence, although lacking in true creativity. He has a need for neat and tidy systems in which every detail finds its appropriate place. His writing is rather dull and mechanical, occasionally enlivened by somewhat corny puns and by flashes of imagination of the sci-fi type. He has a strong drive for competence. He seems to have little feel and little sympathy for other people and does not enjoy interacting with others. Self-centered, he nonetheless has a deep moral sense." The personality sketch was said to be written during Tom's senior year in high school by a psychologist, on the basis of projective tests.

One group of subjects (the prediction group) was asked to rank order nine fields of graduate specialization in terms of which field Tom W. might now be studying. The top-ranked fields were computer science and engineering. Another group of subjects (the similarity group) was asked to rank the nine fields in terms of how similar Tom is to the typical graduate student in each field. Again, computer science and engineering were the top-ranked fields. A final group of subjects (the base rate group) was not shown the personality sketch but was asked to guess what percentage of graduate students in the United States are actually in each of these nine fields. For this study conducted in the early 1970s, the fields of computer science and engineering fell near the bottom of the list (note that this would not be true today). In other words, the judgments of likelihood corresponded much closer to judgments of similarity (correlation = .97) than to estimated percentages (correlation = –.65).

BOX 8.2

Studying Judgment Strategies (Heuristics)

Most recent studies of probabilistic thinking have attempted to describe how the underlying judgmental processes vary as a function of task demands and limitations of the thinker. These limitations have been shown to take the form of simplifying strategies or heuristics by which people make predictions and judgments under uncertainty. Three judgmental heuristics—representativeness, availability, and anchoring—have been studied extensively by Kahneman and Tversky. These heuristics, while efficient and sometimes valid, can lead to biases that have serious implications for decision making. The first example in the text showed that overreliance on the heuristic representativeness can lead to serious errors in career guidance.

Experiments designed to study the use of heuristics typically have two major features: (1) The observed judgment or decision can be linked directly to the choice of a specific heuristic; and (2) other factors that could have influenced the judgment or decision can be ruled out. (Note how this meets one of the major objectives of the scientific method: to narrow down the possible interpretations of a research finding.) Results of the "Tom W." study were consistent with the choice of a representativeness heuristic and, at the same time, ruled out the subjects' use of base rate and information relia-

bility considerations. Kahneman and Tversky (1973) also presented a real-world example of the consequences of failure to consider reliability. Instructors in a flight school adopted a policy of verbally reinforcing successful flight maneuvers. After some experience with this policy, the instructors claimed that contrary to psychological doctrine, high praise for good performance typically resulted in a decrement of performance on the next try. Rather than indicting the reinforcement policy, the instructors should have realized that performance in this complex task is not perfectly reliable and that "regression effects" were inevitable. (See discussion of regression to the mean in chapter 3.) That is, pilots who did exceptionally well on one trial are likely to deteriorate on the next (toward their mean performance level), regardless of the instructor's reaction to the initial success.

Here's another recent example from the sports pages. It has been noted that high salaries for baseball players do not generally lead to better performance. When players are rewarded with a high raise in salary for an especially good year, their performance the following year typically declines. It has been suggested that such players are "spoiled" and that high raises—often leading to increased ticket prices—are a waste. What do you think?

The authors concluded that the subjects in their prediction group relied exclusively on how representative the personality sketch was of each field. They apparently ignored the possible unreliability or invalidity of the projective personality test. They also did not take into account the fact that there were probably more students who fit that description in fields other than computer science and engineering simply because there were so many more students in these other areas. A similar effect may occur when a high school or college athlete overestimates his or her chances of a successful career in professional sports. Box 8.2 includes another example.

Overreliance on the **availability** heuristic can also lead to judgmental biases. Evidence for the use of this heuristic is claimed when the likelihood or frequency of an event is overestimated when that event is easy to imagine or when it is easy to recall relevant instances of that event. In one demonstration of this effect, subjects heard a list of celebrity names of both sexes and were later asked to judge whether there were more male or female names on the list. (Actually, the numbers were equal.) Some subjects received a list where the men were relatively more famous than the women and some received a list where the women were more famous than the men. In each case, the subjects erroneously judged the "more famous sex" as the more numerous. While availability is often a valid cue for the assessment of frequency and probability (e.g., the relative number of men and women in different occupations), availability can be affected by subtle factors unrelated to likelihood such as personal familiarity, recency, and emotional saliency. International travel decreases dramatically following a single well-publicized instance of airplane hijacking or bombing. Buying of earthquake insurance increases *after* an earthquake.

Anchoring is a heuristic in which the judge uses a natural starting point or anchor as a first approximation to the judgment. The anchor is then adjusted following the presentation of new information. The adjustment is typically imprecise and insufficient, resulting, for example, in overreliance on "first impressions." When a group of subjects was asked to make an intuitive estimate of the product $1 \times 2 \times 3 \times 4 \times 5 \times 6 \times 7 \times 8$, the median estimate was 512. By contrast, when another group was asked to estimate the product $8 \times 7 \times 6 \times 5 \times 4 \times 3 \times 2 \times 1$, the median was 2,250. Starting with a large number led to significantly higher estimates than starting with a smaller number (although both groups greatly underestimated the true product: 40,320). The general effect of all of these heuristics is to make people *overconfident* in their judgments.

Risky Decision Making and Perceptions of Risk

One special type of task that may be subject to heuristics and biases has been called **risky decision making.** Risky decision making involves decisions with potential losses in which the possible outcome (gain or loss) varies considerably over choice alternatives, but where the likelihood of achieving the best outcome is typically low. The notion of risky decision making is, of course, closely related to gambling. Apart from being of interest in its own right, the study of risks people take in gambling may also be representative of other risk-taking behavior such as investment decisions and career choices. Judgment and decision researchers have thus long been

interested in gambling behavior. The "gambler's fallacy" is a well-established phenomenon whereby people predict the end of a run of successive identical events even though each new event is independent of previous occurrences. If "heads" comes up four times in a row, most people would bet "tails" on the next flip. (When you flip a coin, the coin has no "memory" for past flips. So, it's just as apt to come up "heads" or "tails" regardless of what's happened on previous tosses.) There's a story—probably apocryphal—that a baseball manager took out a player who had gotten four hits in a row because he surely couldn't get five hits in a row.

Gambling tasks have provided a variety of evidence for the suboptimality of human judgment and decision making. For example, Lichtenstein and Slovic (1973) conducted a controlled study of gambling behavior in a Las Vegas casino. Volunteers were presented with pairs of bets. A typical example would be Bet A: 11/12 chance to win 12 chips, 1/12 chance to lose 24 chips; Bet B: 2/12 chance to win 79 chips, 10/12 chance to lose 5 chips, where each chip had a fixed value (e.g., 25 cents). In this example, Bet A offers a much better chance of winning but Bet B offers a much higher possible payoff. Subjects were asked to evaluate the alternate bets in two ways: First they made a simple choice, A or B. Later, they were asked to assume they owned a ticket to play each bet and they were to state the lowest price for which they would sell the ticket. Presumably, both responses should be governed by the subjective attractiveness of each bet and they should state a higher selling price for the bet they selected in the choice situation. Subjects, however, often chose one bet but stated a higher price for the other bet, a phenomenon called "preference reversal." Lichtenstein and Slovic presume that people chose Bet A because the choice response calls attention to risk level, but they set a higher price for Bet B because selling price calls attention to payoff amount.

Another factor shown to affect risk taking has been referred to as "sunk costs" (Arkes & Blumer, 1985). Sunk costs are past expenditures of money, time, and effort that may (irrationally) affect future decisions. Bettors who have lost on earlier races are more apt to play a long shot on later races in an attempt to recoup their losses; investors are apt to hang on to losing stocks too long in hope that they will rebound. A U.S. senator was recently quoted as saying, "To terminate a project in which $1.1 billion has been invested represents an unconscionable mishandling of taxpayers' dollars." In reality, it may be best to "cut one's losses" rather than risk additional losses on a bad investment.

One study of risk perception involves the use of automobile seat belts. The public has been criticized for their poor perception of driving risks and the benefits of seat belts. Risk perception research helps provide an explanation for this and a prescription for increased seat belt use. Research has shown that people often disregard very small probabilities. There is in fact a very small probability of a fatal accident (1 in 3.5 million) or a disabling injury (1 in 100,000) on a single automobile trip. From this perspective, refusing to buckle one's seat belt may seem quite reasonable. However, if a lifetime of driving is considered, the picture changes considerably. Over a period of 50 years of driving (about 40,000 trips), the probability of being killed is about 1 in 100 and the probability of experiencing at least one disabling injury is about 1 in 3. Experiments by Slovic, Fischhoff, and Lichtenstein (1978) showed that people induced to consider this lifetime perspective responded more favorably toward the use of seat belts than did people asked to consider a trip-by-trip perspective.

One form of risk assessment that affects almost all of us at one time or another is the assessment of medical risk. These assessments lead to decisions that affect our health and well being, such as whether or not to undergo a particular medical treatment. Thus, it is not surprising that researchers have used a medical setting to investigate variables that affect risk taking. One such variable is **information frame.** Recent research has shown that the way in which information regarding possible outcomes is presented or "framed" can have a substantial effect on these decisions. For example, Meyerowitz and Chaiken (1987) showed an effect of message framing on breast self-examination in college women. Subjects were given a pamphlet on breast self-exam (BSE) where information was framed positively or negatively for different subjects as follows:

"By [not] doing BSE now, you (can) [will not] learn what your normal, healthy breasts feel like so that you will be (better) [ill] prepared to notice any small, abnormal changes that might occur as you get older. Research shows that women who [do not] do BSE have (an increased) [a decreased] chance of finding a tumor in the early, more treatable stage of the disease. You can (gain) [lose] several potential health benefits by (spending) [failing to spend] only 5 minutes each month doing BSE. (Take) [Don't fail to take] advantage of this opportunity."

Immediately following administration of the pamphlet, subjects who received the loss pamphlet expressed more positive attitudes toward BSE than did subjects who received the gain pamphlet. More importantly, the validity of this effect was demonstrated four months later when subjects in the loss condition reported a larger number of times they had actually performed BSE than did subjects in the gain condition. The negative framing condition was thus particularly potent in demonstrating the need for breast self-examination. The key feature of the experiments on seat belt use and breast self-examination was the ability to use a between-subjects design where different subjects were presented the same objective information framed differently. (Why would it be difficult to do a good study of this type using a within-subject design?)

In a related example, a medical treatment was found to have a higher level of endorsement when it was described as having "a 50 percent success rate" than when it was described as having "a 50 percent failure rate" (Levin, Schnittjer & Thee, 1988). Other examples of decisions based on perceptions of risk include buying insurance, consumption of food and tobacco known to contain cancer-causing agents, considering job hazards, and locating in areas with weather dangers or potentially hazardous nuclear or waste materials. According to Slovic, Fischhoff, and Lichtenstein (1984), perceptions and attitudes concerning risk are determined not only by objective statistical data, but also by characteristics of hazards such as controllability, catastrophic potential, equity, and threat to future generations. And, of course, we now know the importance of the manner in which information about risk is communicated. Because of such subjective influences, it has been suggested that findings from decision-making research can and should be used in designing public information programs.

Decision Rules

In studies of heuristics and risk taking it was sufficient to demonstrate that a simple principle or rule applied in the majority of individual cases. However, there are many other situations in which a great deal of variation might be expected. For example, choice of mode of transportation may depend mostly on cost factors for some people and time factors for other people. Researchers can observe an individual or group of individuals making judgments or decisions across a variety of situations with identifiable variables so that they can discover the laws or **decision rules** governing these behaviors.

Studying Individual Differences

As in many other areas of psychology, large individual differences can often be found in response to judgment and decision-making tasks. In order to better understand these individual differences, researchers may attempt to identify subject variables that interact with task variables. The area of consumer decision making provides examples.

In one such study by the present author and his colleagues (Levin, Jasper, Mittelstaedt, & Gaeth, 1993), subjects were asked to respond to the current controversy over the relative merits of buying an American or a Japanese car. They were told that complicating matters is the fact that Japanese auto

manufacturers often have some of their parts made or assembled in the United States by U.S. workers, while U.S. auto manufacturers often have some of their work done in other countries. In the main task, subjects were asked to rank-order their likelihood of buying a given model of car from each of six companies. The six companies were described by combining in a factorial design two levels of national manufacturer (American or Japanese) and three levels of percentage of American workers employed (80, 50, or 20).

After completing this task, subjects were asked a series of questions, including whether they agreed or disagreed with the statement, "Buy America first." Responses in the rank-ordering task were then compared for those responding differently to this question. Those subjects who agreed with "Buy America first" showed a clear preference for American companies and companies that employed a high percentage of American workers, while subjects who disagreed with "Buy America first" tended to show the opposite pattern. This occurred even for subjects who indicated that Japanese cars are superior to American cars. In this case, nationalistic feelings represented an important factor in explaining individual differences in car preferences.

Studies of consumer decision making have sometimes focused on individual differences in consumers' familiarity with and knowledge of the class of products being judged. A typical finding is that more knowledgeable consumers are less reliant on price information in picking out superior brands. Other attempts to understand individual differences in response based on distinguishing subject characteristics will be described in the chapters on Social Psychology and Clinical Psychology.

In addition to measuring individual differences, some researchers have devised manipulations that mimic the action of subject variables. For example, Isen (in press) creates a positive affective state or mood in a decision-making or problem-solving task by giving subjects a bag of candy for agreeing to participate. This unexpected gift makes subjects feel good and this has measurable effects on their performance. Compared to subjects who don't receive candy, subjects in a positive state exhibit more thoughtful deliberations in reaching a decision and more creative solutions to problems.

Judgments by Children

One subject variable known to influence many judgments is age. A number of contemporary researchers are interested in the *development* of human judgment and decision-making capabilities. The typical research strategy here is to compare the performance of different age groups on the same or parallel tasks.

A study by Anderson and Cuneo (1978) demonstrated the information integration capabilities of young children. Children at three different age levels (5 years, 8 years, and 11 years) were given a variety of judgment tasks, including the judgment of areas of rectangles. The methodology for obtaining such judgments from children was interesting. Rectangles of varying area were formed by factorially manipulating height and width. The rectangles were said to be cookies of varying size. Each child judged each rectangle. The response scale was a graphic rating scale with smiling and frowning faces pictured at the extremes to indicate "very happy" and "very sad." The child was instructed to select a point along the scale on each trial to indicate how happy or sad a child would be "with that much cookie to eat." Perceptions of area followed the correct height × width rule in older children, but a reliable tendency was found for judgments by the 5-year-olds to follow the additive rule, height + width. While the younger children did not use the correct rule, they demonstrated the ability to integrate information from more than one dimension. Earlier theories had suggested that children of this age were not capable of integrating information from several dimensions, but instead concentrate on a single dimension in their judgments. This study refuted those theories.

This study serves as a good illustration of how repeated-measures designs can control differences in perception between individuals. One child may require larger cookies than another child before giving "happy" ratings. As long as each child is consistent in how their judgments vary across trials, the same decision rule may be discovered for different children who use different parts of the scale.

Decision Aids

Sometimes even a simple arithmetic rule can be used as an aid in future decisions. Dawes (1988) points out the advantages of rule-based decision making in the allocation of scarce resources, such as job hiring, selection of graduate students, and administration of medical procedures. These rules generally take the form of a linear equation that specifies how selected variables are weighted and combined. For example, the psychology department at the University of Illinois has used the following equation for screening applicants for graduate school: 10 × selectivity of undergraduate institution + 700 × undergraduate grade point average + 2 × Graduate Record Exam-Quantitative + 2 × Graduate Record Exam-Advanced + 100 × whether math taken + 100 × research experience.

Here is how these weights (multipliers) are derived: Data concerning the relative success or failure of the decision maker's previous choices were used as the Y-variable (criterion variable) in a multiple regression equation (see chapter 3) and the various possible predictor variables were entered as X-variables. The weight of each X-variable is a measure of the degree of correlation of that X with Y. The net effect of a variable in the multiple regression equation is the product of its weight and its range of variation. Thus, the weights of the Graduate Record Exam scores were much less than that of grade point average simply because the former values have a much wider range. You may have noticed that Graduate Record Exam-Verbal was not included in the University of Illinois equation. Evidently this factor did not discriminate between good and poor graduate students, but this could be because only students with a restricted range of scores on this factor were in the sample. The outcome could be different at other schools. This method can only be used when you have previous data for correlating predictor variables with criterion variables.

The first thing to notice about a rule like this is that it represents a "divide and conquer" strategy. By breaking down a possible choice alternative into component parts or factors, effort can be taken to obtain relevant information about each component and evaluations can be revised as information is updated. Indeed, the use of such rules has sometimes been cited as the distinguishing feature between "expert" and "novice" decision makers (Shanteau, 1990).

The advantages of using such a rule include the following: (1) Rules treat all people in the same manner. (2) Variables are chosen a priori, thus avoiding post hoc criteria that can be used to bias a decision. (3) The basis of judgment is known so that accountability or responsibility is clearly defined. (4) Applicants can determine on which critical dimensions they are particularly high or low, and can perhaps work to change the low ones. (5) Objective rules eliminate human errors such as inconsistent weighting or imperfect memory of past decisions, contrast effects, mood effects, fatigue, and "illusory correlations" (using factors such as physical attractiveness, which may bear no relationship to the criteria of interest). The result is that even a model based on a decision maker's own prior judgments, when applied uniformly to all future judgments, will generally do better in predicting some criterion or implementing the judge's personal values than will the judge him- or herself. This phenomenon has been termed **bootstrapping** and has been demonstrated in situations ranging from predicting student grades to diagnosing neurosis vs. psychosis (Dawes, 1988).

Box 8.3 shows how you can use this method to construct your own decision aid. The advantages and possible disadvantages of this particular illustration are discussed.

Issues of Experimental Design and Methodology

This section will describe how researchers use various methods to determine the rules by which specific judgments and decisions are made.

Observational vs. Experimental Methods

Virtually all of the examples so far in this chapter used the experimental method. The basic orientation of this chapter has been to provide a research model in which the factors of interest are systematically varied while remaining factors are carefully controlled. This model can best be achieved in the laboratory (loosely defined here as any setting in which the researcher can achieve experimental control). The major criticism of laboratory research on judgment and decision making is that the laboratory situation may be so contrived that it has no **external validity,** in other words, it bears little relationship to real-world problems. "Unrealism" is a pitfall to be avoided in such research.

Levin and his colleagues (1983) suggest in their review of external validity tests of laboratory results (use of laboratory results to predict real-world decisions) that validity can be increased by taking into account differences between the laboratory setting and the natural environment. For instance, Gaeth and his associates (1991) studied consumers' preferences for products like personal computers and VCRs by using a preset experimental design to select products with various combinations of features, but they also allowed consumers to inspect the real products possessing these features before responding. Table 8.2 summarizes some of the examples of external validity tests described by Levin and associates (1983).

While the majority of studies on human judgment and decision making use the experimental method, there is sometimes reason to use observational or correlational methods. For example, the author recently participated in a large-scale telephone survey (over 2,000 respondents from a

BOX 8.3

Construction of a Personal Decision Aid

You can use the bootstrapping principle to help you make choices. Suppose, for example, that you are having difficulty in choosing between Class A and Class B for next semester's schedule. First, write down the most important ways (to you) in which the two classes differ. These may be your expected interest in the course material, the relevance of the course for your career objectives, the reputation of the teacher, the convenience of the class meeting time, and the nature of the course assignments. Assign a weight or importance to each of these features. For convenience, you might constrain these weights to sum to 100. Then, consider each feature separately and assign a value to that feature for each of the two classes. The values might vary, say, from 1 to 5. For example, you might have great interest in the course material for Class A and assign it the value 5 on "interest" and have only moderate interest in the course material for Class B and assign it the value 3. Let's say, however, that Class B is a required course in your major area but Class A has only slight relevance to your career goals. Class A then gets a 2 and Class B gets a 5 on "relevance." A sample set of weights and values is shown below.

Feature	Weight	Value Class A	Class B
Interest	30	5	3
Relevance	20	2	5
Teacher	15	5	4
Convenience	25	4	3
Assignments	10	3	4
Weighted Sum		395	365

You compute a weighted sum for each class by multiplying the weight of each feature by its value and then summing over features. The sum for A is $(30 \times 5) + (20 \times 2) + (15 \times 5) + (25 \times 4) + (10 \times 3) = 395$. The sum for B is $(30 \times 3) + (20 \times 5) + (15 \times 4) + (25 \times 3) + (10 \times 4) = 365$. The outcome in this case favors Class A and if you used this rule you would choose Class A.

The advantages of this method are its objectivity, its relative ease of computation, and its ability to allow the decision maker to independently apply his or her own value system (assignment of feature weights) and assessment of facts (assignment of numbers to each alternative for each feature). There are some drawbacks. The most general of these is the limited accuracy of assigning numerical values to each feature of each alternative. Another possible disadvantage is that a new feature may come up for one particular alternative that wasn't part of your original list. Class A may require a field trip that you can't fit into your schedule. Or, one of the features that was already on your list may reach such an extreme value that it suddenly takes on new importance. You may have heard such bad things about the teacher of a particular course that nothing else matters. Arriving at a choice that seems counterintuitive to the decision maker can be a sign of unreliability.

Because multidimensional decisions are typically the most difficult ones to make, these weighted-sum decision aids may be helpful. Try one and see how the outcome fits your prior expectation.

---

seven-state area) of political and economic attitudes and decisions. Researchers from different disciplines contributed items of particular interest to them. Typical survey items included to determine the sociodemographic characteristics of respondents and their household were: age, sex, marital status, education, employment status of self and spouse,

household income, and so forth. Our interest was in economic decisions. Respondents were asked to indicate whether they saved or invested money on a regular basis, the number of credit cards they used, and whether they typically paid their credit card balances in full or carried charges over to the next month. (Note that telephone surveys require questions that

TABLE 8.2 Summaries of Studies Containing External Validity Tests

Content Area	Stimulus Variables	Response Scale	Subjects	Evidence of External Validity
Residential Location Choice	Commuting distance, gasoline cost, rural vs. urban locations	"Bids" for a fixed home under varying circumstances	Recent home buyers	Individual differences in distance gradients in the laboratory task were predictive of individual differences in commuting distance for actual home purchases.
Shopping Location Choice	Price and variety of purchases, convenience of location	Rated likelihood of shopping at hypothetical locations	College students	$r = .93$ between predictions of laboratory-derived model and patronage of actual supermarkets.
Transportation Mode Choice	Cost difference and time difference between car and bus	Degree of preference for car or bus	Local commuters	95% correct classification of car-users and bus-users.
Occupational Choice	Kinds of outcomes (salary, locations, etc.) for hypothetical jobs	Satisfaction (utility) and importance ratings of outcomes	Actual job applicants for public school positions	Predicted 18 out of 30 actual job choices (from among a set of desirable jobs) based on a weighted expected utility formulation.
Consumer Decision Making	Attributes of batteries (brand, length of life) and purpose of purchase	Rated likelihood of purchase	Consumers	Derived importance weights and attribute values were logically related to purpose of purchase (e.g., length of life was more important for home usage than for a camping trip).
Expert Judgments	Dimensions used to judge swine (bone structure, muscle trimness, etc.)	Judgments of swine quality	Livestock judges	Information usage (number of dimensions used, use of configural cues) was predictably related to length of experience and type of training.

From Levin et al., 1983.

can be answered in as simple a manner as possible: e.g., "Yes-no" answers, or, in the case of items such as household income and education, choosing a response category from a list read by the interviewer.) In such a survey, researchers not only measure relationships between the various items, but they look for a meaningful pattern that helps describe the structure underlying the data.

In this case, we concluded that saving and spending decisions depend on both the ability to pay bills and the willingness to delay immediate gratification in order to plan for the future (Levin & Kao, 1993). Several factors seemed to be predictive of a "savings attitude." For example, when income was held constant, married couples, especially those with children, were more apt to save or invest than unmarried couples, and younger respondents were more apt than older respondents to carry charges over.

The major criticism of the observational or correlational research strategy is that the relationships obtained between environmental factors, respondent characteristics, and observed judgments and decisions are circumstantial rather than causal (see chapter 1). Was the expensive car bought for its safety record or for its prestige value? Postpurchase interviews can provide some insight but are subject to biases inherent in justifying one's choices to others. (This will be discussed in more detail in the chapter on Social Psychology.) Systematic observations of sales records and performance records, however, may reveal that differences in auto safety bear little relationship to sales.

Variants of the observational approach have proved useful in understanding judgment processes. For example, an approach that attempts to apply the analytic capabilities of the experimental method to naturalistic observation is the **quasi-experimental design.** An attempt is made to approximate a true experiment in a naturalistic setting by systematically eliminating alternative explanations of the observed phenomenon. This often involves before-and-after observations centered around an event of interest. Such observations are sometimes referred to as "interrupted time-series."

Campbell (1969) reported observations before and after a crackdown on speeding in Connecticut in 1955 to determine if, in fact, driving decisions were altered. While these changes were not observed directly, the number of traffic fatalities was found to decrease following the crackdown. A strong inference about the causal relationship between the crackdown on speeding and altered driving behavior was made only when it was shown that: (1) Several years of data both before and after the crackdown revealed a marked discontinuity in the number of traffic fatalities only following the crackdown on speeding, and (2) Data from comparable states (controls) did not exhibit a similar effect. Such control groups are referred to as **nonequivalent controls** because lack of random assignment to conditions prevents precise equivalence. A number of similar studies were conducted before and after the energy crisis of 1973–74 to show changes in choice of mode of transportation, home heating decisions, and the like. However, in general, such studies lack the control achieved in the Campbell study.

Choice of Factors

The choice of factors to be studied in judgment and decision making will depend on the purpose of the study. If policy implications are of primary concern, then the study must include variables that would be affected by policy decisions. For example, a study of public participation in regional planning in the state of Colorado (Hammond et al., 1977) included variables corresponding to the recreational, agricultural, industrial, and environmental impacts of alternative land use decisions. Participants judged alternatives with a variety of consequences in these factors. The results of this study provided policy makers with information about the different points of view (e.g., different weighting of industrial and environmental factors) of different factions within the community. This permitted a compromise policy to be implemented.

When the study does not fall directly into the category of policy analysis, the choice of factors can rest on a combination of intuition, literature review, and empirical investigation. Empirical investigation to determine relevant factors underlying a particular judgment or decision can be accomplished with a variety of interview techniques. If there are "experts" available, then they can be consulted. Expert judges are particularly good at identifying key variables (remember the "divide and conquer" strategy) and coding or measuring them, but are not necessarily better than the rest of us in integrating diverse sources of information. Thus, for example, interviews with experienced stock brokers can serve as input to a well-designed study of decisions concerning the buying and selling of stocks.

Choice of Response Measures

A variety of response measures have been used to study the judgment or decision process, including discrete choices between a fixed set of alternatives, response latencies, ratings or rankings of alternatives, verbal protocols, eye movements, and estimates of confidence. Some of these are designed to monitor predecisional behavior; some are designed to define the judgment or decision itself; and some are designed as followup measures of postdecisional behavior. This three-fold focus is one of the distinguishing features of judgment and decision making research.

Some researchers have devised methods to track the processing of information before a choice is made, particularly emphasizing *information-seeking,* the selection of facts believed by the subject to aid in making a choice. These include introspective methods in which subjects are asked to think aloud as they choose between alternatives.

The **verbal protocol** method is popular in tracing the processes used by consumers in making their decisions. With this method, the subject is simply asked to give continuous verbal reports, or "to think aloud" while performing a decision task. The object is to identify what information a decision maker has and how it is being processed. This is in contrast to earlier introspective methods, which required subjects to theorize about the causes of their

behavior or perform a "postmortem" of their decision after it has been made. Payne, Braunstein, and Carroll (1978) report the use of verbal protocols in an apartment search task. Table 8.3 gives an example of a protocol that provides information on the sequential (time-ordered) behavior of an apartment seeker. See how your interpretation of this protocol corresponds to the researchers' interpretation. They interpreted it to indicate that the subject initially eliminated alternatives that were unfavorable on some key attributes (e.g., rent is too high, facilities are poor) and then the subject focused on systematically comparing the attributes of the final two choices.

Jacoby, Chestnut, and Fisher (1978) studied the way different consumers gathered information to use in buying breakfast cereal. They used the "information display board" method to keep track of the sequence in which information is sought before a purchase is made. Package information was collected for 16 leading brands of breakfast cereal on each of 35 dimensions (price, net weight, calories, ingredients, etc.) The board consisted of a 16×35 matrix display of actual information values. Each of the resulting 560 cells was represented by a card labeled on the back so that the subject knew, for example, that a particular card told the "net weight" of a package of "Rice Krispies." The subject could remove the card from its holder and read the information. The removal of a card constituted an "acquisition event." Subjects were instructed to "shop as usual" in this simulated shopping task, taking as much or as little time and acquiring as much or as little information as they would in a real-life purchasing situation.

By tracking the sequence in which cards were acquired, inferences were made about the behavioral process used by each subject. Of particular interest here was the distinction between the following transition types: (1) moves from one dimension to another for the same brand, (2) moves from one brand to another on the same dimension, and (3) moves to a different brand and different dimension. Results showed minimal consumer acquisition behavior; the

TABLE 8.3 Protocol for a Subject Selecting among Twelve Apartments

PROTOCOL	RESEARCHER'S INTERPRETATION
Let's just see what the rents are in all the apartments first.	I WILL NOW LOOK AT THE RENT OF EACH ALTERNATIVE.
The rent of A is $140.	THE RENT OF A IS $140.
The rent of B is $110.	THE RENT OF B IS $110.
The rent of C is $170.	THE RENT OF C IS $170.
Um, $170 is too much	ALTERNATIVE C ELIMINATED.
But, if the other ones aren't good. I'll look at them later.	ALTERNATIVE E ELIMINATED (rent of $170 or more).
But right now I'll look at the other ones.	ALTERNATIVE F ELIMINATED (rent of $170 or more).
	ALTERNATIVE G ELIMINATED (rent of $170 or more).
I'm going to look at landlord attitude.	I WILL NOW LOOK AT THE LANDLORD OF EACH ALTERNATIVE.
In H it's fair.	THE LANDLORD OF A IS GOOD.
In D it's poor.	THE LANDLORD OF H IS FAIR.
B it's fair, and	THE LANDLORD OF D IS POOR.
A it's good.	THE LANDLORD OF B IS FAIR.
So, one of them . . . is poor.	ALTERNATIVE D ELIMINATED.
So, that's important to me.	ALTERNATIVE I ELIMINATED (poor landlord).
	ALTERNATIVE K ELIMINATED (poor landlord).
So, I'm not going to live any place where it's poor.	ALTERNATIVE L ELIMINATED (poor landlord).
Kitchen facilities in A are poor.	I WILL NOW LOOK AT THE KITCHEN OF EACH ALTERNATIVE.
In A poor.	THE KITCHEN OF A IS POOR.
In B poor.	THE KITCHEN OF B IS POOR.
In J fair, and	THE KITCHEN OF H IS GOOD.
In H they're good.	THE KITCHEN OF J IS FAIR.
Oh, J and H have better kitchen facilities than A and B	ALTERNATIVE A ELIMINATED.
And everything else about the same.	ALTERNATIVE B ELIMINATED.
So eliminate those two.	SINCE I'VE ONLY GOT TWO ALTERNATIVES I WILL APPLY A COMPENSATORY DECISION PROCESS.
And, decide between these two.	THE CHOICE IS BETWEEN H AND J.
Let's see furniture quality.	LET'S SEE ON FURNITURE.
In H it's below average.	H IS BELOW AVERAGE.
In J it's below average so that's about the same there.	J IS BELOW AVERAGE.
Landlord attitude in J is better than H.	LET'S SEE ON LANDLORD.
	J IS BETTER.
In J the rooms are larger.	LET'S SEE ON SIZE.
So, I guess, J will be better	J IS BETTER.
	I CHOOSE ALTERNATIVE J.

median proportion of available information actually acquired was only 2 percent, with 20 percent of the subjects acquiring no information beyond the brand names. Most information acquisition was limited to price and product composition dimensions such as calories and ingredients. Type 1 (within-brand) transitions characterized heavy searchers, whereas Type 2 (between-brand) transitions characterized light and moderate searchers. Type 3 transitions tended to appear only as search length increased.

According to Bettman, Johnson, and Payne (1989), such methodologies—including equipment for tracking eye movements and computerized versions of the information display board—have generally led to findings that subjects use a variety of rules and strategies en route to a decision. For example, there is evidence that early in the process, subjects tend to compare a number of alternatives on the same key attributes (e.g., cost, in consumer decisions) and thereby reject some alternatives from further consideration. Later in the process, they weigh the advantages and disadvantages of all the attributes of the reduced set of alternatives.

To aid researchers in determining when subjects focus on certain attributes, experimental designs can be constructed that force the decision maker into a trade-off between specific attributes. Consider, for example, the following three options for buying a scientific calculator: Brand 1—price = \$59, quality rating (100-point scale) = 54; Brand 2—price = \$72, quality rating = 70; Brand 3—price = \$85, quality rating = 86. Notice that price-quality combinations are constructed such that no option is favorable on both attributes. If a subject is asked to choose one of the three options, the researcher can determine whether the choice is based on price (Brand 1), quality (Brand 3) or a compromise between the two (Brand 2). Individual differences in choice can then be linked to subject variables such as previous background and knowledge for this type of purchase.

Decisions in the real world usually take the form of discrete choices—whether or not to go shopping, whom to go with, which store to shop at, what mode of transportation to get there, what to buy

once you get there, etc. When discrete choices are employed in laboratory studies of judgment and decision making, the *proportion* of choices of the various alternatives in the choice set are tabulated for each set of conditions and these are analyzed to determine the relative influence of various factors on the choice.

In some cases, such as when there is little variance in choices across situations and individuals, the choice proportions will provide only minimal information about the judgment process. In these cases, additional data may be provided concerning the speed of decision making. Response time or latency measures usually assume a direct relationship between response time and difficulty of the decision—the more information that is considered, or the more complex the process of combining relevant information, or the more similar the various choice alternatives are, the longer the choice will take. Other measures illustrated throughout this chapter are ranking or rating methods aimed at providing quantitative information about the relative evaluation of different choice alternatives.

Follow-up measures of postdecisional behavior often focus on subjects' tendency to seek information that confirms or disconfirms their decision. A common finding is that following a major purchase such as an automobile, consumers will spend more time reading ads about the product they bought than about other makes or brands.

Another common postdecisional measure is *degree of confidence* in the decision made. In a study by Koriat, Lichtenstein, and Fischhoff (1980), subjects were presented with two-alternative general knowledge questions, such as "The Sabines were part of (a) ancient India or (b) ancient Rome." Following each answer, subjects judged the probability that their chosen alternative was correct. There is a general tendency for people to be overconfident in evaluating the correctness of their knowledge (e.g., giving an average estimate of .60 probability of being correct for items whose actual correct response rate was only .50). Subjects, however, markedly improved the appropriateness of their confidence judgments when they were asked to list reasons for and against each of the alternatives before choosing between them. In particular, the listing of contradicting reasons improved the appropriateness of confidence.

Conclusions and Recommendations

There are potential pitfalls in the study of judgment and decision making that could lead to erroneous conclusions or inappropriate applications of research results. Here are some ways to avoid them: (1) Observe judgments and decisions under controlled conditions that allow the separation of the various influences on behavior. (2) In devising experimental tasks, give careful consideration to the task variables and their relationship to judgments and decisions made outside the laboratory. (3) Be careful in generalizing results from tasks specifically designed to elicit errors of judgment. The task may be ideally suited for separating normally confounded factors, but the specific combinations of conditions leading to these errors may be less common in the real world than in the laboratory. (4) Devise tasks and measures that make it possible to identify individual differences rather than assuming that all persons follow the same decision-making rules.

There will continue to be a demand for applying the principles of human judgment and decision making to the critical decisions facing individuals, groups, and institutions in today's complex society. We have seen how behavioral researchers have devised methods for understanding strategies and biases affecting a variety of judgments and decisions. Many of these methods require no more sophisticated paraphernalia than paper-and-pencil tests, poker chips, or information display boards. But most importantly, they require the ingenuity and perseverance of researchers who can endure repeated encounters with judgments and decisions that at first glance may appear completely beyond the bounds of rationality.

Inventive investigation has produced tasks and measures that reveal the processes underlying judgments and decisions and identify the variables affecting these processes. We have even seen some limited applications of decision aids aimed at reducing errors that arise from judgmental biases and suboptimal strategies. Continued expansion of such decision aids is a laudable goal, the attainment of which will clearly depend on the quality of basic research on the judgment process.

Thinking and Problem Solving

Many decision-making tasks possess an element of "problem solving" in the sense that the decision maker is seeking out the best decision or solution from among several alternatives. There is thus a great deal of overlap between research on judgment and decision making and research on thinking and problem solving. Nevertheless, there are some issues and some tasks that were developed to study those issues that are especially emphasized in the "psychology of thinking and problem solving."

Here are some of the major issues addressed by researchers in the area of thinking and problem solving.

1. What is the role of "discovery" in problem solving? That is, how do problem solvers narrow down from a large number of possible solutions to a smaller number that hold greater promise? We will see how word puzzles relying on natural language habits can be used to study this issue.

2. What role does prior experience play in thinking and problem solving? We will describe problem-solving tasks designed to show that prior habits can sometimes inhibit creative thinking.

3. How is expertise developed for skilled performance and problem solving? In this case, researchers developed tasks in which experts could demonstrate how their prior experiences lead to more ready discovery of correct solutions.

4. What developmental processes are necessary for rudimentary reasoning and problem solving? We will include examples of "conservation tasks" designed to study reasoning in children.

The Role of Discovery:
Solving Word Puzzles

The element of "discovery" is a feature of most problem-solving tasks. Among the most popular of these are verbal puzzles.

Suppose you are a contestant on the TV game show "Wheel of Fortune," where your task is to guess the letters in a word and then identify the word. Let's say you have the following sequence to work with: _ _I N_I N_. You could guess letters at random, but this would not be a very good strategy because if you guess a wrong letter before you solve the puzzle, you give up your turn to the next contestant. So, you try to apply what you know about the frequency with which various letters and, more specifically, strings of letters occur in English words. A common word ending is "ING" and, sure enough, your guess of "G" does fit into the last place. At this point there are still many possibilities but common letters like R, S, T are better guesses than letters like X, Z, V. Now let's say that you get lucky—although your knowledge of letter frequencies has increased your chances—and your choice of "T" appears in the first position. Now you can make the odds really work in your favor. There are only a few letters that would fill out the letter string T_I N. By now you've probably identified the word THINKING and won "big money."

Word games have often served as research tools for understanding human thinking and problem solving. Researchers have particularly liked to work with *anagrams*, scrambled letters that can be put in proper sequence to form a word. A popular independent variable manipulation is to vary the letter sequence to either inhibit or facilitate a correct solution based on natural language habits. Thus, KNITGHIN will be harder to unscramble than INGINKTH. Note the variety of dependent variables that can be used: whether or not the puzzle is solved correctly within a fixed time limit, the length of time to solve the puzzle, and the number of "false starts."

Throughout this text we have seen examples of the use of response time or reaction time (RT) as a response measure. Such measures are especially useful in those problem-solving tasks in which almost all subjects will eventually solve the problem. Here, the dependent variable of whether or not the subject solved the problem would not likely discriminate between experimental conditions. In such cases, RT measures are often more illuminating.

One potential—but absurd—strategy for solving an anagram like this would be to generate all possible sequences of the given letters until one is identified as a correct word. This **algorithm** would guarantee a solution but possibly require thousands of attempts. Instead, people use heuristics, rules of thumb such as trying out logical letter strings, which provide shortcut solutions to such problems. (Can you relate the use of heuristics here to the use of heuristics described earlier for judgment and decision making?)

To make things more interesting (and informative) in the anagram task, you could ask the subject to "think out loud" while solving the anagram or move around letters from a Scrabble set. Then you could measure the extent to which the subject used various strategies or heuristics. In this case, the strategies might be identified as a series of intermediate operations whereby the subject tries to first form logical letter strings such as ING, TH, INK and then put these together to form the word. Researchers in this area describe this breaking down of a problem into successive parts as moves from an "initial state" to a "goal state" by way of setting up subgoals.

Verbal Protocols

A major goal of studies of thinking and problem solving is to determine what strategies people use. For tasks in which only a final answer is required, standard dependent variables, such as whether or not a correct solution is reached or time to complete the task, are difficult to translate into analysis of strategies used. Verbal protocols or "think aloud" techniques like those illustrated in table 8.3 for a decision-making task are often used in these cases to supplement the standard measures. Careful analysis of verbal protocols can shed light on mental processes. Consider the following analysis by Lindsay and Norman (1977) of Newell's (1967) earlier research on a problem in "cryptic arithmetic."

> DONALD
> + GERALD
> ROBERT

First, subjects are given the value of one letter, D = 5, and then are told:

"In the above expression, there are ten letters, each representing a different, distinct digit. The problem is to discover what digit should be assigned to each letter, so that when the letters are all replaced by their corresponding digits, the arithmetic is correct. Please speak aloud all that you are thinking as you attempt to solve the problem. You may write down anything you wish."

This is a difficult problem and not all subjects solve it in the allotted time. What is important is not whether the subject solves the problem, but how he or she *attempts* to solve it. Here, the verbal protocols are the data of interest. Here are excerpts from one subject. "Each letter has one and only one numerical value. There are ten different letters and each of them has one numerical value. Therefore, I can, looking at the 2 Ds—each D is 5; therefore, T is zero. Now, do I have any other Ts? No. But I have another D. That means I have a 5 over the other side.

Two Ls equal an R. Of course, I'm carrying a 1, which will mean that R has to be an odd number because the 2 Ls—any two numbers added together has to be an even number and 1 will be an odd number. So R can be 1, 3, (not 5), 7, or 9."

Analysis of these statements reveals some general patterns in this subjects' problem-solving behavior. First, he goes over the overall goal he is trying to reach and the rules for achieving it. Then he breaks down the final goal into smaller steps. He proceeds by trying out simple strategies for achieving these steps. Analysis of the full protocol for this subject revealed that he often had to back up when a strategy didn't work and try something different.

As revealed by verbal protocols, this general description applies to a variety of problem-solving tasks. Based on such findings, the following sequence of steps seems to be a reasonable way of categorizing the problem-solving process: (1) understanding the problem; (2) planning a solution; (3) carrying out the plan; and (4) checking the results.

Verbal protocols are treated like any other data. The researcher tries to analyze and interpret them in ways that make sense. While this may be especially difficult with verbal protocols, they may in some cases be the best data we have. Nevertheless, as described in box 8.4, such methods are not without controversy.

The Role of Set and Functional Fixity

Recall in the chapter on perception and psychophysics that perceptual responses such as interpreting an ambiguous figure are influenced by our expectancies or **set.** In a similar fashion, these influences operate in thinking and problem solving. For example, you may have learned that the correct foil on a multiple-choice test question is often the longest one, and you use this to guess when you don't know the correct answer.

Several classic research paradigms were designed to assess the role of set in problem solving. In Luchins's (1942) "water-jar problems" subjects had to obtain a required amount of water by using three jars that hold specified amounts. Consider the following examples:

Containers			Required
A	**B**	**C**	amount
21	127	3	100
14	163	25	99
18	43	10	5
9	42	6	21

After some trial and error, you might discover that the correct solution to each of these problems is to fill container B, pour out enough to fill A, then pour out enough to fill C twice. What's left in B is the required amount: B – A – 2C. Suppose you were

BOX 8.4

Use of Verbal Protocols: Precautionary Notes

The history of the use of verbal reports is controversial. Attempts to verbally reconstruct the reasons for a particular action after the fact are known to be subject to systematic biases. (Examples of such biases will be discussed in the section on "cognitive dissonance" in the chapter on Social Psychology.) At a more general level, it is possible that the act of thinking aloud can, itself, distort the thought process. For example, the requirement of verbalization may lead people to be more concerned with avoiding silly mistakes than in generating creative ideas.

According to Ericsson and Simon (1993), several precautions must be taken to assure the reliability and validity of the data from verbal protocols. Because we cannot rule out the possibility that the information subjects retrieve at the time of the verbal report is different from the information they used while actually performing the task, concurrent verbal reports should be collected so that processing of information and verbal report coincide in time. It is important to note that subjects' verbalizations reveal the information they attend to while performing a task but do not necessarily explain what they are doing. If subjects are also instructed to explain their thoughts, this instruction may change the sequence of thoughts because the subjects may attend to information not normally needed to perform the task.

Thus, Ericsson and Simon recommend that subjects be told simply to "think aloud" or "talk aloud" while performing the task, rather than being asked to "tell me what you are thinking." Furthermore, they suggest that subjects be given practice problems in which it is easy to verbalize concurrently and from which they can become familiar with the normal content of think-aloud verbalizations. These authors present considerable evidence from problem-solving and decision-making tasks that these simple procedures do not distort the thought processes when subjects instructed to verbalize are compared to subjects in a silent control condition. The examples in the text and in table 8.3 show that, when analyzed carefully, verbal protocols can be quite enlightening.

---

given 5 to 10 problems, all of which could be solved by this equation. Now you're given the following problems:

| Containers | | | Required |
A	B	C	amount
23	49	3	20
15	39	3	18
28	76	3	25

How would you solve these problems? While the first two could be solved by the same B – A – 2C rule, each could be solved by a simpler rule that bypasses B altogether (A – C in the first case, A + C in the second). The last problem can only be solved by the simple rule, A – C.

In Luchins's experiment, one group of subjects (the experimental group) received both sets of problems, while another group (the control group) received only the second set of problems. Almost all the subjects in the experimental group used the long method throughout, whereas the control group used almost exclusively the short method. The phenomenon of "set" defined by this study can be demonstrated whenever a given mode of attacking a problem that has proven successful in the past is shown to persist even when that mode is no longer appropriate.

Note the significance of the phenomenon of "set" for designing studies of problem-solving. Once a method of solving problems has been established,

FIGURE 8.1   The candle problem.

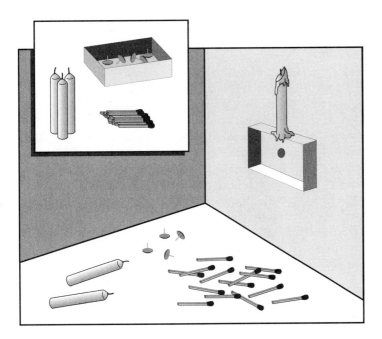

it will affect future similar problems. Thus a study designed to compare two or more problem-solving conditions cannot generally use within-subject designs; independent groups of subjects are almost always required.

A related phenomenon is illustrated in Maier's (1931) "two-string problem." Two strings are suspended from the ceiling and the subject is asked to tie the ends of the strings together. The catch is that the strings are too far apart for the subject to hold on to one and reach the other. A number of objects are available for use, including a pair of pliers. The problem can be solved by using the pliers, not for their usual function, but as a weight to tie to the end of one string to form a pendulum. By swinging the resulting pendulum, the subject can hold onto one string and catch the other. Short of receiving strong hints (e.g., the experimenter "accidentally" starting one string in motion), most subjects had difficulty in

discovering this new use of an old tool. This phenomenon, known as **functional fixity,** has been demonstrated in a variety of contexts. Interestingly, subjects given hints, while performing better than subjects not given hints, are often unaware of the influence of the hint.

A final classic study of this type is the "candle" problem (Duncker, 1945). The subject is given some candles, a box of matches, and some thumbtacks. The task is to mount the candles on the wall in such a way that they can be lighted without burning the wall. Subjects often start by trying to tack the candles to the wall, but this won't work. The correct solution is to use the matchbox, not as a container, but as a platform for the candle, as shown in figure 8.1. Subjects who were presented with an empty matchbox next to a pile of matches were more apt to see the solution than subjects who were presented with a filled matchbox. Note how these examples, where subjects have to learn a new response to an old stimulus, fit the negative transfer paradigm described in the chapter on Human Learning.

The Role of Experience in Problem Solving: Chess Experts

One way to study the range of human thinking and problem solving is to compare "experts" and "novices" on some task. One such task is chess playing. What makes a person an expert at playing chess—superior intellect and memory, different thought processes, better-developed strategies? It had been observed that chess masters had greater memory for chess positions. That is, after viewing a chess board for only a few seconds, masters could reconstruct the board almost perfectly, whereas lesser players could recall only a few pieces. In an often-cited experiment, Chase and Simon (1973) created two versions of the chess board task, one in which the positions of the chess pieces were representative of a real game situation and one in which the pieces were placed on the board randomly. The experts performed significantly better than the nonexperts with meaningful placement of pieces but there was no difference in recall of positions with randomly placed pieces.

Thus, the experts did not possess superior memory per se. However, they were apparently able to use their experience to encode and store meaningful chess positions. In other words, they seemed to be able to organize the information in meaningful ways such that several individual pieces could be remembered as a single unit. Chase and Simon tested this more explicitly by videotaping performance on the memory task and on a perception task in which subjects viewed one chess board and reconstructed the positions on a second board. The time between successive piece placements was used as the dependent variable. In both tasks, the experts showed a pattern of short pauses between placing pieces that formed a meaningful unit or "chunk" and longer

pauses between chunks. The researchers concluded that a master player had more pieces per chunk than a weaker player. As we saw in the memory chapter, "chunking" of individual items into a larger unit is one way to increase memory capacity. Another way to look at the role of expertise in the present case is that among the millions of possible placements, the expert is able to use the heuristic of narrowing down the number of possibilities. Translated into playing ability, the expert can consider possible moves in a very selective fashion. The difference among chess players of different ability appears to lie, not in sheer mental capacity, but in the development through experience of efficient heuristic schemes.

Reasoning in Children

While studying "experts" allows researchers to examine the development of refined problem-solving skills, studying children is the preferred method for examining the development of the foundations for reasoning and problem solving. Interest in the development of reasoning and problem solving has led to the creation of tasks for comparing performance of children of different ages. It is not our purpose here to chronicle these tasks but to describe one famous type of task that has spawned considerable later research—Piaget's **conservation tasks.** Piaget was interested in what tasks requiring the concept of conservation would tell him about the periods or stages of development of the child.

In the prototypical conservation task (Piaget & Inhelder, 1962), a child watches as water is poured from a short, wide container into a tall, narrow one (or vice versa). The child is then asked if there is more water in the second vessel than there was in the first. Children below the age of about 7 fail to see that the quantity of water is unchanged or conserved, and most say that the tall, narrow vessel has more water—probably because the water line is higher.

Similar tasks were developed to examine conservation of other quantities. For example, "conservation of number" is examined by spilling out a number of objects from a compact container so that they spread out on the floor and asking if the number of objects changed. Piaget concluded that children up to a certain age do not yet possess an important intellectual function—the ability to see that certain transformations such as changes in shape do not alter the basic properties of objects.

Are you ready to try a few problem-solving tasks? Several additional tasks are described in box 8.5.

BOX 8.5

A Sampling of Problem-Solving Tasks

Here are a few more problem-solving tasks that researchers have found useful for studying human thought processes. Before you read the solutions, think about how you would solve the problems yourself. Try to analyze your own thought processes. Were you helped or hindered by your past experiences?

The "radiation problem" can be stated as follows: Suppose you are a doctor faced with a patient who has a malignant tumor in his stomach. It is impossible to operate on the tumor, but unless the tumor is destroyed the patient will die. There is a kind of ray that can be used to destroy the tumor. If the rays reach the tumor all at once at a sufficiently high intensity, the tumor will be destroyed. Unfortunately, at this intensity the healthy tissue that the rays pass through on the way to the tumor will also be destroyed. At lower intensities, the rays are harmless to healthy tissue, but they will not affect the tumor either. What type of procedure might be used to destroy the tumor with the rays, and at the same time avoid destroying the healthy tissue? (Gick & Holyoak, 1980).

Most people have trouble solving this problem because of all the constraints imposed. In fact, in the original studies using this problem, only 4 percent of college students came up with the most simple and effective solution: Aim several weak rays at the tumor coming from different directions so that no single ray would be strong enough to damage healthy tissue, but the summative effect of all the rays converging at a single point would be strong enough to destroy the tumor.

Later studies included a condition where subjects first read a different scenario that illustrated in a military setting the principle of a converging attack from different directions. These subjects were able to solve the radiation problem much more readily. This procedure uncovered people's ability to "reason by analogy"—use the same principle in two different, but analogous tasks.

In the "missionaries and cannibals" problem (Newell & Simon, 1977), three cannibals and three missionaries want to cross a river. They have only one boat, which will hold two people, and no other means to cross the river. If there are more cannibals than missionaries on either side of the river, the cannibals will eat the missionaries. The task is to find the most efficient way to get all six people across the river without having any missionaries eaten.

The correct solution is given in figure A. Note the "trick." While most boat trips require two people crossing the river and one returning, one trip requires two people crossing and two returning.

In the "pyramid puzzle" (Gagné & Smith, 1962), the task is to move a set of discs of varying size from one stack to another according to size, with the largest on the bottom. The original stack of five discs is on Circle A and has to be moved to Circle B. Circle C is also available (see figure B). Only one disc may be moved at a time, never placing a larger disc on top of a smaller one. To illustrate this rule, if the smallest disc (from the top of the original stack) is moved to Circle B, then the next smallest disc must be moved to Circle C. Performance is measured by the solution time and the number of moves. "False starts" are common with this problem.

[Continued]

Box 8.5 continued

FIGURE 8.A   The missionaries and cannibals problem.

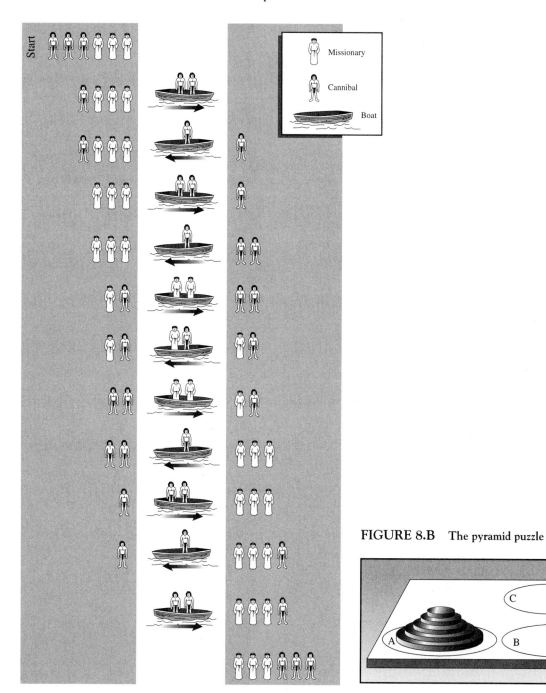

FIGURE 8.B   The pyramid puzzle

Summary and Conclusions

The areas of judgment and decision making and thinking and problem solving are popular among contemporary experimental psychologists because they represent natural extensions of traditional areas such as learning and perception, and because they deal with issues of importance in everyday life. We have discussed several important issues in these areas: Are human judges and decision makers rational? What are the sources of bias in decision making and problem solving? What are the rules or strategies used by decision makers and problem solvers?

We examined the experimental designs and methods used by researchers to address these issues. To address the issue of rationality in decision making, researchers have devised "normative" tasks such as bookbags-and-pokerchips, in which there are mathematically correct answers. In some such studies systematic errors of judgment were discovered such as underestimating the likelihood of a sequence of independent events. Response biases and other sources of error were also uncovered by devising tasks without a correct response but in which the influence of factors such as information reliability and base rate could be separated. These tasks were especially useful in defining simplified strategies or heuristics in which people selectively attend to some kinds of information while giving insufficient attention to others.

In the "representativeness" heuristic, people rely too much on similarity in predicting class membership. In the "availability" heuristic, the memory of specific instances can inflate estimates of the likelihood of a whole class of events. In the "anchoring" heuristic, first impressions play a dominant role. In general, the order in which information is presented can play an important role, as shown in studies of impression formation.

Controlled studies of decision-making processes face the criticism that their findings lack validity if we want to apply them to real-world situations. Evidence is beginning to accumulate that laboratory studies of judgment and decision making are useful for understanding judgment and decision processes in a variety of settings.

Nevertheless, observational or correlational studies of decision making can yield interesting relationships, especially if researchers can detect a meaningful pattern to these relationships. "Quasi-experimental" designs attempt to approximate the experimental method in a naturalistic setting, such as by comparing traffic fatalities before and after a new speed law.

An important class of decision-making situations involves the perception of risk. Because of the subjective nature of risk perception, studies have been able to demonstrate the importance of the manner in which information is presented or "framed." Describing potential outcomes in terms of either positive or negative consequences can affect whether we seek medical treatment or whether we use seat belts.

We presented examples of judgment and decision-making research in areas such as children's judgments, consumer choice, and medical decision making. In addition to facing general issues of experimental design, each individual researcher is faced with his or her own set of judgments and decisions involving selection of stimuli (independent variables) and response measures (dependent variables). These decisions depend on questions such as whether the researcher has theoretical or applied interests and whether there is interest in predecisional and postdecisional behavior.

The study of thinking and problem solving often focuses on how people develop strategies for solving novel and complex problems. These strategies may take the form of testing hypotheses based on prior learning. Anagrams and other word puzzles are used to show how prior language habits can facilitate problem solving, but studies of set and functional fixity show that learned habits can sometimes get in the way when dealing with a novel situation. Expert problem solvers such as chess experts develop heuristics that help them by narrowing down the number of possible solutions.

A controversial issue in the study of decision making and problem solving is the use of verbal protocols or "think-aloud" techniques, in which subjects verbalize their thoughts as they progress through a problem. People may not always be conscious of the influences on their own thought processes. Nevertheless, data provided by verbal protocols often reveal the manner in which people break down a complex problem into smaller parts and deal with each part successively.

Exercises

1. Discuss the pros and cons of studying the "rules" by which people make judgments and decisions, as opposed to examining individual judgments and decisions on a case-by-case basis.

2. Analyze a current major judgment or decision that you are now facing. It could be related to your education, career, health, personal relationships, or financial condition, or some combination of these. List the alternative courses of action you have available, the factors involved, and how these factors vary over the available alternatives. How do you expect to obtain the relevant information and how will you go about weighing the importance of the various factors?

3. How might you design a decision aid to help you in the above situation?

4. Use the "verbal protocol" method on an acquaintance who is facing a major decision-making task. Record the data as in table 8.3 in the text and try to use the table to help you understand the decision-making process.

5. Test an acquaintance on one of the problem solving tasks in box 8.5 and instruct her or him to "think out loud" while performing the task. Use the verbal protocol data to help you construct a summary of the person's thought processes.

6. Devise your own "conservation tasks" and try them out with a young child. Carefully note your observations concerning the child's reasoning ability.

Glossary

algorithm A step-by-step procedure of generating all possible ways to solve a problem. (p. 260)

anchoring Heuristic in which the judge uses a natural starting point as a first approximation to a required judgment. (p. 248)

availability Heuristic in which the likelihood or frequency of an event is estimated on the basis of how easy that event is to imagine or recall. (p. 247)

bootstrapping Using a model based on a decision maker's prior judgments to be applied uniformly to all future judgments. (p. 252)

bounded rationality Choice of the first alternative that satisfies the decision maker's aspiration level, rather than waiting for a possibly better choice. (p. 242)

cognitive psychology The branch of psychology dealing with the acquisition and use of knowledge. (p. 240)

conjunction fallacy The error people make in judging that the likelihood of two things both happening is greater than the likelihood of any one of them happening. (p. 244)

conservation tasks Tasks developed by Piaget to determine the ability of children of different ages to see that transformations such as changes in shape do not alter the basic properties of objects. (p. 264)

decision rules Mathematical formulations for comparing choice alternatives based on weighted combinations of selected variables. (p. 250)

descriptive analysis Describing how judgments and decisions are made, regardless of their accuracy or rationality. (p. 244)

external validity Extent to which laboratory results apply to the "real world." (p. 252)

functional fixity Difficulties experienced in discovering new uses for old tools. (p. 263)

heuristics A variety of simplifying rules or strategies used in judgment, decision making, and problem solving. (p. 246)

information frame Presenting the same information in either positive or negative terms. (p. 249)

nonequivalent controls Control groups in a quasi-experiment that cannot be precisely equated because of lack of random assignments to conditions. (p. 255)

normative analysis Comparing judgments and decisions to a prescribed level of accuracy or optimality. (p. 241)

order effects The effects of order of presentation of information on judgments and decisions. (p. 245)

personality impression formation Tasks in which judgments of likability of persons are related to characteristics such as personality traits. (p. 244)

quasi-experimental design Attempt to approximate a true experiment in a naturalistic setting. (p. 255)

representativeness Heuristic in which people predict the outcome that appears most representative of, or similar to, the evidence. (p. 246)

risky decision making Decisions involving possible losses where the likelihood of achieving the best outcome may be relatively low. (p. 248)

set Subjects' expectancies about which strategies to use in solving problems. (p. 261)

utility maximization Principle stating that a rational decision maker will choose the alternative with the highest "expected value" (probability of a gain times amount to be gained). (p. 241)

verbal protocols "Think aloud" techniques used to analyze the strategies people use while reaching decisions or solving problems. (p. 256)

Suggested Readings

Journals
The following journals regularly publish theoretical and empirical articles on decision making and problem solving: *Organizational Behavior and Human Decision Processes, Journal of Behavioral Decision Making, Journal of Experimental Psychology: Human Perception and Performance, Journal of Experimental Psychology: Learning, Memory and Cognition, Decision Science, Cognitive Psychology,* and *Memory and Cognition.* The following journals occasionally publish major reviews of research in this area: *Annual Review of Psychology, Psychological Review,* and *Psychological Bulletin.*

In addition, journals in particular disciplines include reports of judgment and decision-making research in their area. These include *Econometrica, Management Science, Journal of Risk and Insurance, Journal of Consumer Research, Journal of Economic Psychology, Journal of Marketing Research,* and *Transportation Research.*

Texts (in chronological order)

Von Neumann, J., & Morgenstern, S. (1953). *Theory of games and economic behavior* (3rd ed.). Princeton, N.J.: Princeton University Press.

Simon, H. A. (1957). *Models of man: Social and rational.* New York: Wiley.

Edwards, W. & Tversky, A. (Eds.) (1967). *Decision making.* Baltimore: Penguin.

Bourne, L. E., Jr., Ekstrand, E. R., & Dominowski, R. L. (1971). *The psychology of thinking.* Englewood Cliffs, NJ: Prentice Hall.

Newell, A., & Simon, H. A. (1972). *Human problem solving.* Englewood Cliffs, NJ: Prentice Hall.

Janis, J., & Mann, L. (1977). *Decision making: A psychological analysis of conflict, choice and commitment.* New York: The Free Press.

Kaplan, M. F., & Schwartz, S. (Eds.) (1977). *Human judgment and decision processes in applied settings.* New York: Academic Press.

Lindsay, P. H., & Norman, D. A. (1977). *Human information processing.* New York: Academic Press.

Hogarth, R. (1980). Judgment and choice: *The psychology of decision.* Chichester, England: Wiley.

Wallsten, T. (Ed.) (1980). *Cognitive processes in choice and decision behavior.* Hillsdale, N.J.: Lawrence Erlbaum.

Hammond, K. R., McClelland, G. H., & Mumpower, J. (1980) *Human judgment and decision making: Theories, methods, and procedures.* New York: Hemisphere/Praeger.

Kahneman, D., Slovic, P., & Tversky, A. (Eds.) (1982). *Judgment under uncertainty: Heuristics and biases.* Cambridge: Cambridge University Press.

Arkes, H. R., & Hammond, K. R. (Eds.) (1986). *Judgment and decision making: An interdisciplinary reader.* New York: Cambridge University Press.

Dawes, R. M. (1988). *Rational choice in an uncertain world.* San Diego: Harcourt Brace Jovanovich.

Yates, J. F. (1990). *Judgment and decision making.* Englewood Cliffs, NJ: Prentice Hall.

Social Psychology

Irwin P. Levin

I t is not typical to find a chapter titled "Social Psychology" in an experimental psychology textbook. However, social psychologists have developed many interesting applications of the research methods described in earlier chapters and have, in some cases, contributed their own advances in behavioral research techniques. For example, social psychologists have developed techniques to make laboratory settings more representative of actual social encounters. One of the leading journals in social psychology is called *The Journal of Experimental Social Psychology*, and one of the most influential volumes is *Advances in Experimental Social Psychology*. It thus seems quite appropriate to include social psychology as a relevant content area within experimental psychology.

What makes a topic of particular interest to social psychologists is its emphasis on how social interaction affects the individual. Because of this interest, certain research questions are being addressed primarily by social psychologists. Often, these questions are motivated by observations of actual events. The questions include the following: Why have groups of people stood by while a fellow human being has been violently attacked? Under what circumstances will people comply with a request to harm others? What conditions promote cooperation to conserve environmental resources? How are we affected by having to perform in the presence of others?

We will address these questions with an emphasis on the methods developed to answer them. We want you to pay particular attention to those techniques that are perhaps more common in social psychology than in the other areas described in earlier chapters of this book. These techniques were developed as logical ways of dealing with the issues in social psychology. They include the use of interacting groups, the use of deception as a research tool, the use of confederates who are trained to react in a certain way to elicit certain behaviors from the subject, the use of groups rather than individuals as the unit of analysis, and the combined use of laboratory and field research settings to simulate real-world social processes. These techniques sometimes lead to special problems such as the ethics of manipulating behavior in ways that may lead subjects to perform acts they probably would not have performed otherwise, for example, administering electric shocks to others. The particular research topics to be covered in this chapter are attitudes and attitude change, social roles, person perception, and group processes.

Attitudes and Attitude Change

Social psychologists are particularly interested in the area of attitude change because it represents one way in which an individual is influenced by other individuals within the society. Sometimes the influence is a direct person-to-person influence, as when a friend tries to convince you to try the new Mexican restaurant in town. Sometimes the influence comes from a well-defined group as when other members of a jury try to convince a dissenter to change his or her mind. Sometimes the influence comes from the mass media as when a newspaper editorial tries to convince you to vote for a particular political candidate or when television advertising tries to convince you to change your brand of cola.

The research questions in this area include under what conditions a change in attitude is most likely to occur, which people are most likely to change their attitude, and to what extent changes in attitude lead to changes in behavior. Before such questions can be answered, some fundamental methodological issues must be addressed. These involve *attitude measurement* and validation of the *attitude-behavior relationship*. A necessary condition for understanding the dynamics of attitude change is having reliable and valid measures of attitude strength and, in order to see if changes in attitude do indeed lead to changes in behavior, we must have methods for examining the link between attitudes and behavior.

BOX 9.1

Attitude Measurement

The following is an example of how the semantic differential might be applied to measure attitudes toward building a new nuclear power plant in your community.

Rate on each of the scales below how you feel about building a nuclear power plant in your community.

Bad   __ __ __ __ __ __ __   Good
            –3 –2 –1 0 +1 +2 +3

Economical   __ __ __ __ __ __ __   Uneconomical
                  +3 +2 +1 0 –1 –2 –3

Dangerous   __ __ __ __ __ __ __   Not Dangerous
               –3 –2 –1 0 +1 +2 +3

Desirable   __ __ __ __ __ __ __   Undesirable
             +3 +2 +1 0 –1 –2 –3

There are several things to note about these scales: (1) Both positively scored and negatively scored scales are included (the numbers shown are for scoring purposes and are not seen by the subjects); (2) the combined score on all scales is meant to be more informative than the score on any single scale; and (3) the choice of scales is a decision of the researcher and should be based on the particular issue or item being assessed. (What additional scales would you want to add for the nuclear plant example?)

A simple attitude measure for a given person would be the sum of the scores on the various scales. Try scoring yourself and a couple of friends on the nuclear power issue (including any items you added). How would you assess the *reliability* of this method of attitude measurement? How would you test its *validity*?

Attitude Measurement

The term *attitude* has been defined a number of different ways over the years. For example, Thurstone (1931) defined attitude as "the affect for or against a psychological object." Allport (1935) defined attitude as "a mental and neural state of readiness, organized through experience, exerting a directive or dynamic influence upon the individual's response to all objects and situations with which it is related." Doob (1947) defined attitude as "an implicit, drive-producing response considered socially significant in the individual's society."

For our present purpose of describing research methodology in social psychology, verbal definitions of attitude are not sufficient. As with other psychological variables, we must specify the *operational definitions* of attitude—how attitudes are measured in a given study. The goal is to obtain a reliable, valid index of an individual attitude toward some object, event, or person.

We consider attitude measurement as a special case of psychological scaling and measurement, and as such it was discussed in chapter 4. Let us briefly review a couple of the scaling methods used to operationally define attitudes. The semantic differential (Osgood, Suci, & Tannenbaum, 1957) requires subjects to rate an object or issue on each of several bipolar scales, usually containing 7 points each (other numbers are also used; an odd number permits a zero or neutral point in the middle), with the ends having labels such as "good-bad" and "favorable-unfavorable." Likert scales (Likert, 1932) require subjects to respond to items on a 5-point scale of degree of agreement or approval. With each of these methods, an attitude can be expressed as a profile of responses to specific items or as a total of scores to all items. An example is provided in box 9.1.

Most attitude scaling techniques are examples of rating methods, and variants including 10-point,

20-point, and 100-point scales have sometimes been used to express attitudes. The choice of a scale is often a matter of personal preference by the experimenter. One guiding principle should be that there are enough points on the scale to detect differences in response across levels of the independent variable. For example, if only a 2-point scale ("agree-disagree") were used and almost everyone responded "agree" even though different subjects differ in their extent of agreement, then experimental effects would probably go undetected. Even a nominal 5-point scale reduces to just 3 points if the ends are so extreme that most respondents shy away from using them. In chapter 4 we provided some evidence of the validity of simple rating scales such as these. However, a primary criterion for evaluating the validity of attitude scales is whether differences in attitude are predictive of differences in behavior. In the following pages we will describe research methods for investigating attitude change and ways of detecting that changes in attitude lead to changes in behavior.

Attitude Change

The usual attitude change study is designed along the following lines: Subjects' attitudes toward some item or object are measured at the beginning of an experimental session. During the experiment subjects are exposed to some arguments or communication about the item or object. Attitudes are measured at the end of the session and a change score is computed for each subject. Different experimental conditions (possibly including a control condition with no communication) are compared in terms of differences in mean attitude change score. Factors that may affect changes in attitude include credibility of the source of communication, degree of discrepancy between the position advocated in the communication and the subject's initial attitude, and the use of one-sided versus two-sided arguments.

FIGURE 9.1   Attitude change as a function of discrepancy between subject's initial opinion and opinion advocated, and credibility of the source of the opinion.

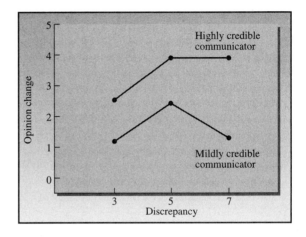

The issue of source credibility effects was investigated by Aronson, Turner, and Carlsmith (1963) by varying both the credibility of the source providing comments about some passages of poetry (T. S. Eliot or an undergraduate student) and the degree of discrepancy between the subject's initial evaluation of the poetry and the source's opinion. When subjects reevaluated the poems after hearing the sources, their attitude change scores reflected an interesting interaction between source credibility and discrepancy. (Recall from chapter 3 that an interaction between two variables means that the effect of one variable differs at different levels of the other variable.) In this case, the effect of varying levels of discrepancy differed for subjects exposed to a source of high credibility and subjects exposed to a source of low credibility. This is shown in figure 9.1. For subjects exposed to a communication from a high-credibility source, attitude change increased as discrepancy increased. In other words, those subjects whose initial opinions deviated most from the stated opinion of the high-credibility source showed the greatest amount of attitude change. However, subjects exposed to a communication from a low-credibility source actually showed less attitude change when discrepancy was large than when it was moderate. Apparently subjects were able to accept and be influenced by an opinion much different from their own only when they believed the opinion to come from a highly credible source.

Notice how much more was learned in this study by including two important independent variables in the same experimental design as opposed to conducting two separate studies each with a single independent variable. For example, if one were examining attitude change as a function of only the degree of discrepancy between the subject's initial attitude and the opinion advocated, then the results would depend on the subject's perception of the credibility of the source of the opinion. Two experimenters could well end up with seemingly conflicting results. The Aronson and associates study avoids this particular source of ambiguity.

Another interesting question in attitude change research is the relative effectiveness of presenting one side versus both sides of an issue. Common sense might say that if we want to change opinions in a particular direction we should present only arguments in that direction, but is it not also possible that it would be more effective to present the other side as well in order to show that our arguments make more sense than theirs? Before turning to a specific example of such research, let's list the important methodological steps in conducting a study of this type: (1) measuring initial attitudes or opinions; (2) selecting one-sided and two-sided arguments that are equivalent to each other in all ways except "one-sidedness vs. two-sidedness"; (3) assigning subjects to experimental conditions; (4) measuring amount of attitude change (perhaps both short-term and long-term) and comparing experimental conditions as well as individuals within a given condition.

A classic study was conducted by the Information and Education Division of the U.S. War Department in 1945 near the end of World War II. As originally reported in a volume by Newcomb and Hartley (1947), this study was set up to provide information on the relative effectiveness of one-sided versus two-sided arguments on American army troops' attitudes concerning the magnitude of the job remaining to be done to defeat the Japanese. (The study was undertaken because of reports that army morale was being adversely affected by overoptimism about an early end to the war.)

Both one-sided and two-sided arguments were presented as radio transcriptions analyzing the war in the Pacific. For both types of argument, the commentator's conclusion was that the job of finishing the war would be tough and that it would take at least two years after V-E day. The one-sided argument consisted only of statements indicating that the war would be long, including statements about distance problems and other logistical difficulties in the Pacific; the resources and stock piles in the Japanese Empire; the strength of the Japanese army; and the determination of the Japanese people.

The two-sided argument included all of the above statements plus statements considering the other side of the picture (i.e., possible reasons for a quick end to the war), including U.S. naval superiority, Japan's manufacturing inferiority, and the U.S. expanding air war. It is important to note that the two-sided argument did not attempt to equate both sides of the argument and it came to the same overall conclusion as the one-sided argument. In effect, the two-sided argument concluded that the job of ending the war would be difficult, even taking into account U.S. advantages and Japanese weaknesses.

Approximately 200 soldiers were assigned at random to the one-sided and two-sided argument conditions and a like number were assigned to a control group, which heard no arguments but was surveyed before and after the same time interval as the other groups. This group was included to control for the influence of other communications the soldiers may have received during this period. (Why do you think this is important?) A preliminary survey was administered one week before the arguments were presented and the final survey was administered. The main measure obtained from each survey was the subject's estimate or "best guess" of the duration of the war. The corresponding dependent variable was whether or not the subject changed to a longer estimate from the initial to the final survey. A change was defined as a difference of one-half year or more between the two estimates. In addition, subjects were classified in terms of their education level and whether their initial estimate of the length of the war was less than two years or was two years or more.

The net effect of each type of argument was assessed by computing the percentage of subjects changing to a longer estimate and subtracting from it the change occurring in the control group. The major results were as follows: (1) Two-sided arguments were more effective than one-sided arguments for individuals who were initially opposed to the point of view (i.e., those whose initial estimate was less than two years). (2) Two-sided arguments were less effective than one-sided arguments for individuals who were already convinced of the point of view being presented (i.e., those whose initial estimate was two years or more). (3) Better-educated persons were more favorably affected by presentation of both sides; poorly educated persons were more affected by one-sided arguments.

This study served as a good example for later research on attitude change for two reasons. First, it showed how an experimental approach might be applied to a real problem of interest to policy makers (e.g., how arguments might be presented most effectively from a lawyer to a jury, depending on the lawyer's knowledge of the characteristics of the jurors). Second, it demonstrated the importance of individual difference factors by showing that the relative effectiveness of one-sided vs. two-sided arguments depends on the person's education level and prior opinion.

Attitude-Behavior Relationship

In most cases, merely demonstrating changes in a person's stated attitude would be insufficient evidence to justify the interest in attitude change research. It is also important to validate evidence for attitude change by demonstrating a parallel change in overt behavior—for example, by showing that subjects choose a new course of action consistent with their changed attitude.

A theory by Fishbein and Ajzen (1975) provides a framework for studying the **attitude-behavior relationship.** According to the theory, most human behaviors can be predicted and explained almost exclusively in terms of individual beliefs and attitudes. The theory assumes that the immediate determinant of a person's overt behavior (B) is the person's intention (I) to perform or not perform that behavior. Intentions are determined by the person's attitude toward the behavior (AB) and the person's subjective norm (SN), which refers to the person's perceptions of the social pressures to perform or not perform the behavior. Translating the theory into empirical tests requires operational definitions of the variables in such a way that we will know that if the theory's predictions are not upheld, one or more of the assumptions must be wrong and needs to be modified.

In one such test, Davidson and Jaccard (1979) attempted to determine whether the decision to have a baby could be predicted from attitudes and subjective norms. A group of 270 women completed a questionnaire assessing their attitudes and subjective norms about having a baby. They rated items such as "making my marriage stronger" and "restricting my freedom" on both their belief (b) that that outcome would occur and their evaluation (e) of how good or bad that outcome would be. According to the model, these beliefs and evaluations combine multiplicatively to determine attitude, i.e., $AB = \sum b_i e_i$ where each i refers to a different outcome.

In addition to rating the various outcomes, the women rated the likelihood that important reference persons (e.g., their husbands) favored the idea of their having a baby in the next two years, and they rated their motivation to comply with each referent. According to the model, these latter two values combine multiplicatively to determine the person's subjective norm (SN).

Two years later, 244 of the women were located again in order to determine whether or not they actually had a child in the intervening period. Multiple regression analysis yielded a correlation of .51 between the model's predictive components (the components of AB and SN) and actual birth. When attempted conception was used as the behavioral measure—including unsuccessful as well as successful attempts—the correlation was even higher (.60). What makes these results particularly impressive is the fact that a number of factors could have intervened during the two-year period to reduce the attitude-behavior relationship.

Because the relationship between attitude and behavior is correlational, we cannot automatically infer that attitude change produces behavior change even in those instances where the correlation is high. Researchers have thus attempted to devise methods that are capable of leading to such an inference. Early introspective attempts relied on subjects' ability to reconstruct the determinants of their behavior. However, it has been established that such procedures can produce biased results that lead to erroneous conclusions about the direction of causality in the attitude-behavior relationship. These distortions have been called **cognitive dissonance** effects.

Cognitive Dissonance

Suppose that you paid $1,000 for a used car that turned out to be a clunker. According to a theory developed by Leon Festinger, you would experience an unpleasant state he labels cognitive dissonance. Festinger's (1957) theory states that cognitive dissonance occurs when we have two cognitions or thoughts that are incompatible or inconsistent with each other. In this case, paying out a substantial sum for a car (cognition #1) is psychologically incompatible with the fact that the car runs poorly (cognition #2). Dissonance is expected to be especially great when the incompatible cognitions reflect badly on us, such as when we appear to act stupidly. According to Festinger, dissonance is a motivational state (like hunger) that energizes and directs behavior aimed at reducing the unpleasant state of tension associated with the dissonance.

Festinger suggests various modes of reducing dissonance. For example, you can try to change one of the elements to make the two elements consistent or consonant. You might try to kid yourself into believing your new car runs pretty well considering its age and price. Alternatively, you can add consonant cognitions to reduce dissonance. The car may not run very well but your friends sure are impressed by the way it looks. Finally, you can reduce cognitive dissonance by changing your attitude concerning the importance of the cognitions. You might decide that you're at the stage of life when career goals and personal relationships are a lot more important than what kind of car you drive.

It is not our intention here to describe in detail cognitive dissonance theory. Rather, our purpose is to show the relevance of the theory for designing behavioral studies and interpreting their results. The theory suggests, for example, that asking a person to retrospectively analyze an earlier behavior or decision can produce a distorted view of the causes of that behavior. A study by Younger, Walker, and Arrowood (1977) illustrates how people's tendency to rationalize their choices can be uncovered. Subjects were interviewed in a naturalistic setting just before and just after placing a bet on a game of chance such as bingo. Subjects were asked to rate their confidence in their bets and indicate how lucky they felt. As predicted by dissonance theory, people were more confident in their bet and felt luckier after making their bet than before making it. The relevance of such results for designing behavioral studies is that an understanding of the processes underlying a particular behavior is difficult if not impossible to achieve "after-the-fact." Subjects' reported feelings of luck and confidence after the bet were not indicative of how they felt before deciding to make the bet.

One implication of the work on cognitive dissonance is that any observed correlation between attitudes and behavior may be due, among other things, to the directive influence of behavior on attitudes as well as the directive influence of attitudes on behavior. You will recognize this as the classic problem facing correlational or observational research. Later in this chapter we will look at ways of dealing with this problem.

Social Roles

One area in which social psychologists have devised novel uses of the experimental method in order to address the issue of causality is the study of **social roles**. Social psychologists are interested in how individuals fulfill their roles in society and how these roles affect them individually. Social roles are sometimes studied in natural settings, but we will emphasize in this section studies in which subjects are placed in unfamiliar settings where these roles are either explicitly prescribed or they are apt to strongly infer that certain roles are expected of them.

You will recall from chapter 1 that an example of this general issue arose in interpreting the results of psychological research. Demand characteristics can lead subjects to perform in ways they think will please the experimenter. In order to eliminate biased responding, good researchers typically avoid revealing to subjects any expectations about their behavior. As we will see in this section, however, researchers studying social roles (as opposed to controlling them) will purposely create such expectations.

Sex Roles

Each society assigns different roles to its female and male members. We all know what these are. It is the purpose of this section to illustrate an experimental method to investigate our ability to play

these roles. In an experiment by von Baeyer, Sherk, and Zanna (1981), female job applicants were scheduled to be interviewed by male interviewers who were described either as valuing the traditional female stereotype of emotionality and deference or as being in favor of more independent, career-oriented women. The experimenters observed each subject's appearance as well as her answers to the interviewer's questions. (Note the need for a "blind" observer here.) The values that the women expected of the interviewer clearly affected their self-presentation strategies. Women who expected a traditional interviewer looked more "feminine" in their demeanor and appearance, including the choice of clothes, makeup, and accessories. These women also tended to give "traditional" answers to questions about marriage and children. In all these respects, these women differed markedly from those who expected an interviewer who valued career-oriented women. The latter group was much less apt to fulfill traditional female stereotypes.

Similar studies with corresponding results have been conducted with men who altered their presentation to fit the presumed values of the person evaluating them. The same is true for role-playing based on racial or ethnic stereotypes. The point is that relatively simple experimental designs can be used to demonstrate how people respond instrumentally to the roles expected of them. The following two examples are particularly revealing.

Compliance: The Milgram Study

A series of experiments conducted in the 1960s by Stanley Milgram (reported in Milgram, 1974) examined people's **compliance** with the roles assigned to them. Milgram's goal was to try to understand acts of brutality during wartime performed in the role of a soldier "taking orders." In the initial study each of 40 men who answered an ad in the newspaper was brought into the laboratory to ostensibly assist in a study of the effects of punishment on learning. The experimenter—a stern-looking "authority figure" in a white lab coat—introduced the subject to another "subject," a rather mild-looking middle-aged man.

One subject in each pair was to play the "teacher" and the other the "learner," where the roles were assigned by drawing slips of paper from a hat. As you may already have guessed, the drawing was rigged and the actual subject became the teacher and the "other subject"—a confederate—became the learner. The teacher's task was to administer electric shocks to the learner by pressing a switch on a realistic-looking shock-generator. Instructions were to increase the level of shock with each successive error on a paired-associates list. The switches were labeled (from left to right) as follows: slight shock, moderate shock, strong shock, very strong shock, intense shock, extreme-intensity shock, and danger: severe shock. In addition, two other switches at the far right were marked XXX.

As the session progressed, the "learner" continued to make errors and reacted in obvious discomfort; moaning, groaning, and pleading as the supposed shock level was increased. If the subject appeared unwilling to go on delivering shocks—as was often the case, as evidenced by sweating, nervous laughter, etc.—the experimenter admonished him to continue. Initial requests were gentle, such as, "Please go on," but progressed to, "It is absolutely essential that you continue," and finally, "You have no other choice. You *must* go on." The result was that 65 percent of the subjects complied with the requests and gave the confederate the full range of shocks. Later experiments in the series verified that "normal" people can be made to comply with such extreme requests by authority figures, with the level of compliance varying slightly as a function of features of the experimental setting, for example, whether it was at Yale University or in an old office building.

However, when the same general experiment was conducted again with two "defiant" confederates, results were different. These confederates who were supposedly associates of the subject-teacher refused to continue after the shock level reached a certain point. With these confederates for support, 90 percent of the subjects stopped before giving the victim the full range of shocks. Other situations contributing to reduced compliance include the close physical proximity of the victim to the subject and the absence from view of the authority figure.

While this study did serve to demonstrate conditions for compliance with the requests of an authority figure and thus helped us understand some of what happened during wartime, it also turned out to be a landmark study in calling attention to ethical issues in the use of deception in research. Milgram's subjects were debriefed at the end of the session and were shown that they had not actually harmed anyone. Still, some subjects were left with the disturbing feeling that they were capable of administering harm to another person, just because they were told to do so.

Compliance with an authority figure need not always take on such a sinister connotation. If the authority figure is a trusted physician who prescribes a regime of diet and exercise to help you deal with your cholesterol problem—an example the present author knows all too well—then compliance may be a wise course of action. Research that helps us understand the dynamics of compliance in this case can lead to improved health care. For example, the demeanor of the authority figure and whether orders are given face-to-face may be important factors.

The Milgram study is our first example of the use of deception as a research tool. Deception in this case was the only way to do this research—short of actually injuring people—but its use is not without controversy. Do the benefits gained from the results of the study outweigh the costs to the research participants? Recall the guidelines presented at the end of chapter 1 for addressing such ethical issues. If such a study were proposed today, it would have to be approved by an ethics committee.

Roles in Society: The Stanford Prison Experiment

A classic study performed in the basement of the psychology building at Stanford University by Philip Zimbardo and his colleagues dramatically demonstrates how we tend to adopt the characteristics expected of us when we are assigned a role in society. In addition to its substantive findings, this study also demonstrates the potential power of the psychology experiment. After screening potential subjects to eliminate those with signs of emotional immaturity, a group of male college students (paid volunteers) was randomly divided into "prisoners" and "guards." The randomization in this case was real, in contrast to the Milgram study. (Recall the discussion in chapter 1 of the importance of randomization in the experimental method.) To create an atmosphere of realism, "prisoners" were "arrested" at their homes, frisked, handcuffed, and booked before being driven blindfolded to the "prison."

For a two-week period subjects were to assume their designated roles, including clothes, confinement, and expected behavior. Guards were allowed to set up their own rules for running the prison, including supervising work shifts, meals, and even toilet visits. The behavior actually exhibited included increased power exerted by the guards, a rebellion by the prisoners, a crushing of the rebellion by the guards, subsequent passivity and depression in most of the prisoners and severe emotional disturbance in several of them (who were promptly "released"), and harassment and dehumanizing treatment of the prisoners by the guards. Because of these dramatic results, the experiment was actually terminated after only six days. The researchers (Haney & Zimbardo, 1977) concluded that the prison setting may actually create the type of behavior—passivity and depression among prisoners, and brutality among the guards—observed in this simulation. Critics have argued that the volunteers knew they were subjects in a prison experiment and adopted the "subject role" expected of them. Many social psychologists, however, feel that role playing in an experiment is in fact a quite useful analog of role playing in occupational, family, and other actual social settings.

It is worthy of note that in later interviews many of the "guards" in the Stanford Prison Experiment expressed great surprise and remorse concerning their own behavior, much as was the case in the Milgram study. This then presents an ethical dilemma for researchers. We may have truly humanitarian motivations for conducting research to better understand the causes of antisocial behavior. But if we need to "create" antisocial behavior in the laboratory, are we not concerned about the psychological effects on participants of performing that behavior? As a brief review of our discussion in chapter 1, let us recall that university departments and government agencies have developed strict guidelines for maintaining ethical standards in psychological research. It is quite likely that some of the studies described in this chapter could not have been conducted under present rules.

Person Perception

Social roles represent only one way in which we judge and react to other people. The area of **person perception** is concerned with the way we categorize persons in terms of their attitudes, behavior, physical appearance, gender, race, occupation, and so forth. The way we categorize a person is an important determinant of the way we act toward that person. If a person is seen as fitting a particular category, there is a tendency to see that person as having all the attributes ascribed to the category. This can have dire consequences, as in racial or ethnic stereotyping or in teachers' expectations of students who happen to score poorly on a standardized intelligence test.

For example, Rubovits and Maehr (1973) showed how expectancies based on racial stereotypes can result in differential behavior toward blacks and whites. White college students enrolled in a teacher training course were to teach a lesson to four junior high school students—two whites and two blacks of comparable ability. Prior to the session the teachers had been given (false) information about the students. One student of each race was randomly assigned a high IQ score and was given the label "gifted" and the other was not. The teacher's behavior during the 40-minute teaching session was coded according to several categories of student-teacher interaction. Analyses of these codings revealed racial biases: black students were given less attention, ignored more, praised less, and criticized more than white students. Furthermore, there was an interaction between race and label. The label "gifted" led to a positive response from teachers only if the student was white. A slight reversal occurred for black students, with giftedness being associated with less positive treatment.

Among the basic questions to be addressed in person perception are the following: Do I like this person? Why did he or she behave that way? These questions are called, respectively, the evaluation question and the causality question (Cantor & Mischel, 1979). Different research paradigms were developed to address each question.

Evaluation

Personality Impression Formation

We have already discussed a method for addressing the evaluation question. The *personality impression formation* paradigm described in the chapter on judgment, decision making, and problem solving used a person perception task to test models of information integration. The desirable features of that task for model testing were that prescaled stimulus values (prior ratings of individual personality trait adjectives) could be combined in sets conforming to specific design requirements (e.g., varying combinations of favorable and unfavorable information), and response requirements (e.g., rating the "likability" of persons defined by each adjective set) were easily understood and could be related to subjects' personal experiences.

For judgment and decision making researchers, this task yielded valuable insights into how information is combined—for example, subjects' evaluations of a person could be described as an average of the values of the individual traits describing that person. Furthermore, the impression formation paradigm yielded substantive results related to the question, Do I like this person? Descriptions provided by sources we trust are weighted more than descriptions provided by other sources. A single negative trait has a disproportionate influence on our impressions of a person. Trait information is less important in evaluating a person who is judged as physically unattractive than in evaluating a person who is judged as attractive.

Attraction

Social psychologists investigating how persons evaluate others sometimes use the term *attraction* to describe their area. Attraction can be defined as an attitude expressing the degree of liking or disliking of another person. A common paradigm for studying attraction is to vary the degree of similarity between the subject and the person being judged.

In general, the more similar you feel to another person the more you will be attracted to that person. The key to addressing this issue experimentally is to formalize the similarity relationship. Byrne and Nelson (1965) operationally defined *similarity* by varying the proportion of shared attitudes held by two people. A group of college students was initially given an attitude scale in which they indicated their opinions about each of a number of topics. At a later date (after their own responses had been scored), they were asked to read an attitude scale supposedly filled out by another student of their same sex. The responses of the "stranger" were actually programmed by the researchers to fit a prearranged proportion of similar attitudes to the subject. Different groups of subjects received proportions of 1.00, .67, .50, and .33. Each subject was asked to rate the stranger on a series of 7-point semantic differential scales with respect to intelligence, knowledge of current events, morality, adjustment, probable liking for the stranger, and probable enjoyment of working with the stranger. The latter two ratings were combined into a single attraction score. The major finding was that attraction scores were positively and linearly related to proportion of similar attitudes. These results were interpreted in terms of a reinforcement theory in which attitude similarity is conceptualized as constituting positive reinforcement.

Rosenbaum (1986) expanded the attraction paradigm by including a control condition in which ratings of attraction are made in the absence of attitudinal information. For example, in one study he imbedded into an array of descriptive traits of a stimulus person either the word *Democrat* or the word *Republican* or no party affiliation was indicated. Ratings of the stimulus person were obtained at Democratic and Republican presidential caucuses. (Note the uniqueness of this research setting. Undergraduate students were sent out to various caucus sites to collect data. This undoubtedly led to the recruitment of subjects who were more involved and opinionated than the general population.) The major differences in response were found between the control condition and the condition in which the subjects' party affiliation was opposite to that of the stimulus person. Ratings were significantly lower in the "opposite party" condition than in the control condition, but ratings were not significantly different in the "same party" condition and the control condition. Rosenbaum thus concluded that dissimilarity was a more potent force in attraction than was similarity.

Attribution of Causality

Research on the causality question of why a person behaved in a certain way has largely been guided by a theory known as **attribution theory** (Kelley, 1972). According to this theory, we attribute causes to persons' actions by deciding whether the behavior was due to: (1) internal factors (something about the persons themselves); (2) external factors (something about the stimuli or environment to which they are reacting); or (3) transient factors (something about the specific situation or particular moment in time). The theory states that in order to reach this decision, we rely on three basic types of information: (1) consensus—the extent to which other persons act in the same manner as the person in question; (2) consistency—the extent to which this person acts in the same manner on other occasions; and (3) distinctiveness—the extent to which this person acts in the same manner in other situations or only in this situation. The theory predicts that we are most likely to attribute another person's behavior to internal causes if consensus is low (i.e., he or she is one of the only people to act this way), consistency is high (he or she tends to act this way on other occasions when this situation arises), and distinctiveness is low (it is not the case that the

person acts this way only in this particular situation). Conversely, we are predicted to attribute another person's behavior to external causes if consensus is high (e.g., most people act this way in this situation), consistency is low (e.g., the person does not always act this way in this situation), and distinctiveness is high (the person acts this way only when this particular situation arises).

There are, of course, times when we do not have information about all three factors: consensus, consistency, and distinctiveness. Consider a subject in the condition of Milgram's (1974) study in which 65 percent of the subjects administered the full range of shocks. If the subject did give the full range of shocks, would you attribute that subject's actions to internal or external factors? What about the subject who refused to comply? How would these subjects judge their own actions?

One interesting application of attribution theory is to compare attributions of the same behavior by those who perform the behavior and those who observe it. The actor may recall that his or her behavior has shown variance in similar situations in the past and thus attribute the behavior to situational influences. On the other hand, observers often lack information about the distinctiveness or consistency of the actor's behavior, and thus they are prone to attribute causality for the same behavior to stable dispositions possessed by the actor. Turnquist, Harvey and Andersen (1988) report several examples of this in the area of illness attributions. Husbands of breast cancer patients are more apt than their wives to attribute the disease to their wives' character. Similarly, wives of heart attack patients are more likely than their husbands to perceive their husbands' personality or overworking as the cause of the attack. Physicians are more apt than patients to attribute heart attacks to patients' habits (e.g., smoking, diet). An exaggerated tendency to attribute behavior to characteristics of the person rather than the environment is sometimes called "the fundamental attribution error."

BOX 9.2

Manipulation Checks

Manipulation checks are attempts to verify operational definitions of independent variable manipulations apart from observing their effects on the dependent variable. In areas such as learning where "amount of prior training" is operationally defined by the number of trials, such checks may not be necessary. However, in other areas manipulation checks can be very useful. They can provide clues as to how an experiment can be modified if the original results were unsatisfactory. For example, studies on animal behavior sometimes require the subjects to be sacrificed so that autopsies can be performed to verify anatomical manipulations such as the location and extent of brain lesions. Such verifications

of independent variable manipulations are important for determining if the lack of a predicted experimental effect is due to a misspecification of levels of the independent variables. In other cases they can be useful in showing that an experimental effect is caused by something other than what was originally presumed.

A key element of studies of audience effects (to be described later in this chapter) is to manipulate whether a performance is being evaluated or merely observed by others. An important manipulation check here would be to ask the subjects if they thought the other people in the room were actually evaluating them.

The consequences of attributions have also been studied. In a simulated medical decision-making task, Levin and Chapman (1990) showed that subjects favored allocation of medical resources to patients whom they perceived to bear little personal responsibility for disease contraction over patients whom they perceived to bear high personal responsibility. Studies whose independent variables are as diffuse as "responsibility for disease contraction" or "attitude similarity" often include assessment of how subjects perceive each level of the independent variable. These assessments are called **manipulation checks.**

Manipulation checks are especially common in social psychology studies involving manipulation of subjective constructs such as attitudes, opinions, and first impressions. Consider the study designed to investigate people's willingness to allocate resources to save the victims of disease as a function of attributions of responsibility for disease contraction (Levin & Chapman, 1990). Two AIDS victim groups were included—intravenous drug users and

hemophiliacs. A pilot study was needed to confirm—through the use of rating scales—that subjects actually did perceive these two groups to differ on degree of responsibility for disease contraction. Higher responsibility for disease contraction was attributed to intravenous drug users than to hemophiliacs. Only then could "perceived responsibility" be assigned a causal influence in allocating medical resources. Box 9.2 provides a further description and examples of manipulation checks.

Group Processes

In addition to being interested in how people perceive and react to others, social psychologists are interested in how individuals are affected by others. These interests are often focused on the groups to which we belong by choice or by circumstance. Do we behave differently when we are in a group compared to when we act alone? How are our attitudes and beliefs affected by those of the other group members? How do we feel when we have to perform in the presence of others? In this section we will examine the methods used to address such questions.

Cooperation and Competition

An attractive way to study group processes is to vary conditions promoting cooperation or competition among group members. Deutsch (1949) reported that reward structures that favored cooperation tended to yield greater group productivity than those that favored competition. Deutsch developed a set of hypotheses concerning the different processes underlying cooperation and competition. For example, in a cooperative setting an action by one person can lead to rewards for all group members, whereas in a competitive setting an action by one person can lead to reward for that person at the expense of others. As a consequence, rewards for competition can lead to obstructive behavior and lack of role differentiation.

Advances in the development of theories of cooperation and competition—especially those that relate to the behavior of individuals within a group—require methods that allow an assessment of the ongoing processes rather than just the products of cooperation and competition. An approach that has received much study is the provision of the opportunity to act cooperatively as opposed to competitively. The most popular task employed in pursuing this approach is the **Prisoners' Dilemma** game. The Prisoners' Dilemma game is patterned after the following potentially real situation: two suspects who are believed to have committed a serious crime together are each arrested and charged. The district attorney does not have enough evidence against either one of them to insure a conviction and therefore tries to get each suspect to confess. Each suspect is interviewed in isolation from the other. The district attorney explains to each of the suspects that they can either confess or stick to their alibi. It is further explained that if both suspects refuse to confess, each will be booked on a relatively minor charge and each will receive a one year sentence. If they both confess, each will be charged with the more serious crime and each will

FIGURE 9.2   The Prisoners' Dilemma and its experimental analog. In the boxes of the upper panel, outcomes below the diagonal are for Prisoner 1 and outcomes above the diagonal are for Prisoner 2. In the boxes of the lower panel, outcomes below the diagonal are for the subject and outcomes above the diagonal are for the subject's opponent (Baron & Byrne, 1987).

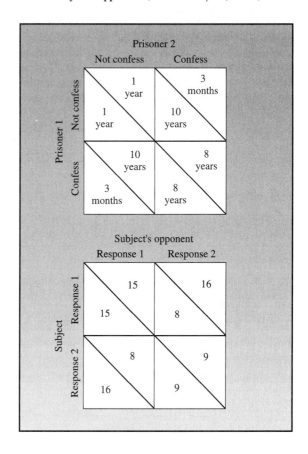

receive a stiffer sentence (8 years). However, if one suspect were to confess while the other does not, then the one who confesses will receive the minimum sentence (3 months) and the one who did not will receive the maximum sentence (10 years). The key to this task is that the outcome of one person's response (confess or not confess) will depend not only on his or her own response but also on the response of the other person. This is shown in the upper panel of figure 9.2.

In the Prisoners' Dilemma, cooperation between the suspects takes the form of neither suspect confessing and each receiving a relatively mild sentence. Competition takes the form of one suspect confessing in hopes that the other suspect will not confess. If the second suspect in fact does not confess, then the first suspect will benefit (receive the minimum sentence). If, however, the second suspect also confesses, then both suspects will receive a stiffer penalty than if neither of them had confessed.

In a generalized form of the Prisoners' Dilemma each of two subjects must independently choose one of two available responses, such as pushing one of two buttons. The rules are as follows: if each subject makes Response 1, the "cooperative" choice, then each will receive a moderate reward. If a subject makes Response 2, the "competitive" choice, then that subject's reward can be maximized at the expense of the other subject. (See lower panel of figure 9.2.) In many experiments, the "partner" is actually the experimenter's preprogrammed sequence of responses. While it would be difficult in many settings to reliably measure cooperative and competitive behavior, operational definitions are simple and straightforward in the Prisoners' Dilemma task. The number of times the subject makes Response 1 and Response 2 is used to examine the relative prevalence of cooperation and competition as a function of reward structures or as a function of cultural and individual differences. Of particular interest is how a subject's responses change over time as a function of the other person's actions. According to Baron and Byrne (1987), competitive persons tend to operate in a self-fulfilling manner. Because they refuse to cooperate with others, they more or less force competition from others. (How would you respond in the Prisoners' Dilemma game if your partner consistently made Response 2?).

The role of cooperative and competitive behavior is a primary focus for a growing number of psychologists interested in environmental issues. Scarcities of crucial public resources such as clean air and water have been attributed in part to unchecked consumption by self-interested individuals at the expense of society as a whole. Individual's responses to such "social dilemmas" may depend on the extent to which they are motivated primarily by concern for their own outcomes or by concern for the collective consequences. Thus, psychologists have developed experimental tasks that serve as analogs for studying conflicts between self-interests and environmental concerns. Such interest is part of a growing area called **environmental psychology.**

Kramer, McClintock, and Messick (1986) developed the following simulated resource conservation task. Groups of six subjects each were told that a resource pool containing 300 points (each worth 5 cents) was available to share between them. On each trial each subject could take from 0 to 10 points. After each trial the remaining pool was increased by 10 percent. Subjects had to decide between taking all that they wanted at the moment—at the risk of quickly using up the resource—or taking a little bit on many occasions, with the possibility of everyone getting more in the long run because the resource was able to replenish itself. False feedback about the other subjects' use of the resource was varied to indicate either that the resource was being sustained or that collective overuse was rapidly depleting it.

Subjects were classified as "cooperators" or "noncooperators" on the basis of prior performance on a two-person task much like the Prisoners' Dilemma. An interaction was found between this classification of subjects and feedback about others' use of the resource. Responses (number of points taken) to the sustained resource condition did not differ between groups, but responses to the depleted resource condition showed that cooperatively oriented subjects exercised greater self-constraint than did noncooperators. Thus the combination of a cooperative attitude and awareness of resource depletion seems crucial in promoting constraint in using common resources.

Bystander Behavior

You are being stalked by a mugger. Out of the corner of your eye you see some people nearby witnessing your plight. Some of them will surely come to your rescue, right? Well, maybe. Several unfortunate real-life incidents showed that bystanders do not always come to the rescue in such cases. What determines whether bystanders will aid another person in distress? Some information can be gained by observation, by collecting and classifying similar cases, and by conducting correlational analyses. However, social psychologists interested in this question generally prefer to bring relevant variables under experimental control. This is a common way in which social psychologists as well as other experimental psychologists get their research ideas: observe a socially significant behavioral phenomenon; search for the relevant variables; then try to bring these variables under experimental control in a laboratory setting.

One potentially important variable is the number of bystanders. Darley and Latané (1968) examined how a subject's response to an emergency situation varied as a function of the number of other bystanders the subject perceived to be there. College students were told that they were to take part in a discussion with other students via an intercom. The subject believed he or she was interacting with one other student, two other students, or five other students. Actually, the subject was alone; the other "students" were just tape recordings. The discussion began with the participants introducing themselves; then suddenly, the person on one of the recordings began to gasp as if he were having an epileptic-like seizure. The behavior of interest was if and when the subject would call for help.

Results were dramatic. The number of perceived bystanders had a large effect on helping behavior. The more bystanders, the less likely the subject was to do anything. The percentage of subjects trying to help the victim decreased from about 85 percent when the subject thought he or she was the only bystander to about 30 percent when he or she thought there were five other bystanders. Furthermore, even when the subject did act, the more bystanders, the more time it took before the subject did anything. This behavior has been called **diffusion of responsibility.** Post-experimental interviews showed that it was not just a matter of apathy or indifference. Subjects were apparently caught in

a conflict between wanting to help others and fearing that they would do the wrong thing and look foolish to the other bystanders.

In addition to the laboratory setting, experimental manipulation of bystander behavior has been conducted in field settings. In a series of studies by the Piliavins, the "field" was the subway of a large city. For example, a study by Piliavin, Piliavin, and Rodin (1975) conducted on the New York subway used confederates to manipulate the unpleasantness of helping in an emergency situation, and whether or not a more able fellow bystander was perceived to be present.

One confederate played the part of the victim, a white male carrying a cane, and either had a physical stigma (a large, unattractive "birthmark" painted on his cheek) or had no physical stigma. Another confederate played the part of a bystander seated near the victim. This bystander either wore a sports coat and tie or he wore a white medical jacket and looked like a medical person. The "emergency" occurred between two subway stops when the "victim" staggered and fell on the floor, and remained there with his eyes closed. To increase generality of results, the study included 166 trials run at all times of the day, with a number of different actors playing the roles of victim and bystander. In the no birthmark condition, a high percentage of bystanders tried to help the victim, and the presence or absence of an available "medical person" had little effect. However, in the birthmark condition, fewer people helped, especially when there was perceived to be an able bystander (medical personnel) present.

Studies like this were designed to see if variables such as perceived need of helping and victim characteristics affect prosocial behavior in a realistic setting. These variables were manipulated in the New York subway study. Studies using the experimental method in a realistic setting are called **field experiments.**

Can you think of other independent variables besides number of bystanders to include in studies of bystander helping behavior? For example, do you think that the degree to which the bystander "identifies with" the victim could be a factor? How would you operationalize this variable? There is precedence for considering such a variable. There can be dramatic differences in reaction to a group with which an individual identifies (the "ingroup") and groups to which an individual does not identify (the "outgroups"). Members of outgroups are generally the recipients of more negative attitudes and less favorable treatment than are members of the ingroup (Brewer, 1979).

Presence of Others

The other side of the coin of being a bystander is having others observe you. Social psychologists have devised tasks and theories aimed at understanding how the presence of others can affect our behavior. What made the need for rigorous experimental investigation apparent was the initial inconsistency of evidence; sometimes persons (and animals) performed better in the presence of others and sometimes they performed worse. After reviewing earlier evidence, Zajonc concluded in 1965 that both facilitation and impairment of performance can be explained by the assumption that the presence of others serves to increase our level of motivation or arousal.

Zajonc's theory is an extension of Hullian drive theory (Hull, 1943), which states that drive or arousal interacts with response strength such that the strongest or most dominant response is more likely to be emitted under conditions of high drive than under low drive. If the dominant response is in fact the correct response, then increased drive facilitates performance; otherwise, it interferes with performance. In order to test a drive theory interpretation of audience effects, it is necessary to find a task with a clearly dominant response and see how the probability of making the response is affected by the presence of others.

In one such study, Zajonc and Sales (1966) varied the frequency of exposure of ten different nonsense words in order to manipulate subjects' familiarity with the different words. Then, in a test session, subjects were told that the words would be flashed on a screen for very brief periods of time

and that their task was to recognize them. In reality, the slides contained only wavy lines. The researchers reasoned that the subjects' guesses would reflect the degree of familiarity of words learned in the first part of the task. This was confirmed in pilot work with varying monetary rewards serving as the drive manipulation. Because the task was shown to be sensitive to more traditional drive manipulations (recall our earlier discussion of manipulation checks), it was then feasible to use this task to examine the drivelike effects of the presence of an audience.

Zajonc and Sales manipulated the presence vs. absence of an audience by having half the subjects work alone and the other half work in the presence of two confederates. As predicted by the theory, subjects emitted more dominant (familiar) responses and fewer subordinate (unfamiliar) responses in the presence of an audience than when alone.

Later experiments manipulated not only the presence vs. absence of an audience but also the function of the audience. Paulus and Murdoch (1971), using a recognition task similar to that used by Zajonc and Sales, included four different audience conditions. Some subjects performed alone and were given no indication that their performance was to be evaluated, and some subjects performed alone but were told that their performance would later be evaluated by two other individuals. Some subjects performed before two other individuals who were said to be evaluating them, and some subjects performed before two others who would not evaluate them. In this case, the **social facilitation effect**—the enhancement of dominant responses—occurred only when evaluation was expected and was not due to the mere presence of others.

The use of theory in this case was particularly interesting, so let's briefly review it. The first thing to note is that the theory was "borrowed" from another area—animal learning—and then applied to social psychology. The most important aspect of the theory is that it deals with intervening variables (drive and response strength) and not just overt behavior. If the presence of others was assumed to have a direct effect on behavior, then it would be predicted to always facilitate or always hinder performance. However, by operationally defining "drive" in terms of the presence or absence of an audience and by hypothesizing that drive interacts with response strength to affect behavior, the theory was able to successfully predict situations when performance would be helped by an audience and when performance would be hindered by an audience. Furthermore, the theory was modifiable in terms of its operational definitions and the two versions of the theory—one defining increased drive by the mere presence of an audience and one defining increased drive by the presence of potential evaluators—could be readily compared.

Crowding

The effects of population density on behavior is an area of interest that has drawn from research using humans and animals in laboratory and naturalistic settings. Contemporary psychologists consider the study of crowding to be a key element in the newly developed area of environmental psychology because it deals with environmental influences on behavior. The key variable in most of these studies is the number of persons or animals per unit of space. Not only is this a readily quantified variable, it also fits the layperson's notion of what crowding is all about. For example, in a naturalistic setting, Baron and associates (1976) measured the attitudes of student dormitory residents differing in number of roommates. For students living in similar sized rooms, students with two roommates were less satisfied with their roommates and perceived them to be less cooperative than students with only one roommate.

Crowding in humans has been considered a form of "environmental stress" produced by overpopulation. Among the realistic observational studies of crowding is Paulus, McCain, and Cox's (1978) examination of crowding in prisons. Observations of prison records for an entire prison system for an eight year period revealed that the death rate (percent of prisoners who died) from various forms of cardiovascular disease was much higher in those years when the prison population was highest. As is typically the case in observational studies, the researchers could

not rule out factors other than crowding (e.g., prison staffing, quality of health care) that may also have varied. A supplemental finding that would not be subject to such confounding factors helps validate the authors' conclusions about the negative health effects of long-term crowding. They examined prisoners *at one point in time* and found those living in the more crowded areas to have elevated levels of blood pressure.

The experimental method has been used to manipulate population density. This can be accomplished by either varying the amount of space for a fixed number of individuals or by varying the number of individuals in a fixed amount of space. For example, Rohe and Patterson (1974) varied density in a children's day care center by subjecting a group of constant size to conditions of both high and low spatial density. Decreased room size led to significant increases in destructive and aggressive behaviors.

Several interesting studies with animals have combined experimental and observational methods by controlling spatial factors and observing their effects on naturally occurring phenomena. Calhoun (1971) reports a study in which rats were contained in an apparatus that could comfortably accommodate 48 rats. The population was allowed to increase unchecked, with adequate food and water but no additional space provided. When the population reached about 80, hyperactivity, sexual aggression, and cannibalism occurred, mortality increased and maternal behavior was disturbed. Physiological disorders such as tumors became common. In short, crowding had adverse effects on rats.

In a study with humans that also combines elements of the experimental and observational methods, Bickman and associates (1973) used the "lost-letter technique" to examine helping behavior as a function of living density. Stamped, addressed envelopes were dropped in public areas of dormitories that were either high, medium, or low in density. Helpfulness was operationally defined as the percentage of letters picked up and mailed by dormitory residents. Low-density dormitories showed the highest rate of return and high-density dormitories showed the lowest rate of return. These latter two studies—which we said involved a combination of experimental and observational methods—are not "true" experiments. For example, students were not assigned at random to dormitories of different density. This makes it a *quasi-experimental* study. Subject variables such as socioeconomic status may differ between more crowded and less crowded dormitories and may be related to helping behavior.

The use of multiple methods and subject populations to investigate a given phenomenon provides **converging evidence** for the reliability of the findings.

Conformity

One interesting phenomenon in the study of group processes is **conformity**—the tendency of individuals to match the behavior of the majority of the group. This is especially apt to occur in situations where the appropriate response is difficult or unclear. Thus, researchers interested in this phenomenon have adopted tasks known to be ambiguous to subjects. Some of the perceptual tasks described in chapter 4 are suitable candidates. Sherif (1937) used the "autokinetic illusion" to study conformity. When a person is placed in a completely dark room and is presented with a single, stationary pinpoint of light, he or she cannot determine precisely where the light is located. The typical subject perceives the stationary light to be moving. After a while, a person who is exposed to the light for a series of trials will settle on a range of locations within which the light is seen as moving. Different persons will have different ranges.

Sherif examined how subjects are influenced by the reported perceptions of other persons. When a group of people mutually report their perceptions, the group tends to establish its own range and each individual tends to report that the light moves within that range. In other words, the members of a group tend to converge in their reported perceptions. Even when confederates make up false reports of how they see the light moving (e.g., they report seeing the light move in an arc), subjects are likely to report seeing the light move in that same way.

Asch (1951) also used a psychophysical task to study conformity. Asch was particularly interested in how an individual will react when confronted with a group that unanimously and incorrectly agrees on a particular judgment. A group of seven to nine students was gathered together in a classroom to participate in what was called a study of visual discrimination. The task required subjects on each trial to match the length of a standard line with one of three comparison lines. One comparison line was the same as the standard while the other two were different. In the experimental condition the group contained only one real subject; the rest were confederates who were instructed to give incorrect responses on two-thirds of the trials. Furthermore, all but one of the confederates gave their responses before it was the real subject's turn. (Note how the use of confederates affords much greater control over the extent of group disagreement than would be the case for an actual group of subjects.) In the control condition there were no confederates giving wrong answers and 95 percent of the subjects made no errors in matching the line lengths. In the experimental condition, 76 percent of the subjects made at least one error by going along with the group. Most of these subjects realized that they differed from the rest of the group but went along with the group because they came to doubt their own perceptions.

Since Asch's early experiments, many other investigations have been carried on along similar lines, with investigators trying to determine what variables affect conformity. Many of these have used a procedural refinement developed by Crutchfield (1955). Rather than employing a group of confederates to create a pressure for conformity, Crutchfield used five real subjects sitting side by side, separated by partitions. Each subject faced a panel supposedly displaying the responses of the other subjects. In reality, the information displayed on the panel was programmed by the experimenter.

Group Decisions

After determining that individuals within a group tend to conform to the behavior of the majority of group members, one might ask how judgments or decisions made by groups as a whole compare to those made by individuals alone. Research of this type requires an assessment of the initial opinions of individual group members, a period of group interaction, and then a final single group decision. The group decision is then examined as a function of the component individual decisions.

As reported by Baron and Byrne (1987), a master's thesis project by James Stoner at MIT uncovered a phenomenon that came to be known as the **risky shift.** In a prototypical task used by Stoner, subjects had to choose between a secure but low-paying job and a less certain but higher-paying position with a new company. In the first phase of the experiment, subjects made their recommendations concerning the decision alone. Then, they met in small groups where they discussed the recommendations and came to an agreement. The agreement in this case and in a number of others studied by Stoner was to choose the risky alternative (e.g., the less certain but higher-paying job) to a greater extent than would be predicted from the prediscussion decisions.

Other studies, however, have found evidence for a "stingy shift"—a group decision that was more conservative than would be predicted from the average of the initial individual opinions. Thus, at a more general level, these phenomena concerning group decisions have been called a "shift toward polarization" (Baron & Byrne, 1987), where group discussion leads individual group members to become more extreme in the same direction as their initial pregroup responses, especially if these responses are seen as socially desirable.

One obvious area of extension of the research on conformity and group decisions is jury decision making. As described in a recent review by MacCoun (1989), experimental research using "mock juries" is crucial because manipulation of the variables of interest is not ethically or legally feasible in actual trial settings and there has been legislation specifically prohibiting attempts to observe or record actual jury deliberation. In the mock jury experiment research participants are randomly assigned to alternative trial conditions and asked to reach a verdict in a simulated case. Manipulations can include the type and strength of evidence presented, the personal characteristics of the defendant and victim, and the degree of agreement/disagreement between jurors. The most robust finding in mock jury research is the majority effect: a faction's influence is a function of its relative size. The result is that even when a jury is ostensibly operating under a unanimity decision rule, its verdict can usually be predicted by an implicit two-thirds majority rule. The pressure to conform to the will of the majority is undoubtedly a factor in why there aren't more "hung" juries.

Mass Media Effects

One informal group that we all belong to is the "audience" of mass media presentations. Researchers have investigated the persuasive effects of mass media advertisements on consumers, the effectiveness of newspaper, magazine, radio, and television editorials in changing our political attitudes, and the extent to which we model the roles portrayed in films and on television.

The effects of television, in particular, have been the object of considerable study by social psychologists (and clinical psychologists as well). Sometimes this study takes the form of analyzing prosocial behavior such as helping others and showing concern for the environment that arises from constructive role models portrayed on television. More often than not, however, these studies focus on antisocial behavior such as prejudice and violence. For example, one common theme is the effect of television violence on aggressive behavior. Because causality is at the heart of this issue, it is common to find studies using the experimental method such as by exposing one group of children to a violent television episode while another group views a nonviolent program. The two groups are then allowed to participate in a play session where they can exhibit varying degrees of aggressiveness and the conclusion is often that viewing violent television causes aggressive behavior. A major problem with such a finding is that it focuses on the short-term effect of

FIGURE 9.3   Correlations obtained in the longitudinal study of TV viewing and aggressive behavior by Lefkowitz, Eron, Walder, and Huesmann (1977).

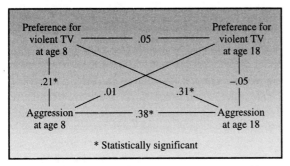

Source: Data from M. M. Lefkowitz, L. D. Eron, L. O. Walder, and L. R. Huesmann, *Growing Up to Be Violent.* Elmsford, New York: Pergamon Press, 1977.

limited exposure to television violence, whereas the real issue is whether or not prolonged exposure to television violence leads to long-term aggressive tendencies.

This has led some researchers to design long-term studies that do not directly manipulate exposure to violence on television but attempt to derive causal inferences from observations of the naturally occurring relationship between television viewing and aggressive behavior. One such example is described below.

A key feature of this study by Lefkowitz and colleagues (1977) is the use of **time-lag** or **longitudinal methods**—in this case, measuring preference for violent television programs and socially significant aggressive behavior (as rated by peers) at age 8 and, ten years later, at age 18 for the same group of boys. Correlations between measures were taken both within a given age level and across age levels. Comparisons between these correlations provide evidence of causality. The correlations obtained in the study are shown in figure 9.3.

Preference for television violence at age 8 was significantly related to aggression at age 8, but the relationship between preference for television violence and aggression was not significant at age 18.

However, there was a significant relationship between preference for television violence at age 8 and aggression at age 18. These significant relationships, in conjunction with a lack of relationship between aggression at age 8 and preference for violent television at age 18, led the researchers to conclude that the most plausible causal hypothesis is that a preference for watching violent television at age 8 contributes to the development of aggressive habits that persist at least to age 18. (Findings for some of the original subjects have now been extended to age 30.)

The status of this causal interpretation is, of course, less firm than if the experimental method had been used. For example, it cannot be ruled out that a factor such as an innate tendency towards aggression affects behavior at both ages 8 and 18 but affects TV viewing preferences only at age 8. However, the causal interpretation has logical appeal and the study certainly contains an element of ecological validity that is not present in most experimental studies of television's effect on behavior. Nevertheless, the less-than-perfect level of predictability of aggressive behavior from preference for violent television suggests that not all people are affected the same way by watching violence on television.

Summary and Conclusions

Taken together, the examples in this chapter are meant to show how the methods of experimental psychology can be integrated into a specific content area with implications for understanding real-world behavior. Furthermore, the examples are meant to show how the development of new research techniques arises from the need to address specific issues. In several instances we saw that the advantages of the experimental method could only be realized by the use of confederates who created varying social situations. In other instances the combined use of experimental, quasi-experimental, and correlational methods provided converging evidence to address a particular issue.

Social psychologists working in universities or other research settings are also experimental psychologists. They use the experimental method in controlled laboratory settings, and they use both experimental and correlational methods in field settings. Their research usually involves human subjects but they sometimes use animals. What makes social psychology a separate content area within experimental psychology is its concern with particular problems dealing with interpersonal relationships and their effect on the individual, and with group behavior as understood at the level of the individual person. The problems discussed in this chapter involved attitudes and attitude change, social roles, person perception, and group interaction.

In the section on attitudes and attitude change we saw that major concerns in studying how attitudes are changed include determining the comparative effectiveness of one-sided vs. two-sided arguments and determining how effectiveness of a communication varies as a function of the difference between the position advocated in the communication and the person's initial attitude. However, changes in attitude would be unimportant unless behavioral changes also occur. Because the prototypical study of the attitude-behavior relationship is correlational in nature, evidence to support the hypothesis that changes in attitude lead to changes in behavior is scarce. Cognitive dissonance theory provides a framework for determining under what conditions attitude change is likely to occur. Studies showed that subjects were likely to change their attitude after performing a behavior in order to make their attitude more consistent with that behavior. These studies also illustrate the difficulty of inferring attitudes "after the fact."

Studies of social roles examine how subjects respond in ways that appear consistent with their classification within society. For example, female job applicants were able to assume traditional or nontraditional sex roles, depending on what they perceived to be the expectations of the evaluators.

A particularly controversial issue that arose when studying social roles is the use of deception in psychological research. This is particularly prevalent in social psychology studies dealing with a person's reaction to the behavior or circumstances of other people. One way to manipulate the perceived behavior of others is to use deception. The use of specially designed simulated environments can also be a powerful tool for studying social roles. A study of compliance with instructions to administer electric shocks as punishment and a study of role-playing in a simulated prison setting each showed that subjects may behave in quite atypical ways if they assume the assigned roles. These studies, however, raise ethical issues concerning their effects on research participants.

Studies of person perception deal with questions such as "Do I like this person?" and "Why did he or she behave that way?" The first question has been addressed with the personality impression formation paradigm and the attraction paradigm. A common result in attraction research is that one's attraction to another person is positively related to similarity of attitudes and negatively related to degree of dissimilarity. The second question is often studied within the framework of attribution theory. Attribution theory is concerned with whether a person's behavior can be attributed to internal or external causes.

A variety of research techniques were described for studying how group interactions affect us. Studies of cooperation and competition try to understand both their causes and their effects. The Prisoners' Dilemma is the model for an experimental game in which one person's rewards depend not only on his or her own responses but on the responses of another person. In many of these tasks the other "person" is either a confederate of the experimenter or a preprogrammed sequence of recorded responses. A simulated social dilemma was used to demonstrate the potential environmental impact on cooperating for the good of the group rather than acting only to promote self-interests.

Other studies of the effect of being with other people have concentrated on how people behave in the presence of others and how they react as part of a group of bystanders. By varying the nature of the task from one in which the correct response is highly familiar to one in which the correct response is unfamiliar, researchers were able to show that the presence of an audience can have either positive or negative effects on performance. Other experimental manipulations showed that audience effects depend on whether the performer believes that he or she is being evaluated by others. Studies of bystander behavior vary the number of perceived bystanders, and a typical result is that the larger the number the less likely any given person is apt to act to help someone in distress. Studies with both rats and humans in naturalistic environments provide converging evidence that crowding can lead to distress and unhappiness. Many of the studies reported here illustrate the importance of providing appropriate operational definitions.

Studies of conformity focus on the tendency of individuals to match the behavior of the majority of the group. In order to control "majority" behavior, extensive use of confederates is made. Perceptions reported by the majority have a powerful effect on how an individual evaluates his or her own perceptions. Studies of group decisions focus on how decisions made by interacting groups such as juries differ from decisions made by individuals acting alone. Group decisions appear to be more extreme (e.g., riskier) than individual decisions. One group we all belong to is the mass media audience. Studies of the effects of the mass media on attitudes and behavior are typically correlational in nature, but a longitudinal or time-lag study of the long-term effects of watching violence on television found support for a model that assumes that viewing violent television can lead to increased aggression, at least in some people.

Exercises

1. Summarize the methodologies described for the first time in this chapter and state why they are more common in social psychology than in other areas.

2. List the pros and cons of conducting a study such as the Stanford Prison Experiment? Concentrate on the ethical issues and the potential benefits to society.

3. Describe a possible observational or correlational study of cooperation vs. competition in a real-world setting. What could be learned from this study that could not be learned in the experimental studies described in the text, and what could be learned using the experimental tasks that could not be learned in the observational study?

4. Describe how you would use attribution theory to investigate the breakup of a close personal relationship. How would you operationally define the three key constructs: consensus, consistency, distinctiveness?

Glossary

attitude-behavior relationship Validating a measure of attitude by seeing if it predicts behavior. (p. 276)

attribution theory Theory describing how we attribute causes to a person's actions. (p. 282)

cognitive dissonance State of tension that occurs when one's behavior is inconsistent with one's beliefs, values, or goals. (p. 277)

compliance Extent to which a person acts in accordance with others' expectancies or orders. (p. 278)

conformity The tendency of individuals in a group to match the behavior of the majority. (p. 289)

converging evidence The use of multiple methods and subject populations to investigate a given phenomenon. (p. 289)

diffusion of responsibility In studies of bystander helping behavior, the larger the number of bystanders, the longer it took for an individual to act. (p. 286)

environmental psychology Study of environmental influences on behavior. (p. 285)

field experiments Use of the experimental method in realistic settings. (p. 286)

manipulation checks Attempts to verify operational definitions of independent variable manipulations. (p. 283)

person perception The way we categorize persons in terms of their attitudes, behavior, physical appearance, etc. (p. 280)

Prisoners' Dilemma Experimental analysis of cooperation vs. competition in which one person's rewards or punishments depend on another's as well as on his or her own responses. (p. 284)

risky shift Tendency for an interacting group to choose a risky alternative more often than expected from prediscussion individual decisions. (p. 290)

social facilitation The enhancement of a dominant response when other people are present. (p. 287)

social roles Roles assigned according to society's expectations of a person with a particular job, sex, race, age, etc. (p. 278)

time-lag methods Studying changes in attitude and behavior across a relatively long period of time (also known as *longitudinal methods*). (p. 291)

Suggested Readings

There are a number of journals specifically devoted to publishing original research in social psychology and related areas. These include *Journal of Personality and Social Psychology, Journal of Experimental Social Psychology, Journal of Applied Social Psychology, Basic and Applied Social Psychology, Personality and Social Psychology Bulletin,* and *Social Cognition.* In addition, specialized journals cover topics of interest to social psychologists such as attitudes and attitude change, environmental psychology, and psychology and the law. Because most psychology majors will take at least one course in social psychology, we won't single out any general textbooks. Many fine introductions to social psychology are available, as well as more advanced books in specialized areas.

Clinical Research Methods

Don C. Fowles and John F. Knutson

Diagnosis
>   The Categorical Approach
>   Anxiety
>   Affective Disorders
>   Schizophrenia
>   Reliability and Validity

Psychopathology
>   Schizophrenia
>   Abused Children
>   Phobias
>   Depression

Psychotherapy
>   Therapy Control Groups
>   Analog and Clinical Trials
>   Measuring Change due to
>   Psychotherapy

Summary and Conclusions

Exercises

Glossary

Suggested Readings

Boxes
>   1. Categorical vs. Dimensional
>   Approaches
>   2. Subtypes
>   3. Further Analyses of the
>   Adoption Study Data: Rejection
>   of Alternative Hypotheses
>   4. Analog Studies
>   5. Defining Psychotherapy
>   6. Waiting List Controls
>   7. The Hawthorne Effect
>   8. Psychophysiological Assessment

To the best of the authors' knowledge, this chapter is the first to focus on clinical research methods in a textbook of experimental psychology. The historical absence of such chapters undoubtedly reflects the perception of a sharp distinction between the experimental method and the correlational method, and a value judgment favoring the former. Historically, the very essence of experimental psychology has been the use of experimental manipulations. The inherent reliance on correlational research in most clinical contexts—not to mention the methodological compromises that are often imposed by practical considerations—has made clinical research appear to be an inappropriate topic.

On the other hand, a case can be made for a chapter on clinical research methods on several counts. First, experimental manipulations are employed in many clinical studies. It is often of interest to determine whether the effect of a manipulation differs in clinical and nonclinical populations. For example, do anxious patients or clients show a greater response than control subjects to stressful stimuli but not to neutral stimuli? You will recognize this example as an interaction between an independent variable and a subject variable (also known as a subject by treatment effect). Such a finding would support the hypothesis that anxious clients are more vulnerable to stress but are not simply chronically anxious. A second reason for examining research methods in a clinical context is that theories of psychopathology often draw on concepts from the basic areas of experimental psychology described in earlier chapters. Just as physiology and biochemistry are relevant to understanding pathology in physical medicine, basic psychological theories often are used to understand psychopathology. Thus, basic experimental psychology is highly relevant to clinical psychology. For example, concepts from the field of animal learning have been applied to depression, which has been attributed to a reduction in positive reinforcement (Eastman, 1976; Ferster, 1973; Lewinsohn & Libet, 1972). A third consideration is that,

in a few cases, something very close to an experimental manipulation is possible (e.g., in the genetic studies of schizophrenia discussed below). Fourth, there are some research methods—for example, assessment of individual differences, twin studies, treatment outcome research—that have seen their greatest development within the area of clinical psychology. These research methods are likely to be neglected in the absence of a chapter on clinical research methods.

Finally, students should learn that complete experimental control is seldom possible in many areas of applied research. Applied researchers, being keenly aware of the disdain for such "sloppy" research sometimes expressed by experimental psychologists, are fond of an old joke that offers a different perspective:

One night a policeman comes upon a drunk apparently searching for something under a lamppost. In response to the policeman's enquiry, the drunk explains that he is looking for his key. Making conversation, the policeman asks if he dropped it here under the lamppost. To his surprise, the drunk replies "No, I lost it over there in the dark, but I'm looking for it under the lamppost because that's where the light is."

Clinical researchers make the point that to disdain clinical research because rigorous experimental methodology cannot always be applied is rather like restricting the search for the key to the lighted area. The point here is that it is legitimate to conduct clinical research in spite of the difficulties. It is a pleasure to be able to expose students to representative examples of the ways in which clinical researchers have struggled with some of the inherent methodological problems in this area.

It is, of course, impossible to cover all clinical research methods in a single chapter, but it is possible to present a broad range of examples. In order to ensure this breadth of exposure, we will cover the major topics of diagnosis, psychopathology, and treatment/remediation, and we will include examples that cut across diagnostic groups (e.g., schizophrenia, anxiety disorders, depression). Diagnosis involves the description and classification of different forms of psychopathology. Psychopathology refers to subjective distress (e.g., anxiety), maladaptive behavior (e.g., compulsive rituals), and bizarre behavior (e.g., hallucinations, incoherent speech) that are both statistically infrequent and severe enough to impair functioning. Under the heading of psychopathology in this chapter we will be especially concerned with etiology and process.

Etiology refers to the causal development of a disorder. Obviously, researchers would not be able to conduct research that produces a disorder. Thus, etiological research typically attempts to study distinguishable samples of subjects to test hypotheses about possible etiology. For example, to assess the possible role of child abuse in the etiology of child behavior problems, investigators have compared abused and nonabused children drawn from the same population (e.g., George & Main, 1979; Goldston, Turnquist, & Knutson, 1989; Kolko, Moser, & Weldy, 1988). The term *process* refers to an examination of the psychological processes that are disturbed in a given form of psychopathology—for example, distorted cognitive processes in depression that lead to a negative interpretation of one's experience (Abramson, Seligman, & Teasdale, 1978; Beck, 1967, 1974). Treatment and remediation, of course, refer to attempts to cure the psychopathology, or at least to ameliorate the symptoms. These topics address the fundamental questions in psychopathology: (1) How is it to be described and assessed (diagnosis)? (2) How did it arise (etiology)? (3) What is its nature (process)? and (4) What can one do about it (treatment)?

Diagnosis

The discussion of research methods will include applications to anxiety disorders, affective disorders, and schizophrenia. Before proceeding, therefore, it is necessary to provide brief descriptions of each of these groups of patients. More complete descriptions can be found in the *Diagnostic and Statistical Manual of the American Psychiatric Association* (4th ed.), (American Psychiatric Association, 1994), usually abbreviated as DSM-IV. DSM-IV is the official nomenclature or diagnostic system for psychiatric disorders used in the United States.

The Categorical Approach

Because of its origins largely within the field of psychiatry, DSM-IV tends to adopt a medical model and to talk about "diseases." One important consequence of embracing a medical model is that a categorical approach is usually adopted, in which psychiatric disorders are viewed as either "present" or "absent." Psychiatrists, in particular, are inclined to view a psychiatric disorder as qualitatively different from normal adjustment (again, a categorical distinction). In contrast, many psychologists would expect that diagnosable psychiatric disorders are sometimes an extreme form of normal psychological problems— that is, that there is a continuum from normal to pathological conditions. In the present chapter, the term psychiatric disorder will be used in a neutral sense—without any assumption as to whether it represents a disease or an extreme normal reaction. Box 10.1 illustrates the difference between the categorical approach and the assumption of a continuum of degree of disorder, as applied to depression.

As a general requirement for diagnosis, the person's behavior and/or emotional reaction must be unusual for the current circumstances. This is known as the statistical deviance criterion. The best example to illustrate this point is bereavement—the emotional reaction to the death of someone dear to you, such as a spouse. Depression during bereavement often is severe enough to meet the diagnostic criteria for major depressive disorder (Bruce et al., 1990). Because such depression is common during bereavement, it does not meet the statistical deviance criterion and is not considered pathological. Only if the depression is unusually severe (disabling) or prolonged is it considered abnormal. Some clinically significant depressions are seen as reactive to life events, but as involving an atypically severe reaction. Other depressions can be severe without any obvious precipitant.

BOX 10.1

Categorical vs. Dimensional Approaches

To illustrate the difference between the categorical and dimensional approaches, consider depression. Depression can be elicited by a number of serious life events—bereavement, divorce, loss of a job, failures of many types, and so on—and possibly by psychological problems that are not as obvious as life events such as disappointment with one's career or one's marriage. On the other hand, many individuals present with severe depression in the absence of any major life event or other severe psychological problem. The dimensional approach assumes that, due to a variable combination of differences in situational factors and personal vulnerability, there is a wide variation in the severity of the depressive reaction. Some people will meet the criteria for diagnosis, others will come close but fall short, while still others will exhibit a depression much too mild to meet

diagnostic criteria. The categorical approach assumes, in contrast, that those who meet diagnostic criteria become depressed as a result of a pathological process that is *qualitatively different* from the mechanisms that produce normal depression. These different theoretical approaches have a major impact on how one thinks about psychopathology. As a general principle, the more severe and bizarre the behavior, the more easily it is seen as outside the range of normal behavior and as manifesting a pathological process. Examples are schizophrenia and mania, which have few counterparts within the normal range of behavior. In contrast, many (but not all) forms of anxiety and depression appear to have much in common with normal anxiety and depression and thus are more readily seen as exaggerations of normal emotional problems.

Anxiety

Within broad diagnostic categories, researchers often attempt to improve precision by creating subtypes (see box 10.2). The anxiety disorders are subdivided into phobias, panic disorder, generalized anxiety disorder, and obsessive-compulsive disorders. *Phobias* involve acute anxiety reactions to the phobic stimuli. The most serious phobia is agoraphobia, a fear of open places such as streets and shopping centers. People with agoraphobia tend to avoid leaving home, which is quite disruptive and handicapping. Simple phobias refer to fears of specific stimuli: heights, enclosed places, small animals, and so on. *Panic disorder* involves brief, severe anxiety attacks in the absence of any obvious precipitant. *Generalized anxiety disorder* involves chronic, mild anxiety and worry that is unrealistic and excessive—for example, about family problems or financial difficulties. In many cases, the person does not identify any specific stimulus or situation that causes the anxiety, in which case it can be called "free-floating" anxiety. Psychological causes

for this anxiety may or may not be reported by the patient, but the degree of anxiety must be out of proportion to the size of the problem involved. *Obsessions* consist of recurrent thoughts that are distressing and ego-dystonic (not something the person wants to think about). Examples are impulses to kill a loved child or recurrent blasphemous thoughts in a religious person (DSM-IV, p. 418). *Compulsions* are repetitive behaviors that the person feels compelled to engage in, such as handwashing or checking (e.g., checking to see if the oven is turned off). Anxiety becomes acute when the person tries to resist these compulsions, but it diminishes if the person gives in to the compulsion.

Affective Disorders

The affective disorders are divided into depression and mania. *Mania* consists of euphoric mood, a high level of activity and speech, an excess of energy combined with little need for sleep, and a tendency to engage in activities that have disastrous outcomes (e.g., poorly planned business schemes that

BOX 10.2

Subtypes

In clinical research, the purpose of diagnosing patients is to create groupings that are likely to have similar features. However, the broad diagnostic categories such as anxiety disorders, affective disorders, and schizophrenia result in groups characterized by large within-group variance. To reduce that variance and improve the prospects of answering research questions, subtype diagnoses have been developed. The subtyping of anxiety and depressive

disorders is discussed in some detail in the text to illustrate the strategies adopted in subtyping. It is generally believed that subtyping will create greater homogeneity with respect to presenting problems, course, outcome, etiology, and response to treatment and will, therefore, facilitate research progress. Thus, the student exploring the clinical research literature should attend carefully to subtype diagnoses being investigated.

lead to bankruptcy). *Depression* often involves the sad (dysphoric) mood familiar to all of us, but sometimes there is only a profound loss of interest in usually pleasurable activities—leaving more of an empty feeling than the strong discomfort associated with dysphoric mood. In addition to this central feature of depressed mood and/or loss of interest, a number of additional symptoms are associated with depression severe enough to meet diagnostic criteria. These include disturbance of sleep (usually insomnia but sometimes hypersomnia), fatigue, weight loss (sometimes weight gain), loss of appetite, psychomotor agitation or retardation, feelings of guilt, and so on. It is often argued that some of the more severe symptoms define a form of depression called melancholia that is attributable to a dysfunction of the neurochemical substrate involved in mood, but this plausible hypothesis has yet to be proven. One major subtyping that does have considerable validity is the unipolar versus bipolar distinction. Bipolar affective disorder refers to individuals with both manic and depressive episodes, whereas individuals with only depressive episodes are said to have unipolar depression. Unipolar depression is further subdivided into dysthymia (chronic, mild depression) versus major depression (acute, severe depression).

Schizophrenia

The term *schizophrenia* is applied to clients manifesting severe symptoms, especially hallucinations, delusions, thought disorder, and bizarre behavior. All of these symptoms are outside the normal range of behavior. Hallucinations are usually auditory—for example, hearing two voices conversing even though no one is there. Delusions are distorted beliefs, such as a belief that one is being persecuted (e.g., someone is trying to poison you), an exaggerated sense of one's importance (e.g., a belief that one is Christ), or a belief that one's thoughts are being broadcast, allowing others to monitor them as they occur. Thought disorder means speech that is impossible to understand. Syntax and grammar are normal, but the content of the speech makes little sense. Examples of bizarre behavior include such things as maintaining a rigid posture for an extended period of time and stereotyped and purposeless motor movements. These symptoms are sometimes called "positive" or "florid" or "active" symptoms and are contrasted with "deficit" or "negative" or "residual" symptoms. The latter symptoms usually refer to the absence of normal behavior, such as social withdrawal; a marked lack of initiative, interests, or energy; poverty of speech (absence of normal speech); and blunted or flat affect (an absence of emotional facial expression).

Reliability and Validity

You should be aware that the clinical interview and the complex decision process involved in making a clinical diagnosis constitute a method of assessment. As such, it is subject to the need to establish reliability and validity—a demand applied to all assessment procedures. The concepts of reliability and validity have been discussed in other chapters (see, for example, box 4.4) but require further discussion here.

In the simplest terms, **reliability** refers to replicability, whereas validity refers to whether an instrument actually measures the designated variable. Basically, reliability refers to the degree to which a researcher has a variable that measures anything, and **validity** refers to whether the variable measures what it is believed to measure. As you might expect, the concept of validity is more complicated than that of replicability. These concepts can be examined with that most familiar of all assessments, the intelligence test or IQ test, and an example from clinical research on anxiety.

The concept of reliability can be illustrated with a type of reliability known as test-retest reliability. Test-retest reliability refers to the agreement between two test scores from the same test obtained with a specified intervening time period—for example, six months. Imagine that you have IQ test scores on 100 individuals tested twice with six months between the testing sessions. By computing a Pearson correlation (see chapter 3) for the association of the two scores among the 100 individuals, you obtain an estimate of the test-retest reliability. Note that there is opportunity for error variance (i.e., variance due to chance factors) from such factors as lack of sleep, illness, emotional disturbance, and so on. Additionally, there may be real changes in measured IQ over six months for some individuals due to educational experiences or, in children, to rapid maturation or other developmental factors. Nevertheless, if the Pearson correlation is not high, then the test cannot be considered reliable over the time period in question. In the case of IQ scores, low reliability over a six-month period is a serious problem.

There is an important point to understand about test-retest reliability: how reliable a test score must be over a given time period depends strongly on one's theory about the characteristic being measured. In the case of IQ or personality traits, we generally expect a relatively high degree of stability over a period of weeks or months, with the reliability declining as the interval increases. An additional consideration with respect to IQ is that the stability is greatly affected by the age at initial testing. For example, one study showed that the one-year retest reliability was only 0.47 when the initial testing was at age one year, with the three- and six-year retest reliabilities falling even further to 0.23 and 0.13. In contrast, when the initial testing was at age six years, the one-, three-, and six-year retest reliabilities were 0.86, 0.84, and 0.81, respectively (Cronbach, 1970, p. 231). Similarly, a Swedish study reported a correlation of 0.72 for IQ scores obtained from third-grade children and again ten years later (Anastasi, 1988, p. 337). Thus, as long as one waits until a reasonable age for the initial testing, test-retest reliabilities for IQ are quite high even over a period of years. As indicated by these correlations, IQ is the most stable trait measured by psychologists. In sharp contrast to intelligence, a measure of state anxiety or of depressed mood is not expected to show temporal stability. Our concept of state anxiety is such that it can change dramatically over a period of minutes. Depressed mood is, perhaps, somewhat more stable, but it too can change substantially over a period of hours, and certainly over days or weeks. Thus, although high test-retest reliability is essential for some measures, it is not for others.

If test-retest reliability cannot be used to estimate the reliability of tests in some cases, what can? This question brings us to a second type of reliability, known as internal consistency and most simply measured by *split-half reliability*. Again, imagine that you have an IQ test with 120 items and that you administer this test to 100 individuals. Next imagine that you divide the test into two 60-item tests by assigning the odd-numbered items to one test and the even-numbered items to the other test. You would then have two scores for each subject, each ostensibly measuring the same thing. Application of a Pearson correlation to the association between the scores on the two 60-item tests among the 100 individuals yields an estimate of the split-half reliability. If this correlation is not high, then the test has considerable error variance and cannot be considered reliable or internally consistent—even for variables such as state anxiety that may change substantially over short periods of time. Also note that by using alternate items (odd vs. even) you have controlled for or eliminated many effects correlated with time during the test, such as practice effects, fatigue effects, changes in motivation, and so on. That is, these factors will equally affect both halves of the test, whereas in test-retest reliability they are uncontrolled. For these reasons, split-half reliability is a useful index of test reliability. However, more sophisticated approaches (i.e., Kuder-Richardson Formula 20 and Coefficient Alpha) are available and are more common than the split-half procedure for assessing internal consistency (Anastasi, 1988, pp. 122–124).

Establishing the validity of an IQ test inherently requires assumptions or hypotheses as to the nature of intelligence. There is wide agreement that intelligence involves abilities that are important in academic performance. Consequently, it is expected that IQ scores should correlate significantly with school grades, achievement test scores, teachers' ratings of students' academic ability, receipt of special academic honors and awards, probability of promotion or graduation, and so on. Because school grades and teachers' ratings are influenced by other factors (e.g., motivation or effort is also important

for school performance; teachers may be influenced by children's actual performance, by their appearance and manners, by their family's social class, etc.), we do not necessarily expect an extremely high correlation between IQ and these indications of validity, but the correlations should be moderately high.

As with reliability, there are different types of validity. Two of the most important are *criterion-oriented validity* and *construct validity*, the former being by far the simpler of the two. If one has a satisfactory criterion and all that is needed is to predict that criterion, then criterion validity applies. For example, if for some purpose an investigator needs to select individuals who meet criteria for a specific clinical diagnosis, he or she could develop a self-report screening test (or employ an existing test) to select individuals likely to receive that clinical diagnosis. If individuals selected on the basis of the test do, in fact, receive that clinical diagnosis at a higher rate than that in the population from which they were drawn, then the test has criterion validity. Note that no theory need be involved in this type of validity—it is simply an empirical matter as to whether the test predicts the criterion.

Construct validity is needed when a test is asserted to measure some psychological construct that has theoretical meaning. To establish that the test measures the presumed construct requires testing many predictions based on the theory. To the extent that the predictions are confirmed, the test is found to have construct validity. In a classic text on assessment, Cronbach (1970) used the concept of anxiety as an example. The construct of anxiety is embedded in a psychological theory, which makes predictions about the effects of anxiety:

> The theory of "anxiety" accepted by the tester might include such expectations as the following: anxiety increases when subjects are exposed to a threat of electric shock; neurotics are more anxious than nonneurotics; anxiety is lowered by a certain drug; anxious persons set high goals for themselves (p. 123).

Construct validity requires extensive research (and often theoretical development), through which the nature of the construct measured by the test becomes clarified and/or the test is modified to more accurately capture the construct of interest. The complexity of the process of construct validation is indicated by Cronbach's (1970, p. 142) conclusion that it is the same as the process by which scientific theories are developed. The central importance to clinical psychology can be seen in the observation that all clinical diagnoses (e.g., schizophrenia, manic-depressive disorder, panic disorder) involve assessments whose validity must be established through the process of construct validity (Morey, 1991).

To return to our IQ test example, a test of general ability could be used either in the context of criterion validity or of construct validity. If the sole purpose is to predict grades in school, then criterion validity can be established and the test score has no additional meaning. On the other hand, if the test user wants to claim that the trait being measured is that of "general intelligence" with implications for being *the* index of intellectual functioning applicable in a wide range of situations (e.g., performance in many different occupations, leadership ability in the military, selection of hobbies, influence on choice of spouse), then the test is being placed in a theoretical context and construct validity is required.

Finally, the relation between reliability and validity is important: it is axiomatic that reliability sets the upper limit for validity. This statement means that an unreliable test cannot be a valid test. Students should know that the statement reflects a fixed statistical relation rather than a pronouncement by researchers. That is, because the unreliability in a test is error variance, it cannot contribute to the assessment of the validity of a test. Obviously, the more error there is in a test, the less accurate information is available to relate to other measures. For example, if alternate forms of an IQ test yield largely random scores, the scores are effectively meaningless and, therefore, cannot predict anything. On the other hand, high reliability does not necessarily assure greater validity—only that greater validity is possible.

Psychopathology

Schizophrenia

Schizophrenia is a severe, often chronic, disorder that afflicts approximately 1 percent of the population. Because of its severity and chronicity, it has been the object of a vast amount of research. Research on genetic influences on schizophrenia contributed strongly to a major shift toward biological theories of severe forms of psychopathology.

The starting point for this research is the very old finding that schizophrenia runs in families. That is, if you take all schizophrenic patients (called probands or index cases) in a series of consecutive admissions to a hospital and examine the risk of schizophrenia among their relatives, you will find that the risk is well above the population base rate of about 1 percent. In a review of all West European studies, the composite rates were as shown in table 10.1 (Gottesman, McGuffin, & Farmer, 1987).

There is considerable uncertainty as to how to diagnose schizophrenia, especially with respect to the breadth of the concept—that is, whether it should include only clear cases of schizophrenia or should also include milder, less certain cases. For that reason, data are presented for definite schizophrenia only and for the combination of definite plus "probable" schizophrenia (a broader concept). (Note that the need to include milder cases underscores the difficulties that can occur in the categorical approach.) In table 10.1, the figures for a spouse are the same as those for the general population, indicating that there is no increased risk as a result of being married to a person with schizophrenia. The

TABLE 10.1   Lifetime Risk for Schizophrenia among Relatives

Relationship	Definite Schiz (%)	Def + Probable Schiz (%)	
Spouse	1.0	2.3	
Children	9.3	12.8	⎫
Siblings	7.3	9.3	⎬ 1st degree
DZ (Fraternal) Twins	12.1	13.7	⎭
MZ (Identical) Twins	44.3	45.6	
Half-Sibs	2.9	6.0	⎫
Nieces, Nephews	2.6	3.5	⎬ 2nd degree
Grandchildren	2.8	5.0	⎭
First Cousins	1.6	2.4	3rd degree

From Gottesman et al., 1987

rates for first-degree relatives (parent, child, sibling), who share 50 percent of their genes in common with the schizophrenic proband, are substantially above the population base rate and are also higher than the rates for second-degree relatives (grandparent, aunt, uncle, nephew/niece, half-siblings), who share 25 percent of their genes in common with the proband. To a biologically oriented theorist, these data appear to support a genetic contribution to schizophrenia. On the other hand, environmentally oriented theorists pointed out that psychosocial environments are more similar within families than for people taken at random. Thus, during the critical early periods of a child's development, familial environmental factors would be more similar within families than between families. It is easy to imagine, further, that first-degree relatives share more similar environments than second-degree relatives, and so on.

You will immediately recognize this as a classic case of confounded variables. If schizophrenia could be studied in animals (it cannot, because there are no animal analogs), one would employ the **cross-fostering** methodology to experimentally manipulate these variables: take the offspring of schizophrenic and of nonschizophrenic mothers and switch them immediately after birth, with the result that the schizophrenic mothers raised the offspring of the nonschizophrenic mothers and vice versa. Because we cannot apply the cross-fostering design to humans, we have to find alternative approaches. The two major strategies have been the comparison of twins and the examination of naturally occurring adoptions.

Twin studies take advantage of the existence of two types of twins. In the case of fraternal or dizygotic (DZ) twins, two eggs are fertilized independently by two spermatozoa to form two zygotes (fertilized eggs). From a genetic perspective, these twins are like other siblings, sharing 50 percent of their genes on average. They just happened to share the same intrauterine environment. In sharp contrast, identical or monozygotic (MZ) twins derive from a single fertilized egg or zygote, which splits apart at some time after the first cell division. As a result of this splitting apart, two individuals are created with exactly the same genetic endowment. The two types of twins constitute "an experiment of nature" that allows us to make interesting comparisons, although it is worth noting that we do not have control over the environmental factors.

As with family studies, in conducting a twin study one begins with consecutive admissions of patients who are schizophrenic (index cases or probands) and then assesses the cotwin to evaluate the presence or absence of schizophrenia. In this case, however, the probands must also be twins, greatly reducing the number of eligible patients. In a classic twin study, Gottesman and Shields (1972) were able to sample 16 years of consecutive admissions to a large teaching hospital in London, during which time every patient's twin status had been determined. The use of consecutive admissions ensures that the sample is representative of patients admitted to the hospital (in this case, it also maximized the number of patients studied, but that advantage is not the major methodological consideration). Even with this large number of years, they were able to obtain only 28 monozygotic and 34 dizygotic twin pairs, reflecting the low joint probability of two infrequent events (schizophrenia and twin status). Nevertheless, this sample was large enough to yield impressive results: the risk of schizophrenia in the monozygotic cotwin of a schizophrenic proband was 50 percent, compared to only 12 percent for a dizygotic cotwin. The data strongly suggest that the greater genetic similarity for MZ twins has produced greater risk for schizophrenia, supporting the genetic interpretation over the environmental one.

Such data had been reported in earlier studies, but the Gottesman and Shields study was important because of its superior methodology in several respects. The use of consecutive admissions is important to ensure a representative sample and, therefore, to avoid sampling biases. Additionally, the authors managed to find, interview, and obtain blood samples from almost all of the twins. The blood samples were necessary in order to make an objective determination of **zygosity**—that is, to determine whether the twins are truly monozygotic or dizygotic. The interviews are, of course, essential for obtaining as much information as possible for a correct diagnosis. Finally, the authors had other clinicians make "blindfolded" diagnoses—that is, diagnoses of the presence or absence of schizophrenia without knowledge of twin status. This procedure avoided the possibility that clinical diagnosis would

be biased by expecting greater concordance for monozygotic twins. Because of the methodological sophistication of this study, criticisms of previous studies could not be applied, and the findings were accepted as valid.

The inference that the greater concordance for schizophrenia among MZ twins than DZ twins reflects genetic factors is made in the context of assuming that environments are no more similar for MZ than DZ twins. Otherwise, genetic and environmental similarity are still confounded. One might expect, however, that MZ twins might share more similar environments than DZ twins, due to greater similarity of (genetically influenced) physical features (e.g., attractiveness, body build), intelligence, and personality, and evidence was presented to support this expectation by critics of the genetic position. To be sure, the environmentalists' criticism along these lines was a last ditch stand. It would be hard to specify precisely which aspects of the environment are more similar for MZ than DZ twins and to argue that those also can be invoked to account for the familial risk. Familial risk is more readily attributed to factors that are common to twins regardless of their zygosity, such as parental behavior, economic factors, neighborhood, and so on. Nevertheless, this "experiment of nature" is not as pure as would be the case in traditional studies in experimental psychology. In order to complete the case for a genetic hypothesis, it was necessary to turn to **adoption studies** to provide converging evidence.

Although ethical considerations preclude switching babies among parents in the hospital for research purposes, an approximation to this experimental design takes place in connection with adoptions. It is theoretically possible, therefore, to exploit adoptions to determine whether schizophrenia runs in adoptive families (the environmental hypothesis) or biological families (the genetic hypothesis). Again, practical considerations make such studies difficult. Ethical considerations preclude actual experimental control and the time span required for adoptees to live through much of the age

TABLE 10.2   Number of Relatives with Schizophrenic Spectrum Disorder

	BIOLOGICAL RELATIVES		ADOPTIVE RELATIVES	
	Total	Sz Spectrum	Total	Sz Spectrum
Experimental (N = 33)	150	13	74	2
Controls (N = 33)	156	3	83	3
p (one-tailed)	.0072		NS	

From Kety et al., 1968.

of risk for developing schizophrenia (approximately from age 15 to age 45) forces reliance on institutional records concerning birth and adoption. It is also difficult to find the adoptees after such a long time period.

In one of the first and most elegant of the early adoption studies, American investigators collaborated with Danish investigators to exploit the excellent public records in Denmark. Kety and associates (1968; see also a later report in Kety et al., 1978) began by compiling a list of all babies born and placed for adoption (within the first year of life) during the years 1924 to 1947. They then checked these names against a national psychiatric register to find all those who had received psychiatric services for a disorder that might be related to schizophrenia. Again, because we are not certain how to precisely diagnose schizophrenia, these investigators erred on the side of including all possible disorders that might be related to schizophrenia—a concept they called schizophrenic spectrum disorder. With this information they were able to compile a sample of adoptees who became schizophrenic, which they called the experimental group. They also compiled a control group of adoptees matched for date of birth and age at adoption who did not have any psychiatric history. The dependent measure was the number of schizophrenics found among the biological and adoptive relatives of these two groups. The results are shown in table 10.2 (adapted from Kety et al., 1968). This table shows that there were 33 subjects in each group,

that the experimental subjects had 150 identified biological relatives and 74 identified adoptive relatives, and that the controls had 156 biological relatives and 83 adoptive relatives. The key result was that among the biological relatives of the experimental group, 13 out of 150 suffered from a schizophrenic spectrum disorder, compared to only 3 out of 156 for the control group. The one-tailed test, significant at the .0072 level, was justified, because there was no doubt as to the direction of the effect (i.e., if an increased rate of schizophrenia was to be found, it would necessarily be among the relatives of the experimental group). In contrast, there were no differences in the risk of schizophrenia among the adoptive relatives. These results clearly indicated that schizophrenia runs in biological families, consistent with the genetic explanation. (Box 10.3 provides additional findings from this study.) Two other important adoption studies reported the same result (Rosenthal et al., 1968; Heston, 1966), leaving little doubt as to the replicability of this finding.

Even though experimental manipulations and rigorous control over the variables involved (e.g., random assignment to groups) could not be employed, it was possible to exploit enough naturally occurring phenomena to draw clear inferences. The phenomenon of schizophrenia running in families is due to genetic factors, not to psychosocial environmental factors. This conclusion, along with the introduction of antipyschotic drugs for the amelioration of schizophrenic symptoms, created a revolution in thinking

BOX 10.3

Further Analyses of the Adoption Study Data: Rejection of Alternative Hypotheses

You might be interested in further analyses of the Kety and associates (1968) data concerned with greater control over variables of interest. First, psychoanalytic theories at the time emphasized the importance of early mother-child interactions in the etiology of schizophrenia. The authors anticipated an argument that the biological mothers might have caused schizophrenia by virtue of interactions during the first year of life. To forestall this criticism of their study, the authors presented data for a subsample who were adopted within the first month of life:

Results for Probands Separated within 1 Month

	BIOLOGICAL RELATIVES		ADOPTIVE RELATIVES	
	Total	Sz Spectrum	Total	Sz Spectrum
Index Cases (N = 19)	93	9	45	2
Controls (N = 20)	92	0	51	1
p (one-tailed)	.0018		NS	

The results were identical to those for the entire sample. It would be difficult in the extreme to argue that mother-child interactions in the first 30 days of life set an infant on the course to schizophrenia.

These results still left one variable uncontrolled. It was logically possible that pregnancy and birth complications might have caused brain damage to the fetus that, in turn, caused schizophrenia. This is a nongenetic, biological hypothesis concerning the etiology of schizophrenia. To preclude this possibility, the investigators examined the risk for schizophrenia among the biological paternal half-siblings of the probands and found positive results: the risk of schizophrenia was greater among the paternal half-siblings of the experimental group than among those of the controls. This analysis takes advantage of the consideration that children given up for adoption often have biological parents who do not have a long-term, stable relationship and are, therefore, likely to have additional children by different mates—creating a large pool of half-siblings. The advantage of paternal half-siblings in the present context is that they do not share the same intrauterine environment, since only the father is in common. Thus, these results eliminated pregnancy and birth complications as an alternative explanation (note how studies such as this fit the description of "quasi-experimental" designs discussed in previous chapters).

about psychopathology: genetic factors came to be seen as important in creating a "diathesis" or vulnerability which, in combination with environmental stress, produces psychopathology (especially severe forms of psychopathology such as schizophrenia or mania). This view is known as the **diathesis-stress** model (e.g., Fowles, 1992b).

Abused Children

Not all clinically important or interesting phenomena are represented in psychiatric diagnoses. For example, the abuse of children by parents is not a diagnosis in DSM-IV, but it is an important area of clinical service and clinical research. For the purposes of the present discussion of methodological issues in clinical research, some recent research on abuse can be used to illustrate additional points regarding clinical research methodology.

Because some disorders or some symptoms of disorders can be represented in populations that are not identified clinically, occasionally topics of interest to clinical researchers can be effectively investigated using samples that are not obviously clinical. For example, one of the present authors has been conducting research on the long-term consequences of the physical abuse of children. By conducting questionnaire surveys of literally thousands of university undergraduates (e.g., Berger et al., 1988; Knutson & Mehm, 1988; Rausch & Knutson, 1991), it was possible to establish a prevalence rate of physically abusive childhood experiences of about 8 percent. That is, approximately 8 percent of the university students reported lifetime childhood experiences that could be considered physically abusive. By screening large numbers of undergraduates, it was possible to identify sufficiently large groups of young adults who were abused and then contrast them with other young adults whose childhoods reflect nonabusive disciplinary experiences. Thus, samples of physically abused subjects (a clinical problem) could be obtained from among university students (a nonclinical population).

Since the ultimate goal of this research was to assess possible consequences of physical maltreatment, subjects from abusive and nonabusive backgrounds were assessed with respect to their own likely parenting behavior (Zaidi, Knutson, & Mehm, 1989). To assess parenting patterns in persons who were not yet parents, the young adult subjects viewed slides that depicted many different potentially irritating child behaviors, such as spilling grape juice on the carpet or burning papers. Then subjects selected disciplinary strategies they would use to alter the depicted child's behavior. This approach to studying parenting is an **analog** procedure (see box 10.4). The results of this research indicated that childhood disciplinary histories did influence the disciplinary strategies selected by the subjects. Persons from more punitive backgrounds were more likely to endorse potentially injurious disciplinary responses, such as striking the child with an object. Thus, this work is an example of obtaining clinical samples from a nonclinical population and testing hypotheses with an analog procedure.

Phobias

Phobias consist of an acute anxiety reaction to a clear phobic stimulus, as opposed to panic disorder and generalized anxiety disorder where an eliciting stimulus is either absent or difficult to detect. Because of the clear eliciting stimulus, the etiology of phobias would appear to be the easiest for psychologists to explain. That is, a phobia looks like a classically conditioned fear response to a conditioned stimulus, and early theories hypothesized a developmental history of (CS-UCS) pairing between the phobic stimulus and some unconditioned stimulus (see chapter 5 for a description of Pavlovian conditioning procedures and recall the story of "Little Albert" in chapter 2). However, attempts to find evidence for such a conditioning history were successful only in a minority of clients suffering from phobias. Two modifications of this hypothesis greatly expanded its scope and explanatory power.

BOX 10.4

Analog Studies

Very often in clinical research, the clinical setting or population may not be accessible or even suitable for experimentation. In such a circumstance, the researcher often attempts to approximate the clinical setting or population in a nonclinical context. Such research is typically referred to as "clinical analog" research. That is, the research does not directly test a clinical hypothesis in a clinical context; rather, it is designed to test a clinical hypothesis in a nonclinical context that is seen as analogous to the clinical context. Often this approach is taken to achieve the advantage of direct experimental control or to have the benefit of larger sample sizes. Clinical analog studies are usually conducted with human subjects, but there are circumstances when a clinical hypothesis cannot be tested directly with human subjects. If an investigator were interested in testing hypotheses by actually producing psychopathology, such work would clearly not be acceptable in humans, but it could be acceptable with nonhuman subjects. For example, in analog studies of the importance of childhood experiences on the development of aggression in adulthood, Knutson and Viken (1984) conducted a series of experiments that manipulated the early aggressive experiences of rats and then tested them

as adults. Animal analog studies of anxiety (e.g., Levis, 1979) and depression (e.g., Seligman, 1975; Suomi & Harlow, 1977) have also been conducted. Thus, clinical analog studies are tests of clinical hypotheses in a nonclinical context or with nonclinical samples.

Clinical analog studies can also be conducted with human subjects. For example, often studies of human fears or phobias have used as subjects undergraduate students who are fearful of snakes or rats (e.g., Lang, Lazovik, & Reynolds, 1965). These studies are analogs of clinical phenomena because there are significant differences between the subjects studied and the characteristics of patients who actually seek services. That is, animal phobias usually have an earlier onset, are less incapacitating than other phobias, and persons with animal phobias do not often seek services at clinics (see Marks & Gelder, 1966). However, it is important to note that these subjects also share many similarities with persons who actually seek services (see Levis, 1970). Thus, if studies of the fear of snakes were conducted with undergraduates who describe themselves as intensely fearful of snakes, as in the Lang, Lazovik, and Reynolds study, the work may be clinically relevant but it still is an analog of a clinical phenomenon.

First, it was suggested that fears can be acquired via *observational learning* or vicarious classical conditioning (e.g., Bandura, 1969; Marks, 1969). This means that direct experience with the UCS is not required. Second, the *preparedness* hypothesis (Seligman, 1971) proposed that we inherit a genetic predisposition to learn fears to some stimuli more readily than to others: clinical researchers have noted that phobic stimuli often involve potentially dangerous objects—for example, snakes, spiders, and heights rather than flowers and mushrooms.

In the observational learning approach, it is argued that we need not be exposed to an unconditioned stimulus (being bitten by a snake or spider)

but may acquire a fear as a result of observing others acting in a fearful manner. Obviously, there are far more opportunities to learn fears in this manner, and it is much safer than actually being exposed to the UCS of a snake or spider bite (i.e., observational learning has adaptive value). Although few snakes and spiders actually pose any danger to humans, avoidance of all of them is easier than determining which are dangerous.

The preparedness hypothesis states that we are, as a result of our evolutionary history, biologically prepared to learn some fears more readily than others. In areas of the world in which snakes and spiders are poisonous, it is adaptive to fear and, therefore, to avoid them. Consequently, it has been hypothesized that there is a selective advantage for those individuals who inherited a readiness to learn and to retain (resist extinction of) a fear of snakes and spiders. The evolutionary contribution is further supported by the observation that fears of such modern objects as guns, knives, electrical outlets, and hammers are uncommon, even though these objects may well be paired with traumatic episodes in our past experience (e.g., Marks, 1969; Mineka et al., 1984).

Attractive though this preparedness/observational learning hypothesis is, proving it from clinical studies is difficult. Retrospective reports are subject to many distortions, as well as to simple failures to recall important events. Experimental induction of phobias in children is prohibited by ethical considerations. In an elegant series of experiments, Mineka and her colleagues solved this methodological problem by studying observational learning of snake phobias among primates (rhesus monkeys), where all the advantages of experimental manipulations and experimental control were available. That is, snake phobias among rhesus monkeys were viewed as an adequate animal analog for phobias seen in clinical populations. It is often difficult to find suitable animal analogs for clinical phenomena, but in this case the primate fears seem similar enough to justify the generalization to the clinical setting.

In an early study, Mineka and her associates (1984) demonstrated acquisition of a snake phobia in six adolescent or young-adult lab-reared rhesus monkeys following exposure to a fearful model. The authors employed three snake stimuli: (1) a live boa constrictor; (2) a 24-inch long (1-inch diameter) toy snake that jiggled slightly when moved by the experimenter; and (3) a nonmoving, 20-inch long (0.5-inch diameter) lifelike model resembling a grass snake. The monkeys were tested in two situations. In the Wisconsin General Test Apparatus (WGTA; see fig. 5.12) the monkey must reach past any objects placed in the box in order to retrieve food at the rear. Latency of the food-reaching response during 60-second trials served as one index

of fear of the objects placed in the box. In addition, the experimenters rated the presence/absence of 12 fear-related behaviors known to occur in this situation among fearful monkeys. In the Sacket Circus the monkeys entered a center compartment and then were free (for a period of five minutes) to remain in the center compartment or to explore four outer cage stimulus compartments that surrounded the center compartment. Time spent in each outer compartment was an index of the fear of the stimulus object placed in the compartment. Prior to observational learning, the six young laboratory-reared monkeys showed no differences in response to the snake stimuli compared to neutral stimuli in either apparatus. In contrast, wild-reared monkeys, who had acquired a fear of snakes prior to their capture, showed very long latencies (maximum or very near maximum) to the three snake stimuli compared to neutral stimuli in the WGTA situation and spent essentially no time in the outer compartments containing snake stimuli in the Sacket Circus situation. The wild-reared, but not the laboratory-reared, monkeys also exhibited fearful behavior when presented with snake stimuli in the WGTA. This part of the experiment established that exposure to snakes is required for the development of the phobia, as the laboratory monkeys had not been exposed and showed no fear.

In the second part of the experiment, the young, laboratory-reared monkeys were exposed to adult monkeys (models) acting fearfully in the WGTA. As a result of this experience, the young monkeys acquired a snake phobia, as indicated by their behavior in the WGTA. This fear generalized to snake stimuli presented in the Sacket Circus situation, in spite of their not having observed fearful adults in this situation. Finally, three months after the vicarious conditioning trials ended, the laboratory-reared monkeys showed an undiminished phobic reaction to snake-related stimuli.

More recently, Cook and Mineka (1989) provided a critical test of the preparedness hypothesis. Prior to this study, the experimenters had found that young monkeys would watch televised videotapes of fearful models and would acquire snake phobias as a result of this form of observational conditioning. This finding permitted the experimenters to videotape fearful responses of adult monkeys to snake stimuli and then to edit the videotapes in such a way that they preserved the model's fearful behavior but replaced the snake stimulus with artificial flowers. By this means, they created videotapes with models showing identical fearful behaviors either to hypothetically prepared stimuli (snakes) or to hypothetically nonprepared stimuli (flowers). There were also videotapes of models responding calmly to neutral stimuli (wood blocks of different shapes and colors). The originally nonfearful observers were exposed either to the snake and neutral stimuli videotapes or to the flower and neutral stimuli videotapes. As predicted, monkeys exposed to models reacting fearfully to snake stimuli acquired a snake phobia, whereas those exposed to models reacting fearfully to flower stimuli did not acquire a flower phobia. This result strongly supports the preparedness hypothesis, as the models' fear responses and the videotapes presenting nonfearful responses to the wooden blocks were identical for the two groups. In a further study, observers acquired a fear of crocodiles when exposed to models reacting fearfully to a toy crocodile stimulus (a hypothetically prepared stimulus) but did not acquire a fear of rabbits when exposed to models reacting fearfully to a toy rabbit stimulus (a hypothetically nonprepared stimulus). Again, the results strongly support the preparedness hypothesis.

These studies illustrate several points. First, they show that the usual procedures of experimental psychology can be employed for clinically relevant research. In this case, their application depended on the availability of an adequate animal analog of an important clinical phenomenon. The phobic responses of rhesus monkeys have been considered to be sufficiently similar to human phobias to be of value in understanding human phobic behavior. Further, it is reasonable to assume that, if primates can acquire phobias via observational conditioning, humans (with even greater intellectual abilities) can also do so, especially in view of the many

demonstrations of observational learning in humans (Bandura, 1969; Marks, 1969). Second, this line of research demonstrates the continuity between the traditional methods of experimental psychology and theories of psychopathology, inasmuch as the theory and research derive from concepts of classical conditioning taken from the experimental literature. Third, as is usually the case, it is not *just* a matter of applying basic concepts from experimental psychology. The clinical focus pushed basic research in the direction of more interest in observational conditioning than might have developed solely within traditional experimental psychology, and it stimulated interest in genetic influences on fear conditioning. Similarly, the need for an adequate animal analog strongly encouraged research with primates, whose responses are more readily related to human clinical responses than are those of more common laboratory animals such as rats. Thus, at least in some cases, clinical research may enrich experimental psychology.

Depression

We all recognize that certain life events are likely to produce depression in many individuals. The most potent of these life events is bereavement—the response to the death of a loved one. Studies of widows have shown that a considerable percentage of widows meet diagnostic criteria for depression (Bruce et al., 1990). Divorce and loss of a job also constitute potentially depressogenic life events. However, many clients present with depression in the clinic without such major life events. To the extent that their depression is reactive to life events, it is an exaggerated reaction to relatively ordinary stressors that the majority of people face without clinically significant depression. Still other depressed clients cannot identify any significant life event at all, but rather report that their depression "just happened." In view of the frequent inadequacy of traumatic life events as a sufficient explanation for the onset of depression, many theories focus on vulnerability within the individual. Often this approach is couched in terms of an interaction model, in which vulnerable individuals are said to develop clinically significant depression in response to only moderately severe life events.

Cognitive approaches have occupied front stage in psychological theories of vulnerability to depression. The essence of these theories is the hypothesis that it is the person's *distorted interpretation* of negative life events that is the proximal cause of the depression. There are two highly overlapping, major cognitive theories of depression. The research concerned with these theories illustrates a number of methodological issues.

The older theory is Beck's cognitive theory of depression (e.g., Beck, 1967, 1974). Beck's theory was based on observations when treating already depressed clients, and it was strongly associated with the development of a cognitive therapy for depression. Beck was impressed with the way depressed clients misinterpret their world in a negative direction and argued that this cognitive distortion tends to keep them depressed. That is, his patients made distorted inferences—for example, "I'm a terrible person . . . I don't deserve to live . . . I'm despicable . . . I loathe myself " (Beck, 1967, p. 18). Beck proposed that these individuals have schemata of self-deprecation and self-blame that are used to incorrectly interpret new experience in a *negative* fashion. These schemata are thought to derive from past rejections, losses, criticisms, failures, and so on, although Beck now emphasizes that there may be genetic and personality contributions (Beck, 1983; Beck et al., 1979). The key point is that the schemata are the primary etiological factor. That is, given that experience is interpreted so negatively, depression is a natural consequence. Thus, it is not current losses or life events that account for the depression, but person characteristics in terms of negative schemata.

The more recent theory is Abramson's (Abramson, Seligman, & Teasdale, 1978) hopelessness theory of depression. Like Beck, Abramson and her colleagues were concerned with the interpretation of real events, but they employed concepts from attribution theory (which, as we saw in the preceding chapter, was an influential development in social psychology). They argued that depression develops when failures and losses are attributed to stable, global, and internal factors. For example, a student who fails an exam might attribute the failure to personal stupidity (an internal attribution) with the additional assumption that he/she is stupid in all academic subjects (a global attribution) and that this stupidity is a permanent characteristic (a stable attribution). Such attributions give the student ample reason to be hopeless and, therefore, depressed. Alternatively, the student might attribute the failure to having several deadlines to meet (external attribution) that seldom come at the same time (unstable attribution—not likely to happen again) and having an examination on Russian grammar, a topic that is particularly difficult (specific attribution—does not generalize to other courses or even to other topics in the same course). In this case, the student is unhappy about the grade but is hopeful that future grades will be better.

The differences between these two theories are obviously subtle. They use different language to talk about the cognitive processes presumed to cause depression, but the practical predictions are much the same: a negative attributional style is associated with a vulnerability to depression, and depression-prone individuals greatly exaggerate real events in a negative direction. Consequently, no attempt will be made to differentiate between them but rather they will be treated as more or less a single theory. This chapter cannot begin to do justice to the massive literature on cognitive theories of depression. Instead, the focus will be on some of the major methodological problems that have arisen in attempts to apply these theories to clinically diagnosable depression.

The first, and perhaps most obvious, problem is that the theories are formulated on the basis of correlational data: the cognitions of already depressed individuals. The cognitive theories see the cognitions as causing the depression, but it is also plausible that being depressed causes a negative attributional style (Lewinsohn et al., 1981). The critical assumption for cognitive theories of depression is that the negative attributional style is a stable characteristic of the individual, constituting a trait-like vulnerability to negative life events (e.g., Hamilton & Abramson, 1983). If a negative cognitive style could be shown to be more stable than depression and to predict who will develop depression, the Beck and Abramson theories would be supported. Longitudinal designs, in which subjects are followed over time as in the study of mass media effects described in the last chapter, are valuable in testing this type of hypothesis.

In order to test either theory, one must be able to assess or measure the hypothesized negative cognitive style. Although not a sophisticated psychometric instrument (Hollon, Kendall, & Lumry, 1986), the Dysfunctional Attitudes Scale or DAS (Weissman & Beck, 1978) was developed to get at trait-like cognitive vulnerability in the context of Beck's theory. Similarly, the Attributional Style Questionnaire or ASQ (Seligman et al., 1979) has been widely used to assess negative attributional style in the context of Abramson and her colleagues' (1978) theory. Three important studies, one conducted before the development of these instruments, illustrate attempts to uncouple the confounded variables of negative cognitive style and depression.

In an early test of the etiological formulation, Lewinsohn and associates (1981) employed a **longitudinal design** in which they obtained measures of depressive cognitive style among a large community sample at Time 1 and then interviewed the same individuals after approximately one year (Time 2). On the basis of the interview at Time 2, the investigators were able to make a clinical diagnosis of depression. The critical comparison was between those individuals who were not depressed at Time 1 but became depressed at Time 2 and controls (individuals who were not depressed at either time). The cognitive theories predict that those who became depressed between Time 1 and Time 2 should have manifested a vulnerability to depression (i.e., a depressive cognitive style) at

Time 1. This prediction was not supported: there were no differences in cognitive style at Time 1 between controls and those destined to become depressed. Individuals who were currently depressed at either Time 1 or Time 2 showed a more negative cognitive style when depressed but not when nondepressed—consistent with the depression-causes-negative-cognitions hypothesis.

There was one interesting finding in support of the importance of depressive cognitions: the more severe the negative cognitions at the time the person was depressed, the more likely the person was to remain depressed—that is, negative cognitive style during depression predicted a more prolonged course of depression. Thus, the authors concluded that cognitive style was not related to the etiology of depression but seemed to be related to the course of the disorder. The authors noted that their data had been collected before the availability of the ASQ and the DAS and that, as a result, they had to employ measures of cognitive style that were not specifically developed to test the cognitive theories. They acknowledged the possibility that different results could possibly have been obtained with the ASQ and/or the DAS. Two more recent studies, however, suggest that these original results were valid and were not attributable to the measures of cognitive style that were employed.

Hamilton and Abramson (1983) approached the same question with a different (and more efficient) longitudinal design. Instead of beginning with a large number of nondepressed individuals and waiting for a small portion to become depressed, Hamilton and Abramson tested groups of depressed and nondepressed psychiatric patients, all of whom were newly admitted to a psychiatric hospital (Time 1). These patients were tested again immediately prior to discharge (Time 2), at which time the depressed patients had recovered to a substantial degree. Additionally, a group of "normal" (i.e., nonpsychiatric) controls were tested at Times 1 and 2. The DAS and the ASQ were used as measures of negative cognitive style that should be trait-like. The results showed a significant Groups X Time interaction, in which the depressed patients showed a more negative cognitive style on both the DAS and the ASQ at Time 1 but improved by Time 2 to such a degree that they no longer differed significantly from the two control groups. That is, the negative cognitive style again was found to covary with the state of depression, rather than being trait-like.

Substantially the same findings were obtained with a **cross-sectional** (between-subjects) **design** comparing currently depressed patients, formerly depressed patients who were currently not depressed, and nonpsychiatric controls in two other studies (Dohr, Rush, & Bernstein, 1989; Hollon, Kendall, & Lumry, 1986). Also, the ability of a negative cognitive style to predict duration of depression (reported by Lewinsohn and associates as described above) was confirmed by Dent and Teasdale (1988). Thus, as assessed by the currently available measures, a negative cognitive style was found not to represent a stable cognitive trait, but more severe negative cognitions during depression do predict a prolonged course of the episode of depression. These studies illustrate the way in which investigators in a clinical context attempted to examine the direction of effect of a correlation when ethical considerations precluded an experimental manipulation (researchers cannot cause depression). Longitudinal designs were important in providing a more precise test of the theory, one that had implications for the direction of causality.

In response to these problems for the cognitive theory of depression, cognitive theorists have suggested that the negative cognitive style may be a latent trait that is activated by a negative life event (Beck et al., 1979)—that is, an interaction between the latent vulnerability and a negative life event brings out the negative cognitive style. The implication of this hypothesis is that the trait cannot be measured with the usual methods while it is latent. Obviously, this hypothesis accounts for the failures above, but it makes the theory much more difficult to test. What is required is a longitudinal study with such close monitoring that researchers can assess the development of a negative cognitive style at the

time of the life event but clearly prior to the development of the depression. Such a design is extremely demanding and expensive. Further, skeptics might well argue that the negative cognitive style is simply a manifestation of the early phase of the onset of depression and not a primary cause.

A second methodological issue has arisen in this literature, having to do with the methods used to define or assess "depression." It appears to matter a great deal whether depression is assessed with a self-report measure or with a clinical diagnosis (a clinical interview combined with application of clinical diagnostic criteria). The negative results for the cognitive theories of depression all were based on clinical diagnoses. More positive support for the cognitive theories has been found with self-report measures of depression.

A later report by Lewinsohn, Hoberman, and Rosenbaum (1988) of the longitudinal study initially reported by Lewinsohn and associates (1981) (see above) examined the prediction of depression as assessed by self-report measures and by clinical diagnosis. Again, a negative cognitive style was found not to predict later depression based on clinical diagnosis, although an earlier clinical diagnosis of depression did predict later depression. In contrast, a negative cognitive style did predict later depression assessed with a self-report measure (the Center for Epidemiologic Studies Depression Scale or CES-D scale). That is, a future episode of clinically diagnosed depression was more strongly associated with earlier episodes of clinically diagnosed depression, whereas a future episode of depression measured by a self-report measure was more strongly associated with earlier self-report measures of negative cognitive style.

Other studies have also yielded stronger support for cognitive theories of depression when depression is assessed via self-report measures. Metalsky, Halberstadt, and Abramson (1987) obtained ASQ scores from students before they received their grades on a midterm exam. The ASQ score in combination with the exam outcome (based on the discrepancy between the student's aspiration for the exam result and the actual result) predicted depressed mood two days after receipt of the midterm grades. In this study, the Multiple Affect Adjective Checklist (MAACL) was used to assess depressed mood as the outcome variable.

These results raise important methodological issues concerning the assessment of depression. There are at least two aspects to this problem. One concerns the conceptualization or definition of depression, the other method variance—that is, self-report versus clinical interview. With respect to the first aspect, Lewinsohn, Hoberman, and Rosenbaum (1988) suggest that the CES-D and other self-report depression scales, such as the Beck Depression Inventory (BDI), measure "depressive symptoms," whereas the interview and clinical diagnosis measure "a diagnosable episode of depressive disorder" (p. 260)—that is, a distinction between a cluster of symptoms and a disorder. The Metalsky, Halberstadt and Abramson (1987) study measured only one aspect of depression, depressed mood, which would be only one component of depressive symptoms. The fundamental distinction between depressive symptoms and a depressive disorder was supported in recommendations for the use of the BDI by a group of senior researchers, including Beck himself (Kendall et al., 1987). These authors (like others) note that the term "depression" can be used to refer to a single *symptom* (depressed mood), to a *syndrome* (a collection of symptoms that cluster together), and to a **nosological category** (a disorder that presumably will ultimately prove to be distinguishable from other disorders). They further argue that the BDI is a measure of syndromal depression, whereas clinical diagnosis at least attempts to define nosological depression. By this argument, a negative attributional style is implicated as important in the development of depressive symptoms, but not of depressive disorder.

Psychotherapy

One of the reasons for including a consideration of research on psychotherapy (see box 10.5) within an experimental psychology text is that many of the contemporary forms of psychotherapy have their roots in basic psychological research or they have been developed by psychologists applying the methodologies of experimental psychology. Thus, while many types of psychotherapy derive from clinical experience, other forms reflect extrapolation from basic psychological research.

With respect to the present consideration of experimental methods in clinical psychology, it is important to note that research on psychotherapy can have three foci. The experimental research can be structured to determine whether one or more therapeutic approaches are effective, or whether there is a difference in relative effectiveness. That is, does Therapy A result in improvement of the clients, or does Therapy A have a more favorable outcome than Therapy B? Such research is typically described as **outcome research** because the goal is to determine the outcome of an intervention. The second type of therapy research is usually described as **process research.** This research is designed either to determine which components of a therapy are important or effective, or to determine by what process does the therapy produce an outcome. In other words, if a therapy is effective, why is it effective?

A third, but often ignored, focus of therapy research is when therapy is used in an experiment to test hypotheses about important variables in a psychiatric disorder. For example, in his efforts to understand the contribution of various family characteristics in the development of antisocial behavior in boys, Patterson (1982) has used treatment programs at the Oregon Social Learning Center to test hypotheses about the role of (a) parental supervision

For the purposes of the present discussion, the terms psychotherapy and therapy are used interchangeably and are considered to be generic terms. All forms of psychological interventions such as behavioral therapy, cognitive therapy, psychoanalysis, or systematic desensitization are subsumed under these more general labels. In general, psychotherapy is defined as a structured prescribed series of formal interactions between an identified patient or client and a service provider who is sanctioned by society or a professional body to provide such services. The services are designed to reduce thoughts, emotions, or behaviors of the patient that are distressing to the patient and/or others in the setting. Generally, these distressing emotions, cognitions, or behaviors are those represented in the diagnoses described in the DSM-IV, discussed earlier.

and monitoring and (b) family problem solving in the development of aggressive and antisocial behavior. By systematically training families in effective strategies for monitoring their children's activities, or by training families in problem-solving skills that are related directly to family function, the rates of aggressive and antisocial behavior in children from treated families were reduced. Patterson then used such data to build his theoretical analysis of children's antisocial behavior. In a sense, the Oregon Social Learning Center group has used their treatment program to experimentally manipulate components of parenting to test theoretical notions about the contribution of specific parenting behaviors in the maintenance of deviant and nondeviant child behaviors (see Patterson, Reid, & Dishion, 1992). Sharing much in common with both outcome and process research, the major goal of this type of therapy research is to gain an understanding of psychopathology rather than to merely improve treatment or to determine variables that influence therapy per se. Of course, improving treatment is not ignored in such research. It is important to note that, in actual practice, the distinctions among these three types of therapy research can be blurred. Students, however, should find the distinctions to be heuristically useful as they consider therapy research in the context of the methods of experimental psychology. In this consideration of psychotherapy research, the focus is on the types of control groups that researchers use as they conduct these various types of therapy research. In addition, there is a discussion of the distinction between clinical trials and analog work and some of the measurement difficulties that can arise in studies of psychotherapy.

Therapy Control Groups

As illustrated throughout this book, the inclusion of control or comparison groups is often the *sine qua non* of experimental psychology. Yet, it is the selection of suitable control groups in psychotherapy research that is often one of the most formidable problems confronting the clinical researcher. As in other experimental research, the researcher has to determine the variables that require control so that strong inferences regarding the influence of preselected independent variables can be determined. One of the earliest critiques of psychotherapy outcome research was based on the argument that the degree of change produced by therapy was no greater than would have occurred spontaneously.

BOX 10.6

Waiting List Controls

A number of problems have been associated with the use of the waiting list control group that are worth noting. Firstly, some potential subjects seeking services for a psychological problem may not agree to be placed on a waiting list, and the resulting groups would violate the requirement of random assignment to experimental conditions. Moreover, some subjects who agree to be in the waiting list control condition might be less severely disturbed or less seriously motivated to seek services. Secondly, potential research subjects who are motivated to seek therapy might seek alternative services while they are on the waiting list. Thus, the subjects on the waiting list might actually get services that are unknown to the researcher and, as a result, it becomes a poor control for spontaneous improvement. Thirdly, some have argued that it is unethical to withhold therapy from those who need it. These three arguments have been sufficiently persuasive that contemporary research on psychotherapy infrequently uses a waiting list as a control group.

That is, Eysenck (1952) essentially argued that the psychiatric disorders being treated (primarily neuroses or nonpsychotic disorders) would evidence considerable improvement with the passage of time. According to Eysenck, most clients would improve without formal psychotherapy and, therefore, the influence of therapy was unproven.

As a result of the extremely influential Eysenck paper and similar papers, therapy researchers adopted the use of "waiting list" control groups (see box 10.6). In the waiting list control group, potential research subjects seeking therapy were placed on a waiting list and the start of therapy was delayed for a sufficiently long period of time so the researcher could compare the outcome of the therapy with the outcome for a group that did not receive any services. Such a control group was designed only to control for the **spontaneous remission** of the disorder or spontaneous remission of the targeted symptoms. Of course, to be able to compare a treatment to a waiting list control, it is important to be certain that the subjects in a waiting list control group did not get services from some other source.

An example of a recent therapy outcome study using a waiting list control group was one by Barlow and associates (1984). These therapy researchers were interested in documenting the natural course of panic disorder and generalized anxiety disorder, as well as the possibility of identifying an effective treatment. In this study, clients were randomly assigned to a behavioral therapy condition or a waiting list control condition. (Random assignment, as opposed to, say, a "first-come, first-served" procedure is absolutely essential.) Although the subjects in the waiting list control group did not receive treatment during the 14 weeks when the treated group received therapy, the control subjects were contacted every 2 to 3 weeks to sustain their interest and cooperation in the study. Moreover, subjects in both the treatment and the waiting list conditions maintained daily records of their anxiety. Thus, although the subjects on the waiting list did not receive treatment, they were not merely ignored for 14 weeks.

An important issue in both outcome and process research in psychotherapy has been to control for **nonspecific therapeutic factors.** Nonspecific factors refer to those components of treatment that are common to virtually all therapies and that might be importantly involved in the impact of the therapy (see Strupp & Hadley, 1979). For example, as noted by Frank (1961), personal contact with a professional might have an impact on psychological problems. Additionally, research has suggested that a client's expectation to improve could positively influence the outcome of a treatment. Thus, it was recognized that experimental conditions in therapy research should be equated with respect to professional contact and the degree to which the therapy was likely to engender an expectation to improve. Obviously, waiting list control groups are not equated with the treatment groups on the dimensions of professional contact and expectations for success.

To develop control groups that were matched on professional contact and expectations for success but would still permit an assessment of change without treatment, psychotherapy researchers borrowed the concept of the **placebo** from pharmaceutical research. A placebo is a treatment that has no active ingredients, but the recipient is led to believe that the treatment has active ingredients and may lead to improvement. It is important to note that, in medicine, the placebo is targeted at psychological attributes of illness and not at core somatic components of illness. For example, a study of the psychological aspects of headache might compare subjects who receive inert pills that taste and look like aspirin (the placebo) with subjects who actually receive aspirin. Applying the placebo concept to psychotherapy research, some investigators have argued that the inclusion of a placebo control group is an essential part of research designed to establish scientifically the effectiveness of psychotherapy (e.g., Prioleau, Murdock, & Brody, 1983).

An influential study that is often described as establishing the importance of the placebo control group was an investigation of therapies for public speaking anxiety by Paul (1966). In this research, the primary focus was the determination of the relative effectiveness (outcomes) of two therapies: one based on helping clients develop insight into their problems and the second based on systematic desensitization, a behavioral therapy developed by Wolpe (1958) and derived from his basic laboratory work. To a large extent, this research reflected the conflict between advocates of traditional psychotherapies and the newer developments of behavior therapies in the late 1960s. In order to establish the relative efficacy of the two therapies, Paul recruited subjects from among university students who were enrolled in public speaking courses *and* who were highly anxious and stressed by public speaking. Subjects who met stringent criteria for public speaking anxiety were randomly assigned to several experimental conditions.

The different experimental conditions were each administered by the same five highly experienced psychotherapists who followed a treatment manual for each of the experimental conditions. For all of the treatment conditions, each subject received five 50-minute contact hours administered by one of the therapists. Subjects assigned to the insight-oriented psychotherapy group were interviewed using the traditional approaches of the experienced therapists in their daily clinical work. The focus of these interviews was to help the subject achieve understanding into the basis of their public speaking anxiety. Subjects assigned to the systematic desensitization condition also received five 50-minute sessions of a modified version of systematic desensitization based on the work of Wolpe. Therapists trained the subjects in progressive relaxation and then exposed them, through visual imagery, to a hierarchy of events related to public speaking anxiety. The pairing of relaxation with images of anxiety-evoking events was designed to reduce or eliminate the public speaking anxiety. Because this therapy was markedly different from the traditional approach ordinarily used by the therapists, and because these therapists were unfamiliar with the systematic desensitization procedures to be used, they were given extensive training in the techniques. Before they commenced the conduct of experimental sessions, they were given opportunities to practice with subjects other than those in the study. Additionally, the therapists' administration of all procedures was monitored through the use of audio tape recordings. Thus, the two different treatment conditions were administered by the same set of therapists who were highly prepared to provide the specific forms of therapy with each experimental condition. The two treatment conditions were closely matched with respect to therapist characteristics (the same therapists administered both therapies), amount of therapist contact by the subject, and other "nonspecific" aspects of treatment.

For the purposes of the present discussion, it was Paul's (1966) inclusion of the **attention-placebo group** that is most important. In this condition, the therapists spent a brief period establishing rapport with the subjects and then discussed the rationale for the placebo treatment condition. This placebo condition involved the administration of a "fast-acting tranquilizer" (actually a 2 gram capsule of sodium bicarbonate, an innocuous chemical that has no psychological effects) and listening to an audio tape of monotonous sounds, which, although described as a highly stressful task, often resulted in drowsiness in listeners. Subjects were told that by taking the fast acting tranquilizer and then exposing themselves to this "highly stressful task," they would eliminate their anxiety in other settings, including public speaking. During the time that the subject listened to the monotonous tape, the therapist, who was present, refrained from interacting with the subject or engaging in any significant interviewing with the subject. Thus, subjects in the attention-placebo condition experienced five 50-minute sessions with the therapist, but they did not receive any actual services from the therapist. Therefore, the attention-placebo control condition was essentially matched to the two treatment conditions with respect to professional contact, expectation for success and other "nonspecific" components of therapy.

The Paul (1966) study also included two additional control groups. Subjects in the no-treatment control condition participated in all of the assessment procedures and they were contacted by telephone at least once. In addition, although they were promised treatment in the future, subjects in that group did not participate in any of the treatment procedures during the course of the research. Thus, this condition was largely a waiting list control group. The second control group consisted of potential subjects who could not be contacted at the start of the study. Because they only provided pretreatment and posttreatment data through the class in which they were enrolled, they had no real involvement in any aspects of the professional contact within the study and could not have been influenced by the telephone calls and the like.

The Paul study is important for many reasons. Initially, it gained prominence because it established the clinical effectiveness of a behavioral therapy. Systematic desensitization was clearly superior to the insight therapy and, although the insight therapy was superior to the waiting list control, insight therapy was not significantly better than the attention placebo. Thus, the Paul study is often credited with stimulating decades of research and practice based on behavior therapy. (It should be noted that later research did not necessarily establish systematic desensitization per se as a superior form of therapy, although many components of desensitization have been supported by later research.) The Paul study not only compared the relative effectiveness of two psychotherapeutic approaches (insight therapy vs. systematic desensitization), it set the stage for many years of therapy research that adopted some sort of attention placebo as a necessary control group. It is for that reason that the study was considered here. Basically, following the Paul (1966) study, the attention placebo became more widely used than the waiting list controls. See box 10.7 for a discussion of phenomena in other concepts resembling the attention placebo.

Although the inclusion of the placebo control condition became an accepted standard for therapy outcome research, the adoption of placebo control groups as *the* standard for psychotherapy research has not gone unchallenged (e.g., O'Leary & Borkovec, 1978; Parloff, 1986; Stiles & Shapiro,

BOX 10.7

The Hawthorne Effect

The Paul (1966) study was not the first psychotherapy study to use a placebo, but the present authors believe it was the most influential. It is important to note, however, that considerations of attentional influences and the inclusion of placebo-like control groups have been important in areas of psychology other than clinical for many years. For example, related to the inclusion of placebo control groups has been the recognition of the **Hawthorne Effect** in studies of human behavior. The term *Hawthorne Effect* derives from a series of studies on worker productivity that were conducted over a 12-year period at the Hawthorne facilities of Western Electric starting in the late 1920s (Dickson & Roethlisberger, 1966; Roethlisberger & Dickson, 1939). Briefly, a variety of single variable experiments were conducted that had positive outcomes, but the outcomes could not be attributable to the direct influence of the physical environment variables that were manipulated. Rather, the outcomes were ultimately seen as the result of the indirect operation of social influences operating in the industrial milieu. For example, one experiment showed that the provision of rest periods enhanced productivity. However, later work also showed the improvement was not attributable to a reduction in fatigue. The productivity benefit achieved with rest periods was later attributed to the social meaning and morale enhancing effects of the rests and not the fatigue reducing effects of rest.

These Hawthorne Effect studies have achieved a position of importance in industrial psychology by calling attention to the operation of social psychological factors in industrial management, and they have been used to expand the domain of psychological research (see Sommer, 1968). However, in the present consideration of experimental methods, these Hawthorne experiments have methodological importance. That is, the Hawthorne studies established the need to design research with human subjects so that the experimenter can assess whether the independent variables directly influence the dependent variables or whether there is an indirect influence due to social and attentional factors. Thus, there is a clear analogy between the inclusion of attention-placebo control groups in psychotherapy research and the need for control groups that will address concerns about the Hawthorne Effect in industrial and social psychological research.

1989). The questions raised about the use of the placebo control have been related to two arguments. Ethical issues have been raised because the placebo involves the use of deception, and deception in psychological research has been increasingly questioned. (See the chapter on social psychology.) Questions have also been raised regarding the conceptual basis of the placebo in psychotherapy research. With respect to the latter, the influence of personal contact, expectations for improvement, and confidence in the clinician are seen as integral and active ingredients in effective therapies, and they are not viewed as presumably "inert ingredients" of psychotherapy. Thus, the "placebo" is seen as an active treatment according to some therapy researchers, and therefore it is worthy of study in its own right.

Perhaps more importantly, a therapy-specific ethical issue was raised by those who questioned the ethics of providing a "treatment" that is presumed to be inert and ineffective to clients who were actively seeking and needing services and, in addition, actually misleading them in an attempt to elicit an expectation that they were receiving an effective treatment. By inducing an expectation of success and thereby reducing the motivation to seek other services, subjects who were actually in need of services might be less likely to seek an effective intervention. Although having subjects who were truly untreated greatly enhanced the utility of the placebo group (i.e., by providing a more veritical estimate of the placebo response), the more effective the placebo was in keeping subjects from seeking alternative services, the more the deception was questioned. Deception was not an acceptable way to recruit and keep potential subjects in an untreated research condition, and it could violate contemporary standards of informed consent. ("Informed consent" as a way of dealing with ethical issues in research was discussed in chapter 1.)

As a result of both ethical and conceptual challenges, the arguments in favor of the placebo control group have been replaced by an argument in favor of using the "best alternative" therapy as the critical control group in psychotherapy outcome studies (e.g., O'Leary & Borkovec, 1978; Parloff, 1986). Basically, the best alternative treatment strategy identifies as the critical control group a treatment that is thought to be at least minimally effective. With this approach, subjects are randomly assigned to two or more treatment conditions that available evidence, or pilot work, would establish as having some efficacy. In addition, according to Parloff (1986), in this approach, the therapists (experimenters) of each condition should work to maximize the influence of the nonspecific elements of their treatment programs. Thus, in the simplest of studies, rather than determining whether a therapy is better than no therapy (i.e., waiting list control) or better than a set of so-called nonspecific therapeutic effects (i.e., placebo control), researchers conduct comparative outcome studies and comparative process studies using one or more different therapies. The studies of parenting by the Oregon Social Learning Center group mentioned earlier used that approach.

Examples of comparative outcome research that incorporated the "best alternative" treatment control strategy are two recent studies by Borkovec and Mathews and their colleagues (Borkovec & Mathews, 1988; Borkovec et al., 1987). The primary focus of this research was on the efficacy of cognitive/behavioral therapy in treating clients with nonphobic anxiety disorders, including generalized anxiety disorder and panic disorder. In the first study (Borkovec et al., 1987), subjects who met stringent diagnostic standards were randomly assigned to a cognitive/behavioral therapy condition or a nondirective therapy condition. Both therapies were provided following standardized protocols and both therapy conditions were matched on number of sessions and therapeutic contact time. Additionally, the two therapies were demonstrated in the research to be equivalent with respect to credibility and client expectations for improvement.

In the first study, the nondirective therapy group was essentially selected to serve as the control against which the cognitive/behavioral therapy would be compared. (It is important to note that in other research contexts, such as the work of Rogers (1951), the nondirective therapy would be the experimental treatment of primary interest.) Because the investigators felt that available evidence indicated that relaxation training was an important factor in treating anxiety disorders, they included relaxation training in both the cognitive/behavioral treatment and the nondirective treatment. Thus, to provide all subjects with a minimally effective therapy, subjects in both the control condition and the experimental condition received the same abbreviated relaxation training as part of the research protocol. In this way, the research was designed to determine whether cognitive/behavioral therapy offered anything beyond relaxation training and the nonspecific influences of professional therapeutic contact and a therapeutic relationship enhanced through nondirective therapy.

After the initial study suggested the superiority of the cognitive behavioral therapy, a follow-up study by Borkovec and Mathews (1988) was designed to assess the importance of several variables that could influence the process of cognitive/behavioral therapy. In particular, Borkovec and Mathews attempted to determine whether there were individual differences among clients in their experiences of anxiety (predominantly cognitive versus somatic symptoms) and their response to the treatment procedure (i.e., relaxation-induced anxiety, a phenomenon where there is a paradoxical increase in anxiety during relaxation training) that would result in differential effectiveness of treatment. This is another example of a possible Subject X Treatment interaction effect. Paralleling the earlier work, subjects with generalized anxiety disorder were randomly assigned to one of three treatment conditions. The nondirective psychotherapy and cognitive/behavioral therapy conditions were again used; the third treatment condition was coping desensitization, where the subject exercised greater personal control over the treatment process. As in the first study, subjects in all treatment conditions were provided relaxation training as a minimally effective treatment. The process measures of expressions of anxiety (cognitive or somatic) and relaxation-induced anxiety were then related to the outcomes of the therapy.

Although the second study did not entirely replicate the superiority of the cognitive/behavioral therapy, the present interest in these two studies from Borkovec's laboratory is not in evaluating the effectiveness of a specific form of therapy but in the approach taken to conduct meaningful and ethical research with clinical populations in a manner that

is methodologically sound. That is, the work permitted a determination of the relative effectiveness of different approaches to therapy while controlling for nonspecific treatment effects that are associated with professional contact. Additionally, all subjects were provided a form of treatment that is recognized as at least minimally effective for the specific disorder. Since other research (e.g., Barlow et al., 1984) had demonstrated the persistence of these anxiety disorders through waiting list control designs, continued use of that control condition in the Borkovec laboratory was not necessary. Students should recognize, however, that some control for possible spontaneous remission is still needed in the context of therapy research with some disorders whose natural course is unknown or unclear. Furthermore, control for professional contact and the nonspecific factors in therapeutic services may still be required in some treatment research contexts. Thus, while the current research climate emphasizes the use of the best alternative treatment strategy in control group design, some researchers still advocate the use of waiting list control groups and some variation of the placebo control. From an ethical perspective, waiting list and placebo controls are most acceptable in instances where a minimally effective treatment has not been established—that is, it is ethically acceptable to withhold treatments that have not been shown to be effective.

So far the discussion of experimental psychological research in the context of psychotherapy research has focused on control group considerations. To a large extent, the adequacy of experimental research in psychotherapy is a function of the establishment of an effective control group. There are, of course, many other considerations that must be made. For example, are the therapists used in the experimental conditions equally matched with respect to amount of experience and training? Can the researcher be confident that the treatment protocol was followed fully in each experimental condition? Are the subjects equally likely to be assigned to the different experimental conditions, or is there some bias in the assignment of subjects to treatment conditions? When such considerations of subjects, therapists, and research protocols are made, a distinction between "analog" studies and "clinical-trials" studies is often offered.

Analog and Clinical Trials

Analog studies are, perhaps, the most common form of experimental research on psychotherapy. In an analog study, the subjects or the treatment conditions are considered to be only approximations of actual clinical populations, settings, or services. In the analog research, in one or more critical ways, the procedures and/or subjects may depart from actual clinical practice. While some have questioned analog studies of therapy, others (e.g., Kazdin, 1978) have argued that virtually all experimental psychological research is an analog, or only an approximation, of the naturally occurring conditions to which investigators hope to generalize.

To some extent, the Paul (1966) study discussed above could be considered an analog study because the subjects were university students who were anxious in a public speaking context. Although anxiety in public speaking might be very unpleasant and might adversely affect one's career plans, relatively few college students are incapacitated by public speaking anxiety. Additionally, the subjects in the Paul research were actively recruited for the study. Thus, although they were extremely anxious, these subjects were only analogs of clients who would actually seek services in clinics. Another way in which the Paul study was an analog is the fact that all therapists were trained to provide all forms of

therapy. In clinical practice, therapists do not typically provide multiple forms of therapy for the same disorder. The research by Borkovec and associates (1987) described above also involved the recruitment of subjects through advertisements and public announcements, but the diagnostic standards of admission to the experiment were consistent with clinical diagnostic standards. Still, in the context of how clients present for services, this research by Borkovec and colleagues would also be considered an analog. In contrast, because subjects in the Borkovec and Mathews (1988) study included referrals from mental health agencies (as well as through advertisements as in the Borkovec et al., 1987, study), the subjects in that study may be more typical of actual clinic samples.

In **clinical trials** research, the clients who serve as subjects are the same clients who would be seeking services at a clinical site. The therapists are the clinicians who would be providing therapy at those sites, and all of the procedures are followed in an actual clinical context. An excellent example of an experimental clinical trial study of psychotherapy was the National Institute of Mental Health (NIMH) collaborative multisite study of the treatment of depression (Elkin et al., 1989). In this research, at each of three different treatment sites, clinical patients who met research diagnostic criteria (Spitzer, Endicott, & Robins, 1978) for a major depressive episode and who did not evidence other psychiatric diagnoses (e.g., antisocial personality disorder, panic disorder, alcoholism, schizophrenia) were randomly assigned to one of four different treatment conditions. The two forms of psychotherapy were cognitive behavioral therapy and interpersonal psychotherapy. Both of these treatment programs were provided by highly trained therapists who followed very specific treatment manuals. Thus, the researchers attempted to ensure that the treatments were properly delivered at all sites as intended.

Two control conditions were included in this research. The imipramine-clinical management control provided subjects with antidepressant medication and supportive and encouraging personal contact, together with direct advice when necessary. Subjects assigned to the placebo-clinical management condition received the same services as the subjects in the imipramine-clinical management condition, except that the medication they received did not have active ingredients. In both of these two groups, the patient and the therapists were uninformed as to whether the subject was receiving the antidepressant medication or a placebo. As you may recall from an earlier chapter, this is known as the **double-blind** procedure. Both the subject and the experimenter are uninformed as to the conditions under which the subjects are operating. In this clinical trials procedure, the imipramine-clinical management condition could be considered the "best alternative" therapy against which the two psychotherapies could be contrasted. The comparison between the imipramine-clinical management condition and the placebo-clinical management condition establishes the minimal effectiveness of the drug treatment. Interestingly, although the authors of the NIMH study had considered including a separate placebo control condition for assessing the effectiveness of psychotherapy, they report being unable to develop an ethically acceptable psychotherapy placebo condition. However, because the placebo-clinical management condition included 20 to 30 minutes of professional contact with support, encouragement, and occasional advice (it was described as "a minimal supportive therapy"), it essentially provides the same analytical information that would be expected from an attention placebo. That

is, this condition included contact with a therapist but did not include the specific techniques of psychotherapy employed in the other psychotherapy treatment groups.

In some respects, the results of the NIMH clinical trials research are most interesting because of the relative lack of differences among the treatment conditions. Overall, there was evidence of improvement among recipients of each of the various therapies. However, when initial severity of depression was considered, the placebo-clinical management procedure did not do nearly as well as the imipramine-clinical management approach for severely depressed patients. From the standpoint of methodology in psychotherapy research, the benefits achieved by all four therapy conditions with the less severely depressed subjects underscore the importance of personal professional contact and the "nonspecific" aspects of therapy rather than the importance of the specific therapeutic approaches. Thus, methodologically, the NIMH study also calls attention to the possible importance of the Treatment X Subject interaction that has been noted in this and earlier chapters.

Measuring Change due to Psychotherapy

The NIMH clinical trials study also demonstrated that not all outcome measures yielded the same results. In all experimental psychological research, documenting that an experiment had an effect on the subjects requires that the experimenter select useful dependent measures. In psychotherapy research, it is critically important that the researcher select dependent measures that are appropriate and useful. In this context the reader should recall the earlier discussion of reliability and validity of assessment instruments. For outcome measures in psychotherapy research to be useful and appropriate, it is essential that the investigators select measures that have established reliability and validity. Very often the utility of the psychotherapy research will hinge more on the dependent measures selected than on the incorporation of specific types of control groups. That is, whether experimental treatments are seen as having different outcomes will be a function of the measures used to demonstrate outcome differences.

You might have heard the common statement: "Statistical significance is not clinical significance." This statement refers to a common observation that researchers in psychotherapy might demonstrate that there are statistically significant differences among treatment groups, but if the dependent measures are not practically important or if they are not reflective of clinically important changes in the patients, then the fact that groups may differ statistically may not be sufficient to truly establish the effectiveness of a therapy. For example, if an experimental treatment for snake phobia caused some treated subjects to report significantly less fear in response to pictures of snakes, but if those same treated subjects still refuse to camp or engage in outdoor activities because of a fear of snakes, the treatment would not have been clinically effective.

In the context of the statement, "Statistical significance is not clinical significance," it is important to remind students that statistical significance refers to the reliability or replicability of a finding. Thus, statistical significance means that a finding is likely to be replicated if the experiment were repeated. In the absence of statistical significance, the replicability of the finding is uncertain, or even unlikely. Therefore, although an experimenter could fail to obtain clinically significant outcomes with statistically significant results, in the absence of statistical significance the research would also not demonstrate clinical significance. Poorly chosen dependent variable measures could lead to statistically nonsignificant and clinically insignificant results.

There are many different approaches to measuring change in experimental tests of psychotherapy, and space precludes covering them all. It is, however, important to call attention to the fact that researchers designing studies of the effect of psychotherapy should not limit themselves to self-reports by the clients. Although the reports of clients can provide important information regarding outcome of a treatment program, very often when persons experience a treatment to which they may have committed a great deal of time and energy, they might respond favorably even when there is no bona fide change. (Recall the discussion of "cognitive dissonance" effects in the preceding chapter.) This is, of course, why therapy researchers included placebo controls. It is also why contemporary researchers include many different outcome measures, especially measures that are not limited by the self-reports of the client. Ideally, the outcome measures would be obtained using several different procedures and from independent sources that are unaware of the treatment conditions to which the subjects were exposed. The Borkovec studies noted above used a psychiatric assessor, standardized questionnaires, and daily diaries as outcome measures. The NIMH clinical trials study used standardized questionnaires as well as semistructured interviews administered by a clinical evaluator. Of course, reports by the therapists from the treatment conditions would not be above question, and contemporary therapy research should not use global ratings by the subjects' therapists as the exclusive measure of change.

Ideally, research on psychotherapy would use a variety of outcome measures. For example, Lang (1968, 1977) noted that the construct of anxiety can be assessed in three different domains: self-reports, behavioral measures, and physiological measures. Most importantly, Lang demonstrated that these three different indices of anxiety do not necessarily evidence a high degree of concordance. Thus, therapy targeted at anxiety might show different outcomes as a function of the measurement system used. In all therapy research, self-reports obtained through standardized questionnaires can be useful. However, self-report measures do have limitations. Clients are not always accurate in describing clinically important information. Additionally, self-report measures can be reactive to and influenced by the assessment context. Client subjects can report improvement to please experimenter therapists, or they can respond in a manner that they believe is expected. Sometimes self-reports from questionnaires are not entirely consistent with self-reports in interviews (recall the earlier discussion of assessment in depression research). As a result, direct observations of the behaviors of the treated subjects can be important. For example, working with families of aggressive children, experimental treatment conditions conducted by researchers at the Oregon Social Learning Center (see Patterson, 1982) use direct observations made in the homes of the subjects to assess change. In research with treatment for antisocial behavior, arrest records can also provide objective information on outcome. For the treatment of some disorders, psychophysiological indices of reactions to stress or anxiety could be used as an outcome measure (e.g., Barlow, Mavissakalian, & Schofield, 1980) or a process measure (e.g., Borkovec & Fowles, 1973) (see box 10.8). In any case, you should keep in mind that experimental research on psychotherapy should incorporate multiple measures that are not restricted to self-reports by the treated subjects and their therapists.

Regardless of the reliability and validity of the measures used to assess the effectiveness of therapy, and regardless of the control group strategy adopted, sometimes efforts to replicate therapy outcome research are unsuccessful. The Borkovec research noted above is just one of many examples. This and other failures to replicate call attention to one of the major problems in clinical research—namely that it is extremely difficult to exactly duplicate an earlier study with respect to therapist characteristics, subject characteristics, and perhaps the exact characteristics of the therapy. The widespread use of standardized therapy manuals has increased confidence in the duplication of the administration of therapy across experiments or across research settings. Nevertheless, exact duplication is difficult. Because of this difficulty in replication, some might question the whole enterprise, but others recognize that in clinical research, such as therapy research, there are many variables that simply cannot be controlled as readily as in a basic laboratory context. Although the replicability of any research cannot be assumed and must be demonstrated, the complexity of clinical research can add to the usual difficulties. Because clinical research is specifically targeted to providing services, it is incumbent upon clinical investigators to demonstrate the replicability of a finding.

In this consideration of replications, the distinction between direct replication and systematic replication made by Sidman (1960) is probably worth noting. In a direct replication, all possible aspects of an earlier experiment are duplicated exactly. Such a procedure clearly establishes the replicability of a finding, but it does not extend the research in new directions or offer new developments. In systematic replications, while most of the experiment would be duplicated exactly, some important component is changed. In clinical research or therapy research, the change could involve the addition of a new control condition or a new treatment condition. To a large extent, the Borkovec and Mathews (1988) study could be considered a systematic replication of the Borkovec and associates (1987) study. Both direct

BOX 10.8

Psychophysiological Assessment

The student who knows that psychiatric disorders have traditionally been viewed as emotional disorders might naturally assume that psychophysiological measures (especially assessment of autonomic nervous system responses) might offer a simple and attractive solution to assessing psychopathological emotional states (and, therefore, assessing outcome in psychotherapy). Unfortunately, such attempts have largely revealed the complexity of the problem, centering especially around two major issues. First, **somatic activity** (activity of the voluntary or striated musculature) has a major influence on physiological responding, usually overwhelming the influence of emotional states. This muted "exercise response" is most easily understood in the use of heart rate to infer emotional states. From a biological perspective, a primary function of the heart is to deliver blood (containing oxygen) to active muscles and to carry away carbon dioxide and other metabolic products of muscle activity. A large literature has amply documented the expectation that follows from this perspective: heart rate covaries strongly with somatic activity, justifying cardiac-somatic coupling as the first hypothesis to consider in understanding changes in heart rate (e.g., Obrist, 1976; Obrist et al., 1974). Although less obvious, physical activity also has an effect on measures of electrodermal activity (often called the galvanic skin response or GSR)—recordings taken from the palm of the

hand that reflect psychologically responsive sweat gland activity (Fowles, 1986). Consequently, any attempt to infer emotional states from psychophysiological measures must first ensure that somatic activity is not responsible for any results obtained—that is, the experimenter must control the level of somatic activity (usually, although not always, keeping it to a minimum). For example, if one wanted to study anxiety during public speaking, it would be difficult to disentangle or unconfound the effects of anxiety versus the effects of the physical exertion inherent in giving a speech.

The second issue concerns the *nature of emotional states* and the degree to which psychophysiological responses show patterns that are specific to these states. Early hopes that specific emotions (e.g., depression, happiness, fear, anger, sadness, rage) could be inferred from specific patterns of physiological responding were dashed by negative findings—that is, one cannot assess the presence and degree of depression by measuring a pattern of physiological responses. It was then proposed that physiological measures could serve as an index of the intensity of a dimension of emotional arousal (e.g., Duffy, 1962; Lindsley, 1951; Malmo, 1959). However, further research established that numerous measures used as an index of arousal did not, themselves, covary, and this state of affairs led to a strong criticism of the arousal concept in a

replications and systematic replications are important in advancing clinical knowledge and clinical service, and, perhaps more than other areas of psychology, both types of replications should be seen as useful approaches for doing research within experimental/clinical psychology.

Summary and Conclusions

This chapter provides examples of research methods in clinical psychology, selected to illustrate many of the most important topics in the field. To achieve this end, examples were chosen to cut across diagnostic groups and across questions of the classic paper by Lacey (1967). More recently, Fowles (1980) cited the work of Gray (e.g., 1975, 1976, 1987) as describing two dimensions of motivation inferred from the literature on animal learning and motivation and applied these motivational constructs to psychophysiology. One dimension, the behavioral activation system or BAS, is an appetitive (concerned with appetites) motivational system that activates behavior in response to conditioned stimuli for rewards or for relieving nonpunishment (the absence of an expected punishment). Relieving nonpunishment is seen in active avoidance paradigms, in which an animal can make a response to avoid a punishment that would otherwise occur. Analyses of this paradigm suggest that relief is experienced when the punishment is successfully avoided. The second dimension, the behavioral inhibition system or BIS, is an aversive motivational system that inhibits behavior that would otherwise occur in response to conditioned stimuli for response-contingent punishment or for frustration (the absence of an expected reward during extinction). Activation of the BAS is accompanied by positive affective states (hope, relief), whereas activation of the BIS is accompanied by negative affective states (fear or anxiety, frustration). Activation of either motivational system is said to increase nonspecific arousal. Fowles proposed that heart rate, as might be suggested by cardiac-somatic

coupling, is more strongly associated with activity of the BAS, whereas under some conditions electrodermal activity might serve to index activity of the BIS. Fowles (1988, 1992a, 1992b, 1993) has further argued that these motivational systems do, in fact, help to understand psychopathology, as suggested by their involvement in emotional states. The potential usefulness of constructs of appetitive and aversive motivational systems has been further supported by findings that self-reports of emotional states define two broad factors of positive and negative affect (Tellegen, 1985; Watson & Clark, 1984; Watson & Tellegen, 1985; Watson, Clark, & Carey, 1988; Watson, Clark, & Tellegen, 1988). Thus, evidence from studies of motivation in animals and of self-reported emotional states in humans converges to suggest two broad dimensions of emotion. In spite of this encouraging state of affairs with regard to the nature of emotional states, many questions and difficulties remain with respect to their psychophysiological assessment. Consequently, the student should realize that the psychophysiological assessment of emotional states is a complex and incompletely solved problem involving methodological problems of controlling somatic activity, theoretical problems concerning the nature of emotional states, and insufficient knowledge concerning the many factors influencing physiological responses.

---

description and assessment of psychopathology, etiology, process, and treatment. Under diagnosis, we called attention to the distinction between categorical and dimensional approaches to assessment, to the importance of subtype diagnoses for reducing within group variance, and to the basic concepts of reliability and validity. The clinical groups discussed included schizophrenia, anxiety, depression, and victims of child abuse. Schizophrenia was used

to illustrate research on the genetic contribution to etiology and the way in which genetic factors were separated from environmental influences through twin and adoption studies. Phobic reactions were used to illustrate a direct contribution of theories from traditional areas of experimental psychology (Pavlovian conditioning) and the use of animal analog studies to provide experimental manipulations that are impossible with humans. Cognitive theories of depression provided an example of attempts to measure an underlying diathesis or vulnerability (a negative cognitive style), and they served to underscore the importance of longitudinal designs and of the methods by which depression and the diathesis are defined. The victims of child abuse provided an example of obtaining clinical samples from a nonclinical population and testing hypotheses in an analog procedure.

Within psychotherapy research, outcome studies, process studies, and studies designed to test hypotheses about psychopathology were distinguished. The methodological issues considered in psychotherapy research focused on the challenges of selecting suitable control groups or conditions. The utility and limitations of the waiting-list control for assessing the spontaneous remission of a disorder, and the attention-placebo control for determining the role of nonspecific treatment influences were outlined. These two control conditions were then contrasted with the use of minimally effective therapy as a control condition for evaluating the outcome or process of experimental treatment conditions. The difficulties and issues involved in selecting appropriate measures for evaluating psychotherapy were reviewed, and the distinction between analog studies and clinical trials was made.

The material reviewed in this chapter is not exhaustive. It was selected to provide a sampling of the types of research methodologies that are used in clinical psychology and that are consistent with the methodologies of other areas of experimental psychology. Additionally, the topics covered were selected because they may be useful for advanced undergraduates who are entertaining the possibility of postbaccaulareate careers in psychological research. All areas of research have special problems and difficulties, and all require some procedural compromises; research in clinical psychology is no different. While it often seems that clinical research is more difficult, results in more compromises, and is particularly fraught with special problems, these problems are not insurmountable. As investigators who have conducted research in basic and applied work in analog and clinical contexts and with human and nonhuman subjects, the present authors have direct experience that cuts across research domains. In the context of that direct experience, we have no hesitancy in urging students to consider clinical research as an area that provides the same opportunities for excitement and discovery and the same challenges for methodological rigor as other areas of investigation within psychology. Clinical research is just one of many areas that can benefit from the application of the methodologies of experimental psychology.

Exercises

1. Describe several examples that illustrate why clinical researchers often use the correlational method rather than the experimental method.

2. List the pros and cons of using a categorical approach (the "medical model") for psychiatric disorders rather than considering a continuum from normal to pathological conditions.

3. Discuss how to test the reliability and validity of a test for introversion-extraversion.

4. Briefly summarize the goals and logic of studies of the relatives of schizophrenics (see tables 10.1 and 10.2).

5. Describe several problems of interest to clinical psychologists that could be studied using nonclinical populations such as college students.

6. Describe several examples from this chapter where new research techniques were devised to address specific issues in clinical psychology.

7. Briefly discuss the rationale and needed precautions for each type of control group used in studies of therapy effectiveness.

8. Discuss the pros and cons of analog clinical research.

Glossary

adoption study The use of naturally occurring adoptions to separate the influences of familial environmental factors (adoptive family) from genetic factors (biological family). (p. 304)

analog research Research in which either the subject population or the manipulated independent variables are only approximations of the populations or variables of interest to the researcher. (p. 307)

attention placebo group A control condition in which the subjects are administered a treatment comprised of inert ingredients or no identified effective components but are exposed to the same personal contact and amount of time with a professional as the subjects in the treatment condition that has the putative effective ingredients. In psychotherapy research, the attention placebo is designed to control for nonspecific therapeutic factors and the amount of contact subjects have with a therapist. *See also* Hawthorne Effect, Nonspecific therapeutic factors. (p. 318)

clinical trials The use of research subjects who are drawn from the same population as the clients who would be seeking services at a clinical site for the exact problem(s) that is under investigation. In clinical trials therapy research, the experimental therapists are the same clinicians who would be providing therapy at clinical sites, and all of the procedures are followed in an actual clinical context. (p. 322)

cross-fostering An experimental technique in animal research in which offspring from experimental mothers are switched with those from control mothers in order to uncouple the effects of maternal behavior from the effects of genes. (p. 303)

cross-sectional design A comparison of different groups (e.g., depressed and nondepressed) at one time. (p. 313)

diathesis-stress The etiological model in which psychopathology is seen as arising from a person's vulnerability (diathesis) interacting with stressful environments. (p. 307)

double-blind A procedure in which neither the experimenter who has contact with the subjects nor the subjects themselves are informed as to the experimental condition to which they have been assigned. (p. 323)

etiology The causal development of any form of psychopathology. In psychopathology there are usually multiple factors involved in etiology. (p. 297)

Hawthorne Effect Based on a series of studies on worker productivity that were conducted over a 12-year period at the Hawthorne facilities of Western Electric starting in the late 1920s, the term Hawthorne Effect refers to the influence of social factors that are confounded with independent variables and determine the outcome of a study by altering the social meaning of the independent variables and, perhaps, by enhancing the morale of subjects. (p. 319)

longitudinal design A comparison of a group of individuals over a period of time. (p. 312)

nonspecific therapeutic factors Factors that are likely to influence therapeutic outcome but are not unique to a specific therapy such as professional contact and client expectations to improve. (p. 316)

nosology The study of the classification of diseases. Within psychopathology, it refers to the study of the classification of psychological or psychiatric disorders. Nosological classification systems use a categorical approach rather than a continuum approach to diagnosis and the classification of diseases. (p. 314)

outcome research Research designed to determine the outcome of a clinical intervention, such as determining whether a therapeutic approach is effective or comparing the effectiveness of different approaches. (p. 314)

placebo A control condition in which the subjects are administered a treatment comprised of inert ingredients (such as in a drug study) or no identified effective components but are lead to believe that the treatment has active ingredients. (p. 317)

process research Research designed to determine why a therapy is effective, i.e., what are the important components of the therapy? (p. 314)

reliability An estimate of the replicability of a test score. There are several types of reliability including alternate forms or interrater reliability (agreement between two sources at the same time), test-retest reliability (agreement over a specified period of time), and internal consistency (e.g., split-half reliability). (p. 300)

somatic activity Activity of the voluntary or striated musculature. (p. 326)

spontaneous remission The elimination or alleviation of a disorder in the absence of any active treatment program. In clinical research, it refers to improvement in control-group subjects who are waiting to be treated or diseases that naturally heal without treatment. (p. 316)

twin study The comparison of concordance for a given form of psychopathology in monozygotic twins versus dizygotic twins. *See also* Zygosity. (p. 303w)

validity The degree to which a test measures what it is said to measure. There are several types of validity: in criterion-oriented validity the test need only predict the criterion; construct validity applies when a test is presumed to measure a psychological construct that has theoretical meaning. (p. 300)

zygosity The characteristics of a fertilized egg in sexual reproduction. In twin studies used to distinguish between monozygotic twins, who derive from a single zygote and thus have an identical genetic inheritance, and dizygotic twins, who derive from two different zygotes and thus (like siblings) share 50 percent of their genes on the average. (p. 304)

Suggested Readings

Anastasi, A. (1988). *Psychological testing* (6th ed.). New York: Macmillan.

Kazdin, A. E. (Ed.) (1992). *Methodological issues and strategies in clinical research*. Washington, D.C.: American Psychological Association.

Journal of Abnormal Psychology

Journal of Consulting and Clinical Psychology

Psychological Assessment

SECTION

IV

Concluding Chapters: Looking Back and Looking Ahead

The concluding chapters will address "promissory notes" from the earlier chapters. Chapter 11 will return to some of the basic issues raised at the beginning of this text and review the role and contribution of behavioral research in each of the content areas described in the later chapters.

We had said that "research is not complete until it has been reported in a clear and understandable manner." Chapter 12 will describe a convenient format for reporting results of a research study and several examples will be provided, including a complete student report.

This chapter will also describe the role of research for those who decide to go on to a graduate program in psychology. Procedures (and hints) for applying to graduate school will be described and prospects for a career in behavioral research will be discussed.

Back to Basics

Irwin P. Levin

In this chapter we will return to some of the basic issues addressed throughout this book and review some important questions about research design raised in the initial chapters of this text by summarizing how they have been addressed in the various research areas covered in the later chapters. The chapter begins with a brief restatement of the steps to be followed in designing and conducting a research study and the issues to be addressed at each step.

Review of Steps in Research

Any attempt to capture the essence of the material covered in a book like this and condense it into a single chart is bound to suffer from oversimplification. But here goes anyway.

Idea for the Study
From personal observations
Will anybody else be interested?
Build onto past research
Suggested by theory
Is it likely to yield novel empirical results?
Are there applied implications?
What are the specific research questions or hypotheses?

Experimental or Observational Method?
Need for control
Need for realism
Sources of bias

Choice of Subject Population
Availability
Concern for generalizability
Ethical concerns
Sampling plan

Experimental Design
Choice of independent variables and levels
—Operational definitions
—Within-subject or between-subjects
  manipulations?

Choice of dependent variables
—Operational definitions
Subject variables to be investigated
Subject variables to be controlled
—Matched groups or randomization?
Extraneous variables to be controlled
—How?
Statistical plan for analyzing data

Conducting the Study
Treatment of subjects
—Ethical concerns
Concern for experimenter and subject biases
Objective measurement and scoring techniques

Of course, any line on this chart needs extensive elaboration. How do you know if your idea for a study will build onto past research? Only by gaining a thorough knowledge and understanding of the literature in that area of study. How do you weigh the need for control and the need for realism in deciding between the experimental and the observational methods? That depends on the stage of progress of a particular stream of research. Sometimes a circular approach works best. Use observational techniques at an early stage to pick out behaviors and factors that need to be addressed in a controlled manner; use the experimental method to achieve the control; later test the external validity of results from the laboratory. As you read through the various steps, think of examples from the text and other sources of how each step was achieved in your areas of interest. The remainder of this chapter may help refresh your memory.

Some Basic Issues

Now we'll return to some of the basic research issues introduced in the early chapters and briefly review their application in later chapters. The choice between the method of *correlation* or *observation* and the *experimental* method involves a tradeoff between achieving external validity and obtaining explanations of causality. The search for causes of forgetting in short-term memory and long-term memory led to the use of the experimental method in which different independent variable manipulations affected each process. However, observational findings that different types of errors occurred when recalling recent vs. distant past material undoubtedly led to hypotheses that were later tested with the experimental method. Similarly, observations of animal stereotypic behavior aided in the development of experimental paradigms for studying conditioning and learning, and in the choice of independent and dependent variables.

The area of perception and psychophysics has a similar background. Observations of naturally occurring illusions such as the "moon illusion" were followed by experimental studies aimed at isolating factors that lead to visual illusions. Development of refined measures of threshold and tasks representing the detection of signals embedded in noise allowed common observations of how we perceive the world to be followed up with experiments to uncover causal factors such as "nonsensory" factors.

In some sense, clinical psychology and social psychology owe their existence as areas of research to an interest in tracking the causes of behavior first observed naturalistically. Why do some people hallucinate? Why do many people comply with the requests of an authority figure even when the requests are unreasonable? When the key factor is a subject variable such as clinical diagnosis, experimental manipulation is not possible. Even here, however, manipulation of independent variables such as level of arousal can provide clues to the interactive effects of dispositional and environmental factors.

Field experiments in which independent variable manipulations were conducted in realistic settings were illustrated in the chapter on social psychology (the studies of bystander behavior in the subway). Quasi-experimental designs that mimicked the experimental method but could not use random assignment of subjects to conditions were illustrated in the social psychology chapter ("lost letters" studies) and in the chapter on judgment, decision making, and problem solving (Connecticut speed law study).

An issue basic to all areas of behavioral research is deciding appropriate control procedures. The "obvious" solution of creating a control group in which the experimental treatment is withheld often presents a more difficult problem than appears at first glance. What is the most appropriate control condition for determining the role of contiguity in Pavlovian conditioning? for determining the source of negative transfer? for learning why we are attracted to some people but not to others? for separating genetic and environmental influences on mental illness? for determining why a particular therapy is effective? We have seen these and many other problems of experimental control handled through careful analysis of potential sources of confounding often resulting from the accumulated knowledge of previous research but aided by familiarity with and understanding of basic experimental design techniques.

A key choice with the experimental method is whether to use a between-subjects or a within-subject design. Within-subject designs provide the greater amount of statistical power but raise concerns about carryover effects. Sometimes the carryover effects are of interest in their own right such as in the study of contrast effects in perception. The area of perception and psychophysics makes heavy use of within-subject designs where researchers may obtain a large amount of data from each of a small number of trained observers. The majority of studies we reviewed in other chapters relied on between-subjects designs, implicitly assuming that comparing how *different subjects* respond to different experimental conditions reveals how the *same subject* would respond to the different conditions in the absence of contaminating carryover effects.

A choice to be made when using the between-subjects design is whether to assign subjects to conditions completely at random or to use a "matching" procedure. While the matching procedure reduces the effects of subject variables, the practical difficulties in implementing such a procedure are often the overriding factor. Nevertheless, studies of clinical assessment often match subjects on variables related to the degree of clinical impairment prior to treatment. Twin studies represent the ultimate in matching.

No issue in experimental psychology is more "basic" than the issue of conducting research in an ethical and humane manner. Chapter 1 provided the American Psychological Association's guidelines for dealing with ethical issues in psychological research. Examples cropped up in various later chapters: treatment of animals in studies of learning and conditioning; use of deception and coercion in social psychological studies of human reactions to stressful situations; withholding of clinical treatment for control subjects in studies of the effectiveness of therapy. Current guidelines include the establishment of ethics committees to judge the relative costs to the participant and benefits to the individual and society of the proposed research, and whether there was due consideration of alternative methods to minimize risk and harm to the participants. The concept of informed consent was established to provide sufficient prior information for a potential subject to decide whether to participate in a study. The burden of proof is clearly on researchers to convince their peers of the worthiness and ethics of their research.

As you reach this point in the text, you've covered a lot of material. What do we expect you to retain of all this material? It's certainly not the details of all the studies reported. First and foremost, we hope that you'll come away with a deeper appreciation of what it takes to do good research with due consideration of ethical issues.

There are some pretty basic principles of good research that we hope you'll retain from the initial chapters of this book and from our summary at the beginning of this chapter. We also hope that you become aware of the special research issues that arise in each content area and the manner in which they are addressed. To help you, we have attempted to summarize this material in the following section.

Summary of Research Issues in Different Areas

In this section we will briefly summarize each of the "topical" chapters by highlighting the unique research issues faced by investigators in each area.

Perception and Psychophysics

Research in this area is marked by attempts to describe and understand how we respond to changes in our environment. The special needs in this area of research include measuring sensitivity to small changes in stimulus value, comparing sensitivity across sense modalities, mapping out the function relating magnitude of response to magnitude of stimulus, determining cues that govern our perception of the world and how these cues are integrated, and examining the role of nonsensory or "psychological" factors in perception.

To meet these needs, researchers developed a variety of measurement or scaling techniques, experimental tasks and concomitant statistical tools, and theoretical frameworks within which the factors of interest could be studied. Experimental tasks developed in this area include situations leading to illusions—systematic errors in perception that reveal our sensitivity to cues that govern processes such as depth perception and estimation of size. Variants of these tasks such as the "visual cliff" have been useful in defining the roles of innate and learned components of perception.

Measures of threshold quantify our ability to sense minimal degrees of stimulation and changes in stimulus value. Signal detection tasks, along with a highly formalized theory of signal detection, allow researchers to separate the influence of sensory and nonsensory factors, and this ability has led to many important applications in areas such as medical diagnosis.

Development of a variety of scaling techniques has given researchers alternative methods of measuring responsiveness to quantitative dimensions such as sound intensity. These developments have led to the establishment of "psychophysical laws"— mathematical equations relating magnitude of sensation to stimulus intensity, but have also allowed researchers to measure responsiveness to qualitative dimensions such as "likability."

Multidimensional scaling techniques and stimulus integration tasks requiring responses to different combinations of stimulus values were developed to help us understand how people respond to stimuli with multiple components. The usefulness of the various scaling and measurement techniques can be compared in terms of their scale properties (e.g., is there a constant unit, is there an absolute zero value?), their susceptibility to context effects (how response to one stimulus depends on preceding stimulus values), their reliability (repeatability), and their validity (e.g., do they measure what they're supposed to?). Tests of validity are particularly difficult and controversial.

Animal Learning and Comparative Cognition

Experimental psychologists investigate animal behavior primarily to understand basic laws of behavior and to compare the behavior of humans and animals. Researchers in this area have several advantages. Compared to investigators of human behavior, they can achieve greater control of both the heredity and the environment of their subjects, including their prior history of learning experiences related to the behavior under investigation. Utilizing these advantages, of course, takes considerable knowledge of the species being investigated, as well as great care and patience. Another advantage is fewer constraints imposed on the range of manipulations that can be performed.

There are, however, many unique challenges to these investigators. For example, they must be concerned with determining whether the behaviors they uncover are *species specific* or universal. They must determine—largely through knowledge of the physiology and behavioral repertoire of organisms— which particular behaviors are most suited for studies with a particular species and which are most apt to generalize to humans. The common use of rats and pigeons in psychology laboratories is based on such considerations, as well as cost factors.

Early accounts of animal behavior were based on naturalistic observation by Darwin and others. However, concerns for the causes of an animal's actions led to the establishment of classic experimental methods in the study of animal learning. Pavlov's procedure employed unlearned reflex reactions (e.g., a dog's salivation in the presence of food) to provide the first objective means of studying the formation of learned associations. Later researchers introduced control conditions to ensure that conditioned responses were due to the sequential pairing of a conditioned stimulus (e.g., a bell) and an unconditioned stimulus (food). Thorndike's puzzle box provided the means to study the effects of reinforcers and punishers in situations where subjects (e.g., cats) had to perform the correct response. This work led to the law of effect—the principle that the consequences of an act determine its future probability.

Skinner's variation provided a more controlled environment for studying animal learning than Thorndike's. The "Skinner box" provided an experimental situation in which a number of interesting independent variable manipulations could be studied. Most notable among these were "schedules of reinforcement"—rules that specify how and when rewards can be earned. In order to control for nonassociative contributions to responding in the Skinner box, the "yoked control" procedure was invented. While the experimental subject received outcomes contingent on its behavior (e.g., bar-pressing), its yoked control received outcomes at the same time regardless of its behavior.

Modern animal behaviorists have broadened the range of behaviors studied from simple habituation in earthworms to complex cognitive behavior such as concept learning in pigeons and language in apes. The research on complex cognitive behavior provides good reasons to believe that at least some cognitive processes thought to be solely human may be evidenced by nonhumans as well. A likely direction for future research in comparative cognition is to introduce a variety of independent variables into learning tasks and to compare their effects on humans and animals.

Human Learning

In addition to adopting the basic paradigms developed to study simple learning and conditioning phenomena, researchers have tapped into human language abilities by devising a variety of verbal learning tasks. These include paired-associate learning where subjects have to assign different responses to each stimulus in a list of stimuli; free recall where subjects must learn a list of items in any order; serial learning where subjects must learn a list of items in a specified order; and verbal discrimination where subjects learn to recognize which item is correct within each of a series of item pairs or sets. Each of these tasks is meant to tap different processes that are operative in everyday human learning such as the role of frequency, inter-item associations, and serial cues.

Unlike animal studies where researchers can control genetic and environmental factors prior to experimentation, studies of human verbal learning in the laboratory must account for pre-existing habits and associations. Consequently, following the pioneer work of Ebbinghaus, researchers developed novel stimulus material (e.g., nonsense syllables) to minimize pre-experimental influences and

verbal assessment techniques to scale stimulus material on dimensions such as familiarity, pronounce-ability, and meaningfulness, as well as assessing the degree of association between stimuli. While such assessments need to be periodically updated, researchers can refer to published norms for stimulus selection and categorization rather than "starting from scratch" each time.

Following the development of verbal assessment techniques and suitable tasks, investigators were able to examine the effects of a variety of independent and subject variables on human verbal learning. By examining sequences of correct and incorrect responses over trials, researchers were able to address the issue of whether learning a single stimulus-response association is gradual or all-or-none. By giving subjects more than one task to perform in succession, researchers were able to study the effects of transfer of training. The development of transfer paradigms included control conditions designed to separate the effects of *nonspecific* sources of transfer such as learning to learn (e.g., developing general strategies and attentional devices for dealing with laboratory tasks) and *specific* sources of transfer created by the relationship between new and old stimulus material.

In order to study human conceptual processes as distinct from the learning of individual stimulus-response associations, concept formation tasks were devised in which subjects learned to assign the same response to a whole class of related stimuli (e.g., those with the same shape). Variants of these tasks were constructed to examine the age-related development of conceptual skills. Contemporary research on human learning focuses on the acquisition of skills such as reading comprehension and classroom learning, which apply basic learning principles like positive transfer and mediation. Modern research tools include sophisticated models based on computer simulation, which are an outgrowth of the concept of associations developed in the early stages of philosophical thought about the human mind.

Memory

Studies of memory are distinguished from studies of learning by their emphasis on retention processes rather than acquisition processes. Thus, most studies of memory present only one exposure of the to-be-remembered material, whereas most studies of learning provide multiple exposures (acquisition trials). Nevertheless, tasks such as paired-associates, free recall, and serial recall are used interchangeably in studies of human learning and memory.

The memory researcher's challenge is to develop experimental paradigms and selected independent variable manipulations and dependent variable measures that focus on the process of retention of material. Measures of retention include recognition, recall, and relearning. Manipulation of item similarity shows when recognition is superior to recall and vice versa.

Two key research issues are distinguishing between long-term and short-term memory processes, and separating the influences of decay and interference on forgetting. The usefulness of distinguishing between two presumably distinct psychological processes such as long-term memory and short-term memory depends on researchers' ability to demonstrate that each process is affected by different variables. One such demonstration dealt with the "bowed serial position effect" in free recall. Enhanced recall of the last items on the list (a "recency" effect ascribed to short-term memory) was affected by the length of the retention interval, while enhanced recall of the initial items on the list (a "primacy" effect ascribed to long-term memory) was affected by the rate of presentation of items. Recording of types of errors made for items at different serial positions also shows differences. Observational studies of selective memory loss for brain-damaged individuals further reinforce the distinction that short-term memory loss and long-term memory loss are due to different processes.

Different methods were developed for studying long-term memory and short-term memory. Interference designs, patterned after paradigms for studying negative transfer, were developed for showing how information obtained either before or after the to-be-remembered material was acquired, can interfere with long-term memory. Special control features are needed in these designs. In demonstrating retroactive inhibition (RI), a control group must perform a neutral filler task during the time interval when the experimental group performs an interpolated interfering task. In demonstrating proactive inhibition (PI), experimental and control groups must have equivalent retention intervals.

Methods developed to study short-term memory include single-item and multiple-item tasks. The most common multiple-item task is the "memory span" task, which is a form of free recall where subjects immediately report as many items as possible from a list of items. The most popular single-item tasks are the distractor task, where a filler task designed to prevent rehearsal of the to-be-remembered item is inserted during the retention interval, and the probe task, in which a list or matrix of items is presented and the subject is later tested for recall of a single item or set of items.

Free recall techniques with no restrictions on the order of recall are useful for studying how people organize information for learning and recall. Even when the organizational rules are clear only to the individual, subjective organization appears to facilitate retention. Besides subjective organization, other methods designed to enhance the elaboration of to-be-remembered material such as by generating visual images and by emphasizing the meaning of the material, serve to increase retention and thus provide the basis for memory aids.

Other phenomena investigated to understand memory and forgetting are "tip-of-the-tongue," "flashbulb" memory, memory demonstrations by "experts," and memory-based judgments and decisions.

Judgment, Decision Making, and Problem Solving

Special topics in human cognition such as judgment, decision making, and problem solving are studied in order to understand how knowledge is acquired and used in complex but commonplace situations. There have been several innovations in research design and the selection of independent and dependent variables that characterize work on these topics. Early research in the area of human judgment and decision making stressed the testing of "normative" models and these required the construction of tasks with mathematically correct judgments. Tasks like the "blue cab/green cab" problem were designed to compare subjects' judgments of probability with those derived from Bayes' theorem. Later studies of a more descriptive nature did not rely on tasks with "correct" judgments but were designed to uncover strategies underlying everyday judgments and decisions. Scenarios were constructed such that subjects' responses revealed their use of particular heuristics or simplifying strategies. The search for systematic biases in such tasks often revealed which factors were predominant and which were neglected in decision making. Predecisional measures such as information search and postdecisional measures such as confidence were developed to better understand the dynamics of decision making.

Information integration tasks were constructed to test simple algebraic models of how diverse factors are combined in forming a judgment. Risky decision making is studied by manipulating the degree of risk of choice options while holding expected value constant in gambling-type tasks. This area is marked by large individual differences where some decision makers are motivated primarily to avoid loss while others prefer to go for the "long shot." Nevertheless, researchers have shown that these decisions are affected by the manner in which choice options are presented and by the way in which questions are asked (choose between options vs. assign a monetary value to each option).

Information framing effects were studied by constructing alternative versions of a choice task where objective values were the same in each version but different labels such as "success rate" or "failure rate" were inserted.

While the issue of "external validity" is important in all areas of psychology, it is of particular concern in the area of human judgment and decision making where the goal is to understand the judgments and decisions guiding our everyday lives. Thus, as a complement to highly controlled studies of a particular aspect of judgment and decision making, some researchers in this area strive to make their tasks as realistic as possible. Accumulating evidence of external validity is a slow process, but applications of research findings to areas such as consumer behavior, allocation of scarce resources, and medical decision making are becoming commonplace. In some cases, decision aids have been constructed to eliminate common biases discovered in laboratory research.

Problem-solving tasks were developed to see how prior learning and concept formation play a role in more complex "thought processes." Word games such as anagrams showed how prior learning can facilitate problem solving, and studies of chess experts' memory for structured and unstructured material showed how organizational processes lead to useful heuristics or simplifying strategies for solving problems. Other problem-solving tasks such as the "candle problem" and the "two string problem" were created to show that prior habits can sometimes inhibit creative problem solving.

The area of human problem solving represents a unique challenge to researchers because of the desire to know not just *whether* a problem is solved but *how* it is solved. The use of verbal protocols or "think aloud" techniques helps researchers understand strategies and successive steps underlying attempts to solve problems. Piaget's "conservation" tasks proved useful in understanding the stages of development of reasoning skills.

Social Psychology

Research in social psychology is often characterized by the interplay between experimental and observational techniques. Observations of real-world events concerning group activity and interpersonal relations, especially as they affect the individual, have motivated carefully controlled laboratory studies of phenomena such as conformity, role playing, obedience to authority, crowding, and bystander behavior. Sometimes observational (correlational) studies, experiments conducted in field settings, "quasi-experimental" studies, and laboratory experiments with humans and animals combine to provide converging evidence. Such is the case in the study of the effects of crowding on behavior.

Field experiments in which subjects are assigned at random to conditions in a real-world setting are exemplified by the Stanford prison study of societal role playing. Quasi-experimental studies in which individuals in different circumstances are compared without the luxury of randomization are exemplified by the "lost letter" studies of altruism in college dormitories. Sometimes, observational studies of the same individuals over a long period of time help us understand relationships such as that between TV viewing and aggressive behavior.

Specialized research techniques developed by social psychologists include the use of interacting groups, which may involve deception and trained confederates, to create target social situations such as having a deviant perception from your peers, being asked to punish a stranger, or being in the presence of someone in need of aid. Techniques such as these allow social psychologists to create the conditions they wish to study rather than waiting for these conditions to occur naturally. Deceptive techniques, however, raise ethical concerns for the treatment of research participants. These issues are dealt with through the use of impartial ethics committees whose primary role is to protect the participants and who consider the relative costs and benefits of alternative ways of conducting the research.

Clinical Psychology

Clinical psychology is perhaps the ultimate area of application and refinement of the research methods developed in experimental psychology. Clinical psychologists have developed sophisticated observational techniques, including comparisons of the co-occurrence of mental illness among relatives of different distance in order to test genetic models of schizophrenia. Additional observational studies designed to separate genetic and environmental influences on the etiology of emotional illnesses used twins raised apart and adopted children. Clinical psychologists have used experimental methods with both humans and animals to create situations analogous to those found in clinical settings.

Unique problems facing researchers in this area include limited availability of targeted clinical populations and uncertain operational definitions. What is a schizophrenic? When does a fear reach the level of a phobia? What levels of depression are pathological? As a partial answer to these problems, clinical psychologists have adapted psychological scaling techniques to show the distributional properties of traits such as anxiety and depression. In addition to its use in diagnosing needs for clinical treatment, this approach reveals the continuity of values along these dimensions. Such continuity has been the guiding principle in designing "analog" studies in which samples selected from a "normal" population can be used to compare the behaviors of those who are relatively high or low on a particular scale. Results of such analog studies with normal populations are typically extrapolated to infer behavioral deficits in a particular clinical population.

Theories of the etiology of behavioral problems are often derived from basic studies of conditioning and learning (e.g., learned phobias) and these models may also suggest ways of extinguishing undesired behavior. Knowledge gained from a variety of studies is often used to suggest meaningful intervention techniques, which can then be tested for their effectiveness. Treatment outcome studies must be conducted with special care to control for nonspecific treatment effects such as mere contact with a caregiver, which can be confounded with the influence of specific therapeutic effects.

Clinical psychologists have also learned much from studies comparing the effects of experimental manipulations on different subject populations. Of particular interest in these studies is the interaction between the independent variable and the subject variable. For example, it would be important to know if individuals with high and low levels of trait anxiety react differently to increases in situational stress such as being asked to make a public presentation.

Research psychologists work on both "basic" problems involving the search for understanding of processes that underlie a variety of behaviors in humans and animals, and "applied problems" that are directed at specific behaviors such as recovery from mental illness. The successful accomplishment of research in either domain requires the skillful use of techniques of experimental design and control and statistical inference, as well as mastery of methods that apply to the specific problem and subject population of interest. The initial chapters of this text were meant to lay the foundations for research in all areas, and later chapters were meant to show how specific methods were built onto these foundations to address particular problems within each content area. While we warned you of "pitfalls" to be avoided at various points along the way, our greatest hope is that you gain an appreciation of carefully done research and its products. The final chapter includes some material designed especially for those of you who will continue the study and practice of research in psychology or related disciplines.

Exercises

1. What single study that you learned about in this class impressed you the most? Defend your choice by describing its good features and why it captured your interest.

2. How do you think the "Stanford prison study" and "Milgram's compliance study" could be modified to meet today's ethical standards? Would their main goals still be achieved?

3. Consider any journal article reporting a research study in your area of interest. Try to reconstruct the steps described in the chart at the beginning of this chapter.

Experimental Psychology and You

Irwin P. Levin

We conclude this text with a brief chapter designed to help you in your current study of psychology and in your possible future studies. We start by helping you with something that may already be a pressing need—writing research reports and getting the most out of the ones you read. This section provides us with the opportunity to show you more examples of interesting research.

We also include in this chapter some discussion of what it takes to get into graduate school and pursue a career that utilizes knowledge of the principles of experimental psychology.

How to Write (and Read) a Research Report

The best way to learn about writing a research report is to read a number of them yourself. In fact, one of the goals of this text is to prepare you to read about research from its original source—the journal article. If the report is well written, you will have enough detail and rationale of the study to judge its merits for yourself.

While some flexibility is permitted in the format of a research report (e.g., in reporting a series of experiments versus a single experiment), the format described below has proven useful in many instances. The basic components are the *title, abstract, introduction, method, results,* and *discussion*. Boxes 12.1 to 12.5 provide illustrations from published articles. Box 12.6 reproduces a complete research report written by undergraduate students.

The *title* should be chosen carefully because the potential reader may stop here if the title does not provoke interest in further reading. Occasionally, a flashy title such as "Pygmalion in the Classroom" is selected. In a scholarly journal, however, this is the exception not the rule. The title should be an accurate preview of what is to come and should thus be relatively specific. The title, "A Study of Human Memory" is too vague and ambiguous. The title, "Manipulating Retention Interval to Separate Short-Term and Long-Term Memory Processes" conveys much more information without being overly long.

The *abstract* is a summary that appears at the beginning. If that sounds a bit backward, think of all the times you started a paper by reading the summary to see if you wanted to go through the time and effort to read the whole thing. The abstract should therefore be self-contained, without assuming that the reader knows anything except the title. It should include the purpose of the study, its major predictions, its method and results, and its main conclusions. *Psychological Abstracts* (see chapter 1) and various computerized literature search techniques publish only the titles and abstracts of articles, so that the interested reader can then decide whether to go to the original source. The motivating role of the title and abstract is paramount. Because most psychology journals impose a word limit (e.g., 150 words) on the abstract, it is a real challenge to write a comprehensive abstract.

Two examples—one on postpartum depression and one on classical conditioning in the rabbit—are provided in box 12.1. While a certain background in the content area of the article is useful (e.g., knowing that the rabbit's nictitating membrane response refers to eyeblinking), each abstract can be understood with relative ease.

The body of the article, of course, starts with the *introduction*. The primary function of the introduction is to state the main issue or problem to be addressed in the paper. This typically includes statement of hypotheses or research questions to be tested, along with background material (including literature citations) that provides insight into where the ideas came from. It rarely, if ever, is the case that a study stands in isolation. Almost all research is an evolutionary process with each new study building onto what has come before. The introduction section is

BOX 12.1

Journal Abstracts

1. Source: Philipps, L. H. C., & O'Hara, M. W. (1991). Prospective study of postpartum depression: 4½ year follow-up of women and children. *Journal of Abnormal Psychology, 100,* 63–73.

The consequences of maternal postpartum depression for mothers and children were investigated in a 4½ year follow-up study, which included 70 of 99 women who had participated in an earlier prospective study of postpartum depression. Information regarding maternal adjustment and depression during the follow-up period and child adjustment at age 4½ years was obtained. Women who had experienced a postpartum depression were predicted to be at increased risk for subsequent depression and poor adjustment of their child. Postpartum depression was directly related to subsequent maternal depression but not child problems. Later maternal depression was related to child problems at 4½ years postpartum. It was concluded that postpartum depression may increase risk for child behavior problems. Intervening with women who have experienced a postpartum depression may reduce likelihood of future depressions and child behavior problems.

2. Source: Marshall-Goodell, B., & Gormezano, I. (1991). Effects of cocaine on conditioning of the rabbit's nictitating membrane response. *Pharmacology, Biochemistry and Behavior, 39,* 503–507.

Two experiments were conducted to determine cocaine's (0, 1, 3, and 6 mg/kg) effects on associative, nonassociative, and motor processes in classical conditioning of the rabbit's nictitating membrane response (NMR). In Experiment 1, acquisition training consisted of tone- and light-conditioned stimuli (CSs) each paired on separate trials with a shock unconditioned stimulus (UCS). Cocaine injected prior to each session significantly impaired acquisition of conditioned responses (CRs). In Experiment 2, rabbits received cocaine injections prior to each training session involving explicitly unpaired CS-alone and UCS-alone presentations. Cocaine had no significant effects upon: base rate of NMRs; frequency of NMRs during presentations of the CSs; and frequency, amplitude, and latency of the UCRs. Consequently, cocaine's impairment of CR acquisition could not be attributed to its effects upon the nonassociative processes of base rate, sensitization, and pseudoconditioning, nor upon the sensory processing of the UCS and/or motor function of the UCR. Rather, cocaine's effects upon CR acquisition were mediated by the drug's effect upon associative processes. It appears likely that the drug affected the ability of the CS to enter into the associative conditioning process.

where this process should be made clear. In addition to statement of hypotheses, this section often includes rationale for the procedures, measures, and independent variables used to test the hypotheses.

Box 12.2 provides one example of a paragraph from an introduction section in which the need for a baseline control condition to study attraction and repulsion is made clear. The researcher then includes such a condition in the design of the experiment.

Our second example illustrates how the approach to a new problem—studying how judges' behavior influences jurors—is built on a history of basic research (recall studies of the "Rosenthal effect" from chapter 1 that show how experimenters influence subjects). The third example illustrates the role of theory in generating new research ideas. In this case, the theories were ultimately refuted. Parental discussion style was shown to play an important role in children's moral development.

BOX 12.2

Sample Portions of Introduction Sections

1. Source: Rosenbaum, M. E. (1986). The repulsion hypothesis: On the nondevelopment of relationships. *Journal of Personality and Social Psychology, 51*, 1156–1166.

The procedure of introducing one person to another along with information about attitudes constitutes the very productive attraction paradigm used by Byrne (1971) and many others. After subjects responded to an attitude questionnaire, Byrne provided them with the same questionnaire ostensibly filled out by another person, a stranger. This procedure allowed Byrne to manipulate a variety of variables systematically, especially the degree of similarity between the subject's responses and the responses of the stranger. In a great number of studies, a linear relation has been found to support the generalization that similarity leads to attraction and dissimilarity causes repulsion. However, in this entire line of research, and it certainly is considerable, an adequate control or baseline condition has never been included. What has been lacking is a no-attitude questionnaire

condition. Such a condition would permit determination of the degree to which similarity enhances attraction, dissimilarity decreases attraction, or whether either one has any consequence at all.

2. Source: Hart, A. (1994). Naturally occurring expectation effects. *Journal of Personality and Social Psychology*. In press.

Variously termed expectancy effects, self-fulfilling prophecies, or behavioral confirmation, an interpersonal expectation effect occurs when a person (A), acting in response to a given set of expectations, treats another person (B) in such a manner so as to induce person (B) to behave in a way that confirms the original expectation (Rosenthal & Jacobson, 1968). To investigate self-fulfilling prophecies, social psychological researchers have experimentally manipulated either the perceiver's expectation of a given situation, interaction, or interactant, or have manipulated the behavior that an individual is to perform, or both. Recent investigations

---

The *method* section follows. It should provide sufficient detail of the tasks, procedures and measurements, as well as description of the subject population and samples, that the interested researcher could replicate (repeat) the study. Some judgment must be exercised in deciding just how much detail to include. For some purposes, specification of the subject population as "undergraduate students at University X" is sufficient. In other cases, distributions of subject variables such as age, gender, and socioeconomic status are needed. In some cases, such as standard learning or memory tasks, instructions to subjects can be paraphrased in a short summary.

In cases such as measurement of attitudes, motivational manipulations, or complex problem-solving tasks, verbatim instructions and items may be useful to report. If any section of a paper is lengthy, dividing into subsections can aid the reader. Common subsection headings for the method section include "experimental design," "tasks and material," "equipment," "procedure," and "subjects." (If the equipment or apparatus is unique, a photo might be included.)

An example included in box 12.3 provides an operational definition of the term "social support" in a study designed to assess the health benefits of (e.g., Neuberg, Judice, Virdin & Carrillo, 1993) have re-iterated that confirmation of inaccurate expectancies may result from either biases in cognitive processing or biases in interaction styles.

Section 15 of the California Pattern Jury Instructions titled "Take no cue from the judge" reads:

> I have not intended by anything I have said or done or by any question I may have asked to suggest what you should find the facts to be or that I believe or disbelieve any witness. If anything I have said or done has seemed to suggest my opinion as to the facts, you will disregard it and form your own opinion.

The legal system has assumed that this plea for accuracy can attenuate the influence of such extra legal factors as the judge's opinion. The degree of influence that judges' opinions and behaviors exert on jurors' verdict decisions is an empirical question, however, that has received limited research attention.

3. Source: Walker, L. G., & Taylor, J. H. (1991). Family interactions and the development of moral reasoning. *Child Development, 62,* 264–283.

The research reported in this article is a reaction to the bias against parents in cognitive-developmental theory. Both Piaget and Kohlberg relegated parents to a minimal and nonspecific role as agents in their children's moral development. Piaget (1932/1977, p. 190) concluded that "the sense of justice, though naturally capable of being reinforced by the precepts and the practical example of the adult, is largely independent of these influences, and requires nothing more for its development than the mutual respect and solidarity which holds among children themselves." Similarly, Kohlberg (1969, p. 399) argued that "family participation is not unique or critically necessary for moral development." Thus, these theorists regarded parents as simply a small part of the general social environment that provides "role-taking opportunities," but no especially important or distinctive experiences.

social support on spouses of cancer patients. Note the references to previous studies dealing with the reliability and validity of the scale used to measure social support. The second example, dealing with the interpretation and recall of interpersonal events, conveys the level of detail needed to describe a subtle manipulation using videotaped actors' display of emotions.

Next comes the *results* section. The old adage, "A picture is worth a thousand words" often applies here. As we have seen in various chapters of this text, data summaries in the form of tables and graphs can be very useful. These should be supplemented with carefully worded text that helps guide the reader

in highlighting the important things to be noticed in the tables and figures. And, of course, relevant statistical tests should be summarized to inform the reader of the reliability of the observed trends. If specific hypotheses were proposed in the introduction section, the outcome of the tests of these hypotheses can be summarized in the results section.

The first example in box 12.4 shows how much information may be conveyed in a well-thought-out table or graph. The table depicts subjects' retrospective estimation of the duration of publicly reported events. (The study was conducted in New Zealand, so don't be surprised if some of the events seem unfamiliar to you.) The

BOX 12.3

Sample Portions of Method Sections

1. Source: Baron, R. S., Cutrona, C. E., Hicklin, D., Russell, D. W., & Lubaroff, D. M. (1990). Social support and immune function among spouses of cancer patients. *Journal of Personality and Social Psychology, 59,* 344–352.

Social support. Perceived social support was assessed using the Social Provisions Scale (Cutrona & Russell, 1987; Russell & Cutrona, 1984). This scale was developed to assess the six relational provisions identified by Weiss (1974). The measure asks respondents to rate the degree to which their social relationships are currently supplying each of the provisions (guidance, reliable alliance, reassurance of worth, social integration, attachment, and opportunity to provide nurturance). Each provision is assessed by four items, two that describe the presence and two that describe the absence of the provision. For example, two of the items on the attachment subscale are "I have close relationships that provide me with a sense of emotional security and well-being," and "I lack a feeling of intimacy with another person." Reliability for the total support score in a previous study of elderly adults was .92, with reliabilities of the 4-item subscales ranging from .76 to .84 (Cutrona et al., 1986). Intercorrelations among subscales range from .27 to .74. Several studies provide evidence for the validity of the Social Provisions Scale among adolescent mothers (Cutrona, 1989), the elderly (Cutrona et al., 1986), public school teachers (Russell, Altmaier, & Van Velzen, 1987), and hospital nurses (Constable & Russell, 1986; Cutrona & Russell, 1987). The discriminant validity of the scale has been demonstrated against measures of mood (e.g., depression), personality (e.g., introversion-extraversion, neuroticism), and social desirability (Cutrona & Russell, 1987; in press).

2. Source: Harvey, J. H., Yorkin, K. L., Lightner, J. M., & Town, J. P. (1980). Unsolicited interpretation and recall of interpersonal events. *Journal of Personality and Social Psychology, 38,* 551–568.

The seriousness of the outcome of the event was manipulated by the actors' display of emotion through nonverbal behavior. In the serious-outcome conditions, the amount of eye contact displayed by the couple decreased throughout the episode, their tones of voice became increasingly harsh, and they slowly moved away from each other as the scene progressed. The scene ended with the female sarcastically asking the male if he still loved her and the male replying in a similar way that he did. In the moderate-outcome conditions, the amount of eye contact stayed the same during the episode, the tone of voice displayed was much more even and mellow, and the couple stayed the same distance from each other as the scene progressed. The final part of the scene involved the female laughingly asking the male if he still loved her and the male replying in a similar fashion that he did and gently touching the female's hand.

The actual verbal dialogue was almost identical in the serious and moderate outcome versions. The two versions had been evaluated by a group of 20 pilot subjects as reflecting the intended variations of outcome severity. Also, these pilot subjects rated the two versions as highly and equally naturalistic in terms of their plausibility as real-life events.

BOX 12.4

Sample Portions of Results Sections

1. Source: Burt, C. D. B., & Kemp, S. (1991).
   Retrospective duration estimation of public events.
   Memory & Cognition, 19, 252–262.

Beginning Date, Actual Duration, Median Estimated Duration, Mean Knowledge Rating and Median Percentage, Absolute and Signed Error for Each Public Event Used in Experiment 1

Brief Event Description and Abbreviation	Date Event Began	Actual Duration (Days)	Median Duration Estimate (Days)	Median Percentage Error (Days)	Median Absolute Error (Days)	Median Signed Error (Days)	Mean Knowledge Rating
Aldo Moro kidnapping (AM)	16 March 1978	55	14.0	74.5	41	–41	1.7
Cook Island's election scandal (SAH)	1 April 1978	117	14.0	88.0	103	–103	1.8
Pope John Paul I's reign (PPI)	27 Aug 1978	33	90.0	172.7	57	57	2.8
Pope John Paul II visits Poland (PPII)	2 June 1979	9	7.0	55.6	5	–2	3.1
Carless days in NZ (CD)	30 July 1979	319	240.0	43.6	139	–79	3.9
Abbotsford emergency (A)	6 Aug 1979	36	13.0	72.2	26	–23	3.4
Soviet Airliner held in NY (SB)	26 Aug 1979	3	2.0	66.7	2	–1	1.4
U.S. Embassy occupation (OUE)	4 Nov 1979	442	28.0	93.7	414	–414	2.4
Great Mosque seized (GM)	20 Nov 1979	14	6.0	67.9	9.5	–8	1.5
Paul McCartney arrested (PMC)	14 Jan 1980	12	4.0	66.7	8	–8	2.4
Hostages Iranian Embassy London (IEL)	30 April 1980	7	4.0	57.1	4	–3	2.2
Mangere College play (MP)	3 May 1980	3	7.0	133.3	4	4	1.1
Clark murder trial (TJC)	6 Jan 1981	123	36.5	81.7	100.5	–86	2.7
Walesa visits Rome (LW)	13 Jan 1981	7	7.0	57.1	4	0	1.6
Suspected foot and mouth outbreak (TPF)	11 Feb 1981	11	7.0	45.5	5	–4	3.2
Pacific Charger runs aground (PC)	21 May 1981	15	6.0	66.7	10	–9	2.1
Springbok tour (ST)	19 July 1981	55	21.0	61.8	34	–34	4.5
Rexin Industrial sit-in (RCF)	1 Sept 1981	96	5.0	94.8	91	–91	1.3
Sweden detains Soviet submarine (SS)	27 Oct 1981	11	14.0	63.6	7	3	2.1
Falkland's war (F)	2 April 1982	73	35.0	61.6	45	–38	4.5
Climbers trapped on Mount Cook (MC)	15 Nov 1982	14	6.0	57.1	8	–8	3.8
Dozier kidnapping (JD)	17 Dec 1982	42	21.0	66.7	28	–21	1.4
Australian bushfire (AB)	16 Feb 1983	2	12.5	525.0	10.5	10.5	3.2

[*Continued*]

Box 12.4 continued

BRIEF EVENT DESCRIPTION AND ABBREVIATION	DATE EVENT BEGAN	ACTUAL DURATION (DAYS)	MEDIAN DURATION ESTIMATE (DAYS)	MEDIAN PERCENTAGE ERROR (DAYS)	MEDIAN ABSOLUTE ERROR (DAYS)	MEDIAN SIGNED ERROR (DAYS)	MEAN KNOWLEDGE RATING
Royals visit New Zealand (R)	17 April 1983	13	7.0	46.2	6	−6	3.5
Discovery of Hitler diaries (S)	22 April 1983	17	21.0	64.7	11	4	3.4
Maori protest march (H)	28 Jan 1984	10	5.0	60.0	6	−5	2.2
Search for psychiatric patient (BDC)	22 Feb 1984	9	9.5	50.0	4.5	.5	2.0
Police besiege Libyan Bureau London (YF)	17 April 1984	10	3.0	70.0	7	−7	2.6
Gloria Kong kidnapping (GK)	29 June 1984	3	4.0	66.7	2	1	3.2
John Kirk extradited from U.S.A. (JK)	7 July 1984	448	134.0	70.1	314	−314	3.5
Wizard temporarily resigns (W)	3 Sept 1984	30	21.0	53.3	16	−9	3.1
Baby Fae heart transplant (BF)	26 Oct 1984	22	14.0	59.1	13	−8	2.6
Riots in New Caledonia (NC)	12 Jan 1985	2	10.5	425.0	8.5	8.5	2.1
Achillo Lauro hijacked (AL)	7 Oct 1985	3	5.5	83.3	2.5	2.5	2.3
Daniloff arrested (ND)	29 Aug 1986	13	26.0	100.0	13	13	2.8
Stars & Stripes beats KZ7 (KZ7)	5 Oct 1986	12	28.0	133.3	16	16	4.8
Overall (Means)		58.08	24.6	95.9	43.75	−33.3	2.6

2. Source: Overmyer, S. P., & Simon, J. R. (1985). The effects of irrelevant cues on "same/different" judgments in a sequential information processing task. *Acta Psychologica, 58,* 237–249.

The left panel of the figure shows the mean RTs for same and different responses to color plotted as a function of congruence of stimulus and probe shapes. An analysis of variance revealed that same responses were faster than different responses (387 vs. 408 msec), $F(1,16) = 10.58$, $p < 0.01$. There was no difference in RT between congruent and incongruent trials (400 vs. 395 msec). There was, however, a significant Response × Congruence interaction, $F(1,16) = 13.46$, $p < 0.01$. Planned comparisons indicated that different responses were faster ($p < 0.01$) on incongruent trials than on congruent trials (400 vs. 417 msec), but that, while same responses tended to be faster on congruent trials than on incongruent trials (382 vs. 391 msec), the difference was not significant. Additional planned comparisons indicated that same/congruent trials were faster than different/congruent trials (382 vs. 417 msec) ($p < 0.01$), but that same/incongruent trials did not differ from different/incongruent trials (391 vs. 400 msec).

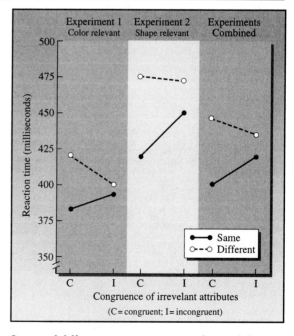

Same and different reaction times to colors and shapes as a function of congruence of irrelevant attributes

second example describes in words and statistical tests the interaction effect depicted in the graph. The graph plots reaction time (RT) for subjects who had to answer as quickly as possible whether a pair of colored shapes was the same or different on a predetermined relevant attribute (e.g., color) irrespective of how they compared on an irrelevant attribute (e.g., shape). The statistical tests are presented in the format prescribed in the American Psychological Association's Publications Manual. $F(1,16) = 10.58$, $p < 0.01$ means that the calculated value of F for "same vs. different responses" was 10.58 with 1 degree of freedom in the numerator and 16 degrees of freedom in the denominator, and that this value is significant with $\alpha = .01$.

The main functions of the concluding section, the *discussion* section (sometimes called the *conclusions* section), are to interpret the results of the study and to discuss their significance. Sometimes interpretation is simple and straightforward. If results support the initial hypotheses, a brief restatement of the rationale of these predictions will probably suffice. If predictions are not upheld, alternative explanations are needed. These are often speculative and refer to literature not cited in the introduction. The discussion section typically ends with suggestions for future research and/or applications that follow from the results of the present study. Sometimes the results of a study raise more questions than they answer. Considering the nature of scientific inquiry and the programmatic approach often used in good research, the number of new studies "spawned" by a research report may be a measure of its success. There is, in fact, a journal called *Citations Abstract*, which lists those later articles that cite a specific earlier paper.

One of the examples in box 12.5 provides some interesting suggestions for inferring causality from observational (correlational) data concerning cultural differences in birth rate. The second example illustrates how results of a study are discussed in terms of their implications for current theories in the area, in this case, theories about imagery and memory. Subjects had to recall word pairs such as MINISTER-BIBLE that were imbedded in common sentences ("THE MINISTER READ THE BIBLE.") or bizarre sentences ("THE MINISTER ATE THE BIBLE."). Our third example provides a succinct description of the relevance of the study's findings to the use of children's testimonies in child abuse court cases.

The very end of a research report consists of a listing, usually in alphabetic order, of the references cited in the paper. The manual published by the American Psychological Association specifies the format used in most psychology journals for citing references. This format was followed in listing the sources for the boxes in this section. The numbers following the authors' names, year of publication, title of article, and name of journal represent, respectively, the volume number and the page numbers.

While we hope you enjoyed the various examples provided in these boxes, we realize that they fail to illustrate one important point: how the different parts of a research paper fit together. So, we provide in box 12.6 a complete research report. This paper was written by a small group of students in an undergraduate experimental psychology laboratory course (which, in our department, follows the lecture course in experimental psychology). With guidance from the professor in charge, students designed their own project—hence, the topic of sexual relations in college students should come as no surprise. They performed their own literature review (introduction section), composed the experimental task and materials (methods section), conducted the statistical analyses and constructed the summary tables (results section), and provided their interpretion of the results and implications (discussion section).

BOX 12.5

Sample Portions of Discussion Sections

1. Source: Randall, W. (1988). A statistical analysis of the annual pattern in white births of maternal age groups in the United States for the years 1973 through 1980. *Journal of Interdisciplinary Cycle Research, 19*, 1–15.

A major problem of delineating cause and effect relationships in the USA is the heterogeneity of the population. The USA total population trend is a mixture of different stable patterns, including different stable regional patterns (Randall, 1987a), racial patterns (Randall, 1987b), and maternal age group patterns. Social class has been suggested as an additional variable (e.g., Pasamanick, et al., 1960; Zelnick, 1969), and other variables in the USA (religious, ethnic, occupational, etc.) also may be involved. Data on small, regional groups of almost any size exist in *Vital Statistics;* the smallest number for black births is in Vermont (approximately 20 per year) and for white births is in the District of Columbia (approximately 1500 per year). Thus intensively focused ethnographic and demographic studies on homogeneous groups may be possible. Several researchers have focused on small, homogeneous populations, and some insight into causation has been obtained. Studies of small agricultural communities (e.g., Malina & Himes, 1977; Ogum & Okorafor, 1979) indicate that the seasonal activities of planting and harvesting are negatively correlated with the peaks in birth. And a total of 29 births that occurred within two years in a village of Abelams in Papua, New Guinea were analyzed by Scaglion (1978). About two-thirds of the fathers participated in the "yam complex," growing ceremonial yams to determine the father's status in the community. The belief is that sex will interfere with the growth of your yams. A trough in the birth rate was present nine months after the growing season only in those families whose husbands engaged in the ceremonial farming. Thus the problem of causation seems considerably more tractable with small homogeneous groups, and this approach may be useful with subgroups of large populations.

2. Source: Riefer, D. M., & Rouder, J. N. (1992). A multinomial modeling analysis of the mnemonic benefits of bizarre imagery. *Memory & Cognition, 20*, 601–611.

The finding that bizarre imagery is retrieved better than common imagery has implications for a number of current theories of the bizarreness effect. For example, McDaniel and Einstein (1986; 1991; Einstein & McDaniel, 1987) have proposed that bizarre images are more memorable because of their distinctiveness within memory, but they also point out that the concept of distinctiveness in itself does not specify which cognitive operations are involved in making these memories distinct. The results of the model's analysis, as well as Einstein et al.'s (1989) finding of superior accessibility for bizarre sentences, seem to provide converging evidence that the effect of distinctiveness is somehow to improve the retrievability of bizarre memory traces. This viewpoint is also consistent with other retrieval-based theories of distinctiveness (see Schmidt, 1991, for a review of theories of distinctiveness).

3. Source: Goodman, G. S., & Aman, C. (1990). Children's use of anatomically detailed dolls to recount an event. *Child Development, 61*, 1859–1871.

Our study is most relevant to the claim that anatomically detailed dolls promote false reports of abuse when no abuse has occurred. Overall, our findings indicate that the use of anatomically detailed dolls in and of itself does not lead children to make false reports of abuse even under conditions of suggestive questioning.

BOX 12.6

A Complete Research Report: Gender Differences in Attitudes Towards Extradyadic Sexual Behavior*

Abstract

Gender differences in moral decision making were studied by asking college students to react to a scenario describing a person who had a one-night stand with someone he or she had just met, even though he or she was already involved in another serious relationship. All scenarios were exactly the same except that the person in the story was identified as either male or female and either a friend or an acquaintance. Even though the means for all subjects were on the unacceptable side of the scale, female subjects judged this type of sexual misbehavior more harshly than did male subjects. Male subjects but not female subjects differentiated between males and females in the scenarios, judging females more harshly than males for the same behavior. It was speculated that males still maintain the outdated "double-standard" that it is more acceptable for men to be sexually promiscuous than women.

Introduction

In the last few decades there has been much research done on issues of morality and the theoretical implications of these issues. In trying to discover whether or not there are differences between males and females in making moral judgments, Gilligan and Attanucci (1988) argued that there are two frameworks in which people make moral decisions: *justice* and *care* perspectives. The justice perspective proposed by Lawrence Kohlberg holds moral development typically to involve the increasing use of universal principles regarding individual rights in solving ethical problems (Sayers, 1987). This theory has been criticized in that it is apparently more representative of how men make moral decisions rather than women.

The care perspective proposed by Gilligan and Attanucci (1988) holds that its basic moral injunction is to not turn away from someone in need. Gilligan and Attanucci conclude that concern with caring and relationship issues typifies women (Sayers, 1987), while men are likely to adopt a less engaged role in their moral judgments (Pratt, Golding, & Kerig, 1987).

Consistent with these theories, Froese, Rumback, and Hard (1990) stated that people's perceptions of sexual behavior may be linked to the dimensions they use to construct their categories of such behavior. For several reasons, men and women may differ in their evaluation of promiscuity. Women emphasize the interpersonal aspects of their decisions to engage in sexual intercourse more than do men. Women typically attempt to establish a personal relationship with a member of the opposite sex before involvement in sexual activity (Froese et al., 1990). This evidence leads to the conclusion that women would look down on promiscuity more than men and subsequently make harsher moral judgments about promiscuous behavior.

In the present study we wanted to see if females really would make a harsher moral judgment than males when evaluating someone else's sexual behavior. In particular, we chose to use a scenario about a person who had a one-night stand when that person was already involved in another relationship. For college students, sexual issues of this type are highly relevant because of the commonality of this type of behavior. We also wanted to investigate whether men and women make different moral judgments about people of the same sex or opposite sex. The reason for this manipulation was to see if the "double standard" (i.e., that it's more acceptable for men to have casual sex than women) is still prevalent in today's generation of college students.

Method

Subjects

One hundred and ninety undergraduate students (102 F, 88 M) were recruited from introductory psychology courses at the University of Iowa.

Material

Four scenarios were constructed that described a person who had a one-night stand. All of the scenarios were exactly the same except that the person in the story was either a young man or woman. Also, the subjects were instructed to imagine that the person was either a close friend or an acquaintance of theirs. The scenario described how this person went to a party and met someone

[Continued]

Box 12.6 continued

visiting for the weekend. Even though the person in the story was already involved in a serious relationship, he or she was attracted to the visitor, and later that night the visitor went back with the person to his or her apartment and they had sex.

Procedure

Each subject received only one of the four versions of the scenario. Subjects were then given a pair of questions that measured reactions to the scenario. The first question asked how acceptable the person's actions were in the subject's opinion on a scale from 1 to 7, 1 being "not acceptable" and 7 being "very acceptable." The second question asked to what extent this would affect the relationship between the subject and the person in the story on a scale of 1 to 7 with: 1 being "large negative effect," 4 being "no effect," and 7 being "large positive effect."

The third part of the questionnaire asked for some demographic subject variables such as gender, age, class (freshman, sophomore, etc.), and personal relationship status (married, involved with someone, or not exclusively involved).

Results

Analysis of variance of data from the first question, which asked for the ratings of acceptability, produced two significant results: Sex of respondent, $F (1,182) = 19.63$, $p < .001$; and the interaction between sex of respondent and sex of person in story, $F (1,182) = 3.94, p < .05$. Figure A shows that males rated the one-night stand as significantly more acceptable than females, even though overall the mean ratings were all on the unacceptable side of the scale. The interaction between sex of respondent and sex of person in the story indicated that men, but not women, judged that when a male person in the story had a one-night stand it was more acceptable than

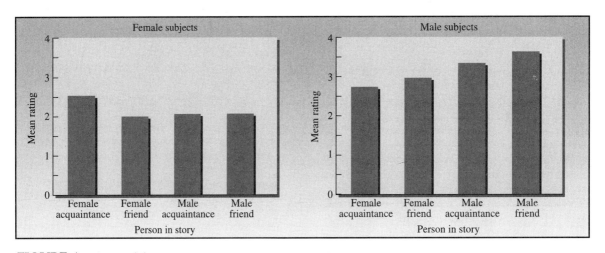

FIGURE A   Acceptability ratings

when a woman in the story had a one-night stand. There were no significant differences between friend vs. acquaintance in acceptability ratings.

Analysis of variance was also used to analyze the question of how the relationship between the respondent and

the person in the story would be affected. Mean responses were on the negative side in all conditions. However, there was a significant interaction between sex of respondent and sex of person in the story, $F (1,182) = 5.26, p < .05$. (See figure B.) Male subjects but not females indicated

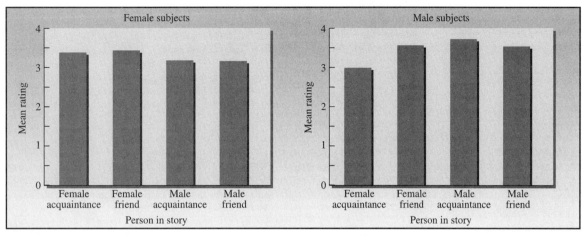

FIGURE B   Effect on relationship.

more negative effect on their relationship with females than with males in the story.

Regression analysis was performed on the subject variables to see which, if any, had an effect on the acceptability ratings. Personal relationship status was the only subject variable that correlated significantly with the first question, and it was significant at the .001 level. This result showed that after collapsing over all the levels of the independent variables, people who were currently involved in a relationship were significantly more unaccepting of the situation than people who were not exclusively involved with anyone.

Discussion

There was a clear gender difference in making moral judgments about someone who had a one-night stand while already involved in a relationship with someone else. Consistent with other studies, females made harsher moral judgments than males about the situation. Theorists have speculated about the reasons for this phenomenon for years, but one possible cause for these differences in attitudes may be differences in sexual behavior. While we did not ask about sexual behavior in our subjects, other studies have shown that male college students are significantly more promiscuous than female college students. Simon (1984) found that after

investigating the number of past sexual partners for nonvirgins, a clear sex difference was found; the mean number was 14.6 for men and 5.6 for women. While it is possible that greater promiscuity leads to more accepting attitudes about sexual behavior, it is also possible that men may somehow already have more accepting attitudes about sexual behavior and this is what leads to greater promiscuity. Even though the direction of causality is not known, there does seem to be a strong correlation between sexual behavior and attitudes about sexual behavior.

The most interesting interaction effects found in this study showed that while women judge males and females alike, men judged female sexual behavior more harshly than male sexual behavior. Male subjects indicated that when females have a one-night stand, the acceptability of this act is lower than when males have a one-night stand, and there is a larger negative effect on the relationship between male subjects and females in the story than male subjects and males in the story. This actually goes against Kohlberg's justice perspective, which says that men are more likely to be disengaged and judge everyone equally and fairly. However, unlike most previous studies, which obtained global attitude measures concerning sexual promiscuity, the current study provided a specific situation for subjects to evaluate. This

[Continued]

Box 12.6 continued

study might thus provide a more valid index of differential responses to females and males engaged in identical behavior.

It is difficult to determine whether the females in this study demonstrated Gilligan's care perspective. We did not take any measures of how empathic they were with the characters in the scenarios, but they certainly did *not* seem to be more empathic with females than with males because they judged all scenarios equally.

This study has shown that men and women do not look at extradyadic sexual relationships equally. This finding contradicts some studies, such as the one done by Clement, Schmidt, and Kruse (1984), that claim that in recent years no differences have been found in sexual attitudes between males and females. Most of the studies done, however, do show that females judge sexual misbehavior more harshly than males, and this is exactly what we also found.

In today's society where equality is striven for in every way, we have shown that males still hold a double-standard where sexual misbehavior is concerned. Even though the males in our study indicated that it was generally unacceptable for anyone to have a one-night stand, it was relatively more unacceptable for females than for males to have an extra-dyadic sexual relationship. An important and inter-esting follow-up study would try to figure out why males persevere in their attitudes about double-standards.

References

Clement, U., Schmidt, G., & Kruse, M. (1984). Changes in sex differences in sexual behavior: A replication of a study on West German students. *Archives of Sexual Behavior, 13*, 99–120.

Froese, A. D., Rumback, K. L., & Hard, L. D. (1990). Sex differences in evaluating heterosexual and homosexual promiscuity. *Psychological Reports, 66*, 579–582.

Gilligan, C., & Attanucci, J. (1988). Two moral orientations: Gender differences and similarities. *Merrill-Palmer Quarterly, 34*, 223–237.

Pratt, M. W., Golding, G., & Kerig, P. (1987). Lifespan differences in adult thinking about hypothetical and personal moral issues: Reflection or regression? *International Journal of Behavioral Development, 10*, 359–375.

Sayers, U. (1987). Freud revisited: On gender, moral development, and androgyny. *New Ideas in Psychology, 5*, 197–206.

Simon, A. (1989). Promiscuity as sex difference. *Psychological Reports, 64*, 802.

*We are indebted to Tonya Sieverding, who took the lead role in writing this paper and made it available to us.

Despite the somewhat personal nature of the task, they were able to secure prior approval to conduct the study from the department's ethics committee by insuring complete confidentiality of responses and by making clear that research participants could withdraw at any time. Note the logical sequence of parts of the paper: a section describing what they wanted to do and why they wanted to do it, a section on how they did it, a section on what they found, and finally, a section describing what they think it all means. We hope that you have a chance to write such a paper with results as interesting as these.

Finally, we should note that the American Psychological Association's Publication Manual contains useful tips on writing. Box 12.7 provides some excerpts, including tips on avoiding sexist language.

It was not our purpose here to stress style over substance. Rather, our intention was to give you a "feel" for what constitutes an efficient and informative way of communicating research results. Progress in psychology, like all science, rests on the ability to communicate and motivate. We hope that some of you will go on to contribute to scientific research and see the fruits of your labor realized in published research articles. For the majority, we hope that you will become informed consumers of research and will continue to seek out and critically evaluate research that affects you professionally and personally. We hope that you now have the confidence to consult original research sources rather than having to rely on secondary sources.

BOX 12.7

Some Guidelines from the Publication Manual of the American Psychological Association: Economy of Expression

Say only what needs to be said. The author who is frugal with words not only writes a more readable manuscript but also increases the chances that the manuscript will be accepted. Editors work with limited numbers of printed pages and therefore often request authors to shorten submitted papers. You can tighten overly long papers by eliminating redundancy, wordiness, jargon, evasiveness, circumlocution, and clumsiness. Weed out overly detailed descriptions of apparatus, subjects, or procedure; gratuitous embellishments; elaborations of the obvious; and irrelevant observations or asides.

Short words and short sentences are easier to comprehend than long ones. A long technical term, however, may be more precise than several short words, and technical terms are inseparable from scientific reporting. Yet the technical terminology in a paper should be understood by psychologists throughout the discipline. An article that depends upon terminology familiar to only a few specialists does not sufficiently contribute to the literature.

The main causes of uneconomical writing are jargon and wordiness. Jargon is the continuous use of a technical vocabulary even in places where that vocabulary is not relevant. Jargon is also the substitution of a euphemistic phrase for a familiar term (e.g., *monetary felt scarcity* for *poverty*), and, as such, it should be scrupulously avoided. Federal bureaucratic jargon has had the greatest publicity, but scientific jargon also grates on the reader, encumbers the communication of information, and often takes up space unnecessarily.

Wordiness is every bit as irritating and uneconomical as jargon and can impede the ready grasp of ideas. Change *based on the fact that* to *because*, *at the present time* to *now*, and *for the purpose of* to a simple *for* or *to*. Change *there were several students who completed* to *several students completed*. *Reason* and *because* often appear in the same sentence; however, they have the same meaning, and therefore they should not be used together. Unconstrained wordiness lapses into embellishment and literary elegance, which are clearly inappropriate in scientific style. Mullins (1977) comprehensively discusses examples of wordiness found in the social science literature.

Writers often become redundant in a mistaken effort to be emphatic. Use no more words than are necessary to convey the meaning. In the following examples, the italicized words are redundant and should be omitted:

They were *both* alike	*one and* the same
a total of 68 subjects	in *close* proximity
Four *different* groups saw	*completely* unanimous
instructions, which were *exactly* the same as those used	*very* close to significance
absolutely essential	*period of* time
has been *previously* found	summarize *briefly*
small *in size*	the reason is *because*

Although writing only in short, simple sentences produces choppy and boring prose, writing exclusively in long, involved sentences creates difficult, sometimes incomprehensible material. Varied sentence length helps readers maintain interest and comprehension. When involved concepts do require long sentences, the components should march along like people in a parade, not dodge about like broken-field runners. Direct, declarative sentences with simple, common words are usually best.

Similar cautions apply to paragraph length. Single-sentence paragraphs may be abrupt. Paragraphs that are too long, a more typical fault in manuscripts, are likely to lose the reader's attention. New paragraphs provide a pause for the reader—a chance to store one step in the conceptual development before beginning another. If your paragraphs run longer than a page in typescript, you are probably straining the reader's thought span. Look for a logical place to make a break or reorganize the material. Unity, cohesiveness, and continuity should characterize all paragraphs.

[Continued]

Box 12.7 continued

Guidelines for Nonsexist Language in APA Journals

EXAMPLES OF COMMON USAGE	ALTERNATIVES
Problems of Designation: Ambiguity of Referent	
1. The *client* is usually the best judge of the value of *his* counseling.	The *client* is usually the best judge of the value of counseling. [Comment: *His* deleted] The client is usually the best judge of the value of *his or her* counseling. [Comment: *Or her* added. (Use sparingly to avoid monotonous repetition.)] *Clients* are usually the best judges of the value of the counseling *they* receive. [Comment: Changed to plural] The best judge of the value of counseling is usually *the client.* [Comment: Rephrased]
2. *Man's search* for knowledge has led *him* into ways of learning that bear examination.	*The search* for knowledge has led *us* into ways of learning that bear examination. [Comment: Rephrased in first person] *People* have continually sought knowledge. The search has led *them* into ways of learning that bear examination. [Comment: Changed to plural and rewritten in two sentences]
3. man, mankind man's achievements the average man man a project man–machine interface manpower	people, humanity, human beings, humankind, human species human achievements, achievements of the human species the average person, people in general staff a project, hire personnel, employ staff user-system interface, person-system interface, human-machine interface work force, personnel, workers, human resources [Comment: Various terms substituted for each example]
4. The use of experiments in psychology presupposes the mechanistic nature of *man.*	The use of experiments in psychology presupposes the mechanistic nature of the *human being.* [Comment: Noun substituted]
5. This interference phenomenon, called learned helplessness, has been demonstrated in rats, cats, fish, dogs, monkeys, and *men.*	This interference phenomenon, called learned helplessness, has been demonstrated in rats, cats, fish, dogs, monkeys, and *humans.* [Comment: Noun substituted]
6. Responsivity in the premature *infant* may be secondary to *his* heightened level of autonomic arousal.	Responsivity in the premature *infant* may be secondary to *the* heightened level of autonomic arousal. [Comment: *His* changed to *the*]

EXAMPLES OF COMMON USAGE	ALTERNATIVES
Problems of Designation: Ambiguity of Referent	
	Responsivity in premature *infants* may be secondary to *their* heightened levels of autonomic arousal. [Comment: Rewritten in the plural]
7. First the *individual* becomes aroused by violations of *his* personal space, and then *he* attributes the cause of this arousal to other people in *his* environment.	First *we* become aroused by violations of *our* personal space, and then *we* attribute the cause of this arousal to other people in *the* environment. [Comment: First-person pronouns substituted for the noun and *he* and *his*: *his* changed to *the*] First *one* becomes aroused by violations of personal space, and then *one* attributes the cause of this arousal to other people in *the* environment. [Comment: *One* substituted: *his* omitted or changed to *the*]
8. Much has been written about the effect that a *child's* position among *his* siblings has on *his* intellectual development.	Much has been written about the relationship between sibling position and intellectual development in *children*. [Comment: Rewritten: plural introduced]
9. Subjects were 16 girls and 16 boys. Each *child* was to place a car on *his* board so that two cars and boards looked alike.	Each child was to place a car on *his* or *her* board so that two cars and boards looked alike. [Comment: *His* changed to *his* or *her* or to *her* or *his* (Use sparingly to avoid monotonous repetition.)]
10. Each person's alertness was measured by the difference between *his* obtained relaxation score and *his* obtained arousal score.	Each person's alertness was measured by the difference between *the* obtained relaxation and arousal scores. [Comment: *His* changed to *the*: plural introduced]
11. The client's husband *lets* her teach part-time.	The client's husband "*lets*" her teach part-time. The husband says he "*lets*" the client teach part-time. The client *says her husband* "*lets*" her teach part-time. [Comment: Punctuation added to clarify that the location of the bias is with the husband and wife, not with the author. If necessary, rewrite to clarify as allegation.]
Problems of Designation: Stereotyping	
12. males, females	men, women, boys, girls, adults, children, adolescents [Comment: Specific nouns reduce possibility of stereotypic bias and often clarify discussion. Use *male* and *female* as adjectives where appropriate and relevant (female experimenter, male subject) Avoid unparallel usage such as 10 *men* and 16 *females*.]
13. Research scientists often neglect their *wives* and *children*.	Research scientists often neglect their *spouses* and *children*. [Comment: Alternative wording acknowledges that women as well as men are research scientists.]

Box 12.7 continued

Examples of Common Usage	Alternatives

Problems of Designation: Stereotyping

14. When a *test developer* or *test user* fails to satisfy these requirements, *he* should . . .	When *test developers* or *test users* fail to satisfy these requirements, *they* should . . . [Comment: Same as Example 13]
15. the psychologist . . . *he* the therapist . . . *he* the nurse . . . *she* the teacher . . . *she*	psychologists . . . *they;* the psychologist . . . *she* therapists . . . *they:* the therapist . . . *she or he* nurses . . . *they:* nurse . . . *he* teachers . . . *they;* teacher . . . *he* [Comment: Be specific, change to plural if discussing women as well as men, or use *he or she.* Do not use *s/he.*]
16. woman doctor, lady lawyer, male nurse	doctor, physician, lawyer, nurse [Comment: Specify sex only if it is a variable or if sex designation is necessary to the discussion ("13 female doctors and 22 male doctors"). *Woman* and *lady* are nouns: *female* is the adjective counterpart to *male.*]
17. mothering	parenting, nurturing (or specify exact behavior) [Comment: Noun substituted]
18. chairman (of an academic department)	Use *chairperson* or *chair:* use *chairman* only if it is known that the institution has established that form as an official title. [Comment: *Department head* may be appropriate; however, the term is not synonymous with *chair* and *chairperson* at all institutions.]
chairman (presiding officer of a committee or meeting)	chairperson, chair, moderator, discussion leader [Comment: In parliamentary usage, *chairman* is the official term and should not be changed. Alternatives are acceptable in most writing.]
19. Only *freshmen* were eligible for the project.	No alternative if academic standing is meant
All the students had matriculated for 3 years, but the majority were still *freshmen.*	No alternative if academic standing is meant [Comment: *First-year student* is often an acceptable alternative to *freshman,* but in these examples, *freshmen* is used for accuracy.]

Where Do You Go from Here?

For many of you, this course and text will mark the end of your formal training in experimental psychology. Perhaps your career and personal life will carry you far afield from behavioral research. Nevertheless, we hope that you have learned something of value: an appreciation of good research; a healthy skepticism concerning extravagant research claims; an increased ability to develop your own personal psychology (understanding your own and others' behavior) by careful observation, making logical inferences, and continuously testing these inferences. The concepts of "experimental control," "placebo effect," "observer bias," and "statistical significance" are quite possibly ingrained in your future thinking about behavior.

For those of you who go on to graduate or professional training in psychology or a related discipline, there is apt to be lots more research in your future. In fact, we suggest that you get as much experience as possible now, such as by volunteering to work in faculty research laboratories. A master's degree—which typically takes 2 or 3 years to complete—may or may not require a thesis reporting the results of original research conducted by the student under faculty supervision. Even when a thesis is not required, a substantial portion of the student's training is apt to involve digesting research results. Ph.D.s in psychology average about 5 years to complete after the bachelor's degree, with an extra year's "internship" for clinical psychologists. A doctoral dissertation definitely requires original research and may be of sufficient quality to merit citation by future researchers. A number of papers cited in this text were based on doctoral dissertations. We suggest that if your psychology department has a graduate program, you ask to see examples of theses and dissertations.

Applying to Graduate School

You ordinarily apply to graduate school in December or January prior to the fall semester when you want to enroll. In a real sense, you're not just applying to a university or a particular department (e.g.,

psychology) within that university, but to a *subarea* within that department. This is because graduate admissions is a matter of "supply and demand." Within a department a certain number of students are admitted each year in each area. The numbers are limited by a desire to maintain a favorable student-to-faculty ratio as well as by a desire to keep apace of job opportunities in the field. So, for example, you are in direct competition with other students applying in clinical psychology, social psychology, cognitive psychology, or the like. In most psychology departments, clinical psychology attracts the most applicants and is thus the most competititive. In other words, your credentials for being admitted into a program of graduate studies in psychology have to be better if you want to pursue a career in clinical psychology. Similarly, Ph.D. programs are more competitive than M.A. programs.

What are the important factors in graduate selection? Grades, of course, are of paramount importance. Grade point average is evaluated in light of the strength of the curriculum you pursued and the perceived quality of your undergraduate institution. Many graduate programs emphasize grades in the last two years, grades in your major area and, if it's a research-oriented program, they may pay special attention to courses like the one for which you're using this book.

Your scores on standardized tests such as the Graduate Record Exam (GRE) are also very important. This test consists of three basic parts—verbal, quantitative, and analytic abilities—plus a specialty test of your knowledge in psychology. *It pays to study for these exams.* Some universities and some private organizations provide special short-term courses. All university bookstores have study guides with sample test items. You should practice these tests under the same time constraints as imposed in the actual testing situation. (In the actual test, you will be under some time pressure and will be penalized for items left out.) GREs are given several times a year; your university will undoubtedly have an office with this information.

Several other factors can enhance your credentials. Undergraduate research experience is always a "plus" when you apply to a research-oriented graduate program. Any other experiences in volunteer work or employment that exhibit your "time management" skills should be looked on with favor. Letters of recommendation from persons who are familiar with the personal qualities that will help you in graduate school are important, especially if they provide information not apparent in your transcripts. (A research supervisor would be an ideal example.)

All applications allow you the opportunity to express your personal qualifications and reasons for pursuing graduate work. It's worthwhile to do your homework and learn about the individual departments to which you're applying; then you can write a personal statement that stresses how you would fit into that particular program. For example, you could refer to specific strengths that a department is known to have, and specific faculty members known for their work in your area of interest.

How many departments should you apply to? There's no easy answer to this question. Faculty advisors at your current institution may be able to look over your records and give you some idea of your chances of getting into specific programs. Brochures from the programs themselves may include information about the range of grades and GRE scores of admitted students. Many departments will have access to the American Psychological Association's guide, *Graduate Studies in Psychology*. Ask to see it. It is not unreasonable to apply to many programs—those that you want the most but may be the hardest to get into, plus those that you may have a better chance with and would be acceptable to you. Remember, it's an investment in your future. Good luck! Figure 12.1 provides an example of an application form and the information requested.

The most direct transfer of what you learned in an experimental psychology course will, of course, occur if you elect graduate work in psychology. But other professional fields such as law, medicine, physical therapy, and business find training in experimental psychology to be relevant and useful. Good research techniques in social psychology can contribute in important ways to our understanding of the judicial system, especially jury decisions. Observational techniques for examining recovery from illness borrow heavily from psychology, and psychological factors themselves are now frequently examined in medicine—from patient's compliance with prescribed medical regimes, to psychological "risk" factors in susceptibility to disease, to physicians' awareness of the importance of "hits," "misses," and "false alarms" in medical diagnosis. Good marketing and advertising techniques follow directly from solid research on perception, learning, attitude formation, and decision making. The study of business organizations is an example of behavioral research that may focus on cooperation vs. competition, negotiation, and group decision making.

Careers in Experimental Psychology

Opportunities to do behavioral research beyond graduate training are many and varied. While universities and colleges provide perhaps the greatest amount of freedom in pursuing one's research interests, different educational institutions differ greatly in the opportunities, facilities, and rewards for research. Chances are, if your college or university includes a rigorous experimental psychology class for its undergraduates, then it must be a research-oriented institution. Some government agencies such as the National Institutes of Health have their own major research facilities. A high percentage of research articles and books comes from major research universities and research institutes. However, as we have illustrated in this text, many important research developments come from the ingenuity of the individual researcher and do not require elaborate facilities and high budgets. Much good behavioral research comes from smaller schools. Furthermore, private agencies employ researchers to address specific problems such as determining the demand for a particular product or service. We encourage you to consult

Application for Admission to The University of Iowa Graduate College

Please read the accompanying instructions before completing this application.

A. PERSONAL DATA

1. Name _____
last   first   middle

2. Maiden Name _____ Should this name be included on your university records? ☐ Yes ☐ No

3. Social Security Number _____/_____/_____   4. Gender (optional) ☐ Male ☐ Female   5. Birth date_____/_____/_____
month   day   year

6. List other name(s) that may appear on transcripts, scores, or other material being submitted _____

7. Residing address _____
street   city   state/country   ZIP   county (if Iowa)

8. Home address _____
street   city   state/country   ZIP   county (if Iowa)

9. Phone number(s) where you can be contacted concerning this application   (_____)_____-_____   (_____)_____-_____
work or school   home

10. Parent or other person to be notified in case of emergency _____
name   relationship

11. _____ (_____)_____
street   city and state   ZIP   county (if Iowa)   telephone number

12. Birthplace _____
city   state/country

13. Country of citizenship   ☐ USA   ☐ Other (specify) _____

14. If you are not a U.S. citizen, are you a permanent resident of the U.S.? ☐ Yes ☐ No

15. If yes, print your Alien Registration Number _____

16. Racial/ethnic information (optional)
   ☐ 1—American Indian or Alaskan Native   ☐ 3—Hispanic/Latino(a)   ☐ 5—White, not of Hispanic/Latino(a) origin
       Tribal/Nation Affiliation: _____
   ☐ 2—African American/Black   ☐ 4—Asian or Pacific Islander

B. EDUCATIONAL DATA

1. Have you previously (or are you currently) registered for courses (on campus, correspondence, extension) at The University of Iowa? ☐ Yes ☐ No

2. Have you previously applied for admission to a UI graduate program? ☐ Yes ☐ No   If yes, for which session?_____

3. List each college or university you have ever attended or are currently attending (see instruction item B3).

Name of institution	Location (city and state)	Dates of attendance (mo/yr to mo/yr)	Type of degree earned or expected	Date or expected date of degree

C. ADMISSIONS DATA

1. For which session are you applying for admission? (check one only and indicate year)
   ☐ Fall (August) 19 _____   ☐ Spring (January) 19 _____   ☐ Summer (June) 19 _____

2. Which specific program (or joint program) should review this application? (see instruction item C2-4) _____

3. Subarea or specialization _____

4. Check (one only) as your immediate objective for enrolling in the Graduate College (see list of Advanced Programs on page 4 of instructions).
   ☐ MA/thesis   ☐ MA/nonthesis   ☐ MFA   ☐ MAT   ☐ MPT   ☐ EdS   ☐ PhD
   ☐ MS/thesis   ☐ MS/nonthesis   ☐ MBA   ☐ MSW   ☐ MPA   ☐ DMA
   ☐ Certificate only   ☐ Professional/personal improvement (an advanced degree is not my current goal)

5. I (took) (plan to take) the Graduate Record Examination in (month and year) _____

6. My GRE scores are: V_____ Q_____ A_____   Subj. Code _____ Subj. Score _____

7. I (took) (plan to take) the Graduate Management Admission Test in (month and year) _____   8. My GMAT scores are: V_____ Q_____ T_____

9. I (have requested) (will request) that my GRE or GMAT scores be sent to The University of Iowa.

G														
C	SES	HC	RES	FOR	ETH	CO	ST	PC	FEE	ORG	COL	DEPT	DEG	WT

[Continued]

FIGURE 12.1   An application for admission to The Iowa Graduate College

FIGURE 12.1 continued

D. STATEMENT IN DETERMINATION OF RESIDENCY

1. Do you consider yourself a resident of the state of Iowa? ☐ Yes ☐ No

2. If you reside in Iowa, when did your present residency begin? _____ / _____
   month   year

3. List the high school from which you graduated _____
   high school name   city   state/country

4. Please give a chronological account of your major activities (including summer activities) for the three years immediately preceding your proposed entry to The University of Iowa.

from (mo/yr) to (mo/yr)	activity (i.e., employment, school, military, etc.)	location (city/state)

E. CERTIFICATION

I certify that to the best of my knowledge all information given on this application is correct and complete, and I understand that any omission or misinformation concerning enrollment in other colleges or universities may void my admission or result in dismissal.

_____   _____
signature of applicant   date

APPLICANTS: Please be sure you have signed your application, then continue to pages 3 and 4.

for office use only

Name: _____   ____/____/____
         last   first   middle   social security number

F. SUPPLEMENTAL DATA *(We will forward this information to your academic department. Please answer questions completely.)*

1. List below three persons familiar with the scope and quality of your past academic or professional work from whom you are requesting letters of recommendation. *(Address these letters to your proposed department of study, The University of Iowa, Iowa City, IA 52242.)*

    Name   *Position*   *Address*

    _____   _____   _____
    _____   _____   _____
    _____   _____   _____
    _____   _____   _____

2. List The University of Iowa faculty with whom you have discussed your plans or whom you know personally. _____
    _____

3. If admitted on this application, your first registration will be:

    ☐ for regular class work on campus: ☐ full-time ☐ part-time

    ☐ for special program or institute on campus: identify _____

    ☐ for off-campus class(es)
       at (site) _____ : course(s) _____

    ☐ for classes through the Saturday and Evening Class Program:
       course(s) _____

4. State your purpose in taking graduate work. _____
    _____
    _____
    _____
    _____
    _____
    _____
    _____

5. What research have you accomplished? _____
    _____
    _____
    _____

6. In what area(s) would you like to do research? _____
    _____
    _____
    _____
    _____

7. For what vocation are you preparing? _____
    _____

8. What was your undergraduate major? _____ Minor? _____

9. What was your graduate major? _____ Minor? _____

10. List your undergraduate and graduate (if applicable) GPA using an A = 4.00 scale.   Undergraduate _____   Graduate _____

11. If your immediate objective is a master's degree, do you plan to continue in a Ph.D. program at The University of Iowa?
    ☐ Yes   ☐ No   ☐ Undecided

[*Continued*]

FIGURE 12.1 continued

12. Give titles of any articles or other publications, inventions, or creative work. _____
_____
_____

13. What preparation and proficiency do you have in foreign languages? *(please be specific)* _____
_____
_____
_____

14. List the academic honors, prizes, or awards you have received. _____
_____
_____
_____
_____

15. List participation in extracurricular activities. _____
_____
_____
_____
_____

16. Work or teaching experience:

Job Classification	Employer	Dates (mo/yr to mo/yr)

17. List any organizations or community activities in which you have been active. _____
_____
_____
_____

18. *(Optional Item)* If you believe that your academic record or test scores do not accurately reflect your ability to do graduate work, you may wish to list below additional factors that you feel merit consideration. Examples might be: experiences that indicate unusual drive, determination, motivation, or leadership characteristics; adverse conditions (e.g., illness); obligations (e.g., employment); or cultural, linguistic, or economic factors in your background.
_____
_____
_____
_____
_____

RETURN APPLICATION MATERIALS PROMPTLY.

the American Psychological Association's pamphlet, *Careers in Psychology*, for more information about employment opportunities. Most departments will have copies or can tell you how to send away for one.

Will you be a good researcher? Of course we cannot answer that question for each of you individually. To overgeneralize, let us say that key factors are (1) a solid knowledge of the fundamentals of good experimental design; (2) proficiency in statistical techniques (at least, knowing what to do and why, even if the computations are done by machine); (3) some knowledge of the background of the area you're investigating, or, at least knowing how to acquire that background; (4) originality (although this may take a while to develop); and (5) enjoyment of the research enterprise. The last may be the most important of all because researchers must often learn to cope with research that "just didn't come out right." And remember, research can be fun!

Exercise

Let's end this book with a bang by making the last exercise a really big one. Arguably, one of the most important issues facing us as we prepare for the twenty-first century is the environment. How will life for us and other species persist with continuing trends of pollution, global warming, deforestation, and depleting natural resources? Consider each of the topical areas represented in this book—animal behavior; human learning and memory; perception and psychophysics; judgment, decision making, and problem solving; social psychology; clinical psychology. We want you to perform a series of "thought experiments" by planning at least one study and anticipating the implications of its results in each of these areas, applying the methods of each area to the study of environmental issues. To be sure, the studies will vary greatly in content and methodology, but what they will have in common is a focus on behavior—how various behaviors are affected by adverse environmental conditions, and possibly the converse as well, how we may learn to behave in ways that might reverse current environmental trends. Our hope is that in addressing this exercise you will see the need for well-designed behavioral research in all these areas and with all the "tools" developed by experimental psychologists, including experimental and correlational studies with humans and animals. Perhaps some of your "thought experiments" will actually become real as you get the "research bug."

Glossary

A

absolute threshold Minimal physical stimulus value that will produce a response 50 percent of the time. (p. 92)

acquisition An increase in the strength of a learned response due to reinforced practice. (p. 125)

adaptation level The value of the stimulus judged "average," to which other stimuli are compared in scaling. (p. 111)

adoption study The use of naturally occurring adoptions to separate the influences of familial environmental factors (adoptive family) from genetic factors (biological family). (p. 304)

algorithm A step-by-step procedure of generating all possible ways to solve a problem. (p. 260)

all-or-none learning Assumption that learning of the associative connection between items occurs on a single trial. (p. 181)

alternative hypothesis Hypothesis that affirms the existence of differences between experimental conditions. (p. 53)

analog research Research in which either the subject population or the manipulated independent variables are only approximations of the populations or variables of interest to the researcher. (p. 307)

anchoring Heuristic in which the judge uses a natural starting point as a first approximation to a required judgment. (p. 248)

anticipation method List learning method in which the subject responds with the succeeding item as each item in the list is presented. (p. 175)

appetitive stimulus One that serves to strengthen responses that produce it and that serves to weaken responses that remove it. (p. 134)

arbitrary concept A tendency for responding to be controlled by stimulus relations—like same, larger, inside—that can be instantiated by objects from many natural classes. (p. 146)

assimilation Context effect in which responses on one trial are positively correlated with responses from earlier trials. (p. 111)

associative learning Behavioral change that results from the contingent occurrence of two classes of events: two classes of stimuli in Pavlovian conditioning and responses and stimuli in Thorndikian conditioning. (p. 140)

associative links Connections between nodes (facts and concepts) represented in semantic network models; used to explain how knowledge is organized. (p. 195)

attention placebo group A control condition in which the subjects are administered a treatment comprised of inert ingredients or no identified effective components but are exposed to the same personal contact and amount of time with a professional as the subjects in the treatment condition that has the putative effective ingredients. In psychotherapy research, the attention placebo is designed to control for nonspecific therapeutic factors and the amount of contact subjects have with a therapist. *See also* Hawthorne Effect, Nonspecific therapeutic factors. (p. 318)

attitude-behavior relationship Validating a measure of attitude by seeing if it predicts behavior. (p. 276)

attribution theory   Theory describing how we attribute causes to a person's actions. (p. 282)

automatic processing   Highly practiced skills that do not require attention to perform. (p. 193)

availability   Heuristic in which the likelihood or frequency of an event is estimated on the basis of how easy that event is to imagine or recall. (p. 247)

aversive stimulus   One that serves to weaken responses that produce it and that serves to strengthen responses that remove it. (p. 134)

B

before-and-after design   Comparing subjects' performance before and after an experimental treatment. (p. 36)

between-subjects designs   Experimental designs in which different subjects are assigned to different levels of the independent variable. (p. 29)

biconditional rule   A concept defined by the joint occurrence or joint nonoccurrence of a specified level of two relevant dimensions (e.g., objects that are striped squares or nonstriped nonsquares); defined by the "if . . . and only if" relationship, as in if "striped" and only if "squares." (p. 189)

bigrams   Two-letter units used in verbal learning studies. (p. 174)

bootstrapping   Using a model based on a decision maker's prior judgments to be applied uniformly to all future judgments. (p. 252)

bounded rationality   Choice of the first alternative that satisfies the decision maker's aspiration level, rather than waiting for a possibly better choice. (p. 242)

bowed-serial-position curve   Plot of recall errors following a single trial on a free recall task; recall of the initial items (a primacy effect associated with long-term memory) and recall of the last items (a recency effect associated with short-term memory) are better than recall of the middle items. (p. 213)

British empiricism   Philosophical school of the eighteenth century that claimed that the study of mind can be linked to physical activity within the brain and that ideas (thoughts) depend on experience. (p. 167)

C

canon of parsimony   (Morgan's canon) The stricture to be extremely conservative in interpreting behavior. (p. 123)

carryover effects   The impact on later behavior of earlier events and reactions to them. (p. 31)

category scaling   The sorting of items into a fixed number of categories. (p. 107)

cause and effect   Identifying factors that determine an observed behavior or change in behavior. (p. 9)

chance sampling effects   Differences in subject variables between samples taken from the same population. (p. 49)

chunking   Reorganizing sequences of items into larger units or "chunks" that may be more meaningful and more easily remembered. (p. 229)

clinical trials   The use of research subjects who are drawn from the same population as the clients who would be seeking services at a clinical site for the exact problem(s) that is under investigation. In clinical trials therapy research, the experimental therapists are the same clinicians who would be providing therapy at clinical sites, and all of the procedures are followed in an actual clinical context. (p. 322)

clustering   In responding to items in free-recall, subjects tend to group the items by category. (p. 225)

cognitive dissonance   State of tension that occurs when one's behavior is inconsistent with one's beliefs, values, or goals. (p. 277)

cognitive economy   Saving memory by storing the attributes of concepts at the highest level to which they generally apply. (p. 195)

cognitive psychology   The branch of psychology dealing with the acquisition and use of knowledge. (p. 240)

comparative cognition   Comparative study of higher forms of learning, memory, and problem-solving. (p. 156)

compliance   Extent to which a person acts in accordance with others' expectancies or orders. (p. 278)

concept formation   Learning to make a common response to each of a class of objects. (p. 188)

conceptual behavior   Responding that extends beyond the conditions of training and that suggests the acquisition of rules or regularities to guide behavior. (p. 145)

conditional probability   The probability of one event given that another event has occurred. (p. 53)

conditional rule   A concept defined by the occurrence of a specified level of one relevant dimension if a second level also occurs (e.g., if the object is striped then it must be a square to be a valid instance); defined by the "if . . . then" relationship, as in if "striped," then "square." (p. 189)

conditioned reinforcement An initially indifferent stimulus may acquire the ability to strengthen responses that produce it. (p. 140)

conditioned response A response to a conditioned stimulus in Pavlovian conditioning that is the product of the pairing of that stimulus with an unconditioned stimulus. (p. 125)

conditioned stimulus A stimulus that is arranged to occur in conjunction with an unconditioned stimulus in Pavlovian conditioning. (p. 125)

confidence intervals Range of values of a statistic such as the mean within which we can establish with a certain degree of confidence that a population parameter will fall. (p. 71)

conformity The tendency of individuals in a group to match the behavior of the majority. (p. 289)

confounding When changes in behavior are due to the influence of two or more variables whose effects on behavior cannot be separated. (p. 28)

conjunction fallacy The error people make in judging that the likelihood of two things both happening is greater than the likelihood of any one of them happening. (p. 244)

conjunctive rule A concept defined by the joint occurrence of specified levels of each of two relevant dimensions (e.g., striped square); defined by the relationship "and," as in "striped" *and* "square." (p. 189)

connectionism An idea or concept is understood through its pattern of associations to other ideas or concepts. (p. 197)

conservation tasks Tasks developed by Piaget to determine the ability of children of different ages to see that transformations such as changes in shape do not alter the basic properties of objects. (p. 264)

context effects The manner in which judgments of individual stimuli are affected by earlier trials with different stimulus values. (p. 111)

contiguity The notion that mere coincidence in time of events is responsible for associative conditioning. (p. 136)

contingency The notion that the relationship between events is responsible for associative conditioning. (p. 137)

contrast Context effect in which responses on one trial are negatively correlated with responses from earlier trials. (p. 111)

control by equation In comparative behavior analysis, the method of equating situational and biological factors in learning problems for two or more species. (p. 158)

control by systematic variation In comparative behavior analysis, the method of varying potential confounding factors to see if they materially change the behavioral differences between or among species. (p. 158)

controlled experimentation The method of carefully changing the situation in order to determine its effect on the phenomenon being observed. (p. 120)

converging evidence The use of multiple methods and subject populations to investigate a given phenomenon. (p. 289)

correlation Measure of the degree of covariation or strength of association between two variables. (p. 72)

correlational method Observations of behavior aimed at yielding quantitative data about the interrelations between events or factors. (p. 7)

counterbalancing Subjects in a within-subject design are assigned to different sequences of experimental conditions such that progressive changes in behavior ("progressive error") are distributed equally across experimental conditions. (p. 31)

critical region Extreme values of the distribution of a statistical test; the probability is α that sample data will lead to these values if the null hypothesis is true (also known as *region of rejection*). (p. 55)

critical test An experiment permitting the comparative testing of alternative hypotheses arising from competing theories. (p. 15)

cross-fostering An experimental technique in animal research in which offspring from experimental mothers are switched with those from control mothers in order to uncouple the effects of maternal behavior from the effects of genes. (p. 303)

cross-sectional study A comparison of different groups (e.g., different age groups or depressed and nondepressed persons) at one point in time. This is to be contrasted with longitudinal studies in which the same group is examined at different points in time. (p. 230)

cuing The use of specific cues to aid in retrieving information. (p. 222)

D

decay   Retention loss assumed to be due to internal biochemical or neurological events independent of intervening behavioral events. (p. 207)

decision rules   Mathematical formulations for comparing choice alternatives based on weighted combinations of selected variables. (p. 250)

declarative learning   Acquisition of factual knowledge that can be stated as specific verbal propositions or clear visual images; compare with procedural learning. (p. 192)

deduction   Process of testing truth or falsity of scientific hypotheses and predictions by going from a general principle (an "if . . . then" statement) to a particular instance. (p. 5)

demand characteristics   Those aspects of an experiment enabling subjects to determine what is expected of them. (p. 10)

dependent variable   Behavior (response) observed by the experimenter. (p. 9)

descriptive analysis   Describing how judgments and decisions are made, regardless of their accuracy or rationality. (p. 244)

descriptive statistics   Statistical summaries of data obtained from a sample of observations. (p. 48)

diathesis-stress   The etiological model in which psychopathology is seen as arising from a person's vulnerability (diathesis) interacting with stressful environments. (p. 307)

dichotic listening task   One message is presented to one ear and a different message is presented to the other ear. The subject is asked to pay attention to one of the messages but is unexpectedly asked to recall the "unattended" message. (p. 230)

difference threshold   Change in value of a physical stimulus that is noticeable 50 percent of the time (sometimes referred to as just-noticeable difference). (p. 92)

diffusion of responsibility   In studies of bystander helping behavior, the larger the number of bystanders, the longer it took for an individual to act. (p. 286)

discrimination   The narrowing of learned behavior to stimuli associated with reinforcement. (p. 127)

dishabituation   Restoration of responding to a habituated stimulus by introducing a new stimulus that does not itself elicit the target response. (p. 142)

disjunctive rule   A concept defined by the occurrence of a specified level of either of two relevant dimensions (e.g., objects that are either striped or square); defined by the relationship "or," as in "striped" *or* "square." (p. 189)

dissyllable   Label applied to both words and nonwords used in verbal learning studies. (p. 174)

distractor techniques   Use of an irrelevant activity (such as counting backwards by 3s) following presentation of the to-be-recalled material; designed to prevent rehearsal during the retention interval. (p. 210)

double-blind   A procedure in which neither the experimenter who has contact with the subjects nor the subjects themselves are informed as to the experimental condition to which they have been assigned. (pp. 10, 323)

E

echoic memory   Information retained in auditory sensory memory. (p. 218)

empiricism   The view that our perceptions are derived from learning experiences. (p. 84)

encoding specificity   The relation between cues at presentation and cues at recall; when the cues are the same, performance is better and when the cues are changed, recall decreases. (p. 222)

environmental psychology   Study of environmental influences on behavior. (p. 285)

episodic memory   The records of an individual's personal experiences. (p. 221)

ethologist   Scientist who specializes in the naturalistic observation of behavior. (p. 123)

etiology   The causal development of any form of psychopathology. In psychopathology there are usually multiple factors involved in etiology. (p. 297)

excitation   Stimulus control that produces learned behavior. (p. 127)

experimental method   Research method characterized by the manipulation of one or more variables and the control of all others. (p. 7)

experimental psychology   Basic methods, procedures, and analytic tools used in the scientific study of behavior; sometimes defined as a set of basic topics such as perception, learning, and memory. (p. 4)

experimenter bias How experimenters' expectations about the results of an experiment may affect the measurement and treatment of data (sometimes referred to as "the Rosenthal effect"). (p. 10)

explicit memory The conscious recollection of specific events in one's life. (p. 228)

explicitly unpaired control A suggested Pavlovian conditioning control procedure in which CSs and USs can never co-occur. (p. 129)

external validity Extent to which the results of a laboratory study apply to conditions that exist in the real world (sometimes referred to as "ecological validity") (pp. 11, 252)

extinction A decrease in the strength of a learned response due to the discontinuation of reinforcement. (p. 126)

extradimensional shift A two-stage concept transfer task in which the relevant dimension is changed from the first task to the second task (e.g., from shape to size). (p. 190)

extraneous variables Variables other than manipulated (independent) variables with potential effects on behavior. (p. 27)

F

factorial design More than one independent variable is manipulated and all combinations of the selected levels of the independent variables are included (e.g., 3×2 design means that 6 combinations are formed by combining 3 levels of Variable A with 2 levels of Variable B). (p. 37)

field experiment Use of the experimental method, including random assignment of subjects to conditions, in a naturalistic setting. (pp. 11, 29, 286)

flashbulb memory The long-term retention of detailed information associated with an event of extreme importance. (p. 230)

food aversion learning A tendency to form a reluctance to eat foods paired with illness—even with long delays between eating the foods and the later sickness that ensues. (p. 148)

formal discipline Early theory of learning stating that simple mental exercise sharpens the mind. (p. 185)

free recall The subject is presented with a list of items and is asked to recall as many of the items as possible in any order. This task is especially useful for studying how subjects organize material. (p. 178)

functional dissociation Distinguishing between different types of memory by showing that they are influenced by different independent variables. (p. 210)

functional fixity Difficulties experienced in discovering new uses for old tools in solving problems. (p. 263)

functional memory How memorial processes affect later impressions, judgments, and decisions. This is to be distinguished from reproductive memory, which is the literal reproduction or recognition of the to-be-remembered material. (p. 231)

G

generalization The spread of learned behavior to untrained stimuli. (p. 127)

H

habituation Reduced reactivity to a repeated stimulus. (p. 141)

Hawthorne Effect Based on a series of studies on worker productivity that were conducted over a 12-year period at the Hawthorne facilities of Western Electric starting in the late 1920s, the term Hawthorne Effect refers to the influence of social factors that are confounded with independent variables and determine the outcome of a study by altering the social meaning of the independent variables and, perhaps, by enhancing the morale of subjects. (p. 319)

heuristics A variety of simplifying rules or strategies used in judgment, decision making, and problem solving. (p. 246)

hypothesis testing Using data from samples to test whether populations are the same or different. (p. 53)

I

iconic memory Information retained in visual sensory memory. (p. 218)

imagery Words that readily evoke distinct images are better remembered because they are easier to encode. (p. 227)

implicit memory Information from the past that can be retrieved without making any conscious effort. (p. 228)

imprinting The formation of a strong attachment to the parents often shown by young birds shortly after hatching. (p. 149)

incremental learning Assumption that learning of the associative connection between items improves gradually over trials. (p. 181)

independent events Events for which the occurrence of one does not change the likelihood of another. (p. 52)

independent random group design Between-subjects design in which subjects are assigned at random to different levels of the independent variable. (p. 34)

independent variable Variable manipulated by the experimenter. (p. 9)

induction Deriving a general principle from a series of specific observations. (p. 5)

inferential statistics The process of inference by which characteristics of populations are learned by analyzing the characteristics of samples taken from the populations. (p. 48)

information frame In judgment and decision making, presenting the same information in either positive or negative terms. (p. 249)

informed consent An ethical principle in research with humans whereby potential participants are informed of the nature of the study before agreeing to participate. (p. 20)

inhibition Stimulus control that reduces learned behavior. (p. 127)

inhibition of delay The hypothesized tendency for the early portion of a long CS-US interval to suppress the incidence of Pavlovian CRs. (p. 127)

instinctive drift The breakdown of well-learned response sequences due to the apparent intrusion of species-typical behaviors. (p. 150)

interaction Statistical measure of the extent to which the effect of one variable differs at different levels of another variable. (p. 38)

interference "Active" component of forgetting; retention loss assumed to be due to other behavioral events such as learning other material. (p. 207)

internal validity Extent to which a study is free of biasing or uncontrolled influences. (p. 10)

interval schedule Consequences follow the first response after finite periods of time. (p. 134)

intervening variable A theoretical or mediating process between manipulated independent variables and recorded dependent variables; e.g., hunger might be hypothesized to bridge changes in food deprivation and amount of food eaten. (p. 158)

intradimensional shift A two-stage concept transfer task in which the relevant dimension is the same for both tasks but the correct attribute of that dimension is changed (e.g., from square to triangle). (p. 190)

isolation effect *See* von Restorff effect. (p. 177)

L

law of constant proportionality The average amount of increase in performance on each trial of a learning task is often approximately a constant fraction of the amount left to be learned. (p. 181)

law of effect Responses in some situations are strengthened or weakened by their consequences. (p. 130)

learned helplessness A hypothesized psychological state that results from the prolonged receipt of aversive stimuli independent of behavior. (p. 139)

learning-memory distinction The study of learning emphasizes the acquisition of new information; the study of memory emphasizes the retention of old information. (p. 166)

learning set A propensity to learn that itself is acquired through specific experience. (p. 144)

level of significance Choice of acceptable Type I error rate (designated α) based on consideration of relative consequences of Type I and Type II errors. (p. 54)

levels of processing The assumption that memory is dependent on the level or depth of information processing; deep processing leads to good memory. (p. 217)

lexical decision task Subjects are asked to decide as quickly as possible whether a string of letters is a word. (p. 196)

longitudinal study Study in which the same individual is followed over a long period of time. (pp. 36, 230, 312)

M

magnitude estimation Scaling method where subjects assign numbers to stimuli such that the ratio of any two numbers corresponds to the ratio of the stimulus magnitude. (p. 109)

manipulation checks Attempts to verify operational definitions of independent variable manipulations. (p. 283)

matched pairs design Assigning subjects to one of two conditions by taking two subjects with approximately the same value on a predetermined subject variable and randomly assigning one member of the pair to one condition and the other to the other condition. (p. 35)

matching Assigning subjects to conditions in a between-subjects design by equating the conditions on selected subject variables. (p. 33)

matching-to-sample A procedure in which the correct choice alternative is the one that matches a prior or present stimulus called the sample. (p. 146)

mean learning curve Plot of mean performance level over successive learning trials, usually showing that absolute improvement in learning scores becomes smaller as the number of trials increases. (p. 181)

meaningfulness A measure of the extent to which a word or syllable evokes associations (e.g., the mean number of associations produced in 60 sec). (p. 173)

mediation Use of an interpolated association learned or naturally occurring to facilitate later learning. (p. 187)

memory scanning Procedure for studying recognition memory in which the experimenter shows a single test item and the subject indicates whether it was one of the items from a previously presented list. (p. 219)

memory span Subjects are asked to recall all of the items on a short list of items. (p. 212)

memory trace A hypothesized process that may link prior presentation of an event with the later behavioral control that it exerts; the trace may grow as stimulus presentation time increases and fade as the time since stimulus offset increases. (p. 159)

memory-based judgments Judgments are required at a later time based on information that the subject does not originally think requires a judgment. This is to be contrasted with on-line judgments, which are made immediately following presentation of the information. (p. 232)

meta-analysis A quantitative method for combining the results of many different studies of the same phenomenon. (p. 57)

method of indirect proof Strategy underlying hypothesis testing, by which the alternative hypothesis is supported when the null hypothesis is discredited. (p. 53)

mnemonics Highly stylized memory aids such as the method of loci, the pegword method, and the keyword method. (p. 229)

mnemonist A memory expert. (p. 228)

modality effect Comparison of recall when items are presented in the auditory or visual mode. (p. 215)

motor fatigue Reduced responsivity of muscles after repeated exertion. (p. 141)

multidimensional scaling Measuring the contribution of each dimension in perceiving and evaluating stimuli that differ along several different dimensions. (p. 109)

multiple correlation coefficient Correlation between the observed values of Y and the values of Y predicted by the multiple regression equation. (p. 77)

multiple regression equation Equation predicting the value of a criterion variable (Y) on the basis of a weighted linear combination of predictor variables (Xs). (p. 77)

multiple-trial free recall (MTFR) Presentation of the same free recall list several times, usually in a different presentation order each time, to study associations and interrelations among words in the list. (p. 178)

multistore models Conceptualization of a multistructure memory storage system, such as a three-component model of sensory register, short-term store, and long-term store. (p. 215)

mutually exclusive events Two events that cannot occur simultaneously. (p. 52)

N

nativism The proposition that our perceptions are guided by innate processes. (p. 84)

natural concept A tendency for responding to be controlled by classes of objects—like cats, flowers, cars, and chairs—that are both broad (they comprise limitless individual influences) and circumscribed (they are readily distinguishable from other categories of objects) and are labeled by humans with simple (unmodified) nouns. (p. 146)

natural language mediators Natural language habits (e.g., learned associations between words) that help subjects in new learning situations. (p. 187)

naturalistic observation Observations of behavior conducted in a naturalistic setting without any intervention on the part of the investigator. (pp. 7, 120)

negative punishment A response is weakened by its removing an event. (p. 134)

negative reinforcement A response is strengthened by its removing an event. (p. 134)

network models Models of learning based on the interconnections between concepts. (p. 195)

nodes Facts and concepts represented within semantic network models. (p. 195)

nonassociative learning Behavioral change that results from the repeated occurrence of only one class of events, as in habituation and sensitization. (p. 140)

nonequivalent controls Control groups in a quasi-experiment that cannot be precisely equated because of lack of random assignments to conditions. (p. 255)

nonparametric tests Statistical tests of significance that do not rely on assumptions about the form of sampling distributions (also called *distribution-free tests*). (p. 70)

nonspecific therapeutic factors Factors that are likely to influence therapeutic outcome but are not unique to a specific therapy such as professional contact and client expectations to improve. (p. 316)

nonspecific transfer Facilitative effects of prior experience on new learning attributed to the acquisition of highly generalizable habits and skills. (p. 185)

normative analysis Comparing judgments and decisions to a prescribed level of accuracy or optimality. (p. 241)

nosology The study of the classification of diseases. Within psychopathology, it refers to the study of the classification of psychological or psychiatric disorders. Nosological classification systems use a categorical approach rather than a continuum approach to diagnosis and the classification of diseases. (p. 314)

null hypothesis Hypothesis initially assumed true; usually the hypothesis of no effect of the variable of interest. (p. 53)

O

one-tailed test The critical region is concentrated at one end of the distribution of a statistical test. (p. 55)

on-line judgments Judgments made immediately following presentation of the relevant information; to be contrasted with memory-based judgments, which are required at a later time. (p 232)

operational definitions Explicit definitions of independent and dependent variables in terms of how they are manipulated or measured. (p. 28)

order effects The effects of order of presentation of information on judgments and decisions. (p. 245)

outcome research Research designed to determine the outcome of a clinical intervention, such as determining whether a therapeutic approach is effective or comparing the effectiveness of different approaches. (p. 314)

P

paired-associate list learning Pairs of items are presented with one item of the pair serving as the stimulus and the other item as the response. This task is especially useful for studying the formation of associations between stimuli and responses. (p. 177)

parallel distributed processing (PDP) In network models of memory based on the principle of "connectionism," a number of nodes must be activated together to represent a particular idea or concept. (p. 197)

parallel processing Hypothesis that the subject can simultaneously examine all of the items in short-term memory at one time. (p. 219)

paralogs Pronounceable syllables that look like words but are not. (p. 174)

Pavlovian conditioning An associative learning procedure in which two different kinds of events are temporally paired with one another irrespective of the organism's behavior. (p. 135)

perceptual constancy Recognizing an object in different perspectives. (p. 84)

person perception The way we categorize persons in terms of their attitudes, behavior, physical appearance, etc. (p. 280)

personality impression formation Tasks in which judgments of likability of persons are related to characteristics such as personality traits. (p. 244)

phonologic loop Hypothesized component of working memory in which sensory information is coded in terms of speech that can be repeated or rehearsed. (p. 219)

pilot study Preliminary data collected to refine materials and procedures before conducting the main study. (p. 17)

placebo A control condition in which the subjects are administered a treatment comprised of inert ingredients (such as in a drug study) or no identified effective components but are lead to believe that the treatment has active ingredients. (p. 317)

placebo effect How subjects' behavior is influenced by their belief that they are being "treated" (e.g., given a drug). (p. 10)

planned comparisons Statistical tests designed to answer specific questions about differences between experimental conditions; trend tests relating mean values on the dependent variable to successive levels of the independent variable are examples. (p. 62)

positive punishment A response is weakened by its producing an event. (p. 134)

positive reinforcement A response is strengthened by its producing an event. (p. 134)

post hoc comparisons Statistical comparisons between experimental conditions that arise after the data have been collected. (p. 62)

precriterion stationarity If learning of a stimulus-response association is all-or-none, then for each item there is a constant (chance) level of probability of being correct prior to the trial of last error. (p. 182)

primacy effect In free-recall, performance is better on the initial items than on later items. (p. 213)

priming Prior exposure to a stimulus item (usually a word) or a closely related associate facilitates later processing (e.g., identification of a word in a lexical decision task) or memory of the item. (p. 196)

Prisoners' Dilemma Experimental analysis of cooperation vs. competition in which one person's rewards or punishments depend on another's as well as on his or her own responses. (p. 284)

proactive inhibition Decrement in recall of a second list attributed to the prior learning of the first list. (p. 208)

proactive interference/facilitation The effect of a prior task on the retention of a second task, studied by comparing the performance of an experimental group that receives both tasks with the performance of a control group that receives only the second task. (p. 185)

probability The long-range likelihood that a particular event will occur. (p. 51)

probe techniques Sampling procedures in which different parts of a list of to-be-recalled material are tested at different times. (p. 211)

procedural learning Acquisition of a skill or action such as typing or juggling; knowledge is demonstrated by performance rather than by descriptive statements; compare with declarative learning. (p. 192)

process research Research designed to determine why a therapy is effective, i.e., what are the important components of the therapy? (p. 314)

programmatic research A series of studies on a given topic. (p. 12)

psychometric scaling Measuring abstract affective dimensions with no well-defined physical values. (p. 105)

psychophysical scaling Measuring the relation between subjective scale values and corresponding physical values. (p. 84)

psychophysics Relation between internal sensations and external properties of stimuli. (p. 92)

punisher A consequence of responding that makes the response less likely to recur. (p. 130)

puzzle box Thorndike's original conditioning apparatus in which performance of the required response permitted the animal to escape from the box and get food. (p. 129)

p-value Probability that the results of a statistical test were due to chance. (p. 55)

Q

quasi-experimental design Attempt to approximate a true experiment in a naturalistic setting. (pp. 9, 255)

R

random control A suggested Pavlovian conditioning control procedure in which CSs and USs are presented independently of one another; unlike the explicitly unpaired control, occasional co-occurrence is possible. (p. 129)

random sample Sample in which each individual in the population has an equal chance of being selected. (p. 49)

randomization Method of assigning subjects to experimental conditions such that each subject has an equal chance of being selected for any given condition. (p. 29)

randomized blocks design Extension of the matched pairs design to more than two experimental conditions. (p. 35)

ratio schedule Consequences follow finite numbers of responses. (p. 133)

reacquisition Acquisition of a conditioned response that follows previous acquisition and extinction. (p. 126)

reaction time (RT) Time between presentation of a test stimulus and the response. (pp. 89, 219)

recall method *See* study-test method. (p. 175)

recall tests Tests of memory in which the subject has to produce the appropriate response. (p. 224)

receiver-operating-characteristic (ROC) curve Plot of hit rate against false alarm rate for varying decision criteria in signal detection. (p. 101)

recency effect In free-recall, performance is better on the last few items than on the preceding items. (p. 213)

recognition tests Tests of memory in which the subject has to pick out the appropriate response from a set of possible responses. (p. 224)

reextinction Extinction of a conditioned response that follows previous acquisition, extinction, and acquisition. (p. 126)

regression line Line that best fits a "scatter diagram" plotting pairs of values on a two-dimensional graph (also known as *prediction line* or *line of best fit*). (p. 72)

regression to the mean When predicting Y from X based on the correlation between X and Y, the predicted value of Y will be less extreme (fewer standard deviation units from the mean) than the value of X. (p. 76)

reinforcer A consequence of responding that makes the response more likely to recur. (p. 126)

reliability An estimate of the replicability of a test score. There are several types of reliability including alternate forms or interrater reliability (agreement between two sources at the same time), test-retest reliability (agreement over a specified period of time), and internal consistency (e.g., split-half reliability). (pp. 40, 107, 300)

representativeness In decision making, heuristic in which people predict the outcome that appears most representative of, or similar to, the evidence. (p. 246)

retention interval The time between the end of the presentation of a to-be-recalled list and the beginning of the test of recall. (p. 215)

retroactive inhibition Decrement in recall of an initial list attributed to the interpolated learning of a second list. (p. 208)

retroactive interference/facilitation The effect of an interpolated task on the later retention of a task learned earlier, studied by comparing the performance of groups that do and do not receive the interpolated task. (p. 185)

risky decision making Decisions involving possible losses where the likelihood of achieving the best outcome may be relatively low. (p. 248)

risky shift Tendency for an interacting group to choose a risky alternative more often than expected from prediscussion individual decisions. (p. 290)

running memory span Subjects, presented with a list of items, are stopped at some point and asked to recall as many items backward in the list as possible. (p. 213)

S

sampling distribution Distribution of values of a statistic such as the mean for different samples from the same population. (p. 51)

savings score Percentage reduction in number of trials to relearn a task that was previously learned. (p. 207)

schedule of reinforcement An explicit rule according to which consequences follow responses. (p. 133)

selective attention Focusing of attention on one channel of information while ignoring others. (p. 84)

semantic differential A measure of the connotative meaning of a word based on ratings of the word on a series of bipolar scales. (p. 174)

semantic memory The accumulated information and rules necessary for the use of language. (p. 221)

sensitive period A period of development during which experiences are particularly likely to change behavior. (p. 149)

sensitization Increased reactivity to a repeated stimulus. (p. 142)

sensory adaptation Reduced responsivity by sensory receptors after repeated stimulation. (p. 141)

serial list learning Task designed to study the acquisition of items in serial order. Subjects have to learn a list of items in the exact order in which the items are presented. (p. 175)

serial position curve The number of errors or correct responses in a serial list learning task is plotted for each serial position. The typical result is a bowed curve where performance is best for the items at the beginning of the list and at the end, and worst for items in the middle. (p. 175)

serial processing Hypothesis that the subject can examine only one item in the memory set at a time. (p. 219)

set Prior expectancy based on repeated experience with a class of stimuli. (pp. 86, 261)

shaping The conditioning of rare behavior through a series of successive approximations to the final act; reinforcement is contingent on responses increasingly like the target topography. (p. 132)

single subject design Each individual subject is treated differently or there is only one subject (this latter instance is sometimes referred to as a "case study"). (p. 36)

Skinner box Skinner's modification of the puzzle box that permitted responses to have consequences without requiring the animal to leave the conditioning chamber. (p. 131)

social facilitation The enhancement of a dominant response when other people are present. (p. 287)

social roles Roles assigned according to society's expectations of a person with a particular job, sex, race, age, etc. (p. 278)

somatic activity Activity of the voluntary or striated musculature. (p. 326)

specific transfer Effects of prior experience on new learning attributed to the similarity between the stimuli or the responses on the two tasks. (p. 185)

spontaneous recovery Resurgence of an extinguished CR without the introduction of CS-US pairings; a period of time away from the conditioning situation may bring about spontaneous recovery. (p. 126)

spontaneous remission The elimination or alleviation of a disorder in the absence of any active treatment program. In clinical research, it refers to improvement in control-group subjects who are waiting to be treated or diseases that naturally heal without treatment. (p. 316)

spreading activation In explaining how information is retrieved in memory, the assumption in network models that when a node is stimulated, nearby nodes are also activated. (p. 195)

standard error Standard deviation of a sampling distribution of a statistic such as the mean. (p. 51)

state dependent retrieval Memory is improved when recall and learning occur in the same context such as the same emotional mood or drug state. (p. 222)

statement of hypothesis Formal expression of a proposal for a research project. (p. 12)

statistically significant Results of a statistical test leading to rejection of the null hypothesis. (p. 55)

steady-state memory test Subjects are required to make repeated continuous demands on memory, such as being presented with a long series of paired-associate items. (p. 213)

stimulus integration Tasks in which the subject has to make a single judgment based on several stimulus values (also known as *information integration* tasks). (p. 112)

study-test method List learning method in which the subject studies each item in the list without responding and is then asked to recall all items in the list without being prompted (also called the *recall method*). (p. 175)

subject bias How subjects' beliefs about what they should do in an experiment affect their responses. (p. 10)

subject population Target group of subjects for a study. (p. 15)

subject variables Extraneous variables pertaining to subject characteristics. (p. 27)

subjective organization (SO) The tendency to recall items in a free-recall list together in the same order even when they are presented in a different order on each trial. (p. 178)

superstitious behavior Apparent Thorndikian conditioning without any real connection between response and consequence. (p. 138)

T

tabula rasa John Locke's assertion that the mind starts out as a blank slate upon which experience writes its messages. (p. 168)

temporal conditioning A Pavlovian conditioning procedure in which the US is delivered at regular temporal intervals without any external CS being given. (p. 127)

theory Explanations or predictions of observable behavior based on unobservable states. (p. 6)

Thorndikian conditioning An associative learning procedure in which an organism's own behavior affects the occurrence of events of potential importance to it. (p. 138)

time-lag methods Studying changes in attitude and behavior across a relatively long period of time (also known as *longitudinal methods*). (p. 291)

"tip of the tongue" When you are unable to recall something that you're sure you know but can't seem to get out. (p. 222)

trigrams Three-letter units used in verbal learning studies. (p. 174)

twin study The comparison of concordance for a given form of psychopathology in monozygotic twins versus dizygotic twins. *See also* Zygosity. (p. 303)

two-process theory The idea that there are two different kinds of learning that eventuate from Pavlovian and Thorndikian conditioning procedures. (p. 139)

two-tailed test The critical region is divided between both ends of the distribution of a statistical test. (p. 55)

Type I error Rejecting a true null hypothesis. (p. 54)

Type II error Retaining a false null hypothesis. (p. 54)

U

unconditioned response A response that is unconditionally elicited by an unconditioned stimulus. (p. 125)

unconditioned stimulus A stimulus that unconditionally elicits a response. (p. 125)

utility maximization Principle stating that a rational decision maker will choose the alternative with the highest "expected value" (probability of a gain times amount to be gained). (p. 241)

V

validity The degree to which a test measures what it is said to measure. There are several types of validity: in criterion-oriented validity the test need only predict the criterion; construct validity applies when a test is presumed to measure a psychological construct that has theoretical meaning. (pp. 40, 108, 300)

verbal assessment Measurement of the characteristics (e.g., frequency) of the materials used to study verbal learning and memory. (p. 169)

verbal discrimination The subject is presented with a set (e.g., a pair) of stimulus items and is asked to pick out the item that the experimenter designates as correct. This task is especially useful for studying the effects of frequency on learning. (p. 179)

verbal protocols "Think aloud" techniques used to analyze the strategies people use while reaching decisions or solving problems. (p. 256)

von Restorff effect A distinctive item within a list (e.g., one printed in a different color from the rest) is generally learned more rapidly than adjacent items (also called the **isolation effect**). (p. 177)

W

Weber's fraction Ratio of the value of a difference threshold to the value of the standard stimulus. (p. 96)

within-subject designs Experimental designs in which each subject receives every level of the independent variable (also known as *repeated measures designs*). (p. 29)

word association tests Used for testing verbal associations to words, usually the first response, e.g., table-chair, black-white, up-down. (p. 173)

working memory Another name for short-term memory store; emphasizes manipulation of current information. (p. 216)

Y

yoked control A control procedure for Thorndikian/Skinnerian conditioning in which the same pattern of stimulation is given to a control subject that is given to a master subject, but without the yoked control subject exerting any influence on the pattern of stimulation. (p. 135)

Z

zygosity The characteristics of a fertilized egg in sexual reproduction. In twin studies used to distinguish between monozygotic twins, who derive from a single zygote and thus have an identical genetic inheritance, and dizygotic twins, who derive from two different zygotes and thus (like siblings) share 50 percent of their genes on the average. (p. 304)

References

A

Abramson, L. Y., Seligman, M. E. P., & Teasdale, J. D. (1978). Learned helplessness in humans: Critique and reformulation. *Journal of Abnormal Psychology, 87,* 49–74.

Allport, G. W. (1935). Attitudes. In C. Muchison (Ed.), *Handbook of Social Psychology* (Vol. 2). Worchester, MA: Clark University Press.

American Psychiatric Association (1994). *Diagnostic and statistical manual of mental disorders* (4th ed., rev.). Washington, D.C.: Author.

Anastasi, A. (1988). *Psychological testing* (6th ed.). New York: Macmillan.

Anderson, J. R. (Ed.). (1981). *Cognitive skills and their acquisition.* Hillsdale, NJ: Erlbaum.

Anderson, J. R. (1983). *The architecture of cognition.* Cambridge, MA: Harvard University Press.

Anderson, J. R. (1990). *Cognitive psychology and its implications* (3rd ed.). New York: Freeman.

Anderson, N. H. (1968). Likableness ratings of 555 personality-trait words. *Journal of Personality and Social Psychology, 9,* 272–279.

Anderson, N. H. (1972). Cross-task validation of functional measurement. *Perception & Psychophysics, 12,* 389–395.

Anderson, N. H. (1991). Functional memory in person cognition. In N. H. Anderson (Ed.), *Contributions to information integration theory. Vol. I: Cognition* (pp. 1–55). Hillsdale, NJ: Erlbaum.

Anderson, N. H., & Cuneo, D. O. (1978). The height + width rule in children's judgments of quantity. *Journal of Experimental Psychology: General, 107,* 335–378.

Anderson, N. S. (1960). Poststimulus cuing in immediate memory. *Journal of Experimental Psychology, 60,* 216–221.

Archer, E. J. (1960). A re-evaluation of the meaningfulness of all possible CVC trigrams. *Psychological Monographs, 74* (1, Whole No. 497).

Arkes, H. R., & Blumer, C. (1985). The psychology of sunk cost. *Organizational Behavior and Human Performance, 35,* 129–140.

Aronson, E., Turner, J. A., & Carlsmith, J. M. (1963). Communicator credibility and communicator discrepancy as determinants of opinion change. *Journal of Abnormal and Social Psychology, 67,* 31–36.

Asch, S. E. (1951). Effects of group pressure upon the modification and distortion of judgment. In H. Guetzkow (Ed.), *Groups, leadership, and men.* Pittsburgh: Carnegie.

Ashmead, D. H., Hill, E. W., & Talor, C. R. (1989). Obstacle perception by congenitally blind children. *Perception & Psychophysics, 46,* 425–433.

Asratyan, E. A. (1953). *I. P. Pavlov: His life and work.* Moscow: Foreign Languages Publishing House.

Astley, S. L., & Wasserman, E. A. (1992). Categorical discrimination and generalization in pigeons: All negative stimuli are not created equal. *Journal of Experimental Psychology: Animal Behavior Processes, 18,* 193–207.

Atkinson, R. C. (1975). Mnemotechnics in second-language learning. *American Psychologist, 30,* 821–828.

Atkinson, R. C., & Shiffrin, R. M. (1965). Mathematical models for memory and learning. Technical Report Number 79, Institute for Mathematical Studies in the Social Sciences, Stanford University.

Atkinson, R. C., & Shiffrin, R. M. (1968). Human memory: A proposed system and its control processes. In K. W. Spence (Ed.), *The psychology of learning and motivation: Advances in research and theory* (Vol. 2, pp. 89–195). New York: Academic Press.

Atkinson, R. C., & Shiffrin, R. M. (1971). The control of short-term memory. *Scientific American, 225,* 82–90.

B

Baddeley, A. D. (1978). The trouble with levels: A re-examination of Craik and Lockhart's framework for memory research. *Psychological Review, 85,* 139–152.

Baddeley, A. D. (1990). *Human memory: Theory and practice.* Boston: Allyn & Bacon.

Bandura, A. (1969). *Principles of behavior modification.* New York: Holt, Rinehart & Winston.

Banks, W. P., & Coleman, M. J. (1981). Two subjective scales of number. *Perception & Psychophysics, 29,* 95–105.

Barlow, D. H., Cohen, A. S., Waddell, M. T., Vermilyea, B. B., Klosko, J. S., Blanchard, E. B., & Nardo, P. A. (1984). Panic and generalized anxiety disorders: Nature and treatment. *Behavior Therapy, 15,* 431–444.

Barlow, D. H., Mavissakalian, M. R., & Schofield, L. D. (1980). Patterns of desynchrony in agoraphobia: A preliminary report. *Behavior Research & Therapy, 18,* 441–448.

Baron, R. A., & Byrne, D. (1987). *Social psychology* (5th ed.). Newton, MA: Allyn & Bacon.

Baron, R. M., Mandel, D. R., Adams, C. A., & Griffen, L. M. (1976). Effects of social density in university residential environments. *Journal of Personality and Social Psychology, 34,* 434–446.

Beck, A. T. (1967). *Depression: Causes and treatment.* Philadelphia: University of Pennsylvania Press.

Beck, A. T. (1974). The development of depression: A cognitive model. In R. J. Friedman & M. M. Katz (Eds.), *The psychology of depression: Contemporary theory and research* (pp. 3–27). Washington, D.C.: Halstead Press.

Beck, A. T. (1983). Cognitive therapy of depression: New perspectives. In P. J. Clayton & J. E. Barrett (Eds.), *Treatment of depression: Old controversies and new approaches* (pp. 265–284). New York: Raven Press.

Beck, A. T., Rush, A. J., Shaw, B. F., & Emery, G. (1979). *Cognitive therapy for depression* (pp. 1–33). New York: Guilford Press.

Beck, A. T., Ward, C. H., Mendelson, M., Mock, J., & Erbaugh, J. (1961). An inventory for measuring depression. *Archives of General Psychiatry, 4,* 561–571.

Berger, A. M., Knutson, J. F., Mehm, J. G., & Perkins, K. A. (1988). The self-report of punitive childhood experiences of young adults and adolescents. *Child Abuse & Neglect, 12,* 251–262.

Bettman, J. R., Johnson, E. J., & Payne, J. W. (1989). Consumer decision making. In H. H. Kassarjian & T. S. Robertson (Eds.), *Handbook of consumer theory and research.* Engelwood Cliffs, NJ: Prentice Hall.

Bhatt, R. S., Wasserman, E. A., Reynolds, W. F., Jr., & Knauss, K. S. (1988). Conceptual behavior in pigeons: Categorization of both familiar and novel examples from four classes of natural and artificial stimuli. *Journal of Experimental Psychology: Animal Behavior Processes, 14,* 219–234.

Bickman, L., Teger, A., Gabriele, T., McLaughlin, C., Berger, M., & Sunaday, E. (1973). Dormitory density and helping behavior. *Environment and Behavior, 5,* 465–490.

Bierce, A. (1941). *The devil's dictionary.* Cleveland: World Publishing, p. 76.

Bijou, S. W., & Baer, D. M. (1967). *Child development: Readings in experimental analysis.* New York: Appleton-Century-Crofts.

Bitterman, M. E. (1960). Toward a comparative psychology of learning. *American Psychologist, 15,* 704–712.

Bitterman, M. E. (1965). The evolution of intelligence. *Scientific American, 212,* 92–100.

Bitterman, M. E. (1965). Phyletic differences in learning. *American Psychologist, 20,* 396–410.

Bitterman, M. E. (1975). The comparative analysis of learning. *Science, 188,* 699–709.

Bjork, R. A. (1972). Theoretical implications of directed forgetting. In A. W. Melton & E. Martin (Eds.), *Coding processes in human memory* (pp. 217–235). Washington, D.C.: V. H. Winston.

Boakes, R. (1984). *From Darwin to Behaviorism: Psychology and the minds of animals*. Cambridge: Cambridge University Press.

Boring, E. G., Langfeld, H. S., & Weld, H. P. (1948). *Foundations of psychology*. New York: Wiley.

Borkovec, T. D., & Fowles, D. C. (1973). Controlled investigation of the effects of progressive and hypnotic relaxation on insomnia. *Journal of Abnormal Psychology 82*, 153–158.

Borkovec, T. D., & Mathews, A. M. (1988). Treatment of nonphobic anxiety disorders: A comparison of nondirective, cognitive, and coping desensitization therapy. *Journal of Consulting and Clinical Psychology, 56*, 877–884.

Borkovec, T. D., Mathews, A. M., Chambers, A., Ebrahimi, S., Lytle, R., & Nelson, R. (1987). The effects of relaxation training with cognitive or nondirective therapy and the role of relaxation-induced anxiety in the treatment of generalized anxiety. *Journal of Consulting and Clinical Psychology, 55*, 883–888.

Bourne, L. E., Jr. (1970). Knowing and using concepts. *Psychological Review, 77*, 546–556.

Bousfield, W. A., & Cohen, B. H. (1953). The effects of reinforcement on the occurrence of clustering in the recall of randomly arranged associates. *Journal of Psychology, 36*, 67–81.

Bousfield, W. A., & Cohen, B. H. (1956). Clustering in recall as a function of the number of word-categories in stimulus-word lists. *Journal of General Psychology, 54*, 95–106.

Bower, G. H. (1961) Application of a model to paired-associate learning. *Psychometrika, 26*, 255–280.

Bower, G. H. (1962). An association model for response and training variables in paired-associate learning. *Psychological Review, 69*, 34–53.

Bower, G. H. (1981). Mood and memory. *American Psychologist, 36*, 129–148.

Bower, G. H., & Hilgard, E. R. (1981). *Theories of learning* (5th ed.). Englewood Cliffs, NJ: Prentice Hall.

Bradshaw, J. L. (1984). A guide to norms, ratings, and lists. *Memory & Cognition, 12*, 202–206.

Breland, K., & Breland, M. (1961). The misbehavior of organisms. *American Psychologist, 16*, 681–684.

Brewer, M. B. (1979). In-group bias in the minimal intergroup situation: A cognitive-motivational analysis. *Psychological Bulletin, 86*, 307–324.

Brookshire, K. H. (1970). Comparative psychology of learning. In M. H. Marx (Ed.), *Learning: Interactions* (pp. 291–364). London: Macmillan Company.

Brown, A. S. (1976). Catalog of scaled verbal material. *Memory & Cognition, 4*, 1S–45S.

Brown, J. (1958). Some tests of the decay theory of immediate memory. *Quarterly Journal of Experimental Psychology, 10*, 12–21.

Brown, R., & Kulik, J. (1977). Flashbulb memories. *Cognition, 5*, 73–99.

Brown, R., & McNeill, D. (1966). The "tip of the tongue" phenomenon. *Journal of Verbal Learning and Verbal Behavior, 5*, 325–337.

Bruce, M. L., Kim, K., Leaf, P. J., & Jacobs, S. (1990). Depressive episodes and dysphoria resulting from conjugal bereavement in a prospective community sample. *American Journal of Psychiatry, 147*, 608–611.

Bryceson, D. (1979). Life and death at Gombe. *National Geographic, 155*, 592–621.

Bugelski, B. R., & Alampay, D. A. (1964). The role of frequency in developing perceptual sets. *Canadian Journal of Psychology, 15*, 205–211.

Byrne, D., & Nelson, D. (1965). Attraction as a linear function of proportion of positive reinforcements. *Journal of Personality and Social Psychology, 1*, 659–663.

C

Calhoun, J. B. (1971). Space and the strategy of life. In A. H. Esser (Ed.), *Environment and behavior: The use of space by animals and men*. New York: Plenum.

Campbell, D. J. (1969). Reforms as experiments. *American Psychologist, 24*, 409–429.

Candland, D. K. (1968). *Psychology: The experimental approach*. New York: McGraw-Hill.

Cantor, N., & Mischel, W. (1979). Prototypicality and personality: Effects on free recall and personality impressions. *Journal of Research in Personality, 13*, 187–205.

Carew, T. J., & Sahley, C. L. (1986). Invertebrate learning and memory. *Annual Review of Neuroscience, 9*, 435–487.

Carter, D. E., & Werner, T. J. (1978). Complex learning and information processing by pigeons: A critical analysis. *Journal of the Experimental Analysis of Behavior, 29*, 565–601.

Chase, W. G., & Ericsson, K. A. (1982). Skill and working memory. In G. H. Bower (Ed.), *The psychology of learning and motivation* (Vol. 16). New York: Academic Press.

Chase, W. G., & Simon, H. A. (1973). Perception in chess. *Cognitive Psychology, 4,* 55–81.

Cohen, N. J., & Squire, L. R. (1980). Preserved learning and retention of pattern-analyzing skill in amnesia: Dissociation of knowing how and knowing that. *Science, 210,* 207–210.

Cohen, N. J., & Squire, L. R. (1981). Retrograde amnesia and remote memory impairment. *Neuropsychologia, 19,* 337–356.

Collins, A. M., & Loftus, E. F. (1975). A spreading-activation theory of semantic processing. *Psychological Review, 82,* 407–428.

Collins, A. M., & Quillian, M. R. (1969). Retrieval time from semantic memory. *Journal of Verbal Learning and Verbal Behavior, 8,* 240–247.

Conrad, R., & Hull, A. J. (1964). Information, acoustic confusion and memory span. *British Journal of Psychology, 55,* 429–432.

Cook, M., & Mineka, S. (1989). Observational conditioning of fear to fear-relevant versus fear-irrelevant stimuli in rhesus monkeys. *Journal of Abnormal Psychology, 98,* 448–459.

Corning, W., & Freed, S. (1968). Planarian behavior and biochemistry. *Nature, 219,* 1227–1230.

Craik, F. I. M. (1968). Short-term memory and the aging process. In G. A. Talland (Ed.), *Human aging and behavior* (pp. 131–168). New York: Academic Press.

Craik, F. I. M., & Lockhart, R. S. (1972). Levels of processing: A framework for memory research. *Journal of Verbal Learning and Verbal Behavior, 11,* 671–684.

Craik, F. I. M., & Tulving, E. (1975). Depth of processing and the retention of words in episodic memory. *Journal of Experimental Psychology: General, 104,* 268–294.

Cronbach, L. J. (1970). *Essentials of psychological testing* (3rd ed.). New York: Harper & Row.

Crowder, R. G. (1976). *Principals of learning and memory.* Hillsdale, NJ.: Erlbaum.

Crutchfield, R. A. (1955). Conformity and character. *American Psychologist, 10,* 191–198.

D

D'Amato, M. R., & Salmon, D. P. (1984). Processing of complex auditory stimuli (tunes) by rats and monkeys (*Cebus apella*). *Animal Learning & Behavior, 12,* 184–194.

D'Amato, M. R., Salmon, D. P., Loukas, E., & Tomie, A. (1986). Processing of identity and conditional relations in monkeys (*Cebus apella*) and pigeons (*Columba livia*). *Animal Learning & Behavior, 14,* 365–373.

Darley, J. M., & Latané, B. (1968, December). When will people help in a crisis? *Psychology Today,* 54–57, 70–71.

Darwin, C. (1859). *On the origin of species by means of natural selection.* London: Murray.

Darwin, C. (1920). *The descent of man; and selection in relation to sex* (2nd ed.). New York: D. Appleton and Company. (Original work published in 1871)

Darwin, C. J., Turvey, M. T., & Crowder, R. G. (1972). An auditory analogue of the Sperling partial report procedure: Evidence for brief auditory storage. *Cognitive Psychology, 3,* 255–267.

Davidson, A. R., & Jaccard, J. J. (1979). Variables that moderate the attitude-behavior relation: Results of a longitudinal survey. *Journal of Personality and Social Psychology, 37,* 1364–1376.

Dawes, R. M. (1988). *Rational choice in an uncertain world.* San Diego: Harcourt Brace Jovanovich.

Day, R. H. (1966). Perception. In J. A. Vernon (Ed.), *Introduction to psychology: A self-selection textbook.* Dubuque, IA: Wm. C. Brown.

Dember, W. N., & Warm, J. S. (1979). *Psychology of perception* (2nd ed.). New York: Holt, Rinehart & Winston.

Dent, J., & Teasdale, J. D. (1988). Negative cognition and the persistence of depression. *Journal of Abnormal Psychology, 97,* 29–34.

Deutsch, M. (1949). An experimental study of the effects of cooperation and competition upon group process. *Human Relations, 2,* 199–231.

Dickson, W. J., & Roethlisberger, F. J. (1966). Counseling in an organization: A sequel to the Hawthorne researches. Boston: Division of Research, Graduate School of Business Administration, Harvard University.

Dohr, K. B., Rush, A. J., and Bernstein, I. H. (1989). Cognitive biases and depression. *Journal of Abnormal Psychology, 98,* 263–267.

Donders, F. C. (1868). Over de snelheid van psychische processen. Onderzoekingen gadaan in het Physiologish Laboratorium der Utrichtsche Hoogeschool, 1868–1869, Tweede reeks, II, 92–120. Translated by W. G. Koster in W. G. Koster (Ed.) 1969. *Attention and performance II. Acta Psychologica, 30,* 412–431.

Doob, L. W. (1947). The behavior of attitudes. *Psychological Review, 54,* 135–156.

Duffy, E. (1962). *Activation and behavior.* New York: John Wiley and Sons.

Duncker, K. (1945). On problem solving. *Psychological Monographs, 58,* 1–112 (Whole No. 270).

E

Eastman, C. (1976). Behavioral formulations of depression. *Psychological Review, 83,* 277–291.

Ebbinghaus, H. (1885). *Über das Gedächtnis: Untersuchungen zur experimentellen psychologie.* Leipzig: Duncker & Humboldt. [Translated by H. A. Ruger & C. E. Bussenius (1913) as *Memory: A contribution to experimental psychology.* New York: Columbia Teacher's College. Reissued by Dover Publications, 1964.]

Edwards, C. A., & Honig, W. K. (1987). Memorization and "feature selection" in the acquisition of natural concepts in pigeons. *Learning and Motivation, 18,* 235–260.

Edwards, C. A., Miller, J. S., & Zentall, T. R. (1985). Control of pigeons' matching and mismatching performance by instructional cues. *Animal Learning & Behavior, 13,* 383–391.

Edwards, W. (1962). Dynamic decision theory and probabilistic information processing. *Human Factors, 4,* 59–73.

Egan, J. P., & Clarke, F. R. (1966). Sensation and perception. In J. B. Sidowski (Ed.), *Experimental methods and instrumentation in psychology.* New York: McGraw-Hill.

Eich, J. E. (1980). The cue-dependent nature of state-dependent retrieval. *Memory & Cognition, 8,* 157–173.

Eisenstein, E. M. (1967). The use of invertebrate systems for studies on the bases of learning and memory. In G. C. Quarton, T. Melnechuk, & F. O. Schmitt (Eds.), *The Neurosciences* (pp. 653–665). New York: Rockefeller University Press.

Eisenstein, E. M., & Cohen, M. J. (1965). Learning in an isolated prothoracic insect ganglion. *Animal Behaviour, 13,* 104–108.

Ekstrand, B. R. (1972). To sleep, perchance to dream. In C. P. Duncan, L. Sechrest, & A. W. Melton (Eds.), *Human memory: Festschrift in honor of Benton J. Underwood* (pp. 59–82). New York: Appleton-Century-Crofts.

Ekstrand, B. R., Wallace, W. P., & Underwood, B. J. (1966). A frequency theory of verbal-discrimination learning. *Psychological Review, 73,* 566–578.

Elkin, I., Shea, M. T., Watkins, J. T., Imber, S. D., Sotsky, S. M., Collins, J. F., Glass, D. R., Plikonis, P. A., Leber, W. R., Docherty, J. P., Fiester, S. J., & Parloff, M. B. (1989). National Institute of Mental Health treatment of depression collaborative research program: General effectiveness of treatments. *Archives of General Psychiatry, 46,* 971–982.

Elstein, A. S., Shulman, L. S., & Sprafka, S. A. (1978). *Medical problem solving.* Cambridge, MA: Harvard University Press.

Epstein, R., Lanza, R. P., & Skinner, B. F. (1981). "Self-awareness" in the pigeon. *Science, 212,* 695–696.

Ericsson, K. A., & Simon, H. A. (1993). *Protocol analysis: Verbal reports as data.* Cambridge, MA: The MIT Press.

Estes, W. K. (1970). *Learning theory and mental development.* New York: Academic Press.

Eysenck, H. J. (1952). The effects of psychotherapy: An evaluation. *Journal of Consulting Psychology, 16,* 319–324.

F

Fantino, E., & Logan, C. A. (1979). *The experimental analysis of behavior: A biological perspective.* San Francisco: Freeman.

Fechner, G. T. (1860). *Elemente der Psychophysik.* Leipzig: Breitkopf und Hartel.

Ferster, C. B. (1973). A functional analysis of depression. *American Psychologist, 28,* 857–870.

Festinger, L. (1957). *A theory of cognitive dissonance*. Evanston, IL: Row, Peterson.

Fishbein, M., & Ajzen, I. (1975). *Belief, attitude, intention, and behavior: An introduction to theory and research*. Reading, MA: Addison-Wesley.

Fowles, D. (1980). The three arousal model: Implications of Gray's two-factor learning theory for heart rate, electrodermal activity, and psychopathy. *Psychophysiology, 17*, 87–104.

Fowles, D. (1986). The eccrine system and electrodermal activity. In M. G. H. Coles, S. W. Porges, & E. Donchin (Eds.), *Psychophysiology: Systems, processes, and applications* (Vol. 1, pp. 51–96). New York: Guilford Press.

Fowles, D. (1988). Psychophysiology and psychopathology: A motivational approach. *Psychophysiology, 25*, 373–391.

Fowles, D. (1992a). A motivational approach to the anxiety disorders. In D. G. Forgays, T. Sosnowski, & K. Wrzesniewski (Eds.), *Anxiety: Recent developments in self-appraisal, psychophysiological, and health research*. London: Hemisphere/Taylor & Francis.

Fowles, D. (1992b). Schizophrenia: Diathesis-stress revisited. *Annual Review of Psychology, 43*, 303–336.

Fowles, D. (1993). A motivational theory of psychopathology. In W. Spaulding (Ed.), *Nebraska Symposium on Motivation: Integrated views of motivation and emotion* (Vol. 41). Lincoln, NE: University of Nebraska Press.

Frank, J. D. (1961). *Persuasion and healing*. Baltimore: The Johns Hopkins University Press.

G

Gaeth, G. J., Levin, I. P., Chakraborty, G., & Levin, A. M. (1991). Consumer evaluation of multi-product bundles: An information integration analysis. *Marketing Letters, 2*, 47–57.

Gagné, R. M., & Smith, E. C., Jr. (1962). A study of the effects of verbalization on problem solving. *Journal of Experimental Psychology, 63*, 12–18.

Gallup, G. G., Jr. (1977). Self-recognition in primates: A comparative approach to the bi-directional properties of consciousness. *American Psychologist, 32*, 329–338.

Gardner, B. T., & Gardner, R. A. (1975). Evidence for sentence constituents in the early utterances of child

and chimpanzee. *Journal of Experimental Psychology: General, 104*, 244–267.

George, C., & Main, M. (1979). Social interactions of young abused children: Approach, avoidance and aggression. *Child Development, 50*, 306–318.

Gescheider, G. A. (1988). Psychophysical scaling. *Annual Review of Psychology, 39*, 169–200.

Gibson, E. J., & Walk, R. D. (1960). "The visual cliff." *Scientific American, 202*, 64–71.

Gibson, J. J. (1950). *The perception of the visual world*. Boston: Houghton Mifflin.

Gibson, J. J. (1979). *The ecological approach to visual perception*. Boston: Houghton Mifflin.

Gick, M. L., & Holyoak, K. J. (1980). Analogical problem solving. *Cognitive Psychology, 12*, 306–355.

Glanzer, M., & Clark, W. H. (1963). Accuracy of perceptual recall: An analysis of organization. *Journal of Verbal Learning and Verbal Behavior, 1*, 289–299.

Glanzer, M., & Cunitz, A. R. (1966). Two storage mechanisms in free recall. *Journal of Verbal Learning and Verbal Behavior, 5*, 351–360.

Glaze, J. A. (1928). The association value of nonsense syllables. *Journal of Genetic Psychology, 35*, 255–267.

Godden, D., & Baddeley, A. D. (1975). Context-dependent memory in two natural environments: On land and under water. *British Journal of Psychology, 66*, 325–331.

Goldston, D. B., Turnquist, D. C., & Knutson, J. F. (1989). Presenting problems of sexually abused girls receiving psychiatric services. *Journal of Abnormal Psychology, 98*, 314–317.

Goolkasian, P. (1980). Cyclic changes in pain perception, an ROC analysis. *Perception & Psychophysics, 27*, 499–504.

Gottesman, I. I., McGuffin, P., & Farmer, A. E. (1987). Clinical genetics as clues to the "real" genetics of schizophrenia (A decade of modest gains while playing for time). *Schizophrenia Bulletin, 13*, 23–47.

Gottesman, I. I., & Shields, J. (1972). *Schizophrenia and genetics: A twin study vantage point*. New York: Academic Press.

Graf, P., & Schacter, D. L. (1985). Implicit and explicit memory for new associations in normal and amnesic subjects. *Journal of Experimental Psychology: Learning, Memory, and Cognition, 11*, 501–518.

Gray, J. A. (1975). *Elements of a two-process theory of learning*. New York: Academic Press.

Gray, J. A. (1976). The behavioral inhibition system: A possible substrate for anxiety. In M. P. Feldman & A. Broadhurst (Eds.), *Theoretical and experimental bases of the behavior therapies* (pp. 3–41). London: Wiley.

Gray, J. A. (1987). *The psychology of fear and stress* (2nd ed.). Cambridge: Cambridge University Press.

Green, D. M., & Swets, J. A. (1966). *Signal detection theory and psychophysics*. New York: Wiley.

Gregg, V. H. (1986). Introduction to human memory. London: Routledge & Kegan Paul.

Griffin, D. R. (1981). *The question of animal awareness*. New York: The Rockefeller University Press.

Groves, P., & Thompson, R. F. (1970). Habituation: A dual-process theory. *Psychological Review, 77*, 419–450.

H

Hamilton, E. W., & Abramson, L. Y. (1983). Cognitive patterns and major depressive disorder: A longitudinal study in a hospital setting. *Journal of Abnormal Psychology, 92*, 173–184.

Hammond, K. R., Rohrbaugh, J., Mumpower, J., & Adelman, L. (1977). Social judgment theory: Applications in policy formation. In M. F. Kaplan & S. Schwartz (Eds.), *Human judgment and decision processes in applied settings*. New York: Academic Press.

Haney, C., & Zimbardo, P. G. (1977). The socialization into criminality: On becoming a prisoner and a guard. In J. L. Tapp & F. L. Levine (Eds.), *Law, justice and the individual in society: Psychological and legal issues*. New York: Holt, Rinehart & Winston.

Harlow, H. F. (1949). The formation of learning sets. *Psychological Review, 56*, 51–65.

Hasher, L., & Zacks, R. T. (1979). Automatic and effortful processes in memory. *Journal of Experimental Psychology: General, 108*, 356–388.

Hastie, R., & Park, B. (1986). The relationship between memory and judgment depends on whether the judgment task is memory-based or on-line. *Psychological Review, 93*, 258–268.

Helson, H. (1964). *Adaptation-level theory*. New York: Harper & Row.

Herman, L. M., & Gordon, J. A. (1974). Auditory delayed matching in the bottlenose dolphin. *Journal of the Experimental Analysis of Behavior, 21*, 19–26.

Heron, A., & Craik, F. I. M. (1964). Age differences in cumulative learning of meaningful and meaningless material. *Scandinavian Journal of Psychology, 5*, 209–217.

Herrnstein, R. J. (1985). Riddles of natural categorization. *Philosophical Transactions of the Royal Society, B 308*, 129–144.

Herrnstein, R. J., & de Villiers, P. A. (1980). Fish as a natural category for people and pigeons. In G. Bower (Ed.), *The psychology of learning and motivation* (pp. 59–95). New York: Academic Press.

Hess, E. H. (1973). *Imprinting*. New York: Van Nostrand Reinhold.

Heston, L. L. (1966). Psychiatric disorders in foster home reared children of schizophrenic mothers. *British Journal of Psychiatry, 112*, 819–825.

Hilgard, E. (1964). Introduction to H. Ebbinghaus, Memory: A contribution to experimental psychology (translated by H. A. Ruger & C. E. Bussenius). New York: Dover Publications.

Hinrichs, J. V., Ghoneim, M. M., & Mewaldt, S. P. (1984). Diazepam and memory: Retrograde facilitation produced by interference reduction. *Psychopharmacology, 84*, 158–162.

Hogarth, R., & Einhorn, H. (1992). Order effects in belief updating: The belief-adjustment model. *Cognitive Psychology, 24*, 1–55.

Hollard, V. D., & Delius, J. D. (1982). Rotational invariance in visual pattern recognition by pigeons and humans. *Science, 218*, 804–806.

Hollon, S. D., Kendall, P. C., & Lumry, A. (1986). Specificity of depressotypic cognitions in clinical depression. *Journal of Abnormal Psychology, 95*, 52–59.

Honig, W. K., & Fetterman, J. G. (Eds.). (1992). *Cognitive aspects of stimulus control*. Hillsdale, NJ: Erlbaum.

Horridge, G. A. (1962). Learning of leg position by the ventral nerve cord in headless insects. *Proceedings of the Royal Society, B 157*, 33–52.

Hull, C. L. (1943). *Principles of behavior*. New York: Appleton-Century-Crofts.

Hulse, S. H., Fowler, H., & Honig, W. K. (1978). *Cognitive processes in animal behavior*. Hillsdale, NJ: Erlbaum.

Hume, D. (1739/1964). *Treatise of human nature* (edited by L. A. Selby-Bigge). London: Oxford University Press.

Hunter, W. S. (1913). The delayed reaction in animals and children. *Behavior Monographs, 2*, 1–86.

I

Inglis, J., & Caird, W. K. (1963). Modified-digit spans and memory disorder. *Diseases of the Nervous System, 24*, 46–50.

Intons-Peterson, M. J., & Roskos-Ewoldsen, B. (1989). Sensory-perceptual qualities of images. *Journal of Experimental Psychology: Learning, Memory, and Cognition, 15*, 188–199.

Isen, A. M. (in press). Positive affect and decision making. To appear in M. Lewis & J. Haviland (Eds.), *Handbook of emotion*. New York: Guilford.

Ittelson, W. H., & Kilpatrick, F. P. (1951). Experiments in perception. *Scientific American, 185*, 50–55.

J

Jacobs, J. (1887). Experiments on "prehension." *Mind, 12*, 75–79.

Jacobson, A., Horowitz, S., & Fried, C. (1967). Classical conditioning, pseudoconditioning, or sensitization in the planarian. *Journal of Comparative and Physiological Psychology, 64*, 73–79.

Jacoby, J., Chestnut, R. W., & Fisher, W. A. (1978). A behavioral process approach to information acquisition in nondurable purchasing. *Journal of Marketing Research, 15*, 532–544.

Johnson-Laird, P. N. (1989). Analogy and the exercise of creativity. In S. Vosniadou & A. Ortony (Eds.), *Similarity and analogical reasoning*. Cambridge, England: Cambridge University Press.

Jones, B. M., & Jones, M. K.(1977). Alcohol and memory impairment in male and female social drinkers. In I. M. Birnbaum and E. S. Parker (Eds.), *Alcohol and human memory* (pp. 127–138). Hillsdale, NJ: Erlbaum.

K

Kahneman, D., Slovic, P., & Tversky, A. (Eds.). (1982). *Judgments under uncertainty: Heuristics and biases*. Cambridge, England: Cambridge University Press.

Kahneman, D., & Tversky, A. (1973). On the psychology of prediction. *Psychological Review, 80*, 237–251

Kaszniak, A. W., Poon, L. W., & Riege, W. (1986). Assessing memory deficits: An information processing approach. In L. W. Poon (Ed.), *Handbook for clinical memory assessment of older adults* (pp. 168–188). Washington, DC: American Psychological Association.

Kausler, D. H. (1974). *Psychology of verbal learning and memory*. New York: Academic Press.

Kazdin, A. E. (1978). Evaluating the generality of findings in analogue therapy research. *Journal of Consulting and Clinical Psychology, 46*, 673–686.

Keith-Spiegel, P., & Koocher, G. P. (1985). *Ethics in psychology*. New York: Random House.

Kelley, H. H. (1972). Attribution in social interaction. In E. E. Jones et al. (Eds.), *Attribution: Perceiving the causes of behavior*. Morristown, NJ: General Learning Press.

Kendall, P. C., Hollon, S. D., Beck, A. T., Hammen, C. L., & Ingram, R. E. (1987). Issues and recommendations regarding use of the Beck Depression Inventory. *Cognitive Therapy and Research, 11*, 289–299.

Kendler, H. H., & Kendler, T. S. (1962). Vertical and horizontal processes in problem solving. *Psychological Review, 69*, 1–16.

Kent, G. H., & Rosanoff, A. J. (1910). A study of association in insanity. *American Journal of Insanity, 67*, 37–96.

Keppel, G. (1965). Problems of method in the study of short-term memory. *Psychological Bulletin, 63*, 1–13.

Keppel, G., & Underwood, B. J. (1962). Proactive inhibition in short-term retention of single items. *Journal of Verbal Learning and Verbal Behavior, 1*, 153–161.

Kety, S. S., Rosenthal, D., Wender, P. H., & Schulsinger, F. (1968). The types and prevalence of mental illness in the biological and adoptive families of adopted schizophrenics. In D. Rosenthal & S. S. Kety (Eds.), *The transmission of schizophrenia* (pp. 345–362). Oxford: Pergamon Press.

Kety, S. S., Rosenthal, D., Wender, P. H., Schulsinger, F., & Jacobsen, B. (1978). The biologic and adoptive families of adopted individuals who became schizophrenic: Prevalence of mental illness and other characteristics. In L. C. Wynne, R. L. Cromwell, & S. Matthysse (Eds.), *The nature of schizophrenia: New approaches to research and treatment* (pp. 25–37). New York: Wiley.

Kimble, G. A. (1961). *Hilgard and Marquis' conditioning and learning* (2nd ed.). New York: Appleton-Century-Crofts.

King, M. C., & Lockhead, G. R. (1981). Response scales and sequential effects in judgment. *Perception & Psychophysics, 30*, 599–603.

Knutson, J. F., & Mehm, J. G. (1988). Transgenerational patterns of coercion in families and intimate relationships. In G. W. Russell (Ed.), *Violence in intimate relationships*. New York: PMA Publishing.

Knutson, J. F., & Viken, R. J. (1984). Animal analogues of human aggression: Studies of social experience and escalation. In D. C. Blanchard, K. J. Flannelly, & R. J. Blanchard (Eds.), *Biological perspectives on aggression*. (pp. 75–94). New York: Alan R. Liss.

Kolers, P. A. (1976). Reading a year later. *Journal of Experimental Psychology: Human Learning and Memory, 2,* 554–565.

Kolko, D. J., Moser, J. T., & Weldy, S. R. (1988). Behavioral/emotional indicators of sexual abuse in child psychiatric inpatients: A controlled comparison with physical abuse. *Child Abuse & Neglect, 12,* 529–541.

Koriat, A., Lichtenstein, S., & Fischhoff, B. (1980). Reasons for confidence. *Journal of Experimental Psychology: Human Learning and Memory, 6,* 107–118.

Kosslyn, S. M. (1975). Information representation in visual images. *Cognitive Psychology, 7,* 341–370.

Kosslyn, S. M. (1983). *Ghosts in the mind's machine.* New York: Norton.

Kramer, R. M., McClintock, C. G., & Messick, D. M. (1986). Social values and cooperative response to a simulated resource conservation crisis. *Journal of Personality, 54,* 576–592.

Kruger, W. C. F. (1934). The relative difficulty of nonsense syllables. *Journal of Experimental Psychology, 17,* 145–153.

Kucera, H., & Francis, W. N. (1967). *Computational analysis of present-day American English.* Providence, RI: Brown University Press.

L

LaBerge, D., & Samuels, S. J. (1974). Toward a theory of automatic information processing in reading. *Cognitive Psychology, 6,* 293–323.

Lacey, J. I. (1967). Somatic response patterning and stress: Some revisions of activation theory. In M. H. Appley & R. Trumbull (Eds.), *Psychological stress: Issues in research.* New York: Appleton-Century-Crofts.

Lang, P. J. (1968). Fear reduction and fear behavior: Problems in treating a construct. In J. M. Shlien (Ed.), *Research in psychotherapy* (Vol. 3). Washington, D.C.: American Psychological Association.

Lang, P. J. (1977). Physiological assessment of anxiety and fear. In J. D. Cone and R. P. Hawkins (Eds.), *Behavioral assessment: New directions in clinical psychology.* New York: Brunner/Mazel.

Lang, P. J., Lazovik, A. D., & Reynolds, D. J. (1965). Desensitization, suggestibility, and pseudotherapy. *Journal of Abnormal Psychology, 70,* 395–402.

Larkin, J., McDermott, J., Simon, D. P., & Simon, H. A. (1980). Expert and novice performance in solving physics problems. *Science, 208,* 1335–1342.

Lashley, K. S., & Russell, J. T. (1934). The mechanism of vision. XI. A preliminary test of innate organization. *Journal of Genetic Psychology, 45,* 136–144.

Leahey, T. H., & Harris, R. J. (1993). *Learning and cognition* (3rd ed.). Englewood Cliffs, NJ.: Prentice Hall.

Lefkowitz, M. M., Eron, L. D., Walder, L. O., & Huesmann, L. R. (1977). *Growing up to be violent.* New York: Pergamon.

Levin, I. P., & Chapman, D. P. (1990). Risk taking, frame of reference and characterization of victim groups in AIDS treatment decisions. *Journal of Experimental Social Psychology, 26,* 421–434.

Levin, I. P., Jasper, J. D., Mittelstaedt, J. D., & Gaeth, G. J. (1993). Attitudes toward "Buy America first" and preferences for American and Japanese cars: A different role for country-of-origin information. In L. McAlister & M. L. Rothschild (Eds.), *Advances in consumer research,* (Vol. XX, pp. 625–629). Provo, Utah: Association for consumer research.

Levin, I. P., & Kao, S. F. (1993). Antecedents of spending and saving habits and use of credit cards in the Midwestern United States. In W. F. van Raaij & G. J. Bamossy (Eds.), *European advances in consumer research* (Vol. 1, pp. 459–466). Provo, Utah: Association for Consumer Research.

Levin, I. P., Louviere, J. J., Schepanski, A. A., & Norman, K. L. (1983). External validity tests of laboratory studies of information integration. *Organizational Behavior and Human Performance, 31,* 173–193.

Levin, I. P., Schnittjer, S. K., & Thee, S. L. (1988). Information framing effects in social and personal decisions. *Journal of Experimental Social Psychology, 24,* 520–529.

Levin, I. P., Wall, L. L., Dolezal, J. M., & Norman, K. L. (1973). Differential weighting of positive and negative traits in impression formation as a function of prior exposure. *Journal of Experimental Psychology, 97,* 114–115.

Levis, D. J. (1970). The case for performing research on nonpatient populations with fears of small animals: A reply to Cooper, Furst, and Bridger. *Journal of Abnormal Psychology, 76,* 36–38.

Levis, D. J. (1979). The infrahuman avoidance model of symptom maintenance and implosive therapy. In J. D. Keehn (Ed.), *Psychopathology in animals: Research and clinical implications.* New York: Academic Press.

Levison, M. J. (1979). Truly random control group in Pavlovian conditioning of planaria (*Dugesia dorotocephala*). *Psychological Reports, 45,* 987–992.

Lewinsohn, P. M., Hoberman, H. M., & Rosenbaum, M. (1988). A prospective study of risk factors for unipolar depression. *Journal of Abnormal Psychology, 97,* 251–264.

Lewinsohn, P. M., & Libet, J. (1972). Pleasant events, activity schedules, and depression. *Journal of Abnormal Psychology, 79,* 291–296.

Lewinsohn, P. M., Steinmetz, J. L., Larson, D. W., & Franklin, J. (1981). Depression-related cognitions: Antecedent or consequence? *Journal of Abnormal Psychology, 90,* 213–219.

Lichtenstein, S., & Slovic, P. (1973). Response-induced reversals of preference in gambling: An extended replication in Las Vegas. *Journal of Experimental Psychology, 101,* 16–20.

Likert, R. (1932). A technique for the measurement of attitudes. *Archives of Psychology, 140,* 1–55.

Lindsay, P. H., & Norman, D. A. (1977). *Human information processing: An introduction to psychology* (2nd ed.). New York: Academic Press.

Lindsley, D. B. (1951). Emotion. In S. S. Stevens (Ed.), *Handbook of experimental psychology.* New York: John Wiley and Sons.

Loftus, E. F., & Palmer, J. C. (1974). Reconstruction of automobile destruction: An example of the interaction between language and memory. *Journal of Verbal Learning and Verbal Behavior, 13,* 585–589.

Lopes, L. L. (1987). Between hope and fear: The psychology of risk. *Advances in Experimental Social Psychology, 20,* 255–295.

Luchins, A. S. (1942). Mechanization in problem solving: The effect of Einstellung. *Psychological Monographs, 54,* 1–95 (Whole No. 248).

Luria, A. R. (1968). *The mind of a mnemonist.* New York: Basic Books.

M

MacCoun, R. J. (1989). Experimental research on jury decision making. *Science, 244 (4908),* 1046–1050.

Mackintosh, N. J. (1974). *The psychology of animal learning.* London: Academic Press.

Macphail, E. M., & Reilly, S. (1989). Rapid acquisition of a novelty versus familiarity concept by pigeons (*Columba livia*). *Journal of Experimental Psychology: Animal Behavior Processes, 15,* 242–252.

Maier, N. R. F. (1931). Reasoning in humans. II. The solution of a problem and its appearance in consciousness. *Journal of Comparative Psychology, 12,* 181–194.

Malmo, R. B. (1959). Activation: A neuropsychological dimension. *Psychological Review, 66,* 367–386.

Mandler, G. (1967). Organization in memory. In K. W. Spence & J. T. Spence (Eds.), *The psychology of learning and motivation* (Vol. 1, pp. 327–372). New York: Academic Press.

Marks, I. M. (1969). *Fears and phobias.* New York: Academic Press.

Marks, I. M., & Gelder, M. G. (1966). Different ages of onset in varieties of phobias. *American Journal of Psychiatry, 123,* 218–221.

Marks, L. E., & Jack, O. (1952). Verbal context and memory span for meaningful material. *American Journal of Psychology, 65,* 298–300.

Matlin, M. W. (1994). *Cognition* (3rd ed.). Fort Worth: Harcourt Brace.

Mazur, J. E. (1990). *Learning and behavior* (2nd ed.). Englewood Cliffs, NJ: Prentice Hall.

McClelland, J. L. (1985). Putting knowledge in its place: A scheme for programming parallel processing structure on the fly. *Cognitive Science, 9,* 113–146.

McClelland, J. L., & Rumelhart, D. E. (1981). An interactive activation model of context effects in letter perception: Part 1. An account of basic findings. *Psychological Review, 88,* 375–407.

McClelland, J. L., Rumelhart D. E., and the PDP Research Group (1986). Parallel distributed processing: Exploration in the microstructure of cognition. *Volume 2: Psychological and biological models.* Cambridge, MA: MIT Press.

McConnell, J. V., & Jacobson, A. L. (1973). Learning in invertebrates. In D. A. Dewsbury & D. A. Rethlingshafer (Eds.), *Comparative psychology: A modern survey* (pp. 429–470). New York: McGraw-Hill.

McCrary, J. W., Jr., & Hunter, W. S. (1953). Serial position curves in verbal learning. *Science, 117,* 131–134.

McFarland, R. A., Warren, B., & Karis, C. (1958). Alterations in critical flicker frequency as a function of age and light:dark ratio. *Journal of Experimental Psychology, 56,* 529–538.

McGeoch, J. A. (1932). Forgetting and the law of disuse. *Psychological Review, 39,* 352–370.

McGeoch, J. A. (1942). *The psychology of human learning.* New York: Longmans, Green.

McGeoch, J. A., & Irion, A. L. (1952). *The psychology of human learning* (2nd ed.). New York: Longmans, Green.

McGinnis, E. (1949). Emotionality and perceptual defense. *Psychological Review, 56,* 244–251.

Mellers, B., & Hartka, E. (1989). Test of a subtractive theory of "fair" allocations. *Journal of Personality and Social Psychology, 56,* 691–697.

Metalsky, G. I., Halberstadt, L. J., & Abramson, L. Y. (1987). Vulnerability to depressive mood reactions: Toward a more powerful test of the diathesis-stress and causal mediation components of the reformulated theory of depression. *Journal of Personality and Social Psychology, 52,* 386–393.

Meyer, D. E., & Schvaneveldt, R. W. (1971). Facilitation in recognizing pairs of words: Evidence of a dependence between retrieval operations. *Journal of Experimental Psychology, 90,* 227–234.

Meyerowitz, B. E., & Chaiken, S. (1987). The effect of message framing on breast self-examination attitudes, intentions, and behavior. *Journal of Personality and Social Psychology, 52,* 500–510.

Milgram, S. (1974). *Obedience to authority.* New York: Harper & Row.

Miller, G. A. (1956). The magical number seven, plus or minus two: Some limits on our capacity for processing information. *Psychological Review, 63,* 81–97.

Miller, G. A., & Selfridge (1950). Verbal context and the recall of meaningful material. *American Journal of Psychology, 63,* 176–185.

Miller, N. E. (1969). Learning of visceral and glandular responses. *Science, 163,* 434–445.

Miller, N. E. (1985). The value of behavioral research on animals. *American Psychologist, 40,* 423–440.

Milner, B. (1966). Amnesia following operation on the temporal lobes. In C. W. M. Whitty & O. L. Zangwill (Eds.), *Amnesia* (pp. 109–133). London: Butterworths.

Mineka, S., Davidson, M., Cook, M., & Keir, R. (1984). Observational conditioning of snake fear in rhesus monkeys. *Journal of Abnormal Psychology, 93,* 355–372.

Minsky, M. (1975). A framework for representing knowledge. In P. Winston (Ed.), *The psychology of computer vision.* New York: McGraw-Hill.

Moore, J. W. (1972). In Black, A. H., & Prokasky, W. F. (Eds.), *Classical conditioning II: Current research and theory.* New York: Appleton-Century-Crofts.

Morey, L. C. (1991). Classification of mental disorder as a collection of hypothetical constructs. *Journal of Abnormal Psychology, 100,* 289–293.

Morgan, C. L. (1896). *An introduction to comparative psychology.* London: Walter Scott, Ltd. (Original work published in 1894.)

Moskowitz, H. R. (1970). Ratio scales of sugar sweetness. *Perception & Psychophysics, 7,* 315–320.

Murdock, B. B., Jr. (1961). The retention of individual items. *Journal of Experimental Psychology, 62,* 618–625.

Murdock, B. B., Jr. (1963). An analysis of the recognition process. In C. N. Cofer & B. S. Musgrave (Eds.), *Verbal behavior and learning* (pp. 10–22). New York: McGraw-Hill.

Murdock, B. B., Jr. (1967). Distractor and probe techniques in short-term memory. *Canadian Journal of Psychology, 21,* 25–36.

N

Newcomb, T. M., & Hartley, E. L. (Eds.). (1947). *Readings in social psychology,* New York: Holt, Rinehart & Winston.

Newell, A. (1967). *Studies in problem solving: Subject 3 on the cryptic-arithmetic task, DONALD plus GERALD equals ROBERT.* Pittsburgh: Carnegie-Mellon Institute.

Newell, A., & Simon, H. A. (1972). *Human problem solving.* Englewood Cliffs, NJ: Prentice Hall.

Noble, C. E. (1952). An analysis of meaning. *Psychological Review, 59,* 421–430.

O

Obrist, P. A. (1976). The cardiovascular-behavioral interaction—as it appears today. *Psychophysiology, 13*, 95–107.

Obrist, P. A., Howard, J. L., Lawler, J. R., Galosy, R. A., Meyers, K. A., & Gaebelein, C. J. (1974). The cardiac somatic interaction. In P. A. Obrist, A. H. Black, J. Brener, & L. V. DiCara (Eds.), *Cardiovascular psychophysiology: Current issues in response mechanisms, biofeedback and methodology* (pp. 136–162). Chicago: Aldine.

Oden, D. L., Thompson, R. K. R., & Premack, D. (1988). Spontaneous transfer of matching by infant chimpanzees (*Pan troglodytes*). *Journal of Experimental Psychology: Animal Behavior Processes, 14*, 140–145.

O'Leary, K. D., & Borkovec, T. D. (1978). Conceptual, methodological, and ethical problems of placebo groups in psychotherapy research. *American Psychologist, 33*, 821–830.

Osgood, C. E., Suci, G. J., & Tannenbaum, P. H. (1957). *The measurement of meaning.* Urbana, IL.: University of Illinois Press.

P

Paivio, A. (1969). Mental imagery in associative learning and memory. *Psychological Review, 76*, 241–263.

Paivio, A., & Csapo, K. (1969). Concrete-image and verbal memory codes. *Journal of Experimental Psychology, 80*, 279–285.

Papini, M. R., & Bitterman, M. E. (1990). The role of contingency in classical conditioning. *Psychological Review, 97*, 396–403.

Parducci, A. (1965). Category judgment: A range-frequency model. *Psychological Review, 72*, 407–418.

Parloff, M. B. (1986). Placebo controls in psychotherapy research: A sine qua non or a placebo for research problems? *Journal of Consulting and Clinical Psychology, 54*, 79–87.

Patterson, G. R. (1982). *Coercive family process.* Eugene, OR: Castalia Publishing Company.

Patterson, G. R., Reid, J. B., & Dishion, T. J. (1992). *Antisocial boys.* Eugene, OR: Castalia Publishing Company.

Paul, G. L. (1966). *Insight vs. desensitization in psychotherapy: An experiment in anxiety reduction.* Stanford, CA: Stanford University Press.

Paulus, P. B., McCain, G., & Cox, V. C. (1978). Death rates, psychiatric commitments, blood pressure, and perceived crowding as a function of institutional crowding. *Environmental Psychology and Nonverbal Behavior, 3*, 107–116.

Paulus, P. B., & Murdoch, P. (1971). Anticipated evaluation and audience presence in the enhancement of dominant responses. *Journal of Experimental Social Psychology, 7*, 280–291.

Pavlov, I. P. (1927). *Conditioned reflexes.* Oxford: Oxford University Press.

Payne, J. W., Braunstein, M. L., & Carroll, J. S. (1978). Exploring predecisional behavior: An alternative approach to decision research. *Organizational Behavior and Human Performance, 22*, 17–44.

Peterson, L. R., & Peterson, M. J. (1959). Short-term retention of individual verbal items. *Journal of Experimental Psychology, 58*, 193–198.

Phillips, L. D., & Edwards, W. (1966). Conservatism in a simple probability inference task. *Journal of Experimental Psychology, 72*, 346–357.

Piaget, J., & Inhelder, B. (1969). *The psychology of the child.* London: Routledge & Kegan Paul.

Piliavin, I. M., Piliavin, J. A., & Rodin, J. (1975). Costs, diffusion, and the stigmatized victim. *Journal of Personality and Social Psychology, 32*, 429–438.

Pollack, I., Johnson, L. B., & Knaff, P. R. (1959). Running memory span. *Journal of Experimental Psychology, 57*, 137–146.

Posner, M. I., & Keele, S. W. (1968). On the genesis of abstract ideas. *Journal of Experimental Psychology, 77*, 353–363.

Posner, M. I., & Snyder, C. R. R. (1975). Attention and cognitive control. In R. L. Solso (Ed.), *Information processing and cognition: The Loyola Symposium.* Hillsdale, NJ: Erlbaum.

Postman, L. (1962). Repetition and paired-associate learning. *American Journal of Psychology, 75*, 372–389.

Postman, L. (1968). Herman Ebbinghaus. *American Psychologist, 23*, 149–157.

Postman, L. (1969). Experimental analysis of learning to learn. In G. H. Bower & J. T. Spence (Eds.), *The psychology of learning and motivation* (Vol. 3). New York: Academic Press.

Postman, L., & Keppel, G. (Eds.). (1970). *Norms of word association.* New York: Academic Press.

Povinelli, D. J. (1993). Reconstructing the evolution of mind. *American Psychologist, 48,* 493–509.

Premack, D. (1978). On the abstractness of human concepts: Why it would be difficult to talk to a pigeon. In S. H. Hulse, H. Fowler, & W. K. Honig (Eds.), *Cognitive processes in animal behavior* (pp. 423–451). Hillsdale, NJ: Erlbaum.

Prioleau, L., Murdock, M., & Brody, N. (1983). An analysis of psychotherapy versus placebo studies. *The Behavioral and Brain Sciences, 6,* 275–310.

Pylyshyn, Z. W. (1981). The imagery debate: Analogue media versus tacit knowledge. *Psychological Review, 86,* 16–45.

Q

Quillian, M. R. (1969). The teachable language comprehender. *Communications of the Association for Computing Machinery, 12,* 459–476.

R

Radloff, L. S. (1977). The CES-D Scale: A self-report depression scale for research in the general population. *Applied Psychological Measurement, 1,* 385–401.

Ratcliff, R., & McKoon, G. (1988). A retrieval theory of priming in memory. *Psychological Review, 95,* 385–408.

Ratner, S. C. (1970). Habituation: Research and theory. In J. H. Reynierse (Ed.), *Current issues in animal learning* (pp. 55–84). Lincoln, NE: University of Nebraska Press.

Rausch, K., & Knutson, J. F. (1991). The self-report of personal punitive childhood experiences and those of siblings. *Child Abuse & Neglect, 15,* 29–36.

Reed, S. K. (1972). Pattern recognition and categorization. *Cognitive Psychology, 3,* 382–407.

Reed, S. K. (1992). *Cognition: Theory and applications* (3rd ed.). Pacific Grove, CA: Brooks/Cole.

Reed, S. K., & Evans, A. C. (1987). Learning functional relations: A theoretical and instructional analysis. *Journal of Experimental Psychology: General, 116,* 106–118.

Reed, S. K., & Friedman, M. P. (1973). Perceptual vs. conceptual categorization. *Memory & Cognition, 1,* 157–163.

Rescorla, R. A. (1978). Some implications of a cognitive perspective on Pavlovian conditioning. In S. H. Hulse, H. Fowler, & W. K. Honig (Eds.), *Cognitive processes in animal behavior* (pp. 15–50). Hillsdale, NJ: Erlbaum.

Revusky, S. H., & Garcia, J. (1970). Learned associations over long delays. In G. H. Bower & J. T. Spence (Eds.), *The psychology of learning and motivation: Advances in research and theory, IV* (pp. 1–84). New York: Academic Press.

Richardson, E. D. (1987). *Long-term neuropsychological, psychiatric and psychosocial sequelae of cerebral malaria.* Unpublished doctoral dissertation, University of Iowa.

Roberts, W. A., & Grant, D. S. (1976). Studies of short-term memory in the pigeon using the delayed matching-to-sample procedure. In D. L. Medin, W. A. Roberts, & R. T. Davis (Eds.), *Processes of animal memory* (pp. 79–112). Hillsdale, NJ: Erlbaum.

Rock, I. (1957). The role of repetition in associative learning. *American Journal of Psychology, 70,* 186–193.

Roediger, H. L. (1990). Implicit memory: Retention without remembering. *American Psychologist, 45,* 1043–1056.

Roethlisberger, F. J., & Dickson, W. J. (1939). *Management and the worker.* Cambridge, MA: Harvard University Press.

Rogers, C. R. (1951). *Client-centered therapy: Its current practice, implications, and theory.* Boston: Houghton Mifflin.

Rohe, W., & Patterson, A. H. (1974). The effects of varied levels of resources and density on behavior in a daycare center. Paper presented at the meeting of the Environmental Design Research Association, Milwaukee.

Roitblat, H. L. (1987). *Introduction to comparative cognition.* New York: Freeman.

Roitblat, H. L., Bever, T. G., & Terrace, H. S. (Eds.). (1984). *Animal cognition.* Hillsdale, NJ: Erlbaum.

Romanes, G. J. (1883). *Animal intelligence.* New York: D. Appleton and Company. [Reprinted in D. N. Robinson (Ed.), *Significant contributions to the history of psychology 1750–1920. Series A: Orientation. Volume VII: G. J. Romanes.* Washington, D.C.: University Publications of America, 1977.] (Original work published in 1882.)

Romanes, G. J. (1889). *Mental evolution in man.* New York: D. Appleton and Company. (Original work published in 1887.)

Roper, K. L., & Zentall, T. R. (1993). Directed forgetting in animals. *Psychological Bulletin, 113*, 513–532.

Rosch, E., & Mervis, C. B. (1975). Family resemblances: Studies in the internal structure of categories. *Cognitive Psychology, 7*, 573–605.

Rosch, E., Mervis, C. B., Gray, W. D., Johnson, D. M., & Boyes-Braem, P. (1976). Basic objects in natural categories. *Cognitive Psychology, 8*, 382–439.

Rosenbaum, M. E. (1986). The repulsion hypothesis: On the nondevelopment of relationships. *Journal of Personality and Social Psychology, 51*, 1156–1166.

Rosenberg, S., Nelson, C., & Vivekananthan, P. S. (1968). A multidimensional approach to the structure of personality impressions. *Journal of Personality and Social Psychology, 9*, 283–294.

Rosenthal, D., Wender, P. H., Kety, S. S., Schulsinger, F., Welner, J., & Ostergaard, L. (1968). Schizophrenic offspring reared in adoptive homes. In D. Rosenthal & S. S. Kety (Eds.), *The transmission of schizophrenia* (pp. 377–391). New York: Pergamon Press.

Rosenthal, R. (1966). *Experimenter effects in behavioral research.* New York: Appleton-Century-Crofts.

Rosenthal, R., & Jacobson, L. (1968). *Pygmalion in the classroom.* New York: Holt, Rinehart & Winston.

Rosenthal, R., & Lawson, R. (1964). A longitudinal study of the effects of experimenter bias on the operant learning of laboratory rats. *Journal of Psychiatric Research, 2*, 61–72.

Rosenthal, R., & Rosnow, R. (1975). *The volunteer subject.* New York: Wiley-Interscience.

Ross, W. D. (Ed.). (1966). *The works of Aristotle* (Vol. 9). London: Oxford University Press.

Rozin, P., & Kalat, J. W. (1971). Specific hungers and poison avoidance as adaptive specializations of learning. *Psychological Review, 78*, 459–486.

Rubovits, P. C., & Maehr, M. L. (1973). Pygmalion black and white. *Journal of Personality and Social Psychology, 25*, 210–218.

Rumelhart, D. E. (1975). Notes on a schema for stories. In D. Bobrow & A. Collins (Eds.), *Representation and understanding: Studies in cognitive science.* New York: Academic Press.

Rumelhart, D. E., McClelland, J. L., and the PDP Research Group (1986). Parallel distributed processing: Explorations in the microstructure of cognition. *Volume 1: Foundations.* Cambridge, MA: MIT Press.

Russell, W. A., & Jenkins, J. J. (1954). The complete Minnesota norms for responses to 100 words from the Kent-Rosanoff Word Association Test. *Technical Report No. 11*, Contract N8 ONR–66216.

S

Sands, S. F., & Wright, A. A. (1980). Serial probe recognition performance by a rhesus monkey and a human with 10- and 20-item lists. *Journal of Experimental Psychology: Animal Behavior Processes, 6*, 386–396.

Santiago, H. C., & Wright, A. A. (1984). Pigeon memory: *Same/Different* concept learning, serial probe recognition acquisition, and probe delay effects on the serial-position function. *Journal of Experimental Psychology: Animal Behavior Processes, 10*, 498–512.

Schiffman, H. R. (1976). *Sensation and perception.* New York: Wiley.

Schwartz, B., & Reisberg, D. (1991). *Learning and memory.* New York: Norton.

Seligman, M. E. P., (1971). Phobias and preparedness. *Behavior Therapy, 2*, 307–320.

Seligman, M. E. P. (1975). *Helplessness: On depression, development, and death.* San Francisco: W. H. Freeman.

Seligman, M. E. P., Abramson, L. Y., Semmel, A., & von Baeyer, C. (1979). Depressive attributional style. *Journal of Abnormal Psychology, 88*, 242–247.

Seligman, M. E. P., Maier, S. F., & Solomon, R. L. (1971). Unpredictable and uncontrollable aversive events. In F. R. Brush (Ed.), *Aversive conditioning and learning* (pp. 347–400). New York: Academic Press.

Shank, R. C., & Abelson, R. (1977). *Scripts, plans, goals, and understanding.* Hillsdale, NJ: Erlbaum.

Shanteau, J. (1990, May). *Decision strategies of experts.* Paper presented at Nags Head Conference on Judgment and Decision Making, Nags Head, NC.

Shanteau, J., & Nagy, G. F. (1979). Probability of acceptance in dating choices. *Journal of Personality and Social Psychology, 37*, 522–533.

Shepard, R. N., & Metzler, J. (1971). Mental rotation of three-dimensional objects. *Science, 171*, 701–703.

Shepard, R. N., & Teghtsoonian, M. (1961). Retention of information under conditions approaching a steady state. *Journal of Experimental Psychology, 62*, 302–309.

Sherif, M. (1937). An experimental approach to the study of attitudes. *Sociometry, 1*, 90–98.

Shettleworth, S. J. (1993). Varieties of learning and memory in animals. *Journal of Experimental Psychology: Animal Behavior Processes, 19*, 5–14.

Shiffrin, R. M., & Schneider, W. (1977). Controlled and automatic human information processing: II. Perceptual learning, automatic attending, and a general theory. *Psychological Review, 84*, 127–190.

Sidman, M. (1960). *Tactics of scientific research: Evaluating experimental data in psychology.* New York: Basic Books.

Simon, H. A. (1956). Rational choice and the structure of the environment: *Psychological Review, 63*, 129–138.

Simon, J. R. (1990). The effects of an irrelevant directional cue on human information processing. In R. W. Proctor and T. G. Reeve (Eds.), *Stimulus-response compatibility*. North-Holland: Elsevier Science Publishers B. V.

Skinner, B. F. (1938). *The behavior of organisms.* New York: Appleton-Century-Crofts.

Skinner, B. F. (1948). "Superstition" in the pigeon. *Journal of Experimental Psychology, 38*, 168–172.

Skinner, B. F. (1950). Are theories of learning necessary? *Psychological Review, 57*, 193–216.

Skinner, B. F. (1964). Behaviorism at fifty. In T. W. Wann (Ed.), *Behaviorism and phenomenology: Contrasting bases for modern psychology* (pp. 79–97). Chicago: University of Chicago Press.

Skinner, B. F. (1977). Why I am not a cognitive psychologist. *Behaviorism, 5*, 1–10.

Slovic, P., Fischhoff, B., & Lichtenstein, S. (1978). Accidental probabilities and seat belt usage: A psychological perspective. *Accident Analysis and Prevention, 10*, 281–285.

Slovic, P., Fischhoff, B., & Lichtenstein, S. (1984). Behavioral decision theory perspectives on risk and safety. *Acta Psychologica, 56*, 183–203.

Sluckin, W. (1965). *Imprinting and early learning.* Chicago: Aldine.

Smith, E. E., & Medin, D. L. (1981). *Categories and concepts.* Cambridge, MA: Harvard University Press.

Smith, M. S., & Glass, A. L. (1977). Meta-analysis of psychotherapy outcome studies. *American Psychologist, 32*, 752–760.

Sommer, R. (1968). Hawthorne dogma. *Psychological Bulletin, 70*, 592–595.

Spence, K. W. (1956). *Behavior theory and conditioning.* New Haven: Yale University Press.

Sperling, G. (1960). The information available in brief visual presentations. *Psychological Monographs: General and Applied, 74*, 1–29.

Spitzer, R. L., Endicott, J., & Robins, E. (1978). Research diagnostic criteria: Rationale and reliability. *Archives of General Psychiatry, 1978, 35*, 773–782.

Stein, L., Xue, B. G., & Belluzzi, J. D. (1993). A cellular analogue of operant conditioning. *Journal of the Experimental Analysis of Behavior, 60*, 41–53.

Sternberg, S. (1966). High speed scanning in human memory. *Science, 153*, 652–654.

Sternberg, S. (1969). Memory scanning: Mental processes revealed by reaction-time experiments. *American Scientist, 57*, 421–457.

Stevens, S. S. (1956). The direct estimation of sensory magnitudes-loudness. *American Journal of Psychology, 69*, 1–25.

Stevens, S. S. (1961). The psychophysics of sensory function. In W. A. Rosenblith (Ed.), *Sensory communication.* New York: Wiley.

Stiles, W. B., & Shapiro, D. A. (1989). Abuse of the drug metaphor in psychotherapy process-outcome research. *Clinical Psychology Review, 9*, 521–543.

Stroop, J. R. (1935). Studies of interference in serial verbal reactions. *Journal of Experimental Psychology, 18*, 643–662.

Strupp, H. H., & Hadley, S. W. (1979). Specific vs. nonspecific factors in psychotherapy. *Archives of General Psychiatry, 36*, 1125–1136.

Suomi, S. J., & Harlow, H. F. (1977). Production and alleviation of depressive behaviors in monkeys. In J. D. Maser & M. E. P. Seligman (Eds.), *Psychopathology: Experimental models.* San Francisco: W. H. Freeman.

Suzuki, K. (1991). Moon illusion simulated in complete darkness: Planetarium experiment reexamined. *Perception & Psychophysics, 49*, 349–354.

Swets, J. A., Pickett, R. M., Whitehead, S. F., Getty, D. J., Schnur, J. A., Swets, J. B., & Freeman, B. A. (1979). Assessment of diagnostic technologies. *Science, 205*, No. 4407, 753–759.

Swets, J. A., Tanner, W. P., Jr., & Birdsall, T. G. (1961). Decision processes in perception. *Psychological Review, 68,* 301–340.

T

Tellegen, A. (1985). Structures of mood and personality and their relevance to assessing anxiety, with an emphasis on self-report. In A. H. Tuma & J. D. Maser (Eds.), *Anxiety and anxiety disorders* (pp. 681–706). Hillsdale, NJ: Lawrence Erlbaum Associates.

Terrace, H. S., Petitto, L. A., Sanders, R. J., & Bever, T. G. (1979). Can an ape create a sentence? *Science, 206,* 891–902.

Tharp, D. A., Levin, I. P., Curry, D. J., & Gray, M. J. (1978, May). *To rate or to rank? Empirical comparisons of two measurement techniques.* Paper presented at meetings of the Midwestern Psychological Association, Chicago.

Thompson, R. F., & Spencer, W. A. (1966). Habituation: A model phenomenon for the study of neuronal substrates of behavior. *Psychological Review, 73,* 16–43.

Thomson, D. M., & Tulving, E. (1970). Associative encoding and retrieval: Weak and strong cues. *Journal of Experimental Psychology, 86,* 255–262.

Thorndike, E. L. (1911). *Animal intelligence.* New York: Macmillan.

Thorndike, E. L., & Lorge, I. (1944). *The teacher's word book of 30,000 words.* New York: Columbia University Press.

Thurstone, L. L. (1927). A law of comparative judgment. *Psychological Review, 34,* 273–286.

Thurstone, L. L. (1931). The measurement of social attitudes. *Journal of Abnormal and Social Psychology, 26,* 249–269.

Tolman, E. C. (1925). Behaviorism and purpose. *Journal of Philosophy, 22,* 36–51.

Tooley, V., Brigham, J. C., Maass, A., & Bothwell, R. K. (1987). Facial recognition: Weapon effect and attentional focus. *Journal of Applied Social Psychology, 17,* 845–859.

Trabasso, T. R., & Bower, G. H. (1968). *Attention in learning: Theory and research.* New York: Wiley.

Treisman, A. M., & Gelade, G. (1980). Feature-integration theory of attention. *Cognitive Psychology, 12,* 97–136.

Tulving, E. (1962). Subjective organization in free recall of "unrelated" words. *Psychological Review, 69,* 344–354.

Tulving, E. (1972). Episodic and semantic memory. In E. Tulving & W. Donaldson (Eds.), *Organization of memory.* New York: Academic Press.

Tulving, E., Schacter, D. L., & Stark, H. A. (1982). Priming effects in word-fragment completion are independent of recognition memory. *Journal of Experimental Psychology: Learning, Memory, and Cognition, 8,* 336–342.

Turnquist, D. C., Harvey, J. H., & Andersen, B. L. (1988). Attributions and adjustment to life-threatening illness. *British Journal of Clinical Psychology, 27,* 55–65.

Tversky, A., & Kahneman, D. (1980). Causal schemes in judgments under uncertainty. In M. Fishbein (Ed.), *Progress in social psychology* (Vol. 1). Hillsdale, NJ: Erlbaum.

Tversky, A., & Kahneman, D. (1983). Extensional versus intuitive reasoning: The conjunction fallacy in probability judgment. *Psychological Bulletin, 90,* 293–315.

U

Underwood, B. J. (1966). *Experimental psychology* (2nd ed.). New York: Appleton-Century-Crofts.

Underwood, B. J., & Freund, J. S. (1969). Verbal-discrimination learning with varying numbers of right and wrong terms. *American Journal of Psychology, 82,* 198–202.

Underwood, B. J., Jesse, F., & Ekstrand, B. R. (1964). Knowledge of rights and wrongs in verbal-discrimination learning. *Journal of Verbal Learning and Verbal Behavior, 3,* 183–186.

Underwood, B. J., Rehula, R., & Keppel, G. (1962). Item-selection in paired-associate learning. *American Journal of Psychology, 75,* 371–373.

Underwood, B. J., & Schulz, R. W. (1960). *Meaningfulness and verbal learning.* Philadelphia: Lippincott.

V

Vaughan, W., Jr., & Greene, S. L. (1984). Pigeon visual memory capacity. *Journal of Experimental Psychology: Animal Behavior Processes, 10,* 256–271.

von Baeyer, C. L., Sherk, D. L., & Zanna, M. P. (1981). Impression management in the job interview: When the female applicant meets the male (chauvinist) interviewer. *Personality and Social Psychology Bulletin, 7,* 45–51.

W

Walster, E., Walster, G., & Berscheid, E. (1978). *Equity: Theory and research.* Boston: Allyn & Bacon.

Warren, J. M. (1973). Learning in vertebrates. In D. A. Dewsbury & D. A. Rethlingshafer (Eds.), *Comparative psychology: A modern survey* (pp. 471–509). New York: McGraw-Hill.

Wasserman, E. A. (1981). Comparative psychology returns: A review of Hulse, Fowler, and Honig's *Cognitive processes in animal behavior. Journal of the Experimental Analysis of Behavior, 35,* 243–257.

Wasserman, E. A. (1982). Further remarks on the role of cognition in the comparative analysis of behavior. *Journal of the Experimental Analysis of Behavior, 38,* 211–216.

Wasserman, E. A. (1993). Comparative cognition: Beginning the second century of the study of animal intelligence. *Psychological Bulletin, 113,* 211–228.

Wasserman, E. A., Kiedinger, R. E., & Bhatt, R. S. (1988). Conceptual behavior in pigeons: Categories, subcategories, and pseudocategories. *Journal of Experimental Psychology: Animal Behavior Processes, 14,* 235–246.

Watson, D., & Clark, L. A. (1984). Negative affectivity: The disposition to experience aversive emotional states. *Psychological Bulletin, 96,* 465–490.

Watson, D., Clark, L. A., & Carey, G. (1988). Positive and negative affectivity and their relation to anxiety and depressive disorders. *Journal of Abnormal Psychology, 97,* 346–353.

Watson, D., Clark, L. A., & Tellegen, A. (1988). Development and validation of brief measures of Positive and Negative Affect: The PANAS scales. *Journal of Personality and Social Psychology, 54,* 1063–1070.

Watson, D., & Tellegen, A. (1985). Toward a consensual structure of mood. *Psychological Bulletin, 98,* 219–235.

Watson, J. B., & Rayner, R. (1920). Conditioned emotional reactions. *Journal of Experimental Psychology, 3,* 1–14.

Waugh, N. C. (1960). Serial position and the memory span. *American Journal of Psychology, 73,* 68–79.

Waugh, N. C., & Norman, D. A. (1965). Primary memory. *Psychological Review, 72,* 89–104.

Weissman, A. N., & Beck, A. T. (1978, November). *Development and validation of the Dysfunctional Attitudes Scale: A preliminary investigation.* Paper presented at the meeting of the American Educational Research Association, Toronto, Canada.

Williams, J. R., Hinrichs, J. V., & Henigbaum, C. (1971). Stimulus functions for constant serial order in paired-associate learning. *Journal of Verbal Learning and Verbal Behavior, 10,* 556–561.

Wolpe, J. (1958). *Psychotherapy by reciprocal inhibition.* Stanford, CA: Stanford University Press.

Woodworth, R. S., & Schlosberg, H. (1954). *Experimental psychology.* New York: Holt.

Wright, A. A., Santiago, H. C., & Sands, S. F. (1984). Monkey memory: *Same/Different* concept learning, serial probe acquisition, and probe delay effects. *Journal of Experimental Psychology: Animal Behavior Processes, 10,* 513–529.

Y

Younger, J. C., Walker, L., & Arrowood, J. A. (1977). Postdecision dissonance at the fair. *Personality and Social Psychology Bulletin, 3,* 284–287.

Z

Zaidi, L. Y., Knutson, J. F., & Mehm, J. G. (1989). Transgenerational patterns of abusive parenting: Analog and clinical tests. *Aggressive Behavior, 15,* 137–152.

Zajonc, R. B. (1965). Social facilitation. *Science, 149,* 269–274.

Zajonc, R. B., & Sales, S. M. (1966). Social facilitation of dominant and subordinate responses. *Journal of Experimental Social Psychology, 2,* 160–168.

Zubin, J., & Spring, B. (1977). Vulnerability: A new view of schizophrenia. *Journal of Abnormal Psychology, 86,* 103–126.

Zuckerman, M., & Lubin, B. (1965). *Manual for the multiple affect adjective check list.* San Diego, CA: Educational and Industrial Testing Service.

Credits

Chapter 1

Box 1.3: From *Ethical Principles of Psychologists and Code of Conduct.* Copyright © 1992 American Psychological Association, Washington DC. Reprinted by permission.

Chapter 4

Figure 4.2: Adapted from "The Role of Frequency in Developing Perceptual Sets" by B. R. Bugelski, D. A. Alampay, 1961, *Canadian Journal of Psychology*, 15, 205–211. Used by permission.

Figure 4.3: Figure from *Psychology of Perception*, Second Edition by William N. Dember and Joel S. Warm, copyright © 1979 by Holt, Rinehart and Winston, Inc., reproduced by permission of the publisher.

Figure 4.8: From N. H. Anderson, "Cross-track validation of functional measurement" in *Perception & Psychophysics*, 12:389–395, 1972. Copyright © 1972 Psychonomics Society, Inc., Austin TX. Reprinted by permission.

Figure 4.9: From S. Rosenberg, C. Nelson, & P. S. Vivikanathan, "A multidimensional approach to the structure of personality impressions" in *Journal of Personality & Social Psychology*, 9:283–4, 1968. Copyright © 1968 American Psychological Association, Washington DC. Reprinted by permission.

Chapter 5

Figure 5.1: From Benjamin B. Lahey, *Psychology: An Introduction*, 3d ed. Copyright © 1989 Wm. C. Brown Communications, Inc., Dubuque, Iowa. All Rights Reserved. Reprinted by permission.

Figure 5.6: From W. N. Dember, et al., *General Psychology*, 2d ed. Copyright © 1984 Lawrence Erlbaum Associates, Hillsdale NJ. Reprinted by permission.

Figure 5.11: Reprinted from *Current Issues in Animal Learning: A Colloquium*, edited by James H. Reynierse, by permission of the University of Nebraska Press. Copyright © 1970 by the University of Nebraska Press.

Figure 5.14: From: *The Experimental Analysis of Behavior: A Biological Perspective* by Edmund Fantino and Cheryl A. Logan. Copyright © 1979 by W. H. Freeman and Company. Used with permission.

Figures 5.15 & 5.16: From E. M. Eisenstein, "The use of invertebrate systems for studies on the bases of learning and memory" in G. C. Quarton, T. Melnechuk, and F. O. Schmitt, (Eds.), *The Neurosciences.* Copyright © 1967 Rockefeller University Press, New York. Reprinted by permission.

Figure 5.17: From R. Boakes, *From Darwin to Behaviourism.* Copyright © 1984 Cambridge University Press, New York NY. Reprinted by permission.

Chapter 6

Figure 6.1: From J. W. McCrary and W. S. Hunter, "Serial Position Curves in Verbal Learning" in *Science*, 117:131–134, 1953. Copyright © 1953 American Association for the Advancement of Science, Washington, DC. Reprinted by permission.

Figure 6.4: From L. R. Peterson and M. J. Peterson, "Knowing and using concepts" in *Psychological Review*, 77:546–56, 1970. Copyright © 1970 American Psychological Association, Washington DC. Reprinted by permission.

Figure 6.6: From S. K. Reed and M. P. Friedman, "Perceptual vs Conceptual Categorization" in *Memory & Cognition*, 1:157–163, 1973. Copyright © 1973 Psychonomics Society, Inc., Austin TX. Reprinted by permission.

Figure 6.7: From P. A. Kolers, "Reading a year later" in *Journal of Experimental Psychology*, 2:554–65, 1976. Copyright © 1976 American Psychological Association, Washington DC. Reprinted by permission.

Figure 6.8: From A. M. Collins and M. R. Quillan, "Retrieval time from semantic memory" in *Journal of Verbal Learning and Verbal Behavior*, 8:240–47, 1969. Copyright © 1969 Academic Press, Inc., Orlando, Florida. Reprinted by permission.

Figure 6.9: From: *Cognitive Psychology and its Implications* by John R. Anderson. Copyright © 1990 by W. H. Freeman and Company. Used with permission.

Page 198 (line art): From J. L. McClelland, "Putting knowledge in its place: A scheme for programming parallel processing structure on the fly" in *Cognitive Science*, 9:1985. Copyright © 1985 Ablex Publishing Corporation. Reprinted by permission.

Page 199 (line art): From J. L. Mc-Clelland and D. R. Rumelhart, "An interactive activation model of context effects in letter perception: Part 1. An account of basic findings" in *Psychological Review*, 88:1959. Copyright © 1959 American Psychological Association, Washington DC. Reprinted by permission.

Chapter 7

Figure 7.2: From L. R. Peterson and M. J. Peterson, "Short-term retention of individual verbal items" in *Journal of Experimental Psychology*, 58:193–98, 1959. Copyright © 1959 American Psychological Association, Washington DC. Reprinted by permission.

Figure 7.3: From B. B. Murdock, Jr., "The retention of individual items" in *Journal of Experimental Psychology*, 62:618–25, 1961. Copyright © 1961 American Psychological Association, Washington DC. Reprinted by permission.

Figure 7.4: From M. Glanzer and A. R. Cunitz, "Two Storage Mechanisms in Free Recall" in *Journal of Verbal Learning and Verbal Behavior*, 5:351–360, 1966. Copyright © 1966 Academic Press, Inc., Orlando FL. Reprinted by permission.

Figure 7.5: From Vernon Gregg, *Introduction to Human Memory*, 1986. Copyright © Routledge, Andover, Hants, England. Reprinted by permission.

Figure 7.6: From R. C. Atkinson and R. M. Shiffrin, "Human Memory" in K. W. Spence, Ed., *The Psychology of Learning and Motivation: Advances in Research and Theory*, Volume 2, 1968. Copyright © 1968 Academic Press, Inc., Orlando FL. Reprinted by permission.

Figure 7.8: From D. Godden and A. D. Baddeley, "Context-dependent memory in two natural environments: On land and under water" in *British Journal of Psychology*, 66:325–31, 1975. Copyright © 1975 British Psychological Society. Reprinted by permission.

Table 7.1: From D. M. Thomson and E. Tulving, "Associative encoding and retrieval: Weak and strong cues" in *Journal of Experimental Psychology*, 86:255–62, 1970. Copyright © 1970 American Psychological Association, Washington DC. Reprinted by permission.

Figure 7.10: From N. H. Anderson, "Evidence for separate judgment and verbal memories," "Functional memory in person cognition" in N. H. Anderson (Ed.), *Contributions to Information Integration Theory, Vol. I: Cognition*. Copyright © 1991 Lawrence Erlbaum Associates, Inc., Hillsdale NJ. Reprinted by permission.

Chapter 8

Table 8.1: From N. H. Anderson, "Likeableness ratings of 555 personality-trait words" in *Journal of Personality & Social Psychology*, 9:272–9, 1968. Copyright © 1968 American Psychological Association, Washington DC. Reprinted by permission.

Table 8.2: From Irwin P. Levin, et al., "External validity tests of laboratory studies of information integration" in *Organizational Behavior and Human Performance*, 31:173–193, 1983. Copyright © 1983 Academic Press, Inc., Orlando FL. Reprinted by permission.

Table 8.3: From J. W. Payne, et al., "Exploring predecisional behavior: An alternative approach to decision research" in *Organizational Behavior and Human Performance*, 22:17–44, 1978. Copyright © 1978 Academic Press, Inc., Orlando FL. Reprinted by permission.

Figure 8.1: From K. Duncker, "On problem solving" in *Psychological Monographs*, 58:1–112, 1945. Copyright © 1945 American Psychological Association, Washington DC. Reprinted by permission.

Page 266 (figure A): From Robert L. Solso, *Cognitive Psychology*. Copyright © 1979 Harcourt Brace Jovanovich, Inc. Reprinted by permission of the author.

Page 266 (figure B): From R. M. Gagne and E. C. Smith, Jr., "A study of the effect of verbalization on problem solving" in *Journal of Experimental Psychology*, 63:12–18, 1963. Copyright © 1963 American Psychological Association, Washington DC. Reprinted by permission.

Chapter 9

Figure 9.1: From E. Aronson, J. A. Turner, and J. M. Carlsmith, "Communicator credibility and communicator discrepancy as determinants of opinion change" in *Journal of Abnormal & Social Psychology*, 67:31–36, 1963. Copyright © 1963 American Psychological Association, Washington DC. Reprinted by permission.

Figure 9.2: From Baron, R. A. and Byrne, D., *Social Psychology*. Copyright © 1987 by Allyn and Bacon. Reprinted by permission.

Chapter 12

Box 12.4: From C. D. B. Burt and S. Kemp, "Retrospective duration estimation of public events" in *Memory & Cognition*, 19:252–262, 1991. Copyright © 1991 Psychonomics Society, Inc., Austin TX. Reprinted by permission.

Page 350 (line art): From S. P. Overmyer and J. R. Simon, "The effects of irrelevant cues on "same/different" judgments in a sequential informtion processing task" in *Acta Psychologica*, 58:237–249, 1985. Copyright © 1985 North-Holland, Subs. Elsevier Science Publishers, B.V., Amsterdam. Reprinted by permission.

Page 354 (figure A): Courtesy of Tonya J. Sieverding, Department of Psychology, Carnegie Mellon University, Pittsburgh PA.

Page 354 (figure B): Courtesy of Tonya J. Sieverding, Department of Psychology, Carnegie Mellon University, Pittsburgh PA.

Box 12.7: This material has been reproduced from the *Publication Manual of the American Psychological Association*, (3rd edition). Copyright © 1983 by the American Psychological Association. Reprinted by permission. Neither the original nor this reproduction can be reproduced or distributed in any form or by any means, or stored in a database or retrieval system, without the prior written permission of the American Psychological Association.

Figure 12.1: Courtesy of The University of Iowa, Iowa City, Iowa.

ILLUSTRATORS

Benoit & Associates
5.1

Wilderness Graphics
2.1, 3.1, 3.2, 3.3, 3.A, 3.B, 3.C, 3.D, 4.2, 4.3, 4.4, 4.5, 4.6, 4.7, 4.8, 4.9, 4.A, 4.B, 5.2, 5.3, 5.4, 5.5, 5.7, 5.9, 5.10, 5.11, 5.12, 5.13, 5.14, 5.15, 5.16, 5.17, 6.1, 6.2, 6.3, 6.4, 6.5, 6.6, 6.7, 6.8, 6.9, 6.A, 6.B, 6.C, 7.1, 7.2, 7.3, 7.4, 7.5, 7.6, 7.7, 7.8, 7.9, 7.10, 8.1, 8.A, 8.B, 9.1, 9.2, 9.3, 12.A, 12.B, 12.C

Name Index

Subject Index

A

Absolute threshold, 92
Abstract, of research report, 344
Abused children, future parenting behavior, 307
Acquisition of learning, 180–184
  all-or-none learning, 181–182
  one-element model, 182–184
Adaptation-level theory, 111
Adoption studies, 7
  schizophrenia, 304–306
Affective disorders
  depression, 299
  diagnosis, 298–299
  mania, 298–299
Aggression, and television viewing, 290–291
Aging, and memory, 230–231
Algorithms, 260
All-or-none learning, 181–182
Alternative hypothesis, 53
American Psychological Association (APA)
  ethical guidelines, 18–20
  guide to graduate studies, 362
  research report writing guidelines, 357–360
Anagrams, 260
Analogies, 194
Analog studies, 307, 308
  parenting of abused children, 307, 308

psychotherapy, 322
Analysis of variance
  multifactor, 65–67
  one-way, 62–64
Anchoring, 248
Animal behavior
  comparative psychology, 118, 119
  reason for study of, 118
Animal research, 15–16
  animal intelligence controversy, 158–159
  comparative cognition, 156–160
  conceptual behavior, 145–148
  ethical issues, 22, 118–120
  experimental method, 122–124
  habituation, 141–142
  language learning in apes, 153–155
  learning in invertebrates, 150–151
  learning sets, 142–145
  myths/facts about, 120–121
  naturalistic observation, 120–122
  Pavlov's research, 124–129, 135–138
  self-concept in apes, 155
  Skinner's research, 130–134

specialized learning, 148–150
  Thorndike's research, 129–130, 138–139
Anticipation method, 175, 177
Anxiety
  diagnosis, 298
  subtypes, 298, 299
Apes
  language learning in, 153–155
  self-concept in, 155
Appetitive stimulus, 134
Arbitrary concepts, 146, 149
Assimilation, 111
Associative learning, 140–141
Associative links, 195
Attention-placebo group, 318
Attitudes, 272–278
  attitude-behavior relationship, 276–277
  attitude change, 274–276
  cognitive dissonance, 277–278
  measurement of, 273–274
Attraction, 281–282
Attribution theory, 282–283, 311
  depression, 311
  fundamental attribution error, 282
Automatic processing, 193–194
Availability heuristic, 247–248
Aversive stimulus, 134

407